National Reading Conference

Officers

Taffy E. Raphael
Oakland University

John E. Readence
University of Nevada, Las Vegas

Donald J. Richgels
Northern Illinois University

Victoria Gentry Ridgeway
Clemson University

Mary Roe
University of Oregon

Nancy Roser
University of Texas, Austin

Martha Rapp Ruddell
Sonoma State University

Robert Rueda
University of Southern California

Ileana Seda-Santana
Universidad Nacional Autonoma de Mexico

Kathy G. Short
University of Arizona

Lawrence R. Sipe
University of Pennsylvania

Wayne H. Slater
University of Maryland

Howard L. Smith
University of Texas at San Antonio

Roger A. Stewart
Boise State University

Jeanne Swafford
Texas Tech University

Barbara Taylor
University of Minnesota

William H. Teale
University of Illinois at Chicago

Diane H. Tracey
Kean University

Julianne C. Turner
University of Notre Dame

Terry Underwood
California State University, Sacramento

Mary Ellen Vogt
California State University, Long Beach

B. Joyce Wiencek
Oakland University

Christopher Worthman
DePaul University

Shelley Hong Xu
Texas Tech University

Josephine Peyton Young
Arizona State University

NRC   *49th Yearbook of the National Reading Conference*

PREFACE

AWARDS

PRESIDENTIAL ADDRESS

NRC ANNUAL REVIEW OF RESEARCH

INVITED ADDRESSES

DIVERSE LEARNERS

INSTRUCTIONAL VARIABLES IN THE CLASSROOM

Teacher Reading in Special Situations

Issues in Literacy Instruction

AUTHOR INDEX

PREFACE

Anyone who even cursorily examines the table of contents of this volume is sure to come away with the notion that the 49th annual conference in Orlando, Florida, was a rousing success. For the first time in years, all of the plenary addresses have been included in the *Yearbook*. We always try to gather all of these, of course, but frequently authors have other ideas for their work or fate intervenes. This year, in spite of—or possibly because of—the high stature of the invited speakers, all have allowed their pieces to be published here. And fine articles they are; several seem certain to be cited frequently in the future.

Additionally, we again had a bumper crop of refereed articles submitted "over the transom," so to speak. The editorial board puzzled (not long—the *Yearbook* publication schedule does not permit that), but hard over these to make sure that only the best were included as in past years, there are some outright gems among those we selected. Others might not be so obviously important on a first read—but they are sure to rise in your estimation when you place them in the context of the "one item in an ongoing series of studies," or "beginnings of a new research line," or "first publication of a budding scholar" that *NRC Yearbook* papers often are.

We thank the authors who submitted 78 papers this year, and the 73 editorial board members who provided 213 timely and thoughtful manuscript reviews. The acceptance rate for this volume was 45%, slightly higher than in past years (and primarily due to the smaller number of submissions this year). We would also like to thank the National Reading Conference and its officers and board members for allowing us the opportunity to edit the *Yearbook* for the past three years. We have enjoyed it and hope that we have contributed something of value to the organization in that time. Our term is up and we proudly hand the reins over to the new team with our best wishes for continued success to James Hoffman, Diane Schallert, Jo Wothy, Beth Maloch, and Colleen Fairbanks from the University of Texas at Austin. As usual, much deserved thanks to Anthony Cheung for his careful—and this year, patient—copyediting work.

Timothy Shanahan and Flora V. Rodriguez-Brown
University of Illinois at Chicago

Lea M. McGee

ALBERT J. KINGSTON AWARD

The 1999 Albert J. Harris Award for outstanding service to the National Reading Conference is given to Lea M. McGee. Lea has been a member of the National Reading Conference since 1978. In that year, she presented her Master's thesis from Old Dominion University ("A Study of Third Grader's Comprehension of a Selected Story Following Listening, Viewing Television, and Reading"). Since that time, Lea has made 21 presentations at NRC, at least one every year since 1978, with the exception of the year that her daughter was born.

Lea has been active in NRC in many other ways throughout the years. One of her earliest contributions was as a Field Council representative. She has served as a reviewer of conference proposals, dozens of papers for the *NRC Yearbook,* and numerous manuscripts for the *Journal of Reading Behavior* (*JRB*) and the *Journal of Literacy Research.* From 1990 to 1992, she served as Associate Editor of *JRB.*

More recently, Lea has served as Chair of NRC's Publications Committee, which oversees the organization's publications and helps set publication policies. In many ways, large and small, Lea has been an important influence in helping the NRC Board to set policies regarding publications. She recommended a joint committee composed of Publication Committee members and Technology Committee members to explore issues related to electronic publishing, helped to establish the new NRC/IRA Research Series, and recommended measures to enable NRC publications to contribute to the organization's strong financial base.

In summary, Lea has contributed to the growth and well-being of NRC in many ways since her first annual meeting in 1978.

Presented by Ronald P. Carver
December 1999

Rebecca Barr

OSCAR S. CAUSEY AWARD

The Oscar S. Causey Award recognizes outstanding contributions to reading research. Dr. Causey was the founder of the National Reading Conference and served as its president from 1952 to 1959.

This year's recipient is highly regarded for her research on the social organization of classroom instruction and beginning reading. Her ground-breaking research in the 1970s was instrumental in legitimizing work that now seems commonplace in our field—the study of what actually happens during classroom reading instruction, and the effects on children's learning to read. We can see in retrospect that this work represented a turning point in our field. I still remember the impression made on me by two of her studies, one entitled, "The Influence of Instructional Conditions on Word Recognition Errors" and the other, "Effect of Instruction on Pupil Reading Strategies," both published in the *Reading Research Quarterly.* Her work offered the hope of understanding children's learning to read not only as a function of individual, psychological processes but also as a function of the social dynamics of curriculum, instruction, and schooling. Her research has been instrumental in broadening the definition of what counts as reading research, to encompass naturalistic along with experimental research, qualitative along with quantitative methodology, and sociological along with psychological perspectives.

This year's recipient is perhaps best known for her studies of the effects of ability grouping on children's reading achievement. Her review entitled, "Grouping Students for Reading Instruction," in the *Handbook of Reading Research, Volume II,* illustrates the breadth, intellectual rigor, and respect for complexity that characterize her work. Here we find not just a review of contemporary studies conducted in the United States but historical thinking about grouping going back to medieval times, as well as cross-national comparisons. The insight she brings to tangled issues is illustrated in this sentence from the conclusion:

> Although it is customary to think of grouping as if it pertained primarily to ability differences found among students in the same school or classroom, grouping is actually a phenomenon of far larger scope that extends to educational provisions based upon major lines of social demarcation in societies at large. (p. 905)

This year's recipient is highly regarded not only for her accomplishments as a scholar, but for her service to the research community. She has been an outstanding leader of the National Reading Conference, having served as president from 1992 to 1993 and as editor of the *Journal of Reading Behavior.* She has been the senior program officer for the Spencer Foundation. She has served as an editor of the *Handbook of Reading Research,* and in 1995 she was elected to the Reading Hall of Fame.

She received her Ph.D. in educational psychology and reading from the University of Chicago, and taught there and at the University of British Columbia before joining the faculty of National-Louis University, where she has been a professor and dean.

Always meticulous in her research, never one to overstate conclusions, a leader whose professional conduct exemplifies the highest ethics—by now the identity of this year's recipient will come as no surprise. It gives me great pleasure to present the 1999 Oscar S. Causey Award to Rebecca Barr.

Presented by Kathryn Au
December 1999

EDWARD B. FRY BOOK AWARD

On behalf of the National Reading Conference, it is my privilege to present the Edward B. Fry Book Award to this year's recipients, David Reinking, Michael McKenna, Linda Labbo, and Ronald Kieffer. Their edited book, *Handbook of Literacy and Technology: Transformations in a Post Typographic World,* aptly reflects our society's current status. At the beginning of this century, our society moved from the agriculture era to the industrial era. At the end of this century, our society is once again moving. We are leaving the industrial era and entering the knowledge era, an era where technology is playing a key role. During the last transition between eras, our way of life dramatically and drastically shifted. It is shifting again. Transformations in how we think, act, teach, learn, and grow are almost overwhelming. Many of us have difficulty in thoroughly understanding the role of technology and its uses, let alone trying to predict its future impact on education. This book offers extraordinary help as we move through our current transition with its accompanying transformations in literacy as it relates to technology.

This book was selected because it best fits the criteria established by the Committee. First, it explicitly advances our knowledge about the uses, values, and potential of technology within literacy. Second, it displays thoughtful inquiry into literacy. The contributing authors and editors are respected leaders in research who examine the intersection of literacy and technology. Third, this book illustrates responsible, intellectual risk taking. This concept is captured in the following quote from their book: "The pace at which the literacy landscape is changing, especially in regard to technological developments, makes conducting meaningful research equivalent to hitting a moving target." These editors have hit the moving target. They took the intellectual risk by trying to understand the impact of technology on literacy and then are helping us to understand what this impact means.

The *Handbook of Literacy and Technology* was initiated at a conference hosted by the National Reading Research Center where 180 researchers and educators explored the relationships between literacy and technology. The editors of this handbook played important roles in this conference and are distinguished scholars in literacy and technology. David Reinking is a Professor of Education and the Head of the Department of Reading Education at the University of Georgia. He is also the editor of the *Journal of Literacy Research.* Michael McKenna is a Professor of Reading at Georgia Southern University. Linda Labbo is an Associate Professor in the Department of Reading Education at the University of Georgia. She is also the section editor of the "Reviews Section" of *Reading On-Line,* the International Reading Association's electronic journal. Ronald Kieffer is an Associate Professor of Reading and Language Arts in the Department of Teaching and Learning at the University of North Dakota. Together, they have book chapters and articles in most of the major literacy journals including our *NRC Yearbooks* and our *Journal of Literacy Research.*

On behalf of the Edward B. Fry Book Award Committee members of Nancy Farnan, Yetta Goodman, Linda Kucan, and Mark Sadowski and the entire NRC membership, it is a distinct pleasure to present the 1999 Edward B. Fry Book Award to David Reinking, Michael McKenna, Linda Labbo, and Ronald Keiffer.

Presented by Laura Roehler
December 1999

Reflections on Literacy Research: The Decades of the 1970s, 1980s, and 1990s*

Linda Gambrell

Clemson University

I n one of my first doctoral classes in the early 1970s, I was given an assignment to read a paper, "Research That Should Have Made a Difference." The paper was authored by Harry Singer, an acclaimed literacy researcher and one of the early leaders of the National Reading Conference (NRC). I found this paper to be a thought-provoking piece, and as a beginning doctoral student, I was impressed with the way Singer identified and described reading research that he believed should have made a difference, but had not had any discernible impact on practice. He also went one additional step and identified research that had made a difference, but should not have. I remember thinking at the time whether others in the reading field would agree with his conclusions about influential research.

With this in mind, I decided to survey NRC members about the research they believed was most influential during the decades of the 1970s, 1980s, and 1990s. There were several reasons why I thought this information might be of value to NRC and the field of literacy. First, several noted scholars have identified influential literacy research, beginning with Russell in 1961, Singer in 1970 and 1976, and more recently, Shanahan and Neuman in 1997. Although these scholars addressed issues related to influential research, they were based on the authors' reflections and reviews of the research, and therefore did not necessarily represent the ideas and opinions of others in the field. Second, NRC will celebrate its fiftieth anniversary in December 2001. Under the recent leadership of Trika Smith-Burke and Norman Stahl, the National Reading Conference has embarked on a historical project to compile databases of oral histories and reminiscences of early NRC scholars and leaders. Our past matters. Part of the maturity of any organization is a realization of the importance of the history of the institution.

According to Moore, Monaghan, and Hartman (1997), "history is not only then, but now, and the quality of historical work done in the future is contingent on the paper trail we leave today" (p. 98). The survey research reported here was designed to explore the perceptions of NRC members about the most influential literacy research of the decades of the 1970s, 1980s, and 1990s, and to identify the work of influential scholars and research trends that have influenced the way literacy is taught.

*Presidential Address, The National Reading Conference, Orlando, FL, December 1999. Appreciation is extended to Yatasha Ballenger, a graduate student in the Clemson University School of Education, for her assistance in coding the data from the survey.

National Reading Conference Yearbook, 49, pp. 1–11.

Historical Background

Four major pieces were identified in our literature that focused on evaluating the impact reading research has made upon instructional practice:

Russell, D. H. (1961). Reading research that makes a difference. *Elementary English, 38,* 74-78.

Singer, H. (1970). Research that should have made a difference. *Elementary English, 47,* 27-34.

Singer, H. (1976). Research in reading that should make a difference in classroom instruction. In S. J. Samuels (Ed.), *What research has to say about reading instruction* (pp. 57-71). Newark, DE: International Reading Association.

Shanahan, T., & Neuman, S. (1997). Conversations: Literacy research that makes a difference. *Reading Research Quarterly, 32,* 202-210.

In 1961 Russell chronicled 10 studies published in books and journals that, in his opinion, significantly influenced the reading curriculum. The studies he identified were published from 1917 to 1956. He referred to these studies as the "Ten Best." Singer, in articles published in 1970 and 1976, built upon Russell's work. In 1970 he identified 5 additional studies that, in his opinion, should have made a difference, but had not. Later, he extended his list to include 2 studies that had made a difference, but that should not have. These 2 studies were the Morphett and Washburn (1931) research that reported a mental age of 6.5 years as necessary for learning to read, and the Cattell (1886) study that suggested configuration was an important clue for word identification.

In 1997, Shanahan and Neuman proposed their list of literacy studies that have made a difference. They identified 13 empirical studies published since 1961 that they believe have had an influence on classroom practice. They pointed to important work done by various people in an area, but selected and highlighted one work as representative. They refer to their list as "a thoughtful 13." Shanahan and Neuman identified common characteristics of the 13 influential studies that they identified: the studies addressed important issues, the studies were theory driven, each study was rhetorically powerful and elegantly executed, and the researchers boldly speculated on broad issues of literacy learning, teaching, and instruction. Clearly, these four papers (Russell, 1961; Singer, 1970, 1976; Shanahan & Neuman, 1997) were designed to inform the field and to stimulate discussion.

In trying to identify the literacy research from the past three decades that had most influenced practice, my work differed from that of Russell, Singer, and Shanahan and Neuman in several ways. Whereas Russell and Singer focused on reading research, like Shanahan and Neuman, I used the broader term "literacy" in order to be as inclusive as possible, particularly with respect to research in areas such as language and spelling. I also used a broader definition of what "counts" as research to include different methodologies and publication outlets. For example, research journals publish most of the current research reports related to literacy, however, books, book chapters, and conference yearbooks also provide a common forum for publishing research, syntheses of research, and theories and models of literacy (Otto, 1992).

Survey of the Membership

Development of the Survey Instrument

A survey instrument was designed to gather information from NRC members about the literacy research of the 1970s, 1980s, and 1990s that, in their opinion, had most influenced practice. A panel of NRC members (Donna Alvermann, James Cunningham, Patricia Cunningham, Susan Neuman, Lesley Morrow, Michael McKenna, Ray Reutzel, and Taffy Raphael) provided feedback about the design of the instrument and the appropriateness of the survey questions. Revisions were made based on their feedback, resulting in a broader emphasis on scholarship and inclusion of diverse methodologies and publication outlets.

The survey asked respondents to answer the following question: What literacy research (using a broad definition of scholarship, including theory, literature reviews, and research methodologies) published in the decades of the 1970s, 1980s, and 1990s do you believe has most influenced literacy practices? Respondents were asked to provide as much information as possible about the published scholarship. The survey informed respondents that complete information was not necessary ("do not feel you must provide complete information for each entry or information for all three decades"). Respondents were asked not to cite their own research. A space was provided for comments about the significance of the research cited so that respondents could share their views about "why" or "how" the work influenced practice.

Respondents were asked to provide the following information: primary area of interest (early childhood, elementary, middle school, high school, college/adult); number of years in the reading field and number of years as an NRC member (1–4 years, 5–12 years, 13–20 years, 20+ years). Finally, respondents were asked to sign the survey if they were willing to give permission to be quoted by name, otherwise their responses would be anonymous. In a letter that accompanied the survey, I promised to donate $1 to NRC for every completed survey returned by the deadline.

Survey Respondents

The current membership list of NRC was used to randomly select 350 members to receive the questionnaire. Of the 350 surveys mailed to NRC members, 119 were returned and 115 were used for analysis, resulting in a return rate of 34%. Four surveys were returned with notes explaining why the individual did not respond (one indicated that the research they were most familiar with did not have direct implications for practice, two indicated that they were "too new" to the field to complete the survey, and one was returned with no explanation).

Those who completed the survey represented a broad cross-section of NRC's membership. The primary areas of interest of the respondents were as follows: early childhood 18%, elementary 42%, middle school 14%, high school 11%, and college/adult 12%. The demographic data from survey reveals that the majority of the respondents (60%) indicated that their primary area of interests are early childhood and elementary. Table 1 displays respondent information regarding the number of years in the reading field and the number of years as an NRC member.

Survey Results

In describing the results of the survey, I will present the findings from each decade and draw from the comments of the survey respondents to provide insights about "why" and "how" the cited literacy research was influential. Individual literacy researchers who were most frequently cited will be highlighted along with the major publications cited by the respondents as being most influential.

Literacy Research That Has Influenced Practice—1970s

The analysis of the data for the 1970s clearly revealed that the work of Dolores Durkin (1978/79) on reading comprehension instruction was identified as the most influential. The next most influential work was that of Kenneth Goodman (1970, 1976) in the area of psycholinguistics. Also frequently mentioned was the work of Marie Clay (1973; 1972, 1979), Louise Rosenblatt (1978), and Frank Smith (1971).

Dolores Durkin and Reading Comprehension Instruction

A clear finding from the survey about research of the 1970s was the dominant influence of the work of Dolores Durkin on classroom observations of reading comprehension instruction. Almost without exception, respondents reported the title and citation for her 1978/79 publication in *Reading Research Quarterly.* The following comments from NRC members describe both the influence and impact of this work on the field of literacy as well as classroom practice:

> "Her work showed that teachers were testing rather than teaching comprehension and laid the groundwork for the wealth of research on strategic comprehension." (Carol Santa)

Table 1

Percentage of Respondents Reporting Years in the Reading Field and Years as an NRC Member

Number of Years	In Reading Field	As NRC Member
1–4	3%	31%
5–12	17%	31%
13–20	27%	27%
20+	50%	8%

"This important classroom study opened our eyes to the reality that we weren't teaching comprehension, just testing . . . we've come a long way in teaching strategic understanding of text." (Barbara Moss)

"This study was the catalyst that ignited the decade of analyzing assessment and evaluation issues in the 1980s." (Cathy Collins Block)

"This work showed how reading instruction often fails to provide comprehension strategies to students. Certainly one of a handful of studies that led to the research in the 1980s looking at the effects of cognitive strategy instruction." (Cecil Smith)

Kenneth Goodman and Psycholinguistics

Kenneth Goodman's early work on reading as a psycholinguistic guessing game was the second most frequently mentioned influential research of the 1970s. Although his paper, "Reading as a Psycholinguistic Guessing Game," was first published in the late 1960s in the *Journal of the Reading Specialist,* it was the publication of a version of this paper in *Theoretical Models and Processes of Reading* that brought Goodman's work to the attention of a wide audience of literacy researchers. Survey respondents noted this work frequently. Respondents commented on the implications of this work for assessment and instruction:

"Goodman's work paved the way not only for a very different kind of assessment paradigm in the form of miscue analysis, but also for the types of instructional accommodations and interventions that miscue analysis suggested would be necessary to help children make the best use of the cueing systems inherent in written language." (Bill Henk)

"As a reading teacher Goodman's work helped me orchestrate strategies around the one simple idea that the mind moves down onto the page rather than the page moving up into the mind." (Jamie Myers)

Marie Clay, Louise Rosenblatt, and Frank Smith

Whereas the survey respondents clearly identified the work of Durkin and Goodman as most influential, the respondents also identified a cluster of influential scholars in the 1970s that deserve mention (presented here in alphabetical order).

Marie Clay's work on early literacy development was frequently cited and two of her publications were specifically identified as influential: *Reading: The Patterning of Complex Behavior* (1973) and *The Early Detection of Reading Difficulties* (1972, 1979):

"*Reading: The Patterning of Complex Behavior* opened our eyes to how children learn to read and write. It was a new view of how to do research in real classrooms. A seminal work." (Margaret Griffin)

"The work of Marie Clay, supported and enhanced by many other researchers, has had a strong influence on the instructional practices of early childhood educators in preschools and the primary grades." (Patricia Koskinen)

The reader response work of Louise Rosenblatt was identified as influential in the 1970s and her book, *The Reader, the Text, the Poem: The Transactional Theory of the Literacy Work* was her most frequently cited publication:

> "Rosenblatt's work empowered individual interpretation, questioned textual authority, and opened the door to new practices that valued students' and teachers' meaning-making in relation to text." (Roberta Hammet)

> "Her work has shaped the ways hundreds of us think about reading. What a relief after New Criticism!" (Patricia Bloem)

> "This seminal work has been a basis for numerous researchers as they have explored reading, writing, discussion, classroom context, curriculum, and culturally relevant instruction." (Janelle Mathis)

Rounding out this cluster of most influential scholars was the work of Frank Smith. Smith's work in the area of psycholinguistics (*Understanding Reading*, 1971) was often cited by respondents as being influential in the 1970s:

> "Smith synthesized a large body of research on the psychology of reading and helped me move into new ways of understanding young readers...away from my behaviorist, phonics only, training. It allowed me to think about teaching from the top down, about children as something other than empty vessels, and eventually transformed my teaching." (Diane Beals)

Literacy Research That Has Influenced Practice—1980s

The survey respondents identified Shirley Brice Heath's (1983) ethnographic study of the families of the Carolina Piedmont as the clear and definitive influential work of the 1980s. The next most influential research was that of Donald Graves (1983) on process writing. In addition, respondents identified the work of Kenneth and Yetta Goodman and Marie Clay as influential during the 1980s.

Shirley Brice Heath and Sociopsycholinguistics

Overwhelmingly survey respondents cited Shirley Brice Heath's *Ways With Words* as the most influential work of the 1980s. This ethnography of communication, based on Heath's 10 years of research in the Carolina Piedmont, compared "Roadville," a white working-class community steeped for four generations in the life of the textile mill, and "Trackton," a black working-class community a few miles away whose older generation grew up farming the land but later worked in the mill. Her close look at the home habits of these two groups indicated that a major difference lies in the amount of narrative or ongoing commentary in which mainstream parents immersed their young children. In tracing the language development of the children, Heath documented how cultural differences between the communities were reflected in the different uses of language:

> "Heath's *Ways with Words* was by far the most important scholarly work of the 80s. She helped us to see the contributions that an anthropological perspective could make on our understanding of and teaching of literacy." (Patricia Anders)

"While I knew the white middle class way of doing literacy with children was not the only way, I couldn't see how to think about this issue. Heath clarified so much . . . made me think about the fit between home and school . . . about the pressures for all students to conform to a middle class model of literacy. She opened the door to the work done by Kathryn Au and Luis Moll and to all kinds of new understandings." (Anonymous)

Donald Graves and Process Writing

Donald Graves's early work on process writing was the second most frequently mentioned influential research of the 1980s. His research on writing as a process began with his dissertation in 1973 on elementary children's knowledge of and behaviors during writing. His work continued into the 1980s and respondents cited many of his publications, but his book, *Writing: Teachers and Children at Work* was noted most often:

"Graves' work transformed classroom practice throughout the country. This book became the bible of process writing in many university classrooms and schoolrooms. Graves' genius was his ability to operationalize theories of writing which were constructivist and translate them in ways that transformed classroom writing practice." (Brenda Shearer)

"This work led to revolutions in elementary classrooms in teaching writing and in bringing reading and writing instruction together." (Jill Fitzgerald)

Marie Clay and Kenneth and Yetta Goodman

In addition to the work of Heath and Graves, survey respondents also recognized the work of Marie Clay and Kenneth and Yetta Goodman as being influential in the 1980s.

Clay's work in the area of Reading Recovery was recognized as influential. Several publications by Clay were mentioned by the respondents, however, none was dominant:

"She changed the way we assess and teach beginning readers. Her influence is seen in the acceptance of observation as an assessment tool. Also, she influenced the shift from the medical model to continuous, naturalistic assessment." (Anonymous)

Kenneth and Yetta Goodman's work in the areas of psycholinguistics, miscue analysis, kidwatching, and whole language were also identified as influential in the 1980s. A number of publications were cited, however, none was dominant.

"Although this work was done in the late 60s and 70s, like a good wine, it had to wait until the right time to reach its full maturity. It did so in the 80s and was foundational to the widespread influence of whole language and emergent literary perspectives." (David Reinking)

"Nationwide whole language changed teacher instructional practices. This work moved us away from teacher-centered classrooms to child-centered classrooms. Teachers no longer felt 'compelled' to follow a 'manual' Both teachers and students were given more ownership in the process of teaching and learning to read." (Christine McKeon)

Literacy Research That Has Influenced Practice—1990s

For the decade of the 1990s, the respondents were in clear agreement that Marilyn Adams's (1990) *Beginning to Read* was the most influential work. The next most frequently mentioned influential scholar was Marie Clay and her work with Reading Recovery.

Marilyn Adams and Beginning Reading

Marilyn Adams's review and synthesis of the research on beginning reading was overwhelmingly the most frequently mentioned influential work of the 1990s. In the introduction to *Beginning to Read,* Adams states: "Before you pick this book up, you should understand fully that the topic at issue is that of reading words. Before you put this book down, however, you should understand fully that the ability to read words, quickly, accurately, and effortlessly, is critical to skillful reading comprehension—in the obvious ways and in a number of more subtle ones. Skillful reading is a whole complex system of skills and knowledge. If the processes involved in individual word recognition do not operate properly, nothing else in the system can either."

Adams's book provided an extensive review of the research on beginning reading, and a comprehensive treatment of the behaviors associated with beginning and expert reading. Adams's work begins with a key assumption—that word recognition is at the base of the language-processing system. She crafted a convincing argument for developing reading instructional programs that help beginning readers see the relationships among orthographic, semantic, syntactical, and phonological patterns in print. Whereas the comments of many survey respondents pointed to the balanced approach of Adam's book, many also pointed to the way the book was interpreted:

> "A very large review of the literature and the first of many 90s reports emphasizing the role of phonics in learning to read . . . heavily influenced our view of reading and how it should be taught." (John Readence)

> "It was an amazing, comprehensive synthesis that has been used for both good and ill." (Cathy Roller)

> "This book-length review of the literature is probably the original impetus for the current emphasis on phonemic (phonological) awareness." (Lois Dreyer)

> "Adams' and the work of others on phonemic awareness pointed attention to this issue, but perhaps more important, fueled an amazing policy-level controversy." (Nancy Padak)

Marie Clay and Reading Recovery

Marie Clay's work related to Reading Recovery was the second most frequently identified research cited by the survey respondents. A number of publications related to Reading Recovery were cited. Clay's research and the Reading Recovery program focus on the importance of observing individual children at work reading and writing, in order to capture evidence of reading progress. Her work is credited with making direct observation more acceptable as a method for data collection, particularly in the years of early childhood education:

> "Reading Recovery has had a direct affect on instruction in the many schools where it has been implemented. It has also had an indirect affect on our perspective about remediating struggling readers. It is also consistent with the tenor of the times politically . . . and remarkable in the sense that it has remained, for the most part, above the fray—inside and outside the field. An instructional practice that has components to which a diverse range of researchers, policy makers, and teachers can relate." (David Reinking)

> "Clay brought a highly successful balance back to literacy instruction." (Anonymous)

> "Clay's work changed our paradigm concerning early literacy. She showed us that 'waiting' was not enough—that teaching concepts of print could enhance, rather than hinder, literacy development." (Cathy Collins Block)

Final Thoughts and Future Directions

The results of this survey provide some insights about the literacy scholarship that NRC members believe has most influenced practice during the 1970s, 1980s, and 1990s. This research is offered as one effort to explore and help define NRC as a research community. The results of the survey related to the 1970s has the virtue of being more distant from the present than the results related to the 1980s and 1990s, and may be more reliable in that the work cited has stood the test of time. It should be acknowledged that the survey results related to the 1980s, and particularly the 1990s, may suffer from the up-too-close view and, therefore, may be somewhat distorted or myopic. The survey results do, however, provide a picture of what NRC members, at this point in time, view as the dominant and most influential scholarly works that have influenced literacy practice across the decades of the 1970s, 1980s, and 1990s.

The results of the survey reveal that the NRC respondents identified the following scholarship as "most influencing practice": Durkin's comprehension work of the 1970s, Heath's socio-cultural ethnographic research of the 1980s, and Adam's synthesis of research on beginning reading in the 1990s. The work of Marie Clay related to Reading Recovery was noted as being influential across all three decades, indicating the high level of recognition of the impact of her work on early intervention. The work of Kenneth Goodman was identified as being influential in both the decade of the 1970s and the 1980s indicating the impact of his research in the areas of psycholinguistics, miscue analysis, and whole language. Clearly, the work of these influential scholars form a major part of the heritage and history of literacy research and practice.

It is noteworthy that there is agreement about the work of several of these influential scholars across the analysis conducted by Shanahan and Neuman (1997) and the results of this study. The Shanahan and Neuman analysis considered empirical research conducted between 1960 and 1995, whereas the current study focused on scholarship, broadly defined, during the decades of the 1970s,

1980s, and 1990s. Both the Shanahan and Neuman article and the NRC survey respondents highlight the influence of the work of Marie Clay, Donald Graves, Delores Durkin, and Kenneth Goodman. Broadening the definition of scholarship to include qualitative research and research syntheses allowed respondents to the NRC survey to recognize the important contributions that the work of Heath and Adams have made to instructional literacy practices.

What do the survey results reveal about definitions of research and literacy within the NRC community? It appears that as a field our conceptualizations of research have broadened. Pressley and Allington (1999) have emphasized the importance of a variety of conceptualizations and methodologies that can complement one another to produce a broader picture than would result from evaluating any one theory or using any one method. Respondents to the NRC survey identified both qualitative and quantitative research as being highly influential, including empirical studies, case studies, ethnographies, and research syntheses. The results of the survey suggest that NRC members appear to favor neither conceptual nor methodological narrowness.

In looking at the results of this survey and thinking about what the results suggest about our definitions of literacy I was drawn to a recent article in the *Journal of Literacy Research* by James Gee. The survey results suggest that, as a field, our view of literacy has broadened and expanded and includes sociocultural dimensions as well as reading and writing. Gee (1999) suggests that a New Literacy Studies perspective is needed to capture the breadth and depth of literacy. This perspective is based on an interdisciplinary effort that takes a sociocultural approach to language and literacy. Gee argues for a wider "literacy and learning" viewpoint, rather than a narrower "reading" one; a viewpoint that disavows dichotomies between, and debates over, phonics and whole language. The New Literacy Studies perspective argues for a focus not on reading, but rather, on oral and written language as composed of diverse but interrelated "tools" for learning.

Interestingly, the results of this study reveal clear evidence of the "pendulum swing" that is frequently referenced in our literacy history and our literature. First, with the swing toward comprehension in the 1970s, followed by the move toward a "middle ground" with the emphasis on socio-cultural aspects of literacy in the 1980s, and then the swing to decoding in the 1990s. The history of literacy suggests that our views will constantly shift and change with the tenor of the times. Times change, as will our future conceptions of literacy. One need only to think about the current implications of technology as compared with the 1970s to realize how quickly our field can change. While the pendulum of literacy will continue to swing, I believe in the "positive sway" of the pendulum swing. As the pendulum swings we do move ever forward in our accumulated knowledge base about literacy.

References

Adams, M. (1990). *Beginning to read: Thinking and learning about print.* Cambridge, MA: MIT Press.

Cattell, J. M. (1886). The time it takes to see and name objects. *Mind, 11,* 63–65.

Clay, M. M. (1973). *Reading: The patterning of complex behavior.* Auckland: Heinemann.

Clay, M. M. (1972, 1979). *The early detection of reading difficulties.* Auckland: Heinemann.

Durkin, D. (1978/79). What classroom observations reveal about reading comprehension instruction. *Reading Research Quarterly, 14,* 481–533.

Gee, J. P. (1999). Critical issues: Reading and the new literacy studies: Reframing the National Academy of Sciences Report on Reading. *Journal of Literacy Research, 31,* 355–374.

Goodman, K. (1970, 1976). Reading: A psycholinguistic guessing game. In H. Singer & R. Ruddell (Eds.), *Theoretical models and processes of reading* (pp. 497–508). Newark, DE: International Reading Association.

Graves, D. (1983). *Writing: Teachers and children at work.* Portsmouth, NH: Heinemann.

Heath, S. B. (1983). *Ways with words: Language, life, and work in communities and class-rooms.* New York: Cambridge University Press.

Moore, D. W., Monaghan, E. J., & Hartman, D. K. (1997). Conversations: Values of literacy history. *Reading Research Quarterly, 32,* 90–102.

Morphett, M., & Washburne, C. (1931). When should children begin to read. *Elementary School Journal, 31,* 46–503.

Otto, W. (1992). The role of research in reading instruction. In S. J. Samuels (Ed.), *What research has to say about reading instruction* (pp. 1–16). Newark, DE: International Reading Association.

Pressley, M., & Allington, M. (1999). Concluding reflections: What should reading instructional research be the research of? *Issues in Education, 5,* 1–35.

Rosenblatt, L. (1978). *The reader, the text, the poem: The transactional theory of the literacy work.* Carbondale: Southern Illinois University Press.

Russell, D. H. (1961). Reading research that makes a difference. *Elementary English, 38,* 74–78.

Shanahan, T., & Neuman, S. (1997). Conversations: Literacy research that makes a difference. *Reading Research Quarterly, 32,* 202–210.

Singer, H. (1970). Research that should have made a difference. *Elementary English, 47,* 27–34.

Singer, H. (1976). Research in reading that should make a difference in classroom instruction. In S. J. Samuels (Ed.), *What research has to say about reading instruction* (pp. 57–71). Newark, DE: International Reading Association.

Smith, F. (1971). *Understanding reading.* New York: Holt, Rienhart & Winston.

Culture in Literacy Education: Thirteen Ways of Looking at a Blackbird

Susan Florio-Ruane
Michigan State University

S eated cross-legged on my living room carpet, I am hosting the first meeting of the Future Teachers' Autobiography Club. The six young women gathered with me around the coffee table are student teachers. The members of this newly formed club are classmates in "The Learning Community," a teacher education program I helped to design. Like most students at my university, these young women come from rural and suburban backgrounds. Despite the December chill, they are flushed with the excitement of solo teaching. Although they have busy lives, each has accepted my invitation to gather monthly for dinner and book talk. Certainly the food and the chance to reconnect with classmates draws them to the club. But they are also drawn by the topic. I have invited them to read and discuss over the remainder of the school year six autobiographies dealing with culture.

In preparation for our meeting, I have asked everyone to read Vivian Paley's book, *White Teacher* (1979/89). Some of us have read excerpts of it before, but reading the entire book and gathering with others to talk about it over dinner is a novel experience. Each young woman arrives with a paperback copy of the book, some with notes scribbled in the margins, others with folded down corners of pages containing memorable passages. In *White Teacher,* the first of many popular books about her teaching, Paley offers a coming-of-age memoir. She describes her novice teaching in a Chicago preschool. Like many of us, Paley is a cultural "pastiche." Middle class, Jewish, female, and from the South, she arrives in Chicago unaccustomed to teaching, confronted with her first African-American pupils, brought up to believe that avoiding mention of race is a way of showing tolerance and politeness.

Deceptively easy to read, Paley's anecdotal memoir lures us into risky, self-searching places. Talk about culture and race does not come easily for Paley. And, even in my cozy living room, it does not come easily for us. But gradually, perhaps warmed by the meal and Paley's engaging prose, we begin to speak and listen in ways less like a seminar or formal dinner, and more like a casual conversation among friends. We begin to talk about Paley's narrative in terms of our own formation and how culture arises in our lives as teachers. In this act of imagination and memory we encircle the idea of culture in personal narrative. Nell's (pseudonym) voice is the first to emerge. Well liked by her peers, she speaks easily and often. So it is not surprising that other voices quiet as Nell begins the story of a

National Reading Conference Yearbook, 49, pp. 12–30.

multicultural festival in which she participated as a child. Almost as if she had started with, "Once upon a time," we settle into story listening and await Nell's problem, its complicating action, and its ultimate resolution.

Nell's Story

> Once upon a time, a little girl named Nell was assigned to prepare an oral report about her cultural background. Nell realized that she did not know very much about hers. What could she say that would give her report the flavor and color of "culture"? Nell felt a wave of panic as she thought about what to show and tell. "I'm not anything," she thought, "I'm just an American." Seeking to impress her teacher and classmates with at least some colorful details of her family's food, dress, and holidays, Nell asked her mother for help. But Nell was disappointed when, barely looking up from the vegetables she was paring for dinner, her mother merely shrugged at the question, "What are we?" She replied, "I don't know. Some mix of Irish and English, I guess. It was a long time ago." When pressed, her mother could summon none of the colorful details Nell hoped to include in her report. Frustrated and desperate for a story, Nell tells us: "I dreaded having to give that report." So, she confesses, to make her cultural background interesting, "I faked being from Poland."

Nell's vignette, which I have tried faithfully to retell, embodies culture's elusiveness in the education of both teachers and children in our society. Whereas its resolution serves the little girl's immediate need for a compelling story, how has Nell's experience shaped her consciousness as an educator? Read one way, it illustrates par excellence a "deficit" model of young white teachers and their education. In this model, Nell is seen to be ignorant of culture—her own or anyone else's. And formal education, personified by her teacher, is seen to trivialize culture associating it only with a static view of culture-as-ethnicity. The child's teacher and mother can be read to personify the white, middle class "culture of power," unreflective about their history and privilege.

However, other readings of Nell's story are also possible. Until this assignment, young Nell has apparently not "hyphenated" her American identity. Her teacher has perhaps posed a less-than-authentic problem for the students. Yet the assignment suggests an awareness that cultural understanding involves self-study and narrative. Nell's mother, like the child, has not thought of herself in terms of her immigrant ancestry. She is similarly nonplussed by the assignment the teacher has made. Yet Nell sets out to fulfill that assignment by creating a good story. She intuitively knows that culture relates to narrative and to history. To understand culture in our own and others' lives is an act of imagination. In that sense, "faking being from Poland" is perhaps only marginally different from imagining a personal cultural narrative tied more closely to "fact."

As we listen to Nell's story, we wonder along with her: What is culture? How do individuals gain access to it? Is culture a label for a group of people? Is culture "one to a customer"? What does culture have to do with history? What does it have to do with literary imagination? What do our cultural stories tell us about others and ourselves. What does culture mean—to the little girl? To the young teacher remembering her schooling? To the profession she is joining?

Defining Culture for Literacy Research and Teacher Education

I sympathize with Nell, her mother, and her teacher. It is hard to think about culture. At best it is a conceptual moving target; even anthropologists contest its definition (Finnan & Swanson, 2000). Most people would agree that culture is far more than "local color." It is more than food, costumes, and festivals. Yet easily saying what it is not, we struggle to learn what it might be. In this paper, I want to make three points about culture—first, like other "big ideas," culture resists easy definition; second, despite its complexity, it is worth our effort as literacy educators and researchers to struggle with the idea of culture; and third, understanding culture involves not only reason, but also creativity.

The late Sylvia Scribner advanced a similar perspective when she wondered about the nature of "literacy" in her essay, "Literacy in Three Metaphors" (1984). She noted that researchers and policy-makers believe that, "literacy is a kind of reality that educators should be able to grasp and explain" and, as such, has an "essence that can be captured through some Aristotelian-like enterprise." This belief leads to the assumption that, "by a rational process of discussion and analysis, the 'true' criterial components of literacy will be identified, and these in turn can become the target of education for literacy" (all quotes from Scribner, 1984, p. 7). Scribner disagreed with this line of reasoning, not only because it oversimplified literacy, but also because it located literacy's power in the hands of a few. An essential definition of literacy would reflect a narrow bandwidth of the world's people and their literate practices. Literacy would be the dominion of those with the power to craft its formal definition.

Scribner was not only a psychologist but also a world traveler. That was probably a good thing. Perhaps it was possible for her to identify metaphors for literacy because she had, in fact, visited and conducted research on literacy in such distant and unlikely places as Liberia, West Africa, and a commercial dairy in the United States. These were places where literacy's different forms and functions were less familiar, and therefore more visible to her. Discovering diverse forms and function of literacy in unfamiliar places helped her to understand her own literate practices as well as those she studied. Perhaps, as well, her brief experience directing the National Institute of Education helped her to recognize the power of particular metaphors for literacy to overwhelm other local meanings, purposes, and values.

The goal of understanding literacy for education, Scribner urged, might be better served by opening ourselves to "differing points of view" about literacy's meaning. These would include diverse experiences of literacy practiced by people in particular local contexts, historical periods, activities, and societies. In short, to understand literacy, we had to be willing to get outdoors and look around. We had to resist comfortable, familiar views and become, if not anthropologists, at least "accidental tourists" entertaining multiple textual representations of literacy. To stir the imagination, Scribner gave us examples. She described, for example, the literate practices of the Vai of Liberia, offering us several new ways of seeing of literacy. These examples encouraged us to inquire, not into literacy's "essence," but into its hows, whys, and wherefores. For purposes of Scribner's analysis, literacy was adaptation to life's functional requirements; it was power with which to transform the conditions of one's life; it was a state of grace, the refinement of human experience in sacred text.

This list of metaphors is not exhaustive. Anthropologist Charles Frake, for example, described to me one community in the Philippines where writing was the primary form of courtship. Young men worked exceedingly hard at their love letters—both their wording and their script. And one need not travel quite so far from home to find other powerful metaphors for literacy. Margaret Finders, for example, sees literacy as the construction of peer group affiliation and identity in the practice of note passing among U.S. adolescents (Finders, 1997). As a parent and former middle school teacher, I was, frankly, relieved. to learn that this was, indeed, a literate practice. We find metaphors for literacy in stories from other unlikely places. LaTour, Woolgar, and Salk's (1986) *Laboratory Life,* for example, depicts literacy as quite literally the process of making knowledge in scientific research.

Scribner urged us to understand literacy interpretively, by examining the metaphors we use when we speak of it. In this way, educators and policy-makers might more insightfully view literacy, not as a unitary content or discrete set of methods, but as an array of forms, functions, practices, and relationships. This insight might foster more locally meaningful and useful curriculum, instruction and assessment. It might also foster greater contact among our world's diversely literate people and practices. Finally, it might reveal our own literate practices as culturally situated. One can see at a glance, then, why literacy researchers and educators need to struggle with the twin concepts of "literacy" and "culture" as they are interwoven and reveal one another. This struggle involves investigating literacy and culture in and through metaphor.

Cultural and the Literate Imagination

"Metaphor," according to Lentriccia and McLaughlin (1990), is thought of by critics as "the master, or central" figure of speech in literature. It can be defined as a "compressed analogy" that involves "a transfer of meaning from the word that properly possesses it to another word which belongs to some shared category of meaning" (p. 83). This transfer of meaning is a powerful process that reveals complexity. Although metaphor is used in its heightened form as a literary figure of speech, we also learn metaphorically in everyday life. This means, as Dewey asserted and as has been revisited in Phillip Jackson's (1998) study of Dewey's aesthetics, that we use metaphor and exercise other powers of the literary imagination as we go about the mundane business of "making sense" in everyday life and as we go about the, perhaps less mundane, business of theorizing. Examples familiar to contemporary literacy researchers and educators would be the instructional "scaffold" and Vygotsky's (1978) "zone" of proximal development—two related metaphors that help us understand and speak about the dynamic process whereby development is supported by and occurs within interactions of more and less knowledgeable others.

Similarly, we use metaphors to capture culture as a complex human process, experience, and characteristic. Prevalent cultural metaphors used by anthropologists conjure up transfer, connection, improvisation, and transformation. (For examples of some metaphors for culture and learning see Anderson-Levitt, 2000; Bruner, 1996; Cole, 1996; Eisnehart, 1995; Geertz, 1983). These are intended to convey the dialectic of culture's conserving meaning while making new meaning possible. To know culture involves both experience and imagination. To know another culturally involves observation and engagement, description and story, other-knowledge and self-knowledge. Thus when we look at anthropologists and their work, for example, we are as likely to see their literary aspirations and pretensions, as we are to see their scientific ones. Ethnography entails imagination—both for the reader and the writer. First of all, an ethnography's author is a "lone ranger" who goes "into the field" and returns to tell the story of what he or she learned there. As such, the ethnographer asks the reader, if not willingly to suspend disbelief, at least to grant him or her some grace. Of this Geertz (1988) says:

> So much of [ethnography] consists in incorrigible assertion. The highly situated nature of ethnographic description—the ethnographer, in this time, in this place, with these informants, these commitments, and these experiences, a representative of a particular culture, a member of a certain class—gives the bulk of what is said a rather take it or leave it quality. (p. 5)

This feature of the ethnography as literature has been both maligned and misunderstood in the past several decades, particularly as ethnography has slipped into the educational research canon. I can vividly recall some two decades ago, for example, a very important educational researcher arriving at the annual meeting of AERA sporting a tee shirt that read, "Real men don't do ethnography." That tee shirt revealed, in my view, a case of mistaken identity. Perhaps this researcher was referring to ethnography's emphasis on description and narrative, what Hymes (1980) refers to as its need for verbal "presentation" of what has been learned by experience in the field (p. 98).

Ethnographies are not the "puff pieces" of social science. Culture is sufficiently hard to know (either one's own experience of it or someone else's) that its description demands literary crafting. We understand it largely in terms of metaphor. Geertz made this observation as he noted that anthropological works tend to be remembered for and cited in terms of who wrote them rather than what the key findings were (Geertz, 1988, p. 8). This, however, does not mean that anthropology lacks criteria for assessing its narratives. Ethnography attempts to illuminate culture in both how it is written and how it is read. There are several ways that the concept of culture is constructed in anthropologists' literate practices. First, ethnography illuminates culture by its textual crafting. It is read critically, not by checking to see if the description offered corresponds to "truth" (presumably yet another description), but with an eye toward the effectiveness of its rhetoric to convey a sense of the author's having been in meaningful contact with others in the setting under study. Much of this rhetorical power rests with the text's coherence as narrative description, in which details "add up" to convey a sense of place, activity, social identity—what anthropologists call local meaning. Thus we read ethnography critically in ways much akin to the critical reading of literature or the experiencing and evaluating of an artistic work.

There is yet another way in which knowledge accrues from ethnographies and in which ethnography, as a genre, is read critically. Anthropologists construct theory in the intertextual reading of multiple ethnographic cases. In this way of reading (and writing) culture, knowledge accrues about general cultural phenomena by looking at varied local particulars. Such reading involves comparison and contrasts across individual cases as they illuminate a more complex whole. In each case, it is important for learners to have access to case descriptions themselves (and not just distillations of "facts" drawn from the cases) and to adopt a critical stance to reading them.

Let us think again about Nell, whom you may recall faked being Polish as a way to complete her assignment. Her education was missing a sense of her life as cultural—in its own terms as well as in its relationship to others' lives and communities. It lacked both texts and contexts for learning about culture. As it currently stands, our curriculum for teacher education does little to help Nell think about culture in her own and others' lives. Research on teachers' learning by researchers such as Zeichner (1993), Paine (1990), and McDiarmid and Price (1990) attest that our curriculum is an exceedingly weak intervention into teacher candidates' thinking about culture. For example, McDiarmid and Price (1990) studied an inservice curriculum on cultural diversity for experienced teachers. They found that both the texts and the means by which they were used to transmit information to teachers about culture encouraged rather than diminished teachers' inclinations to stereotype youngsters on the basis of ethnic and cultural backgrounds.

As much as it involves ethnic food, costume, or holiday practices, cultural identity also involves exploration of subtler aspects of life not typically noted for comment. These include nuances in the styles by which we express ourselves in verbal and nonverbal behavior, family stories echoing across people and generations, and fleeting images of our upbringing in families, neighborhoods, churches, and peer groups. This material is fodder for literary representations of cultural identity. It dominates coming of age narratives as well as immigrant stories of the disorienting and reorienting of self that accompanies movement from one place to another.

Yet, ironically, this is precisely the material framed out of view in academic descriptions of culture. Students of education are rarely taught about culture in terms of searching, evocative questions, and themes. Like the classrooms in which they will teach, their university classes in education are not known, in Harold Rosen's terms, for their "nurture of narrative" (Rosen, 1985). Instead, we teach about teaching—its foundational knowledge and its practices—in decidedly expository ways. Here culture is represented as a static system of knowledge organizing the practices and interpretive frames of a group of people—their idealized "ways of life." This kind of generalized description (e.g., "the Navajo way of life") inevitably stereotypes. It wrings from culture and from individual lives the unique, the particular, the conflictual, and the contradictory. (As an aside, there are times when it is purposeful to use stereotypes to advance, for example, the civil rights of people. But such cases should not be confused with arguing that a "generalized" picture of a group is tantamount to understanding that group's culture, a point that Donna Dehyle has made to me.)

Although done in the spirit of rigorous theorizing about human nature, the rhetorical shift from participant to distanced observer and describer inevitably changes our perspective and hence our text (Pratt, 1986). Relying primarily on generalized description of patterns witnessed in fieldwork, the observer's written report of the field experience as "research" can leave out the detail as well as the drama of the informants' lived experience and also neglect the role of the fieldwork in transforming the researcher's understanding of self and other (Salvio, 1990). Such texts neglect the narrative dimensions of cultural description. Relying on them to learn about culture, teachers are apt to sees others' lives as frozen or lifeless and their own as aloof from cultural forces shaping identity and life chances. This is particularly troublesome in the preparation of literacy educators, since language (both oral and written) is intimately tied to culture. If our understanding of cultural practice is frozen, our understanding of language and literacy development will be as well.

A "Default Mode" for Culture in the Education of Literacy Teachers

Writing about classroom discourse, Courtney Cazden (1988) referred to a default mode in teaching. She observed that, like the default settings in her computer that maintain the characteristics of her printed text, classroom talk is patterned in ways that reproduce the characteristics of oral texts for learning. Teachers ask questions, students respond, teachers evaluate. Questions tend to be testlike, assessing rather than inquiring, and so forth. Each time we turn on the computer the default settings operate, unless we take direct, explicit steps to change them. Likewise, Cazden argued that direct effort is needed to alter the automatic patterns of our teaching so that classroom interactions and the learning possible within them might be changed.

By analogy, we can think of teacher education as having a default mode for teachers' learning about cultural diversity. Teacher educators and U.S. teachers remain at the turn of the century predominantly white, middle class, English speaking, and female (Gay, 1993). Moreover, they are enmeshed in a web of shared knowledge, relationships, and practices historically serving to sustain the profession's status quo (Lortie, 1975). Pre- and in-service curricula tend to reinforce stereotypes, especially when lectures and textbooks are the sole or primary mechanism through which we learn about culture (Duesterberg, 1998). In addition, field experiences, even when they introduce beginners to diverse pupils, rarely offer chances for them to learn from teachers working "against the grain"

(Cochran-Smith, 1991). Even teacher education's contemporary focus on "reflec-tion" tends to strengthen cultural biases if it is not undertaken critically (Dressman, 1998; Smyth, 1992).

Perhaps not surprisingly, then, research finds that beginning teachers cling to two somewhat contradictory explanations for the learning difficulties of di-verse pupils (Paine, 1990). One assumes that the child's intrinsic psychological characteristics determine what is possible for him to learn (e.g., Adam cannot read because he is learning disabled). The second, a cultural explanation, locates re-sponsibility for learning difficulties with the family's culturally patterned child-rearing practices (e.g., Eve could learn to read if her parents were more involved in her schooling). Interestingly, despite the unilateral nature of each explanation, beginning teachers can be observed to speak in terms of both. In each case, the learner's difficulties lie mostly outside the teacher's sphere of influence and are determined by the student's background and the hard wiring of his or her nervous system. The story has already been written.

The cultural explanation is the one we commonly invoke as we attempt to understand the educational difficulties of pupils from racial, ethnic, or language backgrounds different from our own. Following this line of reasoning, differences in background are explanatory of school failure and, as such, are problems rather than resources or even neutral facts of life. There is a wide gulf separating home and school. This gulf is especially difficult to bridge when the child's parents are non–middle class, ethnically or linguistically diverse, or have few years of school-ing. In a painful double bind, the student must become alienated from home and background to succeed in school. Tragically, her or his family must actively sup-port such alienation if school success is to be possible.

One can see at a glance how this cultural explanation (and the assumptions it contains about families' mother tongue, social class, educational levels, and race) serves not to enhance our understanding of others, but to sustain lowered educa-tional expectations for those who are different from ourselves (an insight for which I am indebted to Patricia Edwards). We should recognize that this is but one possible metaphor or narrative trope we might use to interpret cultural experience. Yet this image of culture has become so deeply a part of our collective conscious-ness that it assumes the force of "the truth," and we lose awareness of it as a social and linguistic construction. In short, it comes to shape our experience (Emihovich, 1995; Lakoff & Johnson, 1980).

Many versions of this yarn have been spun in research and in the "common sense" of U.S. educational practice. The image of the child crossing the border from home to school touches us, leveling across a wide range of experiences of loss and change. This image is described in Richard Rodriguez's (1982) educa-tional autobiography, *Hunger of Memory.* Poring over books for his dissertation research in the British Museum, he discovered the trope of the "scholarship boy" in the work of Richard Hoggart. To succeed in school, this boy, "must move between environments, his home and the classroom, which are at cultural ex-tremes, opposed" (Rodriguez, 1982, p. 46). Finding this image in print, Rodriguez experiences self-recognition and a sense that he has not been alone in the feelings of alienation that have accompanied his educational progress and success.

Since, to some extent, we all "leave home" and enter a public world, most teachers can embrace the image of "the scholarship boy," without examining inequality. Readable as both "us" and "them," this trope appears in status quo educational discourse (e.g., kindergarten "round up," school readiness screening) and also in the language of reforms intended to assist diverse youngsters' entry into the school environment (e.g., "mainstreaming," "inclusion"). There are strong reasons why the image pervades educational discourse in the United States. It evokes the romantic, democratic idea of public education as the "balance wheel" rendering outside school experience less important in the determination of a person's futures than his or her education. This value is evident in the writings of founders of education, especially Horace Mann (cited in Gover, 1999) and Cubberly (cited in Sleeter & Grant, 1993). For better and worse, the student's cultural and linguistic background is explicitly framed out of the picture in the pursuit of individual academic achievement and the goals of an educated populace capable of and disposed to sustaining democracy.

However, this trope limits possibilities even as it aims to offer them. This sweeping rendition of going to school, in Kailin's (1999) words, "look(s) at the world from the top down" (p. 81). The omniscient narrator describes the movement of the protagonist between separate, unquestioned worlds. Educational studies of home and school reify this view of culture, as do published memoirs of schooling written for white, middle-class audiences (Florio-Ruane & McVee, 2000). Thus it pervades and reinforces our limiting assumptions about school even as we aim to make education more "accessible." Fredrick Erickson suggests that like the Procrustean Bed, on which occupants wre stretched or cut to fit, school is entered rather than made by its participatns, Of these participants, it is students who are expected to change to fit. Only rarely, and recently, have authors begun to challenge the conventions of this trope, especially its one-dimensional views of home, school, and identity (e.g., Anderson-Levitt, 2000; Lionnet, 1989).

Toward Transformative Texts and Contexts for Understanding Culture

Mary McVee (1999) found in research on the stories young teachers tell about culture that a few master narratives dominate. These are retold and heard uncritically as beginners confront cultural diversity in the classroom. Looking neither inward nor outward for other stories, these appear to suffice—at least in the short run. But teacher candidates ultimately feel isolated and quite literally helpless when their initial attempts at instructing diverse pupils meet with misunderstanding or resistance. Thus a cycle is begun in which, despite or perhaps in virtue of their contact with pupils from diverse backgrounds, teachers experience a hardening sense of the difference between "us" and "them."

Banks (1993) critiques both academic and personal sources of knowledge such as those described above because they offer at best a partial vision of cultural knowledge and, at worst, a distorted, interest-driven one. He argues for a curriculum in which students—and teachers—can learn about culture by means of "transformative" academic texts. These are, in Banks's words, "facts, concepts, paradigms, themes, and explanations that challenge mainstream academic knowledge and expand and substantially revise established canons, paradigms, theories, explanations, and research methods" (p. 7). A hallmark of such a curriculum is its reflexive character, its acknowledgement that cultural study is inevitably partial, interest driven, and value laden.

In U.S. public education of the twentieth century, the lion's share of effort was expended, not to study culture, but to make a well-socialized electorate and workforce. As participants in this socializing mission, pupils and teachers alike experience in school what Barrera referred to as a "culturalectomy" (Jiménez, Moll, Rodriguez-Brown, & Barrera, 1999, p. 217, cited in Walker & MacGillivray, 1999). Educational "culturalectomy" is most clearly visible in the experiences of students of color and those who speak a first language other than English. They rarely find their images reflected in the texts and contexts of school. Some—such as the participants in the "Anthropology at the Crossroads" discussion sponsored by the American Educational Studies Association in November 1999—would elaborate on this metaphor, arguing that what actually happens in school is not only an "ectomy" of one's home culture, but also a "transplant" of mainstream, or what some scholars of color have called "whitestream," cultural values and practices.

School's detachment from culture is also the experience of the descendants of European immigrants. Their collective identity as "white" frames them, not culturally, historically, or economically or even in terms of gender. Rather their identity is constructed racially—with "whiteness" being the normal or unmarked cultural form. As the unmarked form, it seems to require no further reflection or exploration. Nor does it flag a system of identity and identification that rests on oppositions, usually between unequals. Thus the denial of culture in education precludes an historical, contextual analysis that might help us examine how we became the teachers we are—that is, how our histories shape our practices, assumptions, and expectations.

When, for example, I ask my students to write vignettes of their cultural experience as literacy learners, they are usually nonplussed. "I don't have a story," they say. "I'm not anything." Responses like these lack a sense of history or place. The normal or "unmarked" form is the bland, commonsense one. It is the water the fish would be the last to discover. By that designation, it marks the alternative as, perhaps colorful, but also abnormal, nonmainstream. Lack of cultural understanding reinforces these teachers' sense of "us" as normal (mainstream, white or colorless) and "them" as abnormal (minority, of color, nonnative speaking). Yet implicitly the unmarked form is defined in its relationship to the marked form. To be "not anything" is to forget or fail to notice that we are enmeshed in systems in which oppositions are used to define self and other (Frankenberg, 1993; Morrison, 1994). This makes it impossible to remember or notice our forbears' experience of being "outside," the privileged positions we may now occupy, or the access to privilege that is conferred on some and denied to others.

To the extent that European immigrants and their descendants have learned to conflate being "American" with being "white," they participate in the exclusion of non-European immigrants and their descendants from full membership in the national community (Alba, 1990). For this reason, scholars such as Lisa Delpit urge cultural self-study, especially for teachers who will serve as gatekeepers to participation in the wider society. She writes in this regard, "it is vital that teachers and teacher educators explore their own beliefs and attitudes about non-white and non-middle-class people" (1995, p. 179). Yet many if not most teachers believe precisely the opposite. Assuming that it is impolite, even racist, to notice and talk about race, teachers assume they are expected to be "colorblind."

The white teacher's neutrality about race or ethnicity is thought to be fair and a part of offering each pupil the same educational experiences from which to rise or fall on his or her own merit (Ferdman, 1990; Paley, 1979/89). Teachers work toward creating a "level playing field" where all children are treated as if they are the same. Yet to deny racial, linguistic, cultural, and economic background is not to treat all children equally but to retreat from the awareness that differences do make a difference in school, especially as they confer or deny privilege and power. McIntyre (1997) observes that denial of difference has "implications for teaching practice—which include such things as the choice of curriculum materials, student expectations, grading procedures, and assessment techniques—just to name a few" (pp. 14–15). Teachers are an important part of the equation, not neutral observers dismissing, with what Toni Morrison (1992) calls the "generous liberal gesture," inequalities in school and society (pp. 9–10).

Culture, as a static state is not very interesting to teachers. It is rarely integrated with study of children's development. Nor is it studied within the history of schools, conceptions of school improvement and change, or the dynamics of classroom instruction. Finally, culture is often taken out of context, pushed to the margins in a course or two on the foundations of education, typically just prior to or upon completion of the methods courses and field experiences. "Foundation" is an ambiguous metaphor—it is both the underlying strength and structure of a building and also its cellar. Like cellars, literacy teachers often experience their visits to the foundations of education like visiting a dark, musty, basement that is easily ignored as we tend to our busy lives "upstairs." Marginalized this way, culture is not a meaningful, coherent part of what literacy teachers need to understand in order to teach well.

In order to create a profession more reflective of the strengths of our population's history and diversity, we need to transform the texts and contexts of teachers' learning to include multiple voices and stories of culture, literacy, and education. Gazing both inward and outward, and in dialogue with others, we might thus uncover culture not as trait by which to label others, but as a shared human experience of making meaning. Such a process would take, in McHenry's (1997) words, "a conscious step away from the position of contemplation, or observation (of) the student (as) 'separated object'" (p. 349). This change in the curriculum for teacher education would entail a shift of culture from peripheral to central in teachers' thinking about literacy and learning. In so doing, culture would not be defined in its default mode—rather, its meanings would be open to inquiry and discovery. Deborah Meier (1995) calls this "the kind of mental paradigm shift, the 'aha' that is at the heart of learning, [and that] usually requires more than being told by an authority or shown a demonstration" (cited in McHenry, 1997, p. 349).

Vivian Paley exemplifies this kind of "aha" at the heart of learning in *White Teacher*, the book with which this review began. In one vignette, Paley tells of a disturbing discovery in her teaching: the expectations she holds for the white students in her class are higher than those she holds for the black students. (Since Paley used the terms "white" and "black" in her book to refer to those of Caucasian or African American heritage, I have done likewise when paraphrasing her writing.) This discovery brings Paley up short, and she reflects upon her own life as she teaches and observes her pupils. Paley soon realizes that her problem is even more complex than she initially thought: she holds higher expectations for the children of more affluent and highly educated black parents than she does for their counterparts from less educated and affluent homes. As she speculates that her bias may depend on both economic and racial characteristics, Paley sets out to know her students better. In the process, she is surprised also to learn about herself.

Paley's Story

As described in *White Teacher*, Vivian Paley notices a pattern in which the less affluent black girls in her class more frequently use what she calls "ethnic speech" than do their higher achieving, more affluent counterparts. Unexpectedly, Paley learns that one of her struggling black students, Kathy, has a high-achieving older sister in another classroom, Paley reconsiders her low expectations of Kathy, wondering what she may be missing in her interactions with the youngster. Paley decides to engage Kathy in longer conversations. As she talks with Kathy and her friend Charlene, she notices that the girls shift in style from the Black English Vernacular to what Paley calls "middle class school speech." Paley (1979/89) reports:

> I began to realize that many of the black children regularly used different speech patterns when playing with each other and when playing with white children or teachers. They moved in and out of this speech with ease. They had no problems here. *I* had the problem. Actually, I made the same sort of instant transformation with certain Jewish friends. The Yiddish expressions would appear, the inflections, the broken English of the immigrant, all of which resulted in good feelings and frequent laughter. (pp. 28–29)

Yet Paley recollects that not all her Jewish friends received so much pleasure from speaking Yiddish either among themselves or in contact with non-Jewish people. Paley admits that even she, who enjoys the cadence and comfort of Yiddish among Jewish family and friends was, like some of her black students, reluctant to use a private way of speaking in a public setting such as school. She considers that while some of her black students are comfortable using both vernacular and school appropriate speech styles in her classroom, others may be carefully avoiding using ethnic speech styles "in front of a white teacher." She connects the sense her own students are making to her own experience noting:

> As a child, I would never have wished to draw attention to my differences before a non-Jewish teacher. It may seem that I am overdoing my comparison of Jewish feelings and black feelings. But I am talking about feeling different. Perhaps coming to terms with one kind of difference prepares a person for all kinds of differences. At least this is the way it was for me. (Paley, 1979/89, p. 29)

This insight involves not only Paley's observation of her interactions with Kathy, but also her exercise of what anthropologist Michael Fischer (1986) calls "the arts of memory" (p. 194). Early in her book, Paley remembers feeling like an outsider when she was a pupil, despite her mother's repeated insistence that she need not feel this way since there were many other Jewish youngsters in Paley's class and school. Contrasting public and private, Paley does not speak of "minority/majority" distinctions so much as feelings of being an "insider" or an "outsider" to a social system. She therefore is able to focus our attention on the effects that racial and ethnic prejudices might have on an individual speaker's choices for how to express her ideas in a public, institutional setting. When Paley suspends ordinary teacher judgment and adopts a stance of inquiry toward her own and others' lives, she realizes that there is no particular vice or virtue associated with shifting speech styles or preferring not to. Yet although speech style is not an index of students' potential to learn, there are profound consequences for what the teacher makes of the speech behaviors of her students. Paley reasons from the case of Kathy that it is inappropriate and potentially damaging to equate students' preferences for style shifting to their ability to learn in school. Paley learns, and teaches us by her narrative, that the issue of difference—and how both pupils and teachers come to terms with it—lies at the heart of her teaching problem. Discovering that, like Kathy, she is also subject to feeling different and making decisions about how to speak on that basis, Paley makes a connection with Kathy that is new and educationally generative.

Paley raises difficult issues of racial, ethnic, and social class bias in the modest form of a teaching experience retold as a highly crafted narrative vignette. In it she shows us the subtle sociolinguistic adjustments youngsters are expected to make when they leave the private realm of home and family and present themselves in the publicly evaluative realm of the school. She also exposes the damaging consequences of a teacher's unexamined prejudices. Most disturbingly she shows us that even a teacher who has herself experienced feeling like an "outsider" in school can unwittingly hold such biases and project them into the very fabric of her relationships with her students.

In both style and substance, Paley's inquiry breaks the ordinary frame of her (and our) teacher thinking. Adopting the stance of a narrator investigating herself and her students, she does not objectify Kathy or her friend as "others," distanced from the teacher and subject to her judgment. Instead, she makes herself as vulnerable to scrutiny as they have been. Paley draws closer to them even as she considers what differentiates them from herself. Of this experience she says, "it is becoming clear why my experiences with black children have meant so much to me. I have identified with them in the role of the outsider" (Paley, 1979/89, p. 139).

This is more than a good story. Or perhaps it reveals the essence of what good stories can do. In Lee Galda's (1998) words, good literature offers us both "mirrors and windows." Knowledge about others and ourselves is attainable by means of our imaginative engagement with literature.

Paley's writing challenges a tendency in both social science and teacher education to place others at a distance in order to understand them—an act which ironically alienates us from both their experiences and our own. According to Cazden and Mehan (1989) this practice conveys to teachers that we have understood others simply because we have talked about them. They quote Landes (1965) in this regard who asserts:

> Heavy use of this prime tool can fail educators in their goal of attuning instruction to actual processes of learning. This happens when educators talk more *about pupils* than with them and their families. Separateness from the objects of discussion forfeits the experiences words should mirror. (Landes, 1965, p. 64, in Cazden & Mehan, 1989, emphasis added)

Cazden and Mehan note in this regard that books like *White Teacher* offer an alternative to talking about others as a way to understand them. They argue that it is more important for teachers to adopt an inquiring stance toward the cultural experience of the students they meet than to study lists of characteristics of ethnic groups (1989, p. 55). This is a tall order, and considering it stretches our thinking about culture and teacher education.

Transformative Views of Culture for Education:
Thirteen Ways of Looking at a Blackbird

Following Wittgenstein (1953), psychologist Rand Spiro and his associates (1990, 1993/95) have described this kind of learning with the metaphor of the "criss-cross landscape." They theorize that people learn complex concepts and practices not as simple, linear content mastered once and for all and to be applied in new settings, but flexibly and by repeated examination of rich cases. This learning is, in Spiro et al.'s (1993/95) words, "a nonlinear traversal of complex subject matter, returning to the same place in the conceptual landscape on different occasions coming from different directions" (p. 10). It is transformative in that it forces prior, tacit knowledge into the light and changes its nature and content as new cases are encountered. This kind of learning prepares us to solve new and novel problems.

Because flexibility is key to understanding, it is important, in Spiro and Jehng's (1990) words to "use *multiple representations* for advanced knowledge acquisition in ill-structured domains" (p. 175). In this way, a learner investigates two kinds of complexity: (a) each case has sufficient resonance to enable multiple rereadings or revisiting to access the knowledge it represents; and (b) the multiple cases are overlapping, not a set of subtypes of a concept's meaning, but instances of a concept "in use."

Culture is one such complex concept that might be learned by literacy teachers in the ill-structured domain of their practice. It is therefore important for the curriculum of teacher education to examine and re-examine representations of culture—not only canonical ones, but less likely ones, some more distant, others so close to home as to go unnoticed. Thus teachers might continuously explore their own and others' lives as a fundamental part of honing their craft. This idea would radically alter our assumptions about how best to learn about culture for teaching. And it would greatly enrich the questions, images, and genres with which we might explore education in general and literacy education in particular.

I suppose that by now you are wondering what all this has to do with blackbirds. Like the blackbird, culture is at once so ordinary as to go unnoticed and so important as to be idealized. What does culture mean to those who theorize and practice literacy education? Even scholars whose work requires precise definitions can only understand culture indirectly. Scholars employ a profusion of metaphors to envision culture: webs, maps, weavings, artifacts, activities, patterns, schemata, and so forth. As Wallace Stevens (1964) described in the poem, "Thirteen Ways of Looking at a Blackbird," when I think about culture I find myself "of three minds, /Like a tree/ In which there are three blackbirds" (all quotes from Hieatt & Park, 1964, pp. 557–558).

As the stuff of theory, our efforts to fix a definition of culture not only idealize, but frequently also polarize. The tension between the Aristotelian ideal and the scattered examples we encounter was captured in Stevens's poem. Its 13 loosely associated stanzas do not describe "the blackbird" as a stuffed museum piece or taxonomic category. Instead, in ways reminiscent of a Zen koan or of Haiku's terse nature imagery and clipped rhythms, each is a "kernel"' or a "snapshot" of one or several blackbirds in their everyday lives and settings. Some of the stanzas hint at the blackbird's wildness, some at its simplicity of form. Some suggest its great power or its association with danger. Blackbirds thrive in harsh conditions. They can easily cover more ground than the human observer, can even see ("When the blackbird flew out of sight, /It marked the edge/ Of one of many circles.").

Still, ironically, human beings overlook blackbirds and assume dominion over them, the Biblical imperative to name them. Yet naming neither grants power over blackbirds nor confers knowledge of them. Rather, Stevens says, "The blackbird is involved/ In what I know." Moreover, the blackbird is easily missed perhaps disregarded as ordinary, missed from our limited viewpoint or actively avoided as trivial—or menacing. Stevens writes, for example, that "At the sight of blackbirds/ Flying in green light, /Even the bawds of euphony/ Would cry out sharply." Stevens wonders why we do not notice the blackbirds in our midst. He asks, "0 thin men of Haddam, /Why do you image golden birds? /Do you not see how the blackbird/Walks around the feet/Of the women about you?" People are portrayed as "thin men" from Haddam, notable in Stevens's footnote as a place where metal products are made. Riding around in glass coaches, the people of Haddam seem effete, isolated, vulnerable, and afraid to step out into nature. They are focused on creating "golden birds"; the "gold" standard of the idealized blackbird—a taxonomic category. But a bird of gold is a frozen, lifeless copy of the real thing.

In trying to fix the essence of "blackbirdness," we can fail to see and know blackbirds and their power. And because, as Stevens writes, "A man and a woman are one. / A man and a woman and a blackbird are one," by failing to know blackbirds, we also fail to know aspects of ourselves. Like the blackbird of Stevens's poem, it is easy to miss "culture" in our own and others' everyday language and literate practices. Instead, as professional educators, we are pressed, repeating Scribner's words, "to grasp and explain" the essence of literacy or of culture or of learning. Yet, as both the artist and the cultural psychologist show us in their examples, if we look only upward toward a golden bird or "grand theory," when we think about culture, language, or literacy education, we will fail to notice the ordinary human literate motives and practices incessantly "at our feet." To learn about culture for literacy education, as to learn about blackbirds, we need to listen closely and look carefully. If we do not step out of our glass coach and attentively criss-cross the landscape, we will miss the very object of our inquiry— the diversity and complexity of literacy and culture in education.

Author Note

This work was supported, in part, by the Educational Research and Development Centers Program, PR/Award No. R305R70004, as administered by the Office of Educational Research and Improvement, U.S. Department of Education. The comments do not necessarily represent the policies of the National Institute of Early Childhood Development or the U.S. Department of Education. I wish to thank Taffy Raphael, Andrew Topper, Rand Spiro, Jennifer Berne, Jo Lesser, Katie Anderson-Levitt, Kathryn Au, and the students of the Michigan State University Literacy Master's Proseminar for their contributions to my thinking as I developed the paper.

References

Alba, R. D. (1990). *Ethnic identity: The transformation of white America.* New Haven, CT: Yale University Press.

Anderson-Levitt, K. *(2000). Teaching cultures: Knowledge for teaching first grade in France and the United States.* New York: Hampton.

Banks, J. A. (1993). The canon debate, knowledge construction, and multicultural education. *Educational Researcher, June-July,* 4–14.

Bruner, J. (1996). *The culture of education.* Cambridge, MA: Harvard University Press.

Cazden, C. B. (1988). *Classroom discourse.* Portsmouth, NH: Heinemann.

Cazden, C. B., & Mehan, H. B. (1989). Principles from sociology and anthropology: Context, code, and classroom. In M. Reynolds (Ed.), *Knowledge base for the beginning teacher* (pp. 47–57). Oxford, England: Pergamon.

Cochran-Smith, M. (1991). Learning to teach against the grain. *Harvard Educational Review, 6,* 279–310,

Cole, M. (1996). *Cultural psychology: A once and future discipline.* Cambridge, MA: Harvard University Press.

Cubberly, E. P. (1909). *Changing conceptions of education.* Boston: Macmillan.

Delpit, L. (1995). *Other people's children: Cultural conflict in the classroom.* New York: New Press.

Dressman, M. (1998). Confessions of a methods fetishist: Or, the cultural politics of reflective nonengagement. In R. C. Chavez & J. O'Donnell (Eds.), *Speaking the unpleasant: The politics of (non) engagement in the multicultural terrain* (pp. 108–126). Albany, NY: SUNY Press.

Duesterberg, L. M. (1998). Rethinking culture in the pedagogy and practices of preservice teachers. *Teaching and Teacher Education, 14,* 497–512.

Eisenhart, M. (1995). The fax, the jazz player, and the self-story teller: How do people organize culture? *Anthropology and Education Quarterly, 26,* 3–26.

Emihovich, C. (1995). Distancing passion: Narratives in social science. In J. A. Hatch & R. Wisniewski (Eds.), *Life history and narrative* (pp. 37–48). London: Falmer.

Erickson, F. (1986). Qualitative research. In M. C. Wittrock (Ed.), *Handbook of research on teaching* (3rd ed., pp. 119–161). New York: Macmillan.

Ferdman, B. (May, 1990). Literacy and cultural identity. In M. K. Minami & B. P. Kennedy (Eds.), *Language issues in literacy and bilingual/multicultural education* (pp. 347–371). Cambridge, MA: *Harvard Educational Review* Reprint Series No. 22.

Finders, M. (1997). *Just girls: Hidden literacies and life in junior high.* New York: Teachers College Press.

Firman, C., & Swanson, J. D. (2000). *Accelerating the learning of all students: Cultivating culture change in schools, classrooms, and individuals.* Boulder: Westview.

Fischer, M. (1986). Ethnicity and the post-modern arts of memory. In J. Clifford & G. E. Marcus (Eds.), *Writing culture.* Berkeley: University of California Press.

Florio-Ruane, S., & McVee, M. (2000). Ethnographic approaches to literacy research. In M. L. Kamil, R. Barr, P. D. Pearson, & P. Mosenthal (Eds.), *Handbook of reading research* (3rd ed., pp. 153–162). Mahwah, NJ: Erlbaum.

Frankenberg, R. (1993). *White women race matters: The social construction of whiteness.* Minneapolis: University of Minnesota Press.

Galda, L. (1998). Mirrors and windows: Reading as transformation. In T. E. Raphael & K. H. Au (Eds.), *Literature-based instruction: Reshaping the curriculum* (pp. 1–12). Norwood: Christopher-Gordon.

Gay, G. (1993). Building cultural bridges: A bold proposal for teacher education. *Education and Urban Society, 25,* 285–299.

Geertz, C. (1983). *Local knowledge: Further essays in interpretive anthropology.* New York: Basic.

Geertz, C. (1988). *Works and lives: The anthropologist as author.* Stanford, CA: Stanford University Press.

Gover, M. (1999). *Identity is a verb: Transition, learning, and becoming.* Unpublished manuscript.

Hieatt, A. K., & Park, W. (1964). *The college anthology of British and American verse.* Boston: Allyn & Bacon.

Hymes, D. (1980). *Language in education: Ethnolinguistic essays.* Washington, DC: Center for Applied Linguistics.

Jackson, P. W. (1998). *John Dewey and the lessons of art.* New Haven, CT: Yale University Press

Jiménez, R., Moll, L., Rodriguez-Brown, F., & Barrera, R. (1999). Conversations: Latina and Latino researchers interact on issues related to literacy learning. *Reading Research Quarterly, 34,* 217–230.

Kailin, J. (1999). Preparing urban teachers for schools and communities: Anti-racist perspectives. *High School Journal,* 81–87.

Lakoff, G., & Johnson, M. (1980). *Metaphors we live by.* Chicago: University of Chicago Press.

Landes, R. (1965). *Culture in American education: Anthropological approaches to minority and dominant groups in the schools.* New York: Wiley.

LaTour, B., Woolgar, S., & Salk, J. (1986). *Laboratory life.* Princeton, NJ: Princeton University Press.

Lentriccia, F., & McLaughlin, T. (Eds.). (1990).*Critical terms for literary study.* Chicago: University of Chicago Press.

Lionnet, F. (1989). *Autobiographical voices: Race, gender, self-portraiture.* Ithaca, NY: Cornell University Press.

Lortie, D. C. (1975). *School teacher: A sociological study.* Chicago: University of Chicago Press.

McDiarmid, G. W., & Price, J. (1990). *Prospective teachers' views of diverse learners: A study of participants in the ABCD project* (Tech. Rep. No. 90-6). East Lansing: Michigan State University National Center for Research on Teacher Education.

McHenry, H. D. (1997). Education as encounter: Buber's pragmatic ontololgy. *Educational Theory, 47,* 341–357.

McIntyre, A. (1997). *Making meaning of whiteness: Exploring racial identity with white teachers.* Albany, NY: SUNY Press.

McVee, M. B. (1999). *Narrative and the exploration of culture Self, and other in teacher's book club discussion groups.* Unpublished doctoral dissertation. East Lansing: Michigan State University.

Meier, D. (1995). *The power of their ideas: Lessons for America from a small school in Harlem.* Boston: Beacon.

Morrison, T. (1994). *The Nobel lecture in literature: 1993.* New York: Knopf.

Morrison, T. (1992). *Playing in the dark: Whiteness and the literary imagination.* New York: Vintage.

Paine, L. (1990). *Orientation towards diversity: What do prospective teachers bring?* (Research Rep. No. 89-9). East Lansing: Michigan State University National Center for Research on Teacher Education.

Paley, V. G. (1979/89). *White teacher.* Cambridge, MA: Harvard University Press.

Pratt, M. L. (1986). Fieldwork in common places. In J. Clifford & G. E. Marcus (Eds.), *Writing culture: The poetics and politics of ethnography* (pp. 27–50). Berkeley: University of California Press.

Rodriguez, R. (1982). *Hunger of memory: The education of Richard Rodriguez.* New York: Bantam.

Rosen, H. (1985). The autobiographical impulse. In D. Tannen (Ed.), *Linguistics in context: Connecting observation and understanding* (Vol. 29, pp. 69–88). Norwood, NJ: Ablex.

Salvio, P. M. (1990). Transgressive daughters: Student autobiography and the project of self-creation. *Cambridge Journal of Education, 2,* 283–289.

Scribner, S. (1984). Literacy in three metaphors, *American Journal of Education, 93,* 7–22.

Sleeter, C., & Grant, C. (1993). *Making choices for multicultural education: Five approaches to race, class, and gender.* New York: Macmillan.

Smyth, J. (1992). Teachers' work and the politics of reflection. *American Educational Research Journal, 29,* 267–300.

Spiro, R. J., Feltovich, P. J., Jacobson, M. I., & Coulson, R. L. (1993/95). *Cognitive flexibility, constructivism, and hypertext: Random access instruction for advanced knowledge in ill-structured domains.* Urbana, IL: Institute for Learning Technologies.

Spiro, R. J., & Jehng, J. C. (1990). Cognitive flexibility, random access instruction, and hypertext: Theory and technology for the nonlinear and multidimensional traversal of complex subject matter. In D. Nix & R. J. Spiro (Eds.), *Cognition, education, and multimedia* (pp. 163–205). Hillsdale, NJ: Erlbaum.

Stevens, W. (1964). Thirteen ways of looking at a blackbird. In A. K. Hieatt & W. Park (Eds.), *The college anthology of British and American verse* (pp. 557–559). Boston: Allyn & Bacon.

Vygotsky, L. S. (1978). *Mind in society: The development of higher psychological processes.* Cambridge, MA: Harvard University Press.

Walker, N. T., & MacGillivray, L. (1999). *Latina teachers negotiating higher education* (CIERA Research Report). Ann Arbor, MI: Center for Improvement of Early Reading Achievement.

Wittgenstein, L. (1953). *Philosophical investigations* (3rd ed.). (G. E. M. Anscombe, Trans.). New York: Macmillan.

Zeichner, K. (1993). *Education teachers for cultural diversity* (NCRTL Technical Report). East Lansing: Michigan State University.

Reading for Possible Worlds

Jerome Bruner
New York University

I have always been fascinated with the various means available to our species for "going beyond the information given," of making interpretive leaps into possible worlds. Reading a text is, of course, one of the most celebrated ways of making such leaps: a few words on a printed page, an interesting reading, and we are off with hardly any here-and-now to constrain us. But there are many other ways of making leaps beyond the given, even without a written-down text, even when reading in the literal sense is not involved. And I shall want to explore some of them, for I think "text reading" has a long developmental background, one that gives us many hints about what is involved in "good" or "deep" reading—which is mainly what concerns me. Let me confess at the start that reading, for me, is a bit like decoding a message in a bottle you have come upon that has been washed up on the beach. You need a sense of human predicaments to be a good decoder of messages-in-washed-up-bottles. I will have more to say about this later in this essay.

But some will object immediately that it is just this out-of-contextness of written texts that makes reading so difficult for the beginner. No cues or clues as to what it is about, and that is what throws the beginning reader for a loop. But is that really so? Or is it, rather, that we have not given a would-be reader enough opportunity to learn his or her powers at going beyond the bare, decontextualized text to the possible worlds that lie beyond it? But hold on. I think I am going too fast, so let me back up a little and fill in a little.

I want to turn first to something I like to call "scaffolding." Some years ago, David Wood, Gail Ross, and I wrote a paper on the role of scaffolding in early learning (Wood, Bruner, & Ross, 1976). We chose as our medium how children learned to build increasingly elaborate structures with simple wooden blocks, and observed how parents helped their children in their construction efforts. Scaffolding consisted, to put it abstractly first, in reducing the number of degrees of freedom that a child has to cope with in getting blocks to stand on top of or across or leaning on or balanced on each other in the process of construction—getting kids past the troubles they experience getting their block constructions to stand up on their own. What struck us was the skills that parents had in doing just that—not too much help to rob the child of his or her own initiative, and not too little so that a child got frustrated by failure. What they did was very much like what parents do matching the grammatical complexities of their own speech to their children's level of grammatical competence—talking just at or just slightly

National Reading Conference Yearbook, 49, pp. 31–40.

above the level a child was at, neither too babyish nor too grown up (Brown, Cazden, & Bellgui, 1969; Cazden, 1965; McNeill, 1970). It is this sensitivity to matching that underlies all successful apprentice training (Snow & Ferguson, 1977). And it is this that is at the heart of what I am calling *scaffolding*.

So how do we extend this idea of scaffolding to teaching reading comprehension? Note that I am purposely avoiding classic controversies about the raw mechanics of decoding printed symbols into sound, questions like whether it is phonics or whole-word reading. These are obviously important and difficult questions, thought I confess I was long ago converted into an opportunist by Jeanne Chall who convinced me that there were many ways of helping a beginning reader over that first hurdle (Chall, 1967). My concern, rather, is with reading as *comprehending a text*, grasping what it is *about*, becoming a deeper reader and surer traveler beyond the information given.

I want to concentrate on two kinds of scaffolding. One of them is prior to though essential to proper reading. It concerns how we help kids convert oral language into what I shall dare to call "text," text without benefit of print. For there is ample evidence that such a process is a crucial precondition or prolegomenon to dealing effectively with printed text once the child gets to it. But I also want to discuss how, once "bare" print reading begins, kids can be scaffolded to read more deeply what is before them in print—can begin decoding messages in that washed up bottle. This second form of scaffolding derives, interestingly enough, from the child's precocious knowledge of narrative forms.

Let me begin with the second of these. One of the things we surely know is that children know—indeed, know precociously—an extraordinary amount about narrative, its nature and structure, its requirements, its tempting variety. As Joan Lucariello and I argued, discussing the recorded after-being-put-to bed soliloquies of the irrepressible Emmy, is that Emmy by her third birthday was not only well launched into story telling about her daily doings, but even deep into surmises about the proper narrative form for the telling of her experiences of the day: who had done what to whom, why, what possibilities had been foregone, what resulted, what could be done about it (Bruner & Lucariello, 1989). She even concluded, after her first airplane flight, that you had to have luggage to travel on an airplane! Her acquisition of grammatical forms, we suggested, seemed to be driven by her need to get her narratives "right," her way of thinking about things "appropriate" to the occasion (for further elaboration of this point see Bruner, 1991). She filled yards of tape in the recording machine under her bed with the most extraordinary and inventive texts: like the breath-taking use of the timeless present in her out-of-the-blue announcement: "On Sunday we have pancakes." She was plainly shaping her world into narrative structures.

But one must not think of "narrative" as some sort of add-on either to thought or to language. I want to propose, rather, that it expresses the very form of thinking that human beings use for representing human happenings in the intersubjective world characteristic of human cultural adaptation. It is how we make subjective sense of the acts of those with whom we interact—and particularly how we make sense of the shortcomings inherent in our reliance on this human intersubjectivity: the disappointments and wrong guesses we make, the incompletnesses, the failures of things to live up to expectation. Narrative is the shape of being human, fragile though it may be.

But I must take a step even further back. It is now widely appreciated that a necessary condition for human culture is that human beings not only attribute or "recognize" mental states in each other—beliefs, intentions, desires, and the like—but also that they be able to make their own mental states comprehensible to others, even negotiable. Many argue, indeed, that it was this leap forward into negotiable intersubjectivity that made possible the lightning-swift elaboration of semiotic culture in the scant quarter to half-million years since the appearance of *homo sapiens.*

Ontogenetically, we human beings enter into intersubjective sharing right from the start. By 5 or 6 months of age, kids follow an adult's line of regard when the adult turns her gaze outward, and if they find nothing to fix on out there, they turn back to check again where the adult is looking. And very soon afterwards, toward the eighth month, kids begin pointing (the point typically directed to either a strange object in a familiar context or a familiar object in a new one, a matter we will return to presently). Indeed, the kid not only points at that something, but looks back to see whether you "got the message." And after a while, it is not all about the here and now either. Pretending is so reliably human that we now even use its early absence for diagnosing autism.

In a recent book, Michael Tomasello (1999) sums up a widely shared view among paleo-anthropologists when he says that the leap forward of *homo sapiens* was "made possible by a very special form of social cognition, namely, the ability of the individual organism to understand conspecifics as being *like herself* [and] who have an intentional and mental life like herself." I want to propose that this deep, primitive form of human cognition is captured linguistically in the form of narrative. But I had better spell out what that knowledge consists of first. I have to do so in two ways: one is, as it were, a structural way with no arrow of time to it; the other rides athwart the arrow of time, almost defines its personalness.

First the timeless way. Any narrative, like the famous Pentad of Kenneth Burke (1969), requires an Agent, an Action, a Goal, a Means for bringing it all off, and a Setting that constrains what can take place. But that is only the background, what Schank and Abelson refer to as a script—one of those usual things like going to a restaurant, or taking an airplane with the necessary luggage, and so on. What provides the engine to narrative, as Burke long ago noted, is Trouble in the works: some imbalance in the Pentad, some glitch: this Agent and that Action do not fit; or that Action does not belong in this Setting. But that is too abstract and structural. I need a livelier way of characterizing Trouble. So let me shift to the second, the one that rides on the arrow of time.

On this view (based on William Labov's pioneering ideas), a narrative begins with the evocation of a normal, to-be-expected steady state of things. Then, somehow, the canonical expectability of things is violated, upset, put awry. This upset—Aristotle in the Poetics refers to it as the *peripéteia,* although I like the

French *bouleversement* better—this upset then evokes a line of action that either restores or fails to restore the expectable state with which the story began. Stories end with some sort of more or less implicit evaluation of how it came out, and thereby return us to the here and now in which the story is being told.

Please note, by the way, that I have thus far glossed over the very warrant for *telling* a story: that something went wrong, something upset the expectable. Children know and we know what gives a story its point. It is the same thing that gives a point its point, as we have already noted. Something happened that violates expectability—trouble or would-be trouble. According to Peggy Miller's (1982) classic study, children in their preschool years hear and/or tell narratives on average at the rate of about seven an hour. There is a lot of unexpectedness in the world to be told about. Small wonder that our nervous systems are specialized, through the ascending reticular system, to be activated by the unexpected.

So suppose you made the radical decision that you were not only going to have kids tell stories on their own, but let them discuss together the stories they each told. Do they know stories like that? What else could have happened? And so on and so on. I can tell you from my experience with 5-year-olds in the Reggio Emilia preschools, that they love that kind of "close reading" discussion and are astonishingly passionate about their own and the other interpretations offered. I call this radical, because it has the unusual effect of treating the narrative as if it were something to be interpreted, something text-like. Have you ever heard a 5-year-old tell a version of "something like that once happened to me too"? But I am getting ahead of myself again. For I have to return now to that puzzling issue of how kids in oral discourse do something like turning what is said into a "text."

As already noted, there are things to be cultivated in the life of the child well before reading and writing enter the scene with their own challenges. I am referring, of course, to oral preliminaries that make later reading not only easier but also help in the process of narrative scaffolding. All were concerned, strange though the expression may sound, learning to live in a written language before one learns how to read and write it. In the cramped terminology of speech act theory, it is learning to be mindful of *what is said* as well as what might be intended by *what is* said—focusing on a *locution* as well as on its *illocutionary force*. That is one crucial element in what I want to refer to as "text making."

Spontaneous, unreflective language exchanges, full of rough glory though they may be, are not text as I intend the word. Text is *made,* created by an act of attention directed to *what is said.* We make text in the act of attending and reflecting on encountered speech. Or, to take a phrase from Roman Jakobson, text is constructed by a metalinguistic act, by directing attention to speech itself. It is what some scholars are coming to call "linguistic awareness" (Astington, 1993, 1995). Linguistic or metalinguistic awareness converts encountered speech into text. It frees situationally imbedded speech from its immediate context and makes it into a locution that, in some measure, stands on its own. Text is a product of a way of apprehending speech. It does not have to be written down to rank in this sense.

So how is the young child led to convert speech into text? Well, the first and obvious way is by reading favorite stories to the child, or by teaching the child inviolable rhymes and songs whose very life depends upon their being texts—locutions whose locutionary structure matters. We know about the compellingness of such "inscribed," almost ritualized texts. Change the wording of a favorite storybook tale or nursery rhyme, and you are met with a child storm of protest. Sing a song wrong, and it is an occasion for merriment. Knowing there is a text there is a special form of knowing for the preliterate child. Indeed, in most preliterate cultures, to ritualtextualize in this way is not only to make something memorable, but to give it an almost religious significance.

So it is not surprising that the countries with the highest literacy scores in Europe—Hungary, German Switzerland, and Flemish Belgium—all include specifications in their preschool, prereading/writing curricula for songs and rhymes to be memorized, sung, recited. The Hungarian Ministry of Education Kindergarten Handbook, for example, specifies that three-to-fours should be taught to recite six short nursery rhymes, four-to-fives to sing three to four songs with the help of teacher, and five-to-sixes to sing ten of them on their own. But please note that in Hungary (as with the other literacy leaders in the West), the climate in these preschools is highly oral: reading-and-writing in the formal sense does not begin until late—six or seven. Yet these preschools are full of text creating activities.[1] Now obviously, such text creating also cultivates analytic skills useful for eventual literacy: awareness of words, of word order, of phrase structure, and so on. I take this as going with the territory of textuality. Obviously, it will be important in mastering reading later. But it is critical first for grasping *oral text*.

A second route to text making is through cultivating what I want to call *locutionary respect*. It is signaled by people paying attention, being respectful to what is being said. Let me illustrate with an example from life. I spend a month a year in the preschools of Reggio Emilia in the North of Italy. When I first went there to find out what had made them so famous, it was my practice just to sit quietly and observe what went on in those classrooms full of three-to-fours, four-to-fives, and five-to-sixes. Visualize it now: kids, teacher, maybe an *atelierista* in and out with clay and paint, and quite often a pedagogista as well, and me trying to be as inconspicuous as possible. What soon became obvious was that there was something more like a human style than a method at work. Let me describe it. When a teacher asked somebody a question, she waited for an answer. Just that. If an answer were very slow in coming, the teacher rephrased her question or asked whether she had been clear enough about what she was asking. And when an answer came, it got followed up as needed until the teacher understood what the kid intended to say. If there was anything ambiguous about what a kid had

---

1. I am greatly in the debt of Clare and Clare and David Mills whose BBC4 video, "Much Too Early," contains vivid examples of Kindergarten life in the countries noted. Their equally informative Report, "Britain's Early Years Disaster: Part I: The Findings," contains a compendium of findings about the nature and effects of different approaches to early reading. They very kindly made these materials available to me.

said, the teacher typically probed, always operating on the tacit assumption that what people say makes sense, and the burden of proof is as much with you, the listener, as with him, the speaker. Teachers often tried to "follow up" by exploring with the class whether there were other things that were implied by some kid's answer or comment.

In a word, what kids said was taken seriously, respected as locutions to be explored. Never mind whether the topic at hand was about cast shadows and what made them big or small, or about San Prospero, Reggio's patron saint, who had covered the town with a dark cloud to conceal it from the invading Barbarians trooping toward Rome in the fifth century. Answers and comments were taken as intended to mean something, treated as locutions in search of textual interpretation. It was Grice's (1989) Maxim of Relevance at work: assume that what somebody said meant something relevant and take it upon yourself to determine what it might be.

A wry comment: All of this had become so ingrained in those Reggio teachers that they were both puzzled and enchanted when I talked about the dialogically respectful culture of their schools and called it a "little miracle" at a pick-up seminar that began happening on Fridays. But it *was* that, and with what results! In the provincia where Reggio is located, the Emilia Romagna, people stay in school for more years than anywhere in Italy, Reggio has the lowest unemployment rate in Italy, and I know not what else. But Reggiani are not much into computing their league standing on standardized tests. Non molto reggiano! It is enough for them to make jokes about their neighbor rival, Modena, where, they will tell you, the schools are a pale imitation of what they do in Reggio. Modena's preschools, by the way, are also superb, even if they are somewhat of an imitation of Reggio's.

Which brings me finally, and all too briefly, to *interpretive communities* and their role in the leading-up-to-reading process we are discussing. An interpretive community is a collectivity that shares some basis for making sense of things, capable of that form of sharing we refer to nowadays as intersubjectivity. All communication presupposes the presence of an interpretive community. We understand *with* others. And even in contextually imbedded speech, that takes skills—listening, attending jointly, discovering and negotiating differences, knowing where you stand with others, pooling knowledge. All of this is so ubiquitous that we become accustomed to it—and, fatally, sometimes forget that it is as important for our way of getting about in the world as water is for the fish's. Our water is rather like a sea of locutions. And school is where we learn how to deal with it in something other than habitual context-bound ways. And that is why so-called "whole-class" activities are so vital, as with Ann Brown's astonishingly successful school experiments in Facilitating Cooperative Learning in Oakland, California (Brown & Campione, 1996). A whole class becomes an interpretive community. In Oakland, indeed, there were end-of-the-week class meetings to discuss what they had accomplished that week. It is probably the strongly individualistic, each-child-with-her-own-grade culture of our schools that makes effective ones so rare. Each age, each culture has different ways of constituting an interpretive community.

Let me mention one example I like particularly because it is so "text oriented." A whole class makes up a story together orally, in the course of which the teacher "writes it down" so that the class can come back to it a next time to make it even better or scarier or funnier. That is only one example. But there are lots of them you will learn about if you look at David and Clare Mills's new BBC4 film on how those Hungarian, Swiss German, and Belgian Flemish preschools go about it (Mills & Mills, 1997). They all have certain things in common, by the way: all are profoundly oral, all set tasks that give confidence to children engaged in them, all provide occasion for linguistic awareness or metalinguistic reflection, or whatever one wishes to call it. The Millses would also remind us that successful interpretive community building of this oral kind generally keeps kids away from reading until six or seven and concentrates instead on lighter, jollier, less grim-jawed communal approaches to "text" awareness.

And one last comment by way of a note on the Millses' work: They note that there are two familiar troubles that are bypassed by concentrating on oral locutionary skills before launching into reading and writing. The first is tension and pressure. By creating a more relaxed atmosphere, they replace tension with relaxed reflectiveness. Flemish Belgian and German Swiss schools report far less tension about reading not just in the beginners, but also among older kids who have been better prepared in oral textualization. In consequence, secondly, there is less failure and less fear of failure. Starting reading and writing too soon and too little prepared always punishes the less mature and the less socially advantaged. In Hungary, as their leading preschool pedagogical theorist, Joszef Nagy, puts it, the objective is to keep the weaker pupils from falling further and further behind until "at the end of compulsory schooling" they are not "prepared for life" itself. And they succeed. The distance between the top tenth and the lowest tenth of their readers is much less than in other countries—even though their top tenth are literacy high fliers.

Now let me return to the scaffolding provided by a knowledge of narrative in interpreting and comprehending text. I want to begin with a tale about a lively 12-year-old girl, rather rightbrained and artistic, a pupil at an "excellent-rated" state school in Tewkesbury in Gloucestershire, England. In a casual chat she told me that her only boring subject this term in school was a history class she had to take. Why boring? I asked. "Oh it's all about some kings, somebody called Henry, I think." "Henry the Eighth," I inquired? "Yes, that's the one, and we keep having to fill in worksheets with dates when he changed wives and what their names were, and things like that." And then, "I hate history."

So while the world's great historiographers brood over the narrative structures that different periods and different cultures distinctively impose on their past, a teacher in Tewkesbury has managed to denarrativize the whole thing by converting it all into a class test about chronologically ordered names and dates to be entered on work sheets. And we learn from the Millses' exploration of British early education that a kindred disease is beginning to take hold in the teaching of reading (too young and too orally unprepared), as well as science and mathematics (too formal, too lacking in intuitive play). So Britain drops in the European league tables.

But I do not mean to thrash British education, only to illustrate a general principle. If you have some narrative inkling of what you are reading about, you will grasp the text more easily, more deeply, even though perhaps more idiosyncratically. If you even know what *peripéteia* threw things off the track, you are clued for what to look for, to know what usual suspects to call in, to know what makes the thing tellable. How could one possibly comprehend Henry's plight or England's or anybody's as a chronologically ordered and dated list of wives? I am sure the teacher in question had no idea what his work-sheets were doing to that 12-year-old's sense of what was going on in the lessons and in her reading.

I have two suggestions to make with regard to the pedagogy of reading comprehension in light of what I said earlier about the structure of narrative and how that structure might be used to scaffold reading comprehension. Let me try them out in the hope of provoking some discussion.

The first has to do with genres of narrative, a concept that I have been skirting around up to now. Genre gives literature formal shape as well as living excitement. And I do not mean to be fussy about what genre is exactly. It does not matter whether it is Northrop Frye's tragedy, comedy, romance, and irony, or Alistair Fowler's flightier notion that genres are more like pigeons than pigeonholes. It is as plain to kids as to grownups that there are different kinds of stories, that (as we saw earlier) they can "match" stories other kids tell with ones of their own. How I would love to work out a kid version of Aristotle's *Poetics* on those kids—or 10-year-olds or 14-year-olds! I think kids early grasp the idea that a story is not just about things in the world but about how you tell about it too. Even, maybe, they have some inkling about what makes stories well told or not? I think we all would have read more discerningly if we had been exposed to such matters earlier.

The second suggestion also relates to genres of literature and ways of bringing one's narrative knowledge to bear on text. It is an idea I encountered when visiting the fabled high school that had been set up by Frank Brown, the superintendent of schools in Cape Canaveral in Florida, where the federal government had just moved a few trainloads of space scientists and technicians and their families (Bruner, 1964). It was a class of high school freshmen. They were reading plays—actually reading them aloud, acting out the parts. Their teacher, a clever younger woman, mother of two teenagers, gave over a second session on each play to what she called "The Rewrite"—what would you have to do to turn *A Streetcar Named Desire* into a comedy, for example. I have no idea how those kids fared as readers (and playgoers) in the years after, but that session I saw was so radiant with narrative intuition that I wrote about it in *The Saturday Review*, hoping somebody would lift the idea. Perhaps they did.

What can I offer by way of resounding conclusions? The first might be that reading is oral "textual" interpretation carried out in the medium of written text. But that is just too silly, particularly if you have read anything about literacy, anything, for example, like David Olson's (1994) *The World on Paper.* The print medium and the reading style it led to have plainly changed the world, changed the ways our minds operate, even changed the system of laws under which we operate, to take an extreme. What I have been trying to say, rather, is that skill and ease at oral textualization and interpretation constitute a crucial preliminary to literacy. There are ways, easy ways, to introduce a would-be, someday reader into what I have called "speaking a written language." In our eagerness to "train" our kids to become literate reader-writers, we sometimes forget about the importance of these preliminaries. In doing so, we may succeed in getting them alphabetized, but with the high price of making them shallower readers without the habits and inclinations to explore the possible worlds that print makes available to those willing to explore beyond the information given. In emphasizing how we can scaffold kids to read narrative more deeply and discerningly, I do not mean to belittle other forms of printed matter—scientific explanation, legal and normative codes, whatever—but only to urge that since our narrative knowledge is so accessible to cultivation, we might well begin with it. And if it is true that life imitates narrative as much as narrative imitates life, that sort of beginning might, in the long run, make our lives richer.

References

Astington, J. W. (1993). *The child's discovery of the mind.* Cambridge, MA: Harvard University Press.

Astington, J. W. (1995). Talking it over with my brain. *Monographs of the Society for Research in Child Development, 60*(1), Serial No. 243.

Brown, A. L., & Campione, J. C. (1996). Psychological theory and the design of learning environments. In L. Schauble & R. Glaser (Eds.), *Innovations in education: New environments for learning.* Hillsdale, NJ: Erlbaum.

Brown, R. W., Cazden, C. B., & Bellugi, U. (1969). The child's grammar from I to II. In J. P. Hill (Ed.), *Minnesota Symposium on Child Psychology* (pp. 28–73). Reprinted in R. W. Brown, (1970), *Pscholinguistics: Selected papers.* New York: Free Press.

Bruner, J. (1964, January 18). A vivid glimpse of the future. [Review of F. Brown, *The nongraded high school*]. *Saturday Review of Literature,* 71–72.

Bruner, J. (1991). *Acts of meaning.* Cambridge, MA: Harvard University Press.

Bruner, J., & Lucariello, J. (1989). Monologue as narrative recreation of the world. In K. Nelson, *Narratives from the crib* (pp. 73–97). Cambridge, MA: Harvard University Press.

Burke, K. (1969). *The grammar of motives.* Berkeley: University of California Press.

Cazden, C. B. (1965). *Environmental assistance to the child's acquisition of grammar.* Unpublished doctoral dissertation, Harvard University.

Chall, J. (1967). *Learning to read: The great debate.* New York: McGraw Hill.

Grice, P. (1989). *Studies in the way of words.* Cambridge, MA: Harvard University Press.

McNeill, D. (1970). *The acquisition of language.* New York: Harper & Row.

Miller, P. J. (1982). *Amy, Wendy, and Beth: Learning language in South Baltimore.* Austin: University of Texas Press.

Mills, D., & Mills, C. K. (1997). *Paper for British Government's Task Force on the Teaching of Mathematics.* London: BBC Channel Four Television.

Olson, D. R. (1994). *The world on paper.* New York: Cambridge University Press.

Snow, C. E., & Ferguson, C. A. (1977). *Talking to children: Language input and acquisition.* New York: Cambridge University Press.

Tomasello, M. (1999). *The cultural origins of human cognition.* Cambridge, MA: Harvard University Press.

Wood, S. S., Bruner, J. S., & Ross, G. (1976). The role of tutoring in problem solving. *Journal of Child Psychology and Psychiatry, 17,* 89–100.

Language, Literacy, and Culture: Intersections and Implications*

Sonia Nieto

University of Massachusetts, Amherst

Given my background and early life experiences, I should not be expected to write about literacy and learning. According to the traditional educational literature, my home and family situation could not prepare me adequately for academic success. My mother did not graduate from high school, and my father never made it past fourth grade. They came to the United States as immigrants from Puerto Rico and they quietly took their place in the lower paid and lower status of society. In my family, we never had bedtime stories, much less books. At home, we did not have a permanent place to study, nor did we have a desk with sufficient light and adequate ventilation, as teachers suggested. We did not have many toys and I never got the piano lessons I wanted desperately from the age of 5. As a family, we did not go to museums or other places that would give us the cultural capital (Bourdieu, 1985) it was thought we needed to succeed in school. We spoke Spanish at home, even though teachers pleaded with my parents to stop doing so. And when we learned English, my sister and I spoke a nonstandard, urban Black and Puerto Rican version of English: we said "ain't" instead of "isn't" and "mines" instead of "mine" and, no matter how often our teachers corrected us, we persisted in saying these things. In a word, because of our social class, ethnicity, native language, and discourse practices, we were the epitome of what are now described as "children at risk," young people then described when we were coming up as "disadvantaged," "culturally deprived," and even "problem" students.

I was fortunate that I had a family who, although unable to help me with homework, would make sure that it got done; a family who used "Education, Sonia, education!" as a mantra. But they kept right on speaking Spanish (even when my sister and I switched to English), they still did not buy books for our home, and they never read us bedtime stories. My parents, just like all parents, were brimming with skills and talents: they were becoming bilingual, they told us many stories and riddles and tongue twisters and jokes. When my father, 20 years after coming to this country, bought a *bodega,* a small Caribbean grocery store, I was awed by the sight of him adding up a column of figures in seconds, without a calculator or even a pencil. My mother embroidered beautiful and intricate patterns on handkerchiefs, blouses, and tablecloths, a trade practiced by many poor

*Paper presented as a plenary address at the 49th annual meeting of the National Reading Conference, Orlando, FL, December 1999.

National Reading Conference Yearbook, 49, pp. 41–60.

women in Puerto Rico to stock the shelves of Lord and Taylor's and Saks' Fifth Avenue in New York. These skills, however, were never called on by my teachers; my parents were thought of as culturally deprived and disadvantaged, another segment of the urban poor with no discernible competencies.

Sometime in my early adolescence, we bought a small house in a lower middle-class neighborhood and I was able to attend a good junior high and an excellent high school. I did not particularly like that high school—it was too competitive and impersonal and I felt invisible there—but in retrospect I realize that my sister and I got the education we needed to prepare us for college, a dream beyond the wildest imagination of my parents, most of my cousins, and the friends from our previous neighborhood. My new address made a profound difference in the education that I was able to get. I eventually dropped the "ain't" and the "mines" and I hid the fact that I spoke Spanish.

I begin with my own story, not because I believe that autobiography is sacrosanct, or that it holds the answer to all educational problems. My story is not unique and I do not want to single myself out as an "exception," in the way that Richard Rodriguez ended up doing, intentionally or not, in his painful autobiography *Hunger of Memory* (1982). I use my story because it underscores the fact that young people of all backgrounds can learn and that they need not be compelled, as Richard Rodriguez was, to abandon their family and home language for the benefits of an education and a higher status in society. In many ways, I am like any of the millions of young people in our classrooms and schools who come to school eager (although perhaps not, in the current jargon, "ready") to learn, but who end up as the waste products of an educational system that does not understand the gifts they bring to their education. They are the reason that I am concerned about language, literacy, and culture, and the implications that new ways of thinking about them have for children.

Language, literacy, and culture have not always been linked, either conceptually or programmatically. But this is changing, as numerous schools and colleges of education around the country are beginning to reflect a growing awareness of their intersections, and of the promise they hold for rethinking teaching and learning. My own reconceptualized program at the University of Massachusetts, now called Language, Literacy, and Culture, mirrors this trend. I believe the tendency to link these issues is giving us a richer picture of learning, especially for students whose identities—particularly those related to language, race, ethnicity, and immigrant status—have traditionally had a low status in our society. One result of this reconceptualization is that more education programs are reflecting and promoting a sociocultural perspective in language and literacy, that is, a perspective firmly rooted in an anthropological understanding of culture; a view of learning as socially constructed and mutually negotiated; an understanding of how students from diverse segments of society—due to differential access, and cultural and linguistic differences—experience schooling; and a commitment to social justice. I know that multiple and conflicting ideas exist about these theoretical perspectives, but I believe some basic tenets of sociocultural theory can serve as a platform for discussion. I will explore a number of these tenets, illustrating them with examples from my research and using the stories and experiences of young people in U.S. schools.

The language of sociocultural theory includes terms such as *discourse, hegemony, power, social practice, identity, hybridity,* and even the very word *literacy.* Today, these terms have become commonplace, but if we were to do a review of the literature of 20 years ago or less, we would be hard pressed to find them, at least as currently used. What does this mean? How has our awareness and internalization of these terms and everything they imply changed how we look at teaching and learning? Let us look at literacy itself. It is generally accepted that certain family and home conditions promote literacy, including an abundant supply of books and other reading material, consistent conversations between adults and children about the books they read, and other such conditions (Snow, Barnes, Chandler, Goodman, & Hemphill, 1991). I have no doubt that this is true in many cases, and I made certain that my husband and I did these things with our own children. I am sure we made their lives easier as a result. But what of the children for whom these conditions are not present, but who nevertheless "grow up literate" (Taylor & Dorsey-Gaines, 1988)? Should children be doomed to educational failure because their parents did not live in the right neighborhood, were not privileged enough to be formally educated, or did not take their children to museums or attend plays? Should they be disqualified from learning because they did not have books at home?

Tenets of Sociocultural Theory

I began with my story to situate myself not just personally, but socially and politically, a primary premise of sociocultural theory. Given traditional theories, the only way to understand my educational success was to use traditional metaphors: I had "pulled myself up by my bootstraps"; I had "melted"; I had joined the "mainstream." But I want to suggest that these traditional metaphors are as unsatisfactory as they are incomplete because they place individuals at the center, isolated from the social, cultural, historical, and political context in which they live. Traditional theories explain my experience, and those of others who do not fit the conventional pattern, as springing primarily if not solely from our personal psychological processes. Sociocultural theory, on the other hand, gives us different lenses with which to view learning, and different metaphors for describing it. This is significant because how one views learning leads to dramatically different curricular decisions, pedagogical approaches, expectations of learning, relationships among students, teachers and families, and indeed, educational outcomes.

Sociocultural and sociopolitical perspectives are first and foremost based on the assumption that social relationships and political realities are at the heart of teaching and learning. That is, learning emerges from the social, cultural, and political spaces where it takes place, and through the interactions and relationships that occur between learners and teachers. In what follows, I propose five interrelated concepts that undergird sociocultural and sociopolitical perspectives. These concepts are the basis of my own work, and they help me make sense of my experience and the experiences of countless youngsters that challenge traditional deficit views of learning. The concepts are also highly consistent with a critical multicultural perspective, that is, one that is broader than superficial additions to content or "holidays and heroes" approaches.

I will focus on five concepts: (a) agency/co-constructed learning, (b) experience, (c) identity/hybridity, (d) context/situatedness/positionality, and (e) community. Needless to say, each of these words holds many meanings, but I use them here to locate some fundamental principles of sociocultural and sociopolitical theory. These terms are also both deeply connected and overlapping. I separate them here for matters of convenience, not because I see them as fundamentally independent concepts.

Agency

In many classrooms and schools, learning continues to be thought of as transmission rather than as *agency,* or mutual discovery by students and teachers. At the crudest level, learning is thought to be the reproduction of socially sanctioned knowledge, or what Michael Apple (1993) has called "official knowledge." These are the dominant attitudes and behaviors that society deems basic to functioning. The most extreme manifestation of this notion of learning is what Paulo Freire (1970) called "banking education," that is, the simple depositing of knowledge into students who are thought to be empty receptacles. In an elegant rejection of the banking concept of education, Freire instead defined the act of study as constructed by active agents. According to Freire (1985), "To study is not to consume ideas, but to create and re-create them" (p. 4).

Although teachers and theorists alike repudiate learning as the reproduction of socially sanctioned knowledge, it continues to exist in many schools and classrooms. It is the very foundation of such ideas as "teacher-proof curriculum," the need to "cover the material" in a given subject, and the endless lists of skills and competencies "that every student should know" (Hirsch, 1987). This contradiction was evident even near the beginning of the twentieth century when John Dewey (1916) asked:

> Why is it, in spite of the fact that teaching by pouring in, learning by a passive absorption, are universally condemned, that they are still so entrenched in practice? That education is not an affair of "telling" and being told, but an active and constructive process, is a principle almost as generally violated in practice as conceded in theory. (p. 38)

Why does this continue to happen? One reason is probably the doubt among the public that teachers and students have the ability to construct meaningful and important knowledge. Likewise, in low-income schools with students from diverse cultural and linguistic backgrounds, very little agency exists on the part of either students or teachers. In such schools, teachers learn that their primary responsibility is to "teach the basics" because students are thought to have neither the innate ability nor the experiential background of more privileged students. In the case of students for whom English is a second language, the assumption that they must master English before they can think and reason may prevail.

Let me share some examples of agency, or lack of it, from the words of students of diverse backgrounds whom a number of colleagues (Paula Elliott, Haydée Font, Maya Gillingham, Beatriz McConnie Zapater, Mac Lee Morante, Carol Shea, Diane Sweet, and Carlie Tartakov) and I interviewed for my first book (Nieto, 1992, 2000). We found that students' views largely echoed those of educational researchers who have found that teaching methods in most classrooms, especially those in secondary schools and even more so in secondary schools attended by poor students of all backgrounds, vary little from traditional "chalk and talk" methods; that textbooks are the dominant teaching materials used; that routine and rote learning are generally favored over creativity and critical thinking; and that teacher-centered transmission models still prevail (Cummins, 1994; Goodlad, 1984). Students in my study (Nieto, 1992, 2000) had more to say about pedagogy than about anything else, and they were especially critical of teachers who provided only passive learning environments for students. Linda Howard, who was just graduating as the valedictorian of her class in an urban high school, is a case in point. Although now at the top of her class, Linda had failed seventh and eighth grades twice, for a variety of reasons, both academic and medical. She had this to say about pedagogy:

> Because I know there were plenty of classes where I lost complete interest. But those were all because the teachers just, "Open the books to this page." They never made up problems out of their head. Everything came out of the book. You didn't ask questions. If you asked them questions, then the answer was "in the book." And if you asked the question and the answer *wasn't* in the book, then you shouldn't have asked that question! (pp. 55–56)

Rich Miller, a young man who planned to attend pharmacy school after graduation, described a "normal teacher" as one who "gets up, gives you a lecture, or there's teachers that just pass out the work, you do the work, pass it in, get a grade, good-bye!" (p. 66)

The students were especially critical of teachers who relied on textbooks and blackboards. Avi Abramson, a young man who had attended Jewish day schools and was now in a public high school, had some difficulty adjusting to the differences in pedagogy. He believed that some teachers did better because they taught from the point of view of the students: "They don't just come out and say, 'All right, do this, blah, blah, blah.' . . . They're not so *one-tone voice"* (p. 116). Yolanda Piedra, a Mexican student, said that her English teacher "just does the things and sits down" (p. 221). Another student mentioned that some teachers "just teach the stuff. 'Here,' write a couple of things on the board, 'see, that's how you do it. Go ahead, page 25'" (p. 166).

These students did not just criticize, however; they also gave examples of teachers who promoted their active learning. Hoang Vinh, in his junior year of high school, spoke with feeling about teachers who allowed him to speak Vietnamese with other students in class. He also loved working in groups, contrary to conventional wisdom about Asian students' preference for individual work (demonstrating the dangers of generalizing about fixed "cultural traits"). Vinh particularly appreciated the teacher who asked students to discuss important issues, rather than focus only on learning what he called "the word's *meaning*" (p. 143) by writing and memorizing lists of words. Students also offered thoughtful suggestions to teachers to make their classrooms more engaging places. One student recommended that teachers involve more students actively: "More like making the whole class be involved, not making only the two smartest people up here do the whole work for the whole class" (p. 125).

Teaching becomes much more complex when learning is based on the idea that all students have the ability to think and reason. Sociocultural and sociopolitical theories emphasize that learning is not simply a question of transmitting knowledge, but rather of working with students so that they can reflect, theorize, and create knowledge. Given this notion of agency, "banking education" (Freire, 1970) makes little sense. Instead, the focus on reflective questions invites students to consider different options, to question taken-for-granted truths, and to delve more deeply into problems.

Experience

That learning needs to build on experience is a taken-for-granted maxim, based on the idea that it is an innately human endeavor accessible to all people. But somehow this principle is often ignored when it comes to young people who have not had the *kinds* of experiences that are thought to prepare them for academic success, particularly those students who have not been raised within "the culture of power" (Delpit, 1988), or who have not explicitly learned the rules of the game for academic success. The experiences of these students—usually young people of culturally and linguistically diverse backgrounds and those raised in poverty—tend to be quite different from the experiences of more economically and socially advantaged students, and these differences become evident when they go to school.

Pierre Bourdieu (1985) has described how different forms of cultural capital help maintain economic privilege, even if these forms of capital are not themselves strictly related to economy. Cultural capital is evident in such intangibles as values, tastes, and behaviors and through cultural identities such as language, dialect, and ethnicity. Some signs of cultural capital have more social worth, although not necessarily more intrinsic worth, than others. If this is true, then youngsters from some communities are placed at a disadvantage relative to their peers simply because of their experiences and identities. Understanding this reality means that power relations are a fundamental, although largely unspoken, aspect of school life.

We also need to consider the impact of teachers' attitudes concerning the cultural capital that their students do bring to school, and teachers' subsequent behaviors relative to this cultural capital. Sociocultural theories help to foreground these concerns. For example, a 1971 article by Annie Stein cited a New York City study in which kindergarten teachers were asked to list in order of their importance the things a child should learn to prepare for first grade. In schools with large Puerto Rican and Black student populations, socialization goals were predominant, but in mostly White schools, educational goals were invariably first. "In fact," according to Stein, "several teachers in the minority-group kindergartens forgot to mention any educational goals at all" (p. 167). This is an insidious kind of tracking, where educational ends for some students were sacrificed for social aims.

All children come to school as thinkers and learners, aptitudes usually recognized as important building blocks for further learning. But there seems to be a curious refusal on the part of many educators to accept as valid *the kinds* of knowledge and experiences some students bring to school. For instance, teachers often think that speaking languages other than English, especially those languages with low status, is a potential detriment rather than a benefit to learning. Likewise, while traveling to Europe to ski is usually considered culturally enriching, the same is not true of traveling to North Carolina, Haiti, or the Dominican Republic to visit relatives. The reason teachers evaluate these kinds of experiences differently has more to do with their cultural capital than with their educational potential or intrinsic worth.

The reluctance or inability to accept and build on students' experiences is poignantly described by Mary Ginley, a teacher in Massachusetts who taught in a small city with a large Puerto Rican student population. A gifted teacher, Mary also knew that "being nice is not enough," an idea she elaborated on in a journal she kept for a class she took with me:

> Every child needs to feel welcome, to feel comfortable. School is a foreign land to most kids (where else in the world would you spend time circling answers and filling in the blanks?), but the more distant a child's culture and language are from the culture and language of school, the more at risk that child is. A warm, friendly, helpful teacher is nice but it isn't enough. We have plenty of warm friendly teachers who tell the kids nicely to forget their Spanish and ask mommy and daddy to speak to them in English at home; who give them easier tasks so they won't feel badly when the work becomes difficult; who never learn about what life is like at home or what they eat or what music they like or what stories they have been told or what their history is. Instead, we smile and give them a hug and tell them to eat our food and listen to our stories and dance to our music. We teach them to read with our words and wonder why it's so hard for them. We ask them to sit quietly and we'll tell them what's important and what they must know to "get ready for the next grade." And we never ask them who they are and where they want to go. (pp. 85-86)

A case in point is Hoang Vinh, the Vietnamese student I mentioned previously. Vinh was literate in Vietnamese and he made certain that his younger siblings spoke it exclusively at home and they all wrote to their parents in Vietnam weekly. He was a good student, but he was also struggling to learn English, something that his teachers did not always understand. He told how some teachers described his native language as "funny," and even laughed at it. But as he explained, "[To keep reading and writing Vietnamese] is very important. . . . So, I like to learn English, but I like to learn my language too" (Nieto, 1992, 2000, p. 178).

Even more fundamental for Vinh was that teachers try to understand their students' experiences and culture. He explained: "[My teachers] understand some things, just not all Vietnamese culture. Like they just understand some things *outside.* . . . But they cannot understand something inside our hearts" (p. 178). Vinh's words are a good reminder that when students' skills and knowledge are dismissed as inappropriate for the school setting, schools lose a golden opportunity to build on their students' lives in the service of their learning.

Identity/Hybridity

How students benefit from schooling is influenced by many things including the particular individual personalities of students and the values of the cultural context in which they have been raised. Traditional theories, however, privilege individual differences above all other circumstances. As a result, it is primarily through tests and other measures of students' individual abilities that their intelligence is determined. Sociocultural theory goes beyond this limited perspective to include other issues such as students' cultural identities. But culture should not be thought of as unproblematic. Mary Kalantzis, Bill Cope, and Diana Slade (1989) remind us that

> we are not simply bearers of cultures, languages, and histories, with a duty to reproduce them. We are the products of linguistic-cultural circumstances, actors with a capacity to resynthesize what we have been socialized into and to solve new and emerging problems of existence. We are not duty-bound to conserve ancestral characteristics which are not structurally useful. We are both socially determined and creators of human futures. (p. 18)

Culture is complex and intricate; it cannot be reduced to holidays, foods, or dances, although these are of course elements of culture. Everyone has a culture because all people participate in the world through social and political relationships informed by history as well as by race, ethnicity, language, social class, sexual orientation, gender, and other circumstances related to identity and experience.

If culture is thought of in a sentimental way, then it becomes little more than a yearning for a past that never existed, or an idealized, sanitized version of what exists in reality. The result may be an unadulterated, essentialized "culture on a pedestal" that bears little resemblance to the messy and contradictory culture of real life. The problem of viewing some aspects of culture as indispensable attributes that must be shared by all people within a particular group springs from a romanticized and uncritical understanding of culture.

Let me share an example of this with you: Last year, I received an e-mail message with the subject heading "You Know You're Puerto Rican When . . ." The message was meant to be humorous, and it included a long list of experiences and characteristics that presumably describe what it means to be Puerto Rican in the United States (for example, being chased by your mother with a *chancleta,* or slipper, in hand; always having a dinner that consists of rice and beans and some kind of meat; having a grandmother who thinks Vick's Vapor Rub is the miracle cure for everything). I laughed at many of these things (and I shared a good number of these experiences when I was growing up in New York City), but it was also sobering to read the list because it felt like a litmus test for *puertorriqueñidad* (Puerto Ricanness). If you could prove that you had these particular experiences, you could claim to be "authentic"; otherwise, you could not. By putting them to paper, the author was making it clear that these experiences defined the very essence of being Puerto Rican.

Reading the list made me reflect on my own daughters, born and raised in the United States by highly educated middle-class parents. My daughters would likely not pass the Puerto Rican litmus test: their dinner was just as likely to consist of take-out Chinese or pizza as rice and beans; they barely knew what Vick's Vapor Rub was; and I do not remember ever chasing them with *chancleta* in hand. But both of them identify as Puerto Rican, and they speak Spanish to varying degrees and enjoy rice and beans as much as the next Puerto Rican. But they also eat salmon and frog legs and pizza and Thai food. The e-mail message I received made it seem as if there was only one way to be Puerto Rican. The result of this kind of thinking is that we are left with just two alternatives: either complete adherence to one definition of identity, or total and unequivocal assimilation. We are, in the words of Anthony Appiah (1994), replacing "one kind of tyranny with another" (p. 163).

My daughters' identities are complicated. They live in a highly diverse society in terms of race, ethnicity, social class, and other differences, and they enjoy privileges they have received as a result of their parents' social class. The point of this story is to emphasize that culture does not exist in a vacuum, but rather is situated in particular historical, social, political, and economic conditions, another major tenet of sociocultural theory. That is, culture needs to be understood as *dynamic; multifaceted; embedded in context; influenced by social, economic, and political factors; created and socially constructed; learned;* and *dialectical* (Nieto, 1999). Steven Arvizu's (1994) wonderful description of culture as a *verb* rather than a *noun* captures the essence of culture beautifully. That is, culture is dynamic, active, changing, always on the move. Even within their native contexts, cultures are always changing as a result of political, social, and other influences in the environment. When people with different backgrounds come in contact with one another, such change is to be expected even more.

Let me once again use the example of Linda Howard, one of the young women we interviewed for *Affirming Diversity* (Nieto, 1992, 2000). As I have mentioned, Linda was a talented young woman who was graduating as valedictorian of her class. But the issue of identity was a complicated one for her. Being biracial, she identified as "Black American and White American," and she said:

> I don't always fit in—unless I'm in a mixed group. . . . Because if I'm in a group of people who are all one race, then they seem to look at me as being the *other* race . . . whereas if I'm in a group full of [racially mixed] people, my race doesn't seem to matter to everybody else. . . . Then I don't feel like I'm standing out. . . . It's hard. I look at history and I feel really bad for what some of my ancestors did to some of my other ancestors. Unless you're mixed, you don't know what it's like to be mixed. (pp. 51-52)

The tension of Linda's identity was not simply a personal problem. It was evident throughout her schooling, and especially when she reached secondary school. She found that teachers jumped to conclusions about her identity, assuming she was Latina or even Chinese, and identifying her as such on forms without even asking her.

Linda had won a scholarship to a highly regarded university. When discussing her future, she had exclaimed proudly, "I've got it all laid out. I've got a four-year scholarship to one of the best schools in New England. All I've gotta do is go there and make the grade." Linda's future seemed hopeful, overflowing with possibilities. But she did not quite "make the grade." When Paula Elliott, who had interviewed Linda the first time, spoke with her again 10 years later, she found out that Linda had dropped out of college after just a few months, and she had never returned. Over dinner, Linda described her experience at the university in this way: "I felt like a pea on a big pile of rice." Using a sociocultural lens, we can see that identity is not simply a personal issue, but that it is deeply embedded in institutional life. Had there been a way to validate her hybridity, perhaps Linda might have graduated. She certainly had the intellectual training and resources; what she did not have was the support for her identity to ease the way.

In some ways, we can think of culture as having both *surface* and *deep structure*, to borrow a concept from linguistics (Chomsky, 1965). For instance, in the interviews of students of diverse backgrounds that I mentioned previously (Nieto, 1992, 2000), we were initially surprised by the seeming homogeneity of the youth culture they manifested. Regardless of racial, ethnic, linguistic background, or time in the United States—but usually intimately connected to a shared urban culture and social class—the youths often expressed strikingly similar tastes in music, food, clothes, television, and so on. When I probed more deeply, however, I found evidence of deeply held values from their ethnic heritage. For instance, Marisol, a Puerto Rican high school student, loved hip hop and rap music, pizza, and lasagna. She never mentioned Puerto Rican food, and Puerto Rican music to her was just the "old-fashioned" and boring music her parents listened to. But in her everyday interactions with parents and siblings, and in the answers she gave to my interview questions, she reflected deep aspects of Puerto Rican culture such as respect for elders, a profound kinship with and devotion to family, and a desire to uphold important traditions such as staying with family rather than going out with friends on important holidays. Just as there is no such thing as a "pure race," there is likewise no "pure culture." That is, cultures influence one another, and even minority cultures and those with less status have an impact on majority cultures, sometimes in dramatic ways.

Power is deeply implicated in notions of culture and language (Fairclough, 1989). Indeed, what are often presented as cultural and linguistic differences are above all differences in power. Put another way, cultural conflict is sometimes little more than political conflict. Let me give you another example concerning the link between culture and context based on an experience I had that took me by surprise even as a young adult. Rice is a primary Puerto Rican staple. There is a saying in Spanish that demonstrates how common it is: *Puertorriqueños somos como el arroz blanco: estamos por todas partes* (Puerto Ricans are like white rice: we are everywhere), an adage that says as much about rice as it does about the diaspora of the Puerto Rican people, almost half of whom live outside the island. As a rule, Puerto Ricans eat short-grained rice, but I have always preferred long-grained rice. Some Puerto Ricans have made me feel practically like a cultural traitor when I admitted it. I remember my surprise when a fellow academic, a renowned Puerto Rican historian, explained the real reason behind the preference for short-grained rice. This preference did not grow out of the blue, nor is that rice innately better. On the contrary, the predilection for short-grained rice was influenced by the historical context of Puerto Ricans as a colonized people.

It seems that, near the beginning of the twentieth century when Puerto Rico was first taken over by the United States as spoils of the Spanish-American War, there was a surplus of short-grained rice in the United States. Colonies have frequently been the destination for unwanted or surplus goods, so Puerto Rico became the dumping ground for short-grained rice, which had lower status than long-grained rice in the United States. After this, of course, the preference for short-grained rice became part of the culture. As is true of all cultural values, however, this particular taste was influenced by history, economics, and power. This example was a good lesson to me that culture is not something inherent, but often arbitrary and negotiated.

Hybridity complicates the idea of cultural identity. It means that culture is always heterogeneous and complex; it also implies that assimilation or cultural preservation are not the only alternatives. Ariel Dorfman's (1998) autobiography *Heading South, Looking North: A Bilingual Journey* eloquently describes the turmoil he experienced as a child in developing his identity, first in New York City and later in Chile: "I instinctively chose to refuse the multiple, complex, in-between person I would someday become, this man who is shared by two equal languages and who has come to believe that to tolerate differences and indeed embody them personally and collectively might be our only salvation as a species" (p. 42). As an adult, he reflected on the demand to be "culturally pure" that he experienced in the United States as a graduate student:

> Sitting at my typewriter in Berkeley, California, that day, precariously balanced between Spanish and English, for the first time perhaps fully aware of how extraordinarily bicultural I was, I did not have the maturity—or the emotional or ideological space, probably not even the vocabulary—to answer that I was a hybrid, part Yankee, part Chilean, a pinch of Jew, a mestizo in search of a center, I was unable to look directly in the face the divergent mystery of who I was, the abyss of being bilingual and binational, at a time when everything demanded that we be unequivocal and immaculate. (p. 22)

The notion of hybridity, and of culture as implicated with power and privilege, complicates culturally responsive pedagogy. Rather than simply an incorporation of the cultural practices of students' families in the curriculum, or a replication of stereotypical ideas about "learning styles," culturally responsive pedagogy in the broadest sense is a political project that is, according to Gloria Ladson-Billings (1994) about "questioning (and preparing students to question) the struc-

tural inequality, the racism, and the injustice that exist in society" (p. 128). Culturally responsive pedagogy is not simply about instilling pride in one's identity or
boosting self-esteem. It is also about context and positionality, to which I now
turn.

Context/Situatedness/Positionality

When culture is thought of as if it were context free, we fragment people's
lives, in the words of Frederick Erickson (1990), "as we freeze them outside time,
outside a world of struggle in concrete history" (p. 34). Context is also about
situatedness and *positionality,* reminding us that culture includes the social markers
that differentiate a group from others. It is once again the recognition that questions of power are at the very heart of learning. This view of culture also implies
that differences in ethnicity, language, social class, and gender need not, in and of
themselves, be barriers to learning. Instead, it is how these differences are viewed
in society that can make the difference in whether and to what extent young
people learn.

Judith Solsken's (1993) definition of literacy as the "negotiation of one's
orientation toward written language and thus one's position within multiple relations of power and status" (p. 6) brings up a number of questions that have
traditionally been neglected in discussions of reading and writing, questions
such as: How do students learn to use language in a way that both acknowledges
the context in which they find themselves, and challenges the rules of that context? How do young people learn to negotiate the chasm that exists between their
home languages and cultures and those of school? Let me share with you another
example from Linda Howard. What helped Linda go from a struggling student in
junior high to valedictorian of her class several years later? There are probably
many answers to this question, but one ingredient that made a tremendous difference was Mr. Benson, her favorite teacher in high school. He too was biracial, and
Linda talked about some of the things she had learned from Mr. Benson about
positionality and context:

> I've enjoyed all my English teachers at Jefferson. But Mr. Benson, my English
> Honors teacher, he just threw me for a whirl! 'Cause Mr. Benson, he says, I can
> go into Harvard and converse with those people, and I can go out in the street
> and rap with y'all. It's that type of thing, I love it. I try and be like that myself.
> I have my street talk. I get out in the street and I say "ain't" this and "ain't" that
> and "your momma" or "wha's up?" But I get somewhere where I know the
> people aren't familiar with that language or aren't accepting that language, and I
> will talk properly. . . . I walk into a place and I listen to how people are talking,
> and it just automatically comes to me. (p. 56)

Linda's statement is an example of the tremendous intelligence needed by young
people whose Discourses (Gee, 1990) are not endorsed by schools, and who need
to negotiate these differences on their own. Linda's words are also a graphic
illustration of James Baldwin's characterization of language as "a political instrument, means, and proof of power" (p. 68). In the case of African-American discourse, Baldwin suggested—as Linda had learned through her own experience—"It

is not the Black child's language that is in question, it is not his language that is despised: It is his experience" (p. 70). As David Corson (1993) reminds us, "education can routinely repress, dominate, and disempower language users whose practices differ from the norms that it establishes" (p. 7).

What does this mean for teachers? Situations such as Linda Howard's suggest that, "We are faced with essential epistemological questions such as, what counts as important knowledge or knowing?" (Nelson-Barber & Estrin, 1995, p. 178). These questions are at the core of sociocultural theory, and they are neither neutral nor innocent. They are rarely addressed openly in school, although they should be. As Ira Shor (1992) has said, "A curriculum that avoids questioning school and society is not, as is commonly supposed, politically neutral. It cuts off the students' development as critical thinkers about their world" (p. 12).

Sociocultural and sociopolitical perspectives have been especially consequential because they have shattered the perception that teaching and learning are neutral processes uncontaminated by the idiosyncrasies of particular contexts. Whether and to what extent teachers realize the influence social and political context have on learning can alter how they perceive of their students and, consequently, what and how they teach them. A good example of positionality is the status of bilingual education. Bilingualism is only viewed as a problem and a deficit in a context where speakers of a particular language are held in low esteem or seen as a threat to national unity. This is the case of bilingual education in the United States, and especially for children who speak Spanish. That is, there is nothing inherently negative about the project of becoming bilingual (many wealthy parents pay dearly for the privilege), but rather it is the *identities* of the students, and the *status* of the language variety they speak, that make bilingual education problematic. This was clearly explained by Lizette Román, a bilingual teacher whose journal entry for one of my classes reads as follows:

> Unfortunately, most bilingual programs exist because they are mandated by law, not because they are perceived as a necessity by many school systems. The main problem that we bilingual teachers face every day is the misconception that mainstream teachers, principals, and even entire school systems have about bilingual education. . . . As a consequence, in many school districts bilingual education is doubly disadvantaged, first because it is seen as remedial and, second, because little attention is paid to it. Many mainstream teachers and administrators see bilingual education as a remediation program and do not validate what bilingual teachers do in their classrooms even when what they are teaching is part of the same curriculum. . . . The majority think that there must be something wrong with these children who cannot perform well in English. As soon as the children transfer out of the bilingual program, these teachers believe that *this* is the moment when the learning of these children starts. The perception of the majority distorts the importance and the purpose of bilingual education. It extends to bilingual children and their parents. Bilingual children and their parents sense that their language places them in a program where they are perceived to be inferior to the rest of the children. What isolates children in the bilingual program is not the way the program is conducted, but the perceptions the majority has about people who speak a language different from the mainstream. (pp. 87-88)

Lizette's reflections suggest that if teachers believe that intelligence and learning are somehow divorced from context, then they will conclude that the political and economic realities of their students' lives—including their school environments— have nothing to do with learning. In short, teachers can delude themselves by believing that they and the schools in which they work inhabit an "ideology-free zone" in which dominant attitudes and values play no role in learning. When students are asked to give up their identities for an elusive goal that they may never reach because of the negative context in which they learn, students may be quite correct in rejecting the trade.

Community

How we define and describe *community* is of central significance in sociocultural theory. Lev Vygotsky's (1978)) research in the first decades of the twentieth century was a catalyst for the viewpoint that learning is above all a social practice. Vygotsky suggested that development and learning are firmly rooted in—and influenced by—society and culture. Accepting this notion means that it is no longer possible to separate learning from the context in which it takes place, nor from an understanding of how culture and society influence and are influenced by learning.

Vygotsky and others who have advanced the sociocultural foundation of cognition (Cole & Griffin, 1983; Scribner & Cole, 1981) have provided us with a framework for understanding how schools can either encourage or discourage the development of learning communities. Because schools organize themselves in specific ways, they are more or less comfortable and inviting for students of particular backgrounds. Most schools closely reflect the traditional image of the intelligent, academically prepared young person, and consequently, these are the young people who tend to feel most comfortable in school settings. But institutional environments are never neutral; they are always based on particular views of human development, of what is worth knowing, and of what it means to be educated. When young people enter schools, they are entering institutions that have already made some fundamental decisions about such matters, and in the process, some of these children may be left out through no fault of their own. The ability to create community, so important in sociocultural theory, is lost.

Maria Botelho, a doctoral student of mine and a former early childhood teacher and librarian, remembers very clearly what it was like to begin school as a young immigrant student in Cambridge, Massachusetts. After viewing a short video on bilingual education in one of my classes, she felt almost as if she had stepped back in time. The video highlights a number of students, one of them Carla, a young Portuguese student in a bilingual class in Cambridge. Maria reflected on her reactions to the video in the journal she kept for my class:

> I viewed the video "Quality Bilingual Education" twice. I wept both times. The Portuguese-speaking girl, Carla, attended kindergarten in a school that is less than a block from where my parents live in Cambridge; it was too close to home, so to speak. Like Carla, I entered the Cambridge Public Schools speaking only

Portuguese. Unlike Carla, I was placed in a mainstream first-grade class. I still remember my teacher bringing over a piece of paper with some writing on it (a worksheet) and crayons. I fell asleep. There I learned quietly about her world, and my world was left with my coat, outside the classroom door. (Nieto, 1999, p. 110)

Sociocultural theories are a radical departure from conventional viewpoints that posit learning as largely unaffected by context. Traditional viewpoints often consider that children such as Maria who do not speak English have low intelligence. As a result, such children are automatically barred from entering a community of learners. A Vygotskian perspective provides a more hopeful framework for thinking about learning because if learning can be influenced by social mediation, then conditions can be created in schools that can help most students learn. These conditions can result in what Carmen Mercado (1998) has described as the "fashioning of new texts—texts of our collective voices" (p. 92) that emerge as a result of organizing learning environments in which literacy is for sharing and reflecting. Particularly significant in this regard is the notion of the *zone of proximal development* or ZPD (Vygotsky, 1978). But the ZPD is not simply an individual space, but a social one. Thus, according to Henry Trueba (1989), if we accept Vygotsky's theory of ZPD, then failure to learn cannot be defined as individual failure but rather as systemic failure, that is, as the failure of the social system to provide the learner with an opportunity for successful social interactions.

In order to change academic failure to success, appropriate social and instructional interventions need to occur. For teachers, this means that they need to first acknowledge students' differences and then act as a bridge between their students' differences and the culture of the dominant society. The metaphor of a bridge is an appropriate one for teachers who want to be effective with students of diverse backgrounds. This is a lesson I learned from Diane Sweet, a former student who had been an engineer until she fell in love with teaching ESL at the plant where she worked and decided to become a teacher. Diane was well aware of the benefits of bridges, and she applied the metaphor to teaching: a bridge provides access to a different shore without closing off the possibility of returning home; a bridge is built on solid ground but soars toward the heavens; a bridge connects two places that might otherwise never be able to meet. The best thing about bridges is that they do not need to be burned once they are used; on the contrary, they become more valuable with use because they help visitors from *both* sides become adjusted to different contexts. This is, however, a far cry from how diverse languages and cultures tend to be viewed in schools: the conventional wisdom is that, if native languages and cultures are used at all, it should be only until one learns the *important* language and culture, and then they should be discarded or burned. It is definitely a one-way street with no turning back.

The metaphor of the bridge suggests a different stance: you can have two homes, and the bridge can help you cross the difficult and conflict-laden spaces between them. Teachers who take seriously their responsibility for working with students of diverse backgrounds become bridges, or what Díaz, Flores, Cousin, and Soo Hoo (1992) have called *sociocultural mediators*. That is, they accept and validate the cultural symbols used by all their students, not just by those from majority backgrounds. In sociocultural theory, learning and achievement are not merely cognitive processes, but complex issues that need to be understood in the development of community.

Three of my colleagues provide a hopeful example of using students' experiences and identities as a basis for creating community. Jo-Anne Wilson Keenan, a teacher-researcher, working with Judith Solsken and Jerri Willett, professors at the University of Massachusetts, developed a collaborative action research project in a school in Springfield, Massachusetts, with a very diverse student body. The project—based on the premise that parents and other family members of children from widely diverse backgrounds have a lot to offer schools to enhance their children's learning—was distinct from others in which parents are simply invited to speak about their culture and to share food. Instead, their research focused on demonstrating how parents can promote student learning by transforming the curriculum. But engaging in this kind of project is not always easy. Keenan, Solsken, and Willett (1993) pointed out that collaborating with families "requires that we confront our own fears of difference and open our classrooms to discussions of topics that may raise tensions among the values of different individuals, groups, and institutions" (p. 64). Through inspiring stories based on in-depth analysis of the families' visits, they described how they attempted to build reciprocal relationships with parents, and concluded:

> Both the extent and the quality of participation by the parents belies the common perception that low-income and minority parents are unable or unwilling to collaborate with the school. Even more important, our study documents the wide range of knowledge, skills, and teaching capabilities that parents are already sharing with their children at home and that are available to enrich the education of their own and other children in school. (p. 64)

The important work of Moll and Gónzalez (1997) and their colleagues is another well-known example of research that builds on family knowledge.

Conclusion

No theory can provide all the answers to the persistent problems of education because these problems are not just about teaching and learning, but rather are about a society's ideology. Sociocultural theories give us different insights into these problems. While we need to accept the inconclusiveness of what we know, we also need to find new and more empowering ways of addressing these concerns. Maxine Greene (1994), in a discussion of postmodernism, poststructuralism, feminism, literary criticism, and other sociocultural theories, discussed both the possibilities and the limits they have. She wrote: "The point is to open a number of fresh perspectives on epistemology in its connection with educational research" (p. 426). But she added, "no universalized or totalized viewing, even of a revised sort" (p. 426) is possible.

Nevertheless, in spite of this inconclusiveness, we know enough to know that teachers need to respect students' identities and they need to learn about their students if they are to be effective with them. This means understanding the students we teach, and building relationships with them. Ron Morris, a young man attending an alternative school in Boston, described the disappointing relationships he had with teachers before attending the alternative school where he now found himself, a school that finally allowed him to have the relationships he craved. He said:

> When a teacher becomes a teacher, she acts like a teacher instead of a person. She takes her title as now she's mechanical, somebody just running it. Teachers shouldn't deal with students like we're machines. You're a person. I'm a person. We come to school and we all act like people. (p. 265)

Ron reminds us that we do not have all the answers, and indeed, that some of the answers we have are clearly wrong. Ray McDermott (1977) described this fact beautifully: "We are all embedded in our own procedures, which make us both very smart in one situation and blind and stupid in the next" (p. 202). More recently, Herbert Kohl (1994) has suggested that students' failure to learn is not always caused by a lack of intelligence, motivation, or self-esteem. On the contrary, he maintains that "To agree to learn from a stranger who does not respect your integrity causes a major loss of self" (p. 6), or what Carol Locust (1988) has called "wounding the spirit " (p. 315).

Much has been written in the past few years about teachers' reluctance to broach issues of difference, both among themselves and with their students (Fine, 1991; Jervis, 1996; McIntyre, 1997; Sleeter, 1994; Solomon, 1995; Tatum, 1997). This is especially true of racism, which is most often addressed in schools as if it were a personality problem. But prejudice and discrimination are not just personality traits or psychological phenomena; they are also manifestations of economic, political, and social power. The institutional definition of racism is not always easy for teachers to accept because it goes against deeply held notions of equality and justice in our nation. Bias as an institutional system implies that some people and groups benefit and others lose. Whites, whether they want to or not, benefit in a racist society; males benefit in a sexist society. Discrimination always helps somebody—those with the most power—which explains why racism, sexism, and other forms of discrimination continue to exist. Having a different language to speak about differences in privilege and power is the first step in acquiring the courage to confront differences.

Finally, sociocultural and sociopolitical concepts give us a way to confront what Henry Giroux (1992) has called our nation's "retreat from democracy" (p. 4). Paulo Freire (1998), writing a series of letters to teachers, focused on this problem:

> When inexperienced middle-class teachers take teaching positions in peripheral areas of the city, class-specific tastes, values, language, discourse, syntax, semantics, everything about the students may seem contradictory to the point of being shocking and frightening. It is necessary, however, that teachers understand that the students' syntax; their manners, tastes, and ways of addressing

teachers and colleagues; and the rules governing their fighting and playing among themselves are all part of their *cultural identity*, which never lacks an element of class. All that has to be accepted. Only as learners recognize themselves democratically and see that their right to say "I be" is respected will they become able to learn the dominant grammatical reasons why they should say "I am." (p. 49; emphasis in original)

All students are individuals as well as members of particular groups whose identities are either disdained or respected in society. When we understand this, then my own story, and those of countless others, can be understood not simply as someone "pulling herself up by her bootstraps," or "melting," or joining "the mainstream," but as a story that the concepts I have spoken about—agency/co-constructed learning, experience, identity/hybridity, context/situatedness/positionality, and community—can begin to explain. When language, literacy, and culture are approached in these ways, we have a more hopeful way of addressing teaching and learning for all students.

References

Appiah, A. (1994). Identity, authenticity, survival: Multicultural societies and social reproduction. In A. Gutmann (Ed.), *Multiculturalism* (pp. 149–163). Princeton, NJ: Princeton University Press.

Apple, M. W. (1993). The politics of official knowledge: Does a national curriculum make sense? *Teachers College Record, 95,* 222–241.

Arvizu, S. F. (1994). Building bridges for the future: Anthropological contributions to diversity and classroom practice. In R. A. DeVillar, C. J. Faltis, & J. Cummins (Eds.), *Cultural diversity in schools: From rhetoric to reality* (pp. 75–97). Albany: State University of New York.

Bourdieu, P. (1985). The forms of capital. In J. G. Richardson (Ed.), *Handbook of theory and research for the sociology of education* (pp. 241–248). Westport, CT: Greenwood.

Chomsky, N. (1965). *Aspects of the theory of syntax.* Cambridge, MA: MIT Press.

Cole, M., & Griffin, P. (1983). A socio-historical approach to re-mediation. *Quarterly Newsletter of the Laboratory of Comparative Human Cognition, 5*(4), 69–74.

Corson, D. (1993). *Language, minority education and gender: Linking social justice and power.* Clevedon, England: Multilingual Matters.

Cummins, J. (1994). Knowledge, power, and identity in teaching English as a second language. In F. Genesee (Ed.), *Educating second language children: The whole child, the whole curriculum, the whole community* (pp. 33–58). Cambridge, England: Cambridge University Press.

Delpit, L. D. (1988). The silenced dialogue: Power and pedagogy in educating other people's children. *Harvard Educational Review, 58,* 280–298.

Dewey, J. (1916). *Democracy and education.* New York: Free Press.

Díaz, E., Flores, B., Cousin, P. T., & Soo Hoo, S. (1992). *Teacher as sociocultural mediator.* Paper presented at the meeting of the American Educational Research Association, San Francisco.

Dorfman, A. (1998). *Heading south, looking north: A bilingual journey.* New York: Penguin.

Erickson, F. (1990). Culture, politics, and educational practice. *Educational Foundations, 4*(2), 21–45.

Fairclough, N. (1989). *Language and power.* New York: Longman.

Fine, M. (1991). *Framing dropouts: Notes on the politics of an urban high school.* Albany: State University of New York Press.

Freire, P. (1970). *Pedagogy of the oppressed.* New York: Seabury.

Freire, P. (1985). *The politics of education: Culture, power, and liberation.* New York: Bergin & Garvey.

Freire, P. (1998). *Teachers as cultural workers: Letters to those who dare teach.* Boulder, CO: Westview.

Gee, J. P. (1990). *Social linguistics and literacies: Ideologies in discourse.* Bristol, PA: Falmer.

Giroux, H. (1992). Educational leadership and the crisis of democratic government. *Educational Researcher, 21*(4), 4–11.

Goodlad, J. I. (1984). *A place called school.* New York: McGraw-Hill.

Greene, M. (1994). Epistemology and educational research: The influence of recent approaches to knowledge. In L. Darling-Hammond (Ed.), *Review of research in education, 20* (pp. 423–464). Washington, DC: American Educational Research Association.

Hirsch, E. D. (1987). *Cultural literacy: What every American needs to know.* Boston: Houghton Mifflin.

Jervis, K. (1996). "How come there are no brothers on that list?": Hearing the hard questions all children ask. *Harvard Educational Review, 66,* 546–576.

Kalantzis, M., Cope, B., & Slade, D. (1989). *Minority languages.* London: Falmer.

Keenan, J. W., Willett, J., & Solsken, J. (1993). Constructing an urban village: School/home collaboration in a multicultural classroom. *Language Arts, 70,* 56–66.

Kohl, H. (1994). *"I won't learn from you" and other thoughts on creative maladjustment.* New York: New Press.

Ladson-Billings, G. (1994). *The dreamkeepers: Successful teachers of African American children.* San Francisco: Jossey-Bass.

Locust, C. (1988). Wounding the spirit: Discrimination and traditional American Indian belief systems. *Harvard Educational Review, 3,* 315–330.

Mercado, C. I. (1998). When young people from marginalized communities enter the world of ethnographic research: Scribing, planning, reflecting, and sharing. In A. Egan-Robertson & D. Bloome (Eds.), *Students as researchers of culture and language in their own communities* (pp. 69–92). Cresskill, NJ: Hampton.

McDermott, R. P. (1977). Social relations as contexts for learning in school. *Harvard Educational Review, 47,* 198–213.

McIntyre, A. (1997). Constructing an image of a white teacher. *Teachers College Press, 98,* 653–681.

Moll, L., & Gonzalez, N. (1997). Teachers as social scientists: Learning about culture from household research. In P. M. Hall (Ed.), *Race, ethnicity, and multiculturalism* (Vol. 1, pp. 89–114). New York: Garland.

Nelson-Barber, S., & Estrin, E. T. (1995). Bringing Native American perspectives to mathematics and science teaching. *Theory into Practice, 34,* 174–185.

Nieto, S. (1992, 2000). *Affirming diversity: The sociopolitical context of multicultural education.* New York: Longman.

Nieto, S. (1999). *The light in their eyes: Creating multicultural learning communities.* New York: Teachers College Press.

Rodriguez, R. (1982). *Hunger of memory: The education of Richard Rodriguez.* Boston: David R. Godine.

Scribner, S., & Cole, M. (1981). *The psychology of literacy.* Cambridge, MA: Harvard University Press.

Shor, I. (1992). *Empowering education: Critical teaching for social change.* Chicago: University of Chicago Press.

Sleeter, C. E. (1994). White racism. *Multicultural Education, 1*(4), pp. 5–8, 39.

Snow, C. E., Barnes, W. S., Chandler, J., Goodman, I. F., & Hemphill, L. (1991). *Unfulfilled expectations: Home and school influences on literacy.* Cambridge, MA: Harvard University Press.

Solomon, R. P. (1995). Beyond prescriptive pedagogy: Teacher inservice education for cultural diversity. *Journal of Teacher Education, 46,* 251–258.

Solsken, J. W. (1993). *Literacy, gender, and work in families and in school.* Norwood, NJ: Ablex.

Stein, A. (1971). Strategies for failure. *Harvard Educational Review, 41,* 133–179.

Taylor, D., & Dorsey-Gaines, C. (1988). *Growing up literate: Learning from inner-city families.* Portsmouth, NH: Heinemann.

Tatum, B. D. (1997). *"Why are all the Black kids sitting together in the cafeteria?" and other conversations about race.* New York: HarperCollins.

Trueba, H. T. (1989). *Raising silent voices: Educating the linguistic minorities for the 21st century.* Cambridge, MA: Newbury House.

Vygotsky, L. S. (1978). *Thought and language.* Cambridge, MA: MIT Press.

Literacy Education in the Process of Community Development[*]

Kathryn H. Au
University of Hawaii

On June 30, 1995 the Kamehameha Elementary Education Program (KEEP) closed its doors forever. Established in 1971, KEEP had been the nation's longest running educational research and development project dedicated to improving the education of a particular group of culturally diverse students. The students in this case were of Native Hawaiian ancestry, descendants of the original Polynesian inhabitants of the Hawaiian Islands. KEEP had been my professional home for 24 years. In this address I will describe my professional journey since the closing of KEEP, a journey that has profoundly changed my thinking about my work as a literacy researcher.

Throughout my career, my research has focused on the question of how Hawaiian children from low-income families could be helped to attain high levels of literacy in school. In 1994, when it became clear that KEEP would be closed, I took two steps to continue this work. First, I decided to pursue a position at the University of Hawaii. Second, I joined two of my colleagues—Sherlyn Franklin Goo and Alice Kawakami, both educators of Hawaiian ancestry—in setting up a nonprofit corporation for the purpose of carrying on educational projects in Hawaiian communities. Established in 1994, the Institute for Native Pacific Education and Culture, or INPEACE, has fostered the efforts that I will be describing.

When I started my new job at the University of Hawaii in 1995, I began arranging to establish an elementary teacher education cohort for the Leeward Coast of Oahu. The Leeward Coast is a rural area about a 45-minute drive from downtown Honolulu. The majority of its residents are Hawaiians. The Leeward Coast has all the problems of low-income areas throughout the United States: high rates of welfare, unemployment, crime, and drug abuse. Its seven elementary schools enroll about 5,000 students, nearly 60% of them Hawaiians. Students in these schools typically score in the bottom three stanines on standardized tests of reading achievement.

Nani Pai, a former KEEP staff member and longtime resident of the Leeward Coast, named the new teacher education cohort *Ka Lama O Ke Kaiāulu,* which

[*]Oscar S. Causey Research Award Address. Thanks are due to Margaret Maaka and Karen Blake for their contributions to this work, to James Gavelek for introducing me to the work of Etienne Wenger, and to Taffy Raphael for helping me to see the big picture. The research reported in this address was supported by a grant from the Spencer Foundation. The data presented, statements made, and views expressed are solely the responsibility of the author.

National Reading Conference Yearbook, 49, pp. 61–77.

may be translated as "the light of the community." Many Hawaiian expressions have a *kaona,* which is a double or hidden meaning. Thus, *Kaiaulu* is also the name for the gentle breeze that blows along the Leeward Coast. For knowledgeable residents, the term *Kaiāulu* clearly connects the cohort to their community.

We had learned at KEEP that teacher expertise was the key to improving Hawaiian students' literacy achievement. For example, we found that student achievement improved when teachers implemented 90% of the features of writers' and readers' workshops, including portfolio assessment (Au & Carroll, 1997). Obviously, teachers needed time, as well as the opportunities for professional development provided by KEEP, to gain the expertise required to conduct writers' and readers' workshops well.

From my previous work on the Leeward Coast, I knew that one of the barriers to KEEP's success was an exceptionally high rate of teacher turnover. Typical rates of turnover in the schools ranged from 20% to 33% a year but could be as high as 50%. About two-thirds of the graduates of our College of Education receive their first teaching assignments on the Leeward Coast. In 3 years, when they receive tenure, most of these teachers transfer to schools nearer to town.

Our experience at KEEP was that it took 2 to 3 years for most teachers to develop the expertise to conduct effective writers' and readers' workshops. New teachers would spend 3 years receiving inservice consultation from KEEP staff members, steadily gain proficiency in conducting writers' and readers' workshops, and then transfer to other schools. Students in more affluent areas, not those on the Leeward Coast, became the beneficiaries of the expertise these teachers had gained. In turn, in a seemingly endless cycle, those now experienced teachers were replaced by novices. As a headline in the *Honolulu Advertiser* proclaimed, "Neediest students get newest teachers" (Peterson, 1998).

In planning for the cohort, I thought that one way of dealing with the problem of turnover would be to recruit residents of the Leeward Coast, especially Hawaiians, to become teachers. Residents would have a commitment to the community and would likely remain in the schools much longer than 3 years. Such an approach would also address issues of equity. Only about 10% of the teachers in the public schools of our state are Hawaiians, compared to 24% of the students (Office of Accountability and School Instructional Support/Planning and Evaluation Group, 1997). Adults on the Leeward Coast have told me that, apart from substitute teachers, they cannot recall being taught by a single teacher of Hawaiian ancestry.

Fortunately, I was not starting from scratch in establishing the Ka Lama teacher education cohort. Three of the elementary schools on the Leeward Coast had been sites for KEEP, and I had worked with teachers there since 1981. I felt I had a clear understanding of effective literacy instruction in Leeward Coast classrooms that I could bring to language arts methods courses for preservice teachers.

But although I had confidence in my knowledge of literacy instruction and of the schools, I realized that I knew little about the community beyond the schools. If my goal was to recruit residents to become teachers, and to make the Ka Lama teacher education cohort a joint enterprise with the community, I had to better understand the community and the issues it faced.

Two Perspectives on Community

As a literacy researcher who focused on classrooms, my previous thinking about community was primarily in terms of the classroom community of learners (Cairney & Langbien, 1989). When I began the teacher education work described here, I became interested in broader issues of educational change in communities. In this regard, two somewhat different perspectives on community proved valuable.

The first perspective comes from the work of John McKnight (1995), in his book *The Careless Society: Community and Its Counterfeits.* McKnight views community as the site for the relationships among citizens. These relationships lead to care, which McKnight defines as "the consenting commitment of citizens to one another" (p. x). McKnight writes:

> The most significant development transforming America since World War II has been the growth of a powerful service economy and its pervasive serving institutions. Those institutions have commodified the care of community and called the substitution a service. As citizens have seen the professionalized service commodity invade their communities, they have grown doubtful of their common capacity to care, and so it is that we have become a careless society, populated by impotent citizens and ineffectual communities dependent on the counterfeit of care called human services. (pp. ix-x)

McKnight argues persuasively that institutions, by their very efforts to provide services, may hamper the community's efforts to supply care.

On the Leeward Coast, I became acquainted with community leaders working for social, economic, and environmental causes. Themes of sovereignty and the empowerment of Hawaiians run through these efforts. My colleague Puanani Burgess, a Hawaiian community leader and writer, made these themes clear when introducing the preservice teachers to the aquaculture project run by the Wai'anae Coast Community Alternative Development Corporation. The purpose of involving families in aquaculture is not simply to teach them to raise and market fish. Although economic self-sufficiency is an important goal, the ultimate purpose is to give families pride and independence through personal involvement in the community development process and to enable them to contribute to the rebuilding of a vibrant Hawaiian community.

I came to understand that education is just one of several social service systems, including health care and social work, that can work for or against a community's efforts to provide care. I realized that community leaders on the Leeward Coast saw literacy and education not as ends in themselves but as means to an end—a flourishing and self-respecting community in which the cycle of welfare and poverty had been broken. They viewed literacy and education as essential to meeting the community's greatest need—decent jobs.

McKnight does not deny that professionalization brings the advantage of greater expertise due to specialized training, but he stresses that it brings the disadvantage of distance, as service providers are seldom dealing with individuals with whom they share the bonds of community. Although McKnight does not extend his analysis to education, the parallels are easy to see. At present, 80% of the teachers in Leeward Coast classrooms do not reside in the community. Schooling has become the process of educating "other people's children," as Lisa Delpit (1988) puts it. From this first perspective, I knew that my challenge would be to see that our work in teacher education supported the community's efforts to provide care and encouraged community ownership of this and future teacher education efforts.

How best to meet this challenge? This is where the second perspective proved useful. This perspective comes from the work of Jean Lave and Etienne Wenger who have studied what they term "communities of practice." Here I draw upon Wenger's (1998) book, *Communities of Practice: Learning, Meaning, and Identity*. Wenger defines community as "the social configurations in which our enterprises are defined as worth pursuing and our participation is recognizable as competence" (p. 5). Practice is defined as "the shared historical and social resources, frameworks, and perspectives that can sustain mutual engagement in action" (p. 5).

Wenger points out that communities of practice are everywhere and pervasive in everyday life. These groups may overlap with but are not the same as localities such as the Leeward Coast or the urban neighborhoods that are the focus of McKnight's work. Families form communities of practice as they strive to maintain their ways of living. Workers organize with their immediate colleagues to accomplish the tasks at hand. Students join official and unofficial groups to negotiate with or around the agenda imposed by the school. Wenger cites band members rehearsing in garages, computer users congregating in virtual spaces, and youth gangs, all as examples of communities of practice. Communities of practice develop their own routines and rituals, artifacts and symbols, stories and histories. Wenger argues that the learning that individuals find most transformative takes place through membership in communities of practice.

The connection between Wenger's concepts and classroom communities will be obvious to those familiar with the readers' and writers' workshops (Au, Carroll, & Scheu, 1997). Learning is a matter of participating in communities of practice. Students develop as readers and writers as they participate in the workshops, as members of a classroom community of practice.

Wenger (1998) proposes that identity grows from the individual's belonging to communities of practice. He suggests that identity formation and learning be seen in terms of three different modes of belonging (pp. 173–174). Modes of belonging are processes that shape and inspire individuals' learning. I will use the modes of belonging described by Wenger to frame the learning I have done as a researcher over the past 5 years, as I describe three different aspects of my work.

The first mode of belonging is engagement, which Wenger defines as active involvement in mutual processes of negotiating meaning. In this regard I will

discuss case studies of three preservice teachers in the Ka Lama teacher education cohort, and some considerations I have found important in preparing these
teachers to join and contribute to a community of practice in support of educational change on the Leeward Coast. The first and most immediate aspect of my
work is to build this community of practice through my engagement with the
teacher education cohort.

The second mode of belonging is imagination, which Wenger defines as
creating images of the world and making connections across time and space. In
this regard I will discuss historical research on the presence and absence of
Hawaiian teachers in the public schools of Hawaii. This research has helped me to
see our work in teacher education within its broader historical context, to convey
this context to the preservice teachers, and to encourage our mutual imagining of
a future better than the present.

The third mode of belonging is alignment, which Wenger defines as the coor-
dinating of energy and activity to contribute to broader enterprises. In my situation, the broader enterprise is the overall process of community development on
the Leeward Coast. In this regard I will discuss how our work in teacher education
has grown from one component to three, as needs in the setting have been
identified.

Engagement: Case Studies of Preservice Teachers

Preparing case studies is always a daunting prospect, and these case studies
of three preservice teachers in the Ka Lama teacher education cohort were no
exception. We have files about six inches thick for every preservice teacher, including interviews, surveys, videotapes, and written work collected weekly for six
courses and four semesters of field experience, including student teaching. Margie
Maaka and I taught these courses and supervised the field experience and student teaching, so the case studies are informed as well by personal knowing.

The three preservice teachers were enrolled in the first Ka Lama teacher
education cohort. The cohort is part of the elementary education program in the
College of Education at the University of Hawaii. Candidates must have junior
standing to be admitted to this full-time, 2-year program, which leads to a bachelor's
degree in education.

The first of our case studies centers on Carol, a Japanese-American preservice
teacher who graduated from a private school in Honolulu. Carol's case is of interest because many teachers in Hawaii's public schools are Japanese Americans
from middle-class families. The second case study centers on Sarah, a preservice
teacher of Hawaiian ancestry who also graduated from a private school in Honolulu. Sarah's case is of interest because she is a Hawaiian from a middle-class
background, who is an outsider to the Leeward Coast. The third case study centers on Janine, who like Sarah is of Hawaiian ancestry. Unlike Carol and Sarah,
Janine was raised on the Leeward Coast and attended public schools in the area.
In contrast to the other two, she entered the teacher education cohort from a
community college. The point I will be building toward with these case studies is
that preservice teachers with different cultural identities are likely to have differ-

ent concerns as they progress through a teacher education program designed to prepare them to work successfully in a diverse, low-income community.

This discussion of the case studies will be organized around categories of concern evident in the writing of the preservice teachers. First, let us look at the concerns evident in the written work of all three preservice teachers. Not surprisingly, given the emphasis on literacy and the teaching of literacy in the cohort, all three wrote about the value of reading and writing, and about the teaching of reading and writing. Carol had experienced literature discussions for a year in high school, but otherwise the three preservice teachers had had no prior experience with literature-based instruction or the process approach to writing.

In the first of the two language arts methods courses, I had the preservice teachers engage in writers' and readers' workshops. They wrote and revised personal narratives, participating in conferences with me and with their peers, and they shared their pieces in the Author's Chair (Graves & Hansen, 1983). They participated in Book Clubs (Raphael & McMahon, 1994), preparing written responses and discussing the literature with their peers. They learned an array of teaching strategies, including K-W-L (Ogle, 1986), shared and guided reading (Fountas & Pinnell, 1996; Holdaway, 1979), Making Words (Cunningham & Cunningham, 1992), and the experience-text-relationship approach (Au, 1979). They prepared and shared literacy portfolios, following the model developed by Jane Hansen (Hansen, 1992). The three preservice teachers all reported enjoying and learning from these experiences.

The time at which the preservice teachers actually conducted writers' or readers' workshops depended on the circumstances they encountered in their field placements or on the job. Carol's mentor teachers did not fully implement the writers' and readers' workshops, and she did not have the opportunity to work extensively with either of these approaches during her four semesters in the teacher education cohort. However, Carol was hired at a school on the Leeward Coast that favored these approaches. With the help of a resource teacher, Carol established writers' and readers' workshops in her classroom, and during her second year of teaching has continued to use these approaches.

The turning point for Sarah came during the second semester, when she was placed in the kindergarten classroom of a former KEEP teacher who conducted exemplary writers' and readers' workshops. Her experiences during this placement convinced Sarah of the value of these approaches for young children.

Janine spent the third and fourth semesters in the classroom of a mentor teacher who had her take responsibility for introducing and maintaining the writers' workshop in this third-grade class. Janine reported making several mistakes in launching the workshop, but she persisted and every child eventually published a piece that semester. She was the only one of the three preservice teachers to introduce literacy portfolios following Hansen's model. This effort proved successful, in several cases turning into a family project, as children sought help from their parents in assembling the portfolios. In short, the three preservice teachers all came to conduct writers' and readers' workshops in classrooms and to appreciate the value of these approaches.

Now, let us look at the concerns shared by the different pairs of preservice teachers. Carol and Sarah both wrote about instructional strategies. Carol and Janine shared the themes of students' self-esteem or self-confidence and the importance of having a safe classroom environment and building a classroom community. The concerns that Carol and Sarah, and Carol and Janine, had in common might be the concerns of preservice teachers in any setting. In contrast, the concerns that Sarah and Janine shared seemed to grow directly from their role as Hawaiian teachers working with Hawaiian students. They had the following concerns in common: coming to value what it means to be Hawaiian, responsibility for the perpetuation of Hawaiian culture, and social justice.

The differences become more pronounced when we look at the concerns unique to each of the preservice teachers. Concerns expressed by Carol, not evident in the writing of the others, were being a good teacher of all students, and tolerance and not stereotyping students. Sarah was the only one to write about seeking a balance between Hawaiian and Western ways, and to reflect on the privileged nature of her own upbringing. Concerns unique to Janine were quality of education and community involvement, self-improvement, and self-knowledge.

Some differences in the preservice teachers' concerns seem related to their status as outsiders or insiders to the Leeward Coast. Carol and Sarah immediately recognized that Leeward Coast schools represented a different world. Carol described how she had always gone to school and worked with other Asian Americans. During her first semester in the teacher education cohort, as she looked over her mentor teacher's class for the first time, she saw no students who looked like her former classmates. Sarah wrote about how happy she felt to be working in a classroom with many Hawaiian students. However, she was aware of differences in social class and worried about being accepted by the children, even wondering whether she should stop wearing her jewelry to school. Janine, in contrast, felt comfortable in the classroom right from the start. She had the advantage not only of having attended schools in the community but of having held jobs as a tutor and as an instructor at a district park.

Predictably, classroom management posed a greater problem for Carol and Sarah than for Janine. The anthropologist John D'Amato (1988) described the phenomenon of acting, a playful form of misbehavior used by Hawaiian students to test their teachers' mettle. D'Amato noted that, if the teacher does not show the firmness needed to maintain order, students' misbehavior will escalate. D'Amato used the metaphor of the smile with teeth to describe the management style shown by teachers effective in working with Hawaiian students.

Like most preservice teachers, Carol and Sarah thought at first that they could manage the students with more smile and less teeth. In her first field placement, Sarah worked with a Hawaiian mentor teacher who had grown up on the Leeward Coast. At first Sarah found it daunting to discipline the students with any degree of firmness, much less the degree of firmness she saw her mentor teacher using. She felt a sense of accomplishment when she finally managed to establish herself as an authority figure. Janine showed the ability to smile with teeth right from the start. She had no qualms at all about being firm with the children. Twice during university class discussions, she modeled for the other preservice teachers the language and tone of voice she used to show the children she meant business.

Other differences in the preservice teachers' concerns seem related to their ethnicity and cultural identity, and whether they felt a personal connection to Hawaiian issues. In written reflections on her classroom experiences, Carol did not use the word Hawaiian to describe the students. Carol did not have difficulty discussing her own identity as a Japanese American, for example, how she was motivated to be a good student in part by the fear of bringing shame upon her family. In this regard she differed from the mainstream teachers studied by Florio-Ruane, Raphael, Glazier, McVee, and Wallace (1997) who believed that they were "nothing" or "lacking something" when it came to identifying with a particular cultural group. Carol's reflections about culture, however, did not extend to the culture of the students in Leeward Coast classrooms. Her writing indicated that she wanted to be a good teacher for all children. She expressed her commitment in a general fashion without mentioning the needs of any particular group of students. Carol's writing showed that she was gaining an intellectual understanding of issues of social justice as they affected Hawaiians, but that she viewed these issues from a distance. In contrast to Carol, Sarah's writing showed a specific commitment to improving the education of Hawaiian children, rather than the education of all children in general. Sarah wrote:

> Sometimes the challenges of working on the Leeward Coast scare and overwhelm me. . . . I hope that I can face them and work where there are many needs. If nobody ever deals with the hard things in life, we will never put an end to the cycle of poverty and abuse.

In her writing Sarah referred to her experiences growing up as a member of a large Hawaiian family. At the same time, Sarah's work in Leeward Coast classrooms helped her to recognize the privileged nature of her own upbringing. One day, a heavy rainstorm flooded the playground of a Leeward Coast school, causing the school to close for the day. Sarah saw the flooding as one more obstacle to the education of children on the Leeward Coast, and she recalled how such conditions had never affected her own private school. Course readings and discussions appeared simply to be adding momentum and intellectual detail to the process of rethinking already spurred by the experience of working in Leeward Coast classrooms.

As a Hawaiian and insider to the Leeward Coast, Janine showed more awareness than Carol and Sarah of how power relations affected education there. She wrote, "I felt and still feel that most of our kids from kindergarten through the twelfth grade are cheated out of a higher educational standard." Her ability to identify with the children and their struggles in school came from having grown up in the community, rather than from the more abstract notion of a shared Hawaiian heritage, evident in Sarah's writing. Janine wanted to be a role model, raising students' aspirations by demonstrating that Hawaiians from the community could become teachers.

Of the three preservice teachers, Janine appeared to benefit most from the opportunity to read about and reflect on Hawaiian issues. Janine chose to write an autobiography during the writers' workshop, and in this piece she described her childhood and adolescence in terms that corresponded to anthropologists' generalizations about Hawaiian culture (Gallimore, Boggs, & Jordan, 1974). For example, as the oldest child, Janine was assigned responsibility for the day-to-day upbringing of her siblings. She understood the care of her siblings, not her friends or even her schoolwork, to be paramount. This emphasis on the well being of the family or social group over the achievement of the individual is a well-established finding in studies of Hawaiian culture. However, Janine's understanding of this and other aspects of Hawaiian culture was tacit rather than conscious. Her self-perceived lack of understanding led her to write that she felt disconnected from her Hawaiian heritage. For Sarah, the catalyst for thinking seemed to be the experience of being in Leeward Coast classrooms, whereas for Janine, the catalyst seemed to be course readings and opportunities for written reflection. She had a wealth of experience gained by living and attending school on the Leeward Coast, but she had not previously had the opportunity to contemplate these experiences and to situate them in an intellectual framework.

What do these case studies suggest about preparing teachers to teach in diverse communities such as the Leeward Coast? First, participation in a classroom community of readers and writers during their language arts methods courses apparently supported the preservice teachers' learning about literacy instruction. However, it was the combination of coursework and favorable conditions in school settings that helped these preservice teachers to gain confidence in and proficiency with these approaches.

Second, if preservice teachers are from outside the community, they may benefit in particular from spending large amounts of time in the classrooms of mentor teachers. The preservice teachers spent eight hours per week in classrooms during each of the three semesters before student teaching, but reported that they could have used even more time.

Third, the preservice teachers appeared to benefit from opportunities in university courses to explore issues of cultural identity, their own and those of their students. Preservice teachers such as Carol, who as a Japanese American did not share the culture of the students on the Leeward Coast, may adopt the view of wanting to be a good teacher for all children. Class discussions with preservice teachers who hold this attitude could emphasize the importance of students' cultural identity, the role of cultural differences (for example, in the patterning of face-to-face interaction), and culturally responsive pedagogy (Au & Kawakami, 1994; Ladson-Billings, 1995). Even with these activities, however, preservice teachers' attitudes may be slow to change. Preservice teachers such as Sarah, who are of the same ethnicity as the students but from a more privileged background, may benefit in particular from discussions of social class and its relationship to ethnicity and to education. Preservice teachers such as Janine, who are from the community, may value the opportunity to reflect upon their experiences at home and at school and to understand these experiences in a larger cultural and political context.

Imagination: The History of Hawaiian Teachers

I turn now from engagement as a mode of belonging, and my direct work with the preservice teachers, to imagination as a mode of belonging, and the historical research I have been conducting on the rise and fall of Hawaiian teachers in the public schools.

The process of contact with the west has been so destructive to the well being of Hawaiians that I have heard community leaders use the term "genocide" to describe it. When the British explorer James Cook arrived in 1778, Kamehameha I had begun the campaigns that would eventually unite the islands under one ruler. At this time, the islands were inhabited by perhaps 400,000 Hawaiians. A century later, with the coming of whalers, missionaries, traders, and others, the native population had been reduced to about 40,000, in large measure because of the diseases brought by the foreigners. The Hawaiian people suffered further devastation due to the tremendous social, psychological, and economic changes taking place, including the overturning of the native religion and system of land tenure (Kame'eleihiwa, 1992). In 1893, the overthrow of the Hawaiian monarchy, engineered by a group of American sugar planters, brought an end to the last vestige of political control exercised by Hawaiians in their own land. Annexation of the islands to the United States followed in 1898.

The bleakness of this historical backdrop makes the story of the spread of schooling and literacy in Hawaii, and the role of Hawaiian teachers, all the more remarkable. Of course, precontact Hawaii had its own well-established educational and linguistic traditions. Education took place within the extended family, through having children observe and work alongside their elders (Kelly, 1991). In addition, young people who showed special promise participated in courses of formal instruction lasting from 15 to 20 years, for example, to become canoe builders, priests, and dancers of the hula (Dotts & Sikkema, 1994). Hawaiians had a flourishing oral tradition with legends, proverbs, poetical sayings, and lengthy chants memorized to preserve family history and genealogy (e.g., Pukui, 1983) . They delighted in a language celebrated for its subtleties and hidden meanings. They believed in the power of language, that it could bring life, and that it could bring death.

In 1822 American missionaries began translating the Bible into Hawaiian, using a system originally developed for Tahitian (Wilson, 1991). In this way, Hawaiian became a written language. By all accounts, literacy spread rapidly among Hawaiians, as the missionaries taught the king and his chiefs, then other adults. After the early 1830s, when interest among adults began to wane, the missionaries turned their attention to schools for children (Dotts & Sikkema, 1994). These common schools provided children with rudimentary instruction in reading and writing in the Hawaiian language, with Hawaiian adults, mostly men, doing the teaching. In 1840 Kamehameha III signed the general school laws, establishing a system of government schools reaching out to every village in the kingdom. This was the origin of Hawaii's statewide school system. The government common schools, staffed entirely by Hawaiians, taught reading and writing to tens of thousands of children. By the late 1800s, the literacy rate in Hawaii compared favorably to that of any nation in the world (Wilson, 1991). One indication of the high level of readership can be found in the fact that over 100 different Hawaiian-language newspapers were published during the nineteenth century.

Because of my work on the Leeward Coast, I became interested in the question of what had happened to Hawaiians in the teaching force. At one time, 100% of the teachers in the government common schools had been of Hawaiian ancestry. Yet today, fewer than 10% of the teachers in Hawaii's public schools are Hawaiian. In outlining the history of Hawaiian teachers, I would like to highlight three sets of events.

The first set of events that served to displace Hawaiian teachers was the rise of government select schools, which provided instruction in English rather than Hawaiian. With the exception of the High Chief Kekuanaoa, ministers of education in the kingdom were American missionaries and businessmen who promoted the value of English rather than Hawaiian. In 1880 the ministry of education began a concerted effort to phase out the Hawaiian-language schools, replacing them with English-language schools. In 1878 there were 169 Hawaiian-language schools, compared to 11 English-language schools (Board of Education, 1878). In 1888 English-language schools outnumbered Hawaiian-language schools for the first time, 69 to 63. The closing of the last Hawaiian-language school on the major islands took place in 1897, leaving only the tiny school on the remote island of Ni'ihau.

Because Hawaiians spoke English as a second language, most were disqualified from teaching in the select schools, where the pay was ten times higher than in the common schools. Americans filled an increasing number of teaching positions. In 1882, at the beginning of the push for English-language instruction, Hawaiians still constituted 66% of the teaching force, declining to 50% in 1890 (Board of Education, 1890). By 1900 just 28% of the teachers were Hawaiian.

A second set of events affecting the composition of the teaching force in Hawaii was the rising number of Chinese and Japanese teachers from families who had immigrated to Hawaii to provide labor for the sugar plantations. The immigration of the Chinese began in 1851, of the Japanese in 1886. The Territorial Normal School, established to prepare teachers, opened in 1895. From 1895 until 1929, a steadily increasing number of Hawaiians graduated from the Territorial Normal School, as shown in Figure 1 (figures based on Shaw, 1929). The x-axis shows the years, from 1896 to 1928, whereas the y-axis shows the number of Hawaiian graduates.

During the first two decades of the normal school, Hawaiians constituted the majority of graduates. This situation began to change in 1916, when Asian graduates outnumbered Hawaiians for the first time, 15 to 10. By 1929, the Territorial Normal School had graduated 1,981 teachers. About 40% of the graduates were Asian, about 32% Hawaiian, and about 27% Euro-American (Shaw, 1929). In 1926, Hawaiians were still somewhat overrepresented in the teaching force, at 24%, compared to Hawaiian students, at 16%. Gradually, Asians became the largest group, presently accounting for 47% of Hawaii's public school teachers (Office of

Accountability and School Instructional Support/Planning and Evaluation Group, 1997).

The third set of events to be highlighted in the history of Hawaiian teachers began in 1931 when the Territorial Normal School became part of the University of Hawaii. With the establishment of the Teachers College, the teacher preparation program was extended from 2 years to 4, leading to a bachelor's degree. As the Great Depression hit Hawaii and many people were out of work, record numbers of students enrolled at the university, many of them wanting to become teachers. At the same time, the sugar planters feared that the spread of education, in the form of public high schools, would cause potential plantation workers to aspire to other jobs (Dotts & Sikkema, 1994). They lobbied successfully for drastic reductions in the budget for the public schools and for the Teachers College. With these cuts, and little if any demand for teachers, the college raised its admission standards and added a fifth year to its teacher preparation program.

The effect of the changes on Hawaiians can be seen in Figure 2, which shows the contrast to the number of graduates under the normal school. The years from 1932 to 1968 have been added to the x-axis, with the number of Hawaiian graduates during this period indicated. In the 1930s, our estimates indicate that from 4 to 15 Hawaiians appear to have graduated from the Teachers College each year out of graduating classes ranging from 59 to 125. Our estimates for the 1940s are similar. Surprisingly, estimates for the 1950s and 1960s point to even lower numbers, ranging from only 2 to 9 per year out of graduating classes ranging from 88 to 248. Thus, Hawaiians fell from perhaps 15% of graduates with teaching degrees in the 1930s and 1940s to under 5% of graduates in the 1950s and 1960s. The effects on the composition of the teaching force in Hawaii can readily be predicted. In the 1970s, when the first modern data on the ethnicity of teachers in the public schools were compiled, Hawaiians constituted just 7% of the teachers in the public schools.

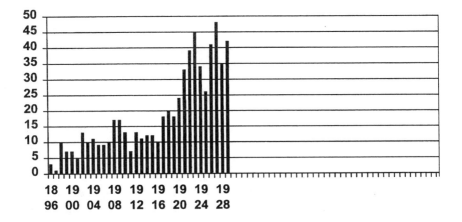

Figure 1. Hawaiian graduates from TNS.

I see some striking modern parallels to these three sets of historical events. First, then as now, powerful groups asserted control over schooling by promoting instruction in one language at the expense of another. Through the imposition of English-language instruction, promoted by the American sugar planters, the assimilation of Hawaiians began long before annexation to the United States. A similar press for assimilation, and against pluralism, can be seen in the movement against bilingual education in the United States today (e.g., Schnaiberg, 1998).

Second, under the guise of higher standards, teacher education became less and less accessible to students from underprivileged groups. In comparison to the Teachers College, the Territorial Normal School had liberal admission policies, along with a shorter program of study, and this allowed Hawaiians to continue to be well represented in the teaching force. Immigrant groups gained ground, but not at the expense of the indigenous group. The raising of admission standards, and the addition of a fifth year to the teacher education program, accompanied by falling demand for teachers, contributed to the near exclusion of Hawaiians from the teaching force. Little change has been seen in this situation for nearly 70 years.

Then as now, steps that appear to contribute to the professionalization of teaching may work against teacher education candidates from diverse groups, such as Hawaiians. For example, a common proposal is to make teacher education part of graduate—rather than undergraduate—education, requiring 5 or 6 years at the university instead of 4. Many of the Hawaiian preservice teachers I know are first-generation college students with limited financial resources. Unlike mainstream candidates from more affluent backgrounds, these Hawaiian preservice teachers would not be able to afford the additional year or two of schooling. As we look at steps to improve teacher education, we should be mindful of providing resources, such as increased financial aid, to ensure that such steps do not further discriminate against teacher education candidates of diverse backgrounds.

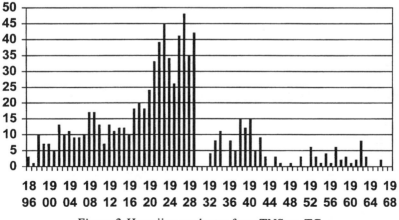

Figure 2. Hawaiian graduates from TNS vs. TC.

Alignment: Three Components of the Ka Lama Teacher Education Initiative

I move now from imagination as a mode of belonging, and my historical research, to alignment as a mode of belonging and the programmatic work that Margie Maaka and I have been doing with the Ka Lama teacher education initiative in the community.

Initial meetings with members of the community made it clear that they were eager to support the teacher education cohort and to work with the preservice teachers. With a grant to INPEACE from the Hawaii Community Foundation, we were able to establish a community advisory board for Ka Lama and to pay honoraria to instructors from the community, to conduct classes on Hawaiian studies and to show the preservice teachers how to connect their teaching to the needs and interests of children on the Leeward Coast.

The first cohort of preservice teachers began classes in August 1996. This cohort consisted of 29 students. Two years later, 27 had successfully completed the program. Sixteen or over half the students were Hawaiian, as compared to 11% in the overall enrollment of the College of Education that fall. The 26 preservice teachers in the second cohort, which includes 10 Hawaiians, will graduate in May 2000.

Our work with the first cohort of preservice teachers had been underway for only a few months when Margie had the idea of adding a second component to the Ka Lama Teacher Education Initiative. Drawing upon her background in Maori education in New Zealand, Margie saw the need not only to prepare Hawaiian teachers but Hawaiian educational researchers and administrators as well. For this reason, she established a graduate studies cohort as a second component to Ka Lama. That cohort, now 14 in number, includes graduates of the teacher education cohort as well as mentor teachers who work with the preservice teachers. Cohort members are admitted to the master's program in elementary education, with an emphasis in language arts. Margie and I teach the courses for this cohort off-campus, at locations convenient for the teachers. In addition, Margie works closely with a subset of graduate students called the *Mana Wahine* (powerful women), Hawaiian teachers whom she is mentoring to write journal articles, give presentations at national and international conferences, and to make connections with colleagues with similar interests in indigenous education.

Whereas Margie had identified one set of issues, I had identified another. Although we had been successful in recruiting a significant number of Hawaiian students, I saw a problem in the composition of our two teacher education cohorts. Only a small number of preservice teachers were residents of, or had close ties to, the Leeward Coast: six in the first cohort and four in the second. Three factors appeared to be contributing to our lack of success in recruiting residents. A first factor was the low rate of high school graduation. One of the Ka Lama preservice teachers who attended school on the Leeward Coast observed in an interview that, of the approximately 300 students in her seventh grade class, only 90 graduated from high school. A second, related factor was the small number of high school graduates who went on to college. Few adults on the coast had the college credits to be admitted as juniors to the College of Education and to our teacher education cohort. A third factor was the paucity of Hawaiian teachers who could serve as role models. As a consequence, few Hawaiian students growing up on the Leeward Coast aspired to be teachers. Larrilynn Holu, a Hawaiian graduate of the Ka Lama teacher education cohort who went to school on the Leeward Coast, recalls believing that only Asians could become teachers, because all the teachers she had ever had were Asian.

Clearly, there was a pipeline problem, severely limiting the pool of Leeward Coast residents who could qualify for admission to our teacher education cohort. I presented the pipeline problem to the community advisory board at its June 1998 meeting. Members believed that the key issue was the lack of support for Hawaiian students attempting to earn associate's degrees at the community college. Such students were likely to be nontraditional students, with family responsibilities, who had been out of school for a number of years. Members argued that these students needed a support system including academic counseling, financial aid, childcare, and a peer support group. In effect, the message was that we could not wait for qualified students to appear—we had to create our own pipeline.

October 1998 saw the opening of the Ka Lama Education Academy, administered by INPEACE at the Wai'anae campus of Leeward Community College, with funding from the Administration for Native Americans and the Office of Hawaiian Affairs. Larrilynn Holu, a graduate of the first Ka Lama cohort quoted earlier, has served as the coordinator and counselor for the Education Academy, with outstanding results. To date, the Education Academy has provided services to 27 residents of the Leeward Coast interested in becoming teachers. Five of these students will receive their associate's degrees in time to be admitted to the third Ka Lama teacher education cohort. We anticipate that about 12 or half the preservice teachers in the fourth teacher education cohort will come through the pipeline created by the Education Academy. The Academy appears to be opening the doors to teaching to some candidates who in all likelihood would not have made it through the system. Some are among the first members of their families to graduate from high school and to enter higher education.

Conclusion

That is where I am with my work as a literacy researcher and educator. I see that I am contributing to the development of a community of practice whose members share the goal of improving education on the Leeward Coast through a commitment to the community. I understand that this contribution is taking place through three modes of belonging (Wenger, 1998): engagement or involvement with an immediately present community of practice, which is the work with the teacher education cohort; imagination or the broadened vision gained through knowledge of communities of practice in other times and spaces, which is the historical research on Hawaiian teachers; and alignment or the coordination of efforts with broader processes at work in the present, which is the expansion of the teacher education initiative from one component to three, to support community development efforts.

The task at hand is still to improve the literacy achievement of Hawaiian students on the Leeward Coast, by increasing the number of Hawaiian teachers who are well prepared to teach them. But I now see this work in a much broader context, in terms of a vertical dimension, or connections to educational efforts now distant in time, as well as in terms of a horizontal dimension, or connections to present community development efforts.

In a letter introducing herself to the preservice teachers, one of the Hawaiian studies instructors from the Leeward Coast, the artist Dalani Kauihou, described what she had learned from teaching fourth-grade students to make *kapa,* the traditional Hawaiian bark cloth. Dalani wrote:

> Being children of our instant gratification society, they are now being taught to go slow, be patient . . . that each step of this process is important to their final product. We discovered that the children feel a closeness to this craft when they learn that as descendants of the Polynesian races, they all had kapa-making ancestors. "This knowledge is already in you," they are taught . . . "You are all kapa makers . . . we are just helping you remember." (Kauihou, 1999, p. 1)

And, I discovered, so it should be with my own work. I want the Hawaiian preservice teachers to remember that they are part of a proud tradition, descendants of an indigenous people who had attained near-universal literacy by the late 1800s. That over 150 years ago their ancestors established a system of common schools, spreading across their island kingdom from the towns to the remote villages. That the teachers in these schools were Hawaiian men and women, who taught reading and writing in their own language. That Hawaiian communities today can raise their own teachers, who will in turn lead their students to high levels of literacy.

References

Au, K. H. (1979). Using the experience-text-relationship method with minority children. *Reading Teacher, 32,* 677–679.

Au, K. H., & Carroll, J. H. (1997). Improving literacy achievement through a constructivist approach: The KEEP Demonstration Classroom Project. *Elementary School Journal, 97,* 203–221.

Au, K. H., Carroll, J. H., & Scheu, J. A. (1997). *Balanced literacy instruction: A teacher's resource book.* Norwood, MA: Christopher-Gordon.

Au, K. H., & Kawakami, A. J. (1994). Cultural congruence in instruction. In E. R. Hollins, J. E. King, & W. Hayman (Eds.), *Teaching diverse populations: Formulating a knowledge base* (pp. 5–23). Albany: State University of New York Press.

Board of Education. (1878). *Report of the president to the Hawaiian legislature, 1878.* Honolulu: Kingdom of Hawaii.

Board of Education. (1890). *Report of the president to the legislature, 1890.* Honolulu: Kingdom of Hawaii.

Cairney, T., & Langbien, S. (1989). Building communities of readers and writers. *Reading Teacher, 42,* 560–567.

Cunningham, P. M., & Cunningham, J. W. (1992). Making words: Enhancing the invented spelling-decoding connection. *Reading Teacher, 46,* 106–115.

D'Amato, J. (1988). "Acting": Hawaiian children's resistance to teachers. *Elementary School Journal, 88,* 529–544.

Delpit, L. (1988). The silenced dialogue: Power and pedagogy in educating other people's children. *Harvard Educational Review, 58,* 280–298.

Dotts, C. K., & Sikkema, M. (1994). *Challenging the status quo: Public education in Hawaii 1840–1980.* Honolulu: Hawaii Education Association.

Florio-Ruane, S., Raphael, T. E., Glazier, J., McVee, M., & Wallace, S. (1997). Discovering culture in discussion of autobiographical literature: Transforming the education of literacy teachers. In C. K. Kinzer, K. A. Hinchman, & D. J. Leu (Eds.), *Inquiries in literacy theory and practice.* Forty-sixth yearbook of the National Reading Conference (pp. 452–464). Chicago: National Reading Conference.

Fountas, I. C., & Pinnell, G. S. (1996). *Guided reading: Good first teaching for all children.* Portsmouth, NH: Heinemann.

Gallimore, R., Boggs, J. W., & Jordan, C. (1974). *Culture, behavior and education: A study of Hawaiian-Americans.* Beverly Hills, CA: Sage.

Graves, D., & Hansen, J. (1983). The author's chair. *Language Arts, 60,* 176–183.

Hansen, J. (1992). Teachers evaluate their own literacy. In D. H. Graves & B. S. Sunstein (Eds.), *Portfolio portraits* (pp. 73–81). Portsmouth, NH: Heinemann.

Holdaway, D. (1979). *The foundations of literacy.* Sydney: Ashton Scholastic.

Kame'eleihiwa, L. (1992). *Native land and foreign desires.* Honolulu: Bishop Museum Press.

Kauihou, D. (1999). *Letter to preservice teachers.* Wai'anae, HI: Cultural Learning Center of Ka'ala.

Kelly, M. (1991). Some thoughts on education in traditional Hawaiian society, *To teach the children: Historical aspects of education in Hawaii* (pp. 4–14). Honolulu: College of Education, University of Hawaii.

Ladson-Billings, G. (1995). Toward a theory of culturally relevant pedagogy. *American Educational Research Journal, 32,* 465–491.

McKnight, J. (1995). *The careless society: Community and its counterfeits.* New York: Basic.

Office of Accountability and School Instructional Support/Planning and Evaluation Group. (1997). *The superintendent's seventh annual report on school performance and improvement in Hawaii, 1996.* Honolulu: Department of Education, State of Hawaii.

Ogle, D. M. (1986). K-W-L: A teaching model that develops active reading of expository text. *Reading Teacher, 39,* 564–570.

Peterson, K. (1998, December 6). Neediest students get newest teachers. *Honolulu Advertiser,* pp. 1, 18.

Pukui, M. K. (1983). *"Olelo No'eau": Hawaiian proverbs and poetical sayings.* Honolulu: Bishop Museum Press.

Raphael, T. E., & McMahon, S. I. (1994). Book Club: An alternative framework for reading instruction. *Reading Teacher, 48,* 102–116.

Schnaiberg, L. (1998, June 3). Prop. 227 to end bilingual education wins. *Education Week on the Web.*

Shaw, R. C. (1929). *The output of the Territorial Normal and Training School.* Unpublished master's thesis, University of Hawaii, Honolulu.

Wenger, E. (1998). *Communities of practice: Learning, meaning, and identity.* Cambridge, England: Cambridge University Press.

Wilson, W. H. (1991). Hawaiian language in DOE unique. *Ke Kuamo'o, 1*(4), 4–6.

Language Matters:
When Is a Scaffold Really a Scaffold?*

Emily M. Rodgers
Ohio State University

One-to-one tutoring is becoming more widely used as part of early intervention programs to prevent reading failure. Just having a tutor is not enough to guarantee a child's success, however. The nature of the specific language interactions between the tutor and the child is critical to learning (Diaz, Neal, & Amaya-Williams, 1990; Pinnell, Lyons, DeFord, Bryk, & Seltzer, 1994).

However, no study has yet attempted to describe in a qualitative manner the nature of the language interaction between child and tutor. Such a study would have the potential to inform us about the nature of effective one-to-one tutoring. For this reason, I conducted a detailed analysis of the patterns of interaction between child and teacher in a one-to-one reading tutorial setting. I used the Reading Recovery program as the context for this study.

The following questions guided my inquiry: What are the patterns of talk between teacher and child when the child reads a new book with teacher support? How do the patterns of interaction between teacher and child change in relation to the child's changing reading behaviors? How do the patterns of interaction during critical learning moments further the child's literacy acquisition?

Theoretical Framework

I use a sociocultural lens to understand cognitive development. From this perspective, it is assumed that children are immersed in the cultural practices into which they are born. Children actively participate with more knowledgeable others in their cultural practices, therefore, social interaction is critical to learning (Vygotsky, 1978).

The difference in the way a child participates in these activities over time mirrors or presages cognitive development. Initially the child requires assistance from more capable others, but gradually, as capacity develops, the child is more able to assist himself or herself. This movement from assisted performance to independence is represented by the notion of the "zone of proximal development" (Vygotsky, 1978).

*Emily M. Rogers was co-recipient of the National Reading Conference Student Research Award in 1999.
National Reading Conference Yearbook, 49, pp. 78–90.

The process by which adults mediate a child's attempts to take on new learning has been termed "scaffolding" (Wood, Bruner, & Ross, 1976). In this process, the adult controls the elements of the task that are beyond the child's ability all the while "upping the ante" in terms of what the child is expected to be able to do next. Speech is a critical tool to scaffold the child's way of thinking and responding (Luria, 1979). Its acquisition plays a crucial role in the development of higher psychological processes (Scribner & Cole, 1981) because it enables thinking to be more abstract, flexible, and independent from the immediate situation (Bodrova & Leong, 1996).

Parents seem to intuitively know how to scaffold their children's efforts to acquire oral language. Mothers, for example, shift what they accept as language from their babies, raising the ante from burps to coos, as their children's attempts become more like speaking (Cazden, 1988). Research suggests that the *type* of assistance provided to the child is important (Wood & Middleton, 1975). Several studies have examined patterns of interaction in literacy learning and found that these interactions provide opportunities for children to have mediated literacy experiences with an expert who can monitor and guide the children's sense-making (Cochran-Smith, 1984; Taylor, 1983).

Reading Recovery is a one-to-one early literacy intervention that provides opportunities for scaffolding. Wong, Groth, and O'Flahavan (1994) examined 5 Reading Recovery teachers and 10 students over 25 lessons as the children read familiar and new books. They identified five types of scaffolding comments made by the teachers: discussing, telling, coaching, prompting, and modeling, and the authors also found that the teachers varied their scaffolding comments as a function of text familiarity. When the reading became more difficult, the teachers increased their modeling, prompting, and discussion comments to provide more assistance to the child.

Hobsbaum, Peters, and Sylva (1996) examined 17 children and 7 Reading Recovery teachers during the writing portion of the lessons and described the nature of the talk between teacher and child as "interactive talk cycles." The authors defined the teacher's role as paramount. They went on to say that, "There is no relaxation of the challenges posed and the teacher is constantly moving to what can be considered as the outer limits of the zone of proximal development" (p. 31).

Evidently, Reading Recovery teachers make deliberate teaching decisions that increase accessibility to the task while supporting the child's performance and maintaining the child's accelerated learning (Clay & Cazden, 1990). What seems to be a casual conversation between child and adult in the context of reading and writing is actually an excellent example of a highly skilled adult moving a child through his zone of proximal development.

In this study, I propose to examine these interactions in a qualitative manner to relate the child's growing literacy understandings to the language interactions between child and teacher. A closer look at the nature of the talk between the child and adult may reveal how the adult is able to scaffold the child's learning.

Method

Design

I used a qualitative case study approach (Patton, 1990) to describe the pattern of interaction between one particular Reading Recovery teacher (whom I shall refer to as Adrienne) and two of her students during one-to-one literacy instruction. Marshall and Rossman (1995) suggest that a case study is a useful research strategy when the purpose of the study is to describe a phenomenon of interest and when the research questions involve describing the "salient behaviors, events, beliefs, attitudes, structures, processes occurring in the phenomenon" (p. 41).

Participants

I selected Adrienne to participate in this study for several reasons. First, I wanted to observe an effective teacher and Adrienne was recommended by her teacher leader. Also, her discontinuation rate was equal or better than the average rate for other Reading Recovery teachers in her state.

The selection of two students was largely left to Adrienne. Adrienne selected John and Nathaniel largely because of her tutoring schedule. She tutored John before recess and Nathaniel afterwards which gave me an opportunity to reset the audio and video equipment between lessons.

Table 1 shows these students' scores on the *Observation Survey of Early Literacy Achievement* (OS) (Clay, 1993). The OS is a set of six literacy tasks, individually administered, and used to determine who qualifies for the program. It measures a child's understanding of print, knowledge of letters, instructional reading level, and ability to hear and record phonemes. The scores show that

Table 1

Pre- and Post-Observation Survey Scores for John and Nathaniel

Observation Survey Tasks	Range of Scores	John Pre	Nathaniel Pre	John Post	Nathaniel Post
Letter Identification	0–54	51	24	53	49
Word Test	0–20	2	0	11	4
Concepts About Print	0–24	12	12	21	Not tested
Writing Vocabulary	Timed task: 10 minutes	6	5	41	24
Hearing and Recording Sounds in Words	0–37	1	5	34	29
Text Reading Level	A–24	1	A	8	3

initially Nathaniel scored lower than John on each task of the OS except Hearing and Recording Sounds in Words (HRSIW) and Concepts about Print (CAP). In analyzing the results, Adrienne noted that Nathaniel was not looking at the print and did not understand the concept of one-to-one matching.

Data Collection: Qualitative Measures

The Reading Recovery lesson activities were organized within three distinct phases: (a) rereading two or three familiar books and working with words, (b) writing a story, and (c) reading a new book with teacher support. This study closely examined the third phase of these lessons using multiple data-collection methods or triangulation to ensure the trustworthiness of the data collected.

Participant observation. Glesne and Peshkin (1992) describe the main outcome of participant observation as understanding the research setting, its participants and their behavior. Participant observation occurs along a continuum from mostly participant to mostly observer (Glesne & Peshkin, 1992; Patton, 1990). The context of my study meant that my role fell further on the continuum as observer than participant. To observe the interactions between an effective Reading Recovery teacher and her students, I could not take part in the teaching. However, I was not strictly an observer. The participants in the study were aware of my presence, and I had many conversations with the teacher about the students.

I videotaped two consecutive Reading Recovery lessons for each student every 3 weeks for 12 weeks. This yielded data from eight lessons for each child. I also observed each child twice a week on consecutive days for the duration of the study. This meant that I observed each child twice during Weeks 1, 2, 4, 5, 7, 8, 10, and 11. During Weeks 3, 6, 9, and 12, I observed the students and videotaped at the same time for a total of 24 observations per child. Each of these lessons was audiotaped daily for the duration of the study.

I also observed each child in his classroom, once every 2 weeks, during a regularly scheduled read-aloud time. Each student was expected to select several books from baskets around the room and to read independently or with a friend for the 30 minutes. During each read aloud session, the student wore a clip-on microphone and waist pack with tape recorder in it.

Document analysis. I photocopied all lesson records for both children. The lesson record contains two forms: teacher's notes as the lesson occurs and a running record; a written notation of the student's oral reading behaviors when he read a book independently that day.

Interviewing. During each of my 24 visits to the school, I conducted unstructured interviews with Adrienne between and after lessons. My purpose was always to hear the teacher's perspective on the students' progress and to understand more about the teacher's decision-making during the lessons. The teacher usually did not need any prompt to begin talking; often she began her own analysis of the lesson as soon as the student left the room.

First Level of Data Analysis: Identifying Talk Cycles

I examined the videotaped lessons looking for cycles of interaction between the teacher and child while the child read a new book. In a pilot study I examined interactions as "talk cycles" that punctuated the student's independent reading of the new book (Rodgers, 1998). Each contribution to a talk cycle by either student or teacher was termed a "move," in keeping with Sinclair and Couthard's (1975) original definition of talk cycle.

Second Level of Data Analysis: Categorizing the Teacher Moves

The next step in data analysis was to identify the categories of teacher talk or moves present in the talk cycles. Examining the teacher moves at first, I used inductive analysis to discern types of moves: demonstrating, questioning, telling, confirming, praising, and directing. These categories of moves were checked against another coder who was a trained Reading Recovery teacher. Agreement was reached on 88% of the codes.

Third Level of Data Analysis: Creating Typologies of Talk Cycles

At this level of analysis, I diagrammed the data contained in the talk cycles to find patterns within the interactions. Analyzing these moves, a theme soon emerged. It appeared to me that most of the teacher's moves were made to propel the student further in his reading of the new book. Initially, I coded the teacher's moves simply as being helpful or non-helpful in getting the student past the difficulty encountered in reading the new book. A helpful move helped resolve the problem, and a non-helpful move appeared to be a "shot in the dark" that was not successful. I diagrammed teacher and student moves to show how they related to one another.

Fourth Level of Data Analysis: Describing the Student's Changing Reading Behaviors

To describe each student's changing reading behaviors, I examined their plans of action at difficulty while reading aloud in their classroom during read-aloud time, and their running records from the days that I videotaped their lessons. My purpose was to describe what the students did at points of difficulty when they were reading independently. I transcribed what they said and did, analyzed each transcription, and looked for patterns of responding. Patterns emerged within each lesson for each student and I was able to construct a picture of each child as a reader at four points in time.

Results

By the end of the study, it became apparent that John had made significantly more progress in reading and writing than Nathaniel. Evidence to support this finding comes from two sources: a comparison of the students' pre- and post-OS scores and an examination of the changes in their text-reading levels over the course of the study. More significantly, differences in the way the teacher and student interacted became apparent.

Pre- and Post-OS Scores

When the OS was first administered, Nathaniel's and John's scores were similar on every task except Letter Identification. However, when the OS was re-administered after 12 weeks of tutoring, there was a marked difference between their scores on nearly every task, though each boy made progress. Table 1 displays both students' pre- and post-OS scores. Further evidence to support this finding comes from both students' records of text-reading levels. These show that John made steady progress every week, whereas Nathaniel sometimes dropped a level and for several weeks stayed at one level.

How can one account for this difference in progress? How is it that John and Nathaniel could work with the same teacher, who used the same framework for lessons and had access to the same resources, yet John was able to make such fast, dramatic progress and Nathaniel made much smaller gains? An analysis of the talk during the lessons may reveal differences in the way Adrienne and the students interacted.

Analyzing the Talk Cycles: The Nature of the Interactions

Ratio of Cycles to words read. One way to characterize the teacher-student interactions is to examine the number of cycles or interactions that occurred during the reading. I counted the number of cycles between Adrienne and each student for two consecutive lessons at four points in time: Weeks 3, 6, 9, and 12 of the study. Then I calculated the ratio of cycles between the teacher and student to the total number of words read in each new book for both lessons, for the 4 focus weeks. "Words read" simply refers to the number of words in the book that the student read during that lesson. Figure 1 offers a comparison of Nathaniel and John's ratio of cycles to words read.

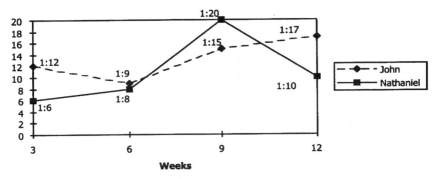

Figure 1. Ratio of cycles to words read: John and Nathaniel.

Even though John read increasingly more difficult text, he read with more and more independence. Evidence to support the view that he is reading with more independence comes from the fact that there are fewer cycles or interactions with his teacher. When the student is not interacting with the teacher, he is either reading accurately or problem solving independently. Therefore, fewer cycles means fewer occasions when the student needs the teacher's support to read.

By contrast, although Nathaniel read with increasing independence, he did not read with as independently as John. At the beginning of the study, John read about 12 words at a time before needing support from his teacher, whereas Nathaniel needed support after reading about 6 words. At the end of the study, John read approximately 17 words without support, whereas Nathaniel required support about every 10 words read. A second critical feature to keep in mind when comparing the ratio of words read to cycles of interactions is that the texts that Nathaniel worked with did not get increasingly difficult throughout the study. At the four focus points of this study (Weeks 3, 6, 9, and 12) John read at Levels 4, 7, 10, and 13, whereas Nathaniel read at Levels 3, 4, 3, and 3.

Division of student moves within cycles. A second way to characterize these teacher-student interactions is to calculate the percentages of moves made by student and teacher during the four points in time: Weeks 3, 6, 9, and 12. This is an interesting dimension to consider because it gives us a feel for who was doing more talking when the student came to difficulty.

To calculate the share of moves made by the teacher and student, I again examined the focus lessons. I totaled the number of moves made by the student and those made by the teacher for the two consecutive lessons during the four points in time. I then calculated the percentages of moves made by the teacher and the student at each point. Figures 2 and 3 compare John's and Nathaniel's percentages of moves in relation to Adrienne's moves.

In Week 3 of John's lessons, there were 10 cycles of interaction between John and his teacher across two consecutive lessons. Within these 10 cycles, the student made 26 moves and the teacher made 19 moves. During two consecutive

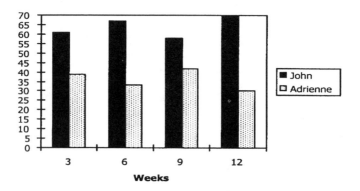

Figure 2. Division of teacher and student moves within cycles: Adrienne and John.

lessons in Week 6, there were 19 cycles. John made 55 moves within these cycles and Adrienne made 28. In Week 9 of John's program, he made 60 moves in 18 cycles whereas his teacher made 46 moves. During the final week of the study, there were 20 cycles of interactions in which John made 59 moves whereas his teacher made only 28.

It is apparent that John always made more contributions to cycles of interactions with his teacher than Adrienne made. This was true at all four points in time that I examined. With the exception of Week 9, John's share of moves increased over time from 61% in Week 3 to 68% in Week 12.

Nathaniel's share of moves within the cycles of interaction did not increase as dramatically as John's over time, nor did he take as large a share of the moves as John. Nathaniel made 40 moves in 14 cycles in Week 3, whereas his teacher contributed 31 moves. In Week 6, Nathaniel contributed 32 moves and his teacher 27 moves in 11 cycles. During Week 9, the week that he read one of his new books completely independently, Nathaniel made 16 moves, as did his teacher in just four cycles. During the last week of the study, Nathaniel made 36 moves and his teacher made 26 in 9 cycles.

Nathaniel and Adrienne usually made about the same number of moves. This remained relatively unchanged over the course of the study. Even though the level of difficulty of texts remained relatively unchanged, the level of support that Adrienne had to give Nathaniel remained about the same. By contrast, it is interesting to note that John made the most moves during the lessons in the last week of the study when the level of text was most difficult.

Analyzing the talk cycles. For each student, I diagrammed every cycle of interaction in two consecutive lessons during Weeks 3, 6, 9, and 12. The total number of cycles diagrammed was 105. These diagrams provided a visual depiction of the kinds of scaffolds that were co-created by the student and teacher during the interaction (see Figure 4 for an example). Three types of scaffolds emerged as a result of this diagramming: continuous, mended, and misleading.

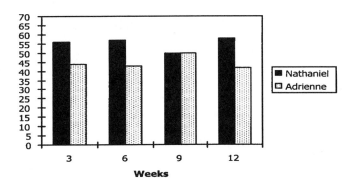

Figure 3. Division of teacher and student moves within cycles: Adrienne and Nathaniel.

Most talk cycles diagrammed in John's lessons were "continuous scaffolds." I defined these scaffolds in this way because every teacher move took the student further along in his problem-solving. A much smaller percentage of the scaffolds in John's lessons was "mended." These were scaffolds that contained at least one move by the teacher that was misleading, but the very next move was helpful. An even smaller number of the scaffolds was "misleading." Misleading scaffolds were those that contained at least two consecutive teacher moves that the student could not use to help himself and had the effect of leading the student away from successful problem-solving.

I expected that I would find a higher percentage of misleading or mended scaffolds in Nathaniel's lessons, than continuous ones; a trend that might explain why he did not make as much progress in reading as John. Surprisingly, I found just the opposite. There was a greater percentage of continuous scaffolds in Nathaniel's lessons. Mended scaffolds occurred less frequently in Nathaniel's lessons, whereas misleading scaffolds occurred no more frequently in Nathaniel's lessons than John's. It appears that the scaffolds created in Nathaniel's lessons were more often helpful than those created in John's lessons. Figure 5 depicts the frequency and types of scaffolds present in John's and Nathaniel's lessons. Adrienne was as responsive to Nathaniel as to John. If frequency and type of scaffold cannot account for progress differences, perhaps the nature of talk within scaffolds can.

Types of teacher talk within the scaffolds. I found six types of teacher contributions to talk cycles in my analyses: Questioning (the teacher asks the student a question), Telling (the teacher reveals or tells the student something), Directing (the teacher directs the student to take a specific action, Demonstrating (the teacher takes the student's role and demonstrates a problem-solving action), Praising (the teacher praises the student), and Confirming (the teacher informs the student when he or she is correct).

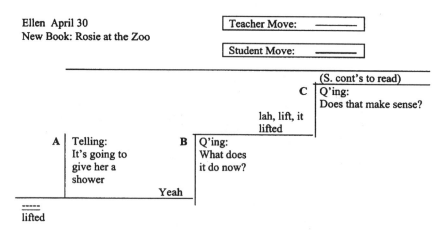

Figure 4. Example of a diagrammed talk cycle.

Figures 6 and 7 display the types and frequency of teacher moves that were present in Adrienne's contributions to the talk cycles in Nathaniel's and John's lessons. The same lessons were analyzed as in the previous figures that showed the students' participation.

It is interesting to note the steady increase in Adrienne's use of directing moves. These moves have the effect of directing the student to take a problem-solving action. For example, John read, "The lion got up," but the text actually said: "The lion looked up." John did not notice the error and Adrienne directed

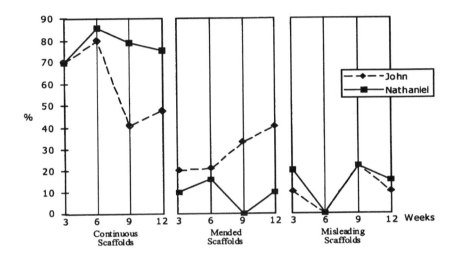

Figure 5. Comparison of the types and frequency of scaffolds in John's and Nathaniel's lessons at Weeks 3, 6, 9, and 12 of the study.

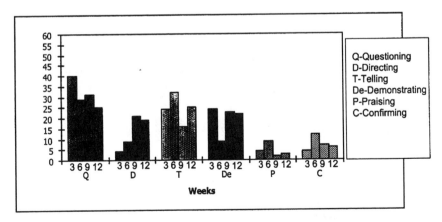

Figure 6. Frequency and type of teacher moves in John's lessons in Weeks 3, 6, 9, and 12.

him to take an action ("Read that again") without actually telling John what was wrong. Such moves by Adrienne were rare initially but became more common later on.

Figure 7 displays Adrienne's moves within cycles of interactions with Nathaniel. The most notable difference between the teacher talk in John's and Nathaniel's lessons is the difference in the frequency of several types of moves. Nearly one-quarter of all Adrienne's moves in John's lessons were demonstrating moves, with the exception of Week 6. Early on in the program she did not direct John to take a specific action, but she increasingly used this move by Weeks 9 and 12. It can be inferred from the frequency and types of moves in the scaffolds in John's lessons that Adrienne demonstrated actions before she directed him to try them himself.

By contrast, Nathaniel's cycles evidenced mostly directing and questioning moves. Although Adrienne used demonstrating moves in Week 3 of the program, these only made up 14% of her moves, compared to 24% in John's program at that time. Thereafter, Adrienne rarely demonstrated for Nathaniel. As a result, because she had not first demonstrated for Nathaniel, she was directing him to take actions that she had not taught him or she was questioning him about things he did not know.

For example, Adrienne often directed Nathaniel to try the first sound, but she rarely demonstrated for him how to reread and articulate the sound of the first letter of the word. This was a common move in John's lessons. In fact, nearly every demonstrating move recorded for John represents this kind of action early on: the teacher reread and articulated the first sound of the word. I suspect that without these demonstrations of what it meant to "try the first sound" then Nathaniel did not know how to do what he was being directed to try.

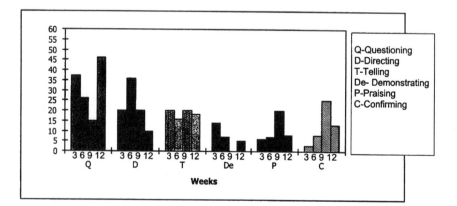

Figure 7. Frequency and types of teacher moves in Nathaniel's lessons in Weeks 3, 6, 9, and 12.

Implications

Rogoff (1990) maintains to understand development from a sociocultural perspective it is necessary to examine how a child's participation in an activity changes over time. Adrienne and John's participation in problem-solving changed over time. John took a greater role in problem-solving, all the while reading more complex text. Adrienne appeared to shift from demonstrating problem-solving action when John needed help, to directing him to take certain actions.

Nathaniel's participation in the reading process did not appear to change. He read text at about the same level of difficulty at the end of the study as he had at the beginning. Likewise, Nathaniel's participation in the problem-solving at difficulty changed very little. He seemed to need help as often and he did not take a greater role in the problem-solving process. Unlike with John, Adrienne did not demonstrate problem-solving actions with Nathaniel as frequently. Instead, she most often directed or questioned Nathaniel. This kind of support seemed not to be helpful because it did not shift Nathaniel's participation in the activity so that he could become a more independent reader like John. There was a difference in the quality of the scaffolds created by Adrienne for John and Nathaniel.

This study supports Wood et al.'s (1976) finding that a critical function of the tutor is to demonstrate the task. They defined demonstrating as imitating "in idealized form an attempted solution" (p. 61). Without the teacher's "imitation" or demonstration of the act to be tried, Nathaniel floundered in his reading attempts. As in the Wood et al. study, it was the role of the tutor to point up discrepancies to the student. I identified how the teacher does that: through her questioning, telling, directing, demonstrating, praising, and confirming moves.

From my perspective, although it is critical to have scaffolds present for learning, not all scaffolds are equal. Is it the kind of assistance that helps children answer more complex questions, while reading independently?

Cazden (1988) and Bliss, Askew, and Macrae (1996) concur that it may be more difficult to scaffold a child's learning in a school setting where specialized knowledge is needed than in the everyday learning that takes place at home. This study suggests why this may be so. The real challenge, at least in a one-to-one literacy tutoring setting, is to scaffold a child's learning so that the child can problem solve with increasing independence on tasks that grow in difficulty. Scaffolds can be provided, as they were to Nathaniel, but they may not move the student beyond the early stages of the zone of proximal development. There is a need to focus on the ways in which the teacher supports him in his problem-solving. This study highlights the importance of asking: What is the nature of the support that the teacher is giving the student? Has the teacher provided clear demonstrations, as needed, of the tasks required of the student? Has the teacher continued to give clear demonstrations even as the task becomes increasingly more difficult? And, is the teacher directing or questioning the student to take a problem-solving move that he does not understand?

References

Bliss, J., Askew, M., & Macrae, S. (1996). Effective teaching and learning: Scaffolding revisited. *Oxford Review of Education, 22,* 37–61.

Bodrova, E., & Leong, D. J. (1996). *Tools of the mind: The Vygotskian approach to early childhood education.* Englewood Cliffs, NJ: Prentice-Hall.

Cazden, C. (1988). *Classroom discourse: The language of teaching and learning.* Portsmouth, NH: Heinemann.

Clay, M. M. (1993). *An observation survey of early literacy achievement.* Portsmouth, NH: Heinemann.

Clay, M., & Cazden, C. (1990). A Vygotskian interpretation of Reading Recovery. In L. Moll (Ed.), *Vygotsky and education* (pp. 206–222). New York: Cambridge University Press.

Cochran-Smith, M. (1984). *The making of a reader.* Norwood, NJ: Ablex.

Diaz, R., Neal, C., & Amaya-Williams, M. (1990). The social origins of self-regulation. In L. C. Moll (Ed.), *Vygotsky and education: Instructional implications and applications of sociohistorical psychology* (pp. 127–154). New York: Cambridge University Press.

Glesne, C., & Peshkin, A. (1992). *Becoming qualitative researchers.* New York: Longman.

Hobsbaum, A., Peters, S., & Sylva, K. (1996). Scaffolding in reading recovery. *Oxford Review of Education, 22,* 17–35.

Luria, A. (1979). *The making of mind.* Cambridge, MA: Harvard University Press.

Marshall, C. M., & Rossman, C. B. (1995). *Designing qualitative research.* Thousand Oaks, CA: Sage.

Patton, M. Q. (1990). *Qualitative evaluation and research methods.* New York: Sage.

Pinnell, G., Lyons, C., DeFord, D. Bryk, A., & Seltzer, M. (1994). Comparing instructional models for the literacy education of high-risk first graders. *Reading Research Quarterly, 29,* 8–39.

Rodgers, E. (1998, February). *Understanding teacher and student talk.* Paper presented at the meeting of the Reading Recovery Conference and National Institute, Columbus, OH.

Rogoff, B. (1990). *Apprenticeship in thinking: Cognitive development in social context.* New York: Oxford University Press.

Scribner, S., & Cole, M. (1981). *The psychology of literacy.* Cambridge, MA; Harvard University Press.

Sinclair, J., & Coulthard, R. (1975). *Towards an analysis of discourse.* New York: Oxford University Press.

Taylor, D. (1983). *Family literacy: Young children learning to read and write.* Portsmouth, NH: Heinemann.

Vygotsky, L. (1978). *Mind in society: The development of higher psychological processes.* Cambridge, MA: Harvard University Press.

Wong, S., Groth, L., O'Flahavan, J., Gale, S., Kelley, G., Leeds, S., Regetz, J., & O'Malley-Steiner, J. (1994). *Characterizing teacher-student interaction in reading recovery lessons* (Reading Research Report No. 17). Athens, GA: National Reading Research Center. (ERIC Document Reproduction Service No. ED 375 392)

Wood, D., Bruner, J., & Ross, G. (1976). The role of tutoring in problem-solving. *Journal of Child Psychology, 17,* 89–100.

Wood, D., & Middleton, D. (1975). A study of assisted problem solving. *British Journal of Psychology, 66,* 181–191.

Borderlands Literacy in a Primary-Grade Immersion Class[*]

Patrick Manyak
California State University, Fullerton

> The Borderlands are physically present wherever two or more cultures edge each other, where people of different races occupy the same territory, where under, lower, middle, and upper classes touch. . . . Living on borders and in margins, keeping intact one's shifting and multiple identity and integrity, is like trying to swim in a new element, an "alien" element. There is an exhilaration in being a participant in the further evolution of humankind. . . . (Anzaldúa, 1987, preface)

A controlled din fills Room 110 as groups of four or five children sort word cards, water bean plants, and share picture books in the class library. At a round table in the back of the room, four first- and second-grade students finish reading a repetitive book in English about a father's daily routine. Their teacher inquires: "What is something you like to do? Sandra?"

Sandra, looking intently at Ms. Page, responds, "Working."

"So, Sandra, do you want to write, 'Sandra is working?'"

Smiling, Sandra gets up, takes a black marker from the teacher, and turns to a large sheet of newsprint clipped to an easel behind the table. The teacher addresses the other three children, "'Sandra is working.' *Ayuden a Sandra escribir las palabras*" (Help Sandra write the words).

Ana declares, "*Primero su nombre, porque ya lo sabe*" (First her name, because she knows it) and then, a second later, "I can't see!" The others watch Sandra write as Ms. Page dictates slowly, "Sandra, Sandra, is—."

When she pauses, Tito offers Sandra a book where she can find the word she needs, "*¿Le doy un libro?*" (Should I give you a book?) Ms. Page continues, "Sandra is work—," and the children echo, "Work."

Eva calls out, "*La doble u*" ("w"), and the children begin to prescribe letters in Spanish. Sandra hesitates on the "k" and Tito leans over, takes the pen, and writes the letter for her. As Sandra finishes her sentence, Ms. Page calls on Ana, "Can you read what Sandra wrote for us? Here is your magic pen." Ana reads, pointing to the words with the marker, and the other children chime in. The lesson continues as Tito, recently emigrated from Honduras, stretches the limits of his English to suggest another sentence: "*Yo quiero escribir* (I want to write), 'Dad is ice cream.'"

*Patrick Manyak was co-recipient of the National Reading Conference Student Research Award in 1999.

National Reading Conference Yearbook, 49, pp. 91–108.

"Working" in an Immersion Class

Whereas the preceding vignette describes activity that appears typical of elementary school classrooms, when situated within historical, cultural, and sociopolitical contexts the focal event raises issues critical to the schooling of English language learners. In California, one-fourth of all students, or 1.4 million children, are English learners (California Department of Education, 1998). The education of these children occurs in a crucible of contested political and pedagogical agendas. After public debate over the relative merits of bilingual and English-only instruction, California voters passed Proposition 227 in June 1998, mandating English-immersion education for a majority of the state's language minority students. Since 80% of California's English learners speak Spanish as their home language (California Department of Education, 1998), the proposition affects a large number of Spanish-speaking children. In view of Latina/o children's persistently low scores on tests of reading achievement (National Center for Educational Statistics, 1994, 1999) and the contention over optimal instructional approaches for Spanish speakers, the new immersion programs warrant close inspection.

During the academic year following the passage of Proposition 227, I investigated the language and literacy development of the native Spanish-speaking children in Room 110, a primary-grade immersion class. Recognizing the diverse contextual influences on language minority students' literacy acquisition (Reyes & Costanzo, 1999), I approached the research from a sociocultural perspective emphasizing the "relationships between human action . . . and the cultural, institutional, and historical situations in which this action occurs." (Wertsch, Del Rio, & Alvarez, 1995, p. 11). Before presenting findings detailing the children's participation in the literacy activities of Room 110, I elaborate the theoretical framework that I drew upon throughout the iterative process of data collection and analysis.

Learning as Participation

Influenced by a number of contemporary scholars (Bloome, 1994; Cook-Gumperz, 1986; Gutierrez, 1995; Myers, 1992), I conceptualize classroom literacy instruction as a set of social practices and not as the simple transmission of isolated knowledge and skills related to print. These practices consist of recurring, teacher-student and student-student interactions involving reading and writing. Through engagement in such interactions, children develop the ability to use written language. This perspective resonates with many theoretical positions critiquing the notion that learning occurs within the heads of individual learners (Lave & Wenger, 1991; Moll, 1990; Rogoff, 1991, 1995; Vygotsky, 1978; Wenger, 1998; Wertsch, 1985, 1991). Constructs such as the zone of proximal development (Vygotsky, 1978), assisted performance (Tharp & Gallimore, 1988), guided participation (Rogoff, Mosier, Mistry, & Artin, 1993), legitimate peripheral participation (Lave & Wenger, 1991) and mediated action (Wertsch, 1998) have increased understanding of how people acquire knowledge, skills, and identities through participation in historically, culturally, and socially constituted practices. In this section, I describe five principles extrapolated from contemporary sociocultural and situated learning theories that constitute my view of learning as participation. I then discuss how these principles have been applied and extended in prior research on the language and literacy development of English learners.

Five Principles of Learning as Participation

Principle one. Learning occurs as newcomers fulfill various peripheral roles alongside more experienced or competent members in community practice. This principle reflects the essence of Lave and Wenger's (1991) theory of legitimate peripheral participation. Lave and Wenger postulate that individuals belong to multiple and overlapping communities of practice constituted by members' mutual engagement in joint enterprises. Within these enterprises, diverse participatory roles and the social relations they entail offer newcomers distinct insights into the nature of the community's practice and opportunities to acquire the knowledge and skills necessary for full participation in the community.

Principle two. Participation in community practice results in the acquisition of new identities. This principle also issues from Lave and Wenger's (1991) monograph. The theory of legitimate peripheral participation accentuates the intrinsic relationship between social relations, learning, and identity. Lave and Wenger state, "Learning implies becoming a different person with respect to the possibilities enabled by systems of relations. To ignore this aspect of learning is to overlook the fact that learning involves the construction of identities" (p. 53). Applied in the context of schooling, this principle underscores the fact that students acquire "institutional biographies" (McDermott, 1987, p. 202) that index the identities they develop as a result of participation in classroom and broader school practices.

Principle three. Historical, cultural, political, and institutional forces constrain the types of practices available to a community. McDermott (1993, p. 295) succinctly articulates the effect of these broad forces on learning: "The question of who is learning what and how much is essentially a question of what conversations they are a part of, and this question is a subset of the more powerful question of what conversations are around to be had in a given culture." McDermott implies that if learning takes place as a result of participation in social practices, the types of practices available in a given community crucially influence what its members can learn and who they can become. Rogoff's (1995) discussion of the community plane of sociocultural activity elaborates on the need to contextualize participation within historical, cultural, political, and institutional contexts. In Rogoff's words, the community plane of activity involves "the institutional structure and cultural technologies of intellectual activity," including "purposes (defined in community or institutional terms), cultural constraints, resources, values relating to what means are appropriate for reaching goals . . . and cultural tools such as . . . linguistic and mathematical systems" (pp. 143-144).

Principle four. The privileging of mediational means extends or limits participants' access to roles in community practice. Lave and Wenger (1991) suggest that unequal power relations frequently influence participation in communities of practice. In particular, they point out that "hegemony over resources for learning" (p. 42) obstructs access to legitimate peripheral participation. Wertsch (1991, 1998) develops the notion of "resources for learning" through his theorizing on mediational means. His discussion of mediated action foregrounds the ubiquity of mediational means or cultural tools in human activity. Wertsch (1991) points out that although many cultural tools may serve to accomplish a task, one tool is often privileged above others. The privileging of a cultural tool within a community hinders those members who use the tool less competently from gaining access to participatory roles even though they may possess other tools that could be employed with equal effect.

Principle five. In the course of community practice complex webs of interaction between participants mediate learning within dynamic, overlapping, and multidirectional zones of proximal development. This principle reflects recent extensions of Vygotsky's concept of the zone of proximal development (ZPD). Vygotsky (1978) conceived of the ZPD as the space between what an individual can do alone and what she can do in collaboration with a more competent other. He posited that social interaction within the ZPD constitutes the genesis of individual cognitive development. Moll (1990) argues that the ZPD has been narrowly interpreted as primarily applying to adult-child dyads in which the adult transmits discreet bodies of knowledge to the child. Based on their research in an elementary classroom, Moll and Whitmore (1993) propose that a "'collective' zone of proximal development" resulting from "the interdependence of adults and children, and how they use social and cultural resources" (p. 20) better captures the dynamic spirit of Vygotsky's concept. Informed by this more expansive understanding of the ZPD, I view collaborative participation in community practice as producing multiple and multidirectional ZPDs that form the basis for socially mediated cognitive development.

English Learners' Participation in Classroom Practices

Taken together, these principles emphasize the socially situated, participatory nature of learning. This theoretical perspective suggests that students' language and literacy acquisition hinges on "the social structures in particular [classroom] communities, on the variety of positionings available for learners to occupy in those communities and on the design and structure of the practices which bound the community" (Norton & Toohey, 1999, p. 10). A number of recent qualitative studies focusing on linguistically diverse students have demonstrated the analytic potency resulting from the foregrounding of these elements (Franquiz & Reyes, 1998; Gutierrez & Larson, 1994; Moll & Dworin, 1996; Moll & Whitmore, 1994; Shannon, 1995; Toohey, 1996, 1998; Willet, 1995). This body of research offers several insights into how the aforementioned principles of learning-as-participation relate to the academic experience of English language learners.

Two studies reveal how the individualizing social structures and interaction routines of classroom practices exclude English learners from the kind of participation important for language acquisition, learning and the development of identities of competence (Toohey, 1998; Willet, 1995). For instance, in the first-grade classroom studied by Toohey (1998), the desks of the English learners were clustered at the front of the room near the teacher where the children had little opportunity to converse with their English-speaking peers. In addition, strict rules regarding copying discouraged the English learners from imitating the speech and writing of fluent English speakers.

Focusing specifically on Latina/o students, Gutierrez and Larson (1994) describe how teachers' hegemonic discursive practices limit children's learning. Many such restrictive practices result from the privileging of English as the obligatory cultural tool for acquiring and enhancing literacy skills. Shannon (1995) suggests that as a result of the hegemonic nature of English, "minority-language speakers take on the burden of an inferior status" (p. 176). Research with Spanish-speaking children indicates that they may internalize the inferior status ascribed to Spanish in society and school. Commins (1989) describes children in a newly formed bilingual class who believed that "English was the language for school," and thus "[opted] for a less well-mastered code even though the possibility existed to work in Spanish" (p. 35).

In contrast to these cases in which language minority students suffered from limited participation in classroom practices and the privileging of English, researchers have documented classrooms in which Latina/o children fulfill diverse participatory roles in literacy practices and utilize a broad variety of cultural tools to mediate their learning (Franquiz & Reyes 1998; Gutierrez, Baquedano-López, Tejada, & Rivera, 1999; Gutierrez & Meyer, 1995; Moll & Dworin, 1996; Moll & Whitmore, 1993; Shannon, 1995). Moll and his colleagues (Moll & Whitmore, 1993; Moll, Tapia, & Whitmore, 1993) describe bilingual classrooms in which learning occurred in social contexts that drew upon children's diverse sociocultural resources, or "funds of knowledge." In these classrooms children focused on the co-construction of meaning as they discussed literature and pursued their own research questions during the study of thematic units. Within these highly collaborative activities students benefited from a variety of socially distributed resources for learning. In particular, bilingual children used their linguistic ability to facilitate interaction between monolingual participants and to access sources of information in Spanish and English.

Franquiz and Reyes (1998) and Gutierrez et al. (1999) portray classroom environments in which the participants' broad linguistic repertoires advance literacy and learning. Franquiz and Reyes (1998) discuss "inclusive learning communities" in which teachers and children employed "a range of language registers and codes (e.g., from standard to more colloquial forms of speech and from monolingual to more mixed language uses)" (p. 213) in the course of classroom activity. The authors particularly emphasize the strategic role codeswitching played in developing the students' linguistic awareness and biliteracy. Gutierrez et al. (1999) focus on a "hybrid learning context" that occurred within a second-third grade bilingual classroom when the teacher and students developed an instructional unit on the human body as a result of the children's name calling. The hybrid language practices of this learning community not only resulted in the commingling of English and Spanish but also redefined the lexicon, humor, and local knowledge of students' informal discourse as important meaning-making resources. Thus, both teams of researchers highlight the increased opportunities for learning in classrooms that refuse to privilege a particular linguistic code or body of cultural capital.

The theoretical perspective framing this study asserts that access to legitimate forms of participation in school activities crucially defines children's opportunities for developing the skills and identities necessary for academic success. The research I have discussed reveals that for English learners such access often hangs in the balance, dependent on the inclusiveness of classroom social practices and the range of cultural tools deemed acceptable as resources for learning. This paper extends such research by examining the experience of Latina/o children in a classroom community established during the new historical moment created by Proposition 227. In particular, the following questions guided my research: (a) What kinds of literacy practices were available to the children in Room 110? (b) How did the students participate in these literacy practices? (c) How did this participation evidence the students' development of language and literacy skills?

Setting

The scene that opens this paper serves as a rudimentary introduction to Room 110, a first- and second-grade English-immersion class at a large urban elementary school in Southern California. The class was comprised of 20 native Spanish-speaking Latina/o children. Several of the students remained with the teacher, Ms. Page, after spending the prior year in her kindergarten and first-grade combination. Others had recently arrived from Mexico or Central America. Ms. Page spoke English and Spanish fluently and had begun teaching the previous year in the school's bilingual program.

I chose Room 110 as my research site for several reasons. First, Ms. Page's class represented the students' initial formal instruction in English literacy. Second, since the students were placed in the class as a result of their low level of English proficiency, I anticipated the opportunity to collect rich data reflecting the processes and problems of children learning to read and write in a relatively unknown language. Third, despite the difficulties created by Proposition 227, Ms. Page maintained a deep commitment to ensuring her English learners access to a full range of research-based, meaning-centered literacy activities.

Data Collection and Analysis

I used an ethnographic approach to data collection and analysis in order to describe and interpret the actions of the members of the classroom community in

Room 110. I collected data for a full school year, acting as a participant observer on the average of two times a week and observed and audio-recorded four literacy activities: Daily News, guided reading, literature study, and author's chair. For a 3-month period beginning in January, I also observed Ms. Page's students when they integrated with children from an English-only first-grade class for 45 minutes after lunch. During integration Ms. Page conducted literature study units involving discussions of and responses to stories read aloud. I occasionally helped the teacher or the children in small ways. However, I primarily sat beside the students, writing notes and audio-recording their interaction.

In addition to many informal talks with Ms. Page, I interviewed her formally in November 1998 and in April and August 1999. I taped the hour-long interviews and simultaneously took handwritten notes. In the last interview I shared my findings from the study and invited her to respond to my analyses. Throughout the year I conducted periodic focus group interviews with the students to elicit their thoughts about the classroom activities. In late February, I led a class discussion in Ms. Page's room, asking children directly about their feelings regarding the integration period, reading and writing in Spanish and English, and the possibility of being in an English-only class the following year. I also interviewed Ms. Garza, Ms. Page's instructional assistant and a parent of one of the students.

As a supplement to these highly contextualized ethnographic data sources, I conducted monthly miscue analyses of six children's reading in English and Spanish and photocopied the same children's classroom writing throughout the year. I also administered an assessment of English proficiency to all of the students at the beginning and end of the school year.

I transcribed all taped lessons and interviews and analyzed fieldnotes and transcripts using methods of constant comparison to code the data and create conceptual categories (Strauss & Corbin, 1990). As I examined the possible linkages between these categories, I identified four interrelated themes that allowed for a "realistic and multilayered description" (Hornberger, 1994, p. 688) of the literacy practices: the struggle over classroom literacy activities, the inclusion of children's life experiences, the collaborative construction of literacy, and the use of hybrid language practices. Returning to the data, I developed a more comprehensive understanding of these themes, the relationships between them, and their bearing on my research questions. In the following sections, I present findings elaborating these four major themes.

The Struggle Over Classroom Literacy Practices

The classroom literacy practices I observed in Room 110 resulted from a contentious commingling of political, institutional, and personal trajectories. Whereas Dixon and Green (1999) point out that a number of recent educational policies in California—including class size reduction, heightened stress on skill-based reading instruction and standardized testing, and the termination of social promotion–cumulatively affect the schooling of language minority children, in this paper I foreground the influence of Proposition 227 on classroom literacy practices. During the 1997–98 school year, Ms. Page taught a kindergarten and first-grade bilingual class at Adams School. Referring to bilingual education, she stated, "I felt it was the best way to [educate] language minority children. I bought into the philosophy behind primary language instruction." Ms. Page's students' achievement reinforced her position: "The kids had a lot of success academically. With the exception of one student, all, including my kindergartners, became competent readers in Spanish. I really believed in what I was doing."

As a result of this experience, Ms. Page opposed Proposition 227 and was deeply disappointed when it passed. The proposition mandated one year of structured-immersion education for English language learners in which "nearly all the classroom instruction is in English" (Unz & Tuchman, 1997) and made teachers who did not follow this dictate liable for damages and legal fees. In spite of the mandate, the implementation of Proposition 227 varied widely from district to district and from school to school within the same district (Garcia & Curry-Rodriguez, 1999). Ms. Page described her district as implementing the proposition "in the most by-the-book fashion." In a meeting with district officials, she was told explicitly that Spanish could "only to be used for support and not for instruction" and that literacy activities could not be done in Spanish. Ms. Page felt that her school exuded linguistic hegemony. In April she stated, "My school is hostile towards Spanish. English is the language of school; English is the language of the test that is going to show our worth. [The message is that] the Spanish stuff is just a waste of time."

In meetings with administrators and parents, Ms. Page immediately brought up the possibility of obtaining parental waivers to allow children to receive bilingual instruction, an alternative granted by the proposition. Attending several parent meetings, she heard school officials announce that the waivers were for parents who wanted their children in a "Spanish class." At a bilingual advisory committee meeting at Adams School, Ms. Page spoke out, informing parents that the waiver was for a bilingual class with instruction in two languages and clarifying that children in immersion classes would not be taught to read and write Spanish. The next day many of the parents expressed interest in waivers, but none could be found in the school office. Ms. Page recalled that by the time the waivers arrived, "the bilingual resource teacher had convinced the parents that I was not going to be the teacher of the bilingual class. And, if there were not 20, they were going to send the children [with waivers] to another school." Although ten parents from Room 110 eventually signed bilingual waivers, Ms. Page and several parents informed me that the school never responded. As a result, Ms. Page felt compelled to offer an English-immersion curriculum.

Early in the year, school officials offered guidelines regarding literacy instruction in first-grade English-immersion classes. They directed teachers to use the kindergarten language arts curriculum and informed them that the immersion classes would focus on promoting oral language development rather than reading. Disregarding these directives, Ms. Page declared, "How can you be a first grade teacher and not teach kids how to read? Reading is still my focus." She then described her instruction as striking a "funny compromise" between the mandates of Proposition 227 and the needs of her students. Referring to the amount of Spanish used in literacy activities, Ms. Page declared:

> I am not doing formal instruction in Spanish reading, but there is definitely informal instruction happening. I am not doing formal writing instruction in Spanish, but there is a lot of Spanish writing going on in my classroom and I do nothing to discourage it. All literacy instruction is supposed to take place in English, and they have hidden the Spanish books. So, I do guided reading in English. But, some kids will not understand me if I explain about reading strategies, do the picture walk, and get [the children] ready to read the book in English. So, I do it in Spanish; yet they read the book in English. The code switching I do is really complicated. I am always trying to speak in a way that the most kids are going to understand at that time.

Whereas the balance between English and Spanish in literacy activities reflected Ms. Page's resistance, the parents and children also influenced the class's literacy practices over the school year. In one instance, Ms. Page consulted with the parents of several children that did not appear to benefit from English reading instruction. After considering Ms. Page's advice, the parents encouraged her to begin providing reading instruction in Spanish to their children. According to Ms. Page, the mother of a struggling second-grade boy told her, "It is better do it the Spanish way. He knows his syllables; he should keep going." As a result of the parental support, Ms. Page conducted a Spanish-language guided reading group.

In the case of the Daily News, the children played a central role in the transformation of one of the class's central literacy practices. Each morning of the first semester, Ms. Page and the children met on the rug for the Daily News. Several children volunteered to share events from their lives, Ms. Page scribed their stories, and then the class read back the news chorally. Although the majority of volunteers shared their news in Spanish, Ms. Page wrote in English, asking students for help in translating the stories. Thus, despite Ms. Page's revolt against the official exclusion of Spanish from literacy instruction, English had a privileged status as the language in which experiences lived and told in Spanish were encoded. This differed markedly from the previous year when Ms. Page conducted the Daily News solely in Spanish to foster the children's acquisition of Spanish literacy.

At the beginning of the second semester, students took responsibility for writing the news. During the class's writing workshop two students served as "reporters" who scribed their peers' news without Ms. Page's supervision. As in all cases of independent reading and writing in the class, the reporters were free to work in English or Spanish. Each morning Ms. Page engaged the class in editing the previous day's news. Since the children frequently wrote in Spanish, these editing sessions became an occasion for Ms. Page to provide consistent instruction in Spanish writing. When I asked Ms. Page about this transformation, she reflected:

The news was a good opportunity to scaffold English language learning because of the shared writing technique. However, it never felt good to do it. I was writing about their lives in the language they do not speak in their lives, and English [was] put up on the wall and not the Spanish they used. So when the kids took up the responsibility of becoming the reporters and they did it in Spanish, [I thought], "I am just going to follow their lead, because I never liked it the other way."

By exercising their freedom to write in Spanish, the children remade the daily news in a way that bolstered their teacher's resistance to the district's implementation of Proposition 227 and that furthered their own biliteracy development.

A Bridge to Participation

Narratives from and references to the children's lives outside of school played a central role in the class's literacy activities. For students in transition to conventional reading and writing, lived experience functioned as a bridge providing access to the relatively unfamiliar world of print and the discourse accompanying it. By grounding activities in the children's sociocultural realities, literacy became an important tool for making sense of the world and a platform for the students' display of knowledge and expertise often ignored in school.

During the class's daily writing workshop, Ms. Page encouraged the children to select exciting or unusual personal experiences as writing topics. At the end of each writing period, a few children shared their work and responded to their classmates' questions from the author's chair. In one typical performance in early November, Juan shared an unconventionally written text in Spanish about his dogs jumping on his bed and biting him. He then called on several of the students stretching their hands high to respond to his story. Smiling broadly, one child inquired, "*¿Dónde te mordieron los perros?*" (Where did the dogs bite you?) Delighting his audience, Juan answered, "*¡En las orejas!*" (On my ears!) The final respondent stated, "*Me gusta tu cuento porque escribiste bien*" (I like your story because you wrote well). Thus, while still struggling to develop conventional reading and writing skills, Juan's familiarity with the content of his text gave him access to the author's chair, enabled him to produce the literate discourse that it required, and earned him praise as a successful author. Although Juan's writing progressed slowly over the course of the year, his ongoing participation in writing workshop and author's chair reinforced his identity as a competent literacy user and provided him important opportunities for development.

In another author's chair performance, Eva read a story that she had written in Spanish about her uncle who was waiting in Tijuana to cross the border. A student then asked her to clarify why her uncle was in Tijuana. Eva responded that the uncle needed a black vest to cross the border because he did not have a passport. Furthering the discussion, Ms. Page stated that she did not understand why the uncle needed a black vest. Eva informed her, "*Es que, va a cruzar la frontera de noche*" (He is going to cross the border at night). Another student, Roberto, inquired again why Eva's uncle was waiting in Tijuana. Eva explained,

"*El está esperando al señor que lo va a traer a través de la frontera a Los Angeles*" (He is waiting for the man to bring him across the border to Los Angeles). This answer did not resolve the matter for Roberto, and his confusion prompted an enthusiastic discussion about border crossing in which several students told stories about family members' border experiences. Juana, the instructional assistant and the mother of a girl in the class, explained in Spanish that people from Mexico and Central America were not free to enter the United States. Eva's story about a family member's experience caused the class to focus on a topic important to the students' lives. During the discussion Eva, other children, and Juana applied their expert knowledge regarding the U.S.–Mexico border to reach an understanding of a complex issue rarely contemplated in primary-grade classrooms.

Additionally, I observed many other instances of children using knowledge from their daily lives in the class's literacy activities. By relying on their personal experiences to produce and interpret texts, the children used their diverse sociocultural resources to further their literacy skills and wove reading and writing into the fabric of their lives.

The Collaborative Construction of Literacy

Literacy events in Room 110 reverberated with the hum of intense collaboration. As the children read and wrote together throughout the day, an atmosphere of enthusiastic sociality emanated from their joint enterprises. The students moved continually between expert and apprentice roles as they negotiated tasks and momentarily displayed their personal expertise. The composition of the Daily News exemplified the zealous participatory spirit that accompanied the class's literacy events. When students took responsibility for the news at midyear, voices, hands, and laughter intertwined in inextricable tangles as the children engaged in joint activity.

The drafting of the Daily News took place in the "office," a rectangular table also used as the class's writing center. The two reporters sat side by side, hovering over a large sheet of lined newsprint, and the newsgiver, when called, sat at the end of the table. Many times I observed the newsgiver straining for a closer view of how the reporters were rendering the words in print. On one such occasion, Diana lay sprawled across the tabletop, face suspended inches from the newsprint, advising the reporters as they worked. Although ardently participatory, the event also resonated with playfulness and humor. In the exchange (see Table 1), Sergio (S) and Roberto (R) scribed Cristian's (C) news about a lowrider car. As the boys stretched out the words for the writer, syllables metamorphosed into the sounds of a lowrider engine and the boys convulsed with laughter.

During these collaborative sessions, assistance flowed in all directions, unimpeded by relative levels of competence or language proficiency. As a struggling writer, Juan received a great deal of support from his partners. However, just as frequently the shifting configurations of joint activity placed him in a position to provide expert help. In one instance, I observed Juan and Lupe sit together to recopy the news they had written after the class had made editorial corrections. They divided the task, deciding that Lupe would write first. As she began to work, Juan leaned over to inspect her words and then dictated to her from the edited paper: "*Ayer–Claudia–fue–a* . . ." (Yesterday–Claudia–went–to . . .) When he reached the unfamiliar name of a restaurant, Juan spelled out the letters for Lupe. Participating as a skilled partner, Juan displayed his own knowledge of print and genuinely contributed to the task at hand.

As collaboration occurred across languages, the children spurred each other's biliteracy development. This appeared throughout the data, but was especially apparent when Susan entered Room 110 in May after spending the majority of the year in a class in which the teacher only taught in English. An English-dominant newcomer, Susan served as an expert in English, prompting and assisting other students to read and write in English. However, she also quickly manifested a keen interest in developing Spanish literacy. A month after her arrival, I observed Susan working as the reporter for the Daily News. When Laura (L) appear to hesitate while beginning to dictate her news in English, Susan (S) promptly told her to speak in Spanish (see Table 2). Susan then received assistance as she attempted to write in Spanish.

Hybrid Language Practices

From the first day of school, a hand-painted poster adorned with a yellow school bus and large letters proclaiming "*¡Bienvenidos! Welcome to . . . Salón 110*" hung on Ms. Page's classroom door. This sign symbolized the linguistic hybridity characteristic of the learning community in Room 110. During the class's

Table 1

Transcript from June 1, 1999

Transcript	Translation

C: El sábado miramos lowriders . . .
    Ssábado
	C: Saturday we saw lowriders . . .
	    Ssaturday

S [Sounding out for Roberto,
    who begins to write]: "El sa"
	S [Sounding out for Roberto,
	    who begins to write]: "El sa"

C: El <u>sa-ba</u>	C: El <u>sa-ba</u>

S: <u>ba-ba-ba-ba-ba</u>
    [Making an engine-like sound]
	S: <u>ba-ba-ba-ba-ba</u>
	    [Making an engine-like sound]

R: Ya, hombre! <u>Sa-</u>	R: Stop, man! <u>Sa-</u>
C: <u>Sa-</u> ba-ba-ba-ba-ba	C: <u>Sa-</u>ba-ba-ba-ba-ba

R: ¡Cómete la ba, ba, ba, ba!
    ¿Ms. Page va a leer,
    "ba, ba, ba, ba"?
	R: Eat the ba, ba, ba, ba!
	    Is Ms. Page going to read,
	    "ba, ba, ba, ba?"

Note. Simultaneous utterances underlined.

literacy activities a kaleidoscopic range of languages, registers, and codes en-twined to produce a uniquely hybrid discourse that served important pedagogical and counterhegemonic functions. The class's hybrid language practices enlisted the participants' "larger linguistic repertoires" (Gutierrez et al., 1999, p. 89) as tools for understanding, participation, and biliteracy development and created a climate that validated the children's bilingual and bicultural identities.

The examples of classroom interaction presented in the prior sections illus-trate how the children's home language, registers, and knowledge provided ac-cess to important participatory roles in literacy events. In the case of the guided reading lesson described at the beginning of this paper, Spanish served as an important resource for accomplishing an English literacy task. First, Ms. Page and the children reviewed the content of the English text they were preparing to read and discussed strategies for interpreting problematic words in Spanish. Next, the children read the book several times in English. Finally, while Ms. Page's mini-lesson focused on writing English words ending with /ing/, the students assisted Sandra in writing her sentence by calling out the letter names in Spanish.

This overlapping of languages had no apparent negative effect on the begin-ning literacy learners. The children demonstrated an impressive awareness of and ability to manipulate the distinct features of English and Spanish. For example, as detailed in the Daily News transcript in the previous section, Susan switched from

Table 2

Transcript from June 8, 2000

Transcript	Translation
L: My sister Daisy-	L: My sister Daisy-
S: Laura's sister. Laura's sister Daisy	S: Laura's sister. Laura's sister Daisy
L: Daisy went—	L: Daisy went—
S: No más dime en español.	S: Just tell me in Spanish.
L: Daisy, mi hermana, hizo la primera comunión.	L: Daisy, my sister, had her first communion.
S: El primero comerción? [sic]	S: Her first comercion? [nonword in Spanish]
L: hizo la primera comunión.	L: Had her first communion.
S: OK.	S: OK.
. . .	. . .
S: Hermana.	S: Sister.
L: Hermana. "H," "h," "e," /er/ – "r," ere. [spells Spanish word using English letter names]	L: Sister. "H," "h," "e," /er/ – "r," ere. [spells Spanish word using English letter names]
S: Lo puedes decir in Spanish.	S: You can say it in Spanish.
L: ere, eme. Eme, eme.	L: ere, eme. Eme, eme. [spells out in Spanish]

English to Spanish after writing "Laura's." As a result, the sentence began "Laura's hermana . . ." When Susan reread her work, she stopped and announced, "Laura's hermana? That don't [sic] make sense. You have to erase the 's.'" With a little negotiation, the two children then produced the correct Spanish form. In addition, of the nine first-grade students in Room 110 that took the SAT 9, six scored above the national median in English reading and on average the group scored at the 63th percentile nationally. These scores are particularly impressive given that the children were placed in Ms. Page's class because of their low levels of English proficiency.

The class's hybrid language practices also supported the children's identities as bilingual and biliterate individuals. Interviews with the children indicated that they prized their unique linguistic ability. Throughout the year many students composed bilingual books or alternated daily between writing in English and Spanish during the class's writing workshop. When I questioned them about their language preferences, the children inevitably responded that they liked to speak, read, and write in both Spanish and English and planned to continue doing so.

When the students from the English-only first grade entered Room 110 for integration, Ms. Page's children demonstrated their linguistic flexibility in hybrid performances that impressed their peers and challenged the hegemonic status of English at Adams School. In a typical activity, Ms. Page called on Juan to sit in the "Hot Seat": to take on the persona of the main character of a story and to answer students' questions from the character's perspective. The book that Ms. Page had read featured Diego, a Latino boy whose family members were migrant workers. Playing the character of Diego, Juan called on peers with outstretched hands who asked questions in both English and Spanish. To meet the needs of his audience, Juan gave bilingual answers. For example, when Antonio asked, "¿Por qué tu estabas agarrando el radio?" (Why are you grabbing the radio?), Juan responded, "Porque me gusta . . . I like to carry the radio."

Such displays inspired the bilingual students from the English-only class to use Spanish when they visited Room 110. Ms. Page reported that these children frequently announced, "Hablo español también" (I speak Spanish too) and that they often asked her in the hallway, "Can we speak Spanish today [in your class]?" The monolingual students also developed an interest in Spanish. One day, Sandra came forward to share a literature response that she had written in English. An African-American boy asked Ms. Page, "Can she read it in Spanish after she reads it in English?" When Ms Page responded, "Yes she can," an African American girl let out an enthusiastic, "Yes!" During Sandra's translation of her writing, the boy from Ms. Jones's class got up on his hands and knees and strained forward, listening intently to the Spanish words.

Borderlands Literacy

To conceptualize my findings from Room 110, I formulated the new theoretical construct of *borderlands literacy*. Although grounded in classroom data, the construct also reflects the theoretical perspectives that informed my study. Borderlands literacy represents a syncretic construct produced from the intersection of sociocultural and situated learning theories and the literacy practices I saw in Room 110. The notion of borderlands literacy owes a particular debt to Chicana scholar Gloria Anzaldúa. Anzaldúa's (1987) work names and maps out the charged physical, psychological, and spiritual space of the borderlands, the juncture between different classes, cultures, and languages. Brimming with images of pluralism, hybridity, and resistance to monological thinking, Anzaldúa's term captures the spirit of the distinctive literacy practices that I documented in this study.

Borderlands literacy emerges when classroom literacy practices depend on children's diverse sociocultural knowledge, life experiences, and linguistic repertoires as resources for reading and writing; view biliteracy as the goal of language minority children's literacy development; provide for inclusive participation in joint activity and social interaction; affirm and extend bilingual and bicultural identities; and challenge monological cultural narratives and oppressive social policies.

Like Anzaldúa's (1987) "new Mestiza consciousness" in which "nothing is thrust out, the good the bad and the ugly, nothing rejected, nothing abandoned" (p. 79), borderlands literacy envisions every element of children's sociocultural experience as a resource for learning. As evidenced in the findings, Ms. Page and her students employed funds of knowledge, life experiences, and hybrid language practices as means for participation in class literacy practices, and consequently, for acquiring reading and writing skills. In conjunction with this inclusive stance on the resources capable of mediating reading and writing, borderlands literacy practices affirm biliteracy as the proper goal of language minority children's literacy development.

Moll and colleagues (Moll & Whitmore, 1994; Moll & Dworin, 1996) have described biliteracy as a powerful cultural tool that enhances children's access and ability to communicate information. In Room 110, many children preferred reading and writing in both English and Spanish as the natural, enjoyable expression of their bilingual, bicultural identities and as a demonstration of special linguistic competence that elicited admiration from their peers. Over the course of the year, I observed children who initially read and wrote only in Spanish begin to write English texts. In Susan's case, she entered the class reading and writing English but quickly demonstrated interest in Spanish literacy. In light of research indicating the bi-directional transfer of reading skills across languages (Verhoeven, 1994), it should not be surprising that Ms. Page's students manifested a high level of achievement in English reading on the SAT 9 exam despite spending time cultivating Spanish reading.

As amply demonstrated in Room 110, borderlands literacy practices are inherently collaborative and broadly participatory. Like the medieval carnivals conjured up by Bakhtin (1984), Daily News, author's chair, literature discussion and the other literacy activities I observed erased the division between participants and spectators and frequently produced informal, humor-laden social interaction. Whereas the class did not ignore traditional literacy skills involving phonics, spelling and punctuation rules, and reading strategies, these skills were developed within a larger framework of collaborative and meaning-centered practices. Notably non-exclusive, the practices offered numerous and shifting participant roles that positioned the children as competent members of a literate community regardless of their language proficiency or skill level. Like the students described by Moll et al. (1993), Ms. Page and the children in Room 110 served as "thinking resources for one another" (p. 160), mediating literacy learning within densely overlapping ZPDs.

Whereas linguistic and cultural differences often earn English Learners "benignly deviant" school identities (Toohey, 1998), borderlands literacy incorporates positively the variegated experiences of bilingual, bicultural children. In Room 110, literacy practices were intricately related to the students' sociocultural experience. Reading and writing continually offered the children opportunities to reflect on or share cultural narratives and to enhance their broad linguistic repertoires. By placing a high value on Spanish and encouraging the development of Spanish literacy, Ms. Page assured that learning to speak, read, and write English was an additive process for her students. Moreover, the children eagerly displayed their growing bilingual and biliterate ability, impressing peers and firmly establishing bilingualism as an emblem of academic competence.

Finally, borderlands literacy represents a public performance of heterogeneity that challenges exclusionary social policy. When set against the monological sociopolitical milieu epitomized by Proposition 227, the literacy practices of Room 110 reflect a "transgressive enunciation of self- and community identities [that] gives . . . 'cultural capital' for dissent" (Amkpa, 1999, p. 100). In this regard, it is significant that Ms. Page, the parents, and the students mutually contributed to the construction of literacy practices that openly resisted the dictates of Proposition 227. The enthusiasm and success of the children as a result of these practices testifies to the shortcomings of a narrowly conceived educational policy and to the potential of multiethnic, multilingual classroom communities to challenge the persistent hegemony of assimilatory "melting pot" ideals.

References

Amkpa, A. (1999). Floating signification: Carnivals and the transgressive performance of hybridity. In M. Sergioph & J. N. Fink (Eds.), *Performing hybridity* (pp. 96–105). Minneapolis: University of Minnesota Press.

Anzaldúa, G. (1987). *Borderlands/La frontera: The new mestiza*. San Francisco: Aunt Lute.

Bakhtin, M. M. (1984). *Rabelais and his world*. Bloomington: Indiana University Press.

Bloom, D. (1994). Reading as a social context in a middle school classroom. In D. Graddol, J. Maybin, & B. Stierer (Eds.), *Researching language and literacy in a social context* (pp. 100–130). Philadelphia, PA: Multilingual Matters.

California Department of Education, Educational Demographics Unit. (1998). *Language census, 1997-98 [Online]*. Available: http://www.cde.ca.gov/demographics/reports/#swlep.

Commins, N. (1989). Language and affect: Bilingual students at home and at school. *Language Arts, 66,* 29–43.

Cook-Gumperz, J. (1986). *The social construction of literacy*. New York: Cambridge University Press.

Dixon, C., & Green, J. (1999, May). *Language use in a policy context: How Proposition 227 and other policy decisions shape language practices and access to academic content.* Paper presented at the meeting of the UC Linguistic Minority Research Institute, Sacramento, CA.

Fránquiz, M., & Reyes, M. de la Luz, (1998). Creating inclusive learning communities through English language arts: From chanclas to canicas. *Language Arts, 75,* 211–220.

Garcia, E., & Curry-Rodriguez, J. (1999, May). *Education of limited English proficient students in California schools: An assessment of the influence of Proposition 227.* Paper presented at the meeting of the UC Linguistic Minority Research Institute, Sacramento, CA.

Gutierrez, K. (1995). Unpackaging academic discourse. *Discourse Processes, 19,* 21–37.

Gutierrez, K., Baquedano-López, P., Alvarez, H., & Chiu, M. (1999). Building a culture of collaboration through hybrid language practices. *Theory into Practice, 38*(2), 87–93.

Gutierrez, K., Baquedano-López, P., Tejeda, C., & Rivera, A. (1999, April). *Hybridity as a tool for understanding literacy learning: Building on a syncretic approach.* Paper presented at the meeting of the American Educational Research Association, Montreal.

Gutierrez, K., & Larson, J. (1994). Language borders: Recitation as hegemonic discourse. *International Journal of Educational Reform, 3*(1), 22–36.

Gutierrez, K., & Meyers, B. (1995). Creating communities of effective practice: Building literacy for language minority children. In J. Oakes & K. Quartz (Eds.), *Creating new educational communities.* 94th yearbook of the National Society for the Study of Education (pp. 35–52). Chicago: University of Chicago Press.

Hornberger, N. (1994). Ethnography. *TESOL Quarterly, 28,* 673–703.

Lave, J., & Wenger, E. (1991). *Situated learning: Legitimate peripheral participation.* New York: Cambridge University Press.

McDermott, R. (1987). Achieving school failure: An anthropological approach to illiteracy and social stratification. In G. Spinder (Ed.), *Education and cultural process* (pp. 173–209). Prospect Heights, IL: Waveland.

McDermott, R. (1993). The acquisition of a child by a learning disability. In J. Lave & S. Chaiklin (Eds.), *Understanding practice: Perspectives on activity and context* (pp. 269–305). Cambridge, England: Cambridge University Press.

Myers, J. (1992). The social contexts of school and personal literacy. *Reading Research Quarterly, 27,* 297–333.

Moll, L. (1990). Introduction. In L. Moll (Ed.), *Vygotsky and education:Instructional implications and applications of sociohistorical psychology* (pp. 1–27). New York: Cambridge University Press.

Moll, L., & Dworin, J. (1996). Biliteracy development in classrooms: Social dynamics and cultural possibilities. In D. Hicks (Ed.), *Discourse, learning, and schooling* (pp. 221–246). New York: Cambridge University Press.

Moll, L., Tapia, J., & Whitmore, K. (1993). Living knowledge: The social distribution of cultural resources for thinking. In G. Salomon (Ed.), *Distributed cognitions: Psychological and educational considerations* (pp. 139–163). Cambridge, England: Cambridge University Press.

Moll, L., & Whitmore, K. (1993). Vygotsky in classroom practice: Moving from individual transmission to social transaction. In E. Forman, N. Minick, & C. A. Stone (Eds.), *Contexts for learning: Sociocultural dynamics in children's development* (pp. 230–253). New York: Oxford University Press.

National Center for Educational Statistics. (1994). *Mini-digest of educational statistics, 1994.* Washington, DC: U.S. Department of Education.

National Center for Educational Statistics. (1999). *The NAEP 1998 reading report card.* Washington, DC: U.S. Department of Education.

Norton, B., & Toohey, K. (1999). *Reconceptualizing the good language learner: SLA at the turn of the century.* Manuscript submitted for publication.

Reyes, M. de la Luz, & Costanzo, L. (1999, April). *On the threshold of biliteracy: A first grader's personal journey.* Paper presented at the meeting of the American Educational Research Association, Montreal.

Rogoff, B. (1991). *Apprenticeship in thinking: Cognitive development in social context.* New York: Oxford University Press.

Rogoff, B. (1995). Observing sociocultural activity on three planes: Participatory appropriation, guided participation, and apprenticeship. In J. Wertsch, P. Del Rio, & A. Alvarez (Eds.), *Sociocultural studies of mind* (pp. 139–164). New York: Cambridge University Press.

Rogoff, B., Mosier, C., Mistry, J., & Artin, G. (1993). Toddlers' guided participation with their caregivers in cultural activity. In E. Forman, N. Minick, & C. A. Stone (Eds.), *Contexts for learning: Sociocultural dynamics in children's development* (pp. 230–253). New York: Oxford University Press.

Shannon, S. (1995). The hegemony of English: A case study of one bilingual classroom as a site of resistance. *Linguistics and Education, 7,* 175–200.

Strauss, A., & Corbin, J. (1990). *Basics of qualitative research: Grounded theory procedures and techniques.* Thousand Oaks, CA: Sage.

Tharp, R., & Gallimore, R. (1988). *Rousing minds to life:Teaching learning, and schooling in social context.* New York: Cambridge University Press.

Toohey, K. (1996). Learning English as a second language in kindergarten: A community of practice perspective. *Canadian Modern Language Review, 52,* 549–576.

Toohey, K. (1998). "Breaking them up, taking them away": ESL students in grade 1. *TESOL Quarterly, 32*(1), 61–84.

Unz, R., & Tuchman, G. M. (1997). *English language education for children in public schools* [online]. Available: http://www.onenation.org/fulltext.html.

Verhoeven, L. (1994). Transfer in bilingual development. *Language Learning, 44,* 381–415.

Vygotsky, L. S. (1978). *Mind in society* (Michael Cole, Trans.). Cambridge, MA: Harvard University Press.

Wenger, E. (1998). *Communities of practice: Learning, meaning, and identity.* New York: Cambridge University Press.

Wertsch, J. V. (1985). *Vygotsky and the social formation of mind.* Cambridge, MA: Harvard University Press.

Wertsch, J. V. (1991). *Voices of the mind: A sociocultural approach to mediated action.* Cambridge, MA: Harvard University Press.

Wertsch, J. V. (1998). *Mind as action.* New York: Oxford University Press.

Wertsch J., Del Rio, P., & Alvarez, A. (1995). Sociocultural studies: history, action, and mediation. In J. Wertsch, P. Del Rio, & A. Alvarez (Eds.), *Sociocultural studies of mind* (pp. 1–34). New York: Cambridge University Press.

Willet, J. (1995). Becoming first graders in an L1: An ethnographic study of L2 socialization. *TESOL Quarterly, 2,* 473–503.

Preparing Reflective Teachers of Reading: A Critical Review of Reflection Studies in Literacy Pedagogy

Kathleen Roskos
John Carroll University

Victoria Risko
Vanderbilt University

Carol Vukelich
University of Delaware

Reflection, as an essential part of teachers' practice, is a strongly held belief among teacher educators, dating back to Dewey (1933) and even earlier (Aristotle's *Ethics*). That teachers should thoughtfully consider the practical and moral implications of their work makes sense intuitively. Yet, a well-researched, common knowledge base that informs and supports the development of reflection in future teachers has not been generated. There are multiple definitions of reflection and multiple ways in which it is invited and displayed. Research findings as to its power are mixed. To assure quality reflection in teaching, a better understanding of the research on reflection is needed—the theoretical frameworks that frame it, the operational definitions that focus it, and the procedures that guide and shape the interpretations of data.

In this paper, we identify a collection of studies on reflection in preservice literacy education and critically review its content for evidence of theory and inquiry that builds a knowledge base for reflection instruction. We also make recommendations that help interpret reflection research in the education of reading teachers and outline new directions for inquiry.

Perspectives

Inspired by Dewey's ideas on reflective inquiry, most teacher educators associate the development of teachers' reflective abilities with their development as accomplished practitioners (e.g., Danielson, 1996). Reflection, it is assumed, stimulates critical thinking about one's own beliefs and practices and leads to adaptations that are indicative of developmental change and growth (Brooks & Brooks, 1993; Clift, Houston, & Pugach, 1990; Hunsaker & Johnston, 1992). Teachers who critically examine their understandings of pedagogy are believed to "continually test and modify these constructions in the light of new experience" (Swandt, 1994,

National Reading Conference Yearbook, 49, pp. 109–121.

pp. 125–126). Reflection goes well beyond what Dewey (1933) describes as "routine thinking," the kind of thinking students do when they adopt traditional stances guided by authority and defer their own deliberations and interpretations. Instead, it enables them to break with tradition, approach learning as problem solvers, and build understandings of diverse and competing viewpoints (Schon, 1987; Slattery, 1995). As Goodman (1984) and others argue, reflection involves logical thinking that includes forming judgments about actions, deductive reasoning, and creative thinking. It is this kind of reflection, sustained over time, that is believed to support prospective teachers' developing understandings of pedagogy (Berliner, 1987) as well as their ability to objectify and learn from their own teaching actions (Jones & Vesiland, 1996).

From both theoretical and practical perspectives, therefore, it makes sense to encourage prospective teachers to become more reflective. Yet, we have limited information about how future teachers acquire and develop their reflective capabilities. Criteria for understanding and evaluating what teachers should be reflecting about, for example, are quite divergent and not well articulated. Zeichner and Liston (1991) describe a literature base that often gives the "impression that as long as teachers [and prospective teachers] reflect about something, in some manner, then whatever they decide to do is okay since they have 'reflected about it'" (p. 24). Even less well specified are instructional methods in professional education that might support and advance reflection as an integral part of the educator's professional role. Kasten and Padak (1997), as a case in point, reveal the lack of explicitness surrounding data collection on reflection in the context of field experiences and the scarcity of reflection studies specific to literacy education.

We, ourselves, faced these same concerns in our efforts to observe qualities of reflective thinking among prospective teachers enrolled in our literacy methods courses (Risko, Roskos, & Vukelich, 1999). Using the popular approach of journal writing to elicit our students' reflections, we examined the mental strategies they recruited to accomplish the task and the intellectual qualities of their thinking. Our results corroborated what others before us had seen: future teachers of reading prefer to reflect at a factual level. They describe, report, and query some, but their responses fall short of meeting our expectations. The essence of reflection, as we briefly sketched above, should go beyond literal levels to involve interpretive, evaluative, critical, and creative thinking if it is to help teachers learn from their own experience. Unfortunately our students did not interpret, evaluate, and critique very much—a troubling observation given the significance of literacy education in society.

Our findings, although not startlingly new, did help us, nonetheless, to identify two major issues about reflective thinking pedagogy that moved us toward a critical review of the literature. The first issue relates to the importance of building a coherent, consistent picture of reflection development among preservice teachers. This requires sorting out what we seem to know and what remains puzzling, if we are to construct a full understanding of the complex processes that support reflection in beginning teachers. The second issue relates to instruction and the role of the teacher educator. How is reflection taught? To what extent do prevailing instructional structures and content elicit and challenge the preservice teacher's reflective abilities? The extent to which existing research informs teacher education is not well articulated nor are routes for discovering more effective approaches well marked.

With these issues pressing on the heels of our earlier study, we saw a critical review of reflection studies as an important step in understanding reflection as a construct in professional literacy education. A critique that examined how reflection is conceived, studied, and applied, we reasoned, would reference where we are in our understanding and also reveal what we yet need to pursue.

Method

Data Collection

We limited our review to empirical studies (quantitative and qualitative) that addressed reflection (e.g., reflective thinking, reflective teaching, reflection process, reflection development) in preservice literacy education published or presented between 1985 and 1999. Seminal works focusing on reflection and teacher education began to appear in the 1980s, starting with Schon's (1983) *The Reflective Practitioner: How professionals think in action.* Many credit this work as a cornerstone to a body of literature and research that ensued and continues to the present day (Schon, 1987, 1991). Correspondingly there was the work by Cruickshank (1987), Calderhead (1989), and Zeichner and Liston (1987), who followed Schon's lead and developed various arguments for reflection development in teacher education. We selected the 1985–1999 time period for analysis to trace the works that followed from Schon's earliest piece and continued to develop during the next 15 years.

Studies were identified through three successive sweeps of the professional literature in teacher education. Initially, the *PsycINFO, Acorn,* and *ERIC* online databases were scanned for articles from 1985 to 1999 that met the inclusion criteria of reflection, teacher education, and preservice education. This search yielded 602 abstracts that included theoretical papers, studies, book chapters, and dissertations. We examined these abstracts to locate any studies pertaining to the teaching of literacy and eliminated all the others. We then surveyed the online databases again, this time adding the term "literacy" as a descriptor to the string. This search produced a total of 82 articles specific to professional education in literacy teaching. In examining this set, we eliminated those articles that did not provide empirical data on the role of reflection in the "learning to teach literacy" process (e.g., position papers, theoretical descriptions, professional essays). In our third sweep, we manually searched the *National Reading Conference Yearbooks* from 1985 to 1999, the *College Reading Association Yearbooks* for this same period, and the full text of retrieved papers for studies that did not emerge from the computer search. This strategy yielded another 12 studies, some that duplicated those found in the prior searches.

The pool of relevant studies was narrowed down to those that *explicitly* dealt with some aspect of reflection as it related to preservice teachers engaged in literacy education coursework and programs. This produced a collection of 30 studies that appeared to offer sufficient descriptive evidence on reflection as a construct in the professional preparation of reading teachers. We grouped the studies into three time periods (1985–1989; 1990–1994; 1995–1999), and each of us assumed responsibility for a time period, agreeing to become an expert in that subset of the collection.

Data Analysis

We analyzed the 30 studies following an inductive paradigmatic analysis process articulated by Polkinghorne (1995). Studies we had gathered were descriptive in nature, relying primarily on qualitative methods and strategies for the treatment of data. Thus, as a staple of qualitative methodology (e.g., Strauss & Corbin, 1990), an inductive paradigmatic analysis seemed well-suited to the fundamental research orientation of the collection.

The basic operation of inductive paradigmatic analysis is classifying a particular instance or event as belonging to a category or concept. The goal is to develop "a categorical schematic *out of* the data" (Polkinghorne, 1995, p. 10), which provides the foundation for inducing relationships that hold between and among the established categories. Such relationships reveal "cognitive networks of concepts" (p. 10) indicative of the formulations held by a culture or group. For our purposes, this approach promised a glimpse of how reflection is conceptualized and studied in the education of future literacy teachers.

For purposes of interrater reliability, we used a two-step analytic procedure to derive categories and features reflective of the knowledge networks embedded in the studies. First, each of us read and reread our respective subset of studies to identify how reflection was conceptualized and systematically examined. We generated detailed summaries of the studies, including the researchers' theoretical perspectives, data collection and analysis techniques, and conclusions. We also analyzed each paper for its methodological strengths and weaknesses by assessing coherence in theoretical stance, method, and findings. Second, all three of us read and reread each other's summaries. We individually recorded emerging concepts and features and discussed and negotiated our observations. From this we created a coding matrix to organize the information we were finding. It consisted of six general thematic categories (author's theoretical frame(s), setting/situation, definitions, influential factors, methodology, recommendations) and related features that represented the information in the papers. We each applied the matrix to a sample study drawn from each time frame to clarify categories and to verify the features. Following further discussion that led to the collapsing of some features, label changes in others, and the addition of new features, we achieved an interrater reliability of 91% on the sample. We then negotiated to resolve any remaining discrepancies.

Using the coding results per the matrix, we next each induced descriptive observations from our original set of studies. We then compared and contrasted these generalizations among us to identify the relationships across and within our emerging "cognitive networks of concepts." These relational links helped us to describe how reflection is understood and treated as an object of study and knowledge in the field of literacy education. This approach also permitted us to derive interpretations as to the scientific quality and pedagogic implications of the body of research, that we cast into recommendations for further consideration.

Results

We begin with descriptive observations derived from the coding matrix we applied to the set of studies, then move to analytic comments that discuss patterned regularities that emerged across the collection. Finally, we offer three recommendations that make the leap to the larger, deeper meanings implied by the research in the collection and point to new directions.

Descriptive Observations

Our first systematic look at the data produced several generalizations about the research collection as a whole, which we detail below.

To a large extent in these studies, *reflection is situated in individual personal experience* that is processed in a monologic matter as opposed to collective or dialogic experience that might involve a study group, an entire class, or a forum. Individually, students are encouraged to probe their own past histories as observers or novice teachers in schools and classrooms as the stimulus for reflective thought. For the most part, however, this thinking occurs out of the mainstream of class activities. Individual thoughts, reactions, and reflective impressions are rarely reported as the impetus for building shared pedagogical knowledge among class members or with the instructor.

Most authors argue that *reflection should widen the understanding of teaching beyond narrow technical concerns to the broader socio-political influences on literacy teaching work.* Yet few provide solid evidence that this actually happens through the reflection tasks students are asked to do. In fact, those studies examining preservice teachers' level of reflective thinking indicate very modest, if any, intellectual advance in this regard with most students remaining preoccupied with the self and the immediate teaching situation (e.g., Kasten & Padak, 1997; Leland, Harste, & Youseff, 1997; Risko, Roskos, & Vukelich, 1999; Smith & Pape, 1990). Beyond this observation, however, there is little evidence of systematic attempts to deepen reflection or to document in detail students' shifts and adaptations in their reflection strategies. Smith and Pape (1990), for example, sketchily describe using their taxonomy to raise the level of students' reflective thinking. They deliberately pitched their responses to students' journal entries at a higher level to "prompt" students' reflective thinking. Unfortunately, the pair did not richly describe links between their responses and students' subsequent responses illustrative of change, reporting only that few students "took the hint" and began reflecting at a higher level. Additionally, most studies offer little practical guidance for teacher educators to expand the value of reflection performance beyond the mere act of reflecting. The extent to which reflection activity impacts the preservice teacher's field experience, for instance, is not probed nor are the influences of different reflection formats (e.g., journals vs. class discussion) on pedagogic reasoning explored.

In a similar vein, almost all the authors discuss *reflection as an intellectual tool for bridging theory and practice,* but virtually none produces the particulars that would suggest how such connections are made. Dewey (1929), for example, argued that it is the educator's "intellectual instrumentalities" that mediate the relationship between theory and practice. The intellectual tools of inquiry (informed observation, systematic analysis, and principled interpretation) shape the educator's "habits of mind" so as to render her everyday practice "more intelligent, more flexible, and better adapted to deal effectively with concrete phenomena of practice" (1929, p. 20). On the whole, however, these studies provide few details and specifics related to the process of reflection wherein lay the interactions that support the habits of mind Dewey describes. Even as the studies collectively contain much descriptive observation of reflection gathered from hundreds of preservice teachers, precious little is devoted to process analyses that might reveal nascent "scientific" habits of mind that build bridges between theory and practice.

Many authors, following Deweyean thinking, suggest that *reflection activities should engage future teachers in an explicit study of their prior experiences as learners and in schools* with the goal of helping students make connections to new learning and to break from traditional ways of "doing" and "seeing." Some authors, for example, use autobiographies (e.g., Danielson, 1989) or interviews (e.g., Bean & Zulich, 1991; Lyons, 1998; Padak & Nelson, 1990) to activate the preservice teachers' prior knowledge for reflection purposes. However, it is not made clear if this helps or hinders the learning goals of reflection. How students are to make their prior knowledge useful as a scaffold for acquiring new ideas and insights is not discussed, leaving the impression that students spontaneously and naturally make connections between the familiar and the new and, moreover, that these connections are always "good" and true. Further there was virtually no tangible evidence that these recollections were formalized or referred to explicitly to help developing teachers resolve conflicts that are inevitable when moving from one tradition to another and to facilitate new learning.

Writing dominates as the preferred mode for eliciting and documenting reflective thinking and practice in the professional education context. The majority of studies in the collection engaged students in reflection through the medium of written text. Preservice teachers are asked to keep journals, respond in writing to portfolios, react in writing to videos, prepare written summaries, and develop written plans for professional growth. Instructional tools such as these appear to give purpose to reflective activity and help guide the construction of personal meaning, that is formulated into writing before being made public to instructor or peers. Relatively few of the 30 articles used oral discourse as the stimulus for reflection either through discussion or role play (e.g., Bruneau, Niles, Slanina, & Dunlap, 1993; Hermann & Sarracino, 1991; Sibbett, Wade, & Johnson, 1998; Wile, 1994). And although dialogue journaling may include student-teacher talk, it is not clear if oral interchange preceded reflection through this means (e.g., Bean & Zulich, 1989; Smith & Pape, 1990). None of the studies, however, take up the matter of linguistic data as either oral or written actualizations of reflective thinking, and the ensuing implications for research design and, relatedly, the knowledge it produces. Some might argue, in fact, that writing as a primary medium is incompatible with educating for reflection-in-action, which relies on careful coaching (showing and telling) in relation to teaching performance (Munby & Russell, 1989; Schon, 1987).

In nearly all of the studies there is an implicit assumption that *reflective abilities are connected to teaching abilities*, and that the development of reflection leads to improvement in teaching practice. This assumption is well-grounded in theory, going back to Dewey (1933), and also is warranted, for it makes sense that in trying to understand the consequences of teaching actions and by contemplating alternative courses of action, teachers expand their repertoire of practice (Ball & Cohen, 1999; Schon, 1987). However, few of the study authors acknowledge this assumption and its complexities in their research designs, thus failing to provide any empirical or theoretical rationale for their endeavor. The authors tell us who reflects, advocate for certain instructional tools and procedures, describe features of reflective thinking, and explore factors that may affect reflection. But most do not articulate why reflection might benefit the student as a developing teacher, nor strive to demonstrate how reflective processes intersect with everyday teaching processes for purposes of professional learning and growth. Also lacking is any exploration of misconceptions and biases that reflection may give rise to and foster, especially for the preservice teacher who must work very hard intellectually to think like a teacher, not a student.

Analytic Comments

Analyzing these observations, once again through the lens of our coding matrix, we identified at least three patterns that characterize this set of 30 reflection studies. Conceptually the collection seems to resemble more a set of unorganized congeries or "heap" than any coherent body of investigative work. The line of inquiry is diffuse and undirected, consisting of disparate studies that do not build on one another. This has a twofold consequence: the research as a whole lacks power because there is no cumulative effect and individual studies lack rigor because there is no press for more sophisticated methods and fine-grained analytic techniques coming from prior work. Every study starts anew at the level of broad-based description. Thus, the assembled collection is a conglomerate, the particulars of which may be pulled together and coalesced into vague thematic images. We must be mindful, however, that such thematic images are highly interpretable and work to highlight their interrelationships, not their particulars, as the basis for future research. Otherwise we may move no further along in building a clearer, truer conceptualization of reflection as it applies to educating future reading teachers.

Second, we can see glimmers in these studies of authors examining reflection as a change agent in the sociopolitical sense and as a way to socialize future teachers into the culture of teaching well equipped with this thinking tool. Although some look at the sociopolitical potential of reflection in preparing literacy teachers, we would argue that this concept must be brought to the forefront and studied systematically. In her recent comments on "recasting" the work of reviewing in relational terms, Livingston (1999) refers to "power" struggles and how these shape learning. Presently the authors of these studies hint at the sociopolitical underpinnings of the power struggles affecting reflection. Wedman and Martin (1986), for example, talk about the dominant culture of the schools being more powerful than methods courses, and how future teachers easily conform to what they see in schools and dismiss what they learned in their literacy courses. Bean and Zulich (1993) describe dialogue journal exchanges that are symmetrical and asymmetrical, alluding to the professor's power, that may dominate and control the student's reflective thinking, even though unintended. Still others nibble around the edges of power in terms of relevance—that ever-present struggle between everyday and scientific thinking that can pit students, cooperating teachers and teacher educators against one another. Although there are prickly instances of exploring reflection as a social, political, and cultural act, and not only a cognitive one, in these studies (e.g., Leland, Harste, & Youseff, 1997), future research should tease out these complexities far more carefully if we are to understand the multifaceted nature of reflection and its development in future professionals.

Third, these studies call into question the pedagogic and structural aspects of preparing teachers to be reflective. Grounded in the constructivist view, descriptions of the pedagogy of reflection from this perspective remain cursory and superficial. Evidence of mediation, for example, is seriously lacking. At this point, the research says very little about the particulars of careful scaffolding that push students' reflective abilities to deeper levels and about the coaching skills that help students develop strategic reflection. The silence on these matters in the research, in fact, is baffling, given the nearly universal acceptance of constructivist ideas linked to Vygotskian theory and the Schonian view of situated reflection. Good coaching goes to the core of constructivist pedagogy yet we do not know very much about it in the important teaching work of preparing reflective literacy teachers. How to effectively and systematically pull students' reflection development from point A to point B in reading methods courses and in larger programmatic contexts must become a high priority on the research agenda. To do otherwise is to run the risk of letting students' beliefs and biases go unchecked and unchallenged, and thus to diminish opportunities for them to develop the kind of thoughtfulness that excellent reading teaching demands.

The instructional tools of reflection (e.g., portfolios, journals, videos) need to be handled more sensitively and scrutinized more closely as mediators of thought and action. Such material artifacts, in the cultural-historical sense, are neither interchangeable nor neutral (Cole, 1996). Rather, these practical tools play a central role in preserving and transmitting modes of action and belief. In this light, they may actually evoke different kinds of reflective thinking and transmit different kinds of conceptual information as to what reflection is and what it means for everyday teaching practice. Evidence is scarce, however, as to systematic attempts to differentiate the effects of different reflection tools. A careful look at the impact of these tools is needed to inform teacher education as it is doubtful that journals, portfolios, role play, and so on will produce the same "reflective outcome." Future research should focus on tracing the influences of these various tools on students' reflective thinking and strategies, and it follows to assess their potential for supporting reflection development and learning.

Discussion

The patterns we identified in the second round of analysis provide a platform for interpreting this research and reveal several of its distinguishing features.

First, we learned that these authors' studies were guided primarily by a constructivist theory of learning; prospective teachers were treated as intellectuals who could learn by doing and thus were invited to examine carefully and write about course activities, classroom observations, and teaching experiences. Second, the authors were guided by their basic assumption that reflection is situational and therefore influenced by individuals' prior knowledge, personal experiences, and beliefs. Third, all viewed reflection as a means to socialize prospective teachers to new traditions and practices; they viewed learning not as static, but as a dynamic process responsive to new experiences and the opportunities to "reflect" on these. The authors, in sum, highlighted the importance of helping prospective teachers analyze the literacy teaching they observe in classrooms, its impact on children's literacy development and achievement, and the need to consider instructional alternatives in the face of classroom diversity.

Yet, we also observed that the research often treated reflection as a monologic process (something done on one's own) rather than a process that could be greatly enhanced and deepened within dialogic and generative learning contexts. For all the interest in the situatedness of reflection activity, we found no evidence of groups coming together to discuss their reflections and to build shared knowledge that could be revisited, probed and made more elaborate when confronted with new experiences and dilemmas. Such dialogic encounters, nonetheless, may be vital for beginners who too often evaluate literacy instruction based on a singular lens and personal perspectives. Considerable scaffolding is also likely required to help these future teachers adopt new perspectives and understandings that respond to learners' many and various needs in literacy instruction. How to teach for students' higher levels of reflection, though, remained ill defined across the entire collection and none of the studies offered evidence that such instruction actually impacted the reading teaching performance of future teachers.

Given these findings, we make three recommendations. One is the need to work toward a consistent line of inquiry that seeks to disentangle the "dynamic simultaneity" of reflection as process and product (Livingston, 1999, p. 10). Not easily separated and traced, it is essential nonetheless to unpack the "how" (mental actions), "what" (tools), and "why" (practical consequences) of reflection if the activity is to make sense in professional literacy education. Better, more precise descriptions of how reflection is accomplished and through what means could generate alternative pedagogical responses to students' strengths and needs on our part. Such responses, embedded in our own professional teaching, might also shed light on the practical consequences of reflective activity for students' conceptual understandings of teaching and consequently their teaching performance.

Another is the need for an expanded view of reflection as a change agent. Beyond what reflection might do for improving individual classroom teaching is the role it can play in shaping the professional person—one who contributes to the school community, is proactive in serving students, challenges negative attitudes, and serves the profession. Cultivating this stance in the formative years of teacher development is a matter that remains thinly described even though it is increasingly seen as part and parcel of professional responsibilities (Danielson, 1996). Tutorials and practica often found in literacy pedagogy coursework, for example, offer rich contexts for reflection that challenges students' preconceived notions of teaching and stimulates new, broader perspectives of professionalism.

And a third is the need to identify proven instructional models and strategies that indeed support and strengthen the reflective abilities of beginning teachers. Presently, there is scant evidence that what is done in the name of reflection actually makes a difference in the knowledge, skills, and dispositions of future reading teachers. For the rich theoretical ideas on the virtues of reflection to become realized in literacy teaching, far more effort needs to be directed to specifying instructional procedures (e.g., coaching, journaling, role playing) and carefully testing them in simulated as well as authentic contexts. At the same time future research should track the beginners' reflective thinking and strategies in teaching contexts, examining relationships and consequences.

Concluding, we are struck by the scarcity of quality empirical work on reflection in preparing future reading teachers. For nearly 15 years the field seems to have been enamored with the idea of reflection, but not moved to harness its potential in the service of improved professional education and literacy teaching. It is time, we think, to push on toward better defined, thickly detailed, and more rigorous inquiry.

References[1]

Afflerbach, P., Bass, L., Hoo, D., Smith, S., Weiss, L., & Williams, L. (1988). Preservice teachers use think-aloud protocols to study writing. *Language Arts, 65,* 693–701.

---

1. References beginning with first author in boldface indicate those studies providing data for the critical review.

Allen, V., Freeman, E., & Lehman, B. (1989). A literacy education model for preservice teachers: Translating observation and reflection into exemplary practice. In S. McCormick & J. Zutell (Eds.), *Cognitive and social perspectives for literacy research and instruction.* Thirty-eighth yearbook of the National Reading Conference (pp. 473–480). Chicago: National Reading Conference.

Ball, D. L., & Cohen, D. (1999). Developing practice, developing practitioners—Toward a practice-based theory of professional education. In L. Darling-Hammond & G. Sykes (Eds.), *Teaching as the learning profession: Handbook of policy and practice* (pp. 3–32). San Francisco: Jossey-Bass.

Bean, T. W., & Zulich, J. (1989). Using dialogue journals to foster reflective practice with preservice, content-area teachers. *Teacher Education Quarterly,* Winter, 33–40.

Bean, T. W., & Zulich, J. (1990). Teaching students to learn from text: Preservice content teachers' changing views of their role through the window of student-professor dialogue journals. In J. Zutell & S. McCormick (Eds.), *Literacy theory and research: Analyses from multiple paradigms.* Thirty-ninth yearbook of the National Reading Conference (pp. 171–178). Chicago: National Reading Conference.

Bean, T. W., & Zulich, J. (1991). A case study of three preservice teachers' beliefs about content area reading through the window of student-professor dialogue journals. In C. K. Kinzer & D. J. Leu (Eds.), *Literacy research, theory, and practice: Views from many perspectives.* Forty-first yearbook of the National Reading Conference (pp. 463–474). Chicago: National Reading Conference.

Bean, T. W., & Zulich, J. (1993). The other half: A case study of asymmetrical communication in content-area reading student-professor dialogue journals. In D. J. Leu & C. Kinzer (Eds.), *Examining central issues in literacy research, theory, and practice.* Forty-second yearbook of the National Reading Conference (pp. 289–296). Chicago: National Reading Conference.

Bednar, M. R. (1991, December). *Teacher cognition: Preservice knowledge and reflections about the reading process.* Paper presented at the meeting of the National Reading Conference. Palm Springs, CA.

Berliner, D. (1987). Ways of thinking about students and classrooms by more and less experienced teachers. In J. Calderhead (Ed.), *Exploring teachers' thinking* (pp. 60–83). London: Cassell.

Brooks, J., & Brooks, M. (1993). *The case for constructivist classrooms.* Alexandria, VA: Association of Supervision and Curriculum Development.

Bruneau, B., Niles, K., Slanina, A., & Dunlap, K. (1993, December). *Exploring preservice students' perceptions of literacy instruction: Listening to students.* Paper presented at the meeting of the National Reading Conference, Charleston, SC.

Calderhead, J. (1989). Reflective teaching and teacher education. *Teaching and Teacher Education, 5*(1), 43–51.

Clift, R., Houston, W., & Pugach, M. (Eds.). (1990). *Encouraging reflective practice: An examination of issues and exemplars.* New York: Teachers College Press.

Cole, M. (1996). *Cultural psychology—A once and future discipline.* Cambridge, MA: Belknap Press of Harvard University Press.

Cruickshank, D. R. (1987). *Reflective teaching: The preparation of students of teaching.* Reston, VA: Association of Teacher Educators.

Danielson, C. (1996). *Enhancing professional practice: A framework for teaching.* Alexandria, VA: Association of Supervision and Curriculum Development.

Danielson, K. (1989). The autobiography as language reflection. *Reading Horizons, 29,* 257–261.

Dewey, J. (1929). *The sources of a science of education.* New York: Liveright.

Dewey, J. (1933). *How we think.* Lexington, MA: Heath. (Original work published 1901).

Goodman, J. (1984). Reflection and teacher education: A case study and theoretical analysis. *Interchange, 15*(3), 9–26.

Gordon, C. J., & Hunsberger, M. (1990). Preservice teachers' conceptions of content area literacy instruction. In J. Zutell & S. McCormick (Eds.), *Learner factors/teacher factors:*

Issues in literacy research and instruction. Fortieth yearbook of the National Reading Conference (pp. 399–407). Chicago: National Reading Conference.

Hermann, B. A., & Sarracino, J. (1991, December). *Restructuring a preservice literacy methods course: Dilemmas and lessons learned.* Paper presented at the meeting of the National Reading Conference. Palm Springs, CA.

Hunsaker, L., & Johnston, M. (1992). Teacher under construction: A collaborative case study of teacher change. *American Educational Research Journal, 29,* 350–372.

Jones, M. G., & Vesiland, E. M. (1996). Putting practice into theory: Changes in the organization of preservice teachers' pedagogical knowledge. *American Educational Research Journal, 33,* 91–117.

Kasten, W. C., & Padak, N. D. (1997). Nuturing preservice teacher's reflection on literacy. In C. K. Kinzer, K. A. Hinchman, & D. J. Leu (Eds.), *Inquiries in literacy theory and practice.* Forty-sixth yearbook of the National Reading Conference (pp. 335–346). Chicago: National Reading Conference.

Leland, C. H., Harste, J. C., & Youssef, O. (1997). Teacher education and clinical literacy. In C. K. Kinzer, K. A. Hinchman, & D. J. Leu (Eds.), *Inquiries in literacy theory and practice.* Forty-sixth yearbook of the National Reading Conference (pp. 385–396). Chicago: National Reading Conference.

Livingston, G. (1999). Beyond watching over established ways: A review as recasting the literature, recasting the lived. *Review of Educational Research, 69,* 9–20.

Lyons, N. (1998). Reflection in teaching: Can it be developmental? A portfolio perspective. *Teacher Education Quarterly,* 115–127.

Munby, H., & Russell, T. (1989). Educating the reflective teacher: An essay review of two books by Donald Schon. *Journal of Curriculum Studies, 21,* 71–80.

Niles, K., & Bruneau, B. (1994, December). *Portfolio assessment in preservice courses: scaffolding learning portfolios.* Paper presented at the meeting of the National Reading Conference. San Diego, CA.

Oropallo, K., & Gomez, S. (1996). Using reflective portfolios in preservice teacher education programs. In E. G. Sturtevant & W. M. Linek (Eds.), *Growing literacy: Eighteenth Yearbook of the College Reading Association* (pp. 120–132). Commerce: Texas A & M University.

Padak, N. D., & Nelson, O. G. (1990). Becoming a teacher of literacy: Novice whole language teachers in conventional instructional environments. In J. Zutell & S. McCormick (Eds.), *Literacy theory and research: Analyses from multiple paradigms.* Thirty-ninth yearbook of the National Reading Conference (pp. 99–107). Chicago: National Reading Conference.

Pape, S. L., & Smith, L. C. (1991, February). *Classroom to classroom: Restructuring to meet field experience needs.* Paper presented at the meeting of the Association of Teacher Educators. New Orleans, LA.

Polkinghorne, D. E. (1995). Narrative configuration in qualitative analysis. In J. A. Hatch & R. Wisniewski (Eds.), *Life history and narrative* (pp. 5–23). London: Falmer.

Rearick, M. L. (1997). *Educational researchers, practitioners, and students of teaching reflect on experience, practice, and theories: Action research in a preservice course "Reading and Literature in the Schools."* Paper presented at the meeting of the American Educational Research Association, Chicago.

Richards, J., & Gipe, J. (1987, April). *Reflective concerns of prospective teachers in an early field placement.* Paper presented at the meeting of the American Educational Research Association, Washington, DC.

Richards, J., Gipe, J., Levitov, J., & Speaker, R. (1989, March). *Psychological and personal dimensions of prospective teachers' reflective abilities.* Paper presented at the meeting of the American Educational Research Association, San Francisco, CA.

Risko, V. J., Roskos, K., & Vukelich, C. (1999). Making connections: Preservice teachers' reflection processes and strategies. *National Reading Conference Yearbook, 48,* 412–422.

Schon, D. (1983). *The reflective practitioner: How professionals think in action.* New York: Basic Books.

Schon, D. (1987). *Educating the reflective practitioner: Toward a new design for teaching and learning in the professions.* San Francisco, CA: Jossey-Bass.

Schon, D. (1991). *The reflective turn: Case studies in and on educational practice.* New York: Teachers College Press.

Schumaker, K. A. (1993, March). *A taxonomy for assisting teacher reflection and growth in reading practice.* Paper presented at the meeting of the Midwest Reading and Study Skills Conference, Kansas City, MO.

Sibbett, J., Wade, S., & Johnson, L. (1998). Preservice teachers' reflective thinking during a case discussion. In D. J. McIntyre & D. M. Byrd (Eds.), *Strategies for career-long teacher education. Teacher education yearbook VI* (pp. 26–39). Reston, VA: Association of Teacher Educators.

Slattery, P. (1995). *Curriculum development in the postmodern era.* New York: Garland.

Smith, L. C., & Pape, S. L. (1990, November). *Reflectivity through journal writing: Student teachers write about reading events.* Paper presented at the meeting of the National Reading Conference, Miami, FL.

Strauss, A., & Corbin, J. (1990). *Basic qualitative research: Grounded theory procedures and techniques.* Newbury Park, CA: Sage.

Sunstein, B. S., & Potts, J. P. (1998). Literacy stories extended: Of reflection and teachers' portfolios. *Teacher Education Quarterly, 25,* 61–71.

Swandt, T. (1994). Constructivist, interpretivist approaches to human inquiry. In N. K. Denzin & Y. S. Lincoln (Eds.), *Handbook of qualitative research* (pp. 118–137). Thousand Oaks, CA: Sage.

Truscott, D., & Walker, B. (1998). The influence of portfolio selection on reflective thinking. In E.G. Stewart, J. Dugan, P. Linder, & W. M. Linek (Eds.), *Literacy and community.* Commerce, TX: College Reading Association.

Wedman, J., & Martin, M. (1986). Exploring the development of reflective thinking through journal writing. *Reading Improvement, 23,* 68–71.

Wile, J. M. (1994, November). *Using portfolios to enable undergraduate pre-service teachers to construct personal theories of literacy.* Paper presented at the meeting of the College Reading Association, New Orleans, LA.

Zeichner, K., & Liston, D. (1987). Teaching student teachers to reflect. *Harvard Educational Review, 57,* 1–22.

Zeichner, K., & Liston, D. (1991). *Traditions of reform in U.S. teacher education.* East Lansing, MI: National Center for Research on Teacher Education. (ERIC Document Reproduction Service No. ED 320 905)

Zulich, J., Bean, T. W., & Herrick, J. (1992). Charting stages of preservice teacher development and reflection in a multicultural community through dialogue journal analysis. *Teaching and Teacher Education, 8,* 345–360.

Lessons Learned While Using Case-based Instruction with Preservice Literacy Teachers

Elizabeth A. Baker and Judy M. Wedman
University of Missouri–Columbia

C ase-based instruction (CBI) is being used successfully in several professional schools (Christensen, Garvin, & Sweet, 1991; Merseth, 1997;
Shulman, 1992; Silverman & Welty, 1992). Although there are many different kinds of CBI, they commonly involve data and a story from a professional
situation. For example, business cases may be stories that include data about how
General Electric or IBM were created and how they have developed. Medical
cases may be about patients and the results of various tests and interviews.
Students in professional schools then analyze and discuss these cases to determine what content they need to learn and what decisions they would make if they
were involved in the case (Barnes, Christensen, & Hansen, 1994). Risko and Kinzer
(1994) argue that CBI can address weaknesses commonly found in teacher education (see also Lundeberg, Levin, & Harrington, 1999). They discuss how theories
of *anchored instruction* (Cognition and Technology Group at Vanderbilt, 1990)
suggest that learners benefit from discussions when they share common experiences. For example, literacy teachers who work in the same classroom benefit from
the ability to discuss their common experience, their shared classroom. Their
classroom becomes the anchor of their discussions. However, providing a similar
anchor during teacher education courses is a challenge. It is difficult to place
20–35 preservice teachers in the same elementary classroom so they will have a
common classroom experience to discuss. With CBI, the learners' common experience is a case. Because the learners are familiar with the same cases, they can
discuss how their different field experiences are similar and dissimilar to the case.
Herein, the learners can gain an understanding of one another's divergent
field experiences and potentially help one another understand each other's field
situations.

For over a decade, researchers and teacher-educators have worked to define
and implement *reflective* practices in preservice teacher preparation. Through the
years definitions of reflection have emerged that include Dewey's (1933) concepts of routine and reflective action, and VanManen's (1977) three levels of
reflection: technical, practical, and critical. Researchers indicate that reflective
thought is necessary for preservice teachers to analyze individual student's learning
needs, explore alternative teaching practices, become familiar with teaching demands, and connect college classroom learning with classroom practice (Schon,
1983; Wedman & Martin, 1991; Zeichner & Tabachnik, 1984). Many teacher prepa-

National Reading Conference Yearbook, 49, pp. 122–136.

ration programs have identified reflection as a desirable characteristic of preservice teachers and have incorporated goals and experiences aimed at fostering reflection. Typically, reflection is addressed through field experiences. However, due to differences in field experiences (i.e., different teachers, classrooms, schools) it is difficult for instructors or peers to give feedback about the nature of preservice teacher's reflective thought. Consequently, preservice teachers are left to develop their own reflection skills. Given CBI, peers can compare their field experiences with the cases and potentially help one another reflect on their divergent field experiences.

Theories of situated cognition argue that "knowledge is situated, being in part a product of the activity, context, and culture in which it is developed and used" (Brown, Collins, & Duguid, 1989, p. 32). In teacher education, just because preservice teachers have the knowledge to pass tests and write papers about teaching children to read does not mean they will be able to teach children to read. Research on situated cognition indicates that if we learn knowledge in situations similar to where we will use the knowledge, we are more likely to transfer the knowledge into practice (Greeno, Smith, & Moore, 1993). Theories of situated cognition imply that field experiences are vital for preservice teachers. However, without anchored situations, preservice teachers are limited to their own insights and making their own connections between coursework and practice. Due to the common experiences provided by CBI, peers can generate and discuss these connections with the possibility of implementing them in the field.

Theories of generative knowledge argue that learners do not often make connections between knowledge that is dispensed to them (i.e., via lectures) and situations where that knowledge can be used (Bereiter & Scardamalia, 1985; Bransford, Franks, Vye, & Sherwood, 1989; Whitehead, 1929). Learners make better connections when they generate knowledge (Risko, McAllister, Peter, & Bigenho, 1994). CBI purposely requires learners to generate their analyses of the cases (Christensen, 1987; Christensen et al., 1991; Merseth, 1997; Shulman, 1992; Silverman & Welty, 1992). Instructors do not lecture about the cases. Rather, the learners are expected to articulate their analyses and challenge one another's analyses.

Teaching is an ill-structured task (Clark & Peterson, 1986; Greeno & Leinhardt, 1986). This means that teachers need to be able to make decisions based on constantly changing sources of information. Field experiences give preservice teachers opportunities to try methods discussed in courses, but may provide limited experience in dealing with the ill-structured, complex nature of teaching. Furthermore, the ill-structured nature of teaching requires preservice teachers to understand the viability of different perspectives. Unlike standard content where there are right and wrong answers, teaching involves different perspectives based on a variety of values, diverse backgrounds, and assorted theories of learning (Ruddell, Ruddell, & Singer, 1994). Preservice teachers must understand and respect perspectives held by parents, administrators, and other teachers in order to communicate effectively with them. Experience with these divergent perspectives is difficult to acquire in traditional education courses and even field placements.

CBI addresses this need by requiring learners to identify alternate explanations to the case and role-play using potential perspectives held by parents, administrators, and other teachers.

Because we wanted to overcome similar weaknesses, we developed and used digital literacy portfolios for CBI in a preservice literacy course for Elementary Education majors. While using these digital literacy portfolios for CBI, we analyzed whether the components of Risko and Kinzer's (1994) rationale were evident in our setting. In other words, we examined if CBI addressed the aforementioned weaknesses. The purpose of this report is to describe unexpected results we encountered while using CBI. These results are being used to alter how we conduct CBI in future courses.

Cases Used In Literacy Education

There are many different types of cases being used in literacy education. One type uses anecdotal stories to highlight dilemmas literacy teachers may encounter (Silverman & Welty, 1992). For example, one of these cases tells of a student teacher who works with a special education cooperating teacher. The school district decides that all students must participate in statewide testing. The cooperating teacher feels that such participation will be detrimental to her special needs students. During the state testing, the student teacher notices that the cooperating teacher gives subtle assistance to her students. Herein the case ends in a dilemma: Should the student teacher report her cooperating teacher for cheating on the statewide tests? The users of such cases are able to discuss multiple perspectives on what the student teacher should do. Although this is only one example, it highlights that these cases end in a dilemma for the users to discuss.

Another type of case consists of stories written by teachers about their experiences (Atwell, 1987; Avery, 1993; Harp, 1993; Routman, 1994). Unlike the anecdotal cases, these cases tell many facets of literacy classrooms. They may include the teacher's philosophy of literacy education, how they deal with children's grapho/phonic development, how they group children, how they arrange their classrooms and schedules, and how they keep track of children's literacy development. These cases are commonly 100–300 pages long. They do not purposely end with dilemmas for discussion. Rather, the readers generate their own topics for discussion. For example, they may discuss whether they would allow children to use invented spelling.

The Reading Classroom Explorer (RCE; Hughes, Packard, and Pearson, 1999) shifts the format from textual to multimedia. "RCE is a searchable (by school, broad theme, and/or keyword) database of digitized video clips" from a video series of five literacy classrooms which represent "students from diverse cultural, linguistic, and intellectual backgrounds" (p. 1). RCE includes voice-overs by the teacher who explains what she is doing in the video and why. RCE also includes interviews with the teachers who discuss such topics as child development, integrated curriculum, communication with parents, and administrative support. Research indicates that the more time literacy teachers spent examining video cases, the better they were able to support their claims about teaching reading (Hughes et al., 1999).

The Multimedia Cases in Teacher Education (MCTE; Kinzer & Risko, 1998) allows users to watch a 20-minute video of a literacy teacher's classroom. The users can then watch video interviews with the teacher in the case, other teachers in the school, the principal, parents of students in the case, and literacy professors who have watched the same video. Herein, the users can watch the same literacy classroom and discuss what they see. They might discuss literacy skills, activities the teacher uses to teach literacy skills, classroom organization, behavior management, and so forth. This series of cases includes different grade levels and different special needs situations (e.g., resource, inclusion). The users are able to compare between and among grade levels and special needs. Risko, Yount, and McAllister (1992) found that literacy teachers who examined multimedia cases during class asked more questions and more high-level questions than students in similar courses that did not use the cases. They also found that the students enrolled in CBI courses developed the ability to take multiple perspectives on various teaching issues and problems much earlier than their peers enrolled in similar non-CBI courses. In another study, Risko, Peter, and McAllister (1996) found that CBI had an impact on students' ability to think flexibly in related field experiences and discussions in other courses.

Digital Literacy Portfolio Series

Distinct from Other Literacy Cases

Whereas anecdotal cases, book cases, RCE cases, and MCTE cases provide valuable opportunities for case-based instruction, they focus on teachers and how they set up literacy programs and provide literacy instruction. We developed the Digital Literacy Portfolio Series (DLPS) in order to foster kidwatching (Wilde, 1996). We wanted to encourage preservice literacy teachers to begin their instructional plans with the needs of children foremost in their minds. Furthermore, first-year teachers are expected to analyze and understand children's literacy growth throughout a school year. However, most preservice teachers have never watched children develop over extended periods of time. Preservice teachers can focus on children's growth during extended field placements (i.e., student teaching). However, the amount of time it takes for a child to make substantive literacy development may extend beyond a college semester—thus limiting preservice teachers' opportunities to identify and analyze children's growth. Unless preservice teachers are given experience with analyzing children's growth, they remain unprepared for their first teaching position. Finally, first-year teachers need to be able to understand their students' diverse language cultures and abilities. One way to develop this understanding is to gain experience with children's literacy development with children who are from diverse language groups. The DLPS includes bilingual Asian children, African-American children, and European-American children.

DLPS Interface

The interface gives users access to video segments of the child as he or she reads and writes with classmates, the teacher, and the principal investigators. Each video segment includes related artifacts. For example, if the video involves a child reading, then the artifact is the book that is being read. This allows the user to see what the child saw while he or she was reading. If the video involves a child writing, then the artifact is the writing sample that the child wrote. Each video also includes a scenario that explains what happened before and after the video. The scenario includes the text from the book in the video so the user can mark what the child says when he or she tries to read the text. The video segments (with corresponding artifacts and scenarios) can be sorted by month and by content area allowing the user to examine literacy growth across these dimensions. The interface also allows users to mark video segments so they can randomly access these segments during case analysis and class discussions.

Method

Setting and Participants

This study occurred in a Midwestern state university in a section of a course entitled "Emergent Literacy for Elementary Teachers." The section was selected because one of the case developers, Dr. Baker, was the instructor. The preservice teachers were first-semester juniors who had taken 8 semester hours of introductory education courses during their freshman and sophomore years. They had also done over 20 hours of classroom observations during their freshman and sophomore years. This was, however, their first semester of taking methods courses. There were 34 preservice teachers in the class, 31 females and 3 males. All the preservice teachers were Elementary Education majors.

The course was part of a block of literacy courses that included 2 semester hours of Children's Literature, 2 semester hours of Emergent Language, and 3 semester hours of Emergent Literacy for Elementary Teachers. These preservice teachers also participated in 2 semester hours of field experience in which they worked with a partner to teach 8–10 literacy lessons to a small group of elementary children. They collaborated with the elementary children's teacher to design, implement, and reflect on their lessons and the progress of the children's literacy abilities. The preservice teachers took this block of literacy courses as a cohort. In other words, the same group of preservice teachers attended Children's Literature, Emergent Language, Emergent Literacy and Literacy Field Experience (9 hours per week) together.

Dr. Baker is a professor of literacy education. At the time of this study, she had taught literacy courses to preservice elementary teachers for 8 years. She had used Multimedia Cases in Teacher Education (Kinzer & Risko, 1998) as well as textbook cases (i.e., Avery, 1993; Harp, 1993; Routman, 1994) for 4 years. This was the first time she used the Digital Literacy Portfolio Series (Baker & Wedman, 1997).

Case-based Instruction

The course met once a week for 3 hours during a 16-week semester. The course was divided into three modules: children's literacy processes, teacher decision-making, and professional development. Case-based instruction was used throughout the semester. Because the block of courses focused on emergent literacy, we used digital portfolios of first-grade children. Specifically, five classes were dedicated to analyzing Julie's digital literacy portfolio. Julie was a first grader who read to and wrote for Dr. Baker in her university office biweekly throughout a school year. Dr. Baker videotaped these sessions and digitized Julie's writings. The instructor showed these videos and writing samples to the class. The preservice teachers were asked to analyze Julie's literacy abilities as they examined the video and writing samples. Another four classes were dedicated to analyzing Zane's digital literacy portfolio. Zane was a first grader whose portfolio was collected in his first-grade classroom. One class session dealt with showing the preservice teachers how to use the digital literacy portfolio interface. For homework, they analyzed Zane's November portfolio samples (over 15 minutes of video and five writing samples which occurred during Literature, Social Studies, Science, and Math). In class, they were asked to develop lessons for Zane that would foster his literacy development. Finally, the preservice teachers used their analyses of the cases to write progress reports about Julie and Zane. In turn, they wrote progress reports about the children they taught during their 10-week field experience.

Data Collection and Analysis

We collected the following data sets: the instructor's reflections about class activities, the instructor's reflections about each rationale for using CBI in teacher education, information about classroom interactions, preservice teachers' answers to study guides as they analyzed the cases, videotapes of each class session, preservice teachers' lesson plans and reflections from their concurrent field experiences, and audiotapes and notes from individual interviews with each student at the end of the semester.

Instructor's reflections about each rationale. After each class, the instructor reflected on the role of anchored instruction, reflective thinking, situated cognition, generative learning, and the ability that CBI had to prepare teachers to deal with the ill-structured nature of teaching. These reflections were the initial data source from which our findings emerged. Other data sets were used to confirm and disconfirm the instructor's perceptions of the role of each rationale for CBI in her course.

Instructor's reflections about the class activities. After each class, the instructor reflected on the activities she used in class, the preservice teachers' apparent grasp of course goals, and conjectures about the effectiveness of the activities she used (including CBI). These reflections were used to identify shifts in instructional focus (i.e., kidwatching, planning for instruction) as well as topics that the preservice teachers generated for discussion.

Classroom Interaction Analysis. To examine preservice teachers' class discussions, we collected data by adapting the Classroom Interaction Analysis system (Flanders, 1970). We established a grid for recording teacher and student questions and responses during class discussions of the cases. Two trained research assistants collected the data by observation, and audio and video recordings. All data were reviewed after each discussion session to establish norms for data analysis. We analyzed the data by sorting and categorizing the discourse initiated by the teacher and the student(s) and by identifying teacher and student interaction patterns.

Study guides. During each case-based discussion, the preservice teachers examined the case and wrote answers to questions we wrote and posed by study guides (Barnes et al., 1994). These study guides evolved throughout the course but included such questions as: What do you notice about the child's reading abilities? If you were this child's teacher what would you plan for tomorrow? Why? If you were this child's teacher, what questions would you ask yourself? What did you like about this lesson? What would you do differently? Why? The preservice teachers worked individually to write responses to study guide questions and then discussed their analysis in small groups as well as whole-class sessions. The preservice teachers referred to their answers in order to discuss the case. We collected these written responses and analyzed them for evidence of using the case as an anchor, ability to reflect and topics of reflection, the generation of questions and topics for class discussion, and their ability to think flexibly about the ill-structured nature of teaching. Triangulation was accomplished by comparing the preservice teachers' written study guide responses to the whole-class discussions during which time all preservice teachers shared their case analyses.

Videotapes. We videotaped the whole-class and small-group discussions that occurred during class sessions. Although one video camera could capture the whole-class discussions, it could not record every small-group discussion. In order to use the dialog that occurred during small-group discussions, we asked for volunteers who would allow us to videotape them. More preservice teachers volunteered than we could videotape, so we randomly selected four of them. Because we had two video cameras, we asked these four volunteers to work in two small groups. We then created a video log of the whole-class and small-group discussions so we could access video for triangulation purposes.

Field experience artifacts. Concurrent to this course, these preservice teachers planned, implemented, and reflected on literacy lessons for small groups of elementary children. We collected their lesson plans and reflections. Their plans were primarily collected so we could understand the context of their reflections. The preservice teachers answered the following questions for their reflections: What did you learn about each child's literacy today? What other information did you learn about each child? What do you need to learn about each child's literacy abilities? What other information do you need to learn about each child? How will you find what you need to learn? If you teach this lesson again, what will you do (the same, differently)? Why? We analyzed their field experience reflections to determine the nature of their views of children's literacy development and their own instruction. Due to logistics and time limitations, we did not observe the preservice teachers during field experiences. They did, however, commonly discuss their field experiences during class and interviews. They also referred to field experiences in response to their study guides.

Interviews. At the end of the semester, each preservice teacher voluntarily participated in an individual interview. A trained research assistant conducted the interviews that were scheduled outside-of-class time and lasted approximately 30 minutes. The interview posed 10 questions that specifically focused on the rationales that served as the basis for the project. These questions included: How has the class used the cases to generate class questions and discussion? How do you think that analyzing Zane and Julie will apply to student teaching and your teaching job? The interviewer took notes and audio-recorded the interviews. The notes were used to analyze each question separately to examine differences in student's perceptions about the relationship of CBI to actual teaching practice and how CBI may have influenced learning. Portions of interviews were transcribed when the notes indicated significant data points. The analysis was used to confirm or disconfirm the instructors' reflections.

We used qualitative data analysis techniques (Glaser & Strauss, 1967; Lincoln & Guba, 1985; Strauss & Corbin, 1990). Specifically, we analyzed the instructor's reflections about each rationale for using CBI in teacher education. We then analyzed data sets to confirm and disconfirm the instructor's perceptions. For example, in order to confirm or disconfirm the instructor's reflections about anchored instruction we reviewed videotapes of class discussions, preservice teachers' answers to the study guide questions, and answers during individual interviews. The videotapes allowed us to examine the role of the anchor in class discussions. The study guides allowed us to examine the relationship between the anchor and the preservice teachers' divergent field experiences. The interviews provided, among other things, information about the preservice teachers' perceptions of how the cases helped them understand one another's field experiences.

Several techniques suggested by Lincoln and Guba (1985) were used to undergird the credibility of data collection and analysis. This inquiry occurred over an extended period of time (16 class sessions during a 5-month period). We triangulated our sources (e.g., instructor, observers, preservice teachers) and our data sets (e.g., classroom interaction analysis, instructor's reflections, study guides, videotapes of class discussions, preservice teachers' field lesson plans and reflections, and individual interviews). Triangulation allowed us to confirm our findings in three or more data sources. During data collection and analysis, Dr.

Baker and observers purposely looked for disconfirming information. These data were used to discard or revise the emergent hypotheses. The instructor debriefed with observers throughout data collection and analysis. By continually generating, refining, and in some cases refuting hypotheses, we developed a systematic way to analyze the data corpus.

Because our findings emerged from a naturalistic study, readers should consider the characteristics of this classroom when relating the findings to other settings. The preservice teachers were junior elementary education majors with over 20 hours of observation in various classroom settings. The instructor had taught literacy courses for 8 years but had used cases for only 4 years. This was also the instructor's first semester of using the Digital Literacy Portfolio Series (Baker & Wedman, 1997). Finally, the course was part of a larger block of courses that focused on emergent literacy. This block included Emergent Literacy, Children's Literature, Emergent Language, and a field experience.

Unexpected Results Encountered While Using CBI

Anchored Instruction

CBI is used in teacher education to overcome difficulties in discussing divergent field experiences during methods courses. It is argued that learners benefit from having a common experience (i.e., case analyses) that they can refer to as they communicate their divergent experiences in their different field placements (Cognition and Technology Group at Vanderbilt, 1990). During data collection and analysis, we found the opposite to be true as well. For example, during class eight, we discussed a writing sample by Julie that included unusual penmanship. Martha (pseudonyms are used for preservice teachers and field experience locations) commented, "We have a student at Clarkton [Elementary] who writes like that so that is how I knew [Julie was using bubble letters]. . . ." Theories of anchored instruction claim that learners can use the anchor to understand their divergent experiences. Although we found this to be true, we also found that preservice teachers used their divergent experiences, field experiences in this instance, to help one another understand the anchor. During class eleven, the study guide asked, "If you were Zane's teacher, what would you plan for him tomorrow? Why?" Laura wrote: "I would want to go over another book with him and help him sound out the words because I have found that the students at Clarkton have really picked up 'sounding out' since Carol and I have worked with them." In this example, Laura used her experience in the field to explain her instructional strategies for the child in the case. In an interview, Joan commented, "When others in the class related their field experience to Julie and Zane, the discussion helped [me] understand. . . ." Here again, the student refers to how classmates' divergent field experiences helped her understand the case. Although this finding does not contradict theories of anchored instruction, it does add a reflexive nature to the rationale for using anchored instruction in teacher education. Instead of the anchor providing a common background for the learners to understand one another's divergent experiences, we found that the learners also used their divergent experiences to understand the anchor.

Reflective Practice

Another reason to use CBI is to foster reflective practice. During data collection and analysis, we found that preservice teachers actively reflected on the cases and their own teaching during field experiences. In particular, they became proficient in their abilities to reflect on children's literacy abilities. Although this proficiency was important and valued by the instructor, it did not contribute to the preservice teachers' abilities to suggest instructional strategies during case discussions.

For example, the preservice teachers examined Zane's portfolio in which he read several pages from a literature book. Afterward, the preservice teachers responded in writing to two study guide questions that asked: (a) What do you notice about the child's literacy abilities? (b) If you were this child's teacher what would you plan for him tomorrow? Why? One preservice teacher, Hanna, exhibited a reflective analysis of Zane's literacy processes by asking questions about his progress, his literacy activities at home, and describing the individual strengths and weaknesses she observed related to word recognition. She identified strengths that enabled the child to decode words by applying knowledge of single consonant sounds, use of pictures clues to identify unknown words, and write using invented spelling. She also identified word recognition weaknesses that may have caused frustration when Zane could not find picture clues to help him identify unknown words, successfully respond to teacher prompts, and use multiple strategies for word identification. Hanna also observed that Zane's lack of word recognition seemed to interfere with meaning construction. However, Hanna did not appear reflective when she described the instruction she might provide for Zane. She identified practice activities that were repetitious and isolated from stories. She did not consider alternative strategies that would engage the child in contextual reading nor the whole act of reading.

Throughout the semester, Dr. Baker had asked the preservice teachers to analyze the cases to determine the child's literacy abilities. During the eighth class session (fourth case discussion), Dr. Baker asked the preservice teachers what they thought about Julie's literacy abilities. The preservice teachers noticed her miscues with double vowels and the sounds of c. They discussed whether she showed signs of dyslexia (due to some letter reversals) and the validity of tests for dyslexia. During the same class session, Dr. Baker also asked a new question: "If you were this child's teacher what would you plan for tomorrow? Why?" Tom stated he would drill her on vowels sounds. Donna said she would drill her on the sounds of c. No one in the class offered an alternative to isolating Julie's weaknesses and creating isolated drills to overcome these weaknesses. Whereas some theoretical perspectives value this instruction, we were interested in whether preservice teachers would offer alternatives and questions. They did not. Herein, the preservice teachers were reflective about alternative explanations about Julie's literacy abilities but not about instructional practices they would use to teach Julie. In other words, we found that although the preservice teachers were reflective in areas we had discussed throughout the semester, they did not transfer this metacognitive habit to new areas of discussion.

Situated Cognition

Theories of situated cognition argue that learners recognize when and how to use knowledge when they learn the knowledge in situations that are similar to where they will use it. Here, case-based instruction appears to be a natural pedagogy that allows the instructor to situate the knowledge and thereby undergird students' abilities to access the knowledge when similar situations arise. Although we found that preservice teachers recognized ways to use the course content in their field experiences, the result we did not expect was the usefulness of situated cognition to the instructor. Specifically, the instructor had been an elementary teacher for seven years. She found that her knowledge of teaching and literacy was in many ways situated in her elementary teaching experiences. For example, while discussing Julie and Zane during CBI, the instructor raised issues of text "friendliness." In her experience as a teacher she learned that a child's reading ability was often determined by the text itself. If children read poorly it could be because they lacked background knowledge or vocabulary; they may have expected certain syntactical structures. However, if they were given a "friendly" text which supported their background knowledge, used their vocabulary and syntactical structures, then they could read well. At the time of this study, the instructor had taught preservice literacy teachers for eight years. She often thought about the importance of discussing "friendly" text but because the instruction was not based on analyzing children's literacy portfolios the topic was typically overlooked. The instructor's knowledge was situated within her own professional experiences as an elementary teacher. With CBI, the case reminded her of her teaching situation and she remembered to cover issues such as the importance of noticing if a text is "friendly" to the reader. Herein we found that situated cognition is not for learners only, but for the instructor too.

Generative Knowledge

We found that CBI effectively gave the preservice teachers ample opportunities to generate discussion. For example, using classroom discourse analysis, we found that within five class sessions, the student-initiated portions of the discussion went from 42% to 100%. Although this dramatic shift occurred during CBI, the instructor encouraged the preservice teachers to generate topics throughout the course (i.e., during literature discussions). Our findings do not indicate that case based instruction *caused* preservice teachers to generate topics of discussion but rather it was used to encourage preservice teachers to generate topics of discussion. Although total student-initiated discussion sounds good, we found that preservice teachers could generate inaccurate conclusions. This finding concurs with other studies (Barnes et al., 1994) that recommend that students engaged in CBI discussions should be given expert guidance. The instructor needs to highlight misconceptions and help the students consider other options.

Ill-structured Knowledge Domain

We found that the preservice teachers gave alternate explanations and analyses of the cases. The individual interviews inquired about the student's perception regarding the ill-structured nature of teaching by asking, "Is there a right and wrong way to teach Zane and Julie? Explain." Student's responses consistently indicated an awareness that there were many ways to provide appropriate instruction:

Stacy: The way they did it was right, but you could also do it differently. And that would have been fine too.

Jill: Everyone has their own way of teaching. You learn by experience and change from there. As long as you see good results there is no right way.

The preservice teachers recognized that one set of explanations was not necessarily right or wrong, simply different. The preservice teachers even commented that they never realized there could be so many instructional alternatives. However, after five classes that used CBI, the preservice teachers asked which epistemological stance was correct for literacy instruction: constructivism or objectivism. Although the preservice teachers were willing to accept different analyses of children's literacy abilities and different instructional methods to teach children, they still wanted to know which epistemology was right and which one was wrong. Their interest in diverse perspectives did not transfer from ideas for Zane's instruction to ideas about epistemologies. The value of divergent perspectives did not transfer from one area of teaching to another.

Discussion

Based on these results, we have made a variety of alterations to how we are currently implementing CBI. We now expect preservice teachers to use the cases as a reflexive anchor. We are sensitive to fostering discussions that focus on how the case/anchor helps them understand the children in their divergent field experience as well as how their field experience helps them understand the case/anchor. Whereas before we might not have asked for preservice teachers to comment on using their divergent experiences to discuss the case/anchor, we now consider this another viable topic for discussion. Future research may be able to examine more closely the reflexive nature of anchored instruction.

We recognize the need to provide further scaffolding to preservice teachers so they will recognize the value of reflection throughout their thought processes as a teacher (not just while kidwatching). We also provide further scaffolding to preservice teachers when considering the value of divergent perspectives beyond kidwatching and planning for instruction. For example, we raise questions about whether there is one correct epistemological stance or one correct approach to literacy instruction. Future research may examine the need for scaffolding in CBI and the transfer of reflective thought and openness to divergent perspectives to non-CBI aspects of teaching.

In terms of generative discussions, we now attempt to ascertain when the instructor should clarify misconceptions. We believe this is the intent of CBI because the information the instructor provides is in direct response to their conceptions. The intervention of the instructor does not cause CBI to revert to inert learning because it is in response to the students' generated topics. We learned that getting students to generate all discussions is not the goal of CBI. Rather, we strive to provide extensive opportunities for preservice teachers to generate the topics but do not expect them to generate all potential solutions. This finding appears to concur with other CBI studies (Lundberg et al., 1999).

When we found that the case situation helped the instructor recall her own professional experiences and metacognition, we were excited. We look forward to preparing for CBI by considering our own experiences and how they relate to the cases and topics that preservice teachers may need to consider while they reflect on the cases and generate discussions. Future studies could examine the impact that CBI has on the instructor's tendency to provide instruction that is situated in their own experiences.

Our findings concur with Risko and Kinzer (1994): CBI may offer exciting possibilities for overcoming common weaknesses in teacher education (Hughes et al., 1999; Lundeberg et al., 1999). There is more to CBI, however, than simply using a set of materials. Like any instructional method, CBI is an amalgamation of the method, materials, instructor, and users. There are many aspects of CBI that need further investigation. For example, would researchers who conduct a study similar to this one have similar or dissimilar findings? Why or why not? Do preservice teachers who use cases that focus on teachers instead of children develop different types of reflective habits? Specifically, do discussions about teacher-based cases shift preservice teachers reflective habits to focus primarily on teachers or do they provide a solid foundation for child-based reflective habits and other reflective habits? Another area for future investigations focuses on multimedia cases. Do multimedia cases provide opportunities for deeper reflection and more exposure to the ill-structured nature of teaching than dilemma-based textual cases? The more we investigate the use of CBI for teacher education, the more we will understand its potentials, limitations, and modes for implementation.

Author Note

This report is part of a grant funded by USED/FIPSE (Project No. P116B71861). The opinions expressed in this paper are the sole responsibility of the authors and do not necessarily reflect the views or policies of USED/FIPSE. We wish to thank the teachers and children who graciously invited us into their classrooms and allowed us to witness the children's literacy growth. We also thank the following colleagues who contributed to the development of DLPS and/or this study: Laurie

Kingsley, Chris Potter, Herbert Remidez, Kyeong-Hee Rha, Karen Sherwood, and Roger Wen.

References

Atwell, N. (1987). In the middle: Writing, reading, and learning with adolescents. Portsmouth, NH: Heinemann.

Avery, C. (1993). And with a light touch: Learning about reading, writing, and teaching with first graders. Portsmouth, NH: Heineman.

Baker, E. A., & Wedman, J. M. (1997). Interdisciplinary multimedia literacy portfolios in elementary classrooms (Application No. P116B71861). Washington, DC: Department of Education, Fund for the Improvement of Postsecondary Education.

Barnes, L. B., Christensen, C. R., & Hansen, A. J. (1994). Teaching and the case method (3rd ed.). Boston: Harvard Business School.

Bereiter, C., & Scardamalia, M. (1985). Cognitive coping strategies and the problem of "inert" knowledge. In S. F. Chipman, J. W. Segal, & R. Glaser (Eds.), Thinking and learning skills: Current research and open questions (Vol. 2, pp. 65–80). Hillsdale, NJ: Erlbaum.

Bransford, J. D., Franks, J. J., Vye, N. J., & Sherwood, R. D. (1989). New approaches to instruction: Because wisdom can't be told. In S. Vosniadou & A. Ortony (Eds.), Similarity and analogical reasoning (pp. 470–497). New York: Cambridge University Press.

Brown, J. S., Collins, A., & Duguid, P. (1989). Situated cognition and the culture of learning. Educational Researcher, 17(1), 32–41.

Christensen, C. R. (1987). Teaching with cases at the Harvard Business School. In C. R. Christensen (Ed.), Teaching and the case method (pp. 16–49). Boston: Harvard Business School.

Christensen, C. R., Garvin, D. A., & Sweet, A. (Eds.). (1991). Education for judgment: The artistry of discussion leadership. Boston: Harvard Business School.

Clark, C. M., & Peterson, P. (1986). Teachers' thought processes. In M. Wittrock (Ed.), Handbook of research on teaching (3rd ed., pp. 255–296). New York: Macmillan.

Cognition and Technology Group (CTG) at Vanderbilt (1990). Anchored instruction and its relationship to situated cognition. Educational Researcher, 19(6), 2–10.

Dewey, J. (1933). How we think. Boston: Heath.

Flanders, N. A. (1970). Analyzing teaching behavior. Reading, MA: Addison-Wesley.

Glaser, B., & Strauss, A. (1967). The discovery of grounded theory. Chicago: Aldine.

Greeno, J. G., & Leinhardt, G. (1986). The cognitive skill of teaching. Journal of Educational Psychology, 78, 75–95.

Greeno, J. G., Smith, D. R., & Moore, J. L. (1993). Transfer of situated learning. In D. K. Detterman & R. J. Sternberg (Eds.), Transfer on trial: Intelligence, cognition, and instruction (pp. 99–167). Norwood, NJ: Ablex.

Harp, B. (1993). Bringing children to literacy: Classrooms at work. Norwood, MA: Christopher-Gordon.

Hughes, J. E., Packard, B. W., & Pearson, P. D. (1999). The role of hypermedia cases on preservice teachers' views of reading instruction (CIERA Rep. No. 3-005). Ann Arbor, MI: Center for the Improvement of Early Reading Achievement.

Kinzer, C. K., & Risko, V. J. (1998). Multimedia and enhanced learning: Transforming preservice education. In D. Reinking, M. McKenna, L. Labbo, & R. Kieffer (Eds.), Handbook of literacy and technology: Transformations in a post-typographic world (pp. 185–202). Mahwah, NJ: Erlbaum.

Lincoln, Y., & Guba, E. (1985). Naturalistic inquiry. Beverly Hills, CA: Sage.

Lundeberg, M. A., Levin, B. B., & Harrington, H. L. (Eds.) (1999). Who learns what from cases and how? Hillsdale, NJ: Erlbaum.

Merseth, K. K. (1997). *Case studies in educational administration.* New York: Longman.

Risko, V. J., & Kinzer, C. K. (1994). *Improving teacher education through dissemination of videodisc-based case procedures and influencing the teaching of future college professionals.* (Application No. P116A40242). Washington, DC: Fund for the Improvement of Postsecondary Education.

Risko, V. J., McAllister, D., Peter, J., & Bigenho, F. (1994). Using technology in support of preservice teachers' generative learning. In E. C. Sturtevant & W. M. Linek (Eds.), *Pathways for literacy: Learners teach and teachers learn* (pp. 155–167). Pittsburg, KS: College Reading Association.

Risko, V. J., Peter, J., & McAllister, D. (1996). Conceptual changes: Preservice teachers' pathways to providing literacy transaction. In E. Sturtevant & W. Linek (Eds.), *Literacy grows* (pp. 103–119). Pittsburg, KS: College Reading Association.

Risko, V. J., Yount, D., & McAllister, D. (1992). Preparing preservice teachers for remedial instruction: Teaching problem solving and use of content and pedagogical knowledge. In N. Padak, T. V. Rasinski, & J. Logan (Eds.), *Inquiries in literacy learning and instruction* (pp. 179–189). Pittsburg, KS: College Reading Association.

Routman, R. (1994). *Invitations: Changing as teachers and learners K–12.* Portsmouth, NH: Heinemann.

Ruddell, R. B., Ruddell, M. R., & Singer, H. (1994). *Theoretical models and processes of reading* (4th ed.). Newark, DE: International Reading Association.

Schon, D. (1983). *The reflective practitioner.* New York: Basic.

Shulman, L. (1992). Toward a pedagogy of cases. In J. Shulman (Ed.), *Case methods in teacher education* (pp. 1–30). New York: Teachers College Press.

Silverman, R., & Welty, B. (1992). *Education: Case studies for teacher problem solving.* New York: McGraw-Hill Primis.

Strauss, A., & Corbin, J. (1990). *Basics of qualitative research: Grounded theory procedures and techniques.* Newbury Park, CA: Sage.

Van Manen, M. (1977). Linking ways of knowing with ways of being practical. *Curriculum Inquiry, 6,* 205–228.

Wedman, J. M., & Martin, M. W. (1991). The influence of a reflective student teaching program: An evaluation study. *Journal of Research and Development in Education, 24*(2), 33–41.

Whitehead, A. N. (1929). *The aims of education.* New York: Macmillan.

Wilde, S. (1996). *Notes from a kidwatcher.* Portsmouth, NH: Heinemann.

Zeichner, K. M., & Tabachnik, B. R. (1984, April). *Social strategies and institutional control in the socialization of beginning teachers.* Paper presented at the meeting of the American Educational Research Association, New Orleans, LA.

Monologic and Dialogic Conversations: How Preservice Teachers Socially Construct Knowledge Through Oral and Computer-Mediated Classroom Discourse

Melissa M. Dodson

University of Texas at Austin

Teachers who use classroom discussion proceed with some intuitive sense of what makes good conversation, yet little has been reported that fully explicates the nature of quality discussion. The literature tends to speak of classroom discussion in contradictory terms. On one hand, teachers and educators speak highly of the value of student-led discussion and argue for the importance of discourse in learning and the importance of students talking and writing to one another. On the other hand, the literature reveals an ambivalence toward student-led discussion. Lurking concerns center on the idea that students left to their own devices may recreate casual conversations, an environment in which the critique of ideas and intellectual reflection are not always welcome.

Today, students and teachers are finding that educational communications have become even more student centered as schools, colleges, and universities increasingly offer online courses using the computer as the medium for class conversation and discussion. What once was a rigorously controlled conversation bound by classroom times and the physical walls of a classroom is now a conversation with no tangible boundaries and with diminished facilitation or control from the teacher. Members of a class can discuss class topics at all hours of the day and night and can carry conversations throughout a week, across a semester, and beyond. These innovations have had an enormous impact on education by forcing us to reexamine the roles of teachers and students in classroom communication. Nonetheless, questions naturally arise concerning the quality of these conversations. Is computer-mediated communication (CMC) an effective form of communication? Can students engage in meaningful conversation through CMC? Do true instantiations of dialogue and interaction occur via CMC?

Theoretical Background

My approach in this study gives explicit recognition to the role of language as a means of constructing knowledge. Specifically, I am interested in examining the talk that is generated by students and their teacher as a means of observing how knowledge develops across the semester. I begin my literature review by

National Reading Conference Yearbook, 49, pp. 137–152.

comparing and contrasting the research on oral and computer-mediated discussion in a classroom.

Oral Classroom Discourse

Over the last 20 years, researchers of classroom discourse have characterized discourse rules, patterns, and cultural practices exhibited by teachers and their students. These studies have noted that student participation in traditional classroom settings from kindergarten to college, is frequently restricted to responding as part of the three-part IRE (initiate-respond-evaluate) sequence that is most common in teacher-led speech acts (Cazden, 1988; Mehan, 1979). These interactions between class members are centralized around the teacher's leadership as the social and evaluative authority.

Recently, however, educators and researchers have come to realize that by dominating the social and interpretive facets of class talk, teachers may actually inhibit students' opportunities to express their thoughts and questions (Au, 1980), thus interfering with the students' attempts to learn. More and more, teachers at all grade levels are supplementing these traditionally centralized structures with decentralized structures such as small-group projects and discussion groups. Still, educators find it difficult to relinquish their authority as the classroom leader and allow their students to take a more active role in the classroom.

Although classroom discussion may be difficult to achieve, there is little debate that when it does occur, participants benefit from the shared multiple perspectives. In recent years, within sociolinguistics, psychology, and education, there has been an increasing interest in classroom talk as social action and as a way to foster the social construction of knowledge (Greene, Weade, & Graham, 1988; Hatano & Inagaki, 1991; Kress, 1989). This research has demonstrated that in classroom talk, as in other kinds of conversations, people use language to pursue their interests and goals, motivated to reach an understanding, using the conversation as a tool for doing so.

Computer-Mediated Communication in Classrooms

By far, the greatest advantage afforded by the use of CMC in the classroom is that it allows for the possibility of increased student communication and interaction (Bump, 1990; Faigley, 1992; Harasim, 1993). Many teachers and researchers have delighted in the medium's more egalitarian nature and its ability to support different power structures, giving students a stronger presence in classroom conversations and discussions.

At their best, CMC classroom discussions are what we hope in-class oral discussions will be, students interacting in dialogue and debate, searching for new ideas and explanations. Not just any interaction will do, however. Simply providing discussion opportunities does not always guarantee that substantive discussion and collaboration will occur. In fact, student network discourse has disappointed and shocked many teachers who have reported that students often write "humorous zingers" and "graffiti-like" messages (Faigley, 1992; Kremers, 1993) and engage in "idle chatter" (Thompson, 1993).

Even when the discussion is civil and on task, the quality of the conversation is not always what we hope it to be. Neuwirth et al. (1993) found that students have difficulty engaging in "appropriate dialogic writing." He viewed their entries as a set of simultaneous monologues—a stance that is often presentational and imposing and does not foster discussion. So, whereas CMC does, in theory, provide more opportunities for student-student interactions, the quality of these interactions must be addressed.

A Dialogical or Monological Stance

In this study, the terms *dialogue* and *monologue* are on a continuum that represents how conversational participants are positioned with regard to each other and their topic. As they communicate, interact, and approach each other, conversational participants take on a stance that is more monologic or dialogic.

My ideas about dialogue are rooted in the sociocultural theories of Vygotsky and Bahktin (Bahktin, 1981; Vygotsky, 1978; Wertsch, 1991). Vygotsky proposed that individuals develop through their interaction with the sociocultural context in which they are situated. In such a view, interaction with more knowledgeable others and the mediating power of language to support change make dialogue a critical factor in how mind develops. In Bahktin's sociocultural theory, utterances voiced by individuals interacting to fulfill their intentions are necessarily echoing other utterances and responsive to the language previously encountered. For Bahktin, all utterances are to some degree dialogic.

Beyond Vygotsky and Bahktin, however, dialogue, and its contrast, monologue, can also represent the psychological stances participants can take toward each other and toward the conversations they create. Participants who take a dialogical stance approach the conversation and its participants with a willingness to hear and entertain other perspectives. Participants taking a monological stance use the conversation as a platform or podium to state opinions. This contrast in stances is similar to the distinction between knowledge transforming and knowledge telling made by Scardamalia and Bereiter (1987) in describing how writers can approach their topic and audience.

Finally, the continuum reflects a range of assumptions about the nature of meaning and how it is created. In monologue, meaning is neither debated nor negotiated; rather, the message itself conveys meaning as fact. In dialogue, participants co-construct meaning through interaction, building a greater understanding from each others' individual and sometimes unique perspectives. Here the message is a means for refining what has been agreed upon previously.

Bruner (1986) discussed the importance of such a stance:

I think it follows from what I have said that the language of education, if it is to be an invitation to reflection and culture creating, cannot be the so-called uncontaminated language of fact and "objectivity." It must express stance and must invite counter-stance and in the process leave place for reflection, for metacognition. It is this that permits one to reach higher ground, this process of objectifying in language or image what one has thought and then turning around on it and reconsidering it. (p. 129)

Thus, the discourse stance that would foster the kind of exchange that would make any discussion, whether it be oral or CMC, a platform or forum for learning would seem to be a dialogical stance. My goal in this study was to explore the effect of a dialogical stance on student learning guided by two research questions: (a) How do student dialogue and discussion develop in oral and computer-mediated conversations? (b) What is the nature of the relationship between knowledge development and dialogue in both mediums of conversations?

Method

My method has been naturalistic (Guba & Lincoln, 1994) rather than experimental in approach, with the goal to explore the nature of classroom conversations rather than to test hypotheses about them. The analyses involve explicit interpretation of verbal descriptions and explanations with quantification playing a subordinate role.

Setting and Students

The data were gathered in the context of an undergraduate teacher-training course in the teacher education department at a major university in the Southwest. The 19 students who enrolled and completed the course, 18 women and 1 man, were college-level seniors training to specialize in various content areas at the middle school level. All the students were native speakers of English. Most students reported they had participated in previous courses that used oral seminar discussion ($M=2.5$ seminar classes). Many had never experienced CMC in a classroom setting ($M=0.63$ classes).

Design of the Course

EDU 338, Applied Human Learning, was a seminar course designed to provide the students with an opportunity to discuss theories of learning and teacher practices as they participated in their last year of preservice teaching-training and as they completed, for the first time, extended, in-class placements and observations in local area schools. The central goal for the course was to give the students an opportunity to revisit what they had learned about theories of learning and development and to consider how these ideas would transfer into practice.

Daily routine. The seminar met once a week for 3 hours, divided into two nearly equal halves, an oral segment and a written CMC segment. Each class day, members of the class met face-to-face in the classroom for the oral segment of discussion, breaking midway to go to a computer lab where they continued the conversation in written format. The teacher had used the Daedalus Interchange for several years as part of her instruction. She reported an appreciation for the alternative format of discussion in which student participation became more evenly distributed and students could introduce questions and topics that they might not have found a way to introduce in the oral segment.

Oral segment. Typically, class discussion focused on the readings for the day, the assignments, and the print-out from the previous day's CMC discussion. The teacher generally refrained from formal lectures, but did, on occasion, talk at length about certain topics.

Written CMC segment. For the written discussion, students met in a lab that had computer monitors linked by a local-area server. When the class members logged on, a split window would appear. In the top two thirds of the window, all comments made by anyone in the class appeared in chronological posts for everyone's perusal. A side bar allowed individuals to read the public conversations at their will. In the lower third of the window, an individual could construct a comment of whatever length and post it to the public conversation by clicking on a small "send" button. After each CMC discussion, the teacher made available printouts to students.

Data Analysis

The data for this investigation included: (a) transcripts of audio tape-recorded oral discussions, (b) printouts of the written conversation, and (c) my daily fieldnotes.

The participants met for 13 class meetings throughout the semester. For detailed analysis, I selected 6 days of discussions spanning the entire semester with 2 from the beginning, 2 from the middle, and 2 from the end of the semester. First, I coded the oral and CMC transcripts to determine the frequency of comments and topics the students created. For the CMC segment, a comment unit was defined as a message sent and posted to the public conversation with the author's name attached. For the oral conversation, I identified the comment units based on a system of turn-taking, in which one uninterrupted turn of talk represented one comment unit. In counting both types of comment units, oral and written, the length or content of the comment was not taken into consideration. A comment such as, "I agree!" and a comment that was three paragraphs long were both coded as one comment unit.

Next, I read the oral and CMC transcripts searching for a global depiction of the various kinds of discussions that developed over the semester. The CMC printouts were diagramed into what Schallert et al. (1996) called coherence graphs. A coherence graph is an analytical tool that allows one to show how the seemingly unconnected mass of "sent" messages to the CMC exchange are connected.

Topic analyses for both oral and computer-mediated discussions proceeded by asking for each comment, "What topic does this comment address?" When a comment seemed to introduce a new topic, comments responding to it were coded as belonging to the same topic. A topic was considered finished when overt references referring back to a topic ceased. A topic was designated whenever at least two or more linked comments about the same subject matter occurred. These could be linked to one another either by explicit markers, such as naming the person being addressed, repetition of a noun phrase, or paraphrased reference, or by implicit indicators such as sequence or obvious content overlap. Using these techniques, topics across six class meetings of oral and CMC discussion were identified noting who had initiated them and contributed to them.

The final set of analyses involved using the topical analyses to locate moments or episodes in the discussion for a microanalysis of the interaction. One obvious feature of the discussion to be explored in this paper concerns the depth of topic development in conversations. Topics that span multiple comments and contributors can be argued to be the product of dialogue. Topics that fail to develop may be the consequence of dialogue-turned-monologue. When describing computer-conferencing discussions, Levin, Kim, and Riel (1990) noted that messages on a topic can either *thread* or *cluster*. In a thread, participants respond to one another, creating iterations on a topic. In a cluster, participants respond to the topic initiation comment rather than to each other directly. Using such a criterion to identify and describe discussion in both oral and computer-mediated discussion, I looked for (a) highly developed topics that included multiple participants who pursued various levels of depth; (b) undeveloped topics and comments that may have deterred their progress; (c) the presence and effects of monological and dialogical stances as indicated by certain key words and phrases in the conversation; (d) points of conflict and how they were negotiated; and (e) episodes in the computer-mediated discussion in which students seemed to shift positions or be persuaded, and episodes when student positions became more unmovable.

Results

The results break down into three sections that identify (a) the class members' participation patterns in both mediums; (b) the topics that developed for each medium across the semester; and (c) the results from a microanalysis of the students' exchanges, interaction, and dialogue. Here, due to the lengthy nature of discourse-protocol data and because of space constraints, I present a summary of these results, highlighting the conversational characteristics that occurred over the semester, and presenting examples from the computer-mediated and oral class discussions.

Participation Patterns Across a Semester

In terms of participation, I included from the six class discussions all oral comments caught on tape and all CMC messages posted and printed. Table 1 offers a depiction of the students' contributions to the semester-long conversation both orally and in CMC.

As one would expect, the teacher played an important role in both conversational mediums, topping the scale in the oral discussions with a total of 667 turns of talk for the six discussions and still maintaining a significant presence in the written CMC with a total of 95 messages. Such a difference demonstrates how her role in the CMC exchange was transformed and became more equal to that of the students'. Compared to classroom participation, most students contributed much more in the CMC segment, supporting the finding that computer-mediated discussions increase participation (Bump, 1990). However, individual participation by the 19 students was uneven in both mediums. Although the means for the students' participation were not considerably different, 46 in the oral and 56 in CMC, there was more variability in the amount of participation in the oral conversations (range=1 to 160) and a more equitable participation among students in the CMC segment (range=27 to 126).

One student, Molly, contributed only one comment across 6 days of oral conversations. In contrast, she contributed a total of 71 messages (considerably higher than the mean) to the computer-mediated discussions. The most oral comments from a student came from Jessica with a total of 160 oral comments. Jessica

Table 1

Class Participation Across 6 Days of Discussion: Oral and CMC

	Oral # Turns	CMC # Comments	Total Comments	Difference CMC-Oral
Donna (teacher)	667	95	762	-571
Noelle (TA)	4	89	93	+86
Allison	19	55	74	+37
Alyssa	29	40	69	+12
Amelia	45	52	97	+08
Brenna	47	37	84	-09
Carrie	73	66	139	-06
Danny	10	104	114	+95
Ginny	20	52	72	+33
Holly	03	46	49	+44
Jessica	160	126	286	-33
Katie	07	34	41	+28
Katrina	136	52	188	-83
Lindsey	42	72	114	+31
Louise	140	74	214	-65
Molly	01	71	72	+71
Muriel	08	27	35	+20
Sally	67	47	114	-19
Stacy	56	57	113	+02
Toni	08	28	36	+21
Valerie	10	28	38	+19
Overall Mean	74	60	133	
Mean Student Participation	46	56	103	

also played a significant role in the CMC segments with a total of 126 messages sent to the computer conversations. This contribution total was the most messages sent to the CMC segments but was a drop in performance compared to her oral contributions. I found that the students who rarely talked in the oral discussions across the semester contributed much more in the CMC segment and students who typically spoke the most in the oral segment dropped somewhat in their relative participation in CMC, supporting theories that point to the equalizing nature of CMC.

Topics Across a Semester

Across the semester, these discussions covered many topics. I identified a total of 104 content-related topics in both the oral and CMC discussions. Overall, the teacher initiated 32 topics, Noelle, the teaching assistant started 4, and the remaining 68 were initiated by the students. There were a total of 33 topics discussed in the oral segments and a total of 71 topics in the CMC segments. This increase reflects the capacity of CMC to allow for multiple topics at the same time. Of the 33 oral topics, the teacher initiated 24 whereas only 9 were student initiated. In contrast, 62 of the CMC topics were student initiated, whereas 8 were started by the teacher and only 4 topics were initiated by the teaching assistant.

In analyzing the development of the various topics within the semester-long conversation, I used the number of comment units addressing a topic as an index of which topics the students were willing to engage. Overall, the topics' lengths across the semester ranged from 2 to 135 comments ($M=21.4$). The mean length of topics for the oral and CMC segments were 39.7 and 12.9, respectively. Because a number of topics are active at once in the CMC segment, discussants can participate in more than one of them but multiple topics also means that topics and their sponsors are competing for attention. As Levin et al. (1990) claimed, what computer-mediated exchange lacks in depth, it makes up for in breadth.

Episodes of Dialogue and Learning

I next turned to a description of the kinds of discourse that make for effective dialogue in CMC. Specifically, I was concerned with what evidence I might garner from these computer exchanges that the students walked away with new understandings and viewpoints. The narrative below illustrates how most of the computer exchanges began each day, with the students responding to the prompt posted at the beginning of the conversation.

This CMC segment was a continuation of the oral discussion devoted to concepts of motivation. In the oral discussion, class members had discussed issues related to the use of extrinsic and intrinsic rewards. These concepts were familiar to most of the students. In addition, the students had read a chapter from Csikszentmihalyi's book on "flow," a concept with which the students were less familiar and had not yet discussed in any real length. The class members decided to use the CMC segment to discuss the concept of flow in contrast to issues related to extrinsic and intrinsic rewards. Note that in the following excerpt and all thereafter, the turns are numbered in terms of when they appeared sequentially in the conversation. With the exception of adding pseudonyms, comments appear just as the students wrote them.

The label I assigned to this topic was "Rewards do/do not foster flow" and it contained a total of 43 comments in all. Because of the topic's length, I present only excerpts. I begin by analyzing the first 6 comments that came as a response to the prompt, What do you think rewards would do to someone who is experiencing flow as she is in an activity?

#4. Stacy:	Rewards I think, would make the flow experience even greater. I think it would make the experience even more exciting.
#8. Amelia:	I think giving an extrinsic reward would just interupt this state of flow and end up just being a barrier to flow.
#9. Allison:	I think a person in flow who is offered extrinsic reward will look at the activity as a task instead of something they want to do.
#10. Jessica:	I think that extrinsic reward can be used to gain intrinsic reward. its like tasting a tomato. You might like it you might not but you have to try. Extrinsic rewards can make them at least try.
#11. Molly:	I agree w/allison
#12. Stacy:	Everyone likes extrinsic rewards, right?

The students began the discussion by responding to the prompt with different opinions and statements. Until Molly's and Stacy's comments, the discussion consisted of a cluster of responses to the prompt and did not yet give the impression of a two-way conversation. Instead, the comments gave the appearance of a set of statements that reflected two sides of an argument but with little acknowledgement of others' comments.

Comments #4 through #10 are written as statements using the phrase, "I think . . ." In this way, the participants seemed to arm themselves with an opinion, but such a statement format, "here's my opinion," does not signal a willingness to discuss or debate, despite the fact that the students are positioning themselves on two sides of a possible argument. Taken together, the comments vaguely reflect a series of factual assertions with very little supportive information such as examples to illustrate their points. Most of the computer exchanges over the semester began in this manner. Often, several conversations continued in this way with students offering their opinions without situating themselves in the stream of thoughts.

Having read some of these responses, Molly and Stacy created a second round of iterations to the discussion. Molly, however, simply agreed with Allison's comment and thus, contributed little new to the conversation. In contrast, Stacy seemed to have recognized that some students had taken an alternative viewpoint. Not certain of this perhaps, she posited, "We all like extrinsic rewards, right?" This received several responses and triggered another iteration:

#13. Jessica:	I do!!
#14. Brenna:	Yep.
#15. Jessica:	The rolls this morning were nice!
#16. Molly:	Yes, but they aren't always necessary.

#18. Katie: I think intrinsic rewards for someone who is experiencing flow
                (praise from the teacher, success) wouldn't hurt, but extrinsic
                might take away from the flow
#19. Valerie: I think rewards might hinder a person from continuing the expe-
                rience of flow while they are in it. Especially if a person has
                already achieved their flow—it's like waking someone up from a
                deep sleep, your interrupting the process of their flow.

At this point, another cluster and a second iteration of comments developed
in response to Stacy's question. Comments #13, 14, 15, and 16 offered some
different viewpoints on the subject. Jessica and Brenna made quick, simple, and
humorous remarks stating that they appreciated extrinsic rewards. Molly also
agreed, but in addition pointed out that they are "not always necessary." In
comments #18 and #19, Katie and Valerie explained that extrinsic rewards could
harm certain learning activities. Having read Comments #16 and #19, and perhaps
others, Stacy then asked for more of an explanation:

#21. Stacy: So then how would receiving one interrupt flow? No they are not
                always necessary, but they are nice to get.
#22. Molly: sometimes when you are offered extrinsic rewards it takes away
                from the sulf fulfilling aspect of the activity
#23. Allison: I just think about when I took an art class, and drawing became
                something I hated instead of something fun
#26. Carrie: I agree with most of you. Giving extrinsic rewards are nice!
#29. Teacher: Stacy. I find it interesting that you think rewards would make
                flow occur even more. Don't you think that rewards might dis-
                tract a person from the activity itself?
#32. Marion: What in the world does a tomato have to do with motivation?
                Just kidding. I agree with whoever said that extrinsic rewards go
                along with flow. Like most things, an extreme of one or another is
                usually unrealistic.
#34. Jessica: Be nice Marion!
#35. Brenna: I think Stacy is right. For example, the ESL class that has a
                reward of watching television on Friday (in English) would see
                that as they learn more English, they understand more on TV
#36. Sally: I think that certain kinds of rewards would slow flow.
#38. Marion: I was just kidding, guys.
#39. Allison: I think that rewards can maybe lead someone into flow, but once
                they are already there, they don't need anything more
#48. Stacy: When I say rewards, I am not talking about, "if you do this then
                you will get . . ." I am saying the personal gratifications that come
                with flow, or say I am climbing a large mountain and I hear about
                an award I could win if I climb to the top first, then I would
                become even more motivated. (The topic continues for a total of
                43 comments and several iterations.)

Using words directly from Valerie's and Molly's comments, Stacy asked, "So
then how would receiving one interrupt flow? No they are not always necessary,
but they are nice to get." From this comment, we see Stacy struggling with her
understanding of extrinsic rewards and the concept of flow. We see her struggling
with the responses offered to her genuine question. This particular move dis-
putes the reliability of the others' comments, and positions Stacy in an argumen-

tative orientation. At the same time, the comment provided a new iteration to the topic and opened it again, for perhaps, a deeper level of discussion.

Molly (in comment #22) is the first to add to this new level of discussion by restating what had been said previously but in different terms. Allison's comment #23 provided a nice example of how an enjoyable flow activity could become less enjoyable after being situated in a classroom environment. However, she made little direct reference to whether rewards influenced her feelings about drawing. Brenna entered the conversation again in comment #35 and announced her general agreement with Stacy emphasizing the benefits of rewards and giving an example from her middle school observations to back it up. But, again, this comment provided support for just one side of Stacy's question and lacked a connection to the concept of flow. Comments #29, 36, and 39 by the Teacher, Sally, and Allison brought back the idea of the relationship between flow and rewards, but only restated comments already offered.

After reading some of these comments, Stacy attempted to clarify her point and position in comment #48. This explanation is difficult to understand. The idea of personal gratification fits with concepts of intrinsic rewards and contradicts the idea of such extrinsic rewards as awards. It does however, illustrate that Stacy was engaging in mental reflection and was prompted by the other comments to evaluate her original idea and comment. This comment received no responses and was her last comment to the exchange. The topic continued for 14 more turns with a few comments providing new iterations but little more new depth or focus.

Dialogic Exchange Patterns

As I analyzed the above exchange and many others across the semester for threads and clusters, I noticed some general characteristics of the conversations that either contributed to the topic's development or detracted from it. For example, comments had different effects on the topic's maintenance. Comments like Stacy's #12 and the teacher's #29, that triggered threads of talk and spurred new and deeper levels of discussion, were stated in a way that invited or solicited participation from other class members. On the other hand, comments that received few or no responses were often stated in a manner that was less inviting.

In this way, the students appeared to take different stances toward the topic and the discussion in general. For example, the students' "I think" comments seem to have had the purpose of transmitting or presenting information rather than being put forward as a basis of exploration or cooperative argumentation. Here we see that the students worked collectively but were not engaged in a discourse exchange. These "monologues" were sometimes difficult to piece together, not just for me, the conversational topographer, but also, I imagine, for the students themselves as they participated in the topical exchange.

In this exchange, we see comments that reflect a monological approach to the conversation, but at the same time, evidence of dialogue and discussion can be identified in Stacy's comments and several of her responders. Stacy signaled a willingness to discuss and hear other viewpoints by asking questions. Other students signaled a reluctance to engage in discussion by offering statements that neither added to the conversation nor fostered its development.

Also apparent from the above exchange is that topic development was influenced by what I call *topic sponsorship*. In the previous example, topic sponsorship was evident when Stacy initiated a new level of discussion and then followed its development, responding to the responses she received. The discussion continued, even after Stacy had left the discussion, only after other participants took on the role as topic sponsor. It appears to be a lack of topic sponsorship that prevented other topics throughout the semester from developing further. The fact that no participant followed these topics' development bespeaks a lack of commitment to the topic and a disinterest in engaging in a dialogical exchange.

What of the epistemic quality of the exchanges? It is doubtful that the students who offered comments from a monological stance learned much from these exchanges. Many of the participants seemed to be proffering information rather than soliciting it. By contrast, because Stacy assumed a dialogical stance toward her topic, viewed it as something worth discussing, her comments revealed a change in perspective. From her comments, we see that she took the responses of the other students under consideration and used them to rethink and reexamine her original understanding of extrinsic rewards and flow. It appears however, that Stacy left the conversation without reaching a firm understanding of the relationship between flow and extrinsic rewards. She does not seem persuaded by the comments offered to her. What is evident from this exchange however, is that Stacy came to recognize that the topic was debatable and that more than one perspective existed.

Dialogue and Monologue in the Oral Segments

Throughout my results I have compared the CMC segments to the oral exchanges. In this way I highlighted each type of discussion's unique and characteristic way of fostering participation and topic development. I found that the characteristics of dialogue that I identified and used to describe "good" computer network discussion work equally well to describe the in-class oral discussion over the semester.

Although we tend to think of oral conversations as developing in a linear manner, there were many occasions in the oral conversations when comments jumped from one topic to another in a somewhat disorderly fashion. Thus, it was possible to consider the oral discourse in terms of threads and clusters. Aspects of topical length and depth in terms of the number and iterations of comments could then be considered within an oral conversation. Throughout the semester-long conversation, I noticed that some participants used explicit markers or implicit, rhetorical signals to indicate that they were open for a discourse exchange. Participants who offered alternative or additional information maintained the topic's life. Others who simply agreed or restated previous comments had less of a maintaining effect. Students revealed a particular stance to the discussion indicating a dialogical pursuit of the topic, or they presented a more monological stance and a seeming unwillingness to consider alternative views. Participants' investment in and dedication to a topic was evident when they returned responses to comments they had received, thereby giving the topic momentum and a deeper sense of dialogical exchange, and helping to create a better learning environment.

There were, of course, some differences to consider in addition. The teacher's more powerful presence in the oral discussions sometimes prevented students from engaging in and producing certain activities that fostered dialogical exchanges. The fact that the teacher initiated most of the oral topics meant that topic sponsorship was mostly her responsibility and concern. Furthermore, her tendency to give a comment following almost every oral student response meant that if threading occurred it was due in part to her decision and direction. In this way, students rarely talked directly to one another in the oral conversations without some mediation from the teacher. When the conversation was set for debate and argumentation, it was mostly contrived by the teacher's preformed agendas for the class.

Another large difference between the two mediums of conversation was evident in the ways students delivered comments to the group. In oral exchange, having the teacher there waiting to respond made it possible for students simply to throw out examples or scenarios to support arguments that were usually teacher created. And, when students offered their comments without explicit links or connection, the teacher generally made the connections for them, constructing and negotiating the meaning. In comparison to the CMC exchanges where the students had to link their comments themselves, create their own arguments, provide their own examples, and then comprehend and respond to other participants' comments in return, the oral participation could be said to require less mental activity and less conversational etiquette.

Perhaps, however, the greatest difference between the two mediums of conversation was due to the differences in the level of the students' participation and the amount of their observable discourse. That the students talked less in the oral does not mean that they constructed less knowledge there. It does mean, however, that we have fewer occasions to witness their knowledge in oral classroom discussion and more verbal or rhetorical evidence of their knowledge change and development in CMC.

Discussion

Results indicated that thoughtful and meaningful discussion occurred in both mediums of conversations when students took a dialogical stance to the topics they introduced and maintained, when one or several participants took on the role of topic sponsorship, and when contributors added new and alternative information that sparked co-argumentation. Topics introduced as statements consisting of well-defined facts seemed to reflect a monological stance to the topic, and invited and received less thoughtful discussion. These comments seemed to have the purpose of transmitting or presenting information rather than being put forward as a basis for explanation or discussion. The lack of topic sponsorship, the failure to contribute additional or alternative viewpoints, and the presence of several monological stances prevented and constrained dialogue and knowledge change.

Oral discourse represents the model of academic discussion to which we grant epistemic weight socially and culturally, and it is the method within which students are expected to work. This does not necessarily mean that dialogue and discussion conducted orally proceeds in a logical fashion or by any strict dialogic method. Faigley (1992) argued that dialectic orderliness is an illusion, even in the realm of lecture and presentational papers. Indeed, I would argue that discussion worth engaging is messy and always under tension, jumping from one topic to another as the conversation progresses, and similar to the kinds often exhibited by the class members of EDU 338. Armed with the analytic tools of CMC research such as coherence graphs, comment groupings, and topic analysis, future studies of oral classroom talk may benefit from a more thoughtful look at dialogue and monologue and their effects on conversation depth and quality.

When we think of a traditional classroom, we tend to view it as a place where argumentation and dialogical interaction is not common. Teacher-led discussion and lecture are usually described as monological. There is no need for debate. His or her speeches and presentations are the final word. Indeed, I have argued that the greatest value of CMC is in its ability to break up traditional conversational practices and to advance a pedagogical reorientation from more monological to dialogical means of knowledge construction.

However, my observations of the teacher, Donna, in EDU 338 and her lectures led me to consider the possibility that a lecture or speech can be dialogical when the stance behind it reflects an appreciation for previous speakers and thinkers and a willingness to debate and hear alternative views. Donna rarely placed her argument or knowledge in monological terms and she rarely ruled out exceptions and alternatives. Even in her long lectures and her typically dominating role in the oral exchanges, the teacher of EDU 338 demonstrated not just a willingness, but a deep desire and commitment to hear and consider the students' ideas and opinions. Research that considers distinctions between monologue and dialogue in traditionally nondialogic settings warrants further research as well.

And so, I return to the question of what makes for good classroom discussion including issues such as how do such discussions proceed in classrooms, under what circumstances do they occur, what might students might gain from them, as well as how and why discussions fail or break down? Another issue embodies the changing nature of classroom communications. I compared and contrasted oral and computer-mediated discussions to shed light on the unique transition we face as classrooms become more "distant" and "text bound" and as definitions of "reading" and "writing" and "discussion" take on new and fresh meanings. Whether or not we use CMC in the classroom, its existence is changing how students and teachers communicate and create knowledge.

This study demonstrates the importance of knowledge of conversational practices and their impact on learning. Students do not all come to electronic classrooms with the kind of practice and understanding of conversational exchange that will serve them well, that will allow them to learn from and with each other. Perhaps, from studies such as this, teachers and students can learn more about communication and how to develop better and stronger ways to communicate and express themselves via CMC.

References

Au, K. (1980). Participation structures in a reading lesson with Hawaiian children: Analysis of a culturally appropriate instructional event. *Anthropology and Education Quarterly, 11,* 91–105.

Bahktin, M. M. (1981). *The dialogic imagination* (M. Holquist, Ed.; M. Holquist & C. Emerson, Trans.). Austin: University of Texas Press.

Bereiter, C, & Scardamalia, M. (1987). *The psychology of written composition.* Hillsdale, NJ: Erlbaum.

Bruner, J. (1986). *Actual minds, possible worlds.* Cambridge, MA: Harvard University Press.

Bump, J. (1990). Radical changes in class discussions using networked computers. *Computers and the Humanities, 24,* 49–65.

Cazden, C. (1988). *Classroom discourse.* Portsmouth, NH: Heinemann.

Faigley, L. (1992). *Fragments of rationality.* Pittsburgh, PA: University of Pittsburgh.

Green, J. L., Weade, R., & Graham, K. (1988). Lesson construction and student participation: A sociolinguistic analysis. In J. L. Green & J. O. Parker (Eds.), *Multiple perspectives analyses of classroom discourse* (pp. 11–47). Norwood, NJ: Ablex.

Guba, E., & Lincoln, Y. S. (1994). Competing paradigms in qualitative research. In N. K. Denzin & Y. S. Lincoln (Eds.), *Handbook of qualitative research* (pp. 105–117). Thousand Oaks, CA: Sage.

Harasim, L. (1990). *Online education: Perspectives on a new environment.* New York: Praeger.

Hatano, G., & Inagaki, K. (1991). Sharing cognition through collective comprehension activity. In L. B. Resnick, J. M. Levine, & S. D. Teasley (Eds.), *Perspectives on socially shared cognition.* Washington, DC: American Psychological Association.

Kremers, M. (1993). Student authority and teacher freedom: ENFI at New York Institute of Technology. In B. Bruce, J. K. Peyton, & T. Batson (Eds.), *Networked based classrooms: Promises and realities* (pp. 161–180). New York: Cambridge University Press.

Kress, G. (1989). *Linguistic processes in sociocultural practice.* Oxford, England: Oxford University Press.

Levin, J. A., Kim, H., & Riel, M. M. (1990). Analyzing instructional interactions in electronic message networks. In L. M. Harasim (Ed.), *Online Education: Perspectives on a new environment* (pp. 185–213). New York: Praeger.

Mehan, H. (1979). *Learning lessons. Social organizations of the classroom.* Cambridge, MA: Harvard University Press.

Neuwirth, C. M., Palmquist, M., Cochran, C., Gillespie, T., Hartman, K., & Hajduk, T. (1993). Why we write together concurrently on a computer network? In B. Bruce, J. Kreeft Peyton, & T. Batson (Eds.) *Networked based classrooms: Promises and realities* (pp. 161–180) New York: Cambridge University Press.

Schallert, D. L., Lissi, M. R., Reed, J. H., Dodson, M. M., Benton, R. E., & Hopkins, L. F. (1996). How coherence is socially constructed in oral and written classroom discussions of reading assignments. In D. J. Leu, C. K. Kinzer, & K. A. Hinchman (Eds.), *Literacies for the 21st century: Research and practice.* Forty-fifth yearbook of the National Reading Conference (pp. 471–483). Chicago: National Reading Conference.

Thompson, D. (1993). One ENFI path: From Gallaudet to distance learning. In B. Bruce, J. K. Peyton, & T. Batson (Eds.), *Networked based classrooms: Promises and realities*

Vygotsky, L. S. (1978). *Mind in society: The development of higher psychological processes.* Cambridge, MA: Harvard University Press.

Wertsch, J. V. (1991). A sociocultural approach to socially shared cognition. In L. B. Resnick, J. M. Levine, & S. D. Teasley (Eds.), *Perspectives on socially shared cognition* (pp. 85–100). Washington, DC: American Psychological Association.

Learning to Teach Literacy in a High-Stakes Testing Environment: Perceptions of Interns and Clinical Faculty in Professional Development Schools

Elizabeth G. Sturtevant, Kristy L. Dunlap, and C. Stephen White
George Mason University

This paper reports on a study of preservice interns and clinical faculty in an elementary/middle-level professional development school (PDS) program. The purpose was to explore how participants perceived the influence of a high-stakes testing environment on the interns' teaching experiences and opportunities. The guiding questions were the following: (a) Were interns' experiences and opportunities related to learning to teach literacy influenced by a high-stakes testing environment in their public school internship placements? If so, how? (b) Did interns and clinical faculty perceive that their instructional beliefs related to teaching literacy were influenced by a high-stakes testing environment? If so, how? (c) Did interns and clinical faculty perceive that their literacy instructional practices were influenced by the high-stakes testing environment? If so, how?

Background

In 1995 the Virginia Board of Education mandated new state "Standards of Learning" in language arts and other subject areas. State tests on these standards (SOL tests) were first given in spring 1998 to all third, fifth, and eighth graders, as well as high school students in classes with end-of-year SOL tests. After the first test administration, the Board of Education set "passing" criteria in fall 1998 without reference to actual student performance. In January 1999, it was reported that 97% of the schools in the state had failed to attain "passing" scores on at least one of the spring, 1998 subject tests. School-by-school results on each of the specific subject tests were reported in local newspapers. Some schools were considered to be in more extreme difficulty than others because they failed to achieve state pass levels on many or all of the tests, or because a lower percentage of their students passed a particular test. Tests were given again in April and May 1999.

George Mason University is a state-supported institution located in a highly diverse urban/suburban region near Washington, DC. For 9 years we have participated in a professional development school partnership with two large local school divisions. In elementary and middle education, approximately 50 graduate students ("interns") per year complete an intensive, full-time program that includes

National Reading Conference Yearbook, 49, pp. 153–164.

teacher preparation courses and internships in these school divisions. The program design, including the methods courses, emphasizes collaboration between the university and schools and a research-based, constructivist approach to teaching and learning. Reading and writing are taught as processes that are affected by sociocultural, cognitive, motivational, and instructional influences. Interns complete two semester-long public school placements in which they are expected to plan and teach integrated units that include teaching strategies taught in the courses, with an emphasis on adaptations for highly diverse student populations (Graduate School of Education, 1996). Communication between university faculty and school-based mentor teachers ("clinical faculty") has been facilitated through required mentoring courses, curricular-planning meetings, university faculty visits to schools, and arrangements in which clinical faculty teach or provide workshops for methods classes.

Since the beginning of the program, curricula in the school divisions connected with the PDS program have been generally consistent with the theories taught in the university methods courses. The new state-mandated SOL tests, however, emphasize a more skills-based view of reading/language arts and a more teacher-directed curriculum than has existed in either the university PDS methods courses or the collaborating school divisions' programs of study.

Anecdotal evidence during the 1998–99 school year indicated that throughout the state, teachers were modifying instruction to include activities that they believed would prepare their students for the tests. In addition, it appeared that expectations for PDS interns may also have been substantially modified, particularly in schools that did not "pass" the tests in 1998. Some interns reported, for example, that they were not permitted to develop and teach integrated units, use writing process approaches, or conduct discussions in their internship placements. Thus, the culture and opportunities for preservice teachers' learning may be changing as mentor teachers and their principals seek to ensure that students pass the state tests.

Theoretical Foundations

The effects of high-stakes testing have been studied in a variety of contexts. For example, it has been found that tests may drive instruction, especially in situations where teachers hold little curricular authority (Stephens et al., 1995). Teachers may drastically reduce attention given to topics or subject areas that are not tested, divert substantial amounts of instructional time to "practicing" for tests, and ultimately leave schools that are identified as "low-performing" (Jones et al., 1999). In addition, high-stakes testing may be related to increased special education identification and grade retention (Allington & McGill-Franzen, 1992).

Studies of teachers' decision-making processes have identified a variety of influences on classroom instruction, including teachers' previously held beliefs and constraints present in the political and cultural environment of the school (Sturtevant, 1996). This environment includes the presence of assessments. The process through which a teacher learns to make instructional decisions has been found to occur over the teacher's lifetime, with the induction period, including student teaching/internship, of particular importance (Kagan, 1992). Influences on the development of beginning teachers' beliefs and knowledge are important to explore since teachers may later continue to follow patterns established in their induction years (Hollingsworth, 1989). The presence of high-stakes tests may affect not only teachers' instructional choices, but also their knowledge and instructional skills, as Smith (1991) asserted: "If exploration, discovery, and integration methods fall out of use because they do not conform to the format of the mandated test, teachers will lose their capacities to . . . use these methods, or even imagine them as possibilities" (p. 11).

This study was designed to explore the effects of state-mandated high-stakes tests on the experiences, instructional beliefs, and decisions of preservice level teacher interns. High-stakes testing in literacy and other areas is becoming increasingly common throughout the United States, as policy-makers become convinced that effective instruction is facilitated through mandated accountability measures. Whereas a number of researchers are investigating the effects of high-stakes testing on children, teachers, and policy, the present study extends this work through a focus on ways high-stakes testing affects the experiences and learning of preservice teachers. Within our own state it recently has been reported that some teachers and school divisions have refused to accept preservice teacher interns or student teachers due to concerns about high-stakes testing (*Washington Post,* February 20, 1999). Although this has not yet occurred at our institution, we hope that documenting the effects of high-stakes tests on the learning environment of preservice teachers will support further research inquiry and policy-makers' attention to this issue.

Methods and Data Sources

Data included anonymous open-ended questionnaires and a focus-group interview. Interns and clinical faculty in grades Pre-K–8 completed questionnaires in spring 1999 related to their perceptions of ways that the state testing program and administration affected the internship experience (see Appendices A and B). Thirty-six interns completed the questionnaires out of a possible 45 in the two PDS intern programs (14 out of 23 early childhood interns, 22 out of 22 middle-grade interns). Twenty-nine clinical faculty completed questionnaires out of a possible 45 teachers (18 out of 23 early childhood teachers, 11 out of 22 middle-grade teachers).

A focus-group interview in fall 1999 explored issues raised in the questionnaires. A purposeful sampling of 12 former interns that had received excellent internship ratings, graduated from both the Early Childhood and Middle Education programs, and were in their first year of teaching were invited to participate in the focus group. Four of these beginning teachers, from two school districts, were able to attend. The focus-group members had taught Grades 1, 3, 4, 5/6 combination, 7 and 8 during their internship year; at the time of the focus group, one was employed in Grade 3 and the others were all employed in Grade 8. The focus-group discussion was guided by interview questions related to how the new teachers would describe and compare the effects of the state testing in their internship and first-year teaching placements. Since the focus group was small, these data were only used to give added dimension to the survey results and to guide development of Year 2 of the larger study.

Data were analyzed using qualitative methodology and descriptive statistics. Questionnaires were transcribed and data were coded using themes that emerged from multiple readings by the three researchers (Merriam, 1988). The focus-group discussion was tape-recorded and analyzed to provide additional insights into the meaning of themes that emerged from the written responses. This study was conducted within a social constructivist theoretical framework that assumes that reality must be described from the perspective of participants in a culture (Berger & Luckmann, 1967).

Results

Responses to Questionnaire Items

Initial analysis of the Likert-scale ratings from the questionnaires included tallying and assigning numeric values to the six categories. Computing means for these values revealed little in terms of patterns of response for either the interns or the clinical faculty. Next, because we wanted to understand the distribution of responses across the scale, we collapsed the six Likert-scale divisions into three categories: *not at all or very little, moderately,* and *strongly,* and again looked at the numbers of responses in each category.

Interns' responses—Ratings. The percentages of responses presented in Table 1 indicate approximately equal proportions of ratings among the categories, particularly for the interns' questionnaire items. Question 2 about the influence of SOL tests on beliefs about literacy experiences in the classroom showed the greatest proportion of interns indicating a rating of "not at all or very little," but the proportion who indicated "moderately" or "strongly" was only slightly less. The proportions were essentially equal for Question 3 regarding the influence of SOL tests on interns' decisions about literacy experiences in the classroom. Interns' responses to Question 4 about conflicts or contradictions between their university courses and classroom practice suggest that the interns experienced a range of classroom placements. Their responses were split between yes and no, with the "mixed" category created for 4 interns who responded "yes" for one semester's placement, but "no" for their other semester's placement. This question was intentionally worded without specifying SOL testing as a factor, and interns did not necessarily refer to SOL tests in their written comments for Question 4.

Table 1

Questionnaire Responses—Percentages of Intern and (Clinical Faculty) Responses by Question and Category

Interns (*n*=36)	Not at all or very little	Moderately	Strongly
Question #2: Have the Virginia Standards of Learning Tests (SOL tests) influenced your *beliefs* about the literacy experiences (activities using language: reading, writing, speaking, critical thinking) that you provide for your students?	39% (41%)	28% (31%)	33% (28%)
Question #3: Have the Virginia Standards of Learning Tests (SOL tests) influenced the *decisions* you make related to teaching literacy in your classroom?	31% (31%)	33% (45%)	36% (24%)
Question #4: Are there *conflicts or contradictions* between the literacy instructional practices that you have learned about in your university literacy courses and the actual literacy activities that you were expected to teach in your internship?	No 42% (54%)	Mixed 11% (32%)	Yes 47% (14%)

Interns' responses—Written comments. Examining the rating categories of the questionnaires led to a closer look at the qualitative information in the interns' written comments. We analyzed these written comments for themes based on issues that the interns and clinical faculty identified: time pressure, beliefs of the clinical faculty versus those of the intern, and beliefs about appropriate literacy-related practice.

For Question 2 about the influence of SOL tests on the interns' beliefs about classroom literacy experiences, ratings were evenly distributed across the categories. The following excerpts from their Question 2 comments give voice to the interns' perceptions about the impact on their teaching time, pacing of instruction, and their curricular choices:

Rating scale—Not at all or very little (39%)

I did not have the time to really delve into literacy, however, because literacy is my priority I tried not to sacrifice it. (Grades K/1)

My beliefs about literacy experiences are founded in what I have been taught, and come to believe, about how children learn best and best use literature to achieve that. I've found no inconsistency between what I believe and the need to satisfy SOL objectives. (Grade 4)

Moderately (28%)

I have found that the creative aspects of literacy experiences are put aside due to the stress of the SOLs; language activities are focused on content. (Grade 2)

It influences the pace at which you cover material. Also, the tests take time out of instruction. In my 7/8 combination class, we had to adjust our instruction since 8th graders were pulled to take tests. (Grades 7/8—language arts)

Strongly (33%)

Yes. This semester the SOL tests have affected my teaching more than last semester. In 4th grade there is a lot of pressure to cover a lot of material in a short amount of time. I had to eliminate a lot of my writing activities in order to stick with a schedule. (Grade 4)

In addition, although some interns and clinical faculty spoke in terms of resistance to changing instruction in response to test pressure, others remarked on improvements they saw in curriculum as a result of the testing program: "[SOL tests] helped me narrow my learning objectives, but they haven't changed my beliefs very much."

The range of interns' responses to the questionnaire and fairly even distribution from high to low impact may indicate that they experienced widely varying classroom environments. However, it may also suggest that their understanding of SOL tests as preservice teachers was less developed than the perceptions of their clinical faculty who experienced accountability pressures more directly.

Clinical faculty responses—Ratings. Twenty-nine clinical faculty completed questionnaires out of 46 possible participants, 18 from the early childhood program, and 11 from middle-level program. Responses of the clinical faculty to Question 2 show a slight pattern in their perceptions of the influence of the SOL tests on their beliefs about literacy experiences. The greatest proportion of respondents (41%) rated the influence on their beliefs as "not at all or very little"; 31% as a moderate influence; and the smallest proportion (28%) rated SOL tests as a strong influence.

Responding to Question 3, clinical faculty rated the influence of the SOL tests on their actual classroom decisions higher than the influence on their beliefs (31% not at all or very little; 45% moderately; 24% a great deal).

Question 4 for the clinical faculty differed from Question 4 for the interns. For each group, we selected an issue that we believed would match their experience and be informed by their perspective. Although the interns would not have been able to reflect on changes over time with respect to literacy activities in classroom environments, the clinical faculty members would be able to contrast the classroom teaching expectations for interns during the SOL testing period with expectations during the pre-SOL era. For Question 4, the clinical faculty's ratings are split: nearly half of the clinical faculty indicated that the SOL tests moderately or strongly changed their expectations of what interns need to teach in literacy. Slightly over half rated the change as low (54% not at all or very little; 32% moderately; 14% a great deal).

Clinical faculty responses—Written comments. Overall, clinical faculty ratings were less ambivalent than the interns'; comments were brief, to the point, and often strongly worded. For example, the clinical faculty, in response to Question #3 about the effect of SOL tests on their classroom decisions, wrote the following remarks to substantiate their ratings of "moderately" and "strongly":

Moderately (45%)

I have to try to make concrete, what is [really] abstract. (Grade 1)

I include even more non-fiction (especially topics related to specific SOL objectives). . . . (Grade 1)

Emphasizing test taking skills. (Grade 3)

Yes, I place more emphasis now on SSR and vocabulary development. (Grade 7/ Social Studies)

90% of my teaching addresses one of the SOL's. (Grade 7/Social Studies)

Strongly (24%)

I am trying to meet with every child every day. (Grades K–1)

We are held responsible for teaching this material to kids! (Grades 1–2)

There is so much required of them to know in Science and Social Studies [that] the primary teams have created 8 new themes to teach over a 2 year period. . . . (Grades 1–2)

More skill and drill of topics that are not always age appropriate. (Grade 2)

More emphasis on reading instruction—more questioning during reading, using context clues, inference, main idea, etc. (Grade 8/English)

Although clinical faculty seldom mentioned the time pressures that interns attributed to SOL test preparation, they more often wrote about conflicts between effective practice and recommended SOL test preparation. Drawing on their own teaching experience and understanding of the curriculum, they pointed to shifts in lesson emphasis, integration of skills practice, or clear links to SOLs in their planning.

Focus-Group Discussion

As noted earlier, in late fall 1999, four former interns met with us to revisit the questions about SOL tests from the spring questionnaire. The focus-group interview indicated that the new teachers had more intensely negative responses to the testing program than had been expressed during the internship year. As one commented, "until you are really responsible for the instruction in that classroom, you have no real idea what it all means." Another who now taught eighth grade, one of the SOL testing levels, wrote, "This year the SOLs are a major pressure. All teachers were told by the principal that we must pass the SOLs this year in all subjects. Teachers must submit lesson plans and unit plans and pacing schedules for everything we teach."

The theme of time pressure that emerged from the interns' comments in the spring was strongly articulated during the focus group. These new teachers focused on the amount of teacher time devoted to "SOL training" and classroom instructional time spent practicing for the tests. One of the eighth grade teachers wrote the following comment about the effect of SOL testing on herself as a new teacher:

> We spent four days last week giving the students practice SOL tests. We also spent 1/2 an hour in one meeting discussing how the Benchmarks would be displayed in my classroom. I believe in standards but am bothered with the obsession over the tests—something gets lost in our teaching when everything has to relate to these tests. . . .

All of the new teachers in the focus group were conscious of the test pressure on their students, an aspect of the SOL testing that went relatively unnoticed during their spring internships. They discussed their students' awareness of the importance of SOL tests although the testing was several months in the future. As one eighth-grade teacher wrote:

> My students feel very pressured and nervous about taking the SOL tests this year. They know they will be accountable this year and in high school for receiving a diploma based on passing the SOL's. The students hear about SOL's in all their classes every day and are beginning to feel "burned out" even before they take the tests.

In summary, the new teachers who participated in the fall interviews felt more negative toward the SOL testing program than had their group as a whole, during the internship. Areas of greatest concern included time pressures for teaching and planning, the restrictions on what was done in the classroom, and the affective impact of the SOL testing program on their students.

Discussion

Conclusions drawn from this study primarily represent a snapshot view of the beliefs, perceptions, and concerns of a group of interns and clinical faculty at a specific point in time, along with follow-up of a small group about 6 months later. As such, the results provide preliminary answers to the research questions and some clear avenues for future inquiry.

Overall, results of this study indicate that both the interns and clinical faculty varied widely in their perceptions of how the high-stakes assessments affected their beliefs, literacy instruction, and the interns' opportunities for learning about literacy teaching. As noted earlier, some interns and clinical faculty perceived strong effects in areas where others perceived very weak effects, with another group in the middle. In terms of the type of effect, although most clinical faculty and interns described negative effects, several positive effects were noted.

The written comments and interview answers provided some clues as to why there was such apparent variation in beliefs and practices. These comments seemed to point partly to differences in contextual conditions, a term we use to broadly indicate effects related to setting, student population, grade level, the grade levels at which the tests were given, and other conditions of instruction. This finding is consistent with previous research about the importance of context on teachers' instructional beliefs and decisions (Moore, 1996; Sturtevant, 1996). One important contextual influence, for example, related to whether a respondent worked at a grade level where testing occurred. For example, a sixth grade (not a testing year) intern wrote: "I had to plan using the SOL guidelines, but I taught in grades where the SOL tests were not being administered, so the teachers did not feel the pressure that others do." By comparison, a third grade (testing year) intern noted: "[The pressure was intense] ... especially at the 3rd grade level where my clinical faculty was teacher-driven in style and SOL panicked. We basically dropped language arts in order to cover social studies content. I felt we were force-feeding facts."

A strong grade-level influence is not surprising, especially since the testing program in Virginia is structured so that elementary and middle school children are tested on 3 years of material at each testing point. Thus, an eighth grade social studies teacher must review content from Grades 6 and 7, in addition to teaching the eighth-grade content. This clear difference in expectation may have a variety of unintended effects on the curriculum, teachers, and students in particular grades.

Another important contextual condition related to how well or poorly the school had done in the previous testing. As noted by one beginning eighth grade teacher in the focus group:

> Our school's like a big focus school because we did so poorly...[we] had to have the [district's] area supervisor come in...we literally looked at scores of every single eighth grade student [from] last year . . . [to see how to get] English scores of 300's to 400's, and 400's to 500's . . . no mention of literacy ever in this meeting. It was strictly numbers.

An area that also requires more exploration is the impact of the high-stakes testing environment on teachers' and interns' beliefs about literacy instruction. In general, our data indicated that clinical faculty and interns tended to perceive that the test program affected their instructional beliefs less than it affected their instruction: that their beliefs were more resilient. Some wrote comments that strongly demonstrated their intention to resist changing their belief systems and to only change their instruction as much as absolutely required. Research over a greater period of time is necessary to explore the long-term impact of high-stakes testing on teachers' beliefs. As noted by Smith (1991), teachers may lose the capacity to use particular methods if they are not permitted to do so, and, as noted by Hollingsworth (1989), the practices used by beginning teachers may set patterns that affect their decisions for many years.

Additional areas that seem important for both researchers and practitioners to address in future work include the longitudinal effects of high-stakes testing on beginning teachers over time; the most appropriate pacing and timing of preservice coursework and field experiences in relation to high-stakes testing; strategies for assisting beginning teachers in addressing time constraints; and ways to help beginning teachers develop an understanding of more complex instructional practices that may help them address high-stakes testing while continuing to meet the individual literacy needs of children.

High-stakes tests, that are becoming prevalent throughout the United States, are a new contextual condition that can have a serious impact on the learning and development of both children and their teachers. This study describes how one group of preservice teacher interns and their clinical faculty perceived the effects of high-stakes testing on their own literacy-related beliefs, practices, and experiences. Future work that explores these issues further is essential to understanding the full effects of tests on teaching and learning.

References

Allington, R. C., & McGill-Franzen, A. (1992). Unintended effects of educational reform in New York. *Educational Policy, 6,* 397–414.

Berger, P., & Luckmann, T. (1967) *The social construction of reality.* Garden City, NY: Doubleday.

Graduate School of Education (1996). *Handbook for early childhood and middle education programs.* Fairfax, VA: George Mason University.

Hollingsworth, S. (1989). Prior beliefs and cognitive change in learning to teach. *American Educational Research Journal, 26,* 160–189.

Jones, M. G., Jones, B. D., Hardin, B., Chapman, L., Yarbrough, T., & Davis, M. (1999). The impact of high-stakes testing on teachers and students in North Carolina. *Phi Delta Kappan, 81,* 199–203.

Kagan, D. M. (1992). Implications of research on teacher belief. *Educational Psychologist, 27*(1), 65–90.

Merriam, S. (1988). *Case study research in education: A qualitative approach.* San Francisco: Jossey-Bass.

Moore, D. W. (1996). Contexts for literacy in secondary schools. In D. Leu, C. Kinzer, & K. Hinchman (Eds.), *Literacies for the 21st century: Research and practice.* Forty-fifth yearbook of the National Reading Conference (pp. 15–46). Chicago: National Reading Conference.

Smith, M. L. (1991). Put to the test: The effects of external testing on teachers. *Educational Researcher, 20*(5), 8–11.

Stephens, D., Pearson, P. D., Gilrane, C., Roe, M., Stallmann, A. C., Shelton, J., Weinzierl, J., Rodriguez, A., & Commeyras, M. (1995). Assessment and decision making in schools: A cross-site analysis. *Reading Research Quarterly, 30,* 478–497.

Sturtevant, E. G. (1996). Lifetime influences on the literacy related instructional beliefs of experienced high school history teachers: Two comparative case studies. *Journal of Literacy Research, 28,* 227–257.

Appendix A

Intern Questionnaire

Questions about Literacy Instruction and the Virginia Standards of Learning Tests

The literacy faculty in the Graduate School of Education at George Mason University would like to know more about current beliefs and attitudes toward literacy instruction in elementary and middle schools in Northern Virginia. Please respond to the following questions. If you wish, you may use the back of this page. Thank you.

(1) Fall placement: grade ___   subject area _____
    Spring placement: grade ___   subject area _____

(2) Have the Virginia Standards of Learning Tests (SOL tests) influenced your beliefs about the literacy experiences (activities using language: reading, writing, speaking, critical thinking) that you provide for your students? (check one box that best indicates your response)

not at all   a great deal

If so, in what ways?

(3) Have the Virginia Standards of Learning Tests (SOL tests) influenced the decisions you make related to teaching literacy in your classroom?

not at all   a great deal

If so, in what ways?

(4) Are there conflicts or contradictions between the literacy instructional practices that you have learned about in your university literacy courses and the actual literacy activities that you were expected to teach in your internship? If so, please explain briefly.

5) In what ways have your teaching experiences been similar or different from your expectations?

Appendix B

Clinical Faculty Questionnaire

Questions About Literacy Instruction and the Virginia Standards of Learning Tests

The literacy faculty in the Graduate School of Education at George Mason University would like to know more about current beliefs and attitudes toward literacy instruction in elementary and middle schools in Northern Virginia. Please respond to the following questions. Thank you.

(1) I have been a clinical faculty/cooperating teacher for ____ interns / student teachers during the last ____ years.
    Currently teaching grade ____   subject area _____

(2) Have the Virginia Standards of Learning Tests (SOL tests) influenced your beliefs about the literacy experiences (activities using language: reading, writing, speaking, critical thinking) that you provide for your students? (check one box that best indicates your response)

not at all   a great deal

If so, in what ways?

(3) Have the Virginia Standards of Learning Tests (SOL tests) influenced the decisions you make related to teaching literacy in your classroom?

not at all   a great deal

If so, in what ways?

(4) Have you changed your expectations of what interns need to teach in literacy this year because of the SOL tests?

not at all   a great deal

If you have changed your expectations, please provide 2–3 examples of literacy instructional practices that you expect interns to demonstrate that are different from previous years.

(5) Do you feel that there are any conflicts or contradictions between what the interns are taught at the university about literacy instruction and what you are expected to teach in your classroom? If so, please explain briefly.

Evolving Partnerships: A Framework for Creating Cultures of Teacher Learning

Ann Potts
Virginia Tech

Sandra Moore
Radford University

Susan Frye and Melissa Kile
Montgomery Co. Public Schools, VA

Carolyn Wojtera
Radford City Public Schools, VA

Donna Criswell
Radford University

I n this paper, we investigate the work of teacher study groups embedded within the context of public school/university partnerships. We examine the history, structure and influence of study groups on teachers' literacy practices situated within two public school/university partnerships. Teacher study groups are defined as educators working as active co-constructors of knowledge engaged in constructing new meanings of literacy practices and professional development. Public school/university partnerships are considered collaborative ventures "that serve as models for inquiry and move beyond finding placements for preservice teachers" (Byrd & McIntyre, 1999, p. viii).

Theoretical Framework

Initiating and sustaining long-term change in public school teaching necessitates an essential shift in how staff development for teachers has been traditionally delivered. The belief that teaching is isolated work is often confirmed by the structures in which teacher-learning has typically taken place (i.e., university coursework or traditional teacher in-service). A promising trend in teacher-learning and partnership literature indicates that the formation of professional learning communities promotes sustained, meaningful change (Barth, 1996; Byrd & McIntyre, 1999; Hargreaves, 1997).

In this paper, we draw upon two theoretical frameworks that characterize successful professional learning settings. The first is learning within a social constructivist community where learners build knowledge through literate activity with knowledgeable others (Spivey, 1997; Vygotsky, 1978), engage in collaborative conversation (Belenky, Clinchy, Goldberger, & Tarule, 1986), and value one another's expertise (Fullan, 1997). The second involves applying tenets of holistic literacy instruction to adult learning. Edelsky (1991) aptly reminds us, "In a whole language classroom, students choose curricular areas to explore, negotiate activi-

National Reading Conference Yearbook, 49, pp. 165–177.

ties with the teachers, collaborate with other students, take risks and chances with the structure and the content of their projects, work with and create texts they control, and learn to value varied readings" (p. 132). Working within study groups strengthens the possibility of teachers creating similar learning environments in their classrooms. The following three questions guide our inquiry: (a) How are teacher's literacy practices influenced by participation in study groups? (b) How do contexts for professional development support and sustain cultures for learning? (c) What are the implications for public school/university partnership work?

Method

Setting and Participants

This study occurs within the setting of two public school/university partnerships that stress collaboration, community building and respect for one another's beliefs and practices. For this paper, we focus on one aspect of the partnership work, study groups. The nature of the study groups involves educators reading, writing, experimenting with and discussing text together in relation to literacy-related instructional practices.

The setting for the study involves faculty and administrators from two elementary schools with similar numbers of students (i.e., approximately 500 students) but in neighboring districts. Tyler Elementary School is a K–3 university-town public school. Augusta Elementary School is a K–5 rural-suburban public school. Since the six researchers are both participants in the project and authors in the paper, actual first names are used. However, the names of the schools and other participants are pseudonyms. At Tyler, 13 Caucasian females currently participate voluntarily in the study group. The group includes classroom teachers, specialists, some of the university elementary education interns, and the lead university faculty member for Tyler. The lead university faculty member is a former elementary school teacher, who has mentored preservice teachers in cohorts, and taught literacy and curriculum courses at the local university. The group holds 45-minute weekly morning meetings before school begins. The members determine what texts they will study and jointly plan the meetings. For academic year 1998–99, the participants read *Build a Literate Classroom* (Graves, 1991) and *Word Matters* (Pinnell & Fountas, 1998).

In contrast, 65 educators participate in the study groups at Augusta Elementary School. Participants include the building administrators, (one male and female Caucasian), K–5 classroom teachers and specialists (all female Caucasian), 18 university interns, 17 females and 1 male (all Caucasian), and the lead university faculty member for Augusta. The lead faculty member has been an elementary school teacher, language arts supervisor, and works with cohorts of preservice teachers from the local university.

The lead university faculty member and central office language arts supervisor facilitate the study groups. Participation was a schoolwide decision based on site-based goals. Meetings occur on designated professional work days and early release days. For academic year 1998–99, the participants read *Teaching Reading in the Content Areas: If Not Me, Then Who?* (Billmeyer & Barton, 1998).

The initiators of the study are the lead university faculty teachers, Sandy and Ann. Three of the teachers will share their narratives of evolving literacy practices. Carolyn is a first-grade teacher at Tyler Elementary School. Melissa teaches kindergarten at Augusta Elementary School. Susan teaches fifth grade at Augusta Elementary School. Ann is the lead university faculty member at Tyler. Sandy is the lead university faculty member at Augusta.

Analysis

Narrative inquiry is being used to study the nature of the learning environments because it represents a viable means for understanding an experience in which the researcher is an active participant (van Manen, 1990). In narrative inquiry, the process of "living, telling, retelling and reliving stories" is the basis for understanding lived experience (Connelly & Clandinin, 1990, pp. 4–5). The stories may describe an individual's or group's work and provide both explanations of actions and rich contextual information.

Six different types of artifacts were used as data in the development of this paper. Artifacts include children's work, teachers' and education interns' work, study group documents, interviews, transcripts of the interviews and field notes. As part of the study group documents we collected a variety of written responses in the form of exit slips completed at the end of the study group meetings.

The lead university faculty, Ann and Sandy, conducted group interviews with the teachers. During the interviews, as the teachers shared their stories they showed examples of children's work, artifacts from the study groups, and shared examples of texts used. After the interviews were transcribed we read and reread the transcripts. We developed a chart, on a large sheet of paper, where we clustered examples of dialogue that we then identified as themes. We then read the exit slips from the study sessions at Augusta, these were categorized into piles that supported the themes. The teachers were sent copies of the transcripts and the themes we had developed. We then met as a group to reconfirm and discuss the stories that illustrated the themes. Sandy and Ann created a draft of the stories to be embedded in the paper. The draft was sent to the teachers and revisions were discussed through e-mail contact, telephone, and on site visit to the teacher's classrooms. This process was maintained as we all, teachers and university faculty, read early drafts of the paper, reread transcripts to engage in member checking the stories, this created a process of dialogical analysis.

This group analysis aids the interpretations, as the data is viewed from multiple perspectives (Denzin & Lincoln, 1994). In this reading and rereading of the transcripts (Erickson, 1986; Hollingsworth, 1994), we adhered to a process of analysis described by Janesick (1994), whereby the researchers make assertions supported by direct quotations from the notes and transcripts of the interviews. The themes emerged from the group's analysis of the data.

This analysis led to the construction of narratives of teachers' stories that characterize the nature of our work. The teachers' narratives illustrate the themes of risk-taking, time, support, commitment and ownership. To establish the trust-worthiness of this study, we used Guba and Lincoln's (1989) criteria: credibility, transferability, dependability, and confirmability. This ongoing process helped us gain insights, raise questions, clarify what we are trying to say and do, and see possibilities for new and different interpretations of our practice.

The Development of Contexts for Teacher Learning

Tyler Elementary School. At Tyler the study group has been ongoing for 6 years and grew out of the mutual need of four teachers (a special education teacher, an art teacher, a first-grade teacher and the speech pathologist) who traveled together to a state reading conference. At the conference, they engaged for the first time in sustained conversations about literacy practices and concerns. As a result, they began to realize the power of their combined knowledge and were excited about maintaining the discourse. Subsequently, they decided to form a study group and invited others to attend.

Carolyn vividly describes the group's history:

> Having been to the conference and having just read Regie Routman's book *Invitations* where Routman writes about teacher collaboration and teachers as learners, we kept asking, "When are we going to find the time to talk like this?" But Routman's words encouraged us to find and formalize a meeting time—to set one up and keep doing it even if no one came. For awhile, no one else did come. It was just the four of us.
>
> When we first met, we really didn't know what we were talking about. We called it "Share our successes." You know, bring your success stories that you had in your classroom and we'll talk about what happened and why. We weren't reading anything at that time. Then we began trying to find articles. In fact once we had a set time and date, we began our more formal study. We would say, "Okay it's your turn to find an article, make copies and put them in everyone's box." And the next time it would be someone else's turn. So it got us digging into our journals and different resources.
>
> Buying books ourselves was a further step into the study group world. I guess because it became an even more formal and more organized group—a more exciting group—we got more out of it! Later on, we applied for and received a "Teacher as Readers" grant from the local reading council. It was our first official funding.

Over time, the group membership has expanded and changed depending upon schedules, interests and other responsibilities. Three of the original members still actively participate. One year ago, the lead university faculty member, who supervised elementary interns at Tyler, was invited to join the study group. The joint involvement of the elementary school faculty and the university faculty member became the impetus for developing a public school/university partnership that is just beginning.

Study groups that grow out of the mutual needs of teachers such as this reveal the long-term need for dialogue and professional development that many teachers desire. As one of the newer members of the Tyler group recently asserted, "Since we have few inservice opportunities and there is little money for attending conferences in our district, we have to make our own learning situations." The context for learning at Tyler Elementary reveals the potential for impacting professional development and literacy practices that build from the grassroots movement of a few teachers. It also reveals what can be accomplished without centralized or site-based staff development support for curriculum and instruction development. In this case, these teachers worked in different ways to create professional development opportunities. However, it takes extraordinary determination, commitment and creativity.

Augusta Elementary School. The context for learning at Augusta is evolving quite differently. While the faculty from both Augusta Elementary and the university are in the second year of a partnership, the study groups are just beginning. The study groups are an outgrowth of complementary work based on the school improvement plan, the site-based committee's call for a shift in staff development, and the partnership work. The elementary faculty made a long-term commitment to the improvement of K–5 literacy practices. Previous site-based goals for professional development focused on understanding and implementing balanced approaches to literacy instruction. For example, kindergarten through second-grade teachers focused on guided reading, whereas third- through fifth-grade teachers emphasized the study of fiction through structures such as "Literature Circles."

For academic year 1998–99, a schoolwide commitment was made to focus on comprehension of nonfiction texts by actively studying content-area reading strategies. This decision represented a critical mass of teachers, specialists, and university interns. It was our hope that this action would help bring about meaningful and enduring change; change that could broaden and deepen children's ability to strategically use reading and writing as learning tools.

Sandy, the lead university faculty member at Augusta, provides background:

> I had been working with the teachers at Augusta for two years in developing our partnership work. When the Augusta faculty decided to focus on content area reading, the principal, Jim, asked me if I would facilitate the study groups with a former colleague, Jennifer, the language arts supervisor from central office. The development of the structure and content of the study groups was a joint endeavor between Jennifer, myself, the principal and Melissa and Susan (who co-chaired the site-based committee for professional development). The five of us became the planning team for the ongoing work of the study group. Funding from both the university and central office was used to buy the texts.
>
> I'll always remember that first work day. It was almost overwhelming, in a good way, to see over 65 people from one school reading, writing and talking about content area reading! We had enough tables that everyone was in a small group of 4–5 people mixed across grade levels and specialty areas. The format for the day included: study groups, separate demonstration lessons for primary and intermediate grades, time to develop lessons within-grade level teams, and across-grade level sharing. The planning team collaboratively designed the work for the study groups so that everyone was getting direct experience in using the

content area strategies as learners themselves. As the day proceeded, we built in opportunities for the study groups to revisit their conceptual understandings of content area reading.

To follow-up, three early release days were designated as times to continue our work. On those days, I led the K–2 group and Jennifer led the 3–5 group. At the end of each study session, we would together select the next chapters to read and the types of strategies the teachers would like to see demonstrated. In between, when I was working in the school, it was exciting to have the teachers stop me in the hall to talk about what they were discovering. It was great for our interns because they were working side-by-side with teachers enthusiastically reading, studying and trying out new ideas. This year (AY99–00) our partnership has an Eisenhower Professional Development Grant for studying and implementing Inquiry-based Science, Content Area Reading Strategies and Technology applications. So it's exciting to see last year's work in content area reading carry forward.

A salient feature of ongoing professional development at Augusta includes long-term study of a common focus. Three early-release days were designated as follow-up sessions for the study groups. Within the study groups, participants select chapters from the content-area reading text by Billmeyer and Barton (1998) *Teaching Reading in the Content Areas: If Not Me, Then Who?* The study group participants discussed ideas that might be confusing to them, or new ideas that help them gain insight into what content-area reading is, points they disagree with, and what seems most important. Decisions on what strategies to explore in their classrooms are determined by the participants as they develop their own questions about content-area reading that meets their particular classroom needs. Recurring meetings provide time for revisiting ideas, sharing, and furthering our study. Working in these ways exposes participants to: (a) multiple interpretations of the text, (b) a wide variety of content reading strategies, (c) different ways teachers adapt strategies for children's developmental levels and needs, and (d) the types of conceptual understandings that the children acquire. Structuring study groups in these ways focuses and stimulates common, schoolwide dialogue. A limitation of the work at Augusta was the amount of time separating the three early release days as some momentum was lost over a 3-month period. Curiously, as the five authors reflected on the processes in which they had been engaged, Susan and Melissa were interested in how the different study groups worked. From this discussion came the impetus to meet more frequently at Augusta. The faculty has now implemented weekly Friday morning voluntary study group meetings. The context for learning at Augusta shows the potential for impacting literacy practices and professional development through the formalization of study groups within a site-based school.

Teachers' Narratives

What follows are three narratives of teachers' who were involved in the study groups. Embedded in each story is how they took risks with instruction and used time and space differently. As a result, their instruction became more focused which enhanced children's learning. Although many stories could be told, the selected narratives best illustrate the major themes of risk-taking, time, support, commitment, and ownership:

Susan's Narrative

I think the focus on content area reading at Augusta has been very powerful—especially for the upper grade teachers. Prior to that work, if you had asked me if there were different types of reading I probably would have said, "No. I don't think so. What do you mean different types?" Realizing the structural differences between the types of reading has been so powerful for us in the upper grades—to really start working on comprehension skills in the content areas. I think the kids tend to have character, setting and plot down pat. But you give them a nonfiction piece and they struggle.

Now I use *more* strategies and *different* strategies. I definitely use the ideas on vocabulary development. What an enlightenment that was for me! I taught vocabulary in that traditional way of, you know you write the vocabulary words up on the board. "Here's the new vocabulary. This is what we'll read in this story. Look out for these words." I realize now that you've given the children absolutely nothing to hook that vocabulary word to. It was like throwing vocabulary words at them. We all have to have some kind of model, hook or demonstration—something that's real to us before we can do it or understand it. [Softer voice] And there the children are, reading [pause] and you just think that because you've written a list up on the board [pause] they're supposed to automatically know what those words mean. I always thought that they were learning the vocabulary well. So the vocabulary strategies from our study of content area reading really focused me.

One of my more exciting days trying out new vocabulary strategies came from combining "brainstorming" with the "Frayer Vocabulary Model" [a word categorization activity in which students analyze a word's essential and nonessential attributes]. We were beginning our study of World War II. I wrote the word "war" on the board and began asking the kids, "What does this mean to you?" "Let's think about everything that this word represents because this is a vocabulary word that really doesn't have a simple visual picture like a cat or a dog. But what visual pictures do you have of war?" They began brainstorming the most powerful words. They talked about weapons, people dying, and opposing teams. They knew a lot of the elements of war and were able to state ideas in their own language. Well I was so excited! *Then,* we began reading about World War II. They were beginning to find their ideas in the readings. It made the reading more meaningful to them because it brought all of their ideas to the forefront. But the children also had time to talk and have someone listen and value what they had to say.

I'm also integrating my social studies and language arts blocks. I always had these little segmented blocks of time. I'd tell the kids, "We are doing language arts right now—this is our literacy block. Now we're shifting gears and we're going to do social studies." By integrating blocks of time, the children not only have more exposure to the material but they're getting more meaningful exposure [pause] which is what these kids need. The day flows better. It just feels like it's a day full of literacy [pause] reading and writing all day long because they're doing a lot of writing in social studies, science and even math. More than I've ever done before.

As I think back on last year, if I had just been handed the content area reading book I never would have read it on my own! You can go to as many workshops and things but if we don't have time [voice trails off]. So our work with content area reading forced us to make time. We knew that when we came back together we would share what we tried. So you're thinking—"Oh—home-work assignment!" I needed that support of teachers around me to talk it out and try it. I've also discovered that if you don't practice and try out ideas you're not going to use them. They won't become a part of you.

In Susan's narrative, we see her integrating her instructional blocks and implementing new curricular innovations. Her focus at the beginning of her unit on World War II illustrates well the important role activating prior knowledge plays in comprehending new material. Her enthusiasm for change is captured in the dialogue of her story. Of greater importance though is her candid acknowledgment that collegial support encouraged her to pursue new knowledge.

Melissa's Narrative

The modeling of lessons at Augusta provided me with the support to try some different instructional strategies. For one of the K–2 teachers' study sessions, Sandy asked me to team with her to demonstrate part of the lesson for the other teachers. Sandy's lesson on teaching about survival used cause/effect strategies with the children's book *Hey, Little Ant* by Phillip Hoose (1998). Together, we dramatized the reading. The illustrations show the tiny ant trembling in the shadow of a very large child and then reverses the roles and the sizes of the characters. The book ends by asking the readers, "Should the boy squish the ant?"

Sandy, didn't know it at the time but I was just getting ready to start a unit on insects. I typically do a two week insect inquiry unit using both fiction and nonfiction texts. I was already familiar with content area reading from completing my master's degree in reading. But from the primary grade study sessions, I decided to try some things in the classroom that I wouldn't have thought would work with kindergartners. So for my culminating activity, I decided to use the "Creative Debate" strategy from the Billmeyer and Barton (1998) text we were all reading and using.

We didn't actually debate but rather had a discussion where everyone brainstormed on a kindergarten level about insects and should we "stomp them out." As I recorded their responses, the children were really coming up with ideas about why we should and should not "stomp them." Some of their responses were ones I expected and have heard before. For example, "Bugs are yucky." "They sting." "They're ugly." "Their families and nestmates need them." "Some are pretty." But this time it was different. Some responses were ones that had not emerged in any previous discussions during our unit—and none were explicitly taught during the unit. For example, "If you stomp a caterpillar, it won't grow into a butterfly." "Some insects give you diseases." "Some insects get rid of dead animals." When I asked for more information about getting rid of dead animals, I discovered the child was talking about flies on roadkill.

I also used the "Semantic Feature Analysis" strategy as a culminating activity for my unit on bats. We studied megabats and microbats, which was something new to me. The semantic feature matrix helped the kids both visually and orally compare and contrast the bats' characteristics. This again, like with the insects, really focused our discussion on distinct points such as size, physical characteristics, and food sources.

So I found out several things. Because my instruction and planning were more focused with specific strategies, there seemed to be higher engagement and interest in the discussion for my kindergartners. Rather than just saying, "We're going to read this and talk about it," instead, there's something specific to follow up with. The topic of insects also has a high level of appeal to kindergartners. They really like "bugs" and they do smash "bugs." So it was real world to them. Higher order thinking came out naturally as they sought examples from their own experiences. As I've thought about all of this, the children had a legitimate outlet for sharing their knowledge.

Melissa's narrative illustrates how an experienced kindergarten teacher takes risks in her practice. Her emphasis on culminating activities for her units provided the children opportunities to synthesize, connect, and make comparisons. We see Melissa expanding her repertoire of developmentally appropriate practices for kindergarten. Her choice of strategies models how primary teachers can adapt strategies sometimes thought to be more appropriate for upper elementary grades. Her actions bring higher order thinking skills into the primary classroom.

Carolyn's Narrative

During one of our morning meetings at Tyler, I was telling Marilyn the art teacher about my philosophy on writing. We realized as we talked that my writing philosophy matched developmentally with her philosophy on drawing. We thought, "How? We can't have anything in common. . . ." Over time, we decided to try team teaching, but realized we needed a longer block of instructional time. To accomplish this, we each gave up a planning period. This gave us two back-to-back periods in which to work with my first graders. We teamed like this for about two years discovering how the children could read or write during art and how they could draw and paint during reading.

One of our best projects was called "Planting a Seed." We wanted to integrate fine arts, literature, and science. We chose to study Georgia O'Keefe first because she looked so closely at flowers. Marilyn would teach about Georgia O'Keefe and have the children study her paintings. I would get out the microscopes. Then with the children, we would look up close at flowers. We would draw and make observations for science. We read about Georgia O'Keefe and wrote stories about her. Then we tried to produce artwork in her style. Later, we did the same thing with Monet. The children's artwork looked like college students had done them. They looked like Monet's work with layers upon layers of oil pastels. We've now borrowed enough from one another and taught each other enough where I can keep art integrated in my class and Marilyn can keep literature integrated in hers. We didn't know the collaboration would help us change our teaching in so many ways.

As other teachers in the study group began to see how we were collaborating, some of them decided, "Well maybe I can do something like that too. Who can I work with?" And now our speech therapist goes into the art classes to teach language instead of pulling those children out for language therapy. She teams with the art teacher and teaches language while Marilyn's teaching art.

Having participated in the study group for six years, I realize how valuable the talk is. We could buy all these books and read and grow a little bit on our own but it was the talking and collaboration that really made the difference and changed the way that we teach. It's been—well I don't know what we would do without it. I don't think our teaching would be the same. I would feel stagnant. You have to have conversation with your colleagues. For us, there's no better way than to clear the calendar and claim Wednesday mornings as ours. People around the school call it the Wednesday Morning Group.

Carolyn's narrative reveals the benefits of taking the risk of working together in what she describes initially as an "unlikely partnership." Working in such reciprocal ways provided support to transform and inform one another's practice.

Emerging Implications

Transformation of Practice

The potential benefits from the actions within the study groups are revealed in the texts of the teachers' narratives. Both Melissa and Susan described the more in-depth conversations that resulted from the study of content-area reading. They observed the children's conversations change as the instruction was structured in more focused ways.

Susan describes both her patience and excitement at listening to the children come to an understanding of "War" in their own language and terms. Her narrative illustrates the importance of starting with the children's understandings and language, before assisting children in developing more complex and critical understandings. The following comment reveals Susan's increased sensitivity to this issue. "It [activating prior knowledge] made the reading more meaningful to the children because it brought all of those ideas to the forefront. But the children also had time to talk and have someone listen and value what they had to say."

Melissa describes, in her narrative, the more complex language that evolved as her kindergartners engaged in the culminating components of her units. She attributed the more in-depth discussion to the children's enhanced opportunities to verbalize multiple connections revealing their prior and emerging knowledge. These changes came about by embedding more structured strategies into her daily practice. As Melissa states in her narrative, "Because my instruction and planning were more focused with specific strategies, there seemed to be higher engagement and interest in the discussion for my kindergartners." Increased responses from the children and their enthusiasm to learn more was paralleled by Melissa's enthusiasm to try out new ideas in her practice acquired from her reading and discussions within the study groups. Together, Susan and Melissa's narratives illustrate how more focused instruction emerged from the study of content-area reading.

For Carolyn, instruction was transformed by working across disciplines with other teachers. Carolyn's narrative shows how teacher collaboration can help children look at a subject from more than one perspective. Together, Carolyn and Marilyn willingly renegotiated their use of instructional and planning time to create a richer experience for the children. As Carolyn asserted, "We teamed like this for about two years—discovering how the children could read or write during art and how they could draw and paint during reading." Collectively, the narratives illustrate the potential benefits to children when teachers willingly change their use of time and curricular engagements.

Qualities That Support and Sustain Teacher Learning

Examining the evolving nature of study groups within two different sites provides, as Cochran-Smith and Lytle (1993) remind us, "insights into the particulars of how and why something works and for whom it works within the content of particular" settings (p. 15). Within both contexts for teacher learning, one site (Tyler) was established as a grass roots beginning for the exploration of literacy practices. The other site (Augusta) was established as a schoolwide, site-based decision to study content-area reading. Commitment of time is a quality that cuts across these settings.

At Augusta, the principal works through site-based committees to make release time for study a priority. At Tyler the commitment for the participating teachers has become an important part of their culture for learning. As one teacher stated, "Wednesday morning is an integral part of my professional life." Not only is the commitment to meet a critical aspect but also the need to have ownership in the process. At both schools the teachers initiated the need for study, committed time for specific professional development that met their needs, and also determined the agendas and the texts to be explored. When ownership of professional development is present a commitment to the work develops and an intrinsic need to share occurs through descriptions of practice, children's work, and stories of dynamic classroom practices as they unfold.

Another essential quality is the need for collegial support. As Carolyn reflects in conversation, "It's so much easier to go to a new place when you've got a friend with you. And I think that is what our group has really been about. That we take our friends with us and help them try new things. We nudge them and they nudge us back. And they show us things through their eyes. Then we show them things through our eyes." Susan also supported this value of collegiality in her comment: "I think I would wither and dry up if I didn't have people to share the excitement with. Because that's a big part of it-being able to share and talk." Inherent in their statements is the power of collaborative learning—learning not just to tolerate, but to appreciate and learn from one another, ultimately creating richer learning environments for children.

Implications for Partnership Work

At the beginning of our paper, public school partnerships are defined as "collaborative ventures that serve as models for inquiry and move beyond finding placements for preservice teachers" (Byrd & McIntyre, 1999). The teachers' narratives and the rich descriptions of the contexts collectively show two very different yet evolving constructions of study groups. The narratives and site descriptions also reveal similar qualities inherent in both—risk taking, time, commitment, ownership, and support. When public school teachers and administrators and university faculty work together in these ways over time, it builds credibility and respect for each other's expertise and practice.

We recognize the dynamic complexity to the process for learning described in this study. Such communities are nonlinear and can be unpredictable. The communities are in a constant process of negotiation and renegotiation, which is developed through trust within the interactions of the participants. Developing the trust necessary for teachers to openly discuss their evolving practice is not easy.

In working with teachers and preservice teachers within the school sites we recognize that each site will be different. Therefore dynamic ways of working will emerge that are best suited to that community. Ideas about how such communities develop can be shared and the successes and problems related, but the sharing does not guarantee successful transfer to another context.

In such dynamic work we are left with loose threads that we will continue to explore. How do we facilitate these communities of teachers and preservice teachers working together to enhance their understanding of literacy practices within the schools? What meaningful resources do teachers need to explore literacy practices? How does the knowledge constructed affect the interns, administrators and university faculty's understanding of literacy practices?

Whereas we have described two distinct sites, it is the willingness to transform practices and the common qualities that support and sustain transformation that make possible the creation of settings where public school teachers, university interns, and faculty can work side-by-side to create centers of inquiry.

References

Barth, R. (1996, April). On common ground: Strengthening teaching through a school-university partnership. *Yale-New Haven Newsletter, 6,* 1, 5–7.

Belenky, M., Clinchy, B., Goldberger, N., & Tarule, J. (1986). *Women's ways of knowing.* New York: Basic.

Billmeyer, R., & Barton, L. M. (1998). *Teaching reading in the content areas: If not me, then who?* Aurora, CO: McREL (Mid-continent Regional Educational Laboratory).

Byrd, D. M., & McIntyre, D. J. (1999). Professional development schools: Promise and practice. In D. M. Byrd & D. J. McIntyre (Eds.), *Research on professional development schools: Teacher education yearbook VII* (p. viii). Thousand Oaks, CA: Corwin.

Cochran-Smith, M., & Lytle, S. L. (1993). *Inside/outside: Teacher research and knowledge.* New York: Teachers College Press.

Connelly, F. M., & Clandinin, D. J. (1990). Stories of experience and narrative inquiry. *Educational Researcher, 19*(5), 2–14.

Denzin, N. K., & Lincoln, Y. S. (1994). *Handbook of qualitative research.* Thousand Oaks, CA: Sage.

Edelsky, C. (1991). *With literacy and justice for all: Rethinking the social in language and education.* New York: Falmer.

Erickson, F. (1986). Qualitative methods in research on teaching. In M. C. Wittrock (Ed.), *Handbook of research on teaching* (3rd ed., pp. 119–161). New York: Macmillan.

Fullan, M. (1997). Emotion and hope: Constructive concepts for complex times. In A. Hargreaves (Ed.), *1997 ASCD Yearbook: Rethinking educational change with heart and mind.* Alexandria, VA: Association for Supervision and Curriculum Development.

Graves, D. (1991). *Build a literate classroom.* Portsmouth, NH: Heinemann.

Guba, E., & Lincoln, Y. (1989). *Fourth generation evaluation.* London: Sage.

Hargreaves, A. (Ed.). (1997). *1997 ASCD Yearbook: Rethinking educational change with heart and mind.* Alexandria, VA: Association for Supervision and Curriculum Development.

Hollingsworth, S. (1994). *Teacher research and urban literacy education: Lessons and conversations in a feminist key.* New York: Teachers College Press.

Hoose, P. (1998). *Hey, little ant!* New York: Random House.

Janesick, V. J. (1994). The dance of qualitative research design: Metaphor, methodolatry, and meaning. In N. K. Denzin & Y. S. Lincoln (Eds.), *Handbook of qualitative research* (pp. 209–219). Thousand Oaks, CA: Sage.

Pinnell, G. S., & Fountas, I. C. (1998). *Word matters: Teaching phonics and spelling in the reading/writing classroom.* Portsmouth, NH: Heinemann.

Spivey, N. N. (1997). *The constructivist metaphor: Reading, writing, and the making of meaning.* San Diego, CA: Academic.

van Manen, M. (1990). *Researching lived experience: Human science for an action sensitive pedagogy.* London, Ontario, Canada: State University of New York Press.

Vygotsky, L. (1978). *Mind in society: The development of higher psychological processes.* Cambridge, MA: Harvard University Press.

Reading and Writing in the Daily Lives of Latino Mothers Participating in an Intergenerational Literacy Project

Gigliana Melzi
New York University

Jeanne R. Paratore
Boston University

Barbara Krol-Sinclair
Boston University/Chelsea Partnership

Several studies have led us to understand that the ways adults and children use literacy at home and in their communities vary widely depending on multiple factors such as culture, language, and social class (Heath, 1983; Purcell-Gates, 1995, 1996; Taylor & Dorsey-Gaines, 1988; Valdés, 1996). Despite ample contrary evidence, the view that economically poor, culturally, and linguistically different households are largely nonliterate settings where parents hold little interest in their own or their children's learning continues to persist. Consider, for example, what teachers told Guadalupe Valdés (1996) in her recent study of the home and school experiences of immigrant families: "'The problem is the parents,' teachers explain. 'They don't care about education. They just won't do for their children what they need to do to help them succeed. They have little education and many are even illiterate'" (p. 191).

This view is commonly held by many educators. Delgado-Gaitan (1996), in her study of Latino families, reported that the most common obstacle to children's success in school identified by teachers was "the parents' lack of time for their children" (p. 111). Purcell-Gates (1995) reported similar findings in her study of an urban Appalachian family. In a survey of teacher attitudes toward urban Appalachian students and their difficulties. Most recently, on our own local radio station, the report of high failure rates of children on the new, high-stakes state assessment drew a comment from the state commissioner that parents are "not doing enough" to support their children's school success. Since the failure rates are highest in the poor, largely nonmainstream communities, this again seems to be a comment on what culturally and linguistically different parents know and value.

Evidence suggests that failure to perceive and understand disparate uses of literacy might lead to inaccurate assessment of the literacy and language knowledge of children and adults, and accordingly, to inappropriate conclusions about

National Reading Conference Yearbook, 49, pp. 178–193.

the roles parents can play in their children's learning. The purpose of this study was to extend our understanding of the types and purposes of literacy embedded within the daily lives of one particular group, Latino mothers and their children who have participated in an intergenerational literacy program (ILP).

Theoretical Foundations

Observing and engaging in home literacy activities has been shown to be a powerful predictor of children's future success in school. For a long time, socio-economic conditions were considered an influential factor in determining the quantity and quality of children's literacy opportunities in the home. Working-class families were found to offer fewer opportunities to read and write than middle-class families (Teale, 1986; Wells, 1985). However, ethnographic studies examining the use of literacy in various communities have shown that literacy is an integral component in the lives of many lower income families.

The work of Shirley Brice Heath (1983) was among the earliest and most influential in helping us to perceive literacy practices in nonmainstream families in different ways. Over a 10-year period, Heath studied the language and literacy behaviors of two communities in the Piedmont Carolinas: Trackton, a working-class African-American community, and Roadville, a working-class White community. Heath observed rich literate traditions in both communities that were intimately tied to the community's needs, goals, and beliefs. The literacy practices of these two communities, however, were unlike those common to a mainstream community she called Maintown. Unlike Maintown children, the children of Roadville did not use reading and writing to "get ready" for school. For example, they were not asked school-like questions as a way of testing or displaying their knowledge; they did not recite rhymes and chants or the alphabet song. They were not asked to speculate about the stories they listened to or to connect them to their own experiences. Rather the children in Roadville were encouraged to stay within the context of the story and to report the factual, whereas children in Maintown were encouraged to associate and move beyond the immediate text and situation. Trackton, too, differed in substantial ways in its literate traditions. In this community, there were few opportunities to interact with written text, such as book reading. However, there were many opportunities to engage in verbal, social interactions. Children in Trackton were praised as they began to demonstrate command of oral language through elaborate storytelling, and use of analogies and metaphors.

Trackton and Roadville children experienced difficulties in school. Children struggled, Heath concluded, not because they were language and literacy deprived, but because they were language and literacy different. Unlike their mainstream peers, the children of Roadville and Trackton did not enter the schoolhouse doors with the knowledge of language patterns and literacy events that are valued and privileged in most classrooms.

Taylor and Dorsey-Gaines (1988), in their study of African-American children living in urban poverty, also found that literacy was an integral part of the children's everyday lives. In their chronicle of daily activities, they observed children reading, writing, and drawing for meaningful purposes. But they, too, found that the ways children used literacy outside of school had little relevance for literacy demands inside the school doors. These children, too, often failed. Taylor and Dorsey-Gaines concluded that it was not because children were literacy impoverished, but rather because there were few, if any, connections between literacy practices in and out of school.

Studies exploring the home literacy practices in various Latino communities offer similar portrayals of Latino households. In various studies, Luis Moll and his colleagues (e.g., Moll, Amanti, Neff, & Gonzalez, 1992), have shown that Latino households have rich "funds of knowledge," that are culturally and historically defined, but whose overall function might not be different from funds of knowledge available in mainstream homes. The portrait of the Mexicano families provided by Vásquez, Pease-Álvarez, and Shannon (1994) also showed that Latino families have ample and varied opportunities to interact with diverse types of texts on a daily basis. More recently, Rodríguez (1999) conducted an ethnographic study of three Dominican families' exposure and use of literacy artifacts. Even though young children in this study did not participate in the structured literacy activities present in mainstream families, oral and written texts were part of their environment. The children had formal interactions with print, but, for the most part, literacy was embedded in their most routine activities.

Although Rodríguez's sample was very small, she also reported differences in literacy practices and availability of literacy artifacts among her families. In particular, she noted that in the two families in which mothers had some college education there were more adult and children's books available. Similar findings were reported by Reese, Goldenberg, Loucky, and Gallimore (1995) in their study of ten working-class, Spanish-speaking Latino families. They found that parent education played a role in the types of literacy opportunities offered to children and in the nature of the interactions with literacy. As they suggested, it is not that parents with higher levels of formal schooling are more interested in their children's education or more able to provide literacy experiences. Rather, parents with higher education use literacy in ways that differentially support their children's literacy development and school success.

The findings reported in these studies point to an important and relatively unexplored area of investigation: variations within the Latino population. Although previous studies have offered rich information about literacy opportunities in Latino homes, few have explored sources of variations within this highly diverse immigrant population. As a preliminary attempt, the present study addressed one possible source of variation within one community of Latino mothers (i.e, those in an intergenerational literacy project). We first examined the incidence and nature of literacy activities reported by these mothers who were receiving explicit guidance in ways to work with their children to support school success. We then explored whether maternal education revealed any systematic variations in the number and types of literacy activities mothers reported.

Method

Setting

The setting for the study was an intergenerational literacy project situated in an early childhood learning center within an urban, largely immigrant community. Parents attend the project four days per week for two hours each day to learn about ways to improve their own English literacy and to learn ways to support their children's success in American schools. Instructional emphasis is on helping parents to situate literacy experiences within the fabric of their daily lives, rather than on the creation of school-like contexts in the home setting. Parents are encouraged to join with their children in multiple uses of literacy, including reading and writing oral histories, composing letters to friends and family members, journal writing, and story writing and publishing. Parents are also taught how to help their children with homework, types of questions they might ask the classroom teacher to learn about their children's progress, and the types of questions they might ask their children to learn about the school day. On a daily basis, parents are asked to record their literacy activities on a Literacy Log. The log is a two-sided form on which parents record their personal literacy activities on one side and literacy activities they share with their children on the other side. Literacy teachers introduce the literacy logs during the first week of instruction during each semester, they explain the logs and provide model entries. At least once a week, parents share and discuss the entries they record in their logs.

Participants

A total of 69 mothers were randomly selected as participants for this study. The sample was drawn from the population of learners who had participated at any time during the Intergenerational Literacy Project's 10-year history. Since its inception, the project has served 1,175 parents and other adult family members. Mothers were the most likely family members to participate, representing 63% of all participants. The most common ethnicity of participants was Latino (79%). Years of formal education varied widely, from learners who never attended school to those who had completed university; the mean years of schooling was 8.0.

To control for gender, ethnicity, and family relationship and to include those participants most representative of the total population, we selected participants for this study from the pool of Latino mothers, comprising 49% of the total population (n=638). We further limited the sample pool to those who had attended school for 12 or fewer years and who were in the program for at least two instructional cycles or semesters (n=411). Potential participants were then divided into two groups based on their years of schooling; a high-education group included learners who had attended school for 9 to 12 years (n=99) and a low-education group was made up of those who went to school for 7 or fewer years (n=312). Thirty-five learners were randomly selected from the low-education pool, and 34 learners were randomly selected from the high-education pool (1 learner was removed because of incomplete literacy logs).

Taken together, learners in our final sample represented 11 different places of origin, including Puerto Rico, Mexico, and countries located in South and Central America. Mean years of schooling of mothers in the low-education group was 4.7; mean years of schooling of mothers in the high-education group was 11.0. Mean number of children of mothers in the low-education group was 2.77; mean age of the children was 5.98 years. Mean number of children of mothers in the high-education group was 2.44; mean age of the children was 6.46 years. Mothers' length of participation for the selected sample averaged 3.5 cycles or approximately 2 years. Mothers in the low-education group had, on average, participated in three instructional cycles in the ILP; mothers in the high-education group had, on average, participated in four instructional cycles.

Data Sources

The data for this study were derived from the literacy logs completed by parents in their family literacy classes. Entries were recorded by parents in the language of their choice. Some were in Spanish, some in English, and, in many cases, in both Spanish and English. Entries were analyzed in the language in which they were written. All literacy logs completed by participants for the entire period of enrollment were collected. In all, 5,427 literacy log entries were analyzed. Of these, 3,434 were recorded by high-education mothers and 1,993 by low-education mothers. Since the length of enrollment varied from two to nine cycles and participants differed in the consistency with which they recorded their literacy activities, the number of literacy log entries varied widely, ranging from as few as 7 to as many as 338 recorded by high-education mothers and as few as 14 to as many as 196 recorded by low-education mothers.

Data Analysis

Data were analyzed first qualitatively and then quantitatively. In the first stage of data analysis, we reviewed entries and sorted them as literacy or nonliteracy related. At this stage, we focused on definitions of what would "count" as literacy. For both the child and adult, we considered literacy-related activities to be any interactions that could reasonably be expected to advance literacy, language, or cognitive development. We agreed to consider each entry only as it was written and without inference. Therefore, we coded *"I sang a song with my children"* as a literacy-related activity on the basis that singing was a form of language play that could serve as a foundation for literacy learning. However, we coded *"I was helping my baby take his little foot to his mouth, an activity that he likes a lot"* as a nonliteracy-related activity since the mother did not explicitly record that she chatted or babbled with the child during the event.

During the initial review on entries, we discovered that mothers commonly embedded multiple literacy activities within a single entry. Therefore, in the second stage of analysis, we calculated the total number of literacy-related activities within each entry. We agreed that events that could stand alone would be counted singly. For example, the entry: *"read a book and talked about a book"* was counted as two activities since reading the book and talking about the book could each have occurred by itself. In contrast, the entry *"I was doing a number book; [we] drew and painted the numbers"* was counted as one activity since the latter phrase described the event but did not add a new activity.

In the third stage of analysis, we coded each literacy activity according to the type of literacy interaction. To accomplish this task, we relied upon the domains of literacy suggested by Teale (1986). During the course of this analysis, we modified Teale's domains in four ways. First, we divided the domain "School-related" into Child's School and Parent's School. We coded as Child's School any activity for which the catalyst was the child's classroom or school activities. We coded as Parent's School any activity for which the catalyst was the parent's schooling. Second, we found several instances in which mothers reported their own reading or writing as leisure activities and we coded them as such. Third, given the nature of the data source, we found entries that represented mothers' reflections on literacy, as in this example: *"When I want to read a book to my son he don't listen only wants to play and pay attention to the color book."* We coded such entries as Literacy Reflections.

Following two team meetings during which sample entries were reviewed jointly and codes were generated, the senior author, a native Spanish speaker, coded all of the data. Upon completion, the research team reconvened, and the coded data from each case were reread and checked until the team agreed that all of the codes accurately reflected the data. Finally, the coded data were organized within three general categories: (a) Literacy for the Sake of Teaching or Learning, (b) Daily Literacy, (c) Literacy in Leisure Activities (see Table 1). After data were coded and clustered, we examined the number and types of reported activities by calculating means and standard deviations for the whole sample. We conducted

Table 1

Domains of Literacy

Literacy for the Sake of Teaching or Learning
    Mother's Schooling and Learning
    Children's Schooling and Learning
    Literacy Reflections
Daily Literacy
    Daily Living
    Information Networks
    Interpersonal Communication
    Work
    Religion
Literacy in Leisure Activities
    Mother's Book Reading
    Storybook Time
    Entertainment

---

correlational analyses investigating whether any available demographic variables influenced maternal reports of daily reading and writing activities. Length of participation, as measured by number of cycles, and years of education were significantly correlated to literacy reports. Therefore, subsequent analyses examined the unique contributions of maternal education and length of participation on number and types of literacy activities reported by mothers. To control for variations in number of entries provided by mothers, all statistical analyses were conducted on percentages of codes over total number of entries.

Results

The first analyses were conducted to determine possible relationships between maternal years of education, number of children, and length of participation, as well as between these variables and literacy activities. As number of children was not significantly correlated to any variable it was removed from future analyses. A moderate significant correlation was obtained between maternal years of education and length of participation ($r=.35$, $p=.01$). Mothers in the higher education group attended more instructional cycles ($M=4.29$, $SD=2.04$) than mothers in the lower education group [$M=2.97$, $SD=1.29$, $t(56)=3.21$, $p<.003$]. Because of this significant difference, multivariate analyses of covariance (MANCOVA), using general linear models for unbalanced designs were conducted. These analyses used length of participation as a covariate, and maternal education as an independent variable. We have divided the presentation of results into two sections, the first related to the number of literacy activities reported by mothers and the second related to the types of literacy activities reported by mothers.

Number of Literacy Activities Reported

As presented in Table 2, during each cycle, mothers provided an average of 20 entries, with approximately two activities per entry. Almost half of the entries per cycle were literacy-related and half of the activities within each entry were literacy events.

Table 2

Means and Standard Deviations for All Quantitative Measures (n=69)

Measures of Literacy Reports	M	SD
Cycles or semesters (#)	3.63	1.82
Entries per cycle (#)	20.73	11.68
Number of activities per entry (#)	1.66	.83
Literacy entries per cycle (%)	46.70	42.18
Literacy activities per entry (%)	50.50	31.28

MANCOVA results showed that length of participation did not significantly influence quantitative measures of literacy. A significant overall trend for maternal education was obtained on two measures: the percentage of entries per cycle that were literacy-related and the percentage of activities within each entry that were literacy-related [$F(2, 65)=2.72, p=.07$]. Mothers in the high-education group tended to focus a significantly higher percentage of entries on literacy-related activities than did mothers in the low-education group. In addition, of the activities reported within each entry, a significantly higher percentage of those reported by high-education mothers were literacy related (see Table 3). We wondered if these results could be explained by differences in writing abilities and the possibility that low-education mothers might compose shorter entries, thereby recording fewer activities than high-education mothers. A post-hoc t-test analysis comparing the number of activities recorded per entry revealed no significant differences. Both low and high-education mothers each recorded approximately two activities per entries ($M=1.57, SD=0.95$, for the low-education group; $M=1.75$, $SD=0.67$, for the high-education group). Differences were in types of activities reported, not in the number of activities reported.

Types of Literacy Activities Reported

We also examined the types of literacy events reported by all participants. Table 4 presents the percentages of types of literacy activities reported. The percentages are based on the total number of literacy and nonliteracy-related entries. Mothers reported more Literacy for the Sake of Teaching or Learning and more Literacy in Leisure activities than Daily Literacy activities. As seen in Table 4, within each general category, mothers reported substantially more activities directly related to their children's schooling and learning than to their own. They also reported more frequently on book reading with their children than on their own. Further, their report of book reading with their children and on their own exceeded their report of entertainment-related literacy activities.

Table 5 presents the breakdown of all literacy categories by mothers' educational levels. Multivariate analyses of covariance showed a significant effect only

Table 3

Means (Adjusted for Length of Participation) for Quantitative Measures by Education Group

	Low-Education (N=35)	High-Education (N=34)	Main Group Differences
Quantitative Measures	*M (SD)*	*M (SD)*	*F* Values
% Literacy entries per cycle	36.60 (20.17)	57.09 (55.10)	3.63**
% Literacy activities per entry	42.53 (24.22)	58.70 (35.08)	2.56*

*$p<.05$. **$p<.10$

Table 4

Mean Percentages of Types of Literacy Reported (n=69)

Type of Literacy Activities	M	SD
Teaching/Learning Literacy	3.53	13.80
Mothers' Schooling/Learning	3.56	4.50
Children's Schooling/Learning	14.13	6.74
Literacy Reflections	3.02	4.36
Other	0.06	0.39
Daily Literacy	6.45	8.97
Daily Living	1.81	3.39
Information Networks	1.74	6.39
Work and Religion	1.30	3.64
Interpersonal Communication	1.61	2.86
Literacy in Leisure Activities	23.07	19.05
Storybook Time	10.59	11.13
Mothers' Book Reading/Writing	7.50	7.79
Entertainment: Play and TV	4.97	6.74
Other	1.17	2.86

Table 5

Mean Percentages (Adjusted for Length of Participation) for Domains and Types of Literacy Reported by Education

Type of Literacy Activity	Low-Education (N=35) M	(SD)	High-Education (N=34) M	(SD)	Group Main Effects F Values
Teaching/Learning Literacy					
Mothers' Schooling/Learning	2.93	(3.71)	4.14	(5.21)	0.31
Children's Schooling/Learning	10.56	(11.19)	17.81	(13.71)	4.96**
Literacy Reflections	3.81	(4.47)	2.22	(4.13)	2.67*
Other	0.03	(0.21)	0.10	(0.52)	0.50
Daily Literacy					
Daily Living	1.49	(2.11)	2.13	(4.28)	2.21
Information Networks	0.13	(1.47)	3.40	(8.86)	2.81**
Work and Religion	1.35	(4.81)	1.27	(1.86)	1.91
Interpersonal Communication	0.63	(1.77)	2.61	(3.47)	7.15***
Literacy in Leisure Activities					
Storybook Time	9.86	(11.88)	11.34	(10.16)	0.28
Mothers' Book Reading/Writing	6.35	(7.21)	8.69	(8.25)	1.34
Entertainment: Play and TV	4.63	(6.07)	5.33	(7.45)	0.16

$*p<.10.$ $**p\leq.05.$ $***p\leq.01.$

for maternal education on Daily Literacy reports [$F(4, 63)=2.79, p<.05$]; length of participation was not significantly related to Daily Literacy. Differences were found in literacy events related to Interpersonal Communication (e.g., letter writing), and for the use of Information Networks (e.g., reading the newspaper). In both cases, mothers in the high-education group reported engaging in these activities to a greater extent than mothers in the low-education group. It is noteworthy that although Information Networks represented the most reported domain of activity by high-education mothers, it was the least reported among mothers in the low-education group. No differences were found between the education groups in their reports of Daily Living (e.g., writing and reading phone bills) or in literacy activities related to Work or Religion.

Similarly, analyses of covariance of the category Literacy for the Sake of Teaching or Learning showed a significant effect of maternal education on literacy reports [$F(4, 63)=2.78, p<.05$]; length of participation was not significantly related to maternal reports in this category. Mothers in the high-education group reported more on their children's schooling and learning than did mothers in the low-education group. An interesting trend was found: mothers in the low-education group reflected more on their own or their children's literacy achievement than did mothers in the high-education group. No differences were found in mothers' report of their own school and learning activities.

Unlike previous categories, MANCOVA results on Literacy in Leisure Activities showed that maternal education did not have any significant effects. No differences were found in low and high-education mothers' reports of reading with their children, personal reading or writing activities, or other entertainment activities, such as playing games or viewing television. Both groups of mothers reported more frequent Leisure-Related Literacy Activities engaged with their children than on their own. However, a trend was found for length of participation and literacy reports in this category [$F(3, 65)=2.30, p=.09$]. In particular, mothers who participated longer in the program increased their reports on storybook reading with their children [$F(1, 68)=3.99, p<.05$].

Discussion

This study was motivated by our interest in whether current understandings about the ways mainstream and nonmainstream families use literacy in the course of their daily lives are consistent with the uses of literacy in this community of Latino mothers who participate in an intergenerational literacy project, many with low levels of formal education. Following the lead of Taylor and Dorsey-Gaines (1988), we hoped that knowing more about the ways families used literacy in their daily lives would allow us to systematically and appropriately "bring the strengths of home learning into the classrooms of the children that we study and teach" (p. xvii). Using self-report data presented by mothers as part of their daily literacy learning routines, we asked what literacy events the mothers engaged in at home alone and with their children, and whether the number and types of literacy activities differed by levels of maternal education. A preliminary analysis showed a confounding relationship between maternal education and length of participation in the project. Mothers who had higher levels of education participated longer in the literacy program than mothers who had lower levels of education. This led us to conduct multivariate analyses of covariance to control for differences in length of participation. In the section that follows, we summarize our findings as they relate to the number and types of literacy activities reported, and we discuss the ways the findings are consistent or inconsistent with earlier studies.

Number of Literacy Activities Reported

In the course of their own literacy classes, high-education mothers were more likely than low-education mothers to report that they engaged alone or with their children in literacy activities and to enumerate the types of activities. Of importance in this finding is the evidence that low-education mothers did not seem to be limited by the act of writing itself—analyses indicated that they wrote as much as their high-education counterparts. Rather, they differed in what they wrote about. Mothers with lower levels of education were more likely to record nonliteracy-related events than mothers with higher levels of education. As these differences were found with length of participation controlled for, it appears that amount of literacy reported is a factor somewhat resistant to change: either low-education mothers had difficulty changing their family routines to increase their uses of literacy or they had difficulty changing the ways they wrote about and reported their uses of literacy. We wondered, but were unable to determine based on the data, whether high-education mothers were, in fact, engaging in greater amounts of literacy at home or whether they were simply better able to grasp the idea that they were being asked to report on all literacy actions.

Types of Literacy Reported

Looking across all mothers, participants were most likely to report on Literacy in Leisure activities. This category included the domains of Storybook Time, which we used to code all instances of mother-child reading and talking about books and storytelling; mothers' book reading and writing; and all activities related to entertainment and play, including, television viewing, painting or coloring activities, singing and fingerplays. Comparing the two groups, we found no significant differences between the report of Literacy in Leisure activities by level of education and no significant differences in the report of particular activities within the larger domain. High-education and low-education mothers engaged in similar amounts of personal reading and writing, and in similar amounts of entertainment-related literacy activities. In addition, they engaged their children in similar amounts of Storybook Time. It is important to note that length of participation in the ILP had a significant effect on Storybook Time reports. With longer participation, mothers report of reading with their children increased. This finding suggests that the literacy program is successful at encouraging mothers from all educational levels to share books with their children. However, this finding is suggestive, as only ethnographic data would provide us with observational evidence to determine whether mothers are, in fact, reading more with their children at home.

In addition to emphasizing Literacy in Leisure activities, all mothers dedicated time and attention to Literacy for the Sake of Teaching or Learning. Within this general category, we included the domains of Mothers' Schooling and Learning, Children's Schooling and Learning, Viewing for Teaching and Learning, and Literacy Reflections. The data indicate that mothers spent a good deal more time attending to their children's learning than to their own, with low-education mothers reporting more than three times as many child-related activities and high-education mothers reporting more than five times as many child-related activities. When the groups were compared, we found that high-education mothers reported significantly more activities related to their children's schooling and learning than did low-education mothers. Interestingly, it was in this analysis where we uncovered the only finding favoring low-education mothers: they tended to report a higher incidence of Literacy Reflections, a domain we used to capture those entries in which the parent commented on the process of reading and writing. We speculated that their own status as beginning readers and writers and the emphasis within the ILP on self-monitoring behaviors might have prompted them to be more reflective of both their own learning and of their children's.

Finally, we were somewhat surprised by the small incidence among all mothers of reporting on Daily Literacy activities. In this general area, we clustered the domains of Daily Living, Information Networks, Work, Religion, and Interpersonal Communication. When we compared mothers by education level and looked within the larger cluster, we found significant differences in two domains, Interpersonal Communication (e.g., letter writing) and Information Networks (e.g., newspaper and magazine reading), favoring high-education mothers. Since activities in these two domains are largely dependent on reasonable proficiency in reading and writing, these differences were predictable.

Connecting What We Learned with What We Knew

How do these findings fit with what we knew at the start of this study? We knew that in low-income, linguistically and culturally different families, children and their parents use literacy in many different ways. Perhaps the evidence across studies was best summarized in the conclusion Teale (1986) drew: "virtually all children in a literate society like ours have numerous experiences with written language before they ever get to school" (p. 192). Our findings are clearly consistent with this conclusion: all participants reported engagement in some forms of literacy interactions during the course of their family lives. Of particular importance is the fact that although maternal education played a role in some categories of literacy reports, the differences between the two groups of mothers were not overwhelming. This finding lends support to the assertion that literacy is present in the lives of Latino families across socioeconomic and educational levels.

However, beyond this general point of agreement, there were areas of difference in our results. Given the differences in the types of studies that have been done, and particularly in the methodologies (i.e., naturalistic observations versus self-reports), comparisons are made with caution and focus on areas where there are particularly notable differences.

Unlike some earlier studies where researchers found little or no storybook reading in some homes (Heath, 1983; Teale, 1986), mothers reported a generally high incidence of storybook reading. Of particular note was that we found no differences between high-education and low-education mothers in the report of Storytime activities. Low levels of education, and correspondingly low levels of literacy proficiency, apparently did not prevent mothers from engaging their children in Storytime activities. Our results were more closely aligned with those of Delgado-Gaitan (1990) and Delgado-Gaitan and Trueba (1991), who found storybook reading present, though in some cases infrequent, in the homes of the Latino families they observed. In each of these studies, and in ours as well, the findings are explained by the emphasis on instruction and modeling of storybook reading in the family literacy program curriculum, as shown by the significant effect of length of participation on Storybook Time reports. Given the importance of storybook reading as preparation for success in school literacy, these are important and positive outcomes of family literacy intervention programs.

We also found differences in the distribution of activities across the various literacy domains. Again, perhaps because of the context of the study and because of the particular data source, mothers reported higher incidences of both Literacy in Leisure activities and Literacy for the Sake of Teaching or Learning than were observed in Teale's naturalistic study. One could argue that the differences are interesting precisely because of the context of the study. In the present setting where parents were explicitly and repeatedly encouraged to read and write with their children, they frequently reported doing so. As well, they were explicitly and repeatedly encouraged and taught how to support their children's school learning, and predictably, they reported doing so with higher levels of frequency than those observed in earlier studies. Several researchers have argued that undereducated parents have the interest in and the capability to support their children's academic learning, but are seldom given explicit guidelines or viewed by teachers as a learning resource (Delgado-Gaitan & Trueba, 1991; Gallimore & Goldenberg, 1993). Our findings, and in particular the evidence that the longer their period of participation, the greater their engagement in family storybook reading, provide support for that claim.

We considered our finding of a very small incidence of reports of Daily Literacy activities from two perspectives. First, we wondered if this domain of literacy was simply underreported, that perhaps parents did not understand that activities such as reading mail, paying bills, and snipping and using coupons represented literacy and were activities they were expected to record. We reviewed what typically happens in the family literacy classes, reviewed the charts and posters that are displayed in classrooms as models for what parents should consider and think about, and we concluded that this explanation was unlikely. Then, we reflected upon the findings that have been reported by some researchers in particular communities. We recalled that Heath (1983), for example, reported that

> Trackton children are enveloped in different kinds of social interactions. They are held, fed, talked about, and rewarded for nonverbal, and later verbal, renderings of events they witness. Trackton adults respond favorably when children show they have come to know how to use language to show correspondence in function, style, configuration, and position between two different things or situations. (p. 120)

Similarly, Purcell-Gates (1996) challenged the notion that "literacy is literally interwoven into all people's lives in a literate society such as ours. Some families in this study, in fact, lived busy and satisfying lives with very little mediation by print" (p. 425). In considering the high incidence of Literacy for the Sake of Teaching or Learning and the low incidence of Daily Literacy, it seemed that, in these households, much of the print literacy that occurred might have been stimulated by the mothers' participation in the ILP and its expectation that parents would take an active role in their own learning and that of their children. As such, the ILP might have changed the roles parents played in their own and their children's learning, but not intruded upon established daily living routines.

Finally, and perhaps most important, results of this study point to variations among a seemingly homogeneous group of mothers—Latino mothers participating in a literacy project. Mothers' years of education significantly influenced literacy reports in three domains: Children's Schooling and Learning, Information Networks, and Interpersonal Communication. For instance, mothers with higher levels of education reported more literacy activities, such as helping children with homework, reading the newspaper, writing and reading personal letters, than mothers with lower levels of education. These findings corroborate those of previous ethnographic studies (Reese et al., 1995; Rodríguez, 1999) demonstrating that uses and types of home literacy activities vary depending on the parents' educational background. Numerous large-scale studies and surveys point to parental education as an important factor influencing children's success in school (Powell, 1995; Zill, Collins, West, & Hausken, 1995). However, as this and other studies show, parental education might lead to distinct uses of literacy in the home and it is this use that might differentially prepare children for success in school (Khandke, Pollit, & Gorman, 1999; Reese et al., 1995).

Further, we found that although lower education mothers participated successfully in the literacy project, they did so for shorter periods of time than their higher education peers. Specifically, mothers in the higher education group participated an average of one more instructional cycle than mothers in the lower education group. The positive relationship between maternal education and length of participation in the literacy project raises a concern about the effectiveness of our literacy program, and perhaps other programs, in retaining and serving mothers from varied educational backgrounds. Most of the lower education mothers in this study were beginning English language learners and beginning readers and writers. Although the learning context is specifically designed to encourage learners to use their first language to support their learning of English literacy, and Spanish-language discussion groups are common during reading and writing activities, all text that is read is in English. It may be that the dual focus—acquiring both English language and English literacy at the same time—is less effective when the adult is learning to read and write for the first time. Alternatively, the participation of low-education mothers may have been influenced by factors such as group size, class heterogeneity, and skill emphasis (i.e., word study, comprehension). Our explanations are only speculative, and this is clearly a finding that deserves careful and systematic study.

Cognizant of the limitations inherent in self-report data, we understand the need to be cautious in drawing conclusions based on our findings. According to our data, these households differed in important ways from those that have been studied previously. If confirmed, the findings would suggest important implications for the ways elementary and adult education teachers plan curriculum for adult and child learners and attempt to bridge the gap between home and school learning. An important next step, therefore, is the collection of naturalistic, observational data to confirm the findings.

References

Delgado-Gaitan, C. (1990). *Literacy for empowerment: The role of parents in children's education*. New York: Falmer.

Delgado-Gaitan, C. (1996). *Protean literacy: Extending the discourse on empowerment*. New York: Falmer.

Delgado-Gaitan, C., & Trueba, H. (1991). *Crossing cultural borders: Education for immigrant families in America*. New York: Falmer.

Gallimore, R., & Goldenberg, C. (1993). Activity settings of early literacy: Home and school factors in children's emergent literacy. In E. Forman, N. Minick, & A. Stone (Eds.), *Education and mind: The integration of institutional, social, and developmental processes* (pp. 315–335). Oxford, England: Oxford University Press.

Heath, S. B. (1983). *Ways with words*. Cambridge, England: Cambridge University Press.

Khandke, V., Pollit, E., & Gorman, K. S. (1999, April). *The role of maternal literacy in child health and cognitive development in rural Guatemala*. Paper presented at the meeting of the Society for Research in Child Development. Albuquerque, NM.

Moll, L. C., Amanti, C., Neff, D., & Gonzalez, N. (1992). Funds of knowledge for teaching: Using a qualitative approach to connect homes and classrooms. *Theory into Practice, 31*, 132–141.

Powell, J. (1995). Parents as early partners in the literacy process. Paper presented at the meeting of the National Conference on Family Literacy. (ERIC Document Reproduction Service No. ED 407 080)

Purcell-Gates, V. (1995). *Other people's words: The cycle of illiteracy*. Cambridge, MA: Harvard University Press.

Purcell-Gates, V. (1996). Stories, coupons, and the TV Guide: Relationships between home literacy experiences and emergent literacy knowledge. *Reading Research Quarterly, 31*, 406–428.

Reese, L., Goldenberg, C., Loucky, J., & Gallimore, R. (1995). Ecocultural context, cultural activity, and emergent literacy: Sources of variation in home literacy experiences of Spanish-speaking children. In S. W. Rothstein (Ed.), *Class, culture, and race in American schools: A handbook* (pp. 199–224). Westport, CT: Greenwood.

Rodríguez, M. V. (1999). Home literacy experiences of three young Dominican children in New York City: Implications for teaching in urban settings. *Educators for Urban Minorities, 1,* 19–31.

Taylor, D., & Dorsey-Gaines, C. (1988). *Growing up literate: Learning from inner-city families.* Portsmouth, NH: Heinemann.

Teale, W. H. (1986). Home background and young children's literacy development. In W. H. Teale & E. Sulzby (Eds.), *Emergent literacy: Writing and reading* (pp. 173–206). Norwood, NJ: Ablex.

Valdés, G. (1996). *Con respeto: Bridging the differences between culturally diverse families and schools.* New York: Teachers College Press.

Vásquez, O., Pease-Álvarez, L., & Shannon, S. M. (1994). *Pushing boundaries: Language and culture in a Mexicano community.* New York: Cambridge University Press.

Wells, G. (1985). Preschool literacy-related activities and success in school. In D. R. Olson, N. Torrance, & A. Hildyard (Eds), *Literacy, language, and learning: The nature and consequences of reading and writing* (pp. 299–255). Cambridge, England: Cambridge University Press.

Zill, N., Collins, M., West, J., & Hausken, E. G. (1995). *School readiness and children's developmental status.* (ERIC Document Reproduction Service No. ED 389 475)

Teachers Connecting and Communicating with Families for Literacy Development

Patricia Ruggiano Schmidt

Le Moyne College

Michael's mother won't come to school to talk. Why would she share her life story or listen to mine?

My child's family is from India. They seem shy. They certainly won't want to talk about their lives.

Talk to families about their life stories. How do you begin? How will this help their children's literacy development?

What does my life story have to do with home/school communication?

I don't even know if Lani's parents speak English. How can I talk to them?

These elementary and secondary teachers expressed their misgivings about new ways to communicate with families from diverse backgrounds in urban and suburban settings. Typical of many teachers in our nation's schools, they have little understanding of the complexity of the family life of children from ethnic and cultural minority backgrounds (Gonzalez et al., 1995). Many teachers have tried newsletters, notes, and parent conferences, but have had little success in creating relationships that foster the home/school communication necessary for literacy development (Edwards, 1999).

One recognized factor that appears to inhibit dialogue is the power relationship that exists between schools representing the dominant White culture and families from minority backgrounds (Banks, 1994; Nieto, 1996). This power relationship often intimidates families, thus preventing them from contributing ideas that might help the teacher work more effectively with students. Furthermore, this intimidation may give the teacher an impression that the families do not understand or do not care about their children's literacy development (Cummins, 1986; Edwards, 1999; Faltis, 1993; Nieto, 1996). Therefore, examining how to help teachers and families connect in ways that eliminate power relationships is important to the education of children from ethnic and cultural minorities. The purpose of this study was to demonstrate how five teachers began to communicate with families from minority backgrounds.

Related Literature

The sociocultural perspective proposes that strong connections between home and school are critical in the literacy development of students from ethnic

National Reading Conference Yearbook, 49, pp. 194–208.

and cultural minority backgrounds (Dyson, 1993; Heath, 1983; Reyhner & Garcia, 1989; Trueba, Jacobs, & Kirton, 1990; Vygotsky, 1978). In order to achieve these connections, researchers refer to culturally responsive pedagogy (Osborne, 1996), culturally relevant teaching (Ladson-Billings, 1995), community collaboration (McCaleb, 1994), joinfostering (Faltis, 1993), and parent stories (Edwards, 1999) as means for bridging home and school. However, widespread implementation of these ideas has not occurred as there is little understanding of the person to person, unstructured conversations that occur between families and teachers as they promote relationships that make strong communication possible (Edwards, 1996, 1999). This is further complicated by the fact that most teachers are females from European-American, middle-class backgrounds and have little experience with diverse groups of people (Paley, 1989; Pattnaik, 1997) and are unaware of the ways in which these families survive in the dominant white culture (Gonzalez et al., 1995). Additionally, they have little knowledge of how to reach out and begin to converse with families from diverse ethnic and cultural minorities (Cochran-Smith, 1995; Nieto, 1996; Schmidt, 1998a, 1999).

Recently, five European-American teachers, who work with urban and suburban elementary and secondary students, began the one-to-one communication necessary to make strong connections with families. They participated in a process associated with the model known as the ABC's of Cultural Understanding and Communication (Schmidt, 1998b) as part of a multicultural literacy course. The teachers' experiences with the ABC's model fostered personal relationships with families that helped both teachers and families understand their students and encourage their literacy development. The power relationships that often develop between teachers and families seemed to disappear.

Methods

This study in the qualitative tradition (Bogdan & Biklen, 1994) used the ABC's model as a framework for the development of home/school communication. Teachers completed the following steps in the ABC's process:

1. An autobiography was written in detail, including key life events related to education, family, religious tradition, recreation, victories and defeats.
2. The biography of a family member of a student who is culturally different from the teacher was written from in-depth unstructured interviews (Spradley, 1979) that include key life events.
3. A cross-cultural analysis of similarities and differences between the life stories was charted (Spindler & Spindler, 1987).
4. Analyses of cultural differences were examined in writing. The teacher reflected on the differences that caused discomfort and admiration.
5. Modifications for classroom practice and communication plans for literacy development and home/school connections based on the preceding process were designed.

After completing their own autobiographies, teachers selected families of students in their classes who were ethnic or cultural minorities. Most teachers began by phoning parents and explaining that they were completing assignments for a college class on effective communication between home and school. They asked if they could meet at least three times at mutually agreed upon locations for the purpose of sharing stories about school experiences.

Informants

Five teachers in a multicultural literacy class of 20 volunteered to be involved in this study, in lieu of a research paper. They selected the family member of a student in their classes who they believed offered academic or emotional challenges. For the entire semester, a father, a grandmother, and three mothers participated in this home/school communication project.

Data Collection and Analyses

Phone calls were made, and notes and letters exchanged before fall curriculum nights and conferences. During the first weeks of school, several teachers visited students' homes; one family member came to school. Data were collected from teachers' journal entries, ABC's assignments, and teacher audiotaped interviews with families. As the course professor, I kept a weekly journal of teacher reports recorded after the multicultural literacy classes.

Data were analyzed from the beginning of the process, using the constant comparative method (Glaser & Strauss, 1967). Each teacher worked with me in the coding and analysis of his or her data. We then met as a group to discuss the dialogue between home and school, sharing patterns of conversations and behaviors. These patterns formed the final themes: (a) teachers discovered that the families wanted to share their stories in the greatest detail; (b) the families were pleased to ask many questions and make positive comments about their similarities and differences when teachers shared their stories; (c) families had many questions and comments which revealed concerns for their children's education; (d) teachers found it easy to ask for help from families in order to understand students' specific behaviors, and families responded with successful ideas for the home and classroom; and (e) the students' dialogue with teachers and classmates and involvement in literacy activities significantly increased.

Results

Each set of informants below, is described under a pseudonym, with their specific responses to home and school communication, and student literacy learning.

Mrs. Diamond, Michael, and Michael's Mother

Mrs. Diamond was in her third year of teaching when she began this project.

She taught English, math, science, social studies, and Spanish to eight students, aged 12–16, in an alternative education program that is the last stop for children before juvenile homes. Six students were from European-American backgrounds, two were half European American and half Native American, and all were from lower socioeconomic levels.

Mrs. Diamond selected Michael, who was 13 years of age and had problems with disruptive language and behaviors. He had negative attitudes toward women and was ashamed of his mother, because of her weight problem. "I don't want people to see her. She's so fat." He saw his father annually when he visited the Algonquin Reservation, something his mother dreaded, since "he gets worse before he goes and comes back out of control." Michael comprehended most reading material at his level, but had poor written expression.

Home and school communication. Mrs. Diamond began her dialogue with Michael's mother by phoning for help. Mrs. Diamond explained that she was working on a college assignment about parent-teacher communication. She asked to visit the home, but Michael's mother immediately refused and volunteered to come to school. Knowing Michael's attitude toward his mother, Mrs. Diamond was surprised and wondered if this meeting would actually take place.

Family stories. The two began their discussion a few days later, after school, after students left the building. Mrs. Diamond started by sharing her autobiography with family pictures and explained the ABC's assignment. Within 10 minutes, Michael's mother began sharing her own life in great detail. She told about her early schooling and the frustrations in her life, especially the separation from Michael's father, an Algonquin who lived in Canada. She talked of the alcoholism in his family, the mental illness in her own family, and the domestic abuse endured on both sides of the family. She added that a few years ago she had traced the family tree back to England in an attempt to understand family problems.

Questions for teacher. Mrs. Diamond discovered that Michael's mother had many questions to ask about her own life. So, she shared many of her own victories and challenges. Mrs. Diamond was able to tell of her own husband's experiences with childhood abuse and how professional help had assisted in breaking the cycle. Soon Michael's mother began to trust Mrs. Diamond. After each meeting, she initiated the next, "When do we meet again? You are helping me understand my son, so I can help him. You are honest with me."

Student's education. Michael's mother and Mrs. Diamond discussed Michael's difficult early school years. When Michael was in second grade, they sneaked out of the house on the reservation, and came to the United States. Their new life was successful at first, because they both liked the second-grade teacher. She cared about Michael and kept his mother informed. Michael's mother continued, "Third, through sixth grades were bad news. The teachers didn't care and were so controlling. Michael repeated sixth grade and then they put him in alternative schools. It has been bad. He doesn't care most of the time. They don't understand me or my son!"

Teacher and family working together. Mrs. Diamond stated:

> My comfort level and openness allowed Michael's mother to share intimate details. These helped me understand Michael, so that I could work more sensitively with him. At first, Michael seemed indifferent to our meetings and then he became down right hostile. He made negative comments and acted out towards me and others. I think he was nervous about his mother sharing so much with me. I told him that if he wanted, he could ask me questions too. This invitation seemed to change his attitude and bring him into a positive frame of mind.

After the sixth meeting, Mrs. Diamond wanted to take Michael and his mother out to supper as a way of saying thanks for their help in understanding the importance of home/school communication, but Michael's mother refused and stated, "I don't want to be seen in a nice place, but come to our house for dinner." Mrs. Diamond agreed with a stipulation that she bring her famous homemade lasagna as the main course. Michael's mother worked long hours at a local factory so this was a welcome compromise.

Student's literacy activities. Mrs. Diamond reported that Michael's writing became distinctly different, shortly after the meetings began. In the past, he dreaded journal writing and often did not participate. Now, he wrote about personal experiences related to family and his interests. Mrs. Diamond also implemented her own version of the ABC's model in the class. The students wrote their autobiographies and interviewed each other. They also created simplified versions of their life stories and shared them with a third-grade class across the hall. The third graders read the stories aloud and with the older students' help, illustrated them to create books. This provided a model for the third grade to write autobiographies and books.

Mrs. Diamond explained the dramatic change in Michael:

> At the beginning of the school year, we had a poor relationship at best, but this has changed! Michael is so positive in the classroom. He seems to have taken control of himself, simply because he knows how much his mother and I care about him.

Mr. DeGenaro, Rishab, and Rishab's Father

Mr. DeGenaro began his first full-time position in an alternative ninth-grade English class in a suburban Northeastern school. Courses were created for students who needed to pass ninth-grade English; they met for 90 minutes two evenings a week. In one of the classes, 15 European-American males, 2 African-American males, 1 Indian-American male, and 3 European-American females from lower socioeconomic levels were enrolled.

Mr. DeGenaro chose Rishab, a student from India. Rishab did not have friends and rarely volunteered comments or questions in class. He appeared to be serious and attentive, but his work was often incorrect. Mr. DeGenaro was curious to find out about Rishab's family history.

Home and school communication. Mr. DeGenaro nervously approached Rishab's father after school one evening to ask for help in completing an assignment for a college class. He told him that the purpose of the assignment was to learn about communication between home and school with families from different cultural backgrounds. To Mr. DeGenaro's surprise, Rishab's father agreed immediately. They decided to meet in Rishab's home to begin the interviews. These took place in a meticulously neat apartment around a dining room table with no other family members present. Each time, Rishab's mother and brother greeted Mr. DeGenaro, but did not become part of the interview process.

Family stories. Mr. DeGenaro described Rishab's father as hungry to discuss his life story and culture. He talked about growing up in India and the close family ties. "One plate, one family. That's our custom. It doesn't mean we have a scarcity of plates. We eat together as a brother, not a separate person, every day. It's about closeness." His wife and he came together as an arranged marriage and had their two sons, Rishab and Raji. They immigrated to the United States because they heard it was the land of opportunity. Rishab's father had received an excellent education from the University of Bombay and believed he could be successful in the United States. The family spoke their native Gujrati at home, but encouraged the sons to speak, read, and write in perfect English.

Questions for teacher. As the interviews progressed, Mr. DeGenaro shared his own life with Rishab's father, telling about his family and early struggles with education. This opened the way for Rishab's father to share his ideas and ask questions about Mr. DeGenaro's life. Mr. DeGenaro revealed, "When I answered questions about my life, I somehow began to gain a greater understanding of my own life as well as Rishab's life." They both discussed family worship and rituals, the value of education and the importance of family meals.

Student's education. Rishab's father prided himself in being what he called "a hands-on parent." He liked to help his sons with homework and encouraged them to study and work long hours. He explained to them, "Although religion is first in our lives, education should be a first priority while young. Religion is always there. Religion can be practiced at a later age. Now is the age to learn."

Rishab's father had some difficulties with his children's educational experiences. When Rishab was in fifth grade, the school psychologist asked to have him tested for learning problems. When the test results came back, the verdict was that Rishab had a learning disability. However, the special education team would not share the test results with Rishab's family. "I don't understand why they hide. They are not telling me the right reasons for my son's troubles." Since Rishab's father did not believe that the school communicated with him, he would not give permission for special help. This caused him to emphasize homework on time and excellent performance in school. He told his sons, "The teachers are your bosses. Take your work seriously."

Teacher and family working together. Mr. DeGenaro had no idea about the learning disability testing. He also did not know that Rishab spoke another language in the home, something that could account for his slower English literacy development. Therefore, Mr. DeGenaro asked Rishab's father for help in understanding how to best work with his son. The father clearly stated, "When Rishab says, 'I guess I understand,' this means he doesn't understand for sure." Mr. DeGenaro explained that he only gave homework for practice, not for new material or ideas not clearly understood. Since Rishab seemed to say that he understood, Mr. DeGenaro assumed that he did. Therefore, homework assignments showed erratic achievement and were sometimes not handed in. Rishab's father did not realize this was happening. From this information, Mr. DeGenaro and Rishab's father decided that Rishab would not get homework until he could independently demonstrate his understanding in class. Mr. DeGenaro would communicate with Rishab's father about specific difficulties, and the father would also try to help Rishab.

Student's literacy activities. This piece of information about Rishab's statement, "I guess I understand," made a dramatic difference. Mr. DeGenaro began to look at Rishab differently. He noticed that Rishab liked to draw ornate designs related to Indian art. So Mr. DeGenaro concentrated on Rishab's reading comprehension and written expression through reading, writing, and drawing to describe key scenes in short stories. Rishab, after reading and discussing a story in class, would draw a particular incident or character. This allowed him to rehearse the writing he would complete in class on the following day. Mr. DeGenaro asked Rishab's father to ask questions about Rishab's drawings and reading. When Rishab completed drafts of his writing in class, he would share them with his father. This evolved into another means for exchange between home and school and encouraged accountability. As a result, Rishab showed some enthusiasm for his work, since the pressure was off. Rishab's father became more conscious of his son's literacy development. And Mr. DeGenaro started seeing real improvement in Rishab's reading, writing, listening, and speaking. Finally, Rishab began to volunteer questions and comments in class and on occasion, smile.

Mrs. Brown, Natoya, and Natoya's Mother

Mrs. Brown reentered the teaching profession after staying home for 10 years to raise her children. She was hired to teach pastry arts to 28 students, Grades 10–12, in a vocational high school in the Northeast. Her students came from county high schools and a wide range of socioeconomic levels. They studied with her and worked as interns at local bakeries. Three students were from African-American backgrounds and the rest were from European-American backgrounds. Mrs. Brown chose Natoya's family in order to learn more about African-American culture.

Home and school communication. When Mrs. Brown phoned Natoya's mother, she asked if she would be interviewed to discuss her thoughts on education. Natoya's mother agreed and offered her home as a convenient place. Since they immediately discovered that they were both working mothers as well as graduate students, Friday evenings were considered the best meeting times. During interviews, Natoya and her sister often wandered in and out of the room to plan their Friday nights.

Family stories. Mrs. Brown began the interviews by telling about some of her early life experiences at home and in school. This stimulated Natoya's mother's memories. She recalled how her parents worked together and sacrificed for their children. This same type of sacrifice continued recently when her husband, Natoya's father, took care of the children for several months while she was trained in New York City by her company.

Mrs. Brown and Natoya's mother discovered similarities and differences. Religion, parents, grandparents, country and city living, losses, challenges, and victories were all discussed in detail with great admiration as the end result for both parent and teacher. Mrs. Brown stated, "I liked talking with Natoya's mother. We have much in common with our course work and family work."

Questions for teacher. Natoya's mother was interested in Mrs. Brown's life from the beginning. One of the first interviews revealed that they both had terrifying stories about family members scalded with boiling water. Both discovered that Sunday dinner was a key family event, but that the food on the table was very different. Mrs. Brown and Natoya's mother were both raised by extended families, but Natoya's mother grew up in the country and Mrs. Brown was a "city girl." Questions arose concerning differences and similarities in religion, family communication, and education. The women shared their fears and hopes for their children.

Student's education. Natoya's mother was concerned about Natoya's math and reading and lack of consistent motivation that had sent her to summer school. "Natoya doesn't try when she's not interested. If she doesn't like it, she won't do it. Math word problems are very difficult for her." Natoya's mother also worried about social aspects in the school. There had been confrontations, such as name calling and physical attacks by White students.

Teacher and family working together. Mrs. Brown and Natoya's mother decided that Natoya would be encouraged to study with her mother in the evenings, since both needed to complete school work. Mrs. Brown also increased the use of word problems and reading and writing in her class. She decided that students would keep journals and read them in class. Additionally, with the math teacher's help, Mrs. Brown helped students create and solve word problems for the pastry class and required in the state's high school math curriculum.

Students' literacy activities. The home visits seemed to have a dramatic impact on Natoya's achievement. Her reading, writing, and math understandings immediately improved in class and on tests. Her teachers and family believed that this was due to her renewed interest in school, encouraged by her teachers' work and family involvement. Additionally, no racial incidents occurred within recent months. As Mrs. Brown explained, "She is comfortable in my room and knows I am an advocate for her. Natoya is acting like a capable, interested student."

Miss Brighten, Shaniqua, and Shaniqua's Grandmother

Miss Brighten began her second year as a music teacher in a suburban junior high school, Grades 7–9. She taught music appreciation and chorus to three hundred students, most from middle to lower socioeconomic levels. About 3% of the students were from minority backgrounds. Miss Brighten selected Shaniqua, a seventh-grade African-American student and her family, for the home/school communication project. She noticed Shaniqua, because she had a bubbly positive attitude, but no friends. Shaniqua was ignored by all students as if invisible. Miss Brighten wondered how this adolescent could maintain such a positive demeanor when no one seemed to care about her. She was average academically and struggled in math.

Home and school communication. Miss Brighten called Shaniqua at home and discovered that her grandmother was raising her. She asked to visit them to learn more about Shaniqua and her family and to help her with school. The neighborhood where Shaniqua lived was 50% African American and 50% Latino and European American. It bordered a mid-sized city in the Northeast. On her first visit, Miss Brighten was uncomfortable wearing her professional dress and felt as though she was intruding on the neighborhood. People stared from their porches and yards as she stepped from her car.

Family stories. Miss Brighten began by telling about her own life as a teen. She described some of the awkward times socially and academically due to a weight problem. She also told stories about her family. When Miss Brighten told her stories, Shaniqua's grandmother began to share her life and Shaniqua's. She explained their strong church affiliation and involvement in the gospel choir and spiritual gatherings. She also proudly played choir recordings.

Miss Brighten interviewed Shaniqua's grandmother five times and was invited to dinner and grocery shopping in the neighborhood. She realized that grandmother was an honored member of the community who greeted all by name as they passed her on the way to the store. She often stopped to talk with individuals and introduced Miss Brighten as Shaniqua's special music teacher.

Questions for teachers. Grandmother asked Miss Brighten about her education and life. Then she wanted to know about Shaniqua's middle school experiences. Miss Brighten talked about Shaniqua's lack of focus on studies and need for help in math and English. She also commented and questioned, "She appears to be happy and positive. Does she have friends in church?" Shaniqua's grandmother explained that Shaniqua had a wonderful social life at church, but probably needed to concentrate on her schoolwork.

Student's education. Shaniqua's grandmother talked about the social and academic difficulties in Shaniqua's early schooling. She never learned times tables or division and on a daily basis, had encountered racial insults. Grandmother helped her deal with the hurts by teaching her to write about them. As a result, Shaniqua regularly wrote letters to her grandmother to share her painful experiences. Grandmother saved all of the letters and gave them to Miss Brighten to read.

Teacher and family working together. Miss Brighten, with grandmother's permission, shared information with Shaniqua's math and English teachers. The English teacher seemed to appreciate Shaniqua's written expression, but was concerned with "atrocious grammar." Shaniqua's math teacher realized that Shaniqua did not have the basics, such as knowledge of the multiplication tables. Shaniqua's grandmother agreed to help Shaniqua by reserving homework time every evening before church. Miss Brighten highlighted Shaniqua's musical abilities by including African-American songs in the school choir. She also decided to help Shaniqua with math and grammar during study hall and after school.

Students' literacy activities. Shaniqua came to Miss Brighten's room on a daily basis to practice multiplication, and division. She also brought drafts of her writing and stories to be read for English class. Other students began joining in to get help from Miss Brighten; an inclusive community developed. Shaniqua was thrilled to be part of a group. Student conversations about classes and after school activities naturally took place and were facilitated by Miss Brighten.

Shaniqua's math and English teachers noticed a complete turn-around in her work and realized that she had the capabilities to learn quickly and easily. Shaniqua's grandmother was pleased with the change in focus toward academics and emphatically stated, "That homework time has to be!"

Miss Clarity, Lani, and Lani's Sister

Miss Clarity was a tenured teacher with 5 years experience in an urban school. Sixty percent of the children were from European-American backgrounds, 30% from Latino and African-American backgrounds, 10% were new arrivals to the United States from Southeast Asia, Ukraine, and Middle East. Sixty percent of the children were from lower socioeconomic levels and qualified for free or reduced breakfast and lunch. The school had been selected as a career exploration and technology center and had extra money for computers, after school programs, and teaching assistants.

Miss Clarity selected Lani from her fourth-grade class, a child born in the United States, whose family emigrated from Jerusalem several years ago. Miss Clarity had no contact with the family and wanted to learn what the family expected from the school. Lani also interested Miss Clarity, because she appeared extremely confident and reserved for a child her age. Lani always wore a head and neck scarf, known as the hijab, but had not been the focus of ridicule. She observed students at play or in conversation and rarely entered into the social circles, but was always offered opportunities to join in group activities by the children. She listened attentively in class and quietly completed her work. She appeared to be more like a little woman than a child.

Home and school communication. Lani's older sister came to the school open house in early September and stated that she was the family representative.

Miss Clarity asked Lani's sister if she could be interviewed about the family culture and explained that she wanted to learn more about the family in order to help Lani with her education. Lani's sister said that she needed permission and requested that Miss Clarity come to their home to meet her mother.

After Miss Clarity's visit to the home, Lani's mother and sister invited her to their mosque. Miss Clarity agreed to go and spent several hours praying with Lani's mother and sister. The interviews began soon after, but Miss Clarity was required to promise that Lani's father would not know about this. "He believes women should not be educated."

Family stories. Lani's sister granted many hours of taped interviews and shared many artifacts in Miss Clarity's fourth-grade class. Among the prized visuals was a videotape of a cousin's Muslim wedding. Also, Miss Clarity was told that Lani was not going to go to high school or college. She would have a husband selected for her by age 15 or 16, and then would be married and bear children. Therefore, Lani's intelligence and potential in a career must not be explored.

When Miss Clarity told the story of her family and how brothers and sisters were encouraged to discover their talents and pursue their goals, Lani's sister expressed sadness. Her father had pulled her out of school when she questioned why she could not wear bell-bottom jeans.

For reading material, Lani's home had the Koran and other Arabic religious books only; the family usually spoke Arabic in the house.

Questions for teacher. Lani's sister wanted to help Lani and herself. She saw Miss Clarity as a person who might help, so she was extremely interested in the school. She asked, "Could I help in your classroom? I am stuck at home waiting for my father to find a husband."

Student's education. Lani's education was not a family priority. She would be married, have children and tend the home. Her brothers also would not go on to college since they would work in the family businesses. The family expected the children to read and write English and understand mathematics. This learning was for survival in this country. Their Arabic customs and traditions would be taught in the home and mosque. Lani's purpose was to maintain these customs and traditions.

Teacher and family working together. Miss Clarity helped Lani share her culture, by encouraging her to bring in artifacts and ideas related to her customs and traditions. The family willingly allowed this and were pleased that their ideas were being reinforced. Miss Clarity hoped that Lani's love of learning would be encouraged and that an appreciation of diversity would take hold. Since the school had a diverse population, it offered many opportunities to study ethnic and cultural minorities through guest speakers, videos, literature, field trips, and class celebrations.

Student's literacy activities. Lani has become more involved with classmates since the interviews with her sister. She shares her family culture with the class and proudly answers their questions. She writes more fluently and asks questions related to her reading material. Finally, Lani can be seen on the playground joining in games and talking privately with friends. However, Miss Clarity had concerns about Lani, "What will become of her? Will she ever be able to know her learning potential? How can she survive in her family or in our country if she experiences such strong cultural conflicts?"

Discussion

The purpose of this study was to understand how teachers connected with the families of their students through the ABC's of Cultural Understanding and Communication (Schmidt, 1998b). For 15 weeks, the five European-American teachers attempted to learn about their students' families and support their students' literacy development. Even though this study contained many limitations, such as the number of informants and amount of time for data collection, the findings seem significant enough to warrant continued exploration of home and school communication through models such as the ABC's of Cultural Understanding and Communication (Schmidt, 1998b). The teachers demonstrated the importance of building more personal connections with families in order to eliminate the power relationships that often exist between the school and homes of students from cultural and ethnic minorities.

Family Stories: Autobiography and Biography

Teachers must be able to develop collaborative relationships with families from diverse backgrounds in an atmosphere of mutual respect, so that their students will have optimal opportunities for literacy development (Faltis, 1993; Goldenberg, 1987; McCaleb, 1994). We know that when present and future teachers explore their own family stories and those of others who are culturally different, sensitivity begins to develop and an appreciation of differences emerges (Banks, 1994; Florio-Ruane, 1994; Schmidt, 1998a, 1998b; Xu, 2000). However, an imbalance of power exists between highly educated teachers and less educated families, or people whose English is a second language. Additionally, educators may fear saying and doing the wrong things with people who are ethnically and culturally different. But, since teachers are in a power position, they are the logical ones to reach out to families and families have knowledge to share that will assist teachers in motivating and promoting literacy development (Edwards, 1999; Gonzalez et al., 1995; Ogbu, 1983).

The teachers in this study were surprised that families were so eager to share their stories. The teachers were also surprised at the ease with which they shared the details of their own life stories and realized that trust was established by doing so. This trust gave teachers and families opportunities to create ways to enhance student's literacy development. The teachers not only better understood the students and their families, but also gained a self-knowledge that was both gratifying and helpful in understanding their own teaching (Pattnaik, 1997; Schmidt, 1998c, 1999). They explained, "This experience helped us understand not only our se-lected students and families, but also helped us see other students in our classes. We think we are better teachers, because of these experiences."

Questions for Teachers: Similarities and Differences

Traditionally, similarities among people have been celebrated and differences have been ignored (Cummins, 1986; Trueba et al., 1990). However, differences can be examined in a positive manner and can be related to the teachers' and family members' personal histories (Banks, 1994; Britzman, 1986; Ladson-Billings, 1994). Therefore, the interview process can serve as a means for sharing life stories and learning about similarities and differences (Spindler & Spindler, 1987). It is em-powering when families' differences are recognized, whether these be physical, academic, or cultural. Such recognition is part of valuing the family and commu-nity in the classroom (Derman-Sparks, 1992; McCaleb, 1994; Paley, 1989).

In this study, the power relationships seemed to disappear when families felt comfortable asking questions about teachers' lives. Teachers questioned them-selves in the process and carefully answered questions while freely expressing their ideas and experiences. Both teachers and families made positive comments about their similarities and differences. The teachers and family members expressed their thoughts: "Trust was built after a few short visits. The questions and an-swers flowed between us." "We could talk about our lives. We had common ground as human beings."

Literacy Development: Home and School Communication

Families are children's first teachers. When communication between teachers and families becomes regular practice, trust in the teacher and school increases (Ladson-Billings, 1994). When families have opportunities to offer perspectives and information about their children, they may become more actively involved in their children's education (Edwards, 1996; Faltis, 1993; Goldenberg, 1987; Kirton, 1990; McCaleb, 1994; Reyhner & Garcia, 1989; Trueba et al., 1994). Conversations between home and school in this study produced literacy activities that were directly related to the sociocultural perspective (Vygotsky, 1978; Heath, 1983) and met students' specific academic and social needs. The resulting cooperative ef-forts enhanced students' literacy learning. Teachers described what they learned:

> I learned how to interpret his behaviors, thanks to his mother!
>
> The family decided on what types of homework were the most helpful.
>
> Her mother learned about ways to work with her daughter at home.
>
> His cultural artistic expression could be used for story comprehension and rehearsal for written expression.
>
> Thanks to her grandmother's information, we realized how important her music and positive group experiences would be for literacy development.

Know Thyself, Understand Others

In this study, teachers and families made a difference in their students' literacy development when they shared portions of their life stories and created working relationships. The ABC's of Cultural Understanding and Communication, based on the premise, "Know thyself and understand others," acted as the means for promoting the authentic communication necessary to connect home and school.

Author Note

A special thanks to five outstanding teachers Aimee Davis, Marilyn Davis, Joe DeChick, Elizabeth Olivia, and Crystal Ponto. They shared their lives and discovered new relationships that supported their students' literacy learning.

References

Banks, J. A. (1994). *An introduction to multicultural education.* Boston, MA: Allyn & Bacon.

Bogdan, R. C., & Biklen, S. K. (1994). *Qualitative research for education: A theory and method* (2nd ed.). Boston, MA: Allyn & Bacon.

Britzman, D. (1986). Cultural myths in the making of a teacher: Biography and social structure in teacher education. *Harvard Educational Review, 56,* 442–456.

Cochran-Smith, M. (1995). Uncertain allies: Understanding the boundaries of race and teaching. *Harvard Educational Review 65,* 541–570.

Cummins, J. (1986). Empowering minority students: A framework for intervention. *Harvard Educational Review, 56,* 18–36.

Derman-Sparks, L. (1992). *Anti-bias curriculum: Tools for empowering young children.* Sacramento: California State Department of Education.

Dyson, A. H. (1993). *Social worlds of children learning to write in an urban primary school.* New York: Teachers College Press.

Edwards, P. (1996). Creating sharing-time conversations: Parents and teachers work together. *Language Arts, 73,* 344–349.

Edwards, P. (1999). *A path to follow: Learning to listen to parents.* Portsmouth, NH: Heinemann.

Faltis, C. J. (1993). *Joinfostering: Adapting teaching strategies for the multilingual classroom.* New York: Maxwell Macmillan International.

Florio-Ruane, S. (1994). The future teachers' autobiography club: Preparing educators to support learning in culturally diverse classrooms. *English Education, 26,* 52–56.

Glaser, B. J., & Strauss, B. (1967). *The discovery of grounded theory.* Chicago: Aldine.

Goldenberg, C. N. (1987). Low-income Hispanic parents' contributions to their first-grade children's word-recognition skills. *Anthropology and Education Quarterly, 18,* 149–179.

Gonzalez, N., Moll, L. C., Tenery, M. F., Rivera, A., Rendon, P., Gonzales, R., & Amanti, C. (1995). Funds of knowledge for teaching in Latino households. *Urban Education, 29,* 443–470.

Heath, S. B. (1983). *Ways with words: Language life and work in communities and classrooms.* Cambridge, England: Cambridge University Press.

Ladson-Billings, G. (1994). *The dreamkeepers: Successful teachers of African American children.* San Francisco: Jossey-Bass.

Ladson-Billings, G. (1995). Culturally relevant teaching. *Research Journal, 32,* 465–491.

McCaleb, S. P. (1994). *Building communities of learners.* New York: St. Martin's.

Nieto, S. (1996). *Affirming diversity: The sociopolitical context of multicultural education.* New York: Longman.

Ogbu, J. (1983). Minority status and schooling in plural societies. *Comparative Educational Review, 27,* 168–190.

Osborne, A. B. (1996). Practice into theory into practice: Culturally relevant pedagogy for students we have marginalized and normalized. *Anthropology and Education Quarterly, 27,* 285–314.

Paley, V. G. (1989). *White teacher.* Cambridge, MA: Harvard University Press.

Pattnaik, J. (1997). Cultural stereotypes and preservice education: Moving beyond our biases. *Equity and Excellence in Education, 30*(3), 40–50.

Reyhner, J., & Garcia, R. L. (1989). Helping minorities read better: Problems and promises. *Reading Research and Instruction, 28*(3), 84–91.

Schmidt, P. R. (1998a). *Cultural conflict and struggle: Literacy learning in a kindergarten program.* New York: Peter Lang.

Schmidt, P. R. (1998b). The ABC's of cultural understanding and communication. *Equity and Excellence in Education, 31*(2), 28–38.

Schmidt, P. R. (1998c). The ABC's Model: Teachers connect home and school. In T. Shanahan & F. V. Rodriguez-Brown (Eds.), *National Reading Conference Yearbook, 47* (pp. 194–208). Chicago: National Reading Conference.

Schmidt, P. R. (1999). Know thyself and understand others. *Language Arts, 76,* 332–340.

Spindler, G., & Spindler, L. (1987). *The interpretive ethnography of education: At home and abroad.* Hillsdale, NJ: Erlbaum.

Spradley, J. (1979). *The ethnographic interview.* New York: Holt, Rinehart & Winston.

Trueba, H. T., Jacobs, L., & Kirton, E. (1990). *Cultural conflict and adaptation: The case of the Hmong children in American society.* New York: Falmer.

Vygotsky, L. S. (1978). *Mind in society: The development of higher mental processes.* Cambridge, MA: Harvard University Press.

Xu, H. (2000). Preservice teachers integrate understandings of diversity into literacy instruction: An adaptation of the ABC's model. *Journal of Teacher Education, 51*(2), 135–142.

Family and Classroom Predictors of Children's Early Language and Literacy Development

Judith Stoep and Ludo Verhoeven
University of Nijmegen, The Netherlands

Research has made clear that a variety of home and school factors determine children's success in early language and literacy development. With respect to home factors, the cultural and socioeconomic background of people can be seen as an important factor. Wells (1990) has shown that a match between linguistic experience in the children's homes and the linguistic demands in the classroom is essential for academic progress. He found that the degree of experience with literate practices in the home had a positive influence on the understanding of the functions and the mechanisms of literacy. In a longitudinal study by Snow, Barnes, Chandler, Goodman, and Hemphill (1991) on the literacy development of lower socioeconomic children, it was shown that home factors predict various literacy skills. The most powerful predictors of children's literacy development were the literacy environment of the home, the mother's education, and the mother's expectations for the child. Other researchers who reported similar findings are, among others, Dickinson and Tabors (1991) and Baker, Sonnenschein, Serpell, Fernandez-Fein, and Scher (1994). These conclusions have been supported by studies by Sonnenschein, Brody, and Munsterman (1996), who also stressed the importance of family beliefs and parenting practices, and Neuman (1996), who focused on storybook reading.

Scaffolding, a conversational strategy in which people build on and extend each other's statements and contributions, can be seen as a major strategy on the part of the teacher. With reference to a Vygotskian approach to development, it is claimed that cultural tools, such as literacy, are optimally learned in social interaction with others. Through experience with literacy tasks in guided participation with skilled partners, the child's repertoire can be gradually expanded (cf. Gee, 1992). There is now substantial evidence that storybook reading in kindergarten plays a significant role in children's early language and literacy development. There is also good evidence that the quality of teacher behavior during book reading has a great impact on children's learning (Dickinson & Smith, 1994). The responsivity of teachers plays an important role in helping children to gain insight into the functions and structure of oral and written language. Scaffolding can be seen as a crucial element of teacher assistance in children's language and literacy learning. For Dutch kindergarten education, the process of scaffolding is discussed in the teacher's guide of *Schatkist* (Treasure-chest), a multimedia method used to activate emergent literacy skills, story awareness, and vocabulary

National Reading Conference Yearbook, 49, pp. 209–221.

(Mommers & Verhoeven, 1989). Realistic stories and fairy tales form the basis of this methodology, and every story relates to a thematic context that can be used by the teacher to enlarge the child's knowledge while making use of the pupils' perceptions of their environment. Children are invited to ask questions about the story line, the characters, and their motives. When a teacher reads a picture book with the children, the phrasing of the story can be adjusted or enriched as a result of the children's questions and remarks. The thematic teaching material can be used to expand the network of notions in the child's memory.

In previous research, the relative contribution of family and school factors received scant attention. In the present study, an attempt was made to relate relevant predictors from the two institutions on the early language and literacy development of children in The Netherlands. Problems that occur in or are related to actual educational practice form the basis of the study. Similar issues have been addressed in earlier pilot research (Stoep & Verhoeven, 1999). A battery of language and literacy tests was administered to 876 children from various sociocultural backgrounds at the end of kindergarten education. Parents completed questionnaires regarding the language and literacy interaction in the home and their levels of school support. Additionally, the following educational factors were examined: class size, teacher attitudes toward early literacy education, time schedule of language and literacy activities, and registers of teacher behavior during storybook reading. By means of correlational and multiple regression analyses, the relevant family and classroom predictors of the early language and literacy development in Dutch and minority children were searched for. The study attempts to answer the following questions: (a) To what extent do the levels of Dutch language and literacy of minority children differ from that of native Dutch children upon entrance to primary school? (b) How can individual variation in Dutch language and literacy achievement within the two groups of children be explained by home and school variables?

Method

A random group of 876 children with a mean age of 6.0 years was selected from 120 kindergarten classes from 77 schools in the urban parts of The Netherlands. The sample included 461 native Dutch children and 415 minority children. The minority children came from many backgrounds, but Turkish, Moroccan, Surinam, and Antillean children made up the greatest number of minority pupils in the sample. Boys and girls were equally represented in the sample (449 boys, 427 girls). The children participated in the study as a part of a standardization survey of the revised version of the *Dutch Language Test for Children*. At the beginning of the study in September 1996, a large number of Dutch schools were approached by the Dutch National Institute for Test Development (Cito). The schools that agreed to participate provided information on all children enrolled in first-year kindergarten at the beginning of that year. Schools with large proportions of low-SES or minority children were overrepresented. Dutch was spoken in all participating classes, though the minority children came from diverse home-language settings. The home language of many of the children was a language different from Dutch (32%), or some Dutch was spoken in the family (31%). A small number of children used Dutch as often as the native language (11%), in some cases Dutch played a larger part in family communication than the native language (7%), and some families used Dutch exclusively in the home setting (nearly 16%). This paper focuses on Dutch language and literacy development; however, in future analyses the home language of the Turkish and Moroccan children will be taken into account.

A broad range of language skills was assessed by the end of the second year of kindergarten. The *Dutch Language Test for Children* (Verhoeven & Vermeer, 1998) was used to measure auditory discrimination and articulation skill, receptive vocabulary, word definition and word formation, sentence comprehension, sentence imitation, text comprehension, and text production. For all tests, Cronbach's alpha was greater than .85. Also, children's scores on the following emergent literacy tasks were collected: book orientation (based on Clay, 1982), phonemic segmentation, and letter knowledge. These literacy measures were taken from a pilot project conducted with 586 native Dutch and minority children (Stoep & Verhoeven, 1999, 2000), and alphas varied from .87 to .96.

The children's parents were interviewed by means of a questionnaire regarding the amount of books and magazines present in the homes, as well as the literacy practices in the home with a special focus on storybook reading to children, and their interest in and support of children's school activities. Questionnaires were provided in Dutch and the home language of the child; the parents could opt for either one. Approximately half of all parents (270 Dutch, 173 minority) returned the questionnaire. The written questionnaires were distributed with assistance from the student's teachers and were not administered personally, which may explain the proportion of parents involved in the analysis. All measures were sufficiently reliable (alphas varying from .58 to .83). In this article, the following constructs are considered: expectations for the child's reading achievement, the reading climate and frequency of reading at home, parental involvement, aid, and the importance parents attach to their contribution to the child's educational support. We also used measures of socioeconomic status, parental education, and the use of Dutch language in the families. Reported data are self-evaluations; nevertheless, the outcomes show a varied answering pattern with which low and high supportive parents could be identified.

In a small-scale study of 42 families, the validity of the data on literacy practices was examined by relating the parent interview data to their actual reports on more in-depth questions and by an observation of an instance of storybook reading to their child. This closely observed sample was constructed to identify the factors that can be held responsible for success in language ability in Dutch monolingual low- and high-SES groups. Four groups of children were distinguished: Dutch low-SES children with high (5 children) or low language scores (6 children) and high-SES pupils with high (23 children) and low language outcomes (8 children). Parents were brought in through the agency of the teachers, and appointments were made in the parents' homes for an elaborate interview, consisting of nearly 100 detailed questions. Following this conversation (average duration of 45 minutes), a storybook reading interaction between caregiver and child was observed and audiotaped. The data supported the validity of the questionnaires used in this study. Because of the relatively small number of parents involved in the in-depth design, and the detailed character of the parents' answers, the outcomes of this related study are not analyzed using statistical measures; instead, quotes have been taken from the transcripts of the interviews to help explain some of the results of the investigation.

Finally, the teachers were interviewed with regards to their attitudes toward adaptive learning and the time scheduled for reading and literacy activities. An inventory was made of the teachers' teaching experience, number of years working at the school and in education in general, and experience with minority pupils. The proportion of minority children in the classroom served as a group characteristic. Moreover, an observation of storybook reading was carried out in each classroom. The books being read during the book-reading sessions were chosen by the teacher. Four trained observers coded the teacher behaviors on-line before, during, and after the reading of the book. All teacher-child interactions were also tape-recorded. Time-sampling (every 20 seconds) was used for coding teacher behavior during the sessions. An attempt was made to classify the teachers' behaviors along the dimension of cognitive demands. A distinction was made between cognitively challenging talk on the one hand and talk with lower cognitive demands on the other, in conformity with classifications suggested by Dickinson and Keebler (1989) and Morrow, Rand, and Smith (1995). Cognitively challenging talk was defined as open questioning and responsivity on the part of the teacher with a focus on activation of background knowledge, text relations, and the prediction of story line. Interrater reliability for the classification of teacher behavior turned out to be reasonable (Cohen's kappa = .81). The sessions had an average duration of 22 minutes (min. 7:30 minutes, max. 40 minutes).

Correlational statistics, including regression analysis, have been used to evaluate the predictive power of the family and classroom variables on children's language and literacy development. Missing data analysis was performed using EM procedures. ANOVA was used to determine the differences between native Dutch and minority pupils. T-tests were used to evaluate the differences between low- and high-SES parents in the in-depth study.

Results

Variation in Language and Literacy Outcomes

Table 1 gives the mean correct scores on the tasks that were used to measure language and literacy skills of Dutch and minority pupils. ANOVAs were used to determine the differences between the groups. Minority children appear to lag behind significantly on all measures. Differences are most striking in the areas of word formation, naming (receptive vocabulary), and definition and sentence imitation skills. For emergent literacy measures, the discrepancy was less alarming in an absolute sense, but still significant.

Clustering of Language and Literacy Tasks

Principal components factor analysis with VARIMAX rotation validated the distinction between language skills as measured by the Dutch Language Test for Children and the literacy scores, as can be seen in Table 2.

Predictors of Language and Literacy Achievement

Dutch children. Table 3 shows correlations between language and literacy tasks and home and school predictors for Dutch children. Language and literacy measures are connected concepts at the end of kindergarten. Regarded separately, they correlate with varying and corresponding home and school predictors. For Dutch children, both language and literacy skills correlated most strongly with socioeconomic status of the child's family and parental education.

Moreover, family literacy evaluations of reading climate, frequency, and reading expectations for the child were related to student outcomes. Parental aid bears an inverted relationship with the child's success: high scores on language and literacy are correlated with low scores on the amount of help provided by parents

Table 1

Means and Standard Deviations of Subtasks of the Dutch Language Test for Children (TAK) and Emergent Literacy Tasks for Minority (N=415) and Dutch children (N=461)

| | Max. | Minority | | Dutch | |
		M	SD	M	SD
Word formation	24	8.27	5.15	15.24	4.52
Text comprehension	24	12.01	5.47	17.44	4.71
Text production	32	15.11	6.46	17.87	5.77
Sentence imitation	40	19.03	10.09	28.63	8.55
Sentence comprehension easy	42	31.44	5.57	35.59	3.94
Sentence comprehension complex	42	28.74	6.09	33.87	4.94
Articulation	45	42.55	4.01	43.65	2.81
Word definition	45	9.30	5.40	18.75	6.03
Auditory discrimination	50	40.92	11.89	45.82	5.43
Receptive vocabulary	96	40.73	14.89	63.80	14.08
Phonemic segmentation	20	2.87	4.51	4.92	5.39
Book orientation	24	10.69	4.94	13.88	4.15
Letter knowledge	34	4.94	6.86	6.82	7.51

Note. All variables significant.

with educational matters. Parental involvement on the other hand, is associated positively with children's test scores. Language skills of the Dutch children are also related to teacher variables such as time spent on book orientation (self-report), and quality of storybook reading in terms of cognitive challenging content of the interaction (as observed during session). Storybook reading is also related to emergent literacy skills, along with teaching experience and amount of time spent on reading in the classroom (as reported in a classroom log).

Regression analysis showed the variables with the strongest relationships with language abilities and emergent literacy. Parental socioeconomic status and education appear to be the most important determinants of Dutch children's language skills at the brink of formal reading education. Observed teacher behavior contributes to success by focusing on challenging content during storybook interaction, and explicitly spending time on book orientation (from logs). Parental contribution to language skills consists of high reading expectations for the child, parental involvement, and pleasure and intensity of reading at the child's home.

Likewise, education and SES together occur to be the most important determinants of literacy outcomes of the Dutch children. The inclusion of other parental predictors such as expectations for future reading results, educational involvement, and reading frequency adds to the proportion of variance accounted for. Parental aid has a significant effect on literacy results as well, but in a counterproductive manner. Teacher storybook reading time (as reported in the classroom journal), and his or her experience with children from minority groups, account for portions of the variance.

Table 2

Rotated Factor Matrix for Confirmatory Factor Model of Language and Literacy

Test	Factor 1 Language	Factor 2 Literacy
Receptive vocabulary	.80	.24
Sentence comprehension complex	.80	.18
Text comprehension	.78	.21
Sentence imitation	.78	.20
Sentence comprehension easy	.78	.25
Word definition	.78	.17
Word formation	.71	.31
Text production	.56	.13
Auditory discrimination	.48	.31
Articulation	.39	.19
Letter knowledge	.18	.86
Phonemic segmentation	.20	.85
Book orientation	.56	.57

Table 3

Correlations Between Language and Literacy Tasks and Home and School Predictors for Dutch Children

	01	02	03	04	05	06	07	08	09	10	11	12	13	14	15	16	17	18	19
01 Language	1																		
02 Literacy	.60*	1																	
Parent:																			
03 Reading expectations	.24*	.28*	1																
04 Reading climate	.21*	.14*	.25*	1															
05 Reading frequency	.19*	.22*	.15*	.29*	1														
06 Involvement	.19*	.16*	.04	.16*	.26*	1													
07 SES	.41*	.32*	.16*	.14*	.14*	.06	1												
08 Education	.41*	.33*	.17*	.18*	.26*	.16*	.67*	1											
09 Aid	-.13*	-.13*	-.06	.01	-.05	.18*	-.14*	-.22*	1										
10 Home language	-.08	.02	-.04	-.06	-.03	-.11*	-.09	-.07	.04	1									
11 Importance aid	-.02	-.01	.09	.25*	.10*	.15*	-.04	-.08	.27*	-.08	1								
Teacher:																			
12 Book orientation	.10*	.04	-.01	.08	.20*	.25*	-.07	.08	.07	-.05	-.09	1							
13 Reading frequency	.05	.20*	.03	.01	.08	.06	-.06	.26*	.03	-.03	-.03	-.08	1						
14 School experience	.09	.15*	-.08	.07	.03	-.14*	-.01	.02	.07	.25*	.08	-.04	.23*	1					
15 Minority experience	-.02	.12*	.02	-.15*	-.14*	-.11*	-.06	-.19*	.19*	.36*	.00	-.23*	-.07	.32*	1				
16 Challenging content	.13*	.17*	.04	-.04	.13*	-.01	.05	.17*	-.08	.01	-.07	-.26*	.23*	.06	-.00	1			
17 Teaching experience	-.06	.09*	-.10*	-.09	.04	-.15*	-.01	-.03	.05	.17*	-.03	-.35*	.15*	.42*	.41*	.37*	1		
18 Prop minority pupils	-.08	-.15*	.04	-.13*	-.30*	-.06	-.09	-.21*	.21*	.07	.03	-.18*	-.29*	-.06	.32*	-.14	-.07	1	
19 Adaptive attitude	-.02	-.05	.06*	-.01	-.12*	.03	-.06	-.05	.06	.08	.13*	-.53*	.03	-.10*	.22	.07	-.02	.23*	1

*p<.05.

Minority children. In Table 4, correlations are displayed for language and literacy tasks for minority children. When we compare Table 4 with Table 3, it is clear that parental variables have weaker correlations with the language and literacy outcomes in the case of the minority children. Nevertheless, most predictors continue to have significant relations with the test scores. Along with SES and parental education, home language is evidently influential: the less Dutch spoken in the family, the lower language and literacy outcomes will be. Parental aid no longer provides significant correlations with the test scores; however, the importance parents attribute to their help is negatively correlated with the literacy results.

In Tables 5 and 6, the regression analysis is summarized. It was performed to explore the relationship between parental and teacher predictors of success in language and literacy of minority children at the end of kindergarten.

In the language domain, again socioeconomic status is the most substantial ingredient. High expectations of the reading success of the child, the amount of time spent on reading by the parent, contribute to the variance explanation. Home language and parental evaluation of the assistance given in the family also are significantly related: language scores are negatively related to the levels of Dutch spoken in the family, and to self-evaluation. The scores on language tasks are negatively related to the proportion of minority pupils in the classroom, as well as to teacher experience with minority students.

Home language, together with SES, judgments on help provided, parental reading frequency, and reading expectations were meaningful factors predicting literacy skills. Subsequently, more teacher background variables mattered in the literacy regression than in the case of language outcomes.

Parent Interview

For a more comprehensive view on parental predictors in a child's literacy learning process, 42 Dutch families were selected for an in-depth interview. In this selected group, children from low- and high-SES homes, and with varying language skills, were equally represented. Following a structured set of questions, the parents reported about the home variables discussed in the previous sections. Almost all parents in our study read to their children: the majority reads every day (67%), some parents read a number of times (7%) or once a week (14%). A small proportion of the parents engage in reading activities with their children only once every 2 weeks (7%) or once a month (over 2%). When talking about reading to their children, low- and high-SES parents did not differ significantly on the aspect of frequency [$t(10.80)=1.12; p=.29$]:

> "I read to them every night before they go to bed. Sometimes, when it is rainy, we tend to do it in the afternoon" (mother of Hendrik, low-SES child with high language ability).

> "It happens quite a lot less than I wish I could. I am a single parent; with two children, my work and the household to take care of, it is hard to find room for reading" (mother of Davey, high-SES child, low language ability).

Table 4

Correlations Between Language and Literacy Tasks and Home and School Predictors for Minority Children

	01	02	03	04	05	06	07	08	09	10	11	12	13	14	15	16	17	18	19
01 Language	1																		
02 Literacy	.64*	1																	
Parent:																			
03 Reading expectations	.14*	.20*	1																
04 Reading climate	.11*	.10*	.26*	1															
05 Reading frequency	.16*	.13*	.13*	.51*	1														
06 Involvement	.13*	.14*	.20*	.26*	.24*	1													
07 SES	.30*	.27*	.07	.09	.06	.03	1												
08 Education	.28*	.26*	.06	.13*	.07	-.02	.69*	1											
09 Aid	-.05	-.07	.19*	.21*	.16*	.33*	-.06	-.05	1										
10 Home language	-.30*	-.17*	-.09	-.06	-.05	-.12*	-.18*	-.19*	.04	1									
11 Importance aid	-.03	-.13*	.10*	.29*	.24*	.21*	-.03	-.08	.29*	-.04	1								
Teacher:																			
12 Book orientation	-.04	-.01	.10*	.01	.09	.17*	.05	-.08	.10*	.12*	.02	1							
13 Reading frequency	.03	.05	.09	.05	.06	.17*	.06	.06	.05	-.09	.01	.24*	1						
14 School experience	.07	.01	-.10*	-.06	.13*	.07	-.06	-.02	.01	.08	-.11*	.08	.21*	1					
15 Minority experience	.15*	.14*	.03	-.17*	.00	.04	-.01	.06	.00	.00	-.15*	.06	.22*	.64*	1				
16 Challenging content	.15*	.06	-.08	.00	.06	-.02	.00	.07	.00	-.06	-.06	-.27*	-.04	.01	.10	1			
17 Teaching experience	.13*	.08	-.13*	-.16*	.04	.00	-.07	.00	-.04	.00	-.17	-.14*	.04	.53*	.77*	.17*	1		
18 Prop minority pupils	-.21*	-.04	.18*	-.20*	-.27*	.05	-.05	-.10	.19*	.03	-.03	-.04	-.07	-.10*	.07	-.19*	-.10*	1	
19 Adaptive attitude	.03	.13*	.10*	-.03	.01	.17*	-.07	-.03	.10	-.01	-.04	-.30*	-.05	-.05	.14*	.03	.11*	.31*	1

*p<.05.

"Bryan really is an outdoor kid. Reading confines itself to later at night. However, by then he is so tired that he prefers to watch television" (father of Bryan, high-SES child, high language ability).

"I do not read a lot to my child, because I actually dislike it" (mother of Ellen, high-SES child with high language ability).

All parents with the exception of one tried to stimulate the emergent literacy and language skills of their children, doing rhyming exercises, singing children's songs, reading storybooks, and assisting with reading, writing, and analyzing words; low-SES parents give evidence of similar activities as high-SES parents [$t(40)$=-.90; p=.37]. Nevertheless, parents have different views on the way they provide support for their child. Some opt for a playful approach:

"Learning to rhyme . . . happens without effort: we make jokes, sing a song, and I give attention to the words" (mother of Raisha, high-SES child, low language skills).

"She writes words herself. When I am ironing, she says, mama you are getting mail! She writes for some time, slips the note under the door. Then I have to look

Table 5

Summary of Stepwise Regression Analysis for Variables Predicting Minority Children's Language Skills at the End of Second-Year Kindergarten (N=348)

Variable	B	SE B	ß*	R²
SES	2.82	.57	.24	
Home language child	-1.22	.25	-.24	
Proportion minority children in classroom	-6.43	1.39	-.22	
Teacher experience with minority pupils	.22	.07	.16	
Parental expectations for reading	1.77	.62	.14	.23

*p<.05.

Table 6

Summary of Stepwise Regression Analysis for Variables Predicting Minority Children's Literacy Skills at the End of Second-Year Kindergarten (N=379)

Variable	B	SE B	ß*	R²
SES	.95	.20	.23	
Parental expectations for reading	.72	.21	.16	
Importance parental aid (self-evaluation)	-.94	.31	-.15	
Reading frequency parents	.16	.06	.13	
Adaptive attitude teacher	.04	.02	.10	
Home language child	-.19	.09	-.11	
Teacher experience with minority pupils	.05	.02	.10	.18

*p<.05.

at it, and I correct her spelling" (mother of Chantal, high-SES child, high language skills).

Others pay attention to language and literacy skills in a more structured setting:

> "I have been trained as a teaching assistant; that is why I know these songs and rhymes, and we do that quite often" (mother of Leon, high-SES child, high language skills).
>
> "He gets guidance from a speech therapist, so I have to practice with him a lot. He was not able to pronounce some sounds at first. He received some tasks, and we have to do them with him at home. We should do it more often, but I cannot force him" (mother of Danny, low-SES child, low language skills).

Some parents do not feel their help is of major importance in this aspect, or find it hard to do it in the right way:

> "We started (to do syllable clapping exercises) now that she has started to learn to read. I do not pounce on it, because I think it is the teacher's responsibility" (mother of Karen, high-SES child, high language scores).
>
> "When they learn new words, I try helping him with naming the sounds in a word. But this is difficult for me, because they learned to say /e - e/ in stead of /i/" (mother of Ferry, low-SES child, low language abilities).
>
> "Regarding language she is far ahead of her peers, so we do not stimulate her anymore (in repeating difficult words)" (mother of Maartje, high-SES child, high language skills).
>
> "She tries to identify letters in the newspaper on her own. I do not get right down to do it with her. We do not teach her (how to write words) because they do it in a special way at school. We would do it differently, and then she would have to unlearn things, while in the same time they think they are skilled. Therefore, we do not do it on purpose" (mother of Fleur, high-SES child, high language scores).
>
> "We do not stimulate him to read words. He can read and write his own name, and that is enough for us" (mother of Geert, high-SES child, high language abilities).

When talking about the effects of their assistance, some parents proved to be skeptical:

> "Now and then he joins me when I am reading a book, pointing out letters and so on. But most of the times he has an attitude like, I do not want to do things like this, because school hours are over" (mother of Adje, high-SES child, low language scores).
>
> "Success is not guaranteed, because I have a daughter who does not like to read at all, and I have been reading to her a lot" (mother of Pieter, high-SES child, high language scores).

Conclusions

The results show that in general there is a strong effect of family characteristics on children's Dutch language development. The difference in sociocultural background of children explained a substantial amount of variance in children's language scores, along with parental education, and expectations for the child's reading success. Children's Dutch literacy development turned out to be related to both family and classroom characteristics. The extent to which parents and teachers succeed and cooperate in engaging children in cognitively challenging conversations and literacy activities strongly predicted children's progress on the literacy-related measures under consideration. This effect was found for children from different linguistic backgrounds. Closer inspection of the effects of teachers' behavior revealed that responsive teachers with a strong focus on text relations and prediction of story line, who spend a considerable amount of time on book orientation and storybook reading, had a strong impact on the learning progress of the native Dutch children. Teacher experience and an adaptive attitude toward kindergarten education in emergent literacy predicted the learning progress of the minority children.

The role of direct parental aid remains unclear. Dutch children do not seem to benefit from explicit instruction on literacy received at home. The "chicken-and-egg" problem seems evident when seeking possible explanations: is parental help responsible for low achievement in language and literacy (which seems unlikely), or are underachievers in need of extra help at home? The negative correlations between importance attributed to parental help and minority student results may be related to the parents' insecurity about factual assistance they can give to children, due to gaps in their own school-related knowledge.

The study has a number of theoretical and practical implications. From a theoretical point of view, it is clear that children's early language and literacy development is guided by both family and school characteristics. The degree to which parents and teachers succeed in engaging children in cognitively challenging practices turns out to be a strong determinant of children learning. From a practical point of view it is important to see that this type of stimulation may help children from diverse backgrounds to extend their oral language repertoire, and to overcome the transition from the use of oral language in social contexts to the use of decontextualized content in written text.

In a detailed study of the pupils considered, questions have arisen for the lack of connections between home and school forces in the language and literacy acquisition process (Stoep, Verhoeven, & Bakker, in preparation). Instruments such as family portfolios (Paratore et al., 1995) may be helpful in bridging the gap between the parents' and teachers' frames of reference.

From the present study there is clear evidence that differences in the home literacy environments of young children are related to their language and literacy development. Similar findings have been presented by Scarborough and Dobrich (1994). It was also found that teacher variables in kindergarten explain a substantial amount of the variation in language and literacy outcomes, as was also shown by Dickinson and colleagues. It can be hypothesized that children from supportive literacy backgrounds continue to make rapid growth in literacy skills. Given the many challenges during the first years of schooling it can be taken for granted that the child's experiences during these years has lasting impact on school performance (cf. Alexander & Entwisle, 1996).

References

Alexander, K., & Entwisle, D. (1996). Schools and children at risk. In A. Booth & J. Dunn (Eds.), *Family-school links: How they affect educational outcomes* (pp. 67–88). Hillsdale, NJ: Erlbaum.

Baker, L., Sonnenschein, S., Serpell, R., Fernandez-Fein, S., & Scher, D. (1994). *Contexts of emergent literacy: Everyday home experiences of urban pre-kindergarten children* (Research Rep. No. 24). Athens, GA: National Reading Research Center.

Clay, M. M. (1982). *Observing young readers.* London: Heinemann.

Dickinson, D., & Keebler, R. (1989). Variation in preschool teachers' styles of reading books. *Discourse Processes, 3,* 353–375.

Dickinson, D., & Smith, M. (1992). Long-term effects of preschool teachers' book readings on low-income children's vocabulary and story comprehension. *Reading Research Quarterly, 29,* 104–123.

Dickinson, D., & Tabors, P. (1991). Early literacy: Linkages between home, school and literacy achievement at age five. *Journal of Research in Childhood Education, 6,* 30–46.

Gee, J. (1992). Socio-cultural approaches to literacy. *Annual Review of Applied Linguistics, 12,* 31–48.

Mommers, C., & Verhoeven, L. (1989). *Schatkist (Treasure-chest).* Tilburg, The Netherlands: Zwijsen.

Morrow, L., Rand, M., & Smith, J. (1995). Reading aloud to children: Characteristics and relationships between teachers and student behaviors. *Reading Research and Instruction, 35,* 85–101.

Neuman, S. (1996). Children engaging in storybook reading: The influence of access to print resources, opportunity, and parental interaction. *Early Childhood Research Quarterly, 11,* 495–513.

Paratore, J., Homza, A., Krol-Sinclair, B., Lewis-Barrow, T., Melzi, G., Stergis, R., & Haynes, H. (1995). Shifting boundaries in home and school responsibilities: Involving immigrant parents in the construction of literacy portfolios. *Research in the Teaching of English, 29,* 367–389.

Scarborough, H. S., & Dobrich, W. (1994). On the efficacy of reading to preschoolers. *Developmental Review 14,* 245–302.

Snow, C., Barnes, W., Chandler, J., Goodman, I., & Hemphill, L. (1991). *Unfulfilled expectations: Home and school influences on literacy.* Cambridge, MA: Harvard University Press.

Sonnenschein, S., Brody, G., & Munsterman, K. (1996). The influence of family beliefs and practices on children's early reading development. In L. Baker, P. Afflerbach, & D. Reinking (Eds.), *Developing engaged readers in school and home communities* (pp. 3-20). Mahwah, NJ: Erlbaum.

Stoep, J., & Verhoeven, L. (1999). Effects of teachers' read alouds on children's early language and literacy development. In T. Shanahan & F. Rodriguez-Brown (Eds.), *National Reading Conference Yearbook, 48* (pp. 86–93). Chicago: National Reading Conference.

Stoep, J., & Verhoeven, L. (2000). *Stimulering van beginnende geletterdheid bij kleuters uit risicogroepen (Stimulation of emergent literacy with at-risk kindergartners).* Apeldoorn, The Netherlands: Garant.

Stoep, J., Verhoeven, L., & Bakker, J. (in preparation). *Parental and teacher commitment in emergent literacy development.*

Verhoeven, L., & Vermeer, A. (1998). *Nederlandse Taaltoets voor Kinderen (Dutch Language Test for Children).* Arnhem, The Netherlands: Cito.

Wells, G. (1990). Talk about text: Where literacy is learned and taught. *Curriculum Inquiry, 20,* 369–405.

Shifting Roles of Responsibility: Scaffolding Students' Talk during Literature Discussion Groups

Beth Maloch

University of Texas at Austin

Although a teacher-led format is the norm for literature discussions in most classrooms, many teachers are experimenting with student-led literature discussions in their literacy curriculum (Eeds & Wells, 1989; Gambrell & Almasi, 1997). This shift is partly in response to researchers' claims (Barnes, 1975; Edwards & Mercer, 1987) that a less teacher-centered discussion format—one that is student led and where the teacher functions as a facilitator—may encourage students to engage in more "problem-solving talk," which in turn leads to a more complete understanding of the literature. In contrast to the IRE (initiation-response-evaluation) pattern characteristic of teacher-led discussions, student-led discussions—specifically literature discussion groups, the focus of this study—often feature participation structures that provide students with more leadership opportunities and more time to talk, which can encourage more complex responses from students (Almasi, 1995).

However, the transition from a teacher-led format to a student-led one entails a significant shift in the roles and demands of all participants. Worthy and Beck (1995) note that moving toward more student-led discussion involves changing the teacher's role from "lesson controller to discussion facilitator, through changes in teacher-student interactions" (p. 313). Teachers making this shift from recitation-style discussions to more democratic ones find that their role in these discussions becomes much more complex.

Researchers such as Lewis (1995) and Evans (1996) note the danger of moving in this direction too quickly or without teacher support. They suggest that literature discussion groups do not always feature the type of equitable dialogue touted by advocates of the approach and sometimes foster inequitable relationships among students—particularly when the teacher is not present. Additionally, Mercer (in press), though not focusing specifically on literature discussions, discovered that students who were engaged in group or partner work rarely utilized "problem-solving" talk. Further, he found little evidence of teachers attempting to raise the quality of the students' talk. Though the work on literature discussion groups is predominately positive, there is evidence that points to a need for further exploration of the dynamics of the discussion process and the teacher's role in supporting students as they shift into new roles of participation.

National Reading Conference Yearbook, 49, pp. 222–234.

Several researchers have provided insights about teachers' support of literature discussion groups (Jewell & Pratt, 1999; Short, Kaufman, Kaser, Kahn, & Crawford, 1999). These researchers indicate that the teacher plays a wide range of roles in the discussions including facilitator, participant, mediator, and active listener. They further indicate the importance of supporting students in both the "how" and "what" of literature discussions. However, few studies have investigated how teachers support students during the interactions evident within these more democratic discussion formats. The shift teachers must make with regard to scaffolding the students' shift in participation structures and task demands is not well known.

The study described here focused specifically on the teacher's role in scaffolding student-led discussions. The central question that this research asks is, What is the relationship between the teacher's role and students' participation in literature discussion groups.

Methods

Overview of the Study

Pseudonyms will be used to refer to all participants. Data analyzed and reported in this paper were collected as part of a 6-month ethnographic study of teacher-student interactions in a third-grade classroom serving 29 students (14 males, 15 females) of varying ethnic and socioeconomic backgrounds (15 Caucasian, 11 African American, 3 Asian). The research procedures were guided by the assumptions of interpretive/constructivist ethnography (Lincoln, 1997; Lincoln & Guba, 1985).

Classroom Context

The classroom explored in this study was in a school located in the suburbs of a mid-size metropolitan city. The school drew its student population from both the surrounding middle-class neighborhoods, as well as from lower-income neighborhoods in the inner city.

Mrs. P, in her fifth year of teaching, was in the process of moving toward a more student-centered classroom. She involved students in such activities as hands-on science, collaborative group-work, novel study, writer's workshop, and sustained silent reading. She held a problem-solving view of learning and social interaction, encouraging students to work through problems or conflicts and providing them with strategies to use in doing so. Out of her belief in the value of student voice and choices in the classroom came the desire to begin using literature discussion groups.

Mrs. P began the implementation of literature discussion groups during the second semester. The implementation process occurred gradually as students engaged in small-group discussions around a shared class novel. After this series of discussions, she introduced the idea of literature discussion groups through a whole-group brainstorming/discussion session centered around the question, "What makes a good discussion group?" Through this session, Ms. P established her expectations of cooperative behavior, substantive responses to topics in their literature response logs, and the responsibility of all participants to contribute to the discussion. She gave students book choices, and organized groups according to the students' interest in these books.

During this study, students participated in two cycles of the literature discussion groups. A cycle included (a) introduction of books by the teacher, (b) expression of student preferences, (c) formation of groups, (d) production of guidelines by individual groups, (e) discussion of literature, usually taking three to four 30-minute sessions, (f) small-group and whole-group self-evaluation, and (g) concluding activities.

Data Collection Techniques

Four phases were used to collect data, as outlined by Rowe (1994): (a) field entry, (b) developing hypotheses, (c) hypothesis refinement, and (d) field exit. Data collection involved ethnographic techniques of participant observation, expanded fieldnotes that included methodological notes (MN) and theoretical notes, videotape, audiotape, interviews with the teacher (TI) and the students (SI), and collection of artifacts. Observations, accompanied by video- and audiotaping, ranged from 2 to 3 days weekly (full-day observations) in the beginning phases of the research to daily observations (2 hours each day) during hypothesis refinement. Approximately 30 literature discussion groups were videotaped across two cycles.

Data Analysis Techniques

Data analysis was ongoing during all phases of data collection using the constant-comparative method (Strauss & Corbin, 1990). Data were reviewed to identify and categorize patterns of participation. Once categories were identified, rules and definitions were developed to identify, delimit, and justify the categories. Negative cases were then sought and analyzed to check and revise categories.

Sociolinguistic microanalyses of student and teacher participation patterns were conducted, both during data collection and more extensively following data collection, to refine and further develop categories. Teacher interventions within the discussions and the student utterances preceding and following those interventions were the focus of the microanalysis. Theoretical sampling guided the selection of videotapes to be transcribed for analysis. To refine hypotheses regarding the teacher's influence on student discourse over time, one group was selected from the first cycle and all sessions for that group were transcribed. During the second cycle, as categories became more refined, representative excerpts of each category were transcribed and analyzed to help further develop and define those categories.

Results

The teacher's role within the literature discussion groups was active, complex, and dynamic. In fact, the teacher was present during the discussions—sitting just outside the circle. She acted as a facilitator and a mediator rather than a leader. Instead of orchestrating the discussion, she responded to the students. This resulted in a back and forth movement, jumping in and out of the discussion, rather than a linear, static mode of participation. The intricacies of this role are discussed here in relation to two salient themes that emerged from the data: (a) the problematic nature of the students' shift in responsibility and (b) the responsive nature of the teacher's interventions relevant to students' difficulties. The first theme—the problematic nature of the students' shift in responsibility—establishes a foundation for the second and most prominent theme, which explores the teacher's response to students' struggle.

Theme 1: The Problematic Nature of Students' Shift in Responsibility

Challenges that resulted from shifting roles of responsibility within the discussions was a major theme. The shift to a student-led discussion was not easily accomplished. The students' struggle with this format is no surprise, given their individual and collective histories, which featured a preponderance of teacher-led activities and discussions. The teacher-led discussion norms were no longer appropriate in the literature discussion groups. As a result, the transition to responsibility for discussion leadership was neither straightforward nor easy.

In the initial literature discussion groups, students and teacher fell back into norms previously established in teacher-led discussions. These norms—raising hands, waiting for the teacher's leadership, looking to the teacher to help solve problems—were evident particularly in the first few literature discussions.

Mrs. P noted these difficulties in her note-taking during the literature discussion groups, and in her review of the videotapes of the discussions. She commented that students were having "difficulty getting going" (Teacher notes, 3/23/98), that they were "not discussing as well" (Teacher notes, 3/25/98), and that they "didn't get it yet" (Teacher notes, 3/23/98). As she reviewed the videotapes, she remarked that students were "not really listening to each other" (3/19/98), that they were "not responding to each other and don't seem to be understanding much of what others are saying" (3/26/98). As noted by Ms. P, students struggled in their discussions in different ways.

In some of the most extreme cases, groups sat in silence, not sure how to begin. When they did begin talking, individual students did not connect their statements to statements made by others, creating a sort of round-robin share time instead of a conversation. The following transcript, taken from the first literature discussion group that met, is representative of several of the initial group meetings (see Table 1 for transcription conventions). All of these excerpts are from the Transcript of 3/16/98. Student comments showed little expression and slow speech with a high frequency of significant pauses and periods of silence.

Table 1

Transcription Conventions

Behavior/Speech Act	Description
Simultaneous speech	Where two people speak at once, the overlapping portion of their utterances are enclosed with slash marks (e.g., *//*).
Interruptions	Where one person interrupts another, the speech ends with two slashes with the first speaker, and begins with two slashes with the second speaker (e.g., "that's like// //that's like adoption").
Tentative transcription	When the exact transcription of speech is difficult, this is indicated by enclosing a probable transcription in parentheses (e.g., "( )").
Omitted conversation	When transcripts have been shortened, this is indicated by an ellipsis (e.g., . . .).
Explanatory comments	When explanatory comments are added to a direct transcription, they are enclosed in brackets, (e.g., "that's just like when you [Ms. P]").
Inaudible speech	Where words or phrases are completely inaudible, this is indicated by a series of asterisks enclosed in parentheses (e.g., (***)).
Emphasis	Where a word or syllable is spoken with extra emphasis, it is underlined (e.g., "There is no love.").

Further, students' body language (e.g., leaning away from others, lack of eye contact, furtive glances around the room) indicated a lack of interest in other's comments. Nonverbal behaviors and contextual notes have been placed in square brackets. Words or phrases that are completely inaudible are indicated by asterisks. The group is discussing, Molly's *Pilgrim,* a novel about a student, Molly, and her family who immigrate to America. In this excerpt, students are discussing Molly's interpretation of the class assignment to make pilgrim dolls.

> Nancy: She wanted to move back where she was from because all the students were making fun of her [pause] and her mother said that they can't go to a certain place because her father had to work very late [pause] and he was working hard and they probably had to look for another house.
>
> Anna: And, they had to make, all take a pin, and [picks up book showing front cover] and make a doll, take a pin and make one.
>
> Evette: Elizabeth was checking everybody's dolls and Molly put her doll in her desk because it didn't [pause] look like a pilgrim in the book [pause] and Elizabeth thought she didn't do her homework [pause] so and Molly said she did and pulled out her bag and pulled out her doll and Elizabeth and her friends laughed.
>
> Anna: She had told her mama about it and *** going to school and her mama said don't worry about it because the teacher might not understand but

> she'll see [silence for almost a minute—Ms. P looks up briefly and looks back down to her notes; students look down and around a little bit].
>
> Anna: Angela? Nancy? [Muffled, hard to hear]
> [Significant pause]
> Nancy: Everybody was singing a song in music that she couldn't read//
> Anna: about her that she couldn't read very well [pause] and they made fun of her because she couldn't read and *** the doll.
> Ms. P: [nods] [silence for about 20 seconds]

In this example, students seem to be retelling the story, simply giving a literal restatement of the text. They did so not to work through confusing details, but because they were not sure what else to do. This confusion becomes more apparent later in the discussion as one of the students remarks, "I don't even know how to have a discussion" (Transcript, 3/16/98). The data clearly indicated that the transition to student-led literature discussion was difficult. Though students began to accept their new responsibilities within the first few sessions, they still struggled with exactly how to function in this type of discussion.

Theme 2: The Responsive Nature of the Teacher's Interventions

Students' lack of interactional expertise often resulted in unfocused, unproductive conversations. In response, the teacher intervened in a number of ways to help students develop these skills. Ms. P suggested or highlighted strategies students could use to become better "discussants." The strategies she highlighted included asking follow-up questions, using names to ask questions, recognizing others' comments, and using evidence. These strategies were consistently aligned with Ms. P's goals for group discussions. Table 2 outlines the strategies and corresponding goals encouraged by Ms. P during this time. An analysis of the data using the constant-comparative method revealed the variety of ways in which she intervened in the discussion to teach participation strategies. Initially, she focused on student difficulties with interaction, but later she shifted her focus to more content-oriented interventions.

An interactional focus. Ms. P acted as a discussion guide by making the discussion process more visible to the students. She helped them build a metacognitive knowledge of discussion. By making these invisible processes explicit, she was able to hold them up for reflection and evaluation. She also made strategies available that the students could use in their discussions. She scaffolded students in the appropriation of these strategies, sometimes in overtly instructional ways, using a variety of interactional pedagogic techniques (i.e., reconstructive recaps, elicitations, reinforcement, extending, refining). Her use of these techniques varied in explicitness and in frequency across groups, individuals, and time.

To illustrate how she used these varying techniques to support students' participation, I will take one strategy (follow-up questions), that was used for various purposes, and demonstrate how it was used and the students' developing understanding of it. The transcript used to illustrate this technique is taken from the same group used in the earlier example. The students, involved in their first literature discussion group, had enacted a stilted discussion that was marked

Table 2

Teacher's Expectations and Associated Strategies

Teacher Goals/Expectations	Further Explanation of Goal	Strategies Associated with Goal
All members are involved and included in the discussion.	(a) Share own responses. (b) Invite others to share. (c) Acknowledge and value	Ask questions, using names, to invite participation. Acknowledge other's comments by: (a) asking follow-up question, (b) restating to check your understanding, (c) thanking person for sharing. Enter conversation by using follow-up question, or by saying "I agree" or "I disagree."
The discussion is cohesive.	(a) Responses or turns are linguistically and/or semantically connected. (b) Cohesive discussions are often characterized by longer amounts of time on a particular topic.	Ask follow-up questions that continue a line of thought. Use phrases such as "I agree/disagree" or "like Nancy said" to connect to another's comment. Make semantic/meaning connections between speakers and between topics.
Discussion participants generate substantive discussion topics.	(a) Students will generate topics for discussion. (b) Discussion topics will be substantive (help generate in-depth conversations).	Refer to literature response log for topics to share. Refer to book (i.e., illustrations, quotes) for topics to share. Generate your own topics that relate to existing discussion.
The discussion focuses on one common topic or text at a time.	(a) Centers around a shared text. (b) Is closely related to book, although personal connections are stressed. (c) Centers on one common topic at a time.	Identify page numbers of section of book that sparked a question. Retell story. When participants are not focusing, alert peers.
Participants support responses by sharing reasoning.	(a) Share reasoning. (b) Invite others to share reasoning.	Ask follow-up questions when participants use one-word or nondescript answers. Include reasoning in your responses. When appropriate, share book quotes to support responses.

by awkward pauses and little in-depth discussion of topics. At that point, Ms. P stepped in to highlight what the students were doing (i.e., retelling) and suggested a question for discussion:

Ms. P: And, how would you have felt if you were Molly walking in, knowing that your pilgrim doll didn't look quite like everybody else's? [Pause]
Nancy: Sad.
Ms. P.: O.K. [moves her hands in a circular motion, trying to get other students to join in] Are you guys going to let her get away with just saying "sad?"
Anna: Sad and
Evette: ***
N: Embarrassed.

Knowing that one-word answers would not facilitate a rich discussion, Ms. P tried to elicit follow-up questions from the student to encourage greater interaction. However, the cues she gave were not explicit enough. First, she tried cueing students through hand gestures. She then indirectly signaled the inadequacy of one-word answers by asking, "Are you guys going to let her get away with just saying 'sad?'" However, this, too, was inadequate. In response, Ms. P became more direct and explicit in her elicitation, quickly following that elicitation with a demonstration of the strategy:

Ms. P: Is somebody going to ask why? Why did you feel sad, Nancy?
Anna: Because//
Nancy: Because everybody's talking about it and it didn't look like the one in the book.
Ms. P.: and that would make you sad because?
N: Because they were making fun of her doll, saying that their doll was best when hers
N: I might want to feel embarrassed//
Anna: Because other people's *** were better than yours?
Evette: I would feel embarrassed because ***, the reason I would feel embarrassed was the doll didn't look like the one in the book.
N: Why would you feel that way?
E: Because it didn't look like a pilgrim. [Nancy nods]

Following the teacher's direct, explicit elicitation and subsequent modeling students began sharing their reasoning, as evidenced by the use of the word "because" and phrases such as "the reason I would." Additionally, students began asking each other follow-up questions. After a few more turns at talk, students returned briefly to using one-word answers with long pauses.

Anna: sad and [pause]
         Ms. P looks at group, kind of looking puzzled that they aren't talking.
Nancy: may feel mad at/ may feel mad
Ms. P: are you gonna//
Evette: Why would you feel mad? [Ms. P smiles, pats Evette on the knee, and says quietly, "Good job, Evette."]
N: because . . . You're kind of sad and you're mad at the girl because she was making fun of you and the doll; get mad

In response to students' use of one-word answers, Ms. P waited, giving them a subtle cue that something was awry by her puzzled expression. Then she repeated her earlier question, "Are you gonna [let her get away with just saying 'mad']?" In the earlier discussion, that cue had been too vague. This time, however, students picked up on it immediately, to the point of interrupting her to ask the follow-up question. The students and teacher had built a shared or common knowledge of this strategy and when to use it (Mercer, 1995). Therefore, the more explicit cue was not necessary. Still, the students were far from being experts at using this strategy.

As the discussion continued, students became overly enthusiastic about the use of the follow-up questioning strategy:

Nancy:	[Turns to Angela] how would you feel?
Angela:	Embarrassed
N:	Why?
A:	because the teacher might think I didn't do my homework [looking at Ms. P as she finishes]
Anna and Evette:	Why?
Ms. P:	O.K., let's try to add instead of asking why. You guys are doing good on that, let's ask a little bit more. Why [to Angela] would you think the teacher might think you didn't do your homework?
A:	Because I didn't have it out on my desk and I was hiding it under something.

In this excerpt, students began using the "why" question after every turn at talk, even when the person had sufficiently explained their reasoning. Students knew to use the strategy but were not clear about when to use it and when not to. In response, Ms. P stepped in to help students refine their understanding of this strategy. Finally, in the last section of this episode, Ms. P steps in to recap what has just occurred in the discussion.

> Ms. P: O.K., you guys are on the right track right here. Nancy shared something and then asked Angela. You guys asked both Nancy and Angela to explain a little bit more. And Anna just felt that she was able to share right after Angela. She didn't have to be asked, she just felt like she could. Anna, thanks for jumping on in. What other things did you think, that stuck out to you in this chapter, in this portion that you read, that you really wanted to share and talk about//

Using a technique that I have labeled a reconstructive recap (term adapted from Mercer, 1995), the teacher recounted what had just occurred. What is notable in this recap is that the teacher did not recap the *content* of the discussion, but the *process*. She remarked on who talked and who questioned and how they entered the conversation. By doing so, she made their discussion process more visible and more understandable to her students. There was also an evaluatory tone in which she positively reinforced this process, encouraging students to engage in these practices in future discussions.

This transcript and analysis illustrates the range of pedagogic techniques used by Ms. P in response to the students' developing understanding of interactional processes and strategies. Starting with a less explicit, less direct cueing technique that was inadequate in eliciting the strategy, she moved to more explicit methods, such as modeling and direct elicitations. Then, as students began to show a tentative understanding of the strategy, she moved back to less explicit cues and focused on extending students' understanding of the strategy. Finally, she recapped the process for the students making it more available for reflection.

This episode was chosen for use here because of the inclusion of so many different intervention techniques, all centering around one particular strategy. It is representative of the data, in that the techniques highlighted here were used consistently across all discussion groups to encourage a variety of strategies according to students needs.

A content/response focus. By carrying the illustration one step further, the teacher's shift from an interactional focus to a content focus can be more clearly demonstrated. Throughout the first cycle of literature discussion groups, students progressed in their understanding of interactional strategies. They used the strategies more often and showed a growing understanding of the discussion process. There was less silence and pausing in the groups as they became more comfortable in their ability to generate appropriate discussion in this situation.

As the shift in student competence occurred, Ms. P's role also began to shift. First, she acted more as a participant than as a guide. Second, she altered her emphasis to focus on the content of the discussion. Specifically, she focused on expanding the students' conversations, pushing them toward greater depth. For example, in the first cycle her focus was on using follow-up questions to generate talk—some sort of fuel for discussion. In the second cycle, as students became more proficient in the discussion process, Ms. P encouraged follow-up questions as a means to deepen or extend the conversation. In the following transcript of a teacher intervention, Ms. P used a reconstructive recap to encourage students to build on each other's questions, adding an emotional element, in an effort to deepen the conversation:

> Ms. P: O.K., see how much that one question had a lot of other questions. What I want you guys to think about. . . . When somebody asks a question and everyone answers it, see if there's another question you can think of that's not necessarily in your book that kind of ties in with that. Like Adam asked, "have you moved?" and Chris didn't have his questions but he tied in with "why did you move?" and then I asked "how did you feel when you moved?" All of those questions are related to Adam's.

Ms. P's intervention here has a very different emphasis than those highlighted earlier. In this episode, she was very interested in building and deepening the content of the discussion. As students' understandings of the discussion process developed, Ms. P's interventions shifted to focus on more content-related needs.

In sum, Ms. P used a variety of intervention techniques within the discussion groups to scaffold students' developing understandings of the discussion process. These techniques included direct and indirect elicitations, modeling, highlighting of strategies, and reconstructive recaps. The length and depth of the interventions had to do with how students responded to interventions. If students understood what they were to do and reacted accordingly, the intervention ended. If there was still confusion, the teacher elaborated or refined the strategy explanation or was more forceful with the request. Further, a pre-established understanding or a shared knowledge of the strategies was necessary before the teacher could use less explicit interventions. Finally, the focus of the teacher's interventions shifted from interactional to content related as students gradually developed more interactional competence.

Conclusion

Although it is widely accepted that one of the aims of education should be the induction of children into ways of using language for seeking, sharing and constructing knowledge, observational studies of classroom life reveal that this induction is rarely carried out in any systematic way. Teachers very rarely offer their pupils explicit guidance on such matters, and researchers have found that pupils commonly lack any clear, shared understanding of the purpose of many of the activities that they are engaged in and the criteria by which they are judged by teachers, and so are often confused (Mercer, in press, p. 2).

Literature discussion groups are promoted as a more equitable way for students to share their responses to literature. However, it is important to note the complex and demanding task that faces participants—teachers and students—when moving from a recitation-style structure to one with decentralized patterns of interaction. This problematic transition is often overlooked by researchers and practitioners in their eagerness to herald the rich, meaningful discussions possible when students lead their own discussions. The research analyzed in this paper reveals some of the problems in this transition and suggests the need for teacher support as students develop new skills related both to the "how" (interaction) and the "what" (content-related emphasis) of literature discussion groups.

The difficulty students can face in student-led groups has also been noted by others. Mercer (in press), for example, found few instances of students engaging in *productive* talk, despite the prevalence of much talk in classrooms. Further, he found few instances of teachers trying to raise the quality of that talk. Other researchers, looking specifically at literature discussion groups, have noted the importance of teachers' interactional support for students (Jewell & Pratt, 1999; Short et. al, 1999). Findings from the research reported here support and extend these results in several ways.

First, shifting from a teacher-led format to a student-led one is not a straightforward process for teachers or students. Shifting expectations of participation can lead to difficulties. This finding supports Mercer's assertion that students often do not engage in productive talk within student groups. Second, in an extension of Mercer's findings, the teacher in this study did attempt to raise the quality of talk. She scaffolded students in their appropriation of strategies, sometimes in overtly instructional ways, using a variety of techniques. Third, concerning teacher support, the metacognitive lens provided by the teacher enabled students to better understand the discussion process which facilitated students' more expert participation and engagement in the dialogue.

The research described here helps develop a theoretical notion of how teachers guide students' progress in the discussion *process* by examining how this is expressed in classrooms. It provides new insights into how teacher language influences students' interactions and learning and explores the notion of scaffolding as it relates to discourse. Although others have noted the importance of providing support for students within student-led discussion groups, few have addressed this process at the point of teacher-student interactions during the actual discussions. This research provides a first look at how a teacher scaffolds students during the moment-to-moment interactions within discussions and illustrates specific ways the teacher supports students' engagement in productive talk. The results of this study provide encouragement to educators who are moving toward more facilitative roles within their classrooms. The findings of this study clearly indicate a progression in students' competency within this new discussion format that is influenced by the teacher's interventions during the discussions.

With the caveat that this is an ethnographic study in one classroom, Table 2, suggests possibilities for future research, as well as practical implications for educators. Items presented in the second column of Table 2 explicate the teacher's expectations for literature discussion groups, and highlights areas for further investigation. Future research, framed around each of these expectations, would offer greater insights into how discussions foster learning. The third column in Table 2 speaks to more practical applications by specifying discussion strategies taught to the students to facilitate their discussions. It provides notions about what this teacher did that worked to cultivate more effective discussions and more competent " discussants." Teachers who wish to move toward using student-led discussion groups may find useful strategies for doing so in the findings reported here.

References

Almasi, J. (1995). The nature of fourth graders' sociocognitive conflicts in peer-led and teacher-led discussions of literature. *Reading Research Quarterly, 30,* 314–351.

Barnes, D. (1975). *From communication to curriculum.* New York: Penguin.

Edwards, D., & Mercer, N. (1987). *Common knowledge: The development of understanding in the classroom.* London: Methuen/Routledge.

Eeds, M., & Wells, D. (1989). Grand conversations: An exploration of meaning construction in literature study groups. *Research in the Teaching of English, 24,* 4–29.

Evans, K. (1996). Creating spaces for equity? The role of positioning in peer-led literature discussions. *Language Arts, 73,* 194–203.

Gambrell, L., & Almasi, J. (Eds.). (1997). *Lively discussions!* Newark, DE: International Reading Association.

Jewell, T., & Pratt, D. (1999). Literature discussions in the primary grades: Children's thoughtful discourse about books and what teachers can do to make it happen. *Reading Teacher, 52,* 842–850.

Lewis, C. (1995, November). *Literature as a cultural practice in a fifth/sixth grade classroom.* Paper presented at the meeting of the National Council of Teachers of English, San Diego, CA.

Lincoln, Y. (1997). What constitutes quality in interpretive research? In C. Kinzer, K. Hinchman, & D. Leu (Eds.), *Inquiries in literacy theory and practice.* Forty-sixth yearbook of the National Reading Conference (pp. 54–68). Chicago: National Reading Conference.

Lincoln, Y., & Guba, E. (1985). *Naturalistic inquiry.* Beverly Hills, CA: Sage.

Mercer, N. (1995). *The guided construction of knowledge.* Bristol, PA: Multilingual Matters.

Mercer, N. (in press). Development through dialogue: A socio-cultural perspective on the process of being gifted. *Cognition and Context.*

Rowe, D. (1994). *Preschoolers as authors. Literacy learning in the social world of the classroom.* Cuskell, NJ: Hampton.

Short, K., Kaufman, G., Kaser, S., Kahn, L., & Crawford, K. (1999). Teacher-watching: Examining teacher talk in literature circles. *Language Arts, 76,* 377–385

Strauss, A., & Corbin, J. (1990). *Basics of qualitative research: Grounded theory and procedures and techniques.* Newbury Park, CA: Sage.

Worthy, J., & Beck, I. (1995). On the road from recitation to discussion in large-group dialogue about literature. In K. Hinchman, D. Leu, & C. Kinzer (Eds.), *Perspectives on literacy research and practice.* Forty-fourth yearbook of the National Reading Conference (pp. 312–324). Chicago: National Reading Conference.

The Role of Text in Peer-Led Literature Circles in the Secondary Classroom

Patricia O. Paterson

Georgia State University

R osenblatt's theory of the reading process as a transaction between the reader and text has been widely studied, and instructional strategies in the classroom have reflected her emphasis on student response (Cooper, 1985; Probst, 1988; Purves, Rogers, & Soter, 1990; Rosenblatt, 1938/1995, 1978, 1994). The social, cultural, cognitive, sociocognitive, and attitudinal aspects of the reader have become important parts of reading research and instruction. However, Rosenblatt also insists on the importance of the text, which she defines as "a set of signs capable of being interpreted as verbal symbols; however, these signs remain simply marks on the paper, an object in the environment, until some reader transacts with it" (1994, p. 1063). She describes this relationship between reader and text as "a to-and-fro interplay between reader, text, and context" (p. 1064). The role of the text, as Rosenblatt sees it, is to channel the reader's thought. Although there are multiple possible readings, Rosenblatt's concept of warranted assertibility outlines the necessity of taking the text into consideration when making interpretations.

An equally important role is that of the text as it is "recontextualized in the minds of readers" (Cazden, 1992, p. 148). Rabinowitz distinguishes two reading activities as different in kind: first reading, in which the readers tend to participate as "narrative audience" in the world of characters and events evoked by the text, and "reading against memory," a process by which second or subsequent readings parallel, vary from, or challenge the memory readers have of the text from the first reading (Rabinowitz & Smith, 1998, pp. 90–91). Smith (Rabinowitz & Smith, 1998) points out that this distinction is similar to the one Rosenblatt (1985) makes between evocation and response, where the lived experience with the text becomes the source for later reflection on themes, meaning, and structure. During both first and second reading, updating interpretations is a crucial part of the literacy act (Iser, 1980).

Literature circles provide an instructional forum in which students share initial readings of the text with each other and then refine, rethink, and substantiate meanings as they reread the text. Literature circles build on Vygotsky's (1962) concept of language-learning as socioculturally based and on the social construction of meaning in which the individual and society interdependently negotiate a text's meaning (Wells & Chang-Wells, 1992). Implementation of literature

National Reading Conference Yearbook, 49, pp. 235–251.

circles can range along a continuum from extensive to minimal teacher control. The stance for this study is one in which the teacher's control over the text is shifted to the students in order to give students increased control over the text and to lessen the authoritative role of the teacher in interpreting literature (Almasi, 1995; Nystrand & Gamoran, 1991; Willinsky, 1990). This type of peer-led discussion of literature provides a complex and rich environment for observing the interplay between students transacting with the text and interacting with one another (Alvermann et al., 1996). Research has shown beneficial results of such peer interactions with text (Goatley, Brock, & Raphael, 1995; Many & Wiseman, 1992; Nystrand & Gamoran, 1991).

Students deal with literature within the contexts of shared cultural values, genre knowledge, intentions, and needs of both reader and writer, and expectations about particular texts; thus, meaning in written texts is shaped by cultural and classroom constraints of rhetorical communities (Fish, 1980; Pappas, 1996). One of the culturally shared expectations about conversation and literature is the belief that assertions can and should be supported with "proof," including, in the case of literature, textual proof. Eeds & Wells (1989) note the prevalence of supported inference and verification comments in fifth- and sixth-grade students' discussion of literature. Other research has focused on modifying instructional handling of text away from narrow, structural, teacher-centered approaches and toward integrated interpretive processes that use intertextual, extratextual, and textual information and rely less on teacher guidance (Hartman, 1994; Rogers, 1991). Peer-led discussions can be used to observe students' ability to put their knowledge into action (Applebee, 1996).

Peer-led literature circles represent an accessible structure for examining reading strategies, especially students' approach to text. As students collaboratively construct meaning, the techniques they use to read and interpret literature are made visible. Research on literature circles has emphasized the contextual frameworks within which meaning is constructed (Almasi, 1995; Alvermann et al., 1996; Burns, 1998; Eeds & Wells, 1989) and the ways in which book clubs support and scaffold the learning of diverse students (Boyd, 1997; Goatley et al., 1995; McMahon & Raphael, 1997; Raphael & McMahon, 1994). Research with more proficient secondary school learners has usually focused on nonliterary texts (Hartman, 1994) or on student perceptions (Alvermann et al., 1996), not on the process of reading a literary text.

Research on Rosenblatt's transactional theory of reading (Cooper, 1985; Cox & Many, 1992; Enciso, 1992; Galda, 1992; Many, 1994; Many & Wiseman, 1992; Probst, 1988; Purves et al., 1990) has focused on students' stances, personal and sociocultural responses, and classroom contexts. Few studies have looked at the role of text in reader response theory. It may be that an examination of the processes used by proficient readers will lead to further insights about the reading process itself and suggest ways in which the reading strategies of both proficient and less proficient readers may be improved. The objective of this study is to examine the role played by the text in peer-led discussions of literature in the secondary school classroom.

Method

Participants

This is a qualitative teacher-researcher study focusing on student discussions of Kafka's (1915/1981) *The Metamorphosis* in student-led literature circles where the teacher's participation was minimal. The participants were the teacher-researcher and 25 students in two sections of a 10th-grade Honors World Literature course. Acceptance into the Honors program was initiated by a student-submitted application and determined on the basis of three teacher recommendations, available reading scores (usually ITBS), class standing, overall GPA, and grade in 9th-grade English. Although the admissions process took all of this information into consideration, the desired criteria included 90+ percentile on reading scores, a minimum grade of 90 in 9th-grade English, a minimum grade in all courses of 85, and class standing in the top 10 percent. The students represented various cultures and ethnicities, including Cambodian, Vietnamese, Chinese, Filipino, Cameroon, Nigerian, Indian, Pakistani, Caucasian, African-American, and students who preferred being classified as "other."

Context

The site for data collection was an urban high school with a diverse student population. Previous instruction had been largely teacher-centered, with periodic individual conferences. Because this class was part of a sequence leading to the 12th-grade Advanced Placement course, instruction had focused on analysis of literature, especially literary terms, archetypes, and textual support of points in written essays.

Prior to this activity, students were informed that a change in instructional method was being implemented in order to investigate its effectiveness but that the usual final assessment of an analytical essay would be given. To impose as few constraints as possible on the interactions, students were told that they would receive a grade for participation in the group, but no further criteria were given. The teacher read aloud two paragraphs of information from the textbook on the author, allowed time for the class as a whole to read the first page, and gave a deadline for finishing the novel. Self-selected groups of students determined their own schedule and discussed the book while the teacher transcribed the discussion. To assess the effect of some teacher guidance, one section of the class was given a one-page, teacher-prepared list of questions to guide the discussion. The other section was given no further teacher assistance. These groups are identified as GQ and No GQ to indicate which were given guide questions.

The text used for this study was Kafka's (1915/1981) *The Metamorphosis*. In this short novel, Gregor Samsa, a traveling salesman for an oppressive company, awakens in his bed at home one morning to find that he has become a "monstrous vermin . . . with a vaulted brown belly, sectioned by arch-shaped ribs . . . and many legs, pitifully thin compared with the size of the rest of him, waving helplessly before his eyes" (pp. 2–3). Kafka situates Gregor's surreal situation in the context of actuality; Gregor thinks, "What's happened to me?" and the text answers "It was not a dream" (p. 3).

Gregor's metamorphosis impacts the rest of his family: his retired father, his passive mother, and his adored sister Grete, all of whom have depended on Gregor's financial support. At first, the father is angry, pelting Gregor with apples and chasing him from the family room; the mother tries weakly to protect Gregor, and Grete reacts sympathetically, cleaning Gregor's room and feeding him. As it becomes clearer that Gregor is now a burden on the family, the other family members adapt, by making money and hiring a charwoman to keep Gregor. Eventually, family pressures build, as indicated by Grete's words to her parents: "Maybe you don't realize it, but I do. I won't pronounce the name of my brother in front of this monster, and so all I say is: we have to try to get rid of it" (p. 51). At the end of the story, Gregor dies, possibly of starvation, and the family takes a holiday to celebrate their "new dreams" (p. 58).

The text is structured into three chapters, with each chapter representing a stage in the family's and Gregor's reactions to his changed form. Although this text is accessible to students in terms of length, vocabulary, and emphasis on family issues, it also presents considerable difficulty in that Gregor's situation is decidedly unrealistic so that the plot does not easily fall into a genre familiar to students.

Data Sources and Analysis

Data include transcripts of each day's discussion by five different groups of 10th-grade Honors World Literature students, photocopies of the essays written subsequent to the discussion, transcripts of student reactions to the activity, and teacher observations. In addition, teacher-constructed overheads and critical commentary about the novel were used to compare student interpretations with the material that would have been presented in the usual teacher-centered approach to this novel. Analysis followed the naturalistic procedures set out by Lincoln and Guba (1985), in which data analysis was ongoing from the first day of data collection. Primary sources were transcripts of literary circles, transcripts of class discussions about the activity, and observations, and secondary sources (essays, teacher-constructed overheads, and critical commentary) were used to triangulate the findings.

Comments focusing on the text (as distinguished from personal experience, group maintenance, social experience, and classroom context) were bracketed, and these were coded using constant-comparative analysis (Glaser & Strauss, 1967) with openness to emergent themes but with background in reading theory as part of the researcher's perspective. The researcher's grounding in theories that stress textual cues and the temporal nature of the reading process (Iser, 1980; Rabinowitz & Smith, 1998; Rosenblatt, 1938/1995, 1978, 1994) helped shape the researcher's identification of themes. Textual comments were then analyzed for emergent categories, and these were revised several times as categories merged or diverged.

Although this process of coding individual comments helped focus the researcher's attention on emergent textual categories, it proved to be inadequate in capturing the holistic nature of the discussions since individual comments were not usually idiosyncratic but were attuned to the dynamic flow of conversation about the story. Using a modification of Almasi's (1995) methodology, the transcripts were again bracketed, this time into dialogue units that were defined as beginning with introduction of a new topic via questions, statements, or emotional reactions and ending with the last comment that could be connected logically to the opening concept. The definition of "logically connected" was derived by close analysis of the transcripts that included transitional comments connecting topics that seemed initially to be incongruent but which linked apparently disparate dialogue segments. Although this methodology limited the ability to include only textual comments, it more adequately captured the holistic flow of the discussions.

Although differences existed among groups in the frequency of use of certain strategies, and in the themes on which they focused, cross-cutting patterns of strategies occurred across groups. In order to display these similarities across groups, the researcher has used excerpts from the discussions of all five groups and has indicated the group number.

Results

Evolving Hypotheses

Analysis indicated that students relied heavily on the text in the group discussion; as they retold the literal "facts" of the story, their retelling frequently led to interpretation as the details of the text gained significance. As these interpretations were shared within the group, students repeatedly returned to the text to clarify plot and action and to support assertions, especially those that were challenged by the group. This process led to new hypotheses as students collaboratively worked to determine meaning:

Victoria: The sister must still love him in some way. Gregor is listening in on the wall to the conversations. It's not the same any more because he can't discuss things any more.

Minh: I think he's close to his sister. She's the only one who knows what he likes—milk and bread?

Nairu: No, he used to like other stuff.

Victoria: The sister used to play the violin, right?

Carolyn: She wanted to go to the Conservatory. From yesterday, we've noticed that they're really dependent on Gregor for income. 'Cause remember all the debt. But see, that's the whole thing, and she says he's going to send her to the conservatory, but the parents want to keep that money so they can keep it instead of spending it on her. . . .

Minh: The father was different before, when Gregor had a job. The father was weak and sickly and had to walk with a stick. And now when Gregor is a roach, he's all slicked down and in a suit.

Carolyn: 'Cause he knew he had to do something. He had to keep the family alive.

Minh: His father was too dependent on Gregor when Gregor had a job.

Nairu: You remember when Gregor walked with his dad and his mom 'cause they walked slow.

Carolyn: That's the whole thing, supporting them. He had to support them when they were walking and he's having to support them financially. When something changes, it throws off the whole balance.

Minh: Like how the family relationships change.

Victoria: They can't stay in the house any longer.

Minh: Maybe his sister was close to him, but maybe since he changes, she's not so close. (Group Two, GQ)

Victoria began with a judgment hypothesis about a character, Gregor's sister Grete: "She must still love him in some way." As support for her assertion, she pointed out that Gregor listens to his sister's conversations through the wall, evidence of a close relationship. Minh agreed with Victoria, pointing out that Grete is "the only one who knows what he likes—milk and bread." The hypothesis ran into trouble, however, when Nairu pointed out that the text contradicts the statement that Gregor likes milk and bread: "No, he used to like other stuff." The group then began discussing the sister, pointing out that Gregor was going to pay her way for school at the Conservatory, the implication being that "they're really dependent on Gregor for income." The discussion thus broadened to include Gregor's relationships with the other family members, especially the father.

In discussing the father's role, the students drew on their memories of the previous day's reading: "The father was different before, when Gregor had a job," a new hypothesis focusing on changes in the characters. Again, the text played a role as Minh used it to support the new hypothesis; to prove that the father was sickly before and now has changed, she mentioned that the father used to walk with a stick but now "he's all slicked down and in a suit." Minh then extended this idea that the father has changed by making a judgment about the father's character and his dependence on Gregor. Nairu and Carolyn joined in with textual support and extension. Shortly thereafter the students arrived at a crucial conclusion: that the change in family relationships has changed the power balance within the family.

Discussion at this point seemed to have veered sharply from Minh's original question about whether Grete loves Gregor. However, the hypotheses about the other characters and the text-derived conclusions led Minh full circle to an answer to her original hypothesis: "Maybe his sister *was* close to him, but maybe since he changes, she's not so close." It is critically important in interpretation that students note the changes that are occurring within the characters; the students have reached this point independently by respecting and responding to the text. Minh wound up disproving her own hypothesis because the text pointed the group in another direction.

During this short dialogue unit, the text served as support for and refutation of hypotheses. The text also enabled students to "read against text," in this case the perceived changes in the family structure due to Gregor's metamorphosis. Thus, the discussion of the text led to a new hypothesis.

The Progression Pattern of the Reading Process

Students also engaged in changing stances and processes as they progressed through the novel. Early discussions were characterized by a proliferation of questions and speculations, quick introductions of issues but few extensions, and short dialogue units. Excluding Group Five, for which only two observations were available, the pattern of questioning is illustrated in Figure 1.

Students focused on elements in the text that needed clarification and that seemed unusual in the context of both the story world and their previous knowledge of story grammar. Many of the factual questions were answered by reference to the text and were disposed of fairly easily. More difficult issues were noted and questioned and preliminary hypotheses made; however, the effort to bring closure to the cognitive conflicts ended in frustration: "It's (the story) cool; it's like cool, but I just want an explanation" (Group Three, No GQ). Despite frustration, student discussion served as a filter to distinguish among questions that could easily be answered, misreadings that could be corrected, and questions still to be resolved.

As the students reached the middle of the novel, they engaged in recursive and predictive processes as they compared new textual material to previous readings, modified understandings, and speculated about future directions. Students began noting changes in the characters even as they tried to define the characters and predict the ending. Thus, students were situated between their past reading and future directions, a position illustrated by the recursive and predictive nature of the following comment:

> Maury: . . . Maybe he's changing both emotionally and mentally. Maybe *it will come up* in Chapter 3 about what he's thinking. *Like we said yesterday,* it's not like he holds any anger toward his father and mother.

As they progressed, students hypothesized explanations for the events in the story:

> Grace: Do you think the medicines changed him?
> Dan: Maybe he was an alien?
> Maury: Maybe he'll change back in the third chapter. (Group Four, No GQ)

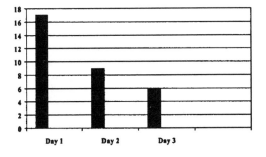

Figure 1. Average number of questions by day for four groups.

In addition, they made predictions about possible directions for the story: "He's supposed to be out of his father's house. Maybe that's not his real father. He shows no love, you know?" Many groups returned to unresolved issues from the first day. For example, Group Two focused extensively on identifying the type of bug Gregor was, and discussion on the second day gave them further evidence.

As students reached the end of the novel, they indicated emotional engagement with the characters. Rather than remaining immersed in the story, however, students' emotional involvement with the characters drove their search for meaning and spurred more analytic approaches to the text. In trying to reconcile the unhappy death of Gregor, a character to whom they had become attached, students reevaluated the other characters, questioned the techniques of the writer, and produced interpretive hypotheses. Students in almost all groups became literary critics, judging the effectiveness of the text as art, a clear move on the continuum from aesthetic to efferent stance:

> Latoya: And then the family tried to kill him and didn't show remorse.
> Rina: And then they just go on with their life. And the charwoman just threw him out.
> Grace: That sucked. And they never said why he wasn't eating.
> Maury: It's because he didn't like what they were giving him.
> Grace: It's like they were putting him in prison. It was all dirty in his room.
> Daniel: And they didn't even care. That's just sad.
> Grace: And they call him an "it." And they locked him in.
> Rina: And his sister of all people.
> Latoya: And they talk about how to get rid of him.
> Grace: I think she's just tired of cleaning up.
> Daniel: She's weak.
> Latoya: But I wouldn't want to get rid of my brother. That was a contrast character.
> Daniel: That was a dynamic character because she changed.
> Rina: Another metamorphosis. (Group Four, No GQ)

The students' identification with Gregor led them to question the motives of the rest of the family and to examine the novel's structure and its effect on the readers. In reflecting on the ultimate meaning of the text for them, they derived a theme that seemed to satisfy the group, and they even playfully wove the symbols of the story into their proposed new theme:

> Daniel: I think she purposely stopped giving him food.
> Grace: It's murder. It's bugicide.
> Latoya: Everybody's attitude changed toward him.
> Rina: Our attitude changed toward the sister, so we've metamorphosized.
> Grace: Maybe he did that to prove a point. We like the sister and then we don't. And that shows us each angle of the book.
> Latoya: Because each of us has our own viewpoint. It shows that people may care for a person and then it rots. So love is for a while and then it rots.
> Daniel: Be kind to insects because you may be one some day.
> Grace: And the apple doesn't fall far from the tree. (Group Four, No GQ)

Questioning the Text

Student analysis hinged largely on the nature and quality of the questions asked. Two types of questions emerged: factual questions and meaning questions. Factual questions were relatively easily answered by reference to students' memories of their reading or by consultation with the text:

Mahari: Who's Grete?
Clarissa: That's the sister. (They consult the text.) (Group Three, No GQ)

Meaning questions, that probed the significance of an event or the motivation of a character, often required more extended discussion and frequently led to long dialogue units. Although they too were answered by the text, the answers often required students to infer meaning from the text rather than retrieve explicit information: "Do you think the father was jealous of him? Or afraid of him?" (Group One, No GQ).

Questioning behavior varied among groups. An interesting phenomenon, possibly reflecting student resistance, occurred with Group Five, which used guide questions. In contrast to groups in which student questions developed into long dialogue units, Group Five's dialogue units were short and choppy, showing little evidence of extending the concepts of the questions. In response to teacher-prepared questions, students gave short, factual answers and even indicated the lack of relevance they saw in the questions:

Kasey: (reading guide questions): "What might the following symbolize? The picture of the woman with the muff."
Zara: What's a muff?
Ashana: It don't matter. That's just what his mother saw him on. (Group Five, GQ)

The group then moved on to the next question, concerning the symbolism of the room:

Zara: His room symbolized privacy.
Alenda: It symbolizes independence.
Ashana: No, he just sleeping there. He likes that furniture a lot. He gets mad when they mess with it. (Group Five, GQ)

Despite unresolved interpretations and some key inferences about meaning, the students dropped the topic to dispose of the next teacher-prepared question. There are other indications of student resistance to some of the emphases of the teacher as when Daniel made the following quip about literary terms: "Isn't turning into a bug while you're asleep an archetype?" (Group Four, No GQ). In addition, the students in Group One were provided the Guide Questions but chose not to use them.

Analysis of question patterns from the first day of discussion to the third day revealed that five groups averaged 11 questions on the third day, down from 17. In particular, the questioning of two groups was drastically reduced (Group Two from 17 to 4 and Group Three from 18 to 8). A possible explanation is that these groups were approaching a negotiated interpretation of the story as shown by Clarissa's statement: "I want to have an ending conclusion" (Group Three, No GQ).

In contrast, Group Five, which had resisted the guide questions, seemed far from interpretive consensus. Their last day of discussion contained 28 questions, many of which reflected unresolved issues from earlier discussion. For example, they were still concerned with the key question of why Gregor metamorphosed, discussed by most groups on the first day:

> Ashana: What was the point of his turning into a bug?
> Kasey: I don't think this story has a point to it, really. It really don't make no sense, it doesn't. I'm not going to sit here and criticize the guy. I think he had some kind of writer's block. What kind of psychotic would sit in his room and write a story about turning into a bug? What do you think the point is? (Group Five, GQ)

However, Kasey's frustration proved to be a catalyst, and the rest of the group's discussion drove for meaning, coming to conclusions that Gregor gives up hope at the end when he discovers that his family doesn't want him: "A lot of people do that" and that the family walk at the end represents "fresh air, calming down, and getting back to normal."

Text as Authority

Students explicitly denoted the text as the arbiter of meaning when debates about points of contention arose. Four variations of this process emerged (italics added):

> *Text Proves a Point.*
> Minh: Let's pick the top three animals you think it is.
> Carolyn: It could be a beetle.
> Victoria: Reads from text. *It says* a brown belly. (Group Two, GQ)
>
> *Omission Allows a Point.*
> Victoria: It could have been a dream, right, since *it never says* what kind of bug it is.
> Minh: *They don't tell us.* It could be a dream. (Group Two, GQ)
>
> *Text Fails to Prove a Point.*
> Janine: She just always brings in dirty stuff.
> Clarissa: Why not? It's a part of life.
> Karen: But sometimes *it's not really there*. It's like when X brings up religious stuff. (Group Three, No GQ)
>
> *Text Disproves a Point*
> Clarissa: That's the dad's money.
> Karen: No, you're wrong.
> Clarissa: *I'll look it up.* (Group Three, No GQ)

The common feature of these sequences is the tendency of students to place final authority for an interpretation on the text.

Significance Cues

Students noticed conflicting or unusual elements in the text, which frequently became clues to meaning. Students' ability to perceive a textual element that didn't make sense led them to further questioning and elaboration of the text's meaning. In one discussion, students in Group Four noticed a contradiction in the text concerning the size of Gregor's room:

> Latoya: His room is nasty now, and he keeps saying it's smaller.
> Daniel: If he's an insect, it would make the room seem smaller.
> Latoya: It's contradictory. He's saying the room is getting smaller, but if you're a bug, it would get larger.
> Daniel: If he's a big bug, but what if he's a medium bug?

This problem with details in the text led the students to examine the size issue more closely; they finally decided that size has a symbolic meaning: "His dad's boots are big. Maybe it's symbolizing the role he's taking now. The story is trying to show that Gregor is outside society" (Latoya, Group Four, No GQ).

Another process students used to interpret text was to make intertext connections, noting parallels between the current text and other texts. Although not required by the teacher, students used intertext connections as part of their meaning-making engagement, going beyond superficial identification of "allusions." Instead, intertext references helped students cue on characterization, structure, or meaning. The unusual plot and structure of *The Metamorphosis* confused students initially, and they relied on previous experiences with literature to explain the magical elements of the plot. Among other possibilities, they suggested that "it could be like the Merlin thing" or "the Wishmaster," or like the "Twilight Zone."

Intertext connections also helped students construct meaning. In a discussion during which students observed that Gregor changes when isolated in his room, a student commented: "Did you read *Lord of the Flies*? It's like the more they're isolated, the more they revert to being primitive." In follow-up discussion, students pointed out that despite being "sensitive and worried about his family," Gregor is powerless to act on these feelings: "But what can he do?" (Group One, GQ). The parallel between the enforced isolation and consequent regression of the British schoolboys in *Lord of the Flies* and Gregor's isolation in his room provided a bridge for students to discover theme.

Another example of use of intertext was a student's comment that Gregor's relationship to his sister is "like Poe, what a weirdo." Although the students did not explore the "weird" aspects of Gregor's relationship, many of the critics do point out the sexual implications. The students' intertext reference in this case offered an entrance to the text that was potentially valuable but which was dropped by the group in the course of the discussion.

Students also noticed patterns or unusual details in the text that led them to awareness of literary devices. The students not only labeled the devices but also hypothesized meaning, a much more sophisticated approach to literary elements than simple recognition and labeling:

> Mahari: There's a lot of imagery. Like in the beginning he can hear raindrops beating. I think that's the idea of the environment. And then they describe the way he looks, a giant insect with armor. So that's giving us the idea of how he looks and how we would feel if we looked like that. (Group Three, No GQ)

Students' awareness of literary elements increased greatly on the last day of discussion, as they recognized that the "facts" of the story carried thematic meaning. After some fruitless discussion of the apples on the second day of discussion, Group Five finally decided to approach this detail as a symbol:

> Ashana: Why did they keep focusing on the apples in his back collecting dust?
> Kasey: It was like a physical scar of the abuse. His father could have abused him for life, not a physical scar but a mental scar. (Group Five, GQ)

Some of these discussions ended without resolution but nevertheless were rich stimuli for student thinking. One group debated at length about the picture in Gregor's room, a detail on which many critics elaborate. Although students never came to consensus about meaning, it was clear that they come close:

> Minh: I don't know why he liked the picture of the lady so much.
> Victoria: Do you think because she's missing two arms she's connected to his family?
> Minh: He's missing his family's support.
> Carolyn: He's missing some warmth. If it was a picture of his sister, I'm surprised that the face is missing. His sister and him were so close, it was almost like losing part of himself. (Group Two, GQ)

In summary, when students recognized literary devices without the aid of the teacher or of supplemental materials, they tended to see them as clues to meaning, not as meaningless terminology to be remembered for a test. Students consistently linked devices such as imagery, symbolism, and allusion to the author's purposes and the corresponding effects on the reader.

Awareness of Author

Students consciously noticed the author as the artist back of the text and examined the motives and purposes of the author. At times, they treated the author as conscious artist, and at other times, they speculated about the ways in which the novel was connected to the author's life. For example, they treated Kafka as a conscious artist in this comment: "I think he (Kafka) has a really creative mind. I mean, he really had to think to come up with this." Because students assumed authorial intention, they looked at textual details as purposeful: "Did you notice that outside the window there's a hospital? The author wouldn't have put in a hospital unless there was a reason." When treating the author as conscious artist, the students often made judgments about the author's skill: "But I think that Kafka gave a lot of superfluous information. He kept telling us information that he didn't tie in."

At other times, however, the students did their own brand of psychoanalysis, trying to determine what psychological forces within the author affected the story. "What could this have to do with Kafka? Like, he didn't like his dad, and this character doesn't like his dad." Students went back and forth between these two camps throughout the discussion, but the most popular reading of the story finally relied on the idea that the author was subconsciously influenced to write about his own life. This approach by the students is certainly congruent with specific lines of literary criticism such as Freudian criticism.

At the end of their discussion, every group appeared driven to make a final assessment of the literary quality of the novel. Although the students did not agree on the value of the novel, they all saw certain merits. Although there was a variety of evaluations, a large number of students finally focused on the idea that the novel represented the author's life:

Ted: The story is far out, but I'm also a believer that real life is more unbelievable than stories. So this could be a story of his life just with different characters but the same meaning. (Group One, GQ)

Clarissa: I want to have an ending conclusion. I think the story was a reflection of Kafka's life and the characters he described as his family, the boarders, etc. were all a description of how he had been treated by society and the bug was the only animal he could relate to because bugs are always being rejected. That was me, CG, and I want to be paid for this. (Group Three, No GQ)

This conclusion is interesting because the classroom instruction in this course, which had been ongoing for 8 months, had largely neglected the author's personal connection to the story. Because they had become interested in this topic, several students chose it for their final paper and voluntarily did research into Kafka's life. An examination of the student essays revealed that four of them explored the topic of the connection between the novel and the author's life.

A comparison between the information that the teacher ordinarily included in the unit on this novel and the student transcripts and essays revealed that students examined most of the issues that would have been part of the teacher-led content. Specifically, the teacher-constructed overheads focused on the tripartite structure of the novel and traced the changes in the family structure during each segment, all issues discussed by the students. Other parallels included the symbolism of the apples, uniform, food, and boots. Students frequently developed similar interpretations to those of the critics. For example, critics frequently cited parallels between the events in the novel and Kafka's life. Like the students, the critics examine the possible sexual implications of Gregor's relationship with his sister, the significance of the family's growing strength as Gregor declines, and the way Kafka uses vermin to symbolize the family's treatment of Gregor.

In a class discussion of their experience with peer-led literature circles, students indicated that these discussions gave them a sense of freedom and the confidence that enabled them to develop and defend their own interpretations.

Richard: It's [the experience] better than what we normally do.
Mrs. P.: Why?

Richard: 'Cause we're thinking. (Group One, GQ)
Clarissa: I can write whatever I think and not whatever you think. (Group Three, No GQ)
G: We weren't within boundaries. (Group Four, No GQ)
D: When we came up with our own ideas, we didn't think, oh, that contradicts what Mrs. P. was saying. (Group Four, No GQ)

Discussion

The major findings from this study revealed that (a) proficient secondary students took the authority of the text seriously and used it extensively in the process of active, engaged reading; and (b) peer-led discussion groups provided a forum in which students could initiate and sustain their own analyses of literature and hone their interpretive skills.

Analysis suggested that students were skillful in engaging in conversations that focused on the text as well as on personal experiences and constructs, illustrating both the transactional relationship between reader and text (Rosenblatt, 1978) and the interactional relationship among readers as they form interpretive communities (Fish, 1980). Students built on the comments of one another as they extended and revised initial hypotheses about characters, plot, and meaning. The extent to which they used the text to spark discussion, sustain and develop hypotheses, and defend interpretations indicated that the text played a consistently strong role in student meaning-making. The instructional design encouraged students to both read and reread the text, promoting a recursive approach (Iser, 1980; Rabinowitz & Smith, 1998). As students returned to text segments they had previously read, they redefined meanings in light of new information.

The group format provided a way for students to address the text according to conventions of literary interpretation that had been reinforced by classroom instruction while encouraging a complex interpretive process that also took into account experiential and cultural knowledge. The degree to which students recognized and used literary elements and terms in their discussion suggested that students had developed the ability to approach literature in the analytical ways encouraged in the classroom and that their approach had been shaped by these classroom expectations. Nevertheless, the results also indicated that students made some efforts to resist or revise the strategies they had been taught as evidenced by Groups One's and Group Five's rejection of the Guide Questions and the emergence of the psychoanalytic approach to interpretation. Students displayed the ability and confidence to put their knowledge into action and to claim ownership of the resulting interpretations (Applebee, 1996). The process by which students hypothesized, theorized, defended, and negotiated their interpretations suggests the value of this strategy for developing critical thinking skills and extends previous research on the ways students resolve conflicts with text in literature circle discussions (Almasi, 1995) and on the empowering effect of peer-led discussion groups and the dampening effect of teacher intervention (Alvermann et al., 1996; Eeds & Wells, 1989).

A possible implication of the parallels between student interpretations and those of the teacher and critic is that substantive features in the written text can lead students—whose classroom experiences have made them knowledgeable of literary conventions—to interpret literature in ways like those of the larger literary community. This finding suggests that a transactive approach to text enables students to attend to genre cues and to become part of the literary tradition shared by writers and interpretive communities.

An important limitation of the study is that the classroom context provided by previous instruction in the class may have had an important function in shaping students' attitude toward text and in providing the scaffolding useful to critical analysis of text; if so, the study would indicate the need for teachers to examine their techniques and strategies closely to see if their approach is one that balances the legitimacy of both the text and the reader. Further, since this study involves only one text, it remains to be seen whether these patterns of text use hold true for different texts. Moreover, this study examines proficient readers still in the middle of their high school careers. More research is needed to determine to what extent older readers and less proficient readers use similar techniques.

This research attempts to focus attention on the role of the text in reading, especially in the context of literature circles, and on the progression of stances which readers take as they read and then reread the text. The study adds to the current model of reading by focusing on the abilities of proficient readers. There are educational implications of these findings for guiding less proficient readers and improving the skills of all readers. Further research in this area will help shed light on the processes by which meaning is constructed and on the complex nature of the reading transaction.

References

Almasi, J. F. (1995). The nature of fourth graders' sociocognitive conflicts in peer-led and teacher-led discussions of literature. *Reading Research Quarterly, 30,* 314–351.

Alvermann, D. E., Young, J. P., Weaver, D., Hinchman, K. A., Moore, D. W., Phelps, S. F., Thrash, E. D., & Zalewski, P. (1996). Middle and high school students' perceptions of how they experience text-based discussions: A multi-case study. *Reading Research Quarterly, 31,* 244–267.

Applebee, A. N. (1996). *Curriculum as conversation: Transforming traditions of teaching and learning.* Chicago: University of Chicago Press.

Boyd, F. B. (1997). The cross-aged literacy program: Preparing struggling adolescents for book club discussions. In S. I. McMahon & T. E. Raphael (Eds.), *The book club connection: Literacy learning and classroom talk* (pp. 162–181). New York: Teachers College Press.

Burns, B. (1998). Changing the classroom climate with literature circles. *Journal of Adolescent and Adult Literacy, 42,* 124–129.

Cazden, C. B. (1992). *Whole language plus: Essays on literacy in the United States and New Zealand.* New York: Teachers College Press.

Cooper, C. R. (Ed.). (1985). *Researching response to literature and the teaching of literature.* Norwood, NJ: Ablex.

Cox, C., & Many, J. E. (1992). Beyond choosing: Emergent categories of efferent and aesthetic stances. In J. Many & C. Cox (Eds.), *Reader stance and literary understanding* (pp. 11–22). Upper Montclair, NJ: Boynton/Cook.

Eeds, M., & Wells, D. (1989). Grand conversations: An exploration of meaning construction in literature study groups. *Research in the Teaching of English, 23,* 4–29.

Enciso, P. (1992). Creating the story world: A case study of a young reader's engagement strategies and stances. In J. Many & C. Cox (Eds.), *Reader stance and literary understanding: Exploring the theories, research, and practice* (pp. 75–102). Norwood, NJ: Ablex.

Fish, S. (1980). *Is there a text in this class? The authority of interpretive communities.* Cambridge, MA: Harvard University Press.

Galda, L. (1992). Evaluation as a spectator: Changes across time and genre. In J. Many & C. Cox (Eds.), *Reader stance and literary understanding: Exploring the theories, research and practice* (pp. 127–142). Norwood, NJ: Ablex.

Glaser, B., & Strauss, A. (1967). *The discovery of grounded theory.* New York: Aldine.

Goatley, V. J. Brock, C. H., & Raphael, T. E. (1995). Diverse learners participating in regular education "book clubs." *Reading Research Quarterly, 30,* 352–380.

Hartman, D. K. (1994). The intertextual links of readers using multiple passages: A postmodern/semiotic/cognitive view of meaning making. In R. B. Ruddell, M. R. Ruddell, & H. Singer (Eds.), *Theoretical models and processes of reading* (4th ed., pp. 616–636). Newark, DE: International Reading Association.

Iser, W. (1980). The reading process: A phenomenological approach. In J. P. Tompkins (Ed.), *Reader response criticism: From formalism to poststructuralism.* (pp. 50–69). Baltimore, MD: Johns Hopkins University Press.

Kafka, F. (1981). *The Metamorphosis.* (S. Comgold, Ed. and Trans.). New York: Bantam. (Original work published 1915)

Lincoln, Y. S., & Guba, E. G. (1985). *Naturalistic inquiry.* Newbury Park, CA: Sage.

Many, J. E. (1994). The effect of reader stance on students' personal understanding of literature. In R. B. Ruddell, M. R. Ruddell, & H. Singer (Eds.), *Theoretical models and processes of reading* (4th ed., pp. 653–657). Newark, DE: International Reading Association.

Many, J. E., & Wiseman, D. C. (1992). The effect of teaching approach on third-grade students' response to literature. *Journal of Reading Behavior, 24,* 265–287.

McMahon, S. I. & Raphael, T. E. (1997). The book club program: Theoretical and research foundations. In S. I. McMahon & T.E. Raphael (Eds.), *The book club connection* (pp. 3–25). New York: Teachers College Press.

Nystrand, M., & Gamoran, A. (1991). Instructional discourse, student engagement, and literature achievement. *Research in the Teaching of English, 25,* 261–290.

Pappas, C. C. (1996). Reading instruction in an integrated language perspective: Collaborative interaction in classroom curriculum genres. In A. Stahl & D. A. Hayes (Eds.), *Instructional models in reading.* Mahwah, NJ: Erlbaum.

Probst, R. E. (1988). *Response and analysis: Teaching literature in junior and senior high school.* Portsmouth, NH: Boynton/Cook.

Purves, A. C., Rogers, T., & Soter, A. O. (1990). *How porcupines make love II: Teaching a response-centered curriculum.* New York: Longman.

Rabinowitz, P. J., & Smith, M. W. (1998). *Authorizing readers: Resistance and respect in the teaching of literature.* Urbana, IL: National Council of Teachers of English.

Raphael, T. E., & McMahon, S. I. (1994). Book Club: An alternative framework for reading instruction. *Reading Teacher, 48,* 102–116.

Rogers, T. (1991). Students as literary critics: The interpretive experiences, beliefs, and processes of ninth-grade students. *Journal of Reading Behavior, 23,* 391–423.

Rosenblatt, L. (1938/1995). *Literature as exploration.* New York: Modern Language Association.

Rosenblatt, L. (1978). *The reader, the text, the poem: The transactional theory of the literary work.* Carbondale: Southern Illinois University Press.

Rosenblatt, L. (1985). Literature—S.O.S.! *Language Arts, 68,* 444–448.

Rosenblatt, L. (1994). The transactional theory of reading and writing. In R. B. Ruddell, M.

R. Ruddell, & H. Singer (Eds.), *Theoretical models and processes of reading* (4th ed., pp. 1057–1092). Newark, DE: International Reading Association.

Vygotsky, L. S. (1962). *Thought and language.* Cambridge, MA: MIT Press.

Wells G., & Chang-Wells, G. L. (1992). *Constructing knowledge together: Classrooms as centers of inquiry and literacy.* Portsmouth, NH: Heinemann.

Willinsky, J. (1990*). The new literacy: Redefining reading and writing in the schools.* New York: Routledge.

Student Engagement in Literature Discussion: An Exploratory Investigation into Small-Group Peer-led and Large-Group Teacher-led Interactive Structures

L. Susan Seidenstricker
University of Maryland

C lassroom culture provides the context in which students construct understandings of text and develop a literary interpretation process. That context can promote understanding of literal aspects of text (Barr & Dreeben, 1991) while restricting the development of multiperspective interpretation processes (Langer, Applebee, Mullis, & Foertsch, 1990). Or it can foster an interpretive process that requires thoughtful reflection and the consideration of conflicting points of view (Almasi, 1995). It is essential that teachers and researchers identify and implement those elements of classroom environment that support the development of a literary interpretation process in which students critically examine text, construct and defend personal interpretations, and consider the multiple viewpoints of an interpretive community.

One traditional classroom context for the construction of literary understanding is the literature discussion in which students and teachers collaboratively interpret text (Alpert, 1987; Alvermann, O'Brien, & Dillon, 1990). Recognizing that social interaction plays a dynamic role in the way knowledge is acquired and organized (Almasi, 1995; Alvermann et al., 1990), this study defines literature discussions as give-and-take dialogues that encourage students to enrich and refine understanding. The structure of those discussions may affect the student's process of meaning construction (Almasi, 1995; Sweigert, 1991). Many forms of literary discussion exist, producing a variety of patterns of interactions between teachers and students. It was the purpose of this study to identify potential factors of literature discussion that may affect the meaning-making process. I also intended to examine and describe the classroom implementation of two widely used discussion contexts: (a) small-group peer-led discussion and (b) large-group teacher-led discussion.

Engagement is defined in this study as strategic and intentional involvement in the social construction of literary understanding. That engagement may occur on three levels: (a) the desire or intent to prepare for, participate in, and interact with other participants in a literature discussion, (b) the personal enjoyment or satisfaction gained from strategic involvement in the social construction of meaning, and (c) cognitive and metacognitive participation in the collaborative meaning-making of a literary discussion group.

National Reading Conference Yearbook, 49, pp. 252–265.

Eeds and Peterson (1995) suggest that students need to develop an aware-ness of literary elements and their functions in a story to nurture the ability to respond imaginatively to text—to go beyond retelling the plot. They claimed that developing an understanding of layers of story meaning, character, place, point of view, time, mood, symbolism, and extended metaphor provides a foundation for building interpretation. Therefore, this investigation examined the development of literary interpretation as seventh-grade readers engaged in thinking, talking, and writing about characters.

Theoretical Perspectives

This study draws upon multiple theoretical and research perspectives: reader response theories of literary interpretation, sociolinguistic theory and research, and sociocognitive theories of learning and development. This study adopts a view of active meaning construction described by Rosenblatt (1978) in which the reader transacts with text and context. The reader shapes and reshapes interpre-tations by connecting new information with previous views.

From a sociolinguistic perspective, this transactional reading process is situ-ated in and dependent on the social and cultural contexts in which it occurs. Situated within a literary discussion, the reader merges and revises interpreta-tions with those of an "interpretive community" (Fish, 1980). In a classroom dis-cussion, teachers and students jointly construct diverse and complex interactive contexts with rule-governed participation structures (Bloome & Green, 1992). Those structures provide a framework in which the reader constructs meaning, displays understanding, and is evaluated.

This study also draws upon the sociocognitive theories of Vygotsky to for-mulate a view of the interpersonal reader. In a literary discussion, the reader makes inner interpretations public, exposing them to the mediating influence of conver-sations with peers and teacher. Vygotsky (1978) suggested that higher mental functions are social in origin, and are learned through interactions with others. Therefore, literary interactions provide a model for how to think about literature as well as a forum for testing and displaying that thinking. Learners develop cogni-tive strategies for understanding and interpreting literature as they use language within the context of literature discussion.

The Vygotskian perspective argues further that for learning to occur, a knowl-edgeable guide is needed to support cognitive development. That support is most appropriately provided at a point in the student's potential development at which he or she can accomplish a task with assistance that could not otherwise be accomplished independently. Within this "zone of proximal development," the teacher or more-knowledgeable peers guide the learner toward increasingly diffi-cult levels of understanding through alternating levels of support/collaboration and independence (Vygotsky, 1978). Vygotsky suggested that those mental func-tions that begin first in a collaborative interpersonal plane subsequently move to an intrapersonal level through "internalization" (1978). Wells (1994) suggested that a learner's zone of proximal development is an expression of a potential for intramental development created by intermental interaction that occurs as the learner and others cooperate in an activity.

This exploratory investigation studied student engagement in literature discussion to identify those interactive factors that promote student engagement and provide appropriate levels of support for the construction of literary understanding and the development of interpretive strategies. Two questions guided this study of small-group peer-led discussion and whole class teacher-led discussion: (a) How do seventh-grade readers engage in literary discussion? and (b) What factors in the interactive contexts affect student engagement in the construction of meaning?

Method

Participants and Procedures

Forty-two seventh graders were drawn from two intact language arts classes in a suburban middle school located in a predominantly white, south-central Pennsylvania community. The sample was comprised of average to low-average readers with a small number of above average readers. The two classes met daily for an 80-minute block of instruction with the same teacher-researcher.

Twenty-one students from each class were matched using pre-study measures of reading achievement (GOALS) and language arts classroom performance (first semester GPA). The two classes were then randomly assigned to a discussion structure. The classes read and discussed trade books as part of a larger unit of instruction on literary characterization. During their study of characterization, the participants (a) developed an extensive vocabulary for character description, (b) learned how to infer character trait, and motives from textual sources, (c) studied methods that authors use to evoke a reader's reaction to characters, and (d) read and wrote fictional short stories with a focus on understanding characterization. At the conclusion of the unit, students in the two classes alternately read and discussed sections of a trade book over a 6-week period with the goals of collaboratively constructing understanding, sharing personal interpretations, and applying characterization learning.

Small-Group Peer-Led Treatment

The small-group peer-led (SGPL) treatment was implemented within an instructional context that used elements of Concept-Oriented Reading Instruction (Guthrie & McCann, 1997) found to promote engaged student literacy learning: (a) a high degree of student self-direction balanced with common goals for all students, (b) instructional support for the acquisition of strategies for learning and constructing understandings, (c) support for learning how to work productively in a collaborative setting, (d) opportunities for students to articulate their understandings in forms and to audiences that are personally and culturally relevant, and (e) instruction that integrates content with strategies for learning in a coherent set of learning tasks.

In the SGPL treatment, the students met in small groups of four to five to collaboratively construct understanding of their readings. Students controlled topic choice, access to conversation, turn-taking, response evaluation, assignment of readings, and participation. The teacher-researcher observed discussions, supporting, facilitating, and participating in interactions when needed. Students discussed their reading with the goals of collaboratively constructing understanding and sharing personal interpretations. The students were instructed to focus on applying their characterization learning.

The SGPL context was characterized by a high degree of student direction. Students selected books from a list of district-approved titles; the teacher-researcher then grouped students with similar selections. Throughout the literature study, the students assessed group interactive processes and set group goals. Each group chose a literary theme for in-depth discussion and study, leading to related research. Each then shared their extended learning with the class, choosing an appropriate mode of expression through negotiation with the teacher. At the conclusion of the 6-week literary study, the students also displayed their learning about a character from their reading using a negotiated mode of expression.

Whole-class instruction focused on collaborative skills needed to build understanding, access group support, and clarify confusions. The use and development of meaning-making strategies were directed by individual student and group need throughout the collaborative process. The teacher-researcher encouraged students to try strategies, evaluate their usefulness, and determine suitable contexts for implementation. Instructional support was provided as needed.

Large-Group Teacher-Led Treatment

In the large-group teacher-led (LGTL) treatment, the teacher-researcher assigned readings followed by whole-class discussion of the passage. The teacher-researcher selected the book to be read and controlled discussion topic choice, access to conversation, turn-taking, response evaluation, and participation. The teacher-led discussion used those practices that researchers suggest promote student engagement in literary interpretation: (a) open-ended questions that seek and place a value on student ideas and feelings (Alpert, 1987), (b) conversation that requires multiple interpretations of text (Almasi, 1995), (c) contiguous discourse in which interactions connect and build upon the ideas of previous exchanges (Nystrand & Gamoran, 1991), and (d) high-level evaluations in which the teacher acknowledges the student contribution and modification to the direction of the discussion (Nystrand & Gamoran, 1991).

Discussions were also characterized by a high degree of teacher scaffolding to encourage student analysis of character traits using evidence from multiple sources. The teacher provided clear explanations and explicit models of characterization thinking. At the conclusion of the 6-week literature study, the LGTL group completed a written character analysis in class in a writers' workshop setting.

Materials

The students in this study read and discussed seven young adult novels. In the SGPL group, student-selected novels included: *Fallen Angels* (1988) by Walter Dean Myers, *Homecoming* (1981) by Cynthia Voigt, *Hoops* (1984) by Walter Dean Myers, *The Bomb* (1995) by Theodore Taylor, *Roll of Thunder, Hear My Cry* (1976) by Mildred Taylor, and *Drivers Ed* (1994) by Caroline Cooney. The teacher-selected title for the LGTL group was *The Lottery Rose* (1976) by Irene Hunt.

Data Collection and Analysis

Data sources for this study included teacher observation notes, informal student interviews, a student survey, and transcribed tapes of discussions. The teacher-researcher observed SGPL groups during their discussions; observational notes of LGTL discussion were recorded immediately following discussions and later from videotapes. Teacher observations focused upon describing student meaning-making behavior that would not be evident on the audiotapes. Observations also noted areas where follow-up instruction could improve strategic meaning-making and questions that could be used to expand understanding of student behavior.

Informal interviews grew from observations, initiated by questions such as, "I noticed that you. . . . Why did you . . .? How did the strategy work? What did you learn about using that strategy? How could you improve that strategy?" A more formal written survey also grew from those observations and informal discussions. On the survey, the students recorded their descriptions of how their group helped them to construct an understanding of their reading, and how they strategically prepared for discussion.

Audio- and videotaped discussions were transcribed and integrated with teacher observation data to identify potential patterns of student engagement. The preliminary patterns were then cross-checked with student descriptions collected from informal conversations and the written survey. Representative excerpts of discussion, teacher observations, and student description were then selected to illustrate identified patterns and build interpretive claims.

Results and Discussion

The final discussions of two SGPL groups provide representative data of small-group discussion. The fourth of five discussions provide representative LGTL data. Table 1 provides a breakdown of student and teacher contributions in each of these three discussions. A meaning unit was defined as a clause or less than a clause—an utterance that contributes meaningfully to the conversation. Meaningful units of conversation were categorized as substantive (sub.), proce-

Table 1

Teacher and Student Meaning Units in Three Representative Discussions

Group	Students Speaking	Teacher Meaning Units				Student Meaning Units			
		Sub.	Proc.	O.T.	Tot.	Sub.	Proc.	O.T.	Tot.
SGPL									
Angels	5 of 5	58	16	0	74	358	103	12	461
Bomb	4 of 5	12	5	0	17	200	22	0	222
LGTL									
Rose	17 of 21	91	19	0	150	115	0	0	115

dural (pro.), or off-task (O.T.). Data collected from these three representative discussions support research that suggests that SGPL discussions are characterized by a greater amount of student engagement than LGTL structures (Almasi, 1995).

The Nature of Seventh-Grade Discussion

SGPL discussion. SGPL groups constructed meaning without the assignment of roles, establishing procedures that met the unique requirements of its collaborating members and the text being read. Interactions were structured around (a) discussion of confusing terms or vocabulary, (b) rehearsal of plot, (c) sharing of favorite passages, and (d) a listing and brief description of characters.

In the beginning of their final discussion, the group reading *Fallen Angels* clarified confusing words encountered during their reading. During their five meetings, this group established a strategic process for working together to construct an understanding of confusing military terminology. Whereas one member located the word in the text, another found it in a dictionary, and the others brainstormed prior experiences with the word. After reading the text passage, the group tested predictions suggested from prior experiences. Next, one student read all of the dictionary meanings, and the group selected the most text-appropriate meaning. Finally, the group paraphrased the passage to verify understanding and recorded understandings in their journals:

JG: Do you have any more words?

JM: Yeah. One of them is spordic. It's some kind of fire. (reading) The visible fire is spordic.

BG: Spell it.

JM: S-P-O-R-A-D-I-C (Students repeat spelling trying to pronounce the word.)

DM: It's sporadic (clarifying pronunciation).

T: What page is it on?

JM: 290 (Students locate the passage.)

JM: (reading) Distant boom of the artillery switched from its sporadic night

rhythm to the pounding of the daylight—
DM: That means fast.
JM: They're not taking good aim.
DM: Fast and constant.
JS: So what is it?
BG: That's sporadic right here. (reading from the dictionary) Occurring at irregular intervals having no pattern or order.
JG: Having no pattern or order.
JM: Is it fast?
JG: No, happening over and over in no pattern or order.
BG: A little bit here, a little bit there. . . .
JG: Yeah.
T: A little bit different than you expected—wasn't it?
DM: Yeah, I thought it was like fast. It's like the firing starts and stops.

In the second part of their discussion, members read sections of the text that they liked or wanted to talk about. Following the reading, group members often shared opinions:

DM: I've got something I want to say. I thought it was nice that one of the guys went to the lunch man and asked him if he had any cake and the guy gave him a cake and some fruit pudding . . . and they celebrated his (Brew's) birthday. He was going to turn nineteen . . . and I thought that was nice.

Sometimes, after the reading of a passage, further clarification was needed:

JS: What's a hamlet? Is that some kind of battle or something?
DM: Isn't that like a village? Yes, It's a village.
JS: Are GIs the good guys or bad guys?
DM: GI's the good guy. Cong's the bad guy.

Students questioned each other until an understanding was reached. Sometimes a passage created a strong emotional reaction. The rereading of a passage describing a mother who threw her baby at a soldier evoked strong student response. The baby blew up upon impact with the soldier:

DM: Why, why did she throw her baby? I'd just take and throw a grenade at them.
T: Because he didn't expect it.
JG: Yeah, anyways, you're not going to hold a baby and it comes up and blows up in your face. I mean you're not going to expect that.
DM: But why would a lady want to blow her baby up? Man, she's dumb.
BG: It's sick.
JS: But she had to do it to save herself.
DM: Well, they ended up being killed, too. Didn't they?
JG: Human life doesn't have much value.

The group sometimes discussed how information contributed to the unfolding plot. At other times a reading was followed with the silent affirmation that no additional words were necessary. The passage describing their flight home included a prayer for the platoon contrasted with the trivial complaint of a man wanting wine with his meal. The stark contrast of two worlds needed no further comment.

The final meeting of the students reading *The Bomb* was also representative of SGPL discussion. It was a chapter-by-chapter rehearsal of the events of the reading. One member began a retelling; others took over the retelling at regular intervals. Participation in the retelling became almost competitive with members vying for opportunities to speak. Conflict arose occasionally over correct sequence of retelling. One member played the self-designated role of correcting errors in the retelling and filling in missed parts of the plot.

The teacher made two unsuccessful attempts to steer the conversation beyond a literal retelling. When the conversation bogged down over a dispute over locating an event in chapter 13 or 14, she suggested that the group consider how the U.S. government reported the Bikini events to the American public:

T: The admiral in Washington told reporters that we're adjusting nicely here. We're all happy.

SC: Yeah but they left the Bikini people out of it.

JG: No, they said that the Bikini people were adjusting nicely and that nothing was wrong. But the reporters didn't go there to see. There wasn't enough food and water. . . . It says in the back of the book . . . that the Bikini people were almost starving on Rongerik until the Navy moved them to Quadulen. . . And they said they started to eat animal's hearts.

T: As far as the American public knew—

JG: Yeah, they thought they (the Bikinians) were adjusting fine, but they weren't.

MM: In chapter 14 Tara had an announcement to make. . . .

The group quickly returned to the retelling without any personal reaction or evaluation of the propaganda process.

LGTL discussion. The teacher orchestrated the discussion in the LGTL group by reacting to and building upon student contributions to a teacher-selected topic. After asking an initial text-based question, the teacher typically guided the conversation by building upon student response. Teacher probes and requests for clarification encouraged multiple and extended student responses. Students responded to and built upon other student responses. Periodically, the teacher tied the multiple responses together, noting important patterns, summarizing student responses, and encouraging further student analysis and evaluation. The result was a highly contiguous discussion, focusing on constructing an understanding of the characters of the novel.

In the selected LGTL discussion, the teacher controlled the topical flow of the discussion. Teacher-selected topics originated from the text and from student responses. The teacher initiated the discussion with a text-based question. "Chapter eight deals primarily with the character Robin. We get a lot of background on him, especially how he interacted with Paul. Who is Robin? What do we find out about Robin?" Thirteen student responses followed, mixed with five teacher probes. The first topic shift grew from a student comment about Robin's tree house. The teacher directed the shift, "Does anyone know what a banyan tree looks like?" Seven student responses followed, including connections to two familiar movies and the sharing of a related poem. Teacher comments included two probes, three informative comments, and a procedural suggestion. The teacher directed the next topic shift by drawing attention to a student comment about finishing the building of a birdhouse. "Let's deal with that for a moment. Kyle said they didn't finish because he (Robin) always interrupted and wanted to go down to see the ducks." The conversation returned to Robin. Eleven student responses were interspersed with three teacher probes, two summarizing statements, and one informative comment.

Throughout this representative discussion, the teacher initiated two text-based topics. All other topic shifts grew from student response. Fifteen teacher questions built upon prior student responses. Eighteen teacher questions and comments probed for further student explanation or multiple responses, nine teacher comments summarized student contributions, four teacher responses provided information, and three teacher comments responded to the acceptability of student response.

LGTL conversation focused on student understanding of the characters Robin and Georgie and how the events of the passage contributed to the dynamic nature of the main character. Conversation rehearsed knowledge about the characters and analyzed how the new insights combined to reflect a developing understanding of Georgie.

Interpretive Thinking About Characters

Transcripts of discussions and student writings were examined for evidence of interpretive thinking about characters in the form of character statements and intertextual support. Analysis identified character statements that describe, evaluate, and show personal reaction. A *description* was defined for this study as a word or group of words that portray the character within a range of text-based acceptability. An *evaluation* contains a student judgment or opinion about the character. Student responses that express an emotion (a) in relation to reading about the character or (b) as a direct result of a character's words or actions, were classified as *personal reactions*. Analysis also determined if the character statements were *supported* or *unsupported*. A *supported statement* was defined as one for which evidence is provided or a connection is made from an intertextual source. An *unsupported statement* is one for which no evidence or connection is made.

In SGPL discussions talk about characters focused on describing physical characteristics and recounting character actions. There were few examples of inferring character traits from character actions or dialogue. The few examples of analytic thinking expressed during discussions did not transfer into individual written character expressions. Collaborative character analysis in the group discussing *Fallen Angels* consisted of building an understanding of how each character coped with wartime survival. The group discussed emotional as well as physical survival techniques. They related character behaviors and thoughts to each individual's attempt to deal with the death and dying around them. As a follow-up project, each group member chose a character to describe (in writing and pictures) for a character book. The descriptions were brief, provided little supportive evidence, and related few of the survival ideas considered during discussion. Highly literal, the paragraphs showed little evidence of in-depth cognitive processing.

In the SGPL group reading *The Bomb,* very little discussion time was allotted to character analysis and evaluation. Teacher attempts to encourage more discussion of the characters went unheeded. Expressions of characterization learning were pictorial representations of characters with captions that retold story events.

Application of characterization learning may not have occurred in the SGPL groups for several reasons. First, the small groups may not have provided the cognitive models needed to illustrate analytic thinking. Without the presence of more knowledgeable peers, these average readers may not have been able to engage in collaborative character analysis. Some groups may not have had members who were willing to take the risk of making initial attempts at characterization talk. Second, at this early stage of learning about characterization, more teacher direction may have been needed. Teacher models, questions, probes, and summary statements may have been needed to scaffold preliminary student attempts at characterization thinking. Finally, the mode of presenting their characterization learning may have limited cognitive processing. Student-chosen formats may not have required in-depth analysis.

In contrast, LGTL students wrote character analyses at the conclusion of the novel unit that displayed evidence of well-developed individual understandings of the main character. Students described Georgie's personality traits at the beginning and end of the story, showing the changes in this character and supporting their descriptions with textual evidence. LGTL talk and writing also included evidence of evaluations of and personal reactions to the characters.

Although the SGPL students had more opportunities to contribute to their discussions, the more highly developed LGTL character analyses suggest that the LGTL discussion may have provided more support for analytic thinking. They may have benefited from a teacher-directed focus on character analysis that guided conversation to a more in-depth consideration of the personalities, contributions, and behaviors of the characters. In the LGTL discussion, the more proficient readers were the risk-takers who initially took advantage of the teacher's support to analyze characters. Those initial attempts, along with teacher feedback, may have provided models of characterization thinking for the less proficient readers. The "hidden" engagement of students listening to and thinking about the modeled processes may have led to the well-developed characterization writing. The LGTL discussion may have provided an effective forum for the acquisition of interpretive processes at a time when instructional support and modeling were critical.

Factors That Influenced Literary Discussions

Three factors appeared to affect the social construction of meaning in the two discussion structures: (a) text requirements, (b) student ability level, and (c) teacher control. The three factors did not appear to operate in isolation; they may have interacted to affect meaning construction.

Text requirements. Each text places unique demands upon the readers who attempt to construct meaning from it. These demands affect discussion topic choice, interactive structure, and strategies chosen to construct meaning. For example, because of the military language of *Fallen Angels*, its readers focused first on clarifying word meanings before constructing understandings of the plot and characters. The word discussions provided a preliminary structure from which a discussion of the assigned reading emerged. The historical nature of *The Bomb* led its readers to structure their discussions around a mapping and recounting of events. In contrast, the five girls reading *Homecoming* focused on their similarities with the teenage main character, making personal connections. The students who read *Roll of Thunder, Hear My Cry* reacted strongly to its depictions of racism. Discussions in this group emerged from reactions to and evaluations of acts of prejudice.

In each case, the character of the text itself may have influenced how its readers constructed meaning both individually and collaboratively in the literature discussion. Interactive structure and topic choice varied with the text discussed.

Student ability. A second factor that may have affected the social construction of meaning is student level of comprehension and interpretive proficiency. In two SGPL groups, discussions were predominantly group retellings of the reading. For those students who struggled to construct a literal understanding of the text, the retellings may have provided a needed rehearsal to test and complete individual comprehension. For those members who comprehended the passage, the retelling provided a forum for practicing and assessing their strategic selection of important events.

In contrast, two highly proficient readers discussing *Roll of Thunder, Hear My Cry* sometimes commented on those author's words that produced powerful images. They related the author's techniques to their own writing. Although these two students read like writers, the other members of their group needed support to correct confusions and fill in gaps in literal understanding. The group therefore spent most of its meeting time checking literal understanding and designing meaning-making strategies.

Preliminary evidence collected in this study suggests that the students' interpretive proficiency may affect how they constructed meaning individually and within the interactive setting. Both interactive structure and topic choice may be affected by students' ability to contribute to the literary interpretation process. Student factors also appear to affect how the reader interacts with text requirements. More proficient readers may have been able to personally reconstruct text events and then collaboratively evaluate character motives and roles in those events. The average readers in this study predominantly reconstructed meaning at a literal level in the SGPL groups with little application of characterization learning. More proficient readers may have orchestrated very different discussions.

Teacher control. In the whole class discussion, the teacher provided support for student interpretation. She collected student ideas, helped students to fill in gaps in understanding, encouraged students to respond to the ideas of others, and urged them to identify patterns emerging in the text. She encouraged multiple responses, yet required that those responses fall within a range of correctness as determined by the text. After directing a literal summary of important events, she urged and supported student analysis and evaluation of those events through probes, questions, and summary statements:

T: Why do you think that Georgie chose Robin to be his friend? Why would Georgie reach out to Robin?

DU: Robin looks at Georgie as his big brother since Paul died.

KM: When he took Robin to the pond, Amanda told him that he had to keep an eye on him like Paul.

T: So, he's watching over him, making sure he's safe, taking him to the pond like Paul used to.

AW: He's helping him with the birdhouse and pushing him to talk.

T: Like Paul.

TD: I think he's treating Robin like he wanted to be treated.

JB: Robin needs him.

DH: Georgie wants to be his brother.

BM: They can both help each other out and be friends.

JH: They both lost someone. They were both hurt badly emotionally.

T: So you see some similarities.

ZD: Robin lost Paul and Georgie lost his family.

AW: He sees himself in Robin, and he wants Robin to have the chances he didn't have.

KM: He wants to help Robin.

T: Extending a hand of friendship requires a risk. Georgie doesn't trust people. Why do you think he can trust this child?

EH: Maybe because Robin can't talk very well. If he tells him stuff, he won't repeat it.

TY: He's different than everyone else.

DH: He's like the rosebush. He won't fight back. He won't hurt Georgie.

For those students who had never considered character behaviors as evidence of character motives, feelings, and personality traits, the structured conversation provided support for their analyses. These supported analyses also provided peer models for nonparticipating students who witnessed examples of group character analysis. The LGTL support and peer models may have produced the positive character analysis results already discussed.

In the small-group peer-led discussions, the teacher played a less direct role. She facilitated the students' ability to control their own discussions by supporting their development of interactive and meaning-making strategies. When needed, she entered conversations with questions to urge students beyond group retelling. Finally, she provided end-of-discussion feedback and follow-up instruction.

Student control of the discussions appeared to have a positive effect on strategy development. Students worked on developing those processes that helped them to successfully construct meaning in their discussion group. Two SGPL groups developed strategies for developing vocabulary meaning; others worked on personal comprehension monitoring strategies. Finally, individuals in each group experimented with the role of writing as a tool for constructing meaning and supporting discussion. SGPL participants wrote questions to raise during discussions; paraphrased important ideas during reading; recorded confusing words and personal hypotheses about their meanings; and marked favorite sections and wrote personal reactions. LGTL students viewed strategic activities as teacher assignments. In contrast, SGPL students developed ownership of the their strategies for collaborative meaning-making. The SGPL discussions appeared to be important forums for the development and practice of meaning-making strategies.

Conclusions

The collaborative meaning-making described in this exploratory study of seventh-grade readers may be limited to the conditions and participants of the SGPL and LGTL discussions studied here. However, the factors that appeared to affect their interactions may be worthy of further study with other young adolescent readers. This preliminary investigation suggests that factors such as text requirements, student ability, teacher control, student choice, and purpose for discussion may affect the nature of student engagement, degree of interactive support, and learning outcomes.

The SGPL students in this study were relatively inexperienced in collaboratively constructing an understanding in a peer-led structure. A more experienced group of readers may have produced very different discussions. However, their inexperience may have also made them more willing to explore meaning-making strategies, to discuss and evaluate their use, and to provide their perspective on the interactive process. They openly shared what they perceived to be factors that affected their meaning-making and developed a collaborative process that they believed to support their needs as active, constructive readers. Their ideas and discussions provide the research community with the perspectives of one group of young adolescent readers about what is important in a literary discussion.

The most important contribution of this exploratory study may lie in the questions it raises about discussion structures. When designing interactive contexts to support literary learning, do we need to more closely consider instructional purpose? Is one interactive context more appropriate for skill acquisition and another more effective for strategy practice and application? If the engagement of highly proficient readers differs from that of less proficient readers, should student ability be considered during interactive design? Can we match student ability with appropriate levels of interactive support to optimize learning outcomes? Could we design new interactive structures that combine the benefits of those currently used? And finally, what other factors affect learning outcomes in literary discussions?

References

Almasi, J. (1995). The nature of fourth graders' sociocognitive conflicts in peer-led and teacher-led discussions of literature. *Reading Research Quarterly, 30,* 314–351.

Alpert, B. (1987). Active, silent, and controlled discussions: Explaining variations in classroom conversation. *Teaching and Teacher Education, 3*(1), 29–52.

Alvermann, D., O'Brien, D., & Dillon, D. (1990). What teachers do when they say they're having discussions of content area reading assignments: A qualitative analysis. *Reading Research Quarterly, 25,* 296–322.

Barr, R., & Dreeben, R. (1991). Grouping students for reading instruction. In R. Barr, M. L. Kamil, P. B. Mosenthal, & P. D. Pearson (Eds.), *Handbook of reading research* (Vol. 2, pp. 885–910). New York: Longman.

Bloome, D., & Green, J. (1992). Educational contexts of literacy. *Annual Review of Applied Linguistics, 12,* 49–70.

Cooney, C. (1994). *Drivers Ed.* New York: Bantam.

Eeds, M., & Peterson, R. (1995). What teachers need to know about the literary craft. In N. L. Roser & M. G. Martinez (Eds.), *Book talk and beyond: Children and teachers respond to literature* (pp. 10–23). Newark, DE: International Reading Association.

Fish, S. (1980). *Is there a text in this class?: The authority of interpretive communities.* Cambridge, MA: Harvard University Press.

Guthrie, J., & McCann, A. (1997). Characteristics of classrooms that promote motivations and strategies for learning. In J. T. Guthrie & A. Wigfield (Eds.), *Reading engagement: Motivating readers through integrated instruction* (pp. 128–148) Newark, DE: International Reading Association.

Hunt, I. (1976). *The lottery rose.* New York: Berkley.

Langer, J. A., Applebee, A. N., Mullis, I. V. S., & Foertsch, M. A. (1990). *Learning to read in our nation's schools: Instruction and achievement in 1988 at grades 4, 8, and 12.* Princeton, NJ: Educational Testing Service.

Myers, W. D. (1984). *Hoops.* New York: Dell.

Myers, W. D. (1988). *Fallen Angels.* New York: Scholastic.

Nystrand, M., & Gamoran, A. (1991). Instructional discourse, student engagement, and literature achievement. *Research in the Teaching of English, 25,* 261–290.

Rosenblatt, L. (1978). *The reader, the text, the poem: The transactional theory of the literary work.* Carbondale: Southern Illinois University Press.

Sweigert, W. (1991). Classroom talk, knowledge development, and writing. *Research in the Teaching of English, 25,* 469–496.

Taylor, M. (1976). *Roll of thunder, hear my cry.* New York: Bantam.

Taylor, T. (1995). *The bomb.* New York: Avon.

Voigt, C. (1981). *Homecoming.* New York: Fawcett Juniper.

Vygotsky, L. (1978). *Mind in society: The development of higher mental psychological processes.* Cambridge, MA: Harvard University Press.

Wells, G. (1994). The complementary contributions of Halliday and Vygotsky to a language-based theory of learning. *Linguistics and Education, 6,* 41–90.

What Happens to Book Talk When the Author Joins the Literature Circle?

Nancy L. Roser
University of Texas at Austin

Miriam G. Martinez
University of Texas at San Antonio

Heather Mrosla
Seattle Public Schools

Carol Junco and Arlene Gorman
Edgewood Independent School District, San Antonio

Jeanette Ingold
Children's Author

A s children's literature has garnered a greater presence in elementary class-rooms during the past decade, researchers and educators have worked to describe and better understand the nature of children's literary meaning making. Building on the work of literary response theorists such as Louise Rosenblatt (1978), recent studies have clearly established that elementary-aged children do "step into" story worlds and bridge their personal experiences with the literature they read (Hancock, 1993; Martinez, Roser, Hoffman & Battle, 1992; Raphael et al., 1992; Sipe, 1998).

There is also evidence that children's literary responses include attention to an author-crafter at work "behind the scenes." Using Langer's (1995) terms, young readers seem to be able to "step out" of the story world as well, and to "objectify" their experience with text. Researchers have documented children's attention to the text as a crafted object (Lehman & Scharer, 1996; Many & Wiseman, 1992; McGee, 1992; Wollman-Bonilla, 1989). Although studies have documented the occurrence of children's responses to the literary craft (Martinez et al., 1992; McGee, 1992), none has systematically described those responses.

Yet, across descriptive accounts of children's language in response to the texts they read, there is evidence that particular classroom procedures may support or enhance readers' "noticings" or awareness of an author at work. Most likely, there have been good reasons for delaying this close inspection of text as a "crafted object" (Cianciolo, 1982). Graves (1998), for example, posits that "character" is the logical focus when children write and read. To a child, it is character (rather than author) who captures attention and glues the story. Giving attention to an author at work making decisions behind the scenes about characters, language, and plot is secondary to a good read and to following characters. Even so,

National Reading Conference Yearbook, 49, pp. 266–276.

it is plausible that children can find and produce more richness in stories if they are gently guided toward the artist behind the art.

Although Edelsky (1988) argues that analyzing the creation of text is part of what people expect of literature study, it has been predominantly secondary teachers who have offered students "literature instruction" with its specialized terminology. For elementary teachers, the language of literature instruction has not been central to instruction. And, although elementary language arts and reading texts designed for preparing elementary teachers are replete with the language of comprehension instruction, they are less sure-footed about the route and lexicon of leading children through narrative discussion.

It is possible that instructional attention paid (at appropriate times and in legitimate amounts) to how an author has shaped a particular text may support students not just in their attempts to note and appreciate craft, but also to write with increasing sensitivity to authors' choices. This study, then, was directed toward eliciting and inspecting craft talk in an attempt to increase our understanding of students' awareness of the literary art. Toward that end, we examined other studies in which the author's craft had been brought front and center for children's consideration, the teacher's role in making the craft evident, and the kinds of instructional supports or "mediators" that could support discussion of the craft.

Bringing the Artist "Front and Center"

Children appear to be more likely to focus on the artistry of literature in contexts in which their attention is directed toward features of craft. Bloem and Manna (1999) involved children in an author study in an attempt to encourage thoughtful literary response. They invited second and fourth graders to pose questions to author/illustrator, Patricia Polacco—questions that would be asked in a phone interview. A central focus of their inquiry was to help students discover "what Polacco actually does as a writer and illustrator to get them to feel and think the way they do" (p. 803). The researchers describe their search for a balance between respecting children's experiences with text, and "celebrating their personal discoveries" with "tracking specific features of Polacco's technique" (p. 803).

Similarly, Madura (1995) approached teaching primary-age children the language arts through author/illustrator studies intended to immerse them in opportunities for aesthetic response to the picture book as "art object." Earlier, Kiefer (1988) had noted that children in the company of picture books seem to develop "a growing awareness of aesthetic factors and of the artist's role in choosing these factors" (p. 264).

Teachers' Role in Craft Talk

The teacher's role in literature discussion may also be an important consideration in nurturing children's responses to literature as a crafted object. Eeds and Peterson (1991) liken the teacher's skillful uncovering of a book's (sometimes hidden) delights to the role of the curator who directs the eye in a museum. Both help their "patrons" see what they would not have seen without such tutelage. As a second metaphor for helping children understand author's craft, Eeds and Peterson selected "shooting literary arrows"—a way of explaining that teachers' volleys of arrows of literary insight may sometimes hit their intended mark. Yet attention to craft may not often occur on initial readings of texts (while readers are still living within the story world), so it may well be important for teachers to read the text more than once and pay attention to their own responses to be sensitive curators. Saul (1989) suggests that book discussion leaders reach for the core of texts with children, so as not to be distracted with trivial questioning and irrelevant talk.

Supporting Craft Talk Through Instructional Materials or "Mediators"

There may be other, more concrete tools as well, that support craft talk. Roser, Strecker, and Ward (1996) found that instructional interventions they called "mediators" seemed to support sustained talk about varied texts. These mediators included children's use of literature response journals, language charts, varied supports for book club discussion, and inquiry charts, among others. Language charts, for example, preserve children's thoughtful reflections, extensions, and creations of meaning in classrooms in which children talk about books (Roser, Hoffman, Labbo, & Farest, 1992). Through their design, these charts can focus students' attention on specific aspects of the text being discussed—including author craft.

Beck and her colleagues (Beck, McKeown, Hamilton, & Kucan, 1997; Beck, McKeown, Worthy, Sandora, & Kucan, 1996) found that an instructional strategy, Questioning the Author, was useful in directing students' attention to what the author is trying to say in a text—a strategy particularly useful for uncovering ambiguity and seeking clarity in informational texts. In their work with aesthetic texts, Bloem and Manna (1999) posted sheets on classroom walls with leading questions (e.g., "How does the author/illustrator make this story happen?" and "Why do you think Polacco told this story?") to support students' explorations of author craft. Similarly, this investigation attempted to document the nature of craft talk that might occur if recording questions intended for the author became a regular part of the responsive talk in the literature circle.

Toward Investigating Craft

Over several studies exploring how teachers and their students work toward insight into authors' craft, we have tried to learn more about what supports and sustains discussion of craft, so that we can better understand how children can be guided toward sharper insights—without being overwhelmed by language, images, and instruction. In this investigation, we explored the following central question: What types of "craft talk" occur during book club when an author is brought "front and center" in book club discussion? We worked to bring the author to the forefront through the use of specific materials and procedures that might help to mediate focused (but not specified) craft talk. Those materials are described in the following section. To probe the central question, we asked: (a) When craft talk occurs, how is it initiated or launched? (b) When craft talk occurs, how is it sustained (to what extent do literary arrows meet their mark)? and (c) What happens to the craft talk when the author visits the literature circle?

Method

This descriptive study of the language of book discussion at two sites involved the teacher participants as co-investigators (with university researchers) in the study.

Setting and Participants

Two groups of six-grade girls in two cities of the Southwest volunteered to participate in book clubs in which they would read and discuss Jeanette Ingold's (1998) work of young adult historical fiction, *Pictures, 1918*. Each book group consisted of six girls. In City A, all six girls were from middle-class families, and attended a parochial school. Three of the girls were Hispanic, two were Caucasian, and one, African American. The girls in City A met with their book club teacher-leader for book club during their lunch period.

In City B, the six Hispanic girls attended a public school, and were from working class families. Their book club met after school, and had been meeting for approximately 6 months prior to this investigation. Two teachers met with this after-school book club: one was the girls' current teacher, whereas the second had been their teacher during the previous year.

The teachers in both settings were interested in reading and learning about book discussions, as well as in discussing the crafting of literary text. Each read research articles and essays about book discussions prior to the study, and each spoke regularly during the study with the university researchers about their plans and reactions to the book club sessions.

Materials

Materials for this investigation included the historical fiction that the students were to discuss, as well as other "mediators" designed and introduced to ease the author's work to the forefront. These materials included student and teacher response journals, language charts, and questions-for-the-author charts. Because the historical novel centers on preserving and creating memories on film, the girls captured their own memories during the study using disposable cameras. They completed photo record forms to track the subjects and reasons for their photographs.

Historical fiction. Each participant in the two book clubs received a copy of Jeanette Ingold's *Pictures, 1918*. The historical fiction, which reveals life in a small Texas town near the close of World War I, is told through the eyes of Asia, a 15-year-old girl who clings to cherished moments, through her keen interest in photography. Asia's special relationship with her grandmother (whose mental condition deteriorates over the course of the novel) is central to her growth in understanding. In addition to her interest in photography, Asia also has a budding romance with Nick Grissom. Nick's cousin, Boy, staying with the Grissom family while his father recovers from a war wound, serves as the antagonist, introducing issues of jealousy and pride. Through this array of characters, Jeanette Ingold immerses readers in life on the Texas home front during World War I. *Pictures, 1918* is filled with references to supporting the war effort, including food rationing, saving peach pits, and buying war bonds. The plot is also suspenseful in that readers try to figure out who is setting fires in the small fictional Texas town of Dust Crossing.

Response journal. Book club members received small, bound journals that they covered with photocopies of turn-of-the-century family photographs. The photographs were used to set the stage for the book, and to encourage the girls to connect with Asia and her interest in preserving memories through pictures. The girls in both groups wrote in the journals during each book club session.

Language charts. Large wall charts were created to help students focus on author craft. One chart was headed, "How Jeanette Ingold . . ." Its three columns invited students to think, talk, and record how the author reveals the emerging themes, sets an authentic time period, and shows characters developing. In addition, a second chart was designed to record the questions the girls raised that they would have liked to address to the author. The second chart was headed "Questions We Would Ask Ms. Ingold If She Were Here." A photograph of Ms. Ingold on the second chart served as still another attempt to bring the author "front and center" and encourage craft talk.

Procedures

In preparation for this study, the teachers read *Pictures, 1918* twice, the first time for enjoyment and the second time paying particular attention to the author's craft. In addition, prior to beginning book club sessions, the teachers met with the students and outlined the book club procedures. Each teacher knew that Jeanette Ingold would meet with the book clubs during their final session. Because meeting with an author to discuss a book is a rare occurrence, the study was designed to approximate more typical classroom book club conditions in City A. Although an author visit to both classrooms was planned, the girls in City A were told that after completing the book they could ask the author their unresolved questions electronically—through e-mail. In contrast, the girls in City B were told from the beginning of the project they would meet the author. In earlier studies with City B's all-girl book club, the university-based researchers had gained their confidence only over time. It seemed reasonable to expect that the presence of the author, if announced ahead of time, might help to mitigate the girls' reticence with a stranger.

The two book clubs met twice a week over a 5-week period. Book club typically began with a read aloud of two or three chapters. The girls had the choice of following along in their own copies or just listening as the teacher read. The read-aloud mitigated the varying reading levels across the participants. To capture the speculative talk that typifies discussion when readers are in the midst of a book, we kept all the copies of the books at school so that no one read ahead.

During book club, reading was sometimes interrupted by questions and attempts to clarify. After the read-aloud, the teachers and students typically took 5 to 8 minutes to write in their journals. An open discussion began when most writers finished, and continued until just before the end of the 50-minute period, when teachers directed the girls' attention to the large, butcher-paper language charts on the wall. There, the girls' observations and wonderings were recorded.

The last book club meeting differed significantly from the first 10 sessions because the author of *Pictures, 1918* visited both groups for the entire final book club session. We had anticipated that Ms. Ingold's presence at the last session would establish her as a "real person" with whom the girls could discuss their conjectures that had arisen in previous sessions about the workings of the story.

Data Collection and Analysis

Data were collected by audiotaping each session. In addition to audiotaping, the university-based researchers videotaped the author visit to each book club. The university researchers also took descriptive notes during the actual discussions, yet participated when questions were asked them, or their opinions sought. All of us collected and examined the girls' journal entries, the language charts, and the question charts. The children's author completed her own language chart individually and apart from the groups, so that she would be prepared for the kinds of directions the students' thinking may have taken. The university researchers and one teacher transcribed the tapes of 6 of the sessions (sessions 1, 2, 5, 6, 9, and 10), as well as the last session—the author visit (session 11). All of the teachers read through the transcriptions while listening to the tapes to determine the accuracy of the transcription and to catch hard-to-hear portions of the conversation. The session in which the author was present permitted comparison with the previous sessions.

Earlier research (Eeds & Wells, 1989) has shown that students are more likely to enter and talk about the story world to a greater extent than to "step out" of the story world to discuss the author at work or the author's messages or themes. We read and reread the 14 transcriptions to identify and highlight those instances of talk (whether by teacher or child) in which the speaker stepped outside the story world to consider the text as a crafted object. An instance of craft talk was considered as either an individual's single observation (offered and unpursued by other participants), or a sustained conversation by two or more participants. Both the noticings of an author at work of a single individual and the sustained talk of a group focused on a particular facet of craft were identified as an instance of craft talk. We grouped related instances of craft talk together, finally identifying six different categories of craft talk that appeared to describe the talk without (too much) ambiguity or overlap. Analysis followed Glaser and Strauss's (1967) constant comparison methodology, with the construction of the six categories followed by further specification and rechecking of the characteristics of the talk within each. We gradually refined categories, checking them against the teachers' perceptions of the book discussions in the two settings, and our expectations for craft talk based on the extant research literature. The six categories and examples are presented in Table 1.

Results

For this investigation, we collapsed the identified instances of craft talk across the two books clubs. Although the children in City A talked more overall and more

Table 1

Types of Craft Talk When the Author Is a Central Focus of Book Discussion

Types of Craft Talk/Defined As	Examples (from Transcripts)
Author as a Crafting Agent Talk that shows awareness that an author has been actively at work beneath a book's surface features, making decisions and leaving imprints.	S: I wonder why she thought of the name, *Pictures, 1918.*
Author's Use of Literary Elements Talk that considers setting, characters, mood, genre, etc. but from outside the story world.	T: A lot of things are kinda coming together, right? C: It's a mystery, kind of, putting it all together (genre traits). C: That doesn't sound like Boy (style).
Awareness of an Impersonal Crafting Agent Talk that indicates awareness that a purposeful, but unspecified, hand has acted upon the text. Whether a "they" or "it," the source of the art is ambiguous.	C: I don't think they've answered it in the book—why does Grandma have Alzheimer's?
Awareness of an Authoring Process Talk that shows awareness that an author has engaged in drafting, revising, editing, researching, etc.	C: I have another question. Did anyone help her write the book?
Awareness of the Author as Karnak Talk indicates that the author knows every nuance of the plot, and every detail that has happened or might happen to characters.	T: We'll ask Ms. Ingold, "Does Boy have a real name?"
Awareness of the Author as a Person Talk indicates awareness that the author lives a life apart from the book.	C: Miss, can we send these questions in to her? C: Where does she live?

about the author's craft than did the children in City B, it was not our immediate purpose to quantify or compare across settings. Rather, we wanted to identify and describe instances of craft talk by confirming categories that held up with different teachers and participants. Thus, the categories of craft talk were constructed and examples drawn from the transcripts from both sites.

To address the major research question (What types of craft talk occur during book club discussion when an author is brought to the forefront in book club discussion?) we identified six categories of craft talk that occurred during regular book sessions, and the proportion of craft talk falling into each category across 6 sessions for each book club (12 sessions in all). The 12 sessions were those that occurred before the author attended the final book club discussion. The categories (and their proportionate share of craft talk) were: (a) awareness of literary elements (31%); (b) awareness of a specific author making crafting moves (43%); (c) awareness of a nonspecific crafting agent (10%); (d) awareness of an author involved in the writing/publishing process (9%); (e) awareness of the author as a person (2%); and (f) awareness of "Author as Karnak," the all-knowing, all-seeing creator of the story world (4%).

To address the question, how is craft talk launched?, we categorized the craft talk by its instigator (i.e., "who shot the literary arrow"?). In the craft talk sessions prior to the author visit, the teachers initiated slightly fewer ($n=44$) craft talk observations, wonderings, or questions than did the students ($n=53$). In the presence of the author, students' craft talk, largely in the form of questions, raised their total initiations of craft talk to 74. Teachers launched no craft talk in the presence of the author.

We then compared the extent to which craft talk instigated by an adult was sustained versus the extent to which craft talk begun by children was picked up on. Of the instances in which a single individual questioned or commented on craft (but the talk was not pursued), both teachers and children initiated the talk 13 times. Children initiated double the instances of craft talk that were sustained by the group (66 instances vs. teachers' 31).

What happens to craft talk when the author visits? Using the same categories of craft talk, we coded the transcripts of the book club in which the author was present. A category that had claimed a relatively modest proportion of book talk in the earlier sessions (author as Karnak) emerged to claim the largest proportion of craft talk (66%). The next most prevalent category of craft talk focused on the author as a person—one with a life outside her writing (14%). Seemingly, the category system values nearly inverted. Those aspects of craft that claimed the least amount of talk outside the author's presence claimed the most attention when the author sat at the book club table (see Figure 1).

Discussion

In this study, children talked about text as a crafted object in the presence of their peers and teachers prepared to steer talk toward awareness of craft. Further, in the presence of mediators chosen to stimulate and support craft talk, these

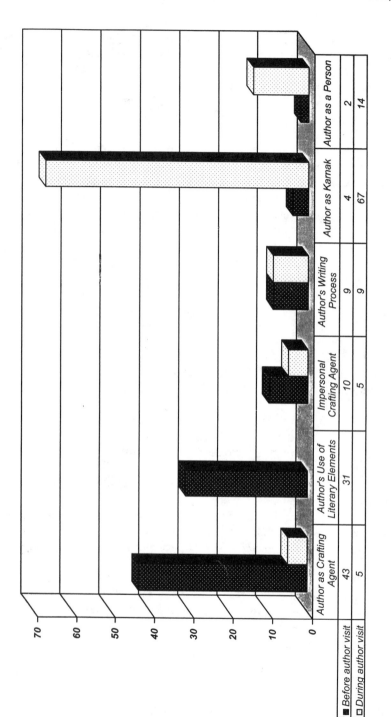

	Author as Crafting Agent	Author's Use of Literary Elements	Impersonal Crafting Agent	Author's Writing Process	Author as Karnak	Author as a Person
Before author visit	43	31	10	9	4	2
During author visit	5		5	9	67	14

Figure 1. Differences in proportions of craft talk in the presence of the author.

children initiated as much or more craft talk than their teachers. Apparently, when teachers are sensitive to the craft talk children initiate, the talk may be sustained to a greater extent than when teachers themselves "shoot the literary arrows."

The actual presence of an author during book club did not encourage craft talk. Rather, children may turn to the author to fill in the gaps and address the wonderings that good stories contain and evoke. In the presence of an all-knowing creator, perhaps readers believe that everything they wish to know about the characters' pasts and futures can be clarified, and all story mysteries can be solved. When the author appeared in person, the children were much less interested in how she worked to draw them in than in finding out the destinies and predilections of what she had crafted.

This "Author as Karnak" talk may not be craft talk at all. Rather, it may be a kind of false understanding that the mysteries created by a pen were not mysteries to the writer, that Iser's (1978) gaps in text are unintentional ones, and all can be made clear in the presence of the text's creator. When the author paused for a long moment to reflect, after being asked a "Karnak" question ("Was Boy abused as a child?"), she subtly showed children that she, too, had unanswered questions about her own creation.

In the presence of the author, talk changes. Intriguingly, in this study, the talk did not necessarily reflect the traditional notions of "craft talk," (i.e., talk of mood, elements, motifs). Instead, and unintentionally, the focus on the author visit took the emphasis away from multiple interpretations constructed by readers through their own transactions with a book to a focus on the meanings intended by the author. Rather than the actual presence of the author, bringing the author to the forefront *through mediators* may be a valuable way to nurture craft talk within the full spectrum of literary response. It was the awareness of an author that the mediators prompted (that the book was a purposefully created object) that did seem to elicit craft talk. To encourage children to assume the rich and varied stances that Langer (1995) and others describe, teachers must offer open-ended invitations to talk about literature, as well as introduce mediators designed to focus attention on literary craft.

References

Beck, I. L., McKeown, M. G., Hamilton, R. L., & Kucan, L. (1997). *Questioning the author: An approach for enhancing student engagement with text.* Newark, DE: International Reading Association.

Beck, I. L., McKeown, M. G., Worthy, J. Sandora, C. A., & Kucan, L. (1996). Questioning the author: A year-long classroom implementation to engage students with text. *Elementary School Journal, 96,* 385–414.

Bloem, P. L., & Manna, A. L. (1999). A chorus of questions: Readers respond to Patricia Polacco. *Reading Teacher, 52,* 802–808.

Cianciolo, P. (1982). Responding to literature as a work of art: An aesthetic literary experience. *Language Arts, 59,* 259–264.

Edelsky, C. (1988). Living in the author's world: Analyzing the author's craft. *The California Reader, 21,* 15–17.

Eeds, M., & Peterson, R. (1991). Teacher as curator: Learning to talk about literature. *Reading Teacher, 45,* 118–126.

Eeds, M., & Wells, D. (1989). Grand conversation: An exploration of meaning construction in literature study groups. *Research in the Teaching of English, 23,* 4–29.

Glaser, B. G., & Strauss, A. L. (1967). *The discovery of grounded theory.* Chicago: Aldine.

Graves, D. (1998, November). Address at the meeting of the National Council of Teachers of English, Nashville, TN.

Hancock, M. R. (1993). Exploring the meaning-making process through the content of literature response journals: A case study investigation. *Research in the Teaching of English, 27,* 335–368.

Ingold, J. (1998). *Pictures, 1918.* San Diego, CA: Harcourt.

Iser, W. (1978). *The act of reading: A theory of aesthetic response.* Baltimore, MD: Johns Hopkins University Press.

Kiefer, B. (1988). Picture books as contexts for literary, aesthetic, and real world understandings. *Language Arts, 65,* 260–271.

Langer, J. A. (1995). *Envisioning literature: Literary understanding and literature instruction.* Newark, DE: International Reading Association and Teachers College Press.

Lehman, B. A., & Scharer, P. L. (1996). Reading alone, talking together: The role of discussion in developing literary awareness. *Reading Teacher, 50,* 26–35.

McGee, L. M. (1992). An exploration of meaning construction in first graders' grand conversations. In C. K. Kinzer & D. J. Leu (Eds.), *Literacy research, theory, and practice: Views from many perspectives.* Forty-first yearbook of the National Reading Conference (pp. 177–186). Chicago: National Reading Conference.

Madura, S. (1995). The line and texture of aesthetic response: Primary children study authors and illustrators. *Reading Teacher, 49,* 110–118.

Many, J. E., & Wiseman, D. L. (1992). The effect of teaching approach on third-grade students' response to literature. *Journal of Reading Behavior, 24,* 265–287.

Martinez, M., Roser, N. L., Hoffman, J. V., & Battle, J. (1992). Fostering better book discussions through response logs and a response framework: A case description. In C. K. Kinzer & D. J. Leu (Eds.), *Literacy research, theory, and practice: Views from many perspectives.* Forty-first yearbook of the National Reading Conference (pp. 303–311). Chicago: National Reading Conference.

Raphael, T. E., McMahon, S. I., Goatley, V. J., Bentley, J. L., Boyd, F. B., Pardo, L. S., & Woodman, D. A. (1992). Research directions: Literature and discussion in the reading program. *Language Arts, 69,* 54–61.

Rosenblatt, L. M. (1978). *The reader, the text, the poem: The transactional theory of the literary work.* Carbondale: Southern Illinois University Press.

Roser, N., Hoffman, J., Labbo, L., & Farest, C. (1992). Language charts: A record of story time talk. *Language Arts, 69,* 44–52.

Roser, N., Strecker, S., & Ward, T. (1996). What I wanna know is why Sam Houston's mom named him after a city: Moving (slowly) toward inquiry in fourth grade. In D. J. Leu, C. K. Kinzer, & K. A. Hinchman (Eds.), *Literacies for the 21st century: Research in practice.* Forty-fifth yearbook of the National Reading Conference (pp. 134-145). Chicago: National Reading Conference.

Saul, W. (1989). "What did Leo feed the turtle?" and other nonliterary questions. *Language Arts, 66,* 295–303.

Sipe, L. (1998). Individual literary response styles of first and second graders. In T. Shanahan & F. V. Rodriguez-Brown (Eds.), *National Reading Conference Yearbook, 47* (pp. 76–89). Chicago: National Reading Conference.

Wollman-Bonilla, J. E. (1989). Reading journals: Invitations to participate in literature. *Reading Teacher, 42,* 112–120.

Using Authentic Assessment for Understanding Emergent Literacy Development: A Case Study

Michele Baker
Lubbock Independent School District

Jeanne Swafford
Texas Tech University

Historically, play was overlooked as a valuable learning experience in class-rooms (Moffett & Wagner, 1993). However, research in emergent literacy development caused researchers to take a closer look at the relationship between play and literacy development (Christie, 1990, 1991). They discovered that as children experiment with reading and writing, they develop an understanding of the concepts and features of print (Clay, 1975, 1986; Schickedanz, 1986). Recognizing that much of children's experimenting occurs in play led researchers to reconsider the role of play in literacy development (Christie & Enz, 1992). During the last decade, there has been a plethora of research related to designing literacy-enhanced play environments that support children's exploration of various aspects of literacy (Christie, 1990, 1991; Christie & Enz, 1992; Morrow, 1990; Morrow & Rand, 1991; Neuman & Roskos, 1990; Rosko, 1990).

Piaget's (1962) and Vygotsky's (1978) theories support the assertion that play performs an integral role in children's cognitive development and that play provides a nonthreatening environment in which children may explore new concepts. Whereas Piaget's work provides insights into the individual nature of children's development through play, Vygotsky's work extends this perspective to provide a deeper understanding of the sociocultural aspects of children's development through play (Nicilopoulou, 1993). Vygotsky (1978) viewed this social dimension of meaning construction as the most significant part of cognitive development. He also introduced the idea that optimal cognitive development occurs within a zone of proximal development, the critical area between what a child can do independently and what a child can do with guidance from more experienced individuals. He also asserted that teaching and learning should occur within authentic, purposeful, child-initiated contexts (Vygotsky, 1978), all of which play provides.

The manner in which Piaget and Vygotsky asserted that play encourages cognitive development is particularly important for literacy development. Both theorists believed that it is through play that children develop symbolic, abstract levels of thought and that play is the primary mechanism through which children learn to develop representational thought. In play, children often use objects to

National Reading Conference Yearbook, 49, pp. 277–290.

stand for something outside of the immediate environment. A child's first experience with the use of symbols is usually within the context of play (Piaget, 1962; Vygotsky, 1978).

The expanded understanding of the role of play for literacy development created an opportunity for educators to utilize literacy-enhanced play environments for emergent literacy assessment. Authentic forms of assessment are consistent with recommendations set forth by the Association for Childhood Education International (Perrone, 1991). These recommendations state that assessment practices should be "related to best practice, and rooted directly in the instructional process itself" (Perrone, 1991, p. 133).

Some research has been conducted to explore the use of literacy-enhanced play environments as a source for emergent literacy assessment. Vukelich and Valentine (1990) found that a literacy-enhanced play environment is an excellent context for teachers to observe young children's emergent literacy behaviors. Vukelich (1994) found that play observations can provide teachers opportunities to discover what children understand about the functions of print. What has not been fully explored is what play observations can reveal about preschool children's general understandings of literacy. Also of concern is whether play observations provide information about children's literacy development that are not revealed through other means of assessment.

Purpose

The purpose of this qualitative case study was to explore the use of play as a context for authentic literacy assessment. The following questions guided the study: (a) What types of emergent literacy demonstrations does a child exhibit while interacting in literacy-enhanced play centers? (b) What do these demonstrations reveal about a child's understandings of literacy? (c) Are play observations a feasible and worthwhile form of literacy assessment for teachers of young children?

Methods

Design of the Study

A qualitative case study design was appropriate for this research for several reasons. First, one child (Amy) was the participant, which delimits the study (Merriam, 1998). Second, the study took place in a naturalistic classroom context, an important consideration when doing research with young children (Sulzby & Teale, 1991). The naturalistic setting also was more likely to provide a holistic view of Amy's literacy development than a contrived setting. Third, the teacher (Michelle) wanted to describe and analyze Amy's literacy understandings over a period of time (Merriam, 1998). Fourth, Michelle wanted to see Amy's play through a new lens. She wanted to view Amy's play with a new curiosity—what Eisner (1991) calls making the familiar strange.

Setting

Data for this study were collected from January through mid-May in Michelle's pre-kindergarten classroom, which was part of a church's kids-day-out program in a mid-sized city in the southwestern United States. Children attended preschool all day, 2 days a week. Ten 4- and 5-year-old children were in Michelle's class. Their birth dates made them eligible to enter kindergarten the next fall. The only required curriculum in the preschool was the *A Beka Book* program (Horton, 1988). The emphasis of the program is on teaching isolated phonics in a structured manner through drill and practice. Michelle met these requirements by spending about 10 to 15 minutes each day on letter-sound drills. Children also did worksheets and sometimes Michelle sent worksheets home for students to complete if they wished. Approximately 75 minutes of the day, children played in literacy-enhanced play centers. Part of the day was also set aside for hands-on activities that expanded children's knowledge of literacy, music, and science. They also played outside and engaged in activities that provided opportunities to improve hand-eye coordination and small motor skills.

Participant

Michelle purposively selected (Lincoln & Guba, 1985) 5-year-old Amy (pseudonym) as the participant in this study for several reasons. After observing Amy's behaviors in formal instructional and assessment contexts and in informal play contexts, Michelle suspected that Amy did not demonstrate her emerging literacy understandings in formal situations. At the beginning of the school year, Michelle used informal assessment procedures to determine students' literacy understandings. Amy identified only eight uppercase and three lowercase letters when Michelle asked her to identify letters on flashcards in a one-on-one context. Amy demonstrated that she could distinguish between numbers and letters and knew some book handling concepts such as the front of a book. Amy did not know, however, where a person would begin reading on a page. She also reported that she could not write any part of her name.

During classroom activities, Michelle noticed that Amy tended not to participate in large- or small-group teacher-directed activities. She seldom attempted any activities that involved a new skill. Amy did not attempt to scribble write or write letter strings on her artwork or in her journal as other children did. When encouraged to do this, Amy said she could not write.

In contrast to Amy's literacy demonstrations in teacher-initiated or teacher-directed activities, Amy seemed to function differently during her play in centers. For example, Amy used emergent writing in literacy-enhanced play centers. Ten days after Amy said she could not write her name, she wrote it in a play center in shaving cream. Amy also wrote many letters in her friend Katie's name in play centers. She also used pretend writing and letter strings when playing in the Kitchen Center. Michelle concluded that Amy knew much more than the literacy assessment or participation in teacher-directed activities indicated. Therefore, Michelle decided to use observation in free play centers to assess Amy's literacy understandings.

Data Collection

Throughout the 19-week period of data collection, Michelle observed Amy twice weekly during the 75-minute free play period in centers that were infused with literacy props. The design of the play centers was consistent with the literature that describes literacy-enhanced play centers (e.g., Morrow, 1990; Morrow & Rand, 1991; Neuman & Roskos, 1990). In addition, themed centers were an extension of large group instruction and concept-building activities. These activities included taking field trips, interacting with guest speakers, participating in hands-on activities, watching videos, and reading books related to a theme. For example, when students were studying about building and construction, they walked to a construction site to watch a building being built. A builder visited the classroom, talked about his job, and described how he used blueprints and particular tools. The class also watched videos and read books about construction. The Block Center included not only blocks but also blueprints, invoices, work orders, tool catalogs, and house plans. Concept-building activities, materials, and literacy props in centers provided children with background knowledge they needed to develop play scenarios using the literacy props as integral parts of their play.

Michelle collected data using participant observation (P-O) guidelines (Bogdan & Biklen, 1992; Glesne & Peshkin, 1992; Lincoln & Guba, 1985). Her roles as P-O varied according to what seemed most appropriate in a given situation (Neuman & Roskos, 1993). As onlooker, Michelle acted as an audience to children's play and did not take an active role. As player, she took on the role of a sensitive partner (Vukelich, 1994). She interacted with children in centers as suggested by Morrow (1990), taking cues from them and playing roles they determined. She also interjected literacy demonstrations when they fit naturally into children's play. On a few occasions, Michelle took the role of leader and assisted children when they needed direction in using literacy props in the centers. Even as a leader, Michelle made sure that children fulfilled their own purposes when playing (Vukelich, 1994).

The primary data source for this study was descriptive fieldnotes (Bogdan & Biklen, 1992). In these notes, Michelle described in detail what Amy did in play centers to demonstrate her literacy understandings. She also kept a reflective journal to record her own biases, questions, ideas, and hunches (Bogdan & Biklen, 1992). Secondary sources of data included audiotaped and videotaped interactions of children in play centers. In addition, Michelle collected artifacts Amy created within the context of play. Michelle used informal interviews with Amy to gain a full understanding of what the artifacts meant to her. She also informally interviewed Amy and her friends during play to gain the children's perspectives about their actions. Prolonged engagement, persistent observation, triangulation, peer debriefing, and member checking were used to insure credibility of this study.

Data Analysis

Inductive data analysis began during data collection as suggested by Bogdan and Biklen (1992). Michelle took time to examine and speculate about the meaning of the data throughout her field work. Initially codes remained open and unstructured and emerged from marginal notes recorded in fieldnotes and in reflective notes. Midway through the study, Michele revisited related literature to help her understand Amy's literacy development more fully. She looked especially at descriptions of the types of literacy understandings children typically develop. She found the terminology Clay (1975) used in her work to be particularly helpful as she coded data.

At the end of data collection, Michelle read the data in their entirety several times, first to get a comprehensive view of the data and thereafter making marginal notes that provided direction for developing her final codes. She also reviewed the videotapes and audiotapes to add clarity and validation to her descriptive fieldnotes. She analyzed data from various sources to get a more complete picture of Amy's literacy understandings.

As Michelle analyzed data, she continually reviewed her research questions. Then she examined the data and tested possible codes. She developed rules to clearly define the codes as suggested by Lincoln and Guba (1985). Then she examined the data to determine patterns or regularities, and finally established categories. The code and category labels were drawn from the work of Clay (1975), Schickendanz (1986), and Vukelich (1994). These sources helped her understand Amy's literacy behaviors and provided labels for those behaviors. By using common terminology, she also hoped that readers would be able to more easily transfer her findings to their own situations.

The codes were organized into two categories: functions of print and concepts of print. To define which data should be included in each category, Michelle developed questions related to each. For example, questions related to the "functions of print" category included: In what ways is Amy using print? How is Amy using print to meet her goals and needs? How is Amy directing others to use print? Questions related to the "concepts of print" category included: What do Amy's actions tell me she knows about how print is organized? What do Amy's actions tell me she knows about the concepts of print? For both categories, Michelle listed literacy demonstrations from her data sources to illustrate the functions and concepts of print Amy understood.

Results

Amy demonstrated an understanding of 14 different functions of print:

1. to gain instruction;
2. to provide others with information;
3. to provide labels;
4. to test skills of others;
5. to organize;
6. to identify ownership;
7. to tell a story;
8. to fill time or entertain;
9. as a resource for information;
10. to influence or direct other's behavior;
11. to gain entrance or reserve space;
12. to designate money;
13. to convey feelings; and
14. to record information.

Table 1 provides examples of Amy's literacy demonstrations that illustrate each function of print delineated above.

Amy demonstrated her understanding of eight different concepts of print:

1. print is made up of separate words;
2. print carries a message;
3. print has its own type of language;
4. print has directionality and orientation;
5. print holds a permanent message;
6. print has punctuation;
7. print and pictures are related; and
8. print has special features.

Table 2 provides examples of Amy's literacy demonstrations that illustrate each concept of print she understood.

Amy demonstrated her understandings of the concepts and functions of print in her play as she worked on projects individually and enacted play scenarios with her friends. In all instances, Amy used literacy for authentic purposes that she or her friends determined. Amy's literacy demonstrations were purposeful, situated, highly interactive, and goal oriented.

In order to help the reader better understand how Amy incorporated literacy into her play, we provide narrative descriptions of her play in two centers: a nonthematic Block Center and a themed play center. Then we describe what Amy's actions revealed about her literacy understandings.

One day in the Block Center, Amy and Katie were building a town with wooden blocks and road signs. Dennis pretended to be a dog and began knocking down their buildings. The girls asked Dennis to stop but when he did not, they went to Michelle for help. She asked them what they could do to keep Dennis from knock-

Table 1

Functions of Print

Code	Illustrative Literacy Demonstrations
Print is used to gain instructions.	Used a map to look for places Used a recipe to prepare food
Print is used to provide others with information.	Wrote an address and drew a map for children who were pretending to be fire fighters Wrote a letter to Katie's sister to tell her when to pick Katie up Wrote a note for medicine while playing in the Animal Hospital Center
Print is used to provide labels.	Labeled rooms on a blueprint Labeled different parts of a picture Asked the teacher to read the words on a puzzle because Amy wanted to "to know all the kids' names"
Print is used to test others' skills.	Gave a friend a letter identification test while playing school Gave an "eye test" to a parrot in the Animal Hospital Center
Print is used to organize.	Reorganized centers by using labels on shelves and tubs Told a peer that he used the wrong folder to examine a dog in Animal Hospital Center
Print is used to identify. ownership	Identified her room on a house plan by putting her name on it Wrote "mom" on an envelope
Print is used to tell a story.	Used sidewalk chalk to draw a picture and write a story about bubbles Asked teacher to record a story to accompany a picture Amy had drawn
Print is used to fill time or entertain.	Read a book when she was "too tired to play" Flipped through magazines while waiting in the Animal Hospital Center Lounged on a sleeping bag and looked through travel brochures
Print is used as a resource for information.	Found the name of a crane in a book Copied words from a book to make a menu Wrote the word *tiger* on her picture by copying it from a friend's shirt
Print is used to influence or direct other's behavior.	Made a *No Dogs* sign so a child would quit pretending to be a dog and stop knocking over her block structure

Table 1 *(continued)*

Code	Illustrative Literacy Demonstrations
	Tried to convince another child to stop crashing her car by writing him a ticket
	Made a *Do Not Touch* sign and placed it on circus toys in the Block Center
Print is used to gain entrance or reserve space.	Made children "sign in" at the "Animal Hospital"
	Told a child to call for an appointment at the "Animal Hospital" so she could write it down
	Wrote her name and placed it beside the typewriter saying "this means I'm next"
Print is used to designate money.	Used play money and checks while playing "store"
	Told a child to write a check when she did not have enough play money to pay for something
Print is used to convey feelings.	Wrote a letter to her mother to tell her she was mad
	Drew a picture of something that made her happy and asked the teacher to write a story
Print is used to record information.	Wrote a report about a fire
	Wrote an order while playing in the Restaurant Center
	Wrote a phone message in the Office Center

ing down their blocks. Amy's first solution was that Michelle should tell Dennis to play in another center. Michelle, however, told the girls they needed to work out the problem themselves.

Katie and Amy proceeded to the Reading Center, sat in comfortable chairs, and discussed different ways they could stop Dennis. All at once Amy declared, "We need to make a sign, just like Mrs. Michelle did for the water!" (Michelle had recently put a "do not touch" sign on the water faucet in the classroom.) Amy and Katie decided to make a sign that said, "No Dogs." Katie was the scribe and Amy dictated. They wrote *NO* with few problems. When they got to the word *dog*, Amy told Katie that the word *dog* started with a *d* and has a *g,* but she could not help Katie write the letter *g.* Katie wrote the letter *d,* and Amy asked Greg how to write a *g.* Then she told Katie to look at the dog poster on the wall and copy the word *dog.* When the girls finished, Michelle asked Amy what the sign said. She replied, "No dogs." Then the girls hung the sign in the Block Center.

In the example above, Amy solved a problem with a classmate by using her knowledge of various concepts of print. She demonstrated her understandings of letter-sound relationships when she determined that the word *dog* begins with the letter *d* and also has a letter *g* in it. She also knew that Greg had the letter *g* in his name. She demonstrated her understanding that particular letters are made by

Table 2

Concepts of Print

Code	Illustrative Literacy Demonstrations
Print is made up of separate words.	Used spaces between letter clusters in a letter string then pointed to each cluster while "reading" what she had written Pointed to 1 word at a time while reading the "Share with friends" rule
Print carries a message.	Asked teacher to read the story Amy had written with a letter string under a picture Told the teacher her picture was not a story because Amy had not written any words
Print has its own type of language.	Asked teacher to "read a book not just tell the pictures" when she paraphrased an unknown story to speed up the reading Began "reading" stories she had written with the phrase "once upon a time"
Print has directionality, orientation, and return sweep.	Pointed at words from left to right and top to bottom while retelling familiar stories Wrote letter strings from left to right, top to bottom
Print holds a permanent message.	Asked teacher to read a poem they had read previously stating, "I know it says 'Jack and Jill' because we read it yesterday." Was upset when the teacher read Amy's letter string differently on two occasions
Print includes punctuation.	Used an exclamation mark in her "Happy Happy Happy" story Stated that a dot means the end
Print and pictures are related.	Stated that she had the wrong cookbook because the pictures showed dinner foods instead of desserts Used pictures on an instruction sheet to figure out how to play a game Used the pictures in a cookbook to decide the ingredients in a cake
Print has special features.	Corrected a child, who had misread *tractor* instead of *snort,* by pointing to a word that began with the letter *s* Identified uppercase letters while playing in the Animal Hospital Center and when playing with an ABC puzzle

certain symbols when she said she did not know how to make the letter *g*. She demonstrated that she understood that the words *no* and *dogs* are two different words when they decided how to spell the words. By suggesting another print source for the word *dog*, Amy displayed her understanding that print can be used as a resource for information. The decision to make the "No dog" sign indicated her awareness that print can function to influence or direct other's behaviors. She also demonstrated her understanding that print carries a message.

In the Fire Station Center, Amy showed still more knowledge of literacy. Several concept-building activities preceded her interactions in the center. A fire-fighter visited the classroom to talk about his job, and Michele read a book about fire-fighters. Because the fire-fighter talked about how maps helped him locate fires, the class also looked at a variety of maps and drew maps of various places. The center contained artifacts and literacy props specific to a Fire Station. Because of the explicit context of the center, it encouraged Amy and her friends to engage in particular play scenarios, rather than more general play as illustrated above in the Block Center.

In this particular example, Amy, Katie, Steven, and Greg were playing together. Steven and Greg were sleeping when the phone rang. Amy answered it and wrote squiggle lines on paper and sketched a map. She woke up the boys, handed them the paper, and told them the address of the fire and a map were written on it. The boys got out all their equipment (pretend hats, coats, hoses) and pushed the toy fire trucks to the fire. When they finished fighting the fire, they put away their equipment in labeled shelves. Amy told Greg that he put his hat in the wrong place on the shelf. Katie told Amy to write a report about the fire (that they had learned about in a book Michelle had read earlier). The girls wrote their reports in spiral notebooks.

While playing in the Fire Station Center, Amy's note, map, and report demonstrated her understanding of three functions of print: to record information, to provide others with information, and to gain instructions. Her admonition to Greg demonstrated her knowledge of two additional functions of print: to organize and to provide labels.

Discussion

Based on Michelle's experience, we believe it is important for teachers of young children to use play observations to assess some children's emerging literacy knowledge, especially those who do not demonstrate their understandings during decontextualized assessment tasks. Michelle found a dramatic difference between what play observations revealed about Amy's literacy development and what was revealed by the *Observation Survey of Early Literacy Achievement* (*OS*) (Clay, 1993), which Michelle administered toward the end of the school year. Below we compare what Amy knew based on play observations with what she knew based on *OS* results.

On the Letter Identification section of *OS*, Amy named 12 uppercase and 6 lowercase letters. When Amy played with an alphabet puzzle, she identified 20 uppercase letters. On another occasion, when giving a "parrot" an "eye test," she identified 17 uppercase letters. On the Hearing Sounds in Words section of the *OS*, Amy made no attempt. This is in sharp contrast to the many times Amy worked diligently to hear the sounds in words as she wrote stories to accompany her art work, wrote a letter to her mom, and made signs.

On the Word Test section of the *OS*, Amy made no attempt to read any words even though it included words, such as *and, I,* and *Mother,* which she often read and could pick out in her favorite books. While playing, Amy read many words that held meaning for her, such as her classmates' names, posters in the Home Living and Animal Hospital Centers, labels posted around the room, and environmental print in games. On the Writing Vocabulary portion of the *OS*, Amy made no attempt to write any words beyond her name. In play, however, Amy often attempted to write words such as *dog, mom,* and *Katie.*

On the Concepts of Print portion of *OS*, Amy demonstrated few concepts of print that she had demonstrated clearly in play. On the *OS*, she did not demonstrate knowledge of directionality, orientation, or return sweep. In play, Amy read simple stories or pretended to read unknown texts and pointed to words demonstrating her knowledge of these concepts. In addition, on the *OS*, Amy was unable to differentiate between a letter, word, or uppercase letter. When Michelle asked her to answer the same kinds of questions during play, Amy demonstrated her understanding of these concepts. She also showed that she understood these concepts in her writing. The above comparisons provide convincing evidence that play observations provided Michelle with important insights into Amy's literacy understandings that were not reflected by the *OS*.

How feasible are play observations in a regular classroom setting? Although Michelle's class had fewer students than most primary grade classrooms, we believe it is feasible to use play observations as one tool to assess students' literacy knowledge. We do not believe, however, that it is feasible to assess every child's literacy development through play observations alone.

To use play for assessment, two major issues need to be resolved. First, how can a teacher observe a few children and, at the same time, fulfill her responsibilities to the other students? Second, how does a teacher know what to record and have time to record students' literacy understandings? One way to overcome the first obstacle is to schedule play observations when another adult is present in the classroom. A teaching assistant, parent volunteer, or university intern could provide assistance during center time. The teacher could focus more on observations and another adult could supervise and assist other students. Ease of recording information during observations is not as difficult as it may seem initially. Teachers can develop simple, systematic ways to record literacy demonstrations. Routman (1994) suggests taking anecdotal records while students work in centers and during other routine classroom activities. Simple, teacher-developed checklists can also be used. Curriculum guidelines or published instruments such as the *OS* provide a good starting point.

Literacy demonstrations, such as Amy's, will not occur in any environment. Centers need to be carefully designed and literacy props need to be integral parts of them. Simply placing literacy props in centers will not guarantee that students will use them. If students are unfamiliar with the props, they will not develop play scenarios that result in rich literacy demonstrations. Teachers must model how literacy props are used within the context of a center, preferably as students initiate their use. When themed centers are used, teachers also need to provide adequate concept-building experiences so students have some knowledge from which to create play scenarios. In addition, teachers must provide children with plenty of time to interact in risk-free, literacy-enhanced play centers.

Theoretical Significance

Michelle's decision to use play observations to assess Amy's literacy development was guided by Piaget's and Vygotsky's assertions that play performs an integral role in cognitive development and, more specifically, literacy development. This study supports the notion set forth by Piaget that play provides a nonthreatening environment in which children can exercise and experiment with emerging literacy skills without the constraint of correctness. Likewise, the study supports Vygotsky's belief that teaching and learning should occur within authentic, purposeful, child-initiated contexts. Michelle designed a classroom environment that included a large block of time for free play in literacy-enhanced centers. This environment supported Amy's ongoing literacy development and supports Vygotsky's (1978) assertion that "teaching should be organized in such a way that reading and writing are necessary for something" and that "reading and writing must be something children need" (p. 117). Furthermore, he wrote that writing must be relevant and meaningful to children's lives and arouse an intrinsic need. These conditions in Michelle's classroom supported Amy's literacy development. Clearly, Amy demonstrated a wider range of literacy skills in child-initiated play settings than in teacher-initiated instructional or assessment contexts. Using literacy for a variety of functions, Amy experimented with her literacy understandings in play and demonstrated her growing knowledge of concepts of print in play settings.

Michelle also designed a classroom environment that encouraged social interactions among students as they constructed meaning and developed their literacy understandings. Vygotsky's theories hypothesize that learning occurs in social situations and that play is inherently social. In this study, play contexts in the classroom community provided Amy with varied opportunities to construct meaning with print. Assessment within these contexts revealed Amy's literacy understandings. Her literacy demonstrations in play exemplify Vygotsky's (1978) assertion that, "In play a child always behaves beyond his average age, above his daily behavior; in play it is as though he were a head taller than himself. As in the focus of a magnifying glass, play contains all developmental tendencies in a condensed form and is itself a major source of development" (p. 102).

The play opportunities in Michelle's classroom also provided contexts in which children with varying literacy understandings could interact. Vygotsky's theories support the notion that when children socialize with more capable individuals in play, they can gain valuable insights that lead to further cognitive development, and in this case literacy development. The narrative descriptions above demonstrate Amy's collaboration with her peers as they used their literacy skills to solve problems and enact play scenarios. No single child was the "shining star," but all children contributed their personal literacy understandings and shone brightly in their own right. In these supportive social contexts within Amy's zone of proximal development, she developed and utilized her growing literacy skills and knowledge in contexts that were meaningful to her. Assessing children's literacy development in play contexts provides teachers with opportunities to glimpse children's developing literacy skills rather than simply evaluating what they have mastered.

Educational Importance

This case study demonstrates the importance of designing classroom environments that provide opportunities for children to interact and use their emerging literacy knowledge in literacy-enhanced play centers. Moreover, it provides indisputable evidence that play observations can offer teachers a clear sense of what students understand about literacy and, subsequently, inform instruction. Goodman (1978) wrote that kid-watching in literacy-enhanced environments can provide teachers with opportunities to observe children engaging in literacy demonstrations that meet a variety of authentic purposes. Furthermore, she wrote that by watching children interact with their peers in supportive environments, teachers can understand and support children's language development. She further asserted that it is the role of school to provide children with environments that can expand their uses of language in a variety of settings and situations (Goodman, 1978).

This study provides evidence that supportive literacy environments give children opportunities to use their developing language skills in a variety of contexts to meet their own goals. Accordingly, the teacher has opportunities to observe children as they explore their environments and exercise their developing literacy skills, assess student learning, and, in response, plan appropriate instruction. This study shows that using less structured, authentic settings for assessment may reveal more accurately what students know about literacy than decontextualized assessments.

This study adds to the literature that supports the use of multiple measures to evaluate student learning. It provides evidence that no single instrument accurately portrays student learning and development. As this case study exemplifies, children may not demonstrate their literacy understandings on decontextualized, inauthentic tasks. Therefore, observations in literacy-enhanced play centers provide alternative opportunities to determine the literacy understandings children construct in context.

References

Bogdan, R., & Biklen, S. (1992). *Qualitative research for education*. Boston: Allyn & Bacon.

Christie, J. F. (1990). Dramatic play: A context for meaningful engagements. *Reading Teacher, 43*, 542–545.

Christie, J. F. (1991). *Play and early literacy development*. Albany: State University of New York Press.

Christie, J. F., & Enz, B. (1992). The effects of literacy play interventions on preschoolers' play patterns and literacy development. *Early Childhood and Development, 9*, 205–220.

Clay, M. M. (1975). *What did I write*. Portsmouth, NH: Heinemann.

Clay, M. M. (1986). Constructive processes: Talking, reading, writing, art, and craft. *Reading Teacher, 39*, 764–770.

Clay, M. M. (1993). *An observation survey of early literacy achievement*. Auckland: Heinemann.

Eisner, E. W. (1991). *The enlightened eye*. New York: Macmillan.

Glesne, C., & Peshkin, A. (1992). *Becoming qualitative researchers*. White Plains, NY: Longman.

Goodman, Y. (1978). Kidwatching: An alternative to testing. *National Elementary Principal, 57(4)*, 41–45.

Horton, B. (Ed.). (1988). *A Beka Book*. Pensacola, FL: A Beka Book.

Lincoln, Y., & Guba, E. (1985). *Naturalistic inquiry*. London: Sage.

Merriam, S. B. (1998). *Qualitative research and case study applications in education*. San Francisco: Jossey-Bass.

Moffett, J., & Wagner, B. J. (1993). What works is play. *Language Arts, 70*, 32–36.

Morrow, L. M. (1990). Preparing the classroom environment to promote literacy during play. *Early Childhood Research Quarterly, 5*, 537–554.

Morrow, L. M., & Rand, M. K. (1991). Promoting literacy during play by designing early childhood classroom environments. *Reading Teacher, 44*, 396–402.

Neuman, S. B., & Roskos, K. (1990). Play, print, and purpose: Enriching the play environment for literacy development. *Reading Teacher, 44*, 214–221.

Neuman, S. B., & Roskos, K. (1993). Descriptive observations of adults' facilitation of literacy in young children's play. *Early Childhood Research Quarterly, 8*, 77–97.

Nicilopoulou, A. (1993). Play, cognitive development, and the social world: Piaget, Vygotsky, and beyond. *Human Development, 36*, 1–23.

Perrone, V. (1991). On standardized testing. *Childhood Education, 67*, 131–142.

Piaget, J. (1962). *Play, dreams, and imitation in childhood*. New York: Norton.

Roskos, K. (1990). Literacy at work in play. *Reading Teacher, 42*, 562–567.

Routman, R. (1994). *Invitations*. Portsmouth, NH: Heinemann.

Schickendanz, J. A. (1986). *More than ABC's: The early stages of reading and writing*. Washington, DC: National Association for the Education of Young Children.

Sulzby, E., & Teale, W. (1991). Emergent literacy. In R. Barr, M. L. Kamil, P. Mosenthal, & P. D. Pearson (Eds.), *Handbook of Reading Research* (Vol. 2, pp. 727–757). New York: Longman.

Vukelich, C. (1994). Effects of play interventions on young children's reading of environmental print. *Early Childhood Research Quarterly, 9*, 153–170.

Vukelick, C., & Valentine, K. (1990). A child plays: Two teachers learn. *Reading Teacher, 44*, 342–344.

Vygotsky, L. S. (1978). *Mind in society*. Cambridge, MA: Harvard University Press.

Opening the Portfolio Again: Conflicting Viewpoints on Assessment in K-12 Classrooms

Rebecca Anderson
University of Memphis

Michael Ford
University of Wisconsin–Oshkosh

Marilyn McKinney
University of Nevada–Las Vegas

Laura Roehler
Michigan State University

Patricia Scanlan
University of Wisconsin–Oshkosh

Beverly Bruneau
Kent State University

> I think they're [portfolios] a really good way to assess and to see the child's growth, and I hope to use them more in the future. We've talked with the other teachers in the school who would like to see the report cards go and just use portfolios. Even our principal doesn't care for report cards, which are something I feel we have to do. But hopefully that will change in the future.
>
> —Angie, third-year teacher, Multiage Grades 1–2

Like Angie, classroom teachers and teacher-educators have become increasingly involved in the use of portfolio assessment, and like Angie, they have conflicting views about how portfolio assessment works in contexts of "real" school settings. As six teacher-educators from various institutions around the country, we have been investigating the use of portfolios in our own classrooms and in the classrooms of former students since 1995. In 1997 (McKinney, Roehler, Anderson, Bruneau, Scanlan, & Ford), we conducted a multisite survey of 260 teachers and found that although over 80% of the respondents preferred portfolio assessment for themselves, only 54% were currently using portfolios with their own students. In 1998 (Scanlan, McKinney, Anderson, Bruneau, Roehler, & Ford), we conducted 60 structured interviews with teachers to gain understanding about what is needed to sustain the use of portfolio assessment. We found that teachers indicated that the assessment of portfolios was a particularly problematic issue for them.

For many educators, portfolio development is a maturing practice. It is critical that we, as teacher-educators, learn from those who have experience with and insight into the assessment of portfolios. We need to learn more about the dilemmas classroom teachers face in order to determine the congruence between what we teach in our literacy classes about assessing portfolios and what teachers are finding that works in K–12 classrooms.

To examine the complexities that make assessment of portfolios problematic, our current study focuses on the following areas: ways portfolios are assessed in K–12 classrooms, means of assessing portfolios that are most (or least) effective,

National Reading Conference Yearbook, 49, pp. 291–304.

advantages and disadvantages associated with each assessment procedure, and K–12 teachers' issues and concerns about assessing portfolios. The purpose of this study was to examine teachers' responses in these areas and explore how experienced K–12 teachers approach the task of assessing student portfolios.

Research Supporting Long-Term Portfolio Use

Although research on the use of portfolio assessment in literacy education courses and programs has been emerging over the last decade (Vogt & McLauglin, 1996), the issue of how best to support ongoing effort in this area has been overlooked by the field. It is quite clear from the evidence that educators have become more familiar with portfolio assessment in recent years. Commeyras and Degroff (1998) completed a national survey of reading professionals that focused in part on views and beliefs about portfolio assessment. Almost 75% of the educators indicated they had had experience with portfolios and 90% indicated their continued interest in the topic. Teacher-educators were among the most enthusiastic subgroup within the survey. Over 90% indicated they had had experience with portfolios. It should not be surprising then that 27% of all educators reported developing a portfolio for at least one of the courses they had taken in their university programs.

Addressing the issue of sustaining portfolio use once teachers leave the university setting, Commeyras and Degroff (1998) found that although staff development was indicated as one vehicle influencing educators' use of portfolios (74%), more educators reported that stronger influences on their understanding of the process were their own reading about portfolios (92%) and implementation of portfolios (86%). Respondents expressed other concerns about portfolios. For example, almost half of all educators believe portfolios should not replace more traditional forms of assessment. Furthermore, most educators still see portfolios primarily as an assessment tool and have yet to embrace them as an essential tool for the learning process. These prevailing views seem to fall short of initial expectations for portfolios to become a viable alternative assessment tool (Tierney, Carter, & Desai, 1991) or a valuable tool to use in altering instruction (Vavrus, 1991). These views also seem to fall short of visions for exemplary practices in the new millennium (Tierney, Johnston, Moore, & Valencia, 2000).

In their recent commentary, Tierney and Clark (1998) discussed existing tensions that can interfere with sustaining individual efforts in portfolio assessment. Although they continued to reaffirm the value in creating a "portfolio pedagogy" in which inquiry and reflection are at the heart of learning and assessment, they also acknowledged the disadvantages inherent within portfolio assessment. They echoed what others have discovered: portfolio assessment is a fairly messy process. Without adequate support, it is easy to abandon the process. In addition, they discussed how recent events have begun to shift the focus of portfolios from a grassroots movement controlled by classroom teachers to a tool for wide scale reform within and beyond classrooms controlled by others. This evolution of portfolio assessment has resulted in a hybrid product that is designed to summarize performance for multiple constituent groups while serving as a means for motivating and engaging students individually. These two goals are not always easily brought together. This concern has been previously voiced by others (Bergeron, Wermuth, & Hammar, 1997; Case, 1994).

The issue of support has surfaced in some recent studies of classroom teachers' use of portfolios. In a case study investigation of portfolio use by elementary teachers across two settings, Valencia and Au (1997) concluded that portfolios could be used effectively to document literacy learning in a way that was both authentic and aligned with classroom practices. The teachers they observed had a high degree of shared understanding and agreement in reviewing evidence within portfolios and stated that through their collaboration they enhanced their understanding of both learning and assessment. Valencia and Au attributed these positive outcomes to the presence of certain supportive internal and external conditions. Teachers were provided time to generate and collect artifacts for the portfolios, support to collaboratively evaluate the portfolios, and opportunities for ongoing staff development. Valencia and Au seemed to be unwilling to generalize similar success for other contexts without these essential conditions in place.

In a similar study of four teachers and their use of portfolio assessment over a 3-year period, Vukelich and Roe (1997) argued for the necessity of ongoing support structures. Their observations revealed that over time changes occurred in teachers' ability to document more effectively, increase student involvement in the process and use the portfolios to drive instructional decisions. Since improvements were noted as teachers had additional opportunities to work with portfolios, support structures that helped teachers sustain their efforts in the initial stages may be critical to prevent abandonment of the process.

Self-studies by teachers seemed to confirm what research on portfolio use has suggested. In telling their story of a 4-year learning experience, Van Wagenen and Hibbard (1998) described an evolutionary enhancement of the portfolio process, discovering the need for goal setting, reflection, growth, documentation, and program improvement outcomes as experiences with the process were sustained over time. Van Wagenen and Hibbard identified district-provided time and administrative support as keys to successfully support the process.

Method

This study of portfolio use in school settings consists of three phases, each of which has built upon previous findings. In order to provide a methodological context for the data reported in this paper, the third phase of the project, we include a brief summary of the previous work. The first phase was a survey of 260 former graduate and undergraduate students in six different sites focusing on how portfolios were being used in school settings and on factors that were influencing teachers' use of portfolio assessment (McKinney et al., 1997). From this survey, we learned that although 80% of these respondents preferred portfolio assessment for themselves, only 54% were currently using portfolios with their own students. The second phase (Scanlan et al., 1998) consisted of structured follow-up interviews with 60 of these teachers. These interviews focused on how portfolios were used in teachers' particular contexts, as well as on factors that either supported or impeded the use of portfolios in their K–12 classrooms. These interviews were tape-recorded, transcribed, and analyzed using the constant comparison method (Glaser & Strauss, 1967). Patterns of response led us as researchers to focus this third phase on teachers who have used portfolio assessment for at least 3 years, how portfolios are assessed, and factors that helped to make portfolios work in the classrooms of these experienced teachers.

Twelve structured interviews were conducted by the team of six researchers located throughout the country. Teachers were asked the following questions with opportunities to elaborate on responses as interviewers deemed necessary:

1. What is your teaching context, and how do you use portfolios?
2. How do you assess portfolios?
3. To what extent are students involved in the process of assessment?
4. How have your assessment practices changed over time?
5. Which portfolio assessment procedures do you find most effective?
6. Which portfolio assessment procedures do you find least effective?
7. How do you feel about the portfolio assessment procedures you are using?
8. What problems/concerns do you have with assessing portfolios?
9. Do you grade portfolios? If so, how?
10. How are parents involved in the assessment process?
11. How does your school/district feel about the portfolio assessment/grading procedures you are using?
12. What have you learned about assessing portfolios?
13. What else would you like to learn about assessing portfolios?

Data sources included tape recordings of interviews and extensive investigator notes. Data were analyzed and triangulated through the following process. Each researcher first analyzed his or her interview tapes and notes by recording responses to the interview questions and supporting quotations. This was followed by analyzing patterns of response at each site using the constant comparison method (Glaser & Strauss, 1967); in addition, anomalous responses were noted. These data were then shared with the other researchers by e-mail in an attempt to define patterns across sites. Themes were developed and refined through ongoing e-mail and phone conversations and by continually returning to the data set for confirmation of the research questions. Triangulation of findings (Lincoln & Guba, 1985) occurred by each researcher analyzing independently each researcher's individual analysis as well as the across-site analyses.

Three Cases

Results are reported within three cases, one each at the elementary, middle, and high school levels. These cases were selected because they best portrayed the patterns that emerged across the cases. Each one includes profiles of the teachers successfully using portfolio assessment at the elementary, middle, and high school levels and the common themes that emerged from the analysis. In reading the profiles, it is evident that although portfolio use is highly variable across grade levels, sites, and teachers, there are also commonalities that have evolved over time and with experience. In order to provide a sense of the practices in use, the profiles include a high level of contextual detail. To ensure anonymity of the participants, names of the teachers are pseudonyms.

Case Profile: An Elementary Teacher's Use of Portfolios

Karen Washington loves to teach and use portfolios with her third-grade students. She teaches in a mid-south, inner-city K–6 school in one of the nation's 20 largest school districts. This district is noted for low achievement scores, with only 10% of third graders reading at grade level. During the past 4 years each school in the district was required to adopt a specific teaching/learning model or program such as Little Red School House, Accelerated Learning Model, or Success for All Reading Program. Two years ago, Karen's school adopted The Co-Nect Model, which emphasizes technology integration and project-based learning. Being a computer enthusiast, Karen finds this model supports her literacy curriculum. Although portfolios are not mandated by the district, teachers in all schools are encouraged to use them. Karen states that teachers are expected to use them in her school, though no one checks to see if they are doing so. It is more "lip service" than follow-up. As a result, teachers are not sure how someone else is using them, nor who to turn to when they have questions and concerns. Regardless, Karen does not feel that she has a lot of questions about portfolios. She feels good about how she is using them as illustrated by her comment, "I'm ahead of myself when it comes to using portfolios with my students."

Karen started using portfolios with her students 4 years ago because she wanted them to "step back and assess what they had done." "In the beginning they were more like scrapbooks than portfolios," she explains. "Now students have to justify in writing why they want to include a piece of work and tell me what they learned." The students have easy access to their portfolios, and are given specific time each week, usually Friday afternoons, to review them. During this weekly time, Karen conferences with individual students while the rest of the class selects pieces for their portfolio and writes their justifications. In addition, students share their artifacts and rationale statements with their peers.

Karen and her students use rubrics to assess the portfolios. She explains that during the conference, she and her students do not give a single overall score but rather they assess individual pieces within the portfolio. Thus, the portfolios are not graded holistically, but students' grades are lowered if they do not complete their portfolio. "If they do not choose something for the portfolio and it isn't up to date, I count off in language arts because I see it as being irresponsible."

Karen uses portfolios with parents during parent/teacher conferences and periodically she sends them home with an attached parent involvement sheet. According to Karen:

It's hard to get your portfolios back when you send them home. I find that parents think it is a good idea when I talk to them about it [during open house and conferences]. But if they don't come to school so I can explain portfolios to them, they definitely don't understand them. And sometimes I go all year without seeing some parents. When I send these portfolios home, they don't understand them. They wonder if it is homework. For these parents, it is very nebulous and misunderstood. Parents understand grades such as an A or F, but they don't understand a 4, 3, 2, or 1 on a rubric. They don't want to see a "1," they want to see an "A" or "B."

Overall, Karen has learned that portfolios are effective in many ways and less so in other ways in her classroom. For instance, Karen acknowledges that students have grown in their abilities to self-assess and take ownership of their learning:

I have been willing to give more control over to the students. Early on I would almost argue with them about which piece to include, and now I am more willing to let them be the judge. The students' assessments of their work are excellent. The more I involve the students in the assessment process, the more the student learns about whatever the task may be.

On the other hand, Karen notes that peer assessment is less effective than self-assessment because "they [students] are new to the idea of going for quality vs. quantity." She continues to add that students "are not diplomatic with one another, they are not good listeners. They are judgmental and they pick each others' work apart." She states that students could help one another on specific tasks such as editing papers but that they cannot provide meaningful feedback to one another from a holistic perspective.

Karen has two unattained goals associated with portfolios. She wants to learn more ways to "pull the students into the assessment process and to deal with time management." She explains, "It's not easy, it takes time, and you must have a game plan worked out in your mind so that it becomes part of your routine." She adds that the pressures to finish the essentials of teaching often conflict with classroom time to work on portfolios. However, Karen will continue to use portfolios with her students because she explains, "I have learned the value and know how important it is for students to look back and reflect on their learning."

Case Profile: A Middle School Teacher's Use of Portfolios

Mary Kay Peterson is an eighth-grade Communication Arts teacher in a medium-sized midwestern city. She is a member of a close-knit eighth-grade team with a Science, Math, and Special Education teacher. Each of the four teachers has a homeroom class, and each integrates the teaching of Social Studies into his or her content-area specialty. The team meets regularly and shares responsibility for all students in the four homerooms; this unit of students and teachers is also referred to as a pod.

Mary Kay was one of the initiators of this alternative eighth-grade experience that began five years earlier. She enthusiastically describes how parents must elect to have their children assigned to this team of teachers; parents also must decide if they want their children to receive letter grades or if they prefer a pass/ fail report. Although there are minor differences in the standards set by each teacher for assigning a "pass" grade, Ms. Peterson requires students to achieve 80% in Communication Arts to get a "pass." Currently, almost 85% of the students in the pod receive pass/fail marks. Students receive a grade report at the end of each quarter that is identical to the grade reports used by all the teachers in this middle school. The report includes a description of the knowledge, skills, and attitudes covered during the quarter, and percentage scores along with a "grade" (letter or pass/fail) in each subject.

Although the portfolios themselves are not graded, Mary Kay penalizes students if work is missing from the portfolio. Putting work into their portfolios is an ongoing process, and it requires students to be organized. Mary Kay reflected that teaching students to be organized is one of the unexpected benefits of portfolio assessment.

With administrative support, Mary Kay's team has a different parent-teacher conference schedule than the rest of the teachers in the building. Traditionally teachers schedule two 15-minute conferences per year. However, this team holds five 30-minute conferences with students and their parents each year. The first conference is held in August just before the beginning of the school year; the purpose of this initial meeting is to get acquainted and set goals. The other four conferences are held at the end of each quarterly reporting period. Mary Kay and her colleagues have used portfolio assessment as a part of the parent-teacher conference since the inception of this alternative eighth grade experience.

Students construct four portfolios throughout each quarter, one each for Communication Arts, Science, Math, and Social Studies. Students are required to share these with their parents at end-of-the-quarter conferences. If a student comes to a conference without his or her portfolio, the conference is rescheduled. Although each teacher in the team approaches the construction of the portfolio a bit differently, they generally expect students to include all their work in the portfolio. Each teacher also requires the students to reflect on their learning. Mary Kay, for example, asks students to focus on four questions: (a) How have you changed as a reader? (b) How have you changed as a writer? (c) A listener? (d) A speaker?

> I gave them the questions, and made them think about it. They did some writing. They did some talking with each other. And I said, "You have to remember that you don't just speak in my class. You speak in Ms. Green's and Mr. Stuart's class." And they did a very incredible job. And I modeled it. And I did one, "Yes, I have changed," and one "No, I haven't changed." And they are very good at putting out something you've modeled. . . . [W]e model it, provide some experience, and then give them time to do it [reflect] again.

Since the portfolios include all work done throughout the quarter, having students focus on particular aspects of their work and their growth can redirect their tendency to discuss every piece. There is little value, the team has learned, to have a student begin with the first piece in the portfolio and describe every single thing he or she has done. Besides that, such a conference is unreasonably time-consuming. Mary Kay speaks candidly about how her use of portfolios has changed. In the beginning, she and her colleagues required their students to save everything, because

> the first year we did this our nightmare was that they would open up a portfolio and there'd be nothing there. And so ours started out as just a collection. They had boxes. It was incredible. . . . [T]hey showed everything. The first year we did this the conferences were an hour to an hour-and-a-half. And, of course, we couldn't sustain that.

Because of the student-centered nature of the instruction teachers provide in this pod, parents of students who have previously experienced limited success in school often request that their children work with this team of teachers. This alternative experience also attracts students who have excelled academically, and whose parents want to ensure that their children are challenged. Mary Kay and her colleagues agree that having students share portfolios with their parents is valuable because it provides an opportunity for dialogue, and enhances the effectiveness of portfolio assessment. Ms. Peterson reports that parents, especially those whose children have had trouble in school, are often amazed at both the quantity and the quality of their child's work. Mary Kay shared several stories about parents who were surprised and pleased with their child's progress. After the first quarter, she had a conference with a parent and her child who unbeknownst to the teachers had

> never done well in school before. And the mom was like, "Oh, I'm so excited." And she started to cry. And we all had said these awesome things about her kid. . . . And I said, "I can't wait to tell my teammates because they won't believe it, because we thought he was always like this. We thought he was always a good student."

As Mary Kay looks ahead to using portfolios again, she wants to secure a video camera that could be available exclusively for use in their pod. This technology would enable students to show work that otherwise could not be represented in a paper folder portfolio. She is also considering the need to use different prompts for promoting student reflection. More specific prompts might allow students to think more critically about both their learning and their growth, as well as facilitate the sharing of particular pieces of the work in their portfolios.

Case Profile: A High School Teacher's Use of Portfolios

Sadie, in her seventh year as a high school composition teacher, is clearly passionate about her work. She teaches mostly Advanced Placement composition classes but characterizes her one "English 4" class (composed of "less proficient, highly transient, and some ELL students") as the one that "keeps me honest." Sadie has a master's degree, is a Southern Nevada Writing Project Fellow, and has recently begun work in a doctoral program. She is chair of the Portfolio Committee in her English Department as well as the Writing Across the Curriculum Committee. She sees herself as a writer, keeps her own portfolio, and views portfolios as a crucial component of her teaching, explaining that "Portfolios would be almost a given in any composition class." Sadie began her career with a strong commitment to their use as a result of her teacher education program and because she kept her own portfolio as a writer. She has also written a number of grants that have supported her work with portfolio assessment.

Sadie smiles as she describes how her portfolio practices have evolved over time. During her first year of teaching, she used a "more random" or "haphazard" approach; students collected pieces of writing, and then they were asked to go through their folders and select a piece to take through the writing process to complete by a final future due date. She would go for long periods of time without doing portfolios and then did not set criteria for what should be included. From this point, she moved to asking students to provide some kind of "guided reflection" about themselves as writers, their thinking process, strengths, and weaknesses. Over time, Sadie says, "I got more organized because the more I used them I saw a pattern and now we keep a variety of things" (e.g., college application, resume, lists of books read, self-evaluations of a favorite piece, metacognitive letter, essays that reflect course requirements for that year). The students keep "working portfolios" that are eventually turned into what Sadie calls "exemplary portfolios." Every quarter, students evaluate their portfolios and write a metacognitive letter to themselves, self-assessing their growth. In characterizing how her practices have changed over time, she says, "I left it more to them [the students]. I used to try to take control of it, and then something clicked and I said I can't keep control of their portfolios. I have enough control."

Portfolios provide opportunities for students to talk with her and each other about their work and their progress over time. The entire English Department has a portfolio system with portfolios passed along from year to year during the "portfolio exchange" that occurs during the second week of the school year. Time is set aside for students to return to their teacher from the previous year, retrieve their portfolios and come back to their current classroom where they can begin to converse about themselves as writers. In Sadie's class, this is the beginning of the metacognitive letters.

Portfolios also provide opportunities for teachers within the English department to have conversations about what they teach each year and how they can build on previous work (e.g., moving from the I-search in one year to working on a Career-Search the following year). Students are helped to build on projects that engaged their interest during one year. Sadie explains:

> We encourage them by asking, "How do you rework projects? Let's say you do something your freshman year, you could do a sort of take-off on it, and use some of that information to build an even better project your senior year." [Students could respond] "Oh, I did that; maybe I could do something with that!"

Teachers new to the school are provided information about the writing sequence for each level and the portfolio system that accompanies it. As part of her work on the Writing Across the Curriculum Committee, Sadie's practice has also been to encourage students to bring papers from content area classes such as math or science to include in their portfolios. In fact, working on these pieces leads to the publication of a "Writing across the Curriculum" anthology each year. Although parent conferences are infrequent at the high school level, the portfolios serve to document student work and provide a vehicle for conversations about performance.

There appears to be an underlying structure that supports the process of portfolio use; this structure is accepted by and used by the majority of the teachers in the English Department and facilitates conversations with teachers from other content areas. However, in spite of support, Sadie reiterates some of the same concerns that resonate across the research literature related to the constraints of process-oriented activities, particularly time: "Time. We never have enough time. Time on my part, time on their part, time taken out of the classroom."

Sadie does not assess the portfolios; she assesses individual pieces and assignments that may end up in the portfolio but not the portfolio per se. "The kids assess them basically. It's just, did they do it? Obviously each of the pieces in there has been assessed, and I give an assignment. This portfolio is for them. It is not for me." However, she delights in the growth she sees:

> At the end of the year I am always so pleased. Even if a student didn't seem to improve in their writing, the way they talk about their writing is much improved. They will talk about their word choice and they will talk about the fact that they tend to be tellers rather than showers. They will talk about how much they have written, how much faster they write.

She finds that the most effective assessment practices are "the ones where the kids are assessing themselves, the ones where they do any kind of metacognitive, reflective kind of thing." Students come to understand the use of the portfolios as tools to facilitate their growth as writers. "That's the structure; it gives the structure and it keeps it all together."

Sadie wants to learn more about electronic portfolios and possibly using rubrics to help students assess themselves, especially if this becomes something more universally done for college entrance. But colleges will need to share what they are looking for in a portfolio. "I think of myself going to school and them wanting to see my portfolio. I would freak. I have no sense of what they would want or what they would look for." She sees portfolios as a more valid form of assessment than the standardized tests now used. But she also sees that there could be a danger if portfolios become more standardized.

Results

Across the representative cases, teachers reported their students' valuing of portfolios and their own valuing and satisfaction with portfolio use. Each of the teachers had been supported as they developed their own use of portfolios. This finding agrees with those of Valencia and Au (1997) and Vukelich and Roe (1997) indicating that support is critical for the sustained successful implementation of portfolios over time. None of the teachers in our study worked in educational settings where either the district or an external agency mandated the use of portfolios. This may have provided a clearer focus for the use of portfolios than for teachers faced with reconciling classroom purposes with external demands (Bergeron et al., 1997). Within the cases, five relevant patterns regarding successful portfolio use emerged.

Portfolios Were Viewed as Tools to Facilitate Growth

All teachers stated that portfolios were a way for parents and teachers to acknowledge student growth. Students, too, could view their growth through self-assessment. In addition, portfolio use provided for the development of student ownership by offering control in terms of choice of artifacts, methods of assessment, opportunities to reflect, and ways to share learning. The portfolios took many shapes in order to facilitate growth. These included types of portfolios developed (e.g., working and exemplary portfolios), the length of time involved for each portfolio, and the role in informing parents and significant others. Finally, teachers saw portfolio use as a way for teachers to work and grow together.

Portfolio Use Was Well Organized and Structured

The teachers indicated that portfolio use required underlying structures that allowed students places to collect their artifacts that were easily accessible. Boundaries for reflection and conversations needed to be understood by students and supported by teachers. The high school teacher offered guided reflection as a means for helping students grow in their uses of reflection. She also provided access to previous years' portfolios so that the students could select artifacts they wished to revise or use for examining growth. The elementary teacher organized times for students to visit their portfolios to select particular artifacts, reflect on their growth, and dialogue with others about elements of their selected artifacts. The middle school teacher provided students ongoing opportunities throughout each quarter to review their work. All teachers modeled a variety of approaches for thinking about and reflecting on the artifacts students had collected.

Freedom to Modify Use Occurred at Each Level

All teachers had freedom to adapt and modify their portfolio use with their students. Parents, students, and teachers were actively involved with portfolio examination and assessment in the elementary and middle school classes. Students and teachers, across subject matters (disciplines), were actively involved with portfolio examination and assessment in the high school class. All teachers had freedom to adjust and modify structures and organizations for portfolio use across the year. The middle school teacher found students' reflective, focused sharing of portfolios with parents to be the heart of the assessment process.

Artifacts within Portfolios Were Assessed, Not Portfolios in Their Entirety

None of the teachers in these cases assessed the entire portfolio. Instead, individual artifacts were assessed in many ways for many purposes. Student self-assessment occurred within all three cases. Students and teachers in the elementary and middle school grades used rubrics during assessment. The high school teacher stated that she has students self-assess through the use of metacognitive letters that they write to themselves. She thought this was the most effective form of assessment for her students. The elementary teacher indicated that artifacts were not an element in student grades but omitted artifacts did lower established grades.

Expertise with Portfolios Grew with Time and Use

As teachers became comfortable with portfolio use in their classrooms, expertise developed. Teachers began with general ideas about portfolio use. The elementary teacher started with the notion of scrapbooks and gradually moved to artifacts that included justification of the selection. The middle school teacher reported a number of ways she and her teammates tried to improve this assessment approach. Thus, as behaviors worked well, teachers built them into structures that supported the increase of expertise for students in terms of growth and for teachers in terms of organization. Over time portfolio use developed in breadth and depth.

Patterns also emerged regarding future goals for portfolio use. Teachers wanted to help parents and other teachers better understand the value and uses of portfolios. All teachers were interested in exploring additional ways to document growth such as videos, electronic portfolios, and software such as Hyper Studio. The high school teacher wanted to add rubrics to strengthen student self-assessment. The middle school teacher wanted to improve her use of prompts to enhance the students' use of reflection. Finally, all three teachers indicated a need to explore time management to better facilitate the use of portfolios and in turn, the valuing of portfolios.

Discussion and Implications

Within and across these three representative cases of successful, long-term portfolio users at the elementary, middle, and high school levels, three major implications have emerged. First, portfolios have an important role as tools for demonstrating growth in the teaching and learning process. They seem to support student awareness of learning and provide ways for conversations to occur among students, teachers, and parents. This awareness of growth is supported by reflection over time and through effort. Reflection and awareness seem to support the internalization of the knowledge, skills/strategies, and dispositions that teachers deem necessary for students to develop expertise in literacy.

Second, teachers who are successful at sustaining portfolio assessment have been able to embrace the complexities of the classroom when using and evolving portfolio practices. Structures develop slowly and need to be modified as teachers and students come to understand how best to teach, to learn, and then to share growth with parents, other students and other teachers. Rather than being constrained by the existence of traditional grading reports and procedures, the teachers we talked with found ways to successfully use portfolio assessment within their professional settings. These teachers actively sought ways to create new structures and routines for assessment that worked alongside the traditional practices. These new structures cannot be "add-ons." Instead, by modifying previous practices in a well-organized and eventually routinized structure, teachers can use time as productively as possible. We know we cannot lengthen time; we can only better use it.

Third, in order to encourage the kind of risk-taking and innovative behavior we saw among the teachers we interviewed, teacher-educators and school administrators need to facilitate an attitude that teachers are learners. When teachers view their own teaching as a means to professional growth and development, when they assume an attitude that "the best is yet to come," and that "change, even in small ways, can make remarkable differences in students," it is easier to initiate and sustain practices such as portfolio assessment. Teachers also need professional opportunities to try new ideas and practices with the support of district administrators, as suggested by other researchers (Valencia & Au, 1997; Van Wagenen & Hibbard, 1998). They need opportunities to have professional conversations with their colleagues, to design alternative programs, and to actively participate in making schools a better place for all students. The increasing pressures of high stakes assessment and accountability, coupled with political calls for standardization of curricula, instruction, and assessments compete with teachers' desires to invest needed time and energy in adopting and adapting effective use of portfolios for classrooms. In his review of assessment for the Association for Supervision and Curriculum Development yearbook, Asp (2000) described a future vision that contrasted sharply with the view of classroom assessment practices such as those we have described in this study. He concluded that attempts to incorporate instructional-friendly assessments "into large-scale efforts have proven quite difficult because of the costs in time and money and the technical issues involved" (p. 146). He suggested that our best hopes for assessment in the future is to focus on bringing coherence between systems that better integrate large-scale and classroom assessments.

Roe and Vukelich (1998) remind us:

> Adopting a portfolio assessment system is challenging. Some challenges begin with the teacher and the understanding he or she possesses about literacy. Others stem from the classroom—too many students and too little time. Still others arise from the wider system—district policies that place teachers' professional beliefs at odds with mandated practices. (p. 153)

These case studies representing educators in a variety of educational contexts also remind us that addressing those dilemmas successfully is possible.

References

Asp, E. (2000). Assessment in education: Where have we been? Where are we headed? In R. S. Brandt (Ed.), *Education in a new era*. Alexandria, VA: Association for Supervision and Curriculum Development.

Bergeron, B. S., Wermuth, S., & Hammar, R. C. (1997). Initiating portfolios through shared learning: Three perspectives. *Reading Teacher, 50*, 552–562.

Case, S. H. (1994). Will mandating portfolios undermine their value? *Educational Leadership, 55*(2), 46–47.

Commeyras, M., & Degroff, L. (1998). Literacy professionals' perspectives on professional development and pedagogy: A national survey. *Reading Research Quarterly, 33*, 434–472.

Glaser, B., & Strauss, A. (1967). *The discovery of grounded theory: Strategies for qualitative research*. Chicago: Aldine.

Lincoln, Y., & Guba, E. (1985). *Naturalistic inquiry*. Beverly Hills, CA: Sage.

McKinney, M., Roehler, L. R., Anderson, R. S., Bruneau, P., Scanlan, P., & Ford, M. P. (1997, December). *Learning from those who do and those who don't: After-effects of portfolio experiences in teacher education programs*. Paper presented at the meeting of the National Reading Conference, Scottsdale, AZ.

Roe, M. F., & Vukelich, C. (1998). Literacy portfolios: Challenges that affect change. *Childhood Education, 74*, 148–153.

Scanlan, P., McKinney, M., Anderson, B., Bruneau, B., Roehler, L., & Ford, M. (1998, December). *Sustaining the use of portfolios: How can we help others and ourselves?* Paper presented at the meeting of the National Reading Conference, Austin, TX.

Tierney, R. J., Carter, M. A., & Desai, L. E. (1991). *Portfolio assessment in the reading-writing classroom*. Norwood, MA: Christopher Gordon.

Tierney, R. J., & Clark, C. (1998). Portfolio: Assumptions, tensions and possibilities. *Reading Research Quarterly, 33*, 474–488.

Tierney, R. J., Johnston, P., Moore, D. W., & Valencia, S. W. (2000). How will literacy be assessed in the next millennium? *Reading Research Quarterly, 35*, 244–250.

Vavrus, L. G. (1991, December). *Connecting literacy assessment and instruction through student portfolios*. Symposium presented at the meeting of the National Reading Conference, Miami Beach, FL.

Valencia, S. W., & Au, K. H. (1997). *Portfolios across educational contexts: Issues of evaluation, teacher development and system validity* (Reading Research Report No. 73). Athens, GA: National Reading Research Center.

Van Waggen, L., & Hibbard, K. M. (1998). Building teacher portfolios. *Educational Leadership, 55*, 26–29.

Vogt, M., & McLauglin, M. (1996). *Portfolios in teacher education*. Newark, DE: International Reading Association.

Vukelich, C., & Roe, M. (1997). That was then and this is now: A longitudinal study of teachers' portfolio process. *Journal of Research on Childhood Education, 12*, 16–26.

Multiple Forms of Evidence: A Longitudinal Case Study of Student Achievement

Rebecca Rogers
Washington University

Virginia J. Goatley
University at Albany, SUNY

Student learning and the assessment of student learning are primarily a social and discursive practice (Johnston, 1997; Moss, 1998). Assessment is a broad range of practices that represent student learning and achievement across domains and over time. This may include both formal (e.g., standardized tests) and documentary (e.g., running records, observations, writing samples) types of assessment. From a social constructivist lens, all assessment practices are essentially interpretive in nature. This view has implications for the consequences of student learning and achievement. With teachers as the primary assessors in the school contexts (Johnston, 1997), educators construct various assessment decisions about students.

The concept of *tension* is prominent in educational research and has strong implications for assessment consequences. Within various domains, tensions occur between the student and the curriculum (Heath, 1983, 1992; Lee, 1996; Michaels, 1981), the student and the teacher (Kos, 1993; Ogbu, 1991), and student's developing literate identity based on gendered or classed curricula (Collins, 1986, 1996; Lee 1996; Shannon, 1995). Research has shown how individual children have difficulty when the instructional contexts do not meet their current base of knowledge or their strategies for constructing knowledge. From within the social constructivist perspective, these sources of mismatch, or tensions, are seen as clashes between the cultural assumptions of the home and the school (Au, 1980; Heath, 1983, 1992; Michaels, 1981). Tension and conflict may result from competing social agendas in the classroom.

This research base suggests tensions are a source for learning about invisible relationships that occur within schools. Assessment of student learning and achievement involves a number of perspectives and foci. Of these, the tension between formal and documentary types of assessment is central (Johnston, 1998). Lipson, Wixson, and Valencia (1994) wrote about the tensions between external and internal assessment systems, and other works have examined the differential value attached to "formal" evidence of student achievement and teacher-based or "documentary" evidence (Hodges, 1997; Johnston, Guice, Baker, Malone, & Michelson, 1995). Given this, the reading and writing difficulties that students

National Reading Conference Yearbook, 49, pp. 305–320.

may face should be thought of in terms of the interactions among participants and social structures (e.g. classroom, district, state and national levels) rather than as a characteristic of the child.

We present a case study of Marty, examining his learning across the elementary grades to address the research question: In what ways is learning in language arts assessed and what are the consequences of these assessments? Marty's profile from first to fourth grade showed persistent tensions based on multiple forms of assessment used during these years. The sources of tensions are located in mismatched assumptions about learning and achievement and how educators talked about and acted upon such assumptions. These tensions in representation of student learning led to instructional consequences.

Method

Description of the Research Context

Marty, the case study student, attended a K–4 elementary school located in a suburban district in upstate New York. Pepper Street school includes a population of students who are primarily Caucasian, though the diversity of the student population is increasing each year. Approximately 10% of the students qualify for free or reduced lunch. The school participated in a federally funded 5-year research project examining the integration of literacy, social studies, and literature in an elementary school.

Marty attended this school beginning in Kindergarten. During first and second grades, he was in a looping situation with a teacher named Jane Larson. For third grade, he attended Linda Barkley's classroom. In fourth grade, he moved to Lucy Grey's class for the 1998–99 school year. Both Jane Larson and Lucy Grey participated in the professional development aspects of the research project, with a focus on integrated instruction. We selected Marty as a case study student when he was in second grade due to his participation in the remedial reading program and his teachers' observation that he was one of the lower students in her class for reading ability. Further, Marty's teachers expressed concern about the complexity of Marty's learning.

Marty is a tall Caucasian boy with blondish-brown hair, who comes from a working-class home. His parents divorced when he was in second grade. Marty and his two older sisters divide their time equally between their mother and father. When Jane Larson suggested to his parents that Marty receive extra tutoring support, his mother told her they did not have the money for it (fieldnotes 3/18/97). Marty is well known by other students for his athletic talents, including his yearly first place finish in a running race.

Data Collection and Analysis

This case study is based on ethnographic data from 4 years, including: (a) formal and informal assessment measures, (b) fieldnotes and audiotapes from classroom observations, (c) student and teacher interviews, (d) copies of student work, and (e) portfolio documents. For Marty's kindergarten and first-grade year, we have only written assessment documents. For both second and fourth grades, we draw on extensive fieldnote observations of thematic units in which Marty participated (e.g., 25 observations over a 2-month period). In addition, for second, third, and fourth grades, researchers observed Marty on a monthly basis during academic instruction in various subjects.

Data analysis involved the examination of fieldnotes, formal records, and interviews with teachers to document the assessment practices in the domains of literature, literacy, and social studies. These included Marty's standardized measures (e.g., California Test of Basic Skills [CTBS] scores, New York state assessments) and informal measures (e.g., district assessments, report cards, teacher observation logs). Next, we analyzed contextual data (e.g. fieldnotes and audiotapes of classroom interactions, student interviews) of classroom instruction, Marty's participation in this instruction, and his ideas about this learning. Further, we coded Marty's writing samples during activities such as journals, process writing, and writing assessments looking for evidence of student learning. We also drew on supporting documents associated with educational experiences (e.g., letters to parents). From this analysis, persistent tensions appeared in Marty's case throughout his elementary school career. One example of such a tension is that despite Marty reading on "grade level" he continued to be defined as a "low reader" and to be placed in a remedial reading class. We organized these tensions into three overlapping categories as they related to Marty's achievement over time.

In order to make sense of these tensions, we turned to the concept of restructuring social theory based on the data that we had collected and analyzed (Burawoy, 1991). The extended case method, as this conceptual and analytic framework is labeled, functions by looking for anomalies or surprises in the data. Working from a framework that views assessment as a socially constructed and represented practice (Johnston, 1997, 1998) along with more recent views of assessment as discursive process (Moss, 1998), we examined the evidence to reconstruct these theories of assessment, rather than construct theories from the "ground up." Part of assessment expertise, as Johnston (1997) reminds us is collecting data that help researchers to confront their own knowledge and restructure ways of thinking about learning and teaching. We focus on the concept of anomalies as producing useful conceptual and practical insight into discussions of assessment and representation of student learning and achievement.

The Case of Marty

In this section, we present multiple lenses from which to look at Marty's achievement over a 4-year period of time. First, we describe the institutional context for Marty's elementary school. Then, we examine the different assessment measures the teachers used.

Classroom Contexts

In first and second grades, Marty was in Jane Larson's classroom. The school had a looping program where Jane moved with her students from first to second grade. Jane described her reading and writing program as student-led in which she placed a strong emphasis on becoming independent learners through collaborative inquiry. Reader's workshop in block periods characterized reading in her classroom, with Jane providing individual instruction and small guided reading groups. She used student-created texts that combined literacy and content area instruction, in both first grade and at the beginning of second grade. Students routinely used these texts to read to each other. In first and second grades, Marty participated in classroom remedial reading instruction when the reading teacher led small-group activities with decodable texts. In second grade, Jane continued with a literature based reading program. She used trade books to supplement her conceptually driven social studies curriculum, using the social studies textbook as a resource.

In third grade, Marty went into Linda Barkley's literature-based classroom. Linda was a teacher who did not participate in the professional development aspect of the research study but was willing to allow researchers into her room to observe the students. Linda described Marty as a low to average student in her classroom who continued to exert effort and a positive attitude across curricular areas (report card 12/98). Mixed in with new students, Marty did not appear to have the same sense of community that he experienced in first and second grades. Linda's social studies program was textbook driven. Analysis of writing samples in student journals and writing portfolios revealed that entries were often connected to content area topics.

Marty participated in reading groups with the Reading Specialist three times a week. In locations outside of the classroom, these students read books that were thematically similar to all students but easier to read. Linda noted that work in content areas was difficult for Marty because of his difficulty with reading. The Reading Specialist said that Marty needed to continue to build his vocabulary, work on medial vowels and use predictions to aid comprehension (report card 12/ 98). By June of third grade, the Reading Specialist indicated that Marty was reading "orally" at a 3.8 grade level according to the informal reading inventory. Marty continued to progress in writing but needed to focus on editing and revising to make his thoughts clear on paper. His standardized test scores, both CTBS and the New York state Pupil Evaluation Program (PEP), showed that he was above grade level. The reading teacher and the classroom teacher recommended reading support for the following year.

In fourth grade, Marty entered Lucy Grey's literature-based program. Lucy organized her Language Arts and Social Studies programs around conceptual ideas. Students read trade books, newspapers, primary documents, and other texts in social studies. They read a range of novels across the year and participated in student-led discussion groups. They participated in extensive writing activities, associated with literature, social studies, other content areas, and story writing. Again, in fourth grade Marty received remedial reading support. Generally, the reading teacher participated with Marty and other students qualifying for remedial services within the classroom, usually in small groups within the regular classroom instruction. Occasionally, at other times of the day, she took him and other students to another room for targeted instruction.

Assessment Measures

Figure 1 outlines Marty's assessment measures at the national, state, district and classroom levels. Marty took the CTBS in reading, language, math, social studies, and science in first through third grades. Within New York State, Marty took the PEP test as a third grader and the English Language Arts test in fourth grade. The PEP test was a series of cloze procedure multiple-choice questions. The new fourth-grade ELA state assessment in 1999 included short passage, multiple-choice questions, and extended writing connected with listening, reading and writing passages. At the district level, Marty's reading and writing growth over time was documented in a K–2 literacy assessment, a 2–4 writing portfolio, and report cards. The K–2 is a documentary assessment that includes running records of Guided Reading according to Pepper Street benchmark books. At the classroom level, there were various performance-based assessments including daily writing, teacher-made exams, anecdotal records, checklists, running records and spelling tests.

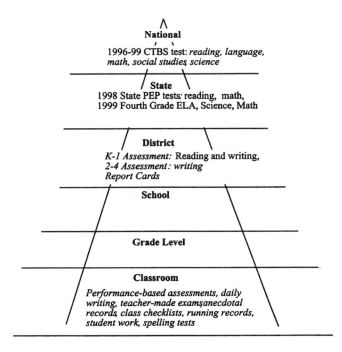

Figure 1. Measures of achievement and assessments.

Based on these assessment measures, three categories emerged that had a substantial impact on the way educators used and interpreted assessments. We framed these categories as tensions that became apparent in Marty's case over a 4-year time period. The tensions are embedded within the categories: (a) individual progress and social expectations, (b) representation of student learning and achievement, and (c) construction of literate identity. These categories stemmed from our analysis and reflect the events and issues that most clearly showed tensions between Marty's progress in his learning and the assessments that indicated his achievement. In the next section, we focus on each one in turn.

Individual Progress and Social Expectations

The first tension involves representations of student growth across assessment measures that extend beyond narrow or surface level indicators. In this category, we focus on the question "What counts as evidence?" to examine the differences between individual progress and social expectations. Assessment is a social achievement. Further, within our current educational system, assessments are normative interpretations. That is, educators often interpret individual progress in comparison to grade-level peers. Marty made substantial growth over time and yet continued to be "at-risk" when he was compared with his peers in reading and writing.

Developing Literacy

Jane Larson, Marty's first- and second-grade teacher, indicated that in the beginning of first grade Marty had difficulty spelling his name and was not able to identify all of the sounds and letters. By January, he was reading level-5 books and had progressed to a level 17 by the end of his first-grade year (Reading Recovery levels). In second grade, he was reading Guided Reading leveled books that were equivalent to a second-grade level (Fountas & Pinnell, 1999, pp. 24) at an instructional level but still was considered below average in terms of the K–2 assessment. Jane noted the significant gains attached to this increase in his reading level. Marty demonstrated strengths as a reader and writer. He showed a range of strategic behaviors in reading and writing and maintained his enthusiasm for reading. Jane reiterated that she believed that rising 22 levels in one and a half years was a remarkable increase (fieldnotes 3/18/97).

When Marty looped with Jane into second grade, she continued literacy instruction based on what she already knew about him. According to teacher comments and report card measures, Marty was reading in grade-level range. He was still learning to be flexible with his strategies and working on fluency and comprehension. By the end of second grade, Marty was reading on grade level at an instructional level. He had increased his fluency in writing, producing more self-chosen writing pieces with increasingly conventional spellings. His teacher noted that his confidence had increased over the 2 years. Despite this growth and his appropriate instructional level at the end of second grade, both the Reading

Specialist and the classroom teacher recommended that he receive reading support the following year. Compared with his peers and the expectations of the class, Marty was considered still to be a "low" reader.

Ongoing Literacy Development

As Marty progressed through the grades, the issue of "what counts as evidence" was compounded with the question of "what counts as reading." By fourth grade, the emphasis was on comprehension of text and reading connections to writing. In many cases, the evidence from previous years (e.g., CTBS, PEP score, K–2 assessment) did not capture the elements of comprehension required for successful reading and extended writing. Comprehension appeared to be a struggle for Marty based on the documentary evidence. For example, on a running record of the novel he was reading in November of fourth grade, *Children of the Longhouse* (Bruchac, 1996), Marty had a 97% accuracy rate. However, when asked to discuss what happened, he identified characters and events but struggled with how to discuss the main points of the book.

Marty's participation in regular classroom instruction appeared to be beneficial to him in focusing on these comprehension and response issues. He participated in small-group discussions, where the main intent was to discuss the ideas and issues raised in the book. Marty started to take an active role in these groups, at one point in October arguing loudly for his interpretation of the book cover that was in contrast to others in his group (fieldnotes 10/28/98). On almost a daily basis, Lucy Grey talked with him, one-to-one at times, to assist him with comprehension and to further encourage his success in the discussion groups.

Although Marty's teacher indicated he made substantial individual growth within fourth grade, this contrasted with his standardized test scores. Marty's writing showed marked improvement within his fourth grade with a clearer expression of his ideas, better organization of his thoughts, and recognizable voice in his writing. Marty's individual progress as a writer was held to social expectations through the standardized English Language Arts exam.

On the fourth-grade New York state English Language Arts (ELA) test given in January, Marty received a holistic score of 2 out of 4. For the independent writing section, he received a 2 out of 3. These meant that Marty passed by state requirements but was required to go to a summer school program for falling below the district cut-off line. However, this score does not reflect the growth as a writer and thinker embedded in these scores for Marty.

Marty's writing on the independent writing part of the assessment that involved looking at a picture of five frogs and writing a story about it, included a narrative structure and writing conventions. Marty wrote:

> One day there were 5 toads. Their names are Marty, Len, Nate Chris and we all can't forget Jake. So the 5 toads need water so they went into a pool. The 5 toads drink all of the water in the pool. They were stuffed. Nate, Len, Marty, Chris and Jake went home. Nate said something bad is going to happen. Jake got hurt. A tree fell on him. But he was ok. So the five toads went home. Look on back. The end.

This writing piece reflected his more in-depth thinking about reading and writing that started to emerge in fourth grade. His voice came across in the passage as he used his friends from his class as examples of frogs in the story. Further, Marty indicated an awareness of audience and an uncertainty if the reader would know to turn the page, he wrote "look on back." Lucy who was trained as a scorer for this state assessment said, "He has a clear beginning, middle and attempted an ending. There is a definite structure to his story."

Though he received a 2/4 on the state ELA assessment, his reading and writing showed significant growth as noted by his classroom teacher and the principal. However, because of the district cut-off he was eligible for summer school. This alongside of an analysis of Marty's other writing showed his growth as a writer in terms of voice and in communicating a point clearly. In an interview (7/99), Lucy noted: "I think as a writer he really grew a lot. He was much more able to . . . make and develop a point." In both of these examples, Marty's learning and a definition of success is contextually bound. This comparison or difference between individual growth and social expectations has consequences on placement and instructional decisions as well as how Marty learns to think about himself within these communities of practice (Wenger, 1998).

Representation of Student Learning and Achievement

Student achievement is a matter of representation (Johnston, 1999; Moss, 1998; Murphy, 1997). Language plays a powerful role in shaping perceptions of student learning and achievement. As McDermott (1996) points out, "language is not a neutral medium; it comes to us loaded with social structure. . . . It comes to us biased with social agendas of a school system that pits all children against all children in a battle for success" (p. 293). We define this category by the different types of language practices (both oral and written) used to make sense of and view Marty's learning and achievement. Examples of such language practices include teacher evaluations, report cards, standardized test scores and how information is communicated to parents. The focus question in this category: How is evidence of student achievement represented?

Marty's Standardized Test Score Data

The CTBS is a standardized achievement test given to all students in the district each spring. The components of the test are reading, language, math, social studies, and science. Table 1 lists Marty's test scores and report card markings across Grades 1 to 4. The district used a combination of standardized test measures, K–2 portfolios and teacher recommendation to make decisions about remedial reading. At the end of both second and third grades, Marty's scores on the CTBS test were on "grade level." Further, his teachers thought he made a lot of growth in terms of his ability to read connected texts with comprehension. However, based on comparison with the overall level of reading in the class, Marty qualified for placement in remedial reading. This decision was based on comparison with his peers, and his proficiency with reading connected texts.

At both the school and the district levels, educators raised concerns about the CTBS test. Consequently, Marty's fourth-grade year was the last time the districts used the tests. These concerns included: the state curriculum and standards extended beyond the CTBS assessment, teachers were familiar with the forms of the CTBS tests leading to concerns of inflated scores, and the need for an assessment that was more closely aligned with the state assessment to monitor student progress across grade levels.

Marty's teachers expressed concerns with Marty's scores. Jane Larson stated she was puzzled by how high his scores were at the end of second grade. Lucy Grey remarked in October of Marty's fourth-grade year upon examining the results of his third-grade test, "these seem much too high for Marty." In July, when Lucy was asked again about the scores she stated, "This was always curious to me. That's not the way he presented himself as a reader and compared to other students with similar scores he seemed much weaker." These numbers seemed most significant because the CTBS did not involve the same assumptions about "what counts as reading" as those of his teachers.

Teachers' Representation of Marty's Learning

As Johnston (1997, 1998) pointed out, teachers are the primary agents of assessment. They are also the primary agents of representing their "findings"

Table 1

Marty's Achievement Data

Assessment Data	Grade Levels			
	1	2	3	4
CTBS—Reading		2.9 GE	4.4 GE	3.1 GE
			55 NCE	37 NCE
CTBS—Social Studies	2.9 GE	6.1 GE	3.8 GE	3.6 GE
			51 NCE	41 NCE
CTBS—Language		5.4 GE	4.6 GE	3.7 GE
			58 NCE	41 NCE
Extra Services	Reading teacher	Reading teacher	Reading teacher	Reading teacher
Teacher Representation	Low	Low	Average/low	Very low
Report Card Reading	C+	B	B+	B
Report Card Social Studies	B+	A	A	B-
Report Card Writing	S	S	G	G
New York (ELA) Assessment				Total SS 632
				Reading SS 630

either in writing or orally about student learning. Marty's second- and fourth-grade teacher knew a lot about Marty that was not included in any of his formal or documentary assessments. Whereas the chart and the numbers present one "snap shot" of Marty, in the following section we illustrate how Marty's teachers represented his learning. Both Jane and Lucy sought out ways to work one-to-one with Marty to nurture his progress and consequently had much to say about his learning.

Second-Grade Teacher

Jane reported that Marty was one of the most complicated students with whom she had ever worked (fieldnotes 1/97). Jane spoke at length about Marty's strategies with literature. During observations and conversations with Jane in her classroom, she consistently called on the texts Marty was reading, pointing out what level of the text and characteristics of the texts that supported Marty as a reader. Jane kept a file on each child with ongoing documentary assessments and completed running records, pointing out where Marty did and did not use strategies, his self-corrections, and the questions and statements he made during and after reading. She showed awareness of his writing, commenting that she was particularly proud of the connections he had made in the piece he wrote about the Underground Railroad because he had used information from social studies and took risks in his writing (summary of fieldnotes 2/97).

Despite Jane's emphasis on his strengths, that he had improved 12 levels in less than a year, and her ongoing articulation of this, he remained one of the lowest readers in the room and as a result continued to need to remedial reading support from the reading teacher. Jane continued to collaborate with the reading teacher throughout first and second grades to provide consistency in their approaches to reading instruction.

Fourth-Grade Teacher

Similar to Jane Larson, Lucy Grey, Marty's fourth-grade teacher, expressed awareness of Marty's progress during several points in the year. In July, reflecting on his growth, Lucy Grey expressed detailed observations of his progress. She stated, "I think he made a lot of progress this year. In the beginning of the year, he literally cried every day for the first month and a half of school. Every day . . . I wouldn't have given the assignment yet and he would cry. I would just say what we would do and show it to him and he would just would shut down and panic. I mean he never articulated this but my thought was that he was thinking, 'I'm not going to be able to be successful. I won't be able to do this'" (interview 7/99). Her first goal was to help Marty realize that he could do the literacy activities and be successful.

Lucy Grey attempted to help Marty with this area by working with him one-to-one at certain points. She said of his early work, "So I would try to get him to that point where I thought if I leave now he will still read and he won't just shut the book. That took a lot of time and I was disappointed at that point in the year,

Marty still needed that kind of a one-to-one, when he was in a book that he was capable of reading independently" (interview 7/99). For Marty, the issue was not whether he could read the books but if he perceived himself as successful with these books and according to Lucy, "interested enough in what he was reading to continue on his own" (interview 11/99).

Both Jane and Lucy focused on a discourse of strengths when they talked about Marty. Further, they both recognized him as a complicated, fragile student who made extensive growth in different areas. Both teachers expressed some uneasiness in placement decisions for Marty. They recognized a need for extra individualized help beyond what they could give him. Like other educators, they struggled with how to provide assistance within current school structures.

Representation to Parents: The English Language Arts Letter

The second area of representation is communication of Marty's test results on the state fourth-grade English Language Arts exam to his parents in a letter. Although Marty's score of 2 placed him above the state cut-off line (1 for failing), he was strongly encouraged to attend summer school classes. Students who scored within the "2" range received the following comments in the State Education report to parents:

> Students demonstrate partial understanding of written and oral text at a literal level. They can recognize basic story elements, make some inferences, and identify some similarities and differences in two related texts, providing limited supporting information. Students' writing shows some focus and basic organization, and uses simple correct spelling, grammar and punctuation, but errors sometimes interfere with readability. (CTB/McGraw-Hill, 1997)

This letter that represented Marty's score on the fourth-grade ELA, stood in contrast to how Lucy talked about his learning and the progress in his writing. The letter referred to Marty's "growth" on the test as a matter of mechanics and readability rather than on the growth in thinking, writing and level of independence embedded in this writing during a test-taking situation. Both Lucy Grey and the principal expressed their recognition of this score as significant progress for Marty.

Representation involves consequences for student learning and achievement in terms of placement decisions and how students and their families make sense of their achievement. The language of documents representing the interpretation of test scores has consequences that extend beyond the education community. These consequences include how students and parents are positioned with regard to knowledge, how these beliefs are internalized, and how this information influences daily lives, including their literate identity. Lucy Grey put it this way, "the harsh realities of the big picture means in many ways losing perspective on the individual child. You are no longer looking at individual growth but a child thrown in with the masses. [It's] the difference between being a number and an individual in the system" (interview 11/99). In New York State, fourth graders are tested on math, science, and language arts, and the scores on these tests make the front page of the newspaper. Lucy regularly struggled with how to make sure students learned what they needed to know while also giving each of them the individual support they needed.

The Construction of Literate Identity

This category is the relationship between the development of literacy and overall achievement in school and the student's developing literate identity. The framing question of this section is: What are the consequences of evidence on student identity? One of the areas that arose in Marty's assessment data over time was his fragile identity. Notions of student literate identity include issues such as developing confidence as a reader, participating in book discussion groups, taking risks in reading and writing and articulating decisions and choices within broader social, cultural, and political contexts. In this section we include examples that represent Marty's literate identity.

Marty's Fragileness

In first, second, third, and fourth grades, each teacher described Marty as a "low" reader. Observations of Marty suggested that he did not want attention brought to the fact that he was struggling with reading. For example, at the start of each thematic unit in fourth grade, Marty often selected the more difficult books that he knew would not be read by the students who saw the reading teacher. Lucy Grey said, "He would be upset about going to sit at the back table with Marianna [Reading Teacher]. He deliberately chose books to read that he thought the other kids that he normally was with wouldn't read. . . . He figured out that if he did that [pick out other books] he wouldn't have to sit back there" (interview 6/ 99). Marty avoided tasks that placed him in situations where he might be perceived as a "low" reader.

Marty's teachers consistently reported that he seemed sensitive and fragile. Jane Larson noted that in second grade it took a whole-class effort to get Marty to answer a question in class (fieldnotes 3/18/97). She reported that Marty would start to cry if she pushed him too hard (fieldnotes 3/18/97). However, at the end of Marty's second-grade year, Jane was confident he had made a lot of growth in terms of seeing himself as a reader and writer (fieldnotes 5/15/97). She was concerned that he would lose the growth he had made if he did not continue to practice reading over the summer.

Similarly, in fourth grade, Marty did not like to be pushed out of his comfort zone. When this happened he would cry (fieldnotes date, interview 7/99). Lucy Grey remarked in an interview (7/99) about her academic expectations for Marty: "And I was always worried about Marty's self esteem because he seemed so fragile to me and I think he is really fragile. . . . He knows that he needs extra help and he hates the fact that he needs extra help." Lucy struggled with whether to make modifications to Marty's work. Lucy further indicated that Marty thought he would not be able to accomplish assignments and was not comfortable in taking a risk to even attempt them.

At the end of fourth grade, Marty wrote in Lucy Grey's class yearbook: "I promise I will start with what I know" (interview 7/99). This quote summarized Lucy Grey's view of Marty at that point, in that he appeared to have conquered many of his struggles. Lucy Grey attributed this quote to what she told him during the school year. She stated, "He told me that at the end of the year, because I would tell him that every time he cried. I would go up to him and say to him '[c]rying is not going to help you here Marty. You need to pull yourself together and start with what you know. You know something. Find out what you know.'"

These strengths and this progress, however, are not reflected on standardized tests of achievement or in the amount of growth he made from the beginning to the end of his fourth-grade year. Further, it is likely that part of the reason Marty was placed in remedial reading classes despite his on "grade level" test scores was his fragileness as a learner. Further, Marty's teachers expressed a concern that he would get "lost in the cracks" if he did not receive additional reading instruction.

Risk-Taking

Marty's literate identity included how he handled risk-taking as a reader and a writer. Marty made substantive growth in this area. For example, being able to articulate his recommendation of a book was a marked improvement from third grade when he was unable to tell, in an interview, what books were his favorite and what books he would recommend (student interview 5/98). In contrast, at the end of fourth grade, Marty wrote about books in a written survey. He wrote:

> I would recommend *Patrick Doyle* because I think kids next year would like this book. I would recommend *Printer's Apprentice* because it was funny. I would not recommend *Mystery in the Sand* because you can't tell right away who it is. I would not recommend *Toliver's Secret* because it did not seem real. (survey 6/99)

Marty could read both *Patrick Doyle is Full of Blarney* (Armstrong, 1997) and *Printer's Apprentice* (Krensky, 1996) at an independent level, whereas *Mystery in the Sand* (Chandler-Warner, 1990) and *Toliver's Secret* (Wood-Brady, 1993) were more difficult for him in terms of comprehension. This seemed to indicate Marty's awareness of when he knew he could read successfully and books he had difficulty understanding.

Lucy stated, "Marty needed to know someone perceived him as capable before he could trust himself to take risks. I really think that for Marty someone believing in his potential, his own confidence and performance are intricately interwoven" (interview 11/99). As Johnston (1998) wrote, "[s]tudents who learn they are, in norm-referenced terms, 'unable' become essentially helpless when they face new performance situations; they fail to use even those strategies that they have, let alone seek new ones" (p. 94). Marty's teachers saw his emerging identity as fragile throughout his elementary school years. Lucy Grey was concerned about his transition into middle school, even with the growth he had made as a risk-taker. How educators talk about, make sense of and communicate children's achievement matters to students. In Marty's case with reminders that he needed to "start with what he knew" and that he could be successful helped him to grow as a reader, writer, and thinker.

Conclusions and Implications

The three themes (i.e., individual versus social expectations, representations of student learning, literate identity) are overlapping rather than disconnected threads for understanding Marty as a learner. One of the striking contradictions in this case study is how the assessments that recognize the social nature of the student and learning (e.g., documentary assessments) are the ones that indicated that he was less "able" than his peers throughout his elementary career. For the most part, the standardized measures indicated he was progressing successfully. This finding seems related to two important issues. First, the assessments differed in terms of "what counts as reading," leading to further complexity in how we could understand Marty. Second, it is clear that the teachers knew Marty better than either formal or documentary evidence. However, the teachers are working with a set of social arrangements that maintain a competitive-comparative notion of ability and learning.

"Snap shot" views of achievement, either formal or documentary, revealed an incomplete portrait of Marty's learning and achievement over time. We cannot understand Marty without also understanding the context, overtime, in which his identity as a struggling reader emerged. Marty's learning was much more complex than the level of book that he was reading. There were issues of confidence and risk-taking that were a part of his placement, his thoughts about himself in relation to texts and contexts, and his achievement. As we saw in his case, students internalize ways of thinking about the relationships between themselves, texts, and contexts. Throughout his schooling, Marty showed troublesome ways of viewing himself in relation to literacy and learning that resulted in an unwillingness to take risks and to avoid tasks that he perceived to be too difficult for him. Nicholls (1989) pointed out that in the culture of normative comparisons, children learn to identify with and develop a comparative-competitive notion of ability. In this framework, students are more apt to reflect on their progress compared with peers rather than if what they are learning makes sense. Without the social arrangements for making something of differential rates of learning, there is no such thing as learning difficulties (McDermott, 1996). However, schools, as they are currently arranged, often focus on individual difference and a comparative-competitive notion of achievement—one that is communicated to students in work expectations, grouping patterns and written assessment measures.

Growth is a more complex representation of what a child can do as well as the logic of his or her errors and the place for assessment. A focus on gains implies a linear sequence between teaching, the curriculum and a student's scores over time. An increase in test scores is generally thought of in terms of positive gains. In the anomalies that appeared in Marty's case, we found growth does not always imply gains on standardized test scores nor do gains imply growth in thinking and reasoning through a domain. Assessment may also involve more subjective understandings such as how Marty grew in terms of his self-confidence and his ability to take risks in both reading and writing. These include a set of literate dimensions not reflected on traditional measures of achievement. This means that educators need to continue to shape different discourses to represent children's literacy learning. It appears that the school district was taking this issue seriously as they changed the assessments toward those that more closely aligned with their views of reading and curriculum. Tensions in student learning and achievement may result in the restructuring of discourse around learning and continued learning for both teachers and students.

These data show that the teachers gave priority to observing literate behaviors in order to understand their students. Often, these observations were in contrast to the types of literacy activities tested on the formal measures. Trajectory of assessment as ethnographic and context-based and issues of validity evolve from an anthropological framework of valuing ways of learning and knowing through observations and theorizing about connections. In this case, the educators were engaging with three constructs of validity. First, teachers may seek to establish and create documentary evidence across time and contexts (Gipps, 1994). Second, student learning and achievement should be viewed from a range of sources. Third, teachers taking an ethnographic approach to assessment may focus both on the confirming and the disconfirming pieces of evidence in student learning. As we have found in this case study, the places of tension in the assessment data are the places that provide useful insight into the complexity of learning. It seems clear that the teachers' knowledge of Marty's literate growth helped him to start to feel secure and confidence in his progress to be more successful in his own views of his literate identity.

References

Armstrong, J.(1997). *Patrick Doyle is full of blarney*. New York: Random House.

Au, K. (1981). Participation structures in a reading lesson with Hawaiian children: Analysis of a culturally appropriate instructional event. *Anthropology and Education Quarterly, 9*(2), 91–115.

Bruchac, J.(1996). *Children of the longhouse*. New York: Puffin.

Burawoy, M. (1991). Reconstructing social theories. In M. Burawoy (Ed.), *Ethnography unbound: Power and resistance in the modern metropolis* (pp. 8–27). Berkeley: University of California Press.

Chandler-Warner, G. (1990). *Mystery in the sand*. New York: Albert Whitman.

Collins, J. (1986). Differential treatment and reading instruction. In J. Cook Gumperz (Ed.), *The social construction of literacy* (pp. 117–137). New York: Cambridge University Press.

CTB/McGraw-Hill (1997). *Complete Battery, TerraNova*. Monterey, CA: McGraw-Hill.

Collins, J. (1996). Socialization to text: Structure and contradiction in schooled literacy. In M. Silverstein & G. Urban (Eds.), *Natural histories of discourse*. Chicago: University of Chicago Press.

Fountas, I., & Pinnell, G. (1999). *Matching books to readers: Using leveled books in guided reading, K–3*. Portsmouth, NH: Heinemann.

Gipps, C. V. (1994). *Beyond testing: Towards a theory of educational assessment.* London: Falmer.

Heath, S. B. (1983). *Ways with words: Language, life and work in community and classrooms.* Cambrodge, England: Cambridge University Press.

Heath, S. B. (1992). Oral and literate traditions among Black Americans living in poverty. In P. Shannon (Ed.), *Becoming political: Reading and writings in the politics of literacy education* (pp. 29–41). Portsmouth, NH: Heinemann.

Hodges, C. (1997). How valid and useful are alternative assessments for decision making in primary grade classrooms? *Reading Research and Instruction, 36,* 157–173.

Johnston, P. (1997). *Knowing literacy.* Portsmouth, NH: Heinemann.

Johnston, P. (1998). The role of consequences. In S. Murphy, P. Shannon, P. Johnston, & J. Hanson (Eds.), *Fragile evidence. A critique of reading assessment.* Mahwah, NJ: Erlbaum.

Johnston, P. (1999). *Unpacking literate achievement* (Tech. Rep. No. 12007). Albany, NY: Center for English Learning and Achievement.

Johnston, P., Guice, S., Baker, K., Malone, J., & Michelson, N. (1995). Assessment of teaching and learning in "literature-based" classrooms. *Teaching and Teacher Education, 11,* 359–371.

Kos, R. (1993). "Nobody knows my life but me!" The story of Ben, a reading disabled adolescent. In R. Donmoyer & R. Kos (Eds.), *At-risk students: Portraits, policies, programs and practices,* (pp. 49–78). Albany: State University of New York Press.

Krensky, S. (1996). *The printer's apprentice.* New York: Yearling.

Lee, A. (1996). *Gender, literacy and curriculum. Re-writing school geography.* London: Taylor & Francis.

Lipson, Wixson, & Valencia (1994).

McDermott, R. P. (1996). The acquisition of a child by a learning disability. In S. Chaiklin & J. Lave (Eds.), *Understanding practice: Perspectives on activity and context* (pp. 269–305). New York: Cambridge University Press.

Michaels, S. (1981)."Sharing time": Children's narrative styles and differential access to literacy. *Language in Society, 10,* 423–442.

Moss, P. (1998). The role of consequences in validity theory. *Educational Measurement: Issues and Practices, 17*(2), 6–12.

Murphy, S. (1997). Literacy assessment and the politics of identities. *Reading and Writing Quarterly, 13,* 261–278.

Nicholls, J. (1989). *The competitive ethos and democratic education.* Cambridge, MA: Harvard University Press.

Ogbu, J. U. (1991). Low school performance as an adaptation: The case of blacks in Stockton, California. In M. A. Gibson & J. U. Ogbu (Eds.), *Minority status and schooling: A comparative study of immigrant and involuntary minorities.* New York & London: Garland.

Shannon, P. (1995). Reading instruction and social class. In P. Shannon (Ed.), *Becoming political: Readings and writings in the politics of education* (pp. 128–138). Portsmouth, NH: Heinemann.

Wenger, E. (1998). *Communities of practice: Learning, meaning and identity.* Cambridge, England: Cambridge University Press.

Wixson, K., Valencia, S., & Lipson, M. (1994). Issues in literacy assessment: Facing the realities of internal and external assessment. *Journal of Reading Behavior, 26,* 315–337.

Wood-Brady, E. (1993). *Toliver's secret.* New York: Random House.

Can a Less Coherent Text Help College Students Evaluate Their Own Understanding?

Ana Claudia Harten

Universidade Catolica de Pernambuco, Brazil

Diane L. Schallert

University of Texas at Austin

One important contributor to being able to learn from what one reads is the ability to assess whether one has comprehended a text at a level that will be adequate for some future use of the material. Although the self-evaluation of comprehension is not the only component of comprehension monitoring, it certainly constitutes an important step in the application of regulatory strategies. When a reader can accurately assess his or her comprehension of a text, he or she can decide whether strategies such as slowing down the rate of reading or rereading a part of the text should be applied in order to resolve comprehension failures. Given the influence on readers' actions, it would seem important to investigate whether readers' evaluations of their own comprehension are routinely satisfactory.

The idea that comprehension monitoring is necessary to the effective use of comprehension strategies has garnered much attention from researchers. One approach within the field of metacomprehension has been to focus on readers' ability to predict test performance over text material, or what Glenburg and Epstein (1985) called the *calibration of comprehension*. The term is often used as both a procedure (a research technique to gather data) and a construct (readers' ability to assess comprehension states). Indeed, a widely used paradigm for examining the accuracy of readers' self-assessed comprehension involves asking students to read a text and to make predictions about their performance on an upcoming comprehension test. Calibration of comprehension refers to the degree of match between readers' predicted and actual performance. The general purpose of this study was to contribute to the literature on readers' calibration of comprehension. In particular, guided by Kintsch's (1988) construction-integration model of text comprehension, we set out to explore the extent to which increasing the processing effort of readers would increase the accuracy of their assessment of their own text comprehension.

Calibration of comprehension is a relatively new area of study, initiated a little more than a decade ago. Although one might expect that college students would be able to predict test performance over text material, researchers initially reported that such students were poor at judging their comprehension. Indeed, early stud-

National Reading Conference Yearbook, 49, pp. 321–330.

ies suggested either that college students cannot accurately judge their comprehension (Glenberg & Epstein, 1985; Glenberg, Wilknson, & Epstein, 1982) or that only some readers can do so moderately well under certain circumstances (Maki & Berry, 1984). Scrutiny of the calibration procedure used in the early studies and more recent attempts (Magliano, Little, & Graesser, 1993; Maki & Serra, 1990; Weaver, 1990) have revealed that college students are somewhat more proficient in calibrating comprehension than earlier studies suggested.

The more recent evidence that college students are able, if only to a moderate degree, to assess their comprehension gave the field of calibration of comprehension a second wind. In recent years, researchers have shown renewed interest in the topic (Lin & Zabrucki, 1998) that has been translated into the pursuit of possible variables that might hinder or facilitate the calibration of comprehension. Although some variables have been shown to influence significantly comprehension calibration, results on the effects of other variables have been inconsistent. Yet, readers' overall calibration ability has generally been reported to be moderate at best (Lin, Zabrucky, & Moore, 1997).

The findings that college students do not show a good calibration of their comprehension seems to contradict the commonsense notion that comprehension monitoring should be routine and fairly accurate among these skilled readers. It is interesting to note that readers' low prediction accuracy contrasts with their accuracy in predicting test results after they take the test (calibration of performance). In addition, such findings seem to present problems for theories of comprehension that emphasize the importance of comprehension monitoring for efficient reading (Baker & Brown, 1982). It is important to consider, however, that young adults' calibration of comprehension has not been extensively studied. An important challenge for this area of research is to determine the basis of readers' calibration of comprehension, and what can be done to improve calibration accuracy. One topic that has received attention is a consideration of the assessment procedure itself. Both the original approach of asking readers to predict how well they will perform on a test as they read and a newer procedure that asks readers to assess the ease with which they feel they are processing the text have been explored. In the research reported here, both approaches are used and compared as a variable in the design.

An important aspect that has been overlooked is the possible role of the transactional relationship between reader and text in the process of calibration. Along the lines argued by Roller (1990) in her analysis of the literature on text effects and reading comprehension, such an oversight may be responsible for the inconsistent results. Research on reading comprehension has reported an interactive effect between text coherence and background knowledge (McNamara, & Kintsch, 1996; McNamara, Kintsch, Songer, & Kintsch, 1996;). In Kintsch's (1988) model of text comprehension, an important effect of such interaction is that whereas low-knowledge readers profit from a fully coherent text, high-knowledge readers may learn better with less coherent text because such text induces more active processing. As increased processing leads to better learning for some learners, it may also lead to more accurate comprehension monitoring because readers can self-assess by accessing a text representation built up from reading that involves more active processing. It was expected in this study that such active processing during reading would, in turn, involve better monitoring strategies that would allow readers to have a more accurate judgment of their text comprehension. On the other hand, the increased processing required by the low-coherence text was not expected to affect the readers' test prediction made after they had taken the test. Here, posttest prediction (calibration of performance) would seem dependent more on latency of response and on whether one can retrieve from memory the needed information for the test question rather than on how well one can construct a coherent meaning.

The research questions addressed by this study were: (a) Would college students self-assess better when they are asked to evaluate their comprehension during reading and prior to comprehension testing (calibration of comprehension) or when they have first completed a comprehension test (calibration of performance)? (b) Would they be more accurate in their predictions when reading less coherent texts than when reading more coherent texts and would background knowledge of the topic interact with text coherence? and (c) Would type of comprehension question (i.e., low-level, text-based questions vs. more knowledge-based, bridging inference questions) influence calibration accuracy?

Method

Participants

Three hundred undergraduate students from an introductory psychology course at a large state university participated in the study as part of a course requirement. Participants were randomly assigned to one of four conditions defined by the combination of two levels of two independent variables (i.e., text coherence and basis of rating). Ultimately, 35 students were excluded from the analyses because they provided exactly the same ratings for all sections of the text, and thus no correlation coefficients could be computed for them between their ratings and test performance.

Materials

Texts. Two versions were used of a description of the events surrounding one of the battles of the Vietnam War. These versions were borrowed from a study by Britton and Gülgöz (1991) who used Kintsch and van Dijk's (1978) model of text comprehension to modify an excerpt from a history textbook to produce a more coherent text. Both versions contained nine paragraphs and had a readability score of 13.5 as measured by the Flesh-Kincaid Index. The low-coherence version was 1,030 words long, and the high-coherence version was 1,302.

In this study, the texts were segmented into four sections, ranging from 200 to 360 words in length. Below each section, a rating scale appeared that either examined comprehension ease ("How easy was the above section to understand?") or the likelihood of answering correctly short-answer questions on the section just read ("How certain are you that you will answer short-answer questions correctly over the above section?"). The comprehension ease scale ranged from "1=not at all easy" to "6=very easy." The prediction scale ranged from "1=not at all sure" to "6=very sure."

Prior-knowledge questionnaire. The prior-knowledge questionnaire consisted of 15 true/false questions (1 point each) about general aspects of the Vietnam War, and 10 specific terms (2 points each) about the war that the participants were asked to define or identify.

Text-comprehension task. The comprehension task consisted of 32 short-answer questions. Sixteen of these questions (text-based questions) queried knowledge of some text detail. The other 16 questions were bridging inference questions and required what Kintsch (1988) calls a situation model understanding. Directly below each question, a rating scale appeared asking participants to rate how certain they were that they had answered correctly on a scale from "1=not at all sure" to "6=very sure."

Procedure

Participants were first given the prior-knowledge questionnaire and then were randomly assigned to one of the four versions of the materials. They read the text at their own pace, recording time when they reached particular portions of the text (at the beginning and at end of each section), as well as completing four Likert-type rating scales. Half of the participants were asked to complete a Likert-type comprehension ease rating scale after reading each section of the text, and the other half were asked to complete the same kind of scales that refer to pretest prediction rating. These ratings represented different ways of measuring participants' comprehension calibration. After reading the text, participants answered the text comprehension questions and rated each question, providing assessment of their comprehension as well as a measure of their performance calibration.

Statistical Analyses

The accuracy of calibration of comprehension was determined by correlating (Gamma correlation) each participant's comprehension or prediction rating performance on a particular section of the text with the participant's actual level of performance on that same section. In the case of posttest calibration (calibration of performance), correlation indices between each participant's question ratings and their scores on the questions were computed. Single-sample t tests were conducted to investigate whether correlations between ratings and test performance exceeded chance. A series of ANOVAs were also performed for each dependent measure. The analyses included between-subjects variables of text coherence (high-coherence, low-coherence), basis of rating (comprehension ease, test prediction), and prior knowledge (used as a continuous variable). The within-subjects variable of question type was included in the analysis for text comprehension, and the within-subjects variable of gamma type was included in the analysis for the accuracy of readers' text assessment. This latter variable included two levels, text-based and bridging inference, which referred to the type of question considered for the computation of the correlation gammas. Simple main effect tests were performed as post hoc analyses whenever pertinent.

Results

Analyses were performed in two steps. First, preliminary analyses tested whether the variables of coherence and background knowledge had been powerful enough to influence processing rate and comprehension outcome. Once these analyses were performed, the tests of the hypotheses related specifically to calibration of comprehension were performed.

Preliminary Analyses

Prior knowledge. It was important to establish that random assignment of participants to condition had resulted in equivalent levels of prior knowledge about the Vietnam War across conditions. As shown in Table 1, mean scores on the prior-knowledge measure were similar across conditions, $F(3, 261)=.41, p=.75$, and showed a low to moderate amount of knowledge about the topic before reading (15 points on average on a 35-point test).

Reading times (sec/word). A significant main effect of text coherence, $F(1, 260)=18.44, p<.001$, indicated that readers who read the low-coherence text spent more time reading ($M=.44$ sec/word) than those who read the high-coherence text

Table 1

Means (and Standard Deviations) for Prior Knowledge, Reading Times, and Text-Comprehension Performance for the Text Coherence × Basis of Rating Conditions

| Measures | High-Coherence Text | | Low-Coherence Text | |
	Ease Ratings	Prediction Ratings	Ease Ratings	Prediction Ratings
Prior Knowledge	15.3	14.7	15.2	14.6
	(4.4)	(4.0)	(4.7)	(4.3)
Reading Rate	.38	.38	.41	.46
(sec/word)	(.10)	(.10)	(.12)	(.12)
Comprehension				
Textbased Questions	12.5	12.6	9.2	9.7
	(6.3)	(5.8)	(4.9)	(5.2)
Inferential Questions	12.8	13.8	9.0	9.1
	(6.2)	(5.2)	(5.2)	(4.5)

(M=.38 sec/word). This finding pointed to a difference in amount of processing required by the two texts, a preliminary assumption needed in order to test for the effect of text coherence on readers' calibration of comprehension. There was also a main effect of prior knowledge on reading times, $F(1, 260)$=10.15, p<.05, indicating that more knowledgeable readers spent less time reading than did less knowledgeable readers. There were no other significant effects.

Text comprehension. Finally, a significant main effect of prior knowledge, $F(1, 260)$=34.62, p<.001, demonstrated that readers with more knowledge of the text topic obtained higher reading comprehension scores than did those with less knowledge. The effect of text coherence on comprehension was also significant, $F(1, 260)$=38.23, p<.001, replicating previous results (McNamara & Kintsch, 1996; McNamara et al., 1996). Readers who read the high-coherence text answered more comprehension questions correctly than did those who read the low-coherence text (see Table 1). No significant main effect for basis of judgment was found, $F(1, 260)$=1.57, p=.211, indicating that the type of rating during reading produced no differential effect on comprehension performance.

There was a reliable ordinal interaction between type of question and text coherence, $F(1, 260)$=4.89, p<.05. Simple main effects tests of the interaction indicated that readers with the high-coherence text received higher comprehension scores than readers with the low-coherence text, for both the text-based questions (M=12.6 and 9.4, respectively), $F(1, 260)$=22.53, p<.001, and the bridging inference questions (M=13.3 and 9.0, respectively), $F(1, 260)$=44.57, p<.001.

Main Analyses: Accuracy of Ratings

In terms of their calibration of performance, participants in all conditions produced mean gammas significantly different from zero (see Table 2), indicating that they did better than chance in predicting the accuracy of their answer to test questions when asked to provide their rating while they answered each question during the test. However, in terms of calibration of comprehension, that is, the accuracy of ratings produced during the reading task itself, participants were much less accurate. Only in the case of correlations between reading ratings and performance on the bridging inference questions, and only for readers of the low-coherence text, was calibration significantly different from zero. Otherwise, calibration accuracy was very low.

Next, gamma coefficients were submitted to analysis of variance to test whether the different text or basis of rating conditions had produced different levels of calibration accuracy. There were no differences found for gammas reflecting calibration of performance but there was a main effect of text coherence detected in the case of calibration of comprehension. This effect indicated that participants who read the low-coherence text were more accurate on their reading ratings than participants who read the high-coherence text. Moreover, in the case of reading judgments, a three-way interaction of gamma type × text coherence × prior knowledge was also significant, $F(1, 257)$=3.92, p<.05 (see Figure 1). Separate analyses for each gamma type demonstrated that there was neither a main effect of prior

Table 2

Means (and Standard Deviations) of Gamma Coefficients for Postreading and Posttesting Ratings by Text Coherence, Basis of Judgment, and Question Type

| | High-Coherence Text | | Low-Coherence Text | |
	Ease Ratings	Prediction Ratings	Ease Ratings	Prediction Ratings
Comprehension Calibration				
Text-based Performance	-.03	.06	.04	.18
	(.81)	(.79)	(.78)	(.73)
Inferential performance	.07	.16	.38*	.33*
	(.74)	(.76)	(.62)	(.70)
Performance Calibration				
Text-based performance	.43*	.48*	.37*	.40*
	(.45)	(.32)	(.43)	(.42)
Inferential performance	.45*	.51*	.40*	.53*
	(.28)	(.28)	(.38)	(.27)

*Significantly different from zero.

knowledge nor interaction effects between prior knowledge and text coherence on readers' reading rating accuracy for text-based questions (see Figure 1, top panel). This result indicates that the calibration involving the text-based questions was not affected by the coherence of the text.

On the other hand, there was a reliable text coherence × prior-knowledge interaction effect on readers' reading-rating accuracy for bridging inference questions, $F(1, 257)=5.10, p<.05$. This interaction effect (see Figure 1, bottom panel) demonstrated that for readers of the low-coherence text, the rating accuracy for bridging inference questions increased as prior knowledge increased. The reverse relationship was detected among readers who read the high-coherence text, indicating that rating accuracy for bridging inference questions seemed to drop as prior knowledge increased among readers. Thus, when it came to the deep comprehension required to answer the bridging inference questions, more knowledgeable readers were more accurate for the low-coherence text, whereas less knowledgeable readers were more accurate with the high-coherence text.

Conclusion

Results demonstrated that increased reading processing seems to foster better calibration of comprehension in college students. The higher postreading prediction accuracy among the readers who read the low-coherence text suggests that the increased processing involved in reading less coherent text must have led students to engage in more evaluative strategies that allowed them to assess better what was and was not understood. Although comprehension calibration seemed to have been influenced by increased reading processing, the performance calibration did not seem to be so influenced. The absence of a main effect of text coherence on posttest rating accuracy seems to suggest that, once a question has been answered, the amount of processing involved during reading is no longer a factor in readers' accurate confidence that the answer is correct.

In addition, the findings on comprehension calibration for the bridging inference questions seem to be in line with Kintsch's (1988) text comprehension model. That is, more knowledgeable readers benefited from the low-coherence text in making accurate assessments of online reading comprehension, whereas less knowledgeable readers benefited from the high-coherence text. Thus, this study

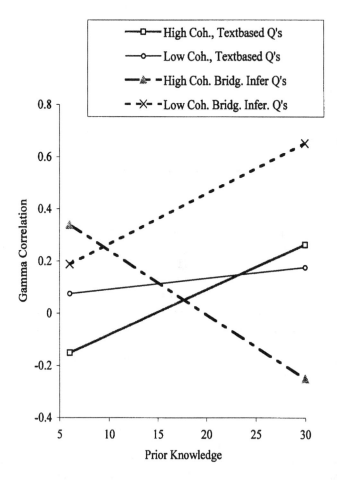

Figure 1. Interaction between coherence, gamma type, and prior knowledge on the accuracy of postreading ratings.

provides an empirical basis for extending the construction-integration model of text comprehension in the area of comprehension monitoring, an important subprocess involved in comprehension that had heretofore not been considered in this model.

Understanding more fully the factors that influence how readers calibrate their comprehension is important, we believe, because such calibration is a first step in encouraging readers to read in more strategic ways. Readers who do not detect that they are having any problem in understanding will not engage in the strategies needed to make their construction of meaning elaborate enough to lead to good performance on an assessment of their comprehension. As well, readers who incorrectly decide that they are not comprehending what they are reading when, in fact, they are, may lose confidence in their reading ability and desist from further attempts at making meaning from text. Our research suggests that a factor that may help improve the calibration of comprehension is the coherence of the text. Although clear coherent prose is reliably easier to understand than less coherent prose, it does bring with it the possibility that readers will become lulled by the ease of processing into thinking that their comprehension is better than it is. Struggling with text may have the unexpected benefit of leading readers to gauge more accurately the level of processing effort that should be deployed. Greater processing effort, likewise, should have the consequence of helping readers monitor their comprehension more accurately.

References

Baker, L., & Brown, A. L. (1982). Metacognitive skills and reading. In P. D. Pearson (Ed.), *Handbook of reading research* (pp. 353–394). New York: Longman.

Britton, B. K., & Gülgöz, S. (1991). Using Kintsch's computational model to improve instructional text: Effects of repairing inference calls on recall and cognitive structures. *Journal of Educational Psychology, 83,* 329–345.

Glenberg, A. M., & Epstein, W. (1985). Calibration of comprehension. *Journal of Experimental Psychology, 11,* 702–718.

Glenberg, A. M., Wilknson, A. C., & Epstein, W. (1982). The illusion of knowing: Failure in the self-assessment of comprehension. *Memory and Cognition, 10,* 597–602.

Kintsch, W. (1988). The role of knowledge in discourse comprehension: A construction-integration model. *Psychological Review, 95,* 163–182.

Kintsch, W., & van Dijk, T. A. (1978). Toward a model of text comprehension and production. *Psychological Review, 85,* 363–394.

Lin, L., Zabrucky, K., & Moore, D. (1997). The relations among interest, self-assessed comprehension, and comprehension performance in young adults. *Reading Research and Instruction, 36,* 127–139.

Lin, L., & Zabrucky, K. (1998). Calibration of comprehension: Research and implications for education and instruction. *Contemporary Educational Psychology, 23,* 345–391.

Magliano, J. P., Little, L. D., & Graesser, A. C. (1993). The impact of comprehension instruction on the calibration of comprehension. *Reading Research and Instruction, 32,* 49–63.

Maki, R., & Berry, S. (1984). Metacomprehension of text material. *Journal of Experimental Psychology, 10,* 663–679.

Maki, R. H., & Serra, M. (1992). The basis of test predictions for text material. *Journal of Experimental Psychology, 18,* 116–126.

McNamara, D. S., & Kintsch, W. (1996). Learning from texts: Effects of prior knowledge and text coherence. *Discourse Processes, 22,* 247–288.

McNamara, D. S., Kintsch, E., Songer, N. B., & Kintsch, W. (1996). Are good texts always better? Interaction of text coherence, background knowledge, and levels of understanding in learning from text. *Cognition and Instruction, 14,* 1–43.

Roller, C. M. (1990). The interaction between knowledge and structure variables in the processing of expository prose. *Reading Research Quarterly, 27,* 78–89.

Weaver III, C. A. (1990). Constraining factors in calibration of comprehension. *Journal of Experimental Psychology, 16,* 214–222.

Creating Contexts for Supporting Word-Meaning Constructions: Dialogues with Struggling Middle-School Readers

Janis M. Harmon
University of Texas at San Antonio

B y the time students reach the middle grades, they need to be well equipped with strategies for figuring out new words encountered in reading. Lipson and Wixson (1997) describe strategic word learners as those who have an "awareness of the variety of methods to acquire word meanings, ability to monitor one's understanding of new vocabulary, and the capacity to change or modify strategies for understanding new words if comprehension is not forthcoming" (p. 558).

Word-learning strategies typically include the use of context clues, attention to word parts, and reference to dictionaries (Cooper, 1997; Graves, Juel, & Graves, 1998). However, Blachowicz and Fisher (1996) closely link vocabulary learning to strategic reading in a manner similar to Lipson and Wixson's description. As learners consider word meanings, they gather data, predict possible meanings, confirm or disconfirm their predictions, make inferences, and monitor their understanding of a new word in the process of comprehending text.

Whereas competent readers automatically approach unfamiliar words in this manner, struggling readers have difficulty addressing new vocabulary encountered during independent reading. As these readers reach the intermediate and middle grades, they are faced with two dilemmas in independent word learning that reflect the complex nature of the reading process (Keene & Zimmerman, 1997). First, many still have difficulty decoding high-frequency words. Second, regardless of pronunciation, these students, like all other students, confront new words with unfamiliar meanings as they read independently. Outcomes of such encounters are strongly influenced by the reader's semantic, schematic, and pragmatic cueing systems for constructing meaning. Struggling readers may not benefit from these encounters with new words because of limited strategic ability in activating appropriate cueing systems. Their reliance on skipping unfamiliar words or asking others severely hinders the opportunities to build important word-learning strategies as they read. These students require instruction and support in how to approach unfamiliar words in a strategic manner.

One possible approach to instruction for helping struggling middle school readers develop more strategic word-learning behaviors is the use of facilitated peer dialogues. A small discussion group, composed of the teacher or some facilitator and two students, meet to talk about unfamiliar words students encounter in

National Reading Conference Yearbook, 49, pp. 331–343.

their reading. The ensuing discussion focuses on constructing functional meanings for student-selected words with an emphasis on developing awareness of strategic actions. The use of discussion to support independent word-learning strategies is drawn from what we know about the importance of discussion for promoting comprehension and about vocabulary learning from naturally occurring contexts.

Current interest in small-group discussions is grounded in a social, constructivist theoretical framework that acknowledges the important role social interaction plays in language development and comprehension (Vygotsky, 1986). In her review of the research on discussions, Gambrell (1996) found evidence across studies suggesting that small-group discussions of texts enabled learners to gain a richer understanding of the text, engage in critical, higher level thinking, and improve their communication skills. Furthermore, recent investigations indicate that we have underestimated the capability of struggling readers to participate in group discussions where they can engage in complex thinking and benefit from interaction with others (Raphael, Brock, & Wallace, 1997). Although studies of discussions have focused mainly on text interpretation, it is also important to consider how these social interactions may impact vocabulary acquisition if the focus of discussion is on word meanings. The social networking that occurs in literacy events, such as small-group discussions, should not be overlooked as a critical element in vocabulary learning (Ruddell, 1994), especially in light of studies that show promising results in how social interactions influence word learning (Drum & Madison, 1985; Stahl & Vancil, 1986).

This study is also grounded in what we know about learning words from context (Baumann & Kamenui, 1991; Beck & McKeown, 1991). Although context clues are important in figuring out word meanings in naturally occurring contexts, many contexts do not provide enough information for students to infer correct word meanings (Beck, McKeown, & McCaslin, 1983). Consequently, by situating word learning in authentic reading events, we need to acknowledge that students may construct partially correct word meanings, they may be uncertain about their understanding of the word, or they may completely misunderstand the author's use of a word (Beck et al., 1983). Students need to understand these limitations of context and be aware that word learning occurs incrementally over time with subsequent exposures to the words. They also need to know that their attempts at meaning construction are important learning tasks for enhancing their vocabulary knowledge.

In regard to supporting independent word-learning strategies, teachers may assume that older learners have the necessary strategies or they may provide direct instruction of strategies, such as the use of context clues and structural analysis. Yet, acquisition of these strategies is problematic in that teachers may not know how these strategies are interpreted and transferred to actual reading events. Small-group discussions hold potential for addressing this issue and may provide a way for teachers to understand the independent word-learning abilities of students. In addition, students can benefit from actively participating in small-group discussions and become more aware of their own strategic actions.

This study focused on the use of facilitated peer dialogues for supporting independent word-learning strategies of struggling middle school readers and for creating contexts to promote metacognitive awareness of word-learning strategies. Two questions guided this study: (a) What is the nature of facilitated peer dialogues for enhancing independent word-learning strategies of struggling middle school students? and (b) What insights can be gained by having students analyze their own talk about unfamiliar words encountered in independent reading?

Method

Participants and Setting

Six students in sixth and seventh grade at a Title I suburban middle school in a metropolitan area in the southwest participated in this study. The students, who were enrolled in developmental reading classes, were 1 to 3 years behind in reading according their performance on standardized tests and informal assessments. These learners, a diverse group of white, African-American, and Asian-American students, were selected and paired according to teacher recommendation and their willingness to participate in the study.

Data Collection and Analysis

Date collection and analysis occurred simultaneously for 3 months from February to April. I facilitated 17 small-group discussions, each lasting approximately 25 minutes. I carefully taped each session and took fieldnotes. I transcribed each session for analysis and triangulation with fieldnotes and observations as well as for later self-analysis by the student participants (Patton, 1990). There were two major sessions: (a) initial discussions about newly targeted words, and (b) later discussions based upon self-analysis of transcripts from the first sessions.

Each pair of participants selected and read the same book. They were in control of each initial discussion session. As the students read silently from their books, they stopped to talk when one or the other found a new word to explore. At that point, I asked the student to pronounce the word and identify its location. After my initial invitation to talk about the word, I used either general or guided prompts to maintain the discussion. General prompts urged the participants to elaborate or support their ideas with such comments as "What gives you that idea?" and "What do you think about that?" When students were unable to make any kind of connection, I then used guided prompts that focused mainly on text-based information.

Through multiple readings of the transcripts and fieldnotes, I focused on three major aspects of these discussions. First, I analyzed the kinds of contributions students made to keep the conversation going. Using categories suggested by Roberts and Langer (1991), I coded the data to capture such actions as predicting, explaining, defining, and clarifying word meanings. Second, I examined the word-learning strategies by systematically coding data based on patterns of strategies observed. Subcategories for strategy selections included emphasis on pronunciation, key words in immediate contexts, references to story events, writing conventions, intertextual connections, and personal ideas that moved beyond the texts. Although these two major categories served as a way to analyze the data, the boundaries between categories became indistinct at times as the students negotiated word meanings.

For the self-analysis section of the study, the students read the transcripts of previous sessions as they listened to themselves on tape. I then prompted the students to talk about their responses using such prompts as "talk about what you did here." I read through these self-analysis transcriptions multiple times searching for patterns of behavior in how the students interpreted their actions during the initial discussions.

Results and Discussion

In this section, I provide descriptions of the sessions for each pair of learners including dialogue moves, independent word-learning strategies, and the self-analyses of selected transcriptions. I also provide a description of the patterns of word-learning strategies exhibited across dialogue pairs.

Description of Dialogue Pairs

Dialogue Pair: Ashley and Tina

Ashley, an African American, and Tina, a white student, were both in sixth grade and at least 2 years behind in reading. The teacher described Ashley and Tina as quiet students with different attitudes toward learning. Ashley seldom participated in class discussions without prompting and struggled continually with comprehension. Tina had a more complacent attitude about reading and showed little interest in classroom activities.

Dialogue moves. Ashley and Tina's talk sessions were a risk-free opportunity to use comprehension strategies. On one level, Ashley and Tina predicted word meanings, explained, clarified, and elaborated meaning constructions, and responded to the story in relation to the targeted words. These strategies were apparent as they collectively negotiated ways to construct legitimate meanings for the self-selected words. Some dialogue moves consisted of agreeing with one another more as a way to keep the conversation going than to expand word meanings. Nevertheless, in those moments where the girls grappled with text ideas, they used necessary comprehension strategies to make sense of the targeted word.

Independent word-learning strategies. The initial sections of all dialogues contained attempts at pronunciation. When one student admitted she could not pronounce the word, the other would offer a pronunciation and sometimes even a meaning. With facilitator prompting, however, the conversations quickly moved on to a focus on word meanings. Tina and Ashley's conversations contained a few instances where they made important connections to formulate acceptable word meanings. Overall, they made four different connections. The most frequent one, used in every dialogue, was references to immediate story events at the sentence level. These connections were typically explanations that recounted the information found in the sentence containing the targeted word. A second connection was references to writing conventions, such as Ashley's comment about the exclamation point in regard to the word "exclaimed." A third connection was references to personal examples. These connections were clearly evident in a conversation about the word "frustrated" where Ashley and Tina talked about what they did when they were frustrated and about how not knowing the meaning of a word was frustrating. In this dialogue, the participants needed little outside support. Although the girls could not specifically articulate a definition for "frustrated," they were able to make references to their own past feelings of frustration. Ashley's lead enabled Tina to understand that this word represented a familiar concept to her. Interestingly, neither girl ever referred back to the text in an attempt to verify their ideas about the word. A fourth connection was references to the broader story line. For the word "suspiciously," Tina felt that the character "looked to me like she was up to something . . . like she was going to do something." To support this meaning, she provided a lengthy retelling of story events prior to the author's use of the word "suspiciously." She situated the meaning of "suspiciously" in a solid context to prove her word-meaning construction. This was the only instance in which these participants made references to the broader story line.

Self-analysis. Analyzing the transcripts was a demanding task for Ashley and Tina to handle independently. They knew when one or the other participant explained something, but in many instances they could not articulate exactly what was being explained. This lack of metacognitive awareness of strategic behavior is described by Garner (1992) who contends that poor readers have limited awareness of their actions and are in need of metacognitive instruction. In spite of these limitations, Ashley and Tina together noticed they read around the word, talked about the word, stated a meaning, and explained the word. These strategic ideas emerged with only general facilitator prompts. Although these strategies seem generalized, the participants still engaged in higher level thinking as they analyzed and confirmed their actions.

In other instances, the analysis of transcripts was overwhelming. As a result, my prompts became more direct and supportive. I showed Ashley and Tina how they used examples, made connections, referred to the whole story, and examined punctuation.

Dialogue Pair: Carl and Thomas

Thomas, an African-American sixth grader, and Carl, an Asian-American sixth grader, were at least 2 to 3 years behind in reading. While displaying an eagerness for school and learning, Thomas was reluctant to read any novel or participate in class discussions. Carl was a quiet student who appeared to enjoy reading even though he struggled with comprehension.

Dialogue moves. These participants relied heavily on my prompts to maintain a dialogue about the targeted words. Overall, their dialogue moves contained a high number of responses to questions and prompts I asked. Thomas never hesitated in providing some kind of definition for the words he targeted. Carl, on the other hand, was reluctant to explicitly state a meaning. He felt more comfortable in explaining a meaning after the conversation was underway. Nevertheless, once they gained some momentum, both boys contributed to the conversation by explaining, clarifying, and supporting some of their ideas about the targeted words. Other dialogue moves consisted of agreeing with one another, admitting no knowledge of the words, restating ideas, and maintaining their newly constructed meanings.

Independent word-learning strategies. Carl and Thomas had difficulty with pronunciation and lacked background knowledge about topics and language structures. Although this limited their ability to negotiate meanings of unfamiliar words independently, the role of pronunciation frequently diminished if one knew how to say the word. Sometimes Thomas even overlooked the correct pronunciation while remaining focused at the word level. For example, for the word "squinting" in this sentence: "He wrinkled his forehead, squinting at her." Thomas totally disregarded the context and correct pronunciation as evident in the following excerpt:

Facilitator: Any ideas how to say the word?
Carl: Squinting [pronounced correctly].
Facilitator: Squinting. O.K. Talk about what you think that word might mean.
Thomas: Sitting down or something.
Facilitator: What gives you that idea?
Thomas: Squan . . . squinting. It's like saying . . . probably the same meaning as squanting . . . squatting.
Facilitator: O.K., but it has to make sense now. Check it out. Words have to make sense in what you're reading. Does it make sense in the sentence?
Carl: I don't think . . . I think like where it said "he wrinkled his forehead, squinting at her," . . . like squinting is like looking at her.
Facilitator: Looking how?
Carl: Looking straight at the eyes. That's what I think.
Facilitator: What gives you that idea?
Carl: Because where it says he wrinkled his forehead squinting *at* her. *At* her means like he's looking at her.
Facilitator: How do you feel about that, Thomas? Do you agree?
Thomas: Yeah. He's probably making a weird face.

With support, Thomas moved beyond the word level to consider how the author's word needed to make sense in the story.

The boys used narrow contexts to construct reasonable word meanings. Their connections were limited mainly to the immediate story events at the sentence level. Sometimes the boys noted key words, made time references such as "brushing your hair in the morning," and considered outside connections as in Thomas's reference to the Scrabble game for the word "scrabbling."

Self-analysis. These boys had a meager understanding of word-learning strategies. They remained focused on sounding out the words and made vague references to sentences, paragraphs, and even the dictionary. Thomas was fixated on the physical aspects of the transcripts and even pointed out where I had misconstrued some of his lines.

In their first independent analysis attempt, Carl and Thomas noted three strategies they used: sound out the words, read the sentence, and check to see if the word looks like a familiar word. I explained some the strategies I saw them use, such as referring to the story line, using key words, looking before and after the word, considering the author's choice of words, and "trying out" the word when the boys demonstrated how to "squint" their eyes. After this initial explanation, the boys followed my lead and in subsequent sessions noted where they gave clues, found examples of clues, stated word meanings, sounded out words, and referred to the Scrabble game.

Dialogue Pair: Michael and Robert

Michael and Robert, both African Americans, were seventh graders who were 1 to 2 years behind in reading. They actively participated in class discussions and exhibited some interest in the reading assignments of the class.

Dialogue moves. Michael and Robert continually searched for ideas to support their word-meaning speculations and did not hesitate to explain, clarify, and elaborate their ideas. Michael, in particular, was not afraid to admit that he had no knowledge of certain words and was also confident enough to ask questions when the discussion did not make sense to him. Overall, the dialogues contained explanations that took the form of giving examples, making references to text passages, raising connected issues, and clarifying previously made points. When their efforts did not produce reasonable explanations, my prompts became more direct in guiding the discussion.

Independent word-learning strategies. Although the boys could not pronounce some of the words, pronunciation was not an issue. They attended mainly to word meanings and made a variety of connections. These connections included references to immediate story events, texts, personal examples, broader story line encompassing events beyond the sentence level, and the ways authors write texts. The boys also made comparisons, tried metaphorical connections, used generalized meanings for words, and worked together to create a meaning for "Astroturf."

Self-analysis. The following points of interest emerged across the self-analysis sessions: (a) Like the other participants, Michael and Robert had difficulty articulating their actions, (b) they were more aware of the strategies they used than the other pairs of participants, and (c) they took this opportunity to continue exploring word meanings.

First, although more vocal than the others, Michael and Robert groped for the right words to express their thoughts about what they analyzed from the transcripts. For example, Robert used the word "connection" to mean synonym in the following discussion about the word "silage":

> Michael: I think on silage I think we like read over the sentence and like read some sentences and the back to like come to a conclusion.
> Facilitator: So you did look all over. What else did you guys do?
> Robert: We like put connections into it.
> Facilitator: What kind of connections, Robert? Can you give me an example?
> Robert: We used other words instead of silage, we put other words in between it.
> Facilitator: You substituted other words. Like what word?
> Robert: Hay.

A second point of interest was their strategy awareness. Michael and Robert noticed that they read the sentence, used synonyms, connected to their prior knowledge, used comparisons and examples, referred to a discussion in another class, talked about the word, examined word parts, looked at key words, and referred to a previous discussion about another word. They never mentioned pronunciation as a strategy, though they could not pronounce some words. Usually if one did not know the word, the other did. As facilitator, I interjected comments periodically where I recapped or summarized the kinds of strategies the participants were describing. I also pointed out other strategic behaviors, such as considering multiple meanings using key words, looking at the ways authors write, examining the actions of the characters, using examples not previously mentioned, and referring to text-based information.

What was unique about these boys was their continual references to how they collaboratively constructed and negotiated word meanings. They were conscious of how they worked together. For example, as the boys analyzed their actions for the word "silage," Robert made a distinctive observation:

> Facilitator: All of these ideas you have said make sense and that's important. What else do you see that you did?
> Robert: Well, on the third page. . . . I know what we did. He put his thoughts with my thoughts so we combined them to make one whole thought.
> Facilitator: Where do you see that, Robert?
> Robert: When I say on it's something that you put on . . . and he says like a seasoning. So he put his thoughts with mine and we made a whole thought.

The boys used these sessions to continue exploring word meanings. After listening to the transcripts for the word "disgust," Robert wanted to change his mind about "disgust" meaning "sarcastic." In their analysis of the word "intricate," Michael explained how girls weave or crochet their hair into "intricate" patterns.

Patterns of Independent Word-Learning Strategies

Students negotiated meanings for their words within the social contexts of facilitated peer dialogues. My own reaction to student responses at times helped them grapple with ideas and at other times constrained their efforts. As a participant in the dialogues, it was difficult to refrain from explaining the word meanings to the students instead of allowing them the opportunity to apply strategies while nudging them in more fruitful directions. Although the findings are only generalizable to the six participants, the patterns of word-learning strategies exhibited across dialogue pairs represent those strategies that students were able to use spontaneously with little or no effort and those which required prompting and support.

Word-Learning Strategies Used Spontaneously

These three dialogue pairs voluntarily employed several independent word-learning strategies for figuring out unfamiliar words at some point during the discussions. Collectively, these strategies consisted of (a) word-level analysis that included both pronunciation and attention to orthographic similarities of words, (b) a search for word-meaning clues in the sentence containing the targeted word, (c) attention to writing conventions, such as punctuation and capitalization, and (d) the use of a dictionary. In those instances where one participant had full or partial knowledge of a targeted word, then the student with this prior knowledge spontaneously confirmed the word meaning and made connections to the sentence context and, at times, to personal experiences.

Word-level analysis. All participants made attempts at pronouncing the words they selected to discuss, and all, at one time or another, had difficulty sounding out the words. However, in many instances, the other participant could pronounce the word correctly. At other times, even the pronunciation did not help the participants with meaning construction. More interestingly, several participants relied on orthographic similarities to identify the words and word meanings. For example, as previously mentioned, Thomas thought "squinting" meant "squatting" with little regard to the context. He also thought that "trumpet" had something to do with "triumphantly." Tina presumed that "exclaimed" and "explained" had the same meaning.

Sentence-level analysis. Another predominant word-learning strategy across all dialogue pairs was the close attention students paid to the sentence containing the word. The paucity of helpful clues in many of these sentences led to unproductive attempts at word-meaning constructions in several of the dialogues. However, there were instances where the sentence did provide enough clues. For example, Carl and Thomas surmised that "peering out the window" meant "looking out the window."

Writing conventions. In some dialogues, participants made references to writing conventions, such as punctuation and capitalization. Ashley used this strategy in her reference of the exclamation point to explain the meaning for the word "exclaimed."

Dictionary. Use of a dictionary occurred only once. Thomas voluntarily looked up the word "shimmering" in the sentence "The blue sky shimmered and became blindingly bright." Both Thomas and Carl had concluded previously that it meant, "The sky was changing colors." After reading the definition "to shine waveringly or tremulously; to glimmer; flash; gleam; glint; sparkle; glitter," Thomas maintained that it meant "to glitter and change colors."

Participants sometimes used several of these unprompted strategies in their discussion of a particular word. For example, in the following excerpt, Michael and Robert, while remaining at the sentence level in their effort to figure out the meaning of the word "Holstein," also used writing conventions to substantiate their word-meaning construction:

Michael: It says "John went to the next cow, Marge, a big Holstein who was an easy milker because she dropped the milk as soon as you started pulling." I think it [Holstein] probably be like a powerful milk cow . . . like milk comes out quicker and easier.
Facilitator: Milk comes out quicker and easier?
Robert: I don't think the milk has anything to do with it. I just think it's like a brand name like a horse. What do they call them big horses?
Facilitator: Clydesdales?
Robert: Yeah. Like a Clydesdale. Because it is a type of horse. And Holstein is a type of cow.
Michael: I didn't know they had names of cows.
Robert: They have different types of everything. Like a different type of dog or cat or something.
Facilitator: That's true. Let's explore what Michael said here that maybe this cow had certain special features.
Michael: Yeah. Probably stronger than other cows.
Robert: Yeah. That's possible. I'm just saying that milk doesn't have nothing to do with it with the cow. I think that it's just a different not special just regular cow because all the Holsteins could not drop milk as fast as she does.
Facilitator: Is there any other clue in there?
Robert: The comma after Marge.
Michael: They got Holstein capitalized.

Michael and Robert were the only ones who spontaneously considered a variety of connections that included making comparisons and talking about the ways in which authors write texts.

Word-Learning Strategies Requiring Support

The participants in this study, especially Ashley, Tina, Carl, and Thomas, needed prompting and support to use other independent word-learning strategies, particularly for referring to story events beyond the immediate sentence level in order to make connections with relevant ideas. Because the students typically focused on sentence-level information, they narrowed the range of possible clues and connections available in the broader story line. On several occasions, I prompted the students to explore ideas about the setting and character actions beyond the immediate context of the targeted word. For example, the following excerpt for the word "corridor" illustrates how Tina and Ashley needed support in making connections to the setting of this event:

Ashley: It says, "Still no one home. 'Where *is* everyone?' I shouted down the empty corridor."
Facilitator: What do you think?
Ashley: I don't know.
Facilitator: Think about what you are reading and what's happening.
Ashley: She's shouting. She's shouting something out.
Facilitator: O.K. What you think, Tina?
Tina: I have no idea.
Facilitator: Think about what the character is doing and where the character is.
Ashley: She's at her house.
Tina: And everybody's gone.
Facilitator: What's happening to her?
Ashley: She's like getting frustrated because no one's home.
Facilitator: What's happening right here? Is she at home?
Ashley: Yeah.
Facilitator: Are you sure she's at home?
Tina: She's at the principal's office.
Facilitator: And what is she doing?
Tina: Calling . . .
Ashley: She's calling home.
Facilitator: She's calling home. It says here, "I dropped a quarter in the pay phone next to the principal's office and called home." So is she in the office?
Both: No.
Tina: She's by the office.
Facilitator: So where is she?
Tina: In school.
Facilitator: Where in school? Where do you see her in the school?
Ashley: In the hallway.
Facilitator: So she's shouting and it says "I shouted down the empty corridor." So corridor is just another word for . . .
Tina: Hallway.

This excerpt is representative of dialogues that occurred with each pair of participants for some of the words they selected to discuss. I also used prompts to help them examine prefixes and suffixes as well as figurative language used by the author.

Conclusion and Implications

Although teaching independent word-learning strategies to struggling learners at the middle school level is a complex, time-consuming task, it is critical in helping them become more proficient independent readers. As the Carnegie Council on Adolescent Development has pointed out, middle school offers many children their "last best chance" for a productive future (cited in Irvin, 1998). Time for independent reading, although necessary, is not sufficient to enable learners to become more proficient readers. Along with the basic tasks and activities associated with current middle school reading programs, these students need intense, explicit support from a knowledgeable teacher for developing effective independent word-learning strategies.

In line with studies that support the use of discussion with diverse learners (Raphael et al., 1997), the students in this study engaged in meaningful talk but with a focus on word meanings. The students saw first hand what it meant to use word-learning strategies. These learner-centered discussions also enabled the learners to experience some metacognitive awareness as they critically examined what they did to make sense of words. Furthermore, these sessions were motivating since the students examined their own contributions to the discussions.

The students employed some strategies easily and used others with difficulty or, in several instances, not at all. As a result, these students need explicit instruction that will explain and clarify how to engage in more fruitful endeavors beyond the word and sentence levels for constructing word meanings. However, explicit instruction alone will not guarantee that students will use the strategies nor even provide assurance that they will be aware of what they are doing as they confront unfamiliar words in their reading.

As Bomer (1998) points out, "struggling readers need both rich conversations about big ideas in texts, which let them participate as full members of a literate community, and interactions that support figuring out the details of the textual world" (p. 32). In reference to word-learning strategies, learners need opportunities to closely examine words in naturally occurring contexts as they talk about text ideas. They also need to examine their own use of independent word-learning strategies in supportive contexts where their voices can be heard. Whereas all students at this age benefit from collaborative activities, struggling readers especially need the help of a teacher in combination with peers. Struggling readers can also benefit from working with their peers in nonthreatening contexts that the learners themselves help to create. The students in this study were more actively engaged with print because of the personalized nature of the sessions.

In conclusion, this study indicates that facilitated peer dialogues have the potential for providing the support students need to enhance their word-learning abilities and to become strategic word learners as described by Lipson and Wixson (1997). These sessions can provide an opportunity for the teacher to assess independent word-learning strategies and an opportunity for on-the-spot instruction in meaningful contexts where students control the content of what is discussed. Although time constraints may be problematic, it is important to consider how small discussion groups can be used to help struggling readers broaden their strategic word-learning behaviors as they learn more about reading and about themselves as readers and independent word learners.

References

Baumann, J. F., & Kameenui, E. J. (1991). Research on vocabulary instruction: Ode to Voltaire. In J. Flood, J. M. Jensen, D. Lapp, & J. R. Squire (Eds.), *Handbook on teaching the English language arts* (pp. 602–632). New York: Macmillan.

Beck, I., & McKeown, M. G. (1991). Conditions of vocabulary acquisition. In R. Barr, M. Kamil, P. Mosenthal, & P. D. Pearson (Eds.), *Handbook of reading research* (Vol. 2, pp. 789–814). White Plains, NY: Longman.

Beck, I., McKeown, M. G., & McCaslin, E. S. (1983). Vocabulary development: All contexts are not created equal. *Elementary School Journal, 83,* 177–181.

Blachowicz, C., & Fisher, P. (1996). *Teaching vocabulary in all classrooms.* Englewood Cliffs, NJ: Prentice-Hall.

Bomer, R. (1998). Conferring with struggling readers: The test of our craft, courage, and hope. *New Advocate, 12*(1), 21–38.

Cooper, J. D. (1997). *Literacy: Helping children construct meaning* (3rd ed.). Boston: Houghton Mifflin.

Drum, P. A., & Madison, J. (1985). Vocabulary instruction: A conversational format. In J. A. Niles & R. V. Lalik (Eds.), *Issues in literacy: A research perspective.* Thirty-fourth yearbook of the National Reading Conference (pp. 59–64). Rochester, NY: National Reading Conference.

Gambrell, L. B. (1996). What research reveals about discussion. In L. B. Gambrell & J. F. Almasi (Eds.), *Lively discussions!: Fostering engaged reading* (pp. 25–38). Newark, DE: International Reading Association.

Garner, R. (1992). Metacognition and self-monitoring strategies. In S. J. Samuels & A. E. Farstrup (Eds.), *What research has to say about reading instruction* (pp. 236–252). Newark, DE: International Reading Association.

Graves, M. F., Juel, C., & Graves, B. B. (1998). *Teaching reading in the 21st century.* Boston: Allyn & Bacon.

Irvin, J. (1998). *Reading and the middle school student: Strategies to enhance literacy* (2nd ed.), Needham Heights, MA: Allyn & Bacon.

Keene, E. O., & Zimmermann, S. (1997). *Mosaic of thought: Teaching comprehension in a reader's workshop.* Portsmouth, NH: Heinemann.

Lipson, M. Y., & Wixson, K. K. (1997). *Assessment and instruction of reading and writing disability: An interactive approach* (2nd ed.). New York: Longman.

Patton, M. Q. (1990). *Qualitative evaluation and research methods* (2nd ed.). Newbury Park, CA: Sage.

Raphael, T. E., Brock, C. H., & Wallace, S. M. (1997). Encouraging quality peer talk with diverse students in mainstream classrooms: Learning from and with teachers. In J. R. Paratore & R. L. McCormick (Eds.), *Peer talk in the classroom: Learning from research* (pp. 176–206). Newark, DE: International Reading Association.

Roberts, D. R., & Langer, J. A. (1991). *Supporting the process of literary understanding: Analysis of a classroom discussion* (Report Series 2.15). Albany, NY: Center for the Learning and Teaching of Literature.

Ruddell M. R. (1994). Vocabulary knowledge and comprehension: A comprehension-process view of complex literacy relationships. In R. B. Ruddell, M. R. Ruddell, & H. Singer (Eds.), *Theoretical models and processes of reading* (4th ed., pp. 414–447). Newark, DE: International Reading Association.

Stahl, S. A., & Vancil, S. J. (1986). Discussion is what makes semantic maps work in vocabulary instruction. *Reading Teacher, 40,* 62–67.

Vygotsky, L. (1986). *Thought and language* (A. Kozulin, Trans.). Cambridge, MA: Massachusetts Institute of Technology. (Original work published 1934)

From University Classroom to Secondary Classroom: An Examination of Two Teachers' Beliefs and Practices About Literacy in the Social Studies

Elizabeth K. Wilson
University of Alabama

R esearch in teacher education has explored the intricate relationships between teachers' beliefs and practices. Clark and Peterson (1986) explained that teaching involves two major processes: (a) teachers' thought processes and (b) teachers' actions. The underlying assumption is that teachers' beliefs and thoughts about different components of the instructional process can substantially influence their classroom plans and behaviors (Armour-Thomas, 1989).

This influence can be seen throughout all phases of the teacher's development. Research indicates that a prospective teacher's beliefs about teaching are well established by the time the student begins the teacher education program (Wilson, 1990). These beliefs which include how teachers and students should behave (Clark, 1988; Nespor, 1987) are developed during what Lortie (1975) characterized as the apprenticeship of observation, which are the years that the teacher is a student. Subsequently, some suggest that the beliefs of preservice teachers change very little during the preservice program (Bennett, 1991) and that it is much more difficult to change established beliefs that they bring into the program (Wilson, 1990). Zeek and Winstrom (1999) suggest that teacher educators can provide preservice teachers with experiences that encourage reflection on and integration of current research and practice as well as connection between theory and practice and their own personal theories of teaching and learning.

Research consistently indicates that teachers teach the way they were taught. Beginning teachers characterize their experiences as a student (Zeek & Wickstrom, 1999) as well as their student teaching experience (Clark, Smith, Newby, & Cook, 1985) as the influential factors in shaping their beliefs, behaviors, and attitudes. Other researchers have concluded that such influences will supplant the information presented in the university program (Palonsky & Jacobson, 1988) particularly when there is a conflict between theory and practice (Britzman, 1991).

Research in social studies education has shown that teachers hold particular beliefs about social studies and instruction and that these beliefs can guide pedagogical decisions and practices (Leming, 1989; Onosko, 1989). Such research (Wilson & Wineberg, 1988) has focused on teachers' thought processes, suggesting that "conceptions and ways of reasoning about curriculum reflect and

National Reading Conference Yearbook, 49, pp. 344–355.

shape how we think about, study, and act on matters of social studies education" (Cornbleth, 1985, p. 2).

In regard to reading in the social studies, Gee and Rakow (1990) surveyed secondary social studies teachers' reading practices and concluded that there was a relationship between the practices that the teachers believed to be valuable, have confidence in, and employ in their classrooms. Case study research of a preservice teacher (Wilson, Konopak, & Readence, 1994) and an inservice teacher (Konopak, Wilson, & Readence, 1995) concluded that both teachers exhibited some inconsistencies between their beliefs and practices about social studies and literacy. In other words, the practice of these two teachers seemed to be mitigated by external factors/constraints (e.g., the cooperating teacher, state mandates).

Theoretical Framework

According to Fang (1996), "the most significant contributions to our understanding of the relationship between teachers' beliefs and practices have, in recent years, taken place in the field of reading/literacy" (p. 52). Research in reading education (e.g., Hinchman, 1987; Moje, 1993; Rupley & Logan, 1984; Stern & Shavelson, 1983) has suggested that teachers' beliefs and practices are filtered through their understanding of the reading process. However, the extent to which teachers' beliefs influence decision-making and practice has been challenged. Investigators (Duffy & Ball, 1986; Lampert, 1985; Wilson et al., 1994) have suggested that external factors such as sociocultural and environmental realities of the classroom can override the teacher's own beliefs. According to Fang (1996), such studies are indicative of the "recurring themes of 'consistency' vs. inconsistency between teacher beliefs and practices in this limited body of research" (pp. 47–48).

In recent years, as research of teachers' beliefs and practices has been expanded, one area is still relatively unexplored in the literature—an ongoing examination of the transition from preservice teacher to classroom teacher. This study will examine the beliefs and practices of two teachers as they moved from preservice teacher into the secondary social studies classroom. This research examines the beliefs and practices and other factors that influence two social studies teachers in the preservice and inservice phases of their development.

Method

The research process for this study was guided by the following research questions: (a) What are the teachers' perceptions of literacy in the social studies classroom during each phase of the study? (b) How have these teachers' changed their instructional planning and decision-making in regard to literacy activities in the social studies classroom during each phase of the study? (c) What factors have influenced these changes? and (d) What are the consistencies and inconsistencies between each teacher's beliefs and practices?

Participants and Setting

The participants for this study were Ann and Betty, two Caucasian females who held their bachelor's and master's degrees in secondary social studies education from a southeastern university. Both teachers had been students in the researcher's undergraduate content literacy and social studies methods courses as well as the graduate-level social studies methods course. Both women received their master's degrees in social science education at the same institution. Ann completed her degree program after beginning her teaching position. Betty worked as a graduate assistant for 2 years as she completed the degree.

The participants were selected for this study because they had taken the researcher's social studies and content literacy courses, received A's in the researcher's courses and the student teaching experience, were easily accessible to the researcher, and were willing to participate.

Ann. At the conclusion of this study (Spring 1999), Ann was completing her sixth year of teaching. For 6 years she had been teaching at a middle school in a suburb of the city in which the university she attended is located. During her first year of teaching, she taught world history to seventh graders; after that, she taught eighth grade U.S. history.

During her preservice program, Ann participated in her methods block and tutoring experiences at a middle school (Fall 1991). For the student teaching experience (Spring 1992), Ann taught world history at a middle school with a Clinical Master Teacher, a member of a team of teachers who supervised the student teachers.

Betty. At the time the study concluded, Betty had completed her fourth year of teaching social studies. The 1998–99 academic year was the third year she taught geography to ninth graders at a large high school. She previously taught several grade levels of social studies at a private school for 1 year.

In her preservice program, for her methods block field experience, Betty and her partner taught at an interdisciplinary school, where innovative practices were encouraged. For the student teaching experience (Spring 1993), like Ann, Betty was placed with a Clinical Master Teacher. Betty taught U.S. history, economics, and government to 11th and 12th graders at an inner city school. For Betty, this experience was a contrast with the innovative experience she had during the methods block.

Descriptions of the Social Studies Methods and Literacy Courses

The social studies methods and content literacy courses taught by the researcher were based on the constructivist approach. Many opportunities were provided for student interaction, class discussion, and hands-on activities. The content literacy course was taken concurrently with the undergraduate social studies methods course the semester prior to the student teaching experience. During the undergraduate "methods" semester, the preservice teachers had two clinical experiences designed to allow for connections between theory and practice to be made and examined. For one experience (social studies methods), each preservice teacher was paired with another methods student and was assigned a social studies unit to teach by the assisting teacher. For the second experience (content reading course), the preservice teacher assisted a social studies teacher with an after-school tutoring program that was associated with a federally funded reading program. Both experiences took place over the course of the semester. Students responded to prompts regarding their experiences in their journals. For both social studies methods courses, the instructor used the literacy strategies (e.g., anticipation reaction guides, journal writing) being presented in the literacy course as part of her instructional practices.

Procedures

Data collection for this study took place over several years, beginning when the researcher had each participant in her undergraduate courses (Ann, 1991 and Betty, 1992). Materials were collected from each participant during her coursework and her inservice teaching through the final phase of the study that was conducted during the 1998–99 academic year. Throughout the study, the researcher visited the participants' classrooms making observations, conducting interviews, and writing fieldnotes.

Researcher positionality. The researcher understands that her constructivist beliefs about content literacy and social studies inevitably affected her own social studies and content literacy instruction. Also, the researcher recognizes her role as instructor to the teachers in this study. The researcher attempted to address this by not asking questions specifically about methods instruction. Rather, open-ended questions were asked that did not necessarily require the participants to discuss the researcher's instruction unless they chose to do so. To address the possible bias created by this relationship, the researcher used multiple data sources and included the assistance of others in the triangulation of the data.

Data Sources and Data Analysis

To study the teachers' actual planning, decision-making, and implementation, multiple data sources were employed. Included were: (a) lesson plans and other materials (e.g., journal entries, unit plans) from each participant's university coursework, (b) evaluations from preservice teaching experiences, (c) lesson plans from inservice teaching assignments, (d) teacher and student materials from preservice teacher experiences as well as inservice teaching experiences, (e), participant interviews, (f) fieldnotes that were collected throughout all phases of the study, and (g) audiotapes and transcriptions.

These data were used to answer the research questions and to identify possible contextual variables related to both teachers. Each participant engaged in member checks of the data collected. Then, the multiple data sources were analyzed by a research team using constant comparative analysis (Glaser & Strauss,

1967; Miles & Huberman 1984). The data were examined for consistency among beliefs, lesson choices, units/daily planning, class materials, coursework materials, class interactions, and interview responses. To produce an accurate representation of the findings and to control for researcher bias, data were triangulated across the research team and all data sources. The research team included a literacy educator and a doctoral student, also a classroom teacher, in teacher education.

Results

Guided by research questions that examined the participants' perceptions of literacy in the social studies classroom, their classroom practices, the consistency/inconsistency between the participants' beliefs and practices, and the factors that influenced them, the analysis of the data indicates that themes have emerged from this process. The following section will present the results according to the two main phases of teacher development examined in this study.

Preservice Phase

As part of their social studies methods and content-area reading coursework, both teachers described reading as important to success in the social studies classroom. Preservice course assignments and teaching experiences included requirements for incorporating a variety of literacy strategies into their instructional planning and classroom teaching experiences. Based on information obtained from class assignments and journal entries, both teachers appeared to be interactive in their views about reading. Their definitions of literacy learning focused on meaning being made by the reader's personal knowledge and the knowledge gleaned from the text. Subsequently, both preservice teachers employed a variety of strategies in their social studies methods course and content reading course assignments and teaching experiences.

Betty used a wide variety of strategies. Her social studies lesson plans included graphic organizers and anticipation reaction guides. During her literacy tutoring experience, she targeted note-taking and organizational strategies and felt successful with them. In her journal she wrote about this experience: "When some of the students told me that they were learning more in their classes because of what I taught them, I knew that this was a worthwhile experience! I am so glad I did it!"

Although Ann employed less variety than Betty, she used multiple forms of text to convey her instruction. For her social studies lessons, she incorporated outside materials (e.g., magazine articles) and developed a reading guide to accompany each article. It is important to note that Ann experienced a shift in her thinking about teaching and learning during this phase of her development. She explained:

> Before methods, I guess the only ideas that I had, the ideas that I had gotten
> from being in the class as the student, the teacher should get up there, give the

information and you were just supposed to take it in. And then from methods I learned that it shouldn't just be giving out information, and the students memorizing that information for a test. I learned that there needs to be so much more, that the information needs to be given in lots of different ways, so that the students can understand it, and that the students need to be more involved in getting the information, not just in one way. . . .

Betty had the same experiences as a student, but she seemed to have thought about this before. Initially, she stated in her journal, that she hoped she would "not teach the way she had been taught."

Although they were required to incorporate literacy activities and strategies into their social studies methods and content literacy coursework and field experiences, neither teacher practiced this as much during the student teaching experiences. This appeared to be a result of the influence of the cooperating teachers. Ann perceived her cooperating teacher as an exemplary role model. Subsequently, she modeled her cooperating teacher and did not use the variety of strategies explored in the university courses. Instead, she followed her cooperating teacher's structured format: relate information to prior knowledge, note-taking, activity (e.g., map activity, reinforcement). Silent reading was assigned during class; occasionally, Ann and her students read the material aloud.

On the other hand, Betty tried to employ a variety of strategies (e.g., semantic mapping, study guides) during her student teaching experience. Frequently, she used anticipation guides and other strategies, but her cooperating teacher characterized them as "cute." As the semester progressed, she focused more on executing classroom discussions (teacher-directed questions followed by student responses) as emphasized in her cooperating teacher's evaluations, rather than emphasizing literacy strategies as she had done previously. Emulating her cooperating teacher, Betty's literacy activity each day was provided in the form of assigning pages to be read that day. Interestingly, after she began to like her cooperating teacher, her cooperating teachers' evaluations characterized her as "too teacher-centered" in her instruction. It is interesting to note, an examination of the cooperating teacher's evaluations showed that, with the exception of comments about Betty's use of "cute" activities, neither teacher wrote suggestions about how to use literacy activities or address reading in their classrooms.

Both Ann and Betty felt driven to act in accordance with the cooperating teachers' philosophies and actions. According to both teachers, they would "teach differently next year." Betty was looking forward to employing her own teaching philosophies which she felt were different from those of her cooperating teacher. Ann looked forward to teaching in her own classroom, but she also discussed emulating many of her cooperating teacher's practices, particularly in the area of classroom management.

Inservice Phase

Both teachers had difficulties, in particular, during their first year of teaching in that they were disappointed in their initial teaching experiences and achievements. Ann explained: "Well, I tried to do things that were interesting to get them involved and often times that would work; they would get involved in those particular activities, but then on the work, keeping up, like when they had to do vocabulary . . . it was hard to motivate them." Betty, commented: "Basically, after the first couple of months, you know I just think they were bored to death, you know." Betty explained how she addressed it:

> I just tried anything, going from giving them some time to get information on their own, talking about it with other people . . . and maybe putting me less in focus or up here, and putting them more in the learning process. . . . Because I thought well maybe if they interact with each other, do some different things, and talk to each other about it, maybe then you know it's just a different way for them to learn and maybe they'll be a little bit more interested in the material.

Throughout their inservice experiences, both teachers expressed frustration that students did not read text materials used in the social studies classroom. Both teachers expressed disappointment that students, overall, were not "excited about learning social studies." Betty discussed the negative attitudes some students possess about social studies: "Some of them were like, 'Oh social studies—all we do is read the book and answer questions.'" Although both teachers felt this way, they seemed to react differently.

In Ann's practice, she seemed to avoid the use of text materials on a regular basis. When Ann did employ text materials during the lessons, she referred to the book and directed students to examine it with her. Ann seemed to struggle with this and other related instructional issues. In an interview, she explained:

> Everyday they turn to a certain page in their textbook, but we don't read the textbook. I guess I started off *not* reading the textbook very much because the seventh grade text was very difficult reading; so, I just didn't have the students do a lot of reading. I tried to give them the information in a way that they could understand, because the textbook didn't present it very well. . . . I don't consider myself to be a textbook teacher, I never wanted to be a textbook teacher. But, we do follow the textbook. You know, I follow it [the textbook] because it follows the course of study so well.

However, Ann felt strongly that the incorporation of writing activities related to a variety of text materials, such as plays, primary documents, and diary entries would strengthen the social studies content information. She explained that this was one way she could motivate and stimulate student learning. In an interview, Ann explained how she used simulated diary entries in her classes:

> It is a simple assignment and they learn so much. . . . They understand that there is no right or wrong answer and so even the students who don't have as much ability can still get involved in the lesson. . . . If they listen to what we talked about in class they can do the assignment well. I love to use diaries and newspapers. . . . I can do a lecture type lesson. . . . I want them to listen while I am talking so they don't have to take notes. Their information will come from the diaries and maybe the questions we did. You can give the information in a way that is interesting to them and getting them involved and asking questions instead of just standing there and giving them the information in lecture.

Despite some positive experiences, in an interview, she explained that the students would not read the book, so she did not "expect it anymore." In dealing with literacy issues, she commented, "I feel like that's something I need to work on."

Similarly, Betty declared that "students don't read." As a result, she gave students questions to answer during reading. She explained this in an interview:

> They would never read through the information. They would look at the questions and then just go back and pick out the answer. They wouldn't read completely or thoroughly. And so, on most things, unless I do something very detailed, where they have to go . . . paragraph by paragraph . . . they're just going to look for the information, which I'm sure we all do it at some point. So, I try and give them something that's very detailed in order to get them to read that information a little more thoroughly, because otherwise to me it doesn't seem like they will take the time to do it.

Although her lessons followed a consistent pattern (e.g., questions, reading assignment, discussion, reinforcement), Betty incorporated a variety of strategies into her practice. In an interview about a geography lesson the researcher observed, Betty explained that, "We really do a lot in terms of getting together . . . and of course doing magazines, graphic organizers, and games" to stimulate students to read and learn. During another interview, she described her reasoning for using certain strategies, in this case the outlines, cloze procedure, and anticipation reaction guides:

> A lot of times we'll do an outline where they have to go through, read and fill in their outlines. Once again, that's just to get them to read because if you asked them just to read the section so we can talk about it, they're not going to do it. So we do that. Sometimes they do it where they can fill in the blank as they read it, or sometimes it's like a regular outline where I give them the topic, and they give the subtopic, and they have to put characteristics, or facts, or information about it. Usually, I use that and I use those questions, and anticipation/reaction guides, are usually my biggest ones that I use.

Factors Influencing Ann's and Betty's Beliefs and Practices

During the inservice phase, both teachers mentioned the influence of state testing and pressures placed on them by the school and community. Betty discussed the dilemma she goes through: "Am I supposed to really focus on something?"; "Am I supposed to teach this for them graduating in the graduation exam?"; "Am I supposed to teach this so they'll know it for World History?" Although important to Ann, the graduation exam was not as daunting since she taught middle school and seemed a little more removed from the pressures on the high school teachers.

For Ann throughout the study, an influence was the methods semester that caused her to reexamine teaching and learning. During her sixth year of teaching, she explained this because she saw that students are "not just getting the information straight from the teacher. . . . I just learned really that you should use different teaching strategies, and I hadn't really seen different teaching strategies before methods." During her methods instruction, she explained that "just thinking about what I had learned in high school, and the way that my professors had taught history in college . . . which was lecturing, I realized from that, what needed to be different."

Betty was also influenced by the level and abilities of her students. Unlike Ann who had only taught middle school students, Betty confronted difficulties when dealing with different grade levels. She found differences in teaching the seniors during student teaching and the middle school students and ninth graders during the inservice phase. Regarding the seniors, she explained that "they were more serious, more focused and it was like they were more interested in the information material part." At the conclusion of the study, she described how she had to modify her instruction for the younger students: "Before it was like no I'm going to teach you this, here's the information and here's what we are doing. And now I kind of think that I am interacting with them more."

Despite the other factors, Ann and Betty were most concerned with the students and motivation as they tried to employ and implement varied strategies and learning activities into their social studies classrooms. According to both teachers, it is student attitudes or capabilities, that influence what they feel they can and cannot do in the classroom. Betty explained this during her second year of teaching:

> They won't ever read what I've got, and on most occasions, they're not going to read it outside of class. So in order to get them to read about it before we talk about it so they have an idea about what we're going to talk about, I usually give them study questions to do so they can read it, get through it, get some of that big information, answer those questions, and tomorrow we'll talk about, we'll talk about that information, and we'll go back over those questions.

Discussion

The purpose of this study was to extend previous findings regarding teachers' beliefs and practices about literacy in social studies classrooms. Based on the analysis, themes emerged from the data. To begin with, struggle was an overlying theme for both teachers. During the preservice phases there was struggle for both teachers in varying degrees. For Betty, during student teaching, she differed from her cooperating teacher in her classroom practices. She struggled to complete the semester. Although, Ann had some differences with her cooperating teacher, she seemed to adapt her instruction to the routine of the cooperating teacher (Wilson et al., 1994).

According to both teachers, their greatest struggles took place with their students. Both teachers recognized the students' lack of motivation and interest in reading and learning about social studies. This influenced their instructional decisions (Ann—writing activities, varied text materials, Betty—reading guides and varied strategies). This struggle seemed to make them connect with their interactive beliefs about literacy. Subsequently they attempted to use a more diverse repertoire of strategies in their efforts to teach the content. Although the teachers stated their greatest struggles were with their students, perhaps, their real struggles were with themselves. That is, each teacher struggled with the ways in which she dealt with the conflicts and constraints present in her own social studies classroom.

Another theme that emerged is the notion of avoidance. Although Betty consistently voiced her ideas about using a variety of literacy strategies, she acknowledged her failure to do this during her first year of teaching. As a new teacher who was addressing her new content and her new students, she avoided implementing instruction consistent with her beliefs. Once she recognized this, she began to incorporate different strategies into her teaching. For Ann, her reflections during the course of this study made her question how she was avoiding addressing literacy in her classroom. Subsequently, she questioned how she viewed herself as a teacher (e.g., Was she a textbook teacher?).

The results of this study indicate support of previous research (Duffy & Ball, 1986) that suggested that teachers are not always consistent in the beliefs they claim to espouse and the instructional practices they demonstrate. In addition, the teachers in this study appeared to be constrained by other influences such as cooperating teachers or students (Duffy & Ball, 1986; Lampert, 1985; Wilson et al., 1994). For example, during her preservice phase, Betty had established notions about teaching and learning that she modified when her cooperating teacher did not value her teaching methods. As inservice teachers, both teachers felt constrained by the apparent refusal or lack of motivation by their students for reading and learning. To handle this, in her first year of teaching, Betty seemed to model the instruction of her cooperating teacher until she recognized that this instruction was not addressing her students' needs. At times, throughout the study, Ann became tied to the text and more text-centered instruction. During an interview, she explained her displeasure with this. Perhaps, each teacher dealt with the conflict by reverting to instruction with which they were familiar (Britzman, 1991). However, both teachers felt the need to alter their instruction to provide a diversity of strategies that were more consistent with their beliefs about teaching and learning.

In sum, both teachers displayed some inconsistencies between their beliefs and instructional intentions and their actual teaching practices at varying degrees. These inconsistencies appeared to be related to the environmental realities of the classroom or school that related to the students, testing, and the text materials.

The results of this study have implications that confront issues outside the four walls of the secondary classroom. First, there are important issues to consider for teacher education programs. Such issues include: (a) How can literacy teacher educators make an impact on content area preservice teachers? (b) How can teacher educators address the future contextual factors that confront beginning teachers during their preservice programs?, and (c) What obligations do teacher educators have to novice teachers once they graduate? Second, how can administrators help new teachers with their development? Particularly, how can they help beginning teachers negotiate the constraints that confront new teachers?

It is hoped that this study will assist inservice and preservice teachers by making them aware that their practice may not always match their beliefs when they get caught in the day-to-day activities and demands in the classroom. Teacher educators should provide opportunities for preservice and inservice teachers to explore ways of providing instruction consistent with their beliefs when there are constraints and conflicts present. Furthermore, teacher educators should assist teachers with reflecting upon and making connections between current theory, practice, and their own theories about teaching and learning (Zeek & Winstrom, 1999). Also, this research should help cooperating teachers understand that student teachers might have different beliefs and practices from their own. Student teachers and inservice teachers should be allowed to make their own pedagogical choices and should be mentored in this process by teacher educators, supervisors, and school administrators.

Educational issues such as teacher testing and higher education assessments will continue to influence the future of the teaching profession at all levels. I hope future research will assist teacher educators, cooperating teachers, school administrators, and classroom teachers through the preservice and inservice phases of development.

References

Armour-Thomas, E. (1989). The application of teacher cognition in the classroom: A new teaching competency. *Journal of Research in Development in Education, 22,* 29–37.

Bennett, C. (1991). The teacher as decision maker program. *Journal of Teacher Education, 42,* 119–130.

Britzman, D. (1991). *Practice makes practice: A critical study of learning to teach.* Albany: State University of New York.

Clark, C. (1988). Asking the right questions about teacher preparation: Contributions of research on teacher thinking. *Educational Researcher, 17*(2), 5–12.

Clark, C., & Peterson, P. (1986). Teachers' thought processes. In M. C. Wittrock (Ed.), *Handbook or research on teaching* (pp. 255–296). New York: Macmillan.

Clark, D., Smith, R., Newby, T., & Cook, V. (1985). Origins of teaching behaviors. *Journal of Teacher Education, 36*(6), 49–54.

Cornbleth, C. (1985). Reconsidering social studies curriculum. *Theory and Research in Social Education, 13,* 31–45.

Duffy, G., & Ball, D. (1986). Instructional decision-making and teacher effectiveness. In J. Hoffman (Ed.), *Effective teaching of reading: Research and practice* (pp. 163–180). Newark, DE: International Reading Association.

Fang, Z. (1996). A review of research on teacher beliefs and practices. *Educational Research, 38*(1), 47–65.

Gee, T., & Rakow, S. (1990) Helping students learn by reading: What experienced social studies teachers have learned. *Social Education, 54*(6), 398–401.

Glaser, B, & Strauss, A. (1967). *The discovery of grounded theory: Strategies for grounded research.* New York: Aldine.

Hinchman, K. (1987). The textbook and three content-area teachers. *Reading Research and Instruction, 26,* 247–256.

Konopak, B. C., Wilson, E. K., & Readence, J. R. (1995). Examining teachers' beliefs, decisions, and practices about content area reading in secondary social studies. In C. Kinzer & D. Leu (Eds.), *Multidimensional aspects of literacy research, theory, and practice*. Forty-third yearbook of the National Reading Conference (pp. 127–136). Chicago: National Reading Conference.

Lampert, M. (1985). How do teachers manage to teach? Perspectives on problems in practice. *Harvard Educational Review, 55*, 178–194.

Leming, J. (1989). The two cultures of social studies education. *Social Education, 53*, 404–408.

Lortie, D. (1975). *School teacher: A sociological study*. Chicago: University of Chicago Press.

Miles, M., & Huberman, A. (1984). *Qualitative data analysis*. Beverly Hills, CA: Sage.

Moje, E. (1993, December). *Life experiences and teacher knowledge: How a content teacher decides to use literacy strategies*. Paper presented at the meeting of the National Reading Conference, Charleston, SC.

Nespor, J. (1987). The role of beliefs in the practice of teaching. *Journal of Curriculum Studies, 19*(4), 34–54.

Onosko, J. (1989). Comparing teachers' thinking about promoting students' thinking. *Theory and Research in Social Education, 17*, 174–195.

Palonsky, S. B., & Jacobson, M. G. (1988, April). *Student teacher perceptions of elementary social studies: The social construction of curriculum*. Paper presented at the meeting of the American Educational Research Association, New Orleans, LA.

Rupley, W. H., & Logan, J. W. (1984). *Elementary teachers' beliefs about reading and knowledge content*. (ERIC Document Reproduction Service No. ED 258–162)

Stern, P., & Shavelson, R. (1983). Reading teachers' judgements, plans, and decision-making. *Reading Teacher, 37*, 280–286.

Wilson, E. K. Konopak, B. C., & Readence, J. R. (1994). A case study of a preservice secondary social studies teacher's beliefs and practices about content area reading. In C. Kinzer & D. Leu (Eds.), *Examining central issues in literacy research, theory, and practice*. Forty-second yearbook of the National Reading Conference (pp. 335–344). Chicago: National Reading Conference.

Wilson, S. (1990). The secret garden of teacher education. *Phi Delta Kappan, 72*, 204–209.

Wilson, S., & Wineburg, S. (1988). Peering at history from different lenses: The role of disciplinary perspectives in the teaching of American History. *Teachers College Record, 89*, 525–539.

Zeek, C., & Winstrom, C. (1999). The making of a teacher: The influence of literacy development on preservice teachers' current teaching practices. *Yearbook of the National Reading Conference, 48* (pp. 479–490). Chicago: National Reading Conference.

Reader Response and Social Action

Arlette Ingram Willis

University of Illinois at Urbana-Champaign

Julia L. Johnson

University of Illinois at Urbana-Champaign

Multicultural literature has come under attack by neoconservative forces within literacy education as a poor source of literature for our nation's children (Stotsky, 1999). In addition, the use of reader response techniques to teach multicultural literature also has come under attack as a questionable school literacy practice (Marshall, Hynds, & Appleman, 1999).

Previous research, using reader response theory with multicultural literature in culturally and linguistically diverse high school English classrooms, has focused on personal responses and student dialogue (Athanses, 1998; Beach, 1994; Henly, 1993; Matthews & Chandler, 1998; Spears-Bunton, 1992). Specifically, this body of research has sought to determine how to improve understanding of multicultural literature; how to improve understandings of self; and how to raise cultural consciousness and change attitudes and behaviors toward racial/ethnic groups. Such approaches leave larger issues of class, culture, gender, history, ideology, race, and society fundamentally unchallenged and unchanged.

This study is part of a larger study that focuses on reader response and multicultural literature as used in culturally diverse high schools. Conceptually, our research project was framed to promote social action—an education that prepares youth to participate in a true democracy. We believe in an education that points to what society should be and currently is not. Moreover, and most importantly, we believe in an education that empowers students to enact, correct, and achieve a more just society (Ayers, Hunt, & Quinn, 1998).

We have critically framed our study of reader response by supplying socio-historical and socio-cultural information not found in the text, but important to understanding the text. In addition, this study allows for the extension of reader response beyond individual written responses and shared dialogue to include performance (i.e., artistic, dramatic, oral interpretative responses). A concerted effort is made to encourage students toward social action. In the phase of the study reported here, we sought to understand how additional socio-historical

National Reading Conference Yearbook, 49, pp. 356–366.

and socio-cultural information encouraged students to engage in social action to promote a more just society.

Review of Related Literature

There is a plethora of research conducted on the use of reader response and a growing body of research on the use of reader response with multicultural literature. The focus of our research project specifically involves using reader response with multicultural literature in diverse high schools. The importance of this smaller subset of research cannot be overlooked for it most specifically addresses the unique circumstances of multicultural literature in secondary settings where canonical literature continues to reign supreme (Applebee, 1992). Research by Appleman and Hynds (1997), Athanses (1998), Beach (1994, 1997), Beach and Hynds (1991), and Spears-Bunton (1992), among others, points to the tension that often exists when multicultural literature is introduced into the curriculum. These research studies identified reader response as a means to understanding the connections students were making to multicultural literature.

As one might expect, using multiple classrooms, texts, and reader response frameworks resulted in a range of findings, possibilities, and tensions. For example, Athanses's (1998) research suggests that secondary students can benefit from reading texts written by diverse authors, and that such readings may in fact help to dispel stereotypes and myths. He concludes that his study "substantiates the promise of teaching multicultural literature and marks the need for redirection in conversations on content integration to the essential nature of instruction" (p. 293).

Willis (1997) also has argued that the teaching and learning of multicultural literature and the use of reader response do little to address the effects of a dominant ideology on the reader, text, author, and context. Moreover, she has argued that teachers need to use reader response approaches that include a critique of the influence of historical, social, political cultural, racial/ethnic, economic, and gendered contexts and how they are revealed and represented by authors, within the literature, and within the classroom contexts (Willis, 2000).

Method

In a semester-long study, an ethnographic approach was used to examine the responses to multicultural literature (e.g., African-American literature) in an untracked and elective high school English class. Data consisted of transcriptions of audiotaped pre-and post-intervention interviews, student written work and artifacts, videotapes of shared dialogue sessions and guest speakers, teacher lesson plans, supporting socio-historical information supplied to the students, and researchers' fieldnotes and reflective journals. In this phase of the study, the content of students' written responses were analyzed by coding for emergent patterns (Glaser & Strauss, 1967). The results and conclusions are descriptive.

Participants

Participants included 24 high school students (15 males, 9 females) in an ability-tracked high school who enrolled in an elective Minority Literature class for seniors (13) and juniors (11). Demographically, the class consisted of 10 European Americans (6 males, 4 females); 12 African Americans (7 males, 5 females); 1 Asian American (male); and 2 African-American and European-American biracial students (1 male, 1 female). The students' academic ability levels ranged from advanced placement college-bound seniors to learning disabled juniors receiving resource teacher support.

Classroom Setting

The study began on January 25, 1999, and ended on May 11, 1999 (with 1 week off for spring break), for a total of 15 weeks. The class met daily for 50 minutes. The classroom was located in a remote section of the building. It also was the classroom and office space of another teacher who moved in and out of the classroom throughout our study.

The classroom English teacher, Mrs. Jude, is a European-American female, who has taught the Minority Literature class at Crescent High School for 10 years. The researchers, two African-American women, are certified teachers, one with over 25 years of experience, and one with 1 year of classroom experience. In addition, due to the classroom teacher's flexible schedule, we held formal and informal meetings, debriefing and planning sessions, and general conversations about issues in the school, community, and the lives of the students.

We established two pedagogical goals: (a) to encourage students to move beyond personal responses to multicultural literature by supplying socio-historical and socio-cultural information not found in texts, and (b) to encourage students toward social action. The entire project was completed in several distinct stages: selection of materials, pilot study, observations, pre-intervention interviews, baseline data collection, intervention, post-intervention interviews, and questionnaire.

First, we collected multicultural titles throughout the spring of 1998, read extensively through the summer of 1998, met with the classroom teacher during the fall, and co-planned the first few weeks of the semester in January 1999.

Next, we began the semester by observing students, writing field notes and reflective journal entries, co-teaching and planning lessons along with the classroom teacher. Thus, from the onset the students had three in-class teachers. Daily we chatted informally following each class and met once a week to review the week's activities, the direction of the project, and to plan for the following week. Then, we conducted a one-on-one interview with each student. The pre-intervention interviews were designed to gain some insight into each student's ideological, historical, social, ethnic/racial, economic, religious, and gendered frames of reference. We also asked students about their reading interests and habits, their favorite and least favorite English teachers, and ways in which they have been asked in past English classes to respond to literature.

The pre-intervention interviews were especially helpful as they allowed us to talk to students outside of the classroom on a one-to-one basis. The interview schedule consisted of questions that allowed us a quick glimpse into the world of each student and it helped us to understand the students' worldviews, reading interests and habits, and past English classroom experiences. For example, the interview data revealed that many students felt their "perfect day" meant getting up late and hanging-out with friends. Students described their "perfect world" as one free of racial and class prejudice, war, hunger, poverty, drugs, and one having great (warm) weather and peace (the interviews were conducted in the coldest and snowiest months). In terms of students' experiences responding to text, students revealed that they were most often asked to discuss a text in class, take quizzes and tests, complete reports, or work on group projects. Few of the students responded by mentioning they had been asked to write about their feelings and thoughts about the reading. Of the few who did supply this answer, most were seniors who had taken Advanced Placement (AP) classes.

The instructional approach to the teaching of this class is drawn from critical literacy theory and pedagogy (Freire, 1970; Shor, 1999) that calls for classrooms in which dialogue is important and students are active participants. We valued the student input as it often allowed us to understand what students were interested in learning more about that they thought would aid their understanding of the text.

Additionally, we extended Bleich's (1978) response heuristic by adding to the information students had available to them before they wrote their response to the literature. Following Bleich's heuristic, students were encouraged to share their initial responses to the novel, *A Lesson Before Dying*. As students shared and negotiated meaning, generative themes were drawn from these conversations and problematized for further discussion. For example, we surmised that students were uncertain about the role of race in murders involving white victims and African-American defendants. Thus, we supplied additional historical information to coincide with the text. This information was drawn from a variety of sources including reference materials, videos, hypermedia, and guest speakers. (It was our hope that students would be able to locate this information themselves, but they were not, due to circumstances beyond our control.) We also used their ideas to help write the prompts used for reader response. In this stage of the research project, we videotaped large and small group sessions during the first 2 and last 2 weeks of the intervention.

During the intervention stage there were several opportunities for students to respond to text in written, oral, dramatic, and artistic ways to the idea of social justice. Since we were using the novel *A Lesson Before Dying,* we expanded the socio-historical and socio-cultural information needed to understand the novel. The information we supplied also helped students to make connections between the legal system in the state of Louisiana in the 1940s and the legal system in the State of Illinois in 1999. We encouraged students to link the injustices of the court system of the Jim Crow south of the 1940s with our contemporary and equally unjust systematic problems of our court system. With the students' help, we identified numerous themes in the novel: freedom, justice, death, family, racism, poverty, human worth, religion, and empathy. The themes were relevant to the lives of our students and at the core of our desire to extend this novel to social action. During the post-intervention stage, we distributed a questionnaire and conducted individual interviews.

In the examples to follow, we used the responses of three students (A, B, C), respectively, as *representative* of the students in the course. The sample written responses below are from students who were in the AP track, held senior status, and were on track to graduate. Demographically, the students were a European-American female who was graduating at the end of her junior year in high school (Student A), an African-American male who was very popular in school (Student B), and a European-American male who was a very strong writer (Student C).

Independently, each researcher read through each student's responses to social justice prompts as well as their final essays to discern themes or categories. Interrater reliability was high (95%), and when raters disagreed, discussions resulted in complete agreement. We divided the students' responses into three broad categories: those against the use of the death penalty, those uncertain of their position, and those in support of the use of the death penalty.

Results

Two weeks into reading and discussing the novel *A Lesson Before Dying*, we surmised that the students knew little about racial relations in the South and how they were manifested in jury trials that involved white victims and African-American defendants. We viewed a video of the famous Scottsboro Boys murder trail. Few students had heard of the trial before viewing the video. The first social justice prompt followed a discussion of the novel and the viewing of the video *Scottsboro Boys Trial*. Students were asked to respond to a prompt written to elicit their thoughts about whether innocent people are currently sentenced to die for crimes they did not commit.

First Written Responses

Student A (Against the death penalty)

I think that it is very possible for someone now to be sentenced to die for crimes they did not commit. An example is the man who was proved innocent in Illinois, and just recently released after spending many years in jail for murder. I'm not sure if the fact that he was black was a factor in the trial, but he was convicted of a crime that he was ultimately proved innocent of. It is obvious that he could have been proved not guilty in appeals court than he could have been proved not guilty in his first trial. Some reason existed for this and if it was present in his trial, it has probably been present in the trials of others.

Student B (Uncertain)

Yes, there are people who have been sentenced to die for crimes they did not commit. A prime example is the Native American activist, Leonard Peltier.

Peltier was falsely accused of murdering two F. B. I. Agents. The Supreme Court even admitted to this false accusation, but declined to drop his sentence.

Student C (Supportive of the death penalty)

In a sense, the people of Kosovo have been sentenced to die. Atrocities are being committed against these innocent people by the Serbians. Though it is not a court case, you could say that these people are sentenced to die.

In each case, the students were willing to admit to injustices, but were not willing to address the cases highlighted in either the novel or the video of the *Scottsboro Boys* as acts of injustice.

Second Written Responses

A week later, another opportunity to respond to issues of social justice arose to questions following further reading in the novel and the viewing of the film, *Dead Man Walking*. In this prompt, students were asked about the "fairness" of the death penalty.

Student A (Against the death penalty)

In some cases perhaps the death penalty is fair and just, but that certainly cannot be an accurate generalization made for every case. Because some people are sentenced to death have later been proved innocent. Capital punishment is too risky and irreversible to completely be "fair and just." Most people assume that because the death penalty has existed forever, there is no other choice in dealing with people convicted of a crime such as murder… I definitely think that rehabilitating a criminal would be more beneficial than killing them, but to do so would require time, money, and energy that many are not willing to invest.

Student B (Uncertain)

If you commit a crime and get caught, then you deserve to be punished and our legal system does this as often as possible…I have always taken a non-committed view of the death penalty. I see both sides as just…Death row inmates appeal for a number of years and usually don't get the death penalty, but it does occur enough to set a legal precedent and that's its purpose.

Student C (Supportive of the death penalty)

I already knew that better lawyers give you better chances of winning a case, and that people who have more money usually win. I still believe in the death penalty, if you kill someone you deserve to die… The death penalty is fair.

Third Written Responses

Several days later, the students were asked to respond to the information offered by one of the guest speakers, the Honorable Judge DeLamar. The judge had recently been asked to serve on a state panel created to review the death penalty in the state of Illinois. He spoke about the current status of the death penalty in the state. In our prompt, we asked the students to compare and contrast the discrepancies between the criminal justice system portrayed in the novel and the criminal justice system described by the judge.

Student A (Against the death penalty)

In the novel, Jefferson was sentenced and given the death penalty in an obviously unfair and racist trial. Now, the justice system has been modified so that defendants are more protected against the type of trial that Jefferson received. But, because the penalty does still exist, there is still room for an irreversible error, such as in Jefferson's case. As Judge DeLemar stated yesterday, of the 17 people given the death penalty, 11 have been set free. This shows that errors have occurred and therefore they could occur again.

Student B (Uncertain)

From a legal standpoint, Jefferson's conviction of murder is justified, according to Judge DeLamar. However, the punishment of execution is not. It is an example of the mistreatment towards Blacks that was abundant during this time period. It seems that in Jefferson's case and the array of cases Judge DeLamar described, that there are many loopholes in our legal system that can have bad results. I do not have the answer to how this problem can be fixed, but it should not be overlooked.

Student C (Supportive of the death penalty)

I think the discrepancies are what caused the states to add more and more guidelines for the death penalty. Instances like Jefferson's trial or other trials similar to Jefferson's but with more publicity make people realize the poor judgement and legal atrocities committed within the courtroom. I think, though, that if we reform too much, and add too many guidelines, that eventually there will be no more death penalty, and I have strong aversions to that notion.

Final Written Response

For the students' final written response to the novel and issues of social justice, they were asked to write an essay in response to the prompt: "What lessons have you learned from your reading of *A Lesson Before Dying*?"

Student A (Against the death penalty)

A lesson I have learned from this book is the importance of believing in yourself and believing that although you may not be a hero, perhaps you may become one through helping others to become heroes. The purpose of life can vary for everyone, as it did for Jefferson and Grant, but that does not mean that some do not have a purpose. . . . Because most people are not always forced into a task that could make heroes, as Grant was, it is important to believe in yourself, to believe that each person does have a purpose in life, and to know that they are important and will make a difference.

Student B (Uncertain)

If I were on trial, would my attorney refer to me as a hog? I would hope that in the case that I was on trial, I would come off as being somewhat intelligent. In Jefferson's case, his racist lawyer had no hopes of getting Jefferson off. The Judge and the jury had no intent in letting this black man go. To them Jefferson really wasn't anything, but a hog. If he had at least a little bit of intellect, it might not have gotten him off, but it would have at least given him his dignity. This ordeal taught me that I must conduct myself in a rational mature manner in every situation possible.

Student C (Supportive of the death penalty)

Another issue that I thought a great deal about after completing this novel, and listening to our guest speakers, is my opinion on the death penalty. While I still firmly believe in capital punishment, incidents such as Jefferson's helped me to see the other view of anti-death penalty. Also the video of The Scottsboro Boys, helped me to consider the opposing view. I learned that it is not a good idea to adamantly support one view, and disregard the opposing opinion without first looking at it from the other point of view. . . . Every time Gaines began to describe the vicious cycle, I would actually get a bad feeling in the gut of my stomach, and I would become simply nauseated because I felt I was part of that vicious cycle, and sometimes I had to put the book down. This is the first time I had ever felt that way about a subject, and it was very odd. Knowing that there was no escape for them (African Americans) and actually almost experiencing it was a totally different thing.

Student responses indicated that students who were not in support of the death penalty learned to better articulate their position often adopting legal terms to make their points. Students who were uncertain tended to remain uncertain throughout the intervention, often vacillating between strong statements of support and nonsupport of the death penalty. And, students who supported the death penalty remained stalwart in their position, however, the final response by Student C illustrates that some students began to reconsider their thinking on issues of social justice.

By triangulating the data (pre-intervention interviews, videotapes, written responses, and post-intervention questionnaires and interviews) a more complex description of the students' thinking emerges. For example, Student A was very quiet in class, seldom volunteering her point of view, but created thoughtful artistic work and was very involved in a dramatic presentation of the novel. She appeared involved in the topic, although silently. Student B was quite outspoken in class, often challenging others' viewpoints. His comments and actions often suggested that he was not willing to address contemporary issues of social justice. Student C, though compliant and respectful throughout the course, often sat quietly with his arms wrapped around himself or placed his head down on his desk, especially during the guest presentations. He appeared to be distancing himself from the information offered in the course. From this data, we surmised that students come to school/class with preconceived notions of social justice. When spaces are created for students to critically reflect on these notions, they can articulate more socially just ideas. We have learned that helping students to think critically about issues of social justice is a slow process.

Post-Intervention Interviews and Questionnaires

Following our intervention, we conducted post-intervention interviews and distributed a post-intervention questionnaire. We transcribed the student post-intervention interviews and tabulated the results of the questionnaires. We found that students believed that the guest speakers and videos were the most influential sources of additional information.

Student responses indicated that the presentations by the Honorable Judge DeLamar and Professor James Anderson were the most impressive. Students mentioned that the Honorable Judge DeLamar told them about things in the law they did not know and about changes in the death penalty in Illinois, while he remained neutral. They also enjoyed Professor James Anderson's description of life in the South, as he lived there shortly after the time of Gaines's fictive story. Professor Anderson shared some of his family and life story as an African-American male teenager who had experienced some of the circumstances depicted in *A Lesson Before Dying*.

Conclusions

Beginning this research project on the first day of a new semester helped students to view us, the two African-American female researchers, as part of the classroom community. Our daily attendance, participant observation, pre- and post-intervention interviews, co-teaching, videotaping, and post-intervention questionnaires were helpful in establishing and maintaining a comfortable learning/teaching climate in which to use reader response and address issues of social justice. The critical literacy framework focuses on literature and ways in which teachers can build knowledge, understanding, and appreciation for the connection among socio-historical and socio-cultural events and current social structures and events in student responses to literature.

Literacy instruction that includes students' responses to literature, and most especially literature written by authors of color, needs to be reshaped to reflect the multiple voices, ways of knowing, expressions, and understandings students bring to the classroom. Our findings are in agreement with Richard Beach and James Marshall (1991), who posit that in secondary English classrooms planning response activities involves ongoing decisions that takes into account a range of factors: student attributes (needs, interests, abilities, attitudes, knowledge, stances), the teacher's own attributes, instructional goals, and related criteria, relevant response strategies and activities, the social/cultural context, and long term planning (cited in Beach, 1993, p. 153).

We agree, and believe that when seeking to understand students' responses multiple factors need to be considered. Our daily attendance, audio and videotaping, and the triangulation of data, allows us to incorporate many of these areas of concern into our data analysis. Moreover, using the constant comparative framework, we argue that information gathered in process, allowed us to make more productive use of student in-class dialogue and written responses as students began to articulate their viewpoints on issues of social justice.

Allen Luke (1998) also writes that "our decisions about how to teach literacy...demand that we undertake a social analysis of the dynamic communities that children live in" (p. 306). Moreover, we maintain, in agreement with Gutierrez, Lopez, and Turner (1997), that as literacy educators we need to begin to "negotiate and push the linguistic and socio-cultural borders of communities" in which literacy is taught (cited in Luke, 1998, p. 307). What we argue here is that by critically framing multicultural literature, we can realize an enriched space for learning. A space where, as Luke (1998) suggests, "we can learn to respect and listen to, speak with, and read and write different voices, cultures, and texts and we enable our students to do the same, blending their community knowledges, practices and voices to reframe and redesign texts" (p. 309).

Clearly, a more complete description and understanding of the classroom context, interpretive community, and student interactions and responses produced a better understanding of the student responses. We do note that if only examining students' written responses, their viewpoints did not appear to change significantly. Ramsey (1987) also found that students' viewpoints change slowly. However, we maintain that to broaden students' understanding and reading of their world, as well as issues of social justice within a text, it is necessary to offer them information that is important to understanding the text, but information that may not be offered by the author. In doing so, students are more able to critique their reading of the novel and their world.

Interestingly, we found that the greatest encouragement to social change were the guest speakers who spoke from their lived experiences about issues of social justice. We suggest that the inclusion of socio-historical and socio-cultural information that students can draw upon helps them to make connections and associations with and beyond the text as well as offers them insights to use as they articulate their concerns.

Author Note

Research support for this project was made possible through funding provided by the Spencer Foundation; the University of Illinois at Urbana-Champaign, College of Education, Faculty Fellows Summer Research Program; and the National Council of Teachers of English.

References

Applebee, A. (1992). Stabilitiy and change in the high school canon. *English Journal, 81*(5), 27–35.

Appleman, D., & Hynds, S. (1997). Walking our talk: Between response and responsibility in the literature classroom, *English Education, 29,* 272–297.

Athanases, S. (1998). Diverse learners, diverse texts: Exploring identity and difference through literary encounters. *Journal of Literacy Research, 30,* 273–296.

Ayers, W., Hunt, J., & Quinn, T. (Eds.). (1998). *Teaching for social justice.* New York: New Press.

Beach, R. (1993). *A teacher's introduction to reader response theories.* Urbana, IL: National Council of Teachers of English.

Beach, R. (1994). *Stances of resistance and engagement in responding to multicultural literature.* Paper presented at the meeting of the American Educational Research Conference, New Orleans, LA.

Beach, R. (1997). Students' resistance to engagement with multicultural literature. In T. Rogers & A. Soter (Eds.), *Reading Across Cultures: Teaching literature in a diverse society,* (pp. 69–94). New York: Teachers College Press.

Beach, R., & Hynds, S. (1991). Research on response to literature. In R. Barr, M. Kamil, P. Mosenthal, & P. Pearson (Eds.), *Handbook of Reading Research* (Vol. 2, pp. 453–489). New York: Longman.

Beach, R., & Marshall, J. (1991). *Teaching literature in secondary school*. New York: Harcourt, Brace, Jovanovich.

Bleich, D. (1978) *Subjective criticism*. Baltimore, MD: John Hopkins University Press.

Freire, P. (1970). *Pedagogy of the Oppressed*. New York: Continuum.

Gaines, E. (1993). *A lesson before dying*. New York: Vintage.

Glaser, B., & Strauss, A. (1967). *The discovery of grounded theory: Strategies for qualitative research*. Chicago: Aldine.

Gutierrez, K., Banquedano-Lopez, R., & Turner, M. (1997). Putting language back into language arts: When the radical middle meets the third space. *Language Arts, 74,* 368–378.

Henly, C. (1993). Reader response theory as antidote to controversy: Teaching *The Bluest Eye. English Journal, 82*(3), 14–19.

Luke, A. (1998). Getting over method: Literacy teaching as work in "New Times." *Language Arts, 75,* 305–313.

Marshall, J., Hynds, S., & Appleman, D. (1999, November). *Reading and teaching differently: Reader response and the challenge of multicultural texts*. Paper presented at the meeting of the National Council of Teachers of English, Denver, CO.

Matthews, R., & Chandler, R. (1998). Using reader response to teach *Beloved* in a high school American studies classroom. *English Journal, 88*(2), 85–92.

Ramsey, P. (1987). *Teaching and learning in a diverse world: Multicultural education for young children*. New York: Teachers College Press.

Shor, I. (1999). What is critical literacy? *Journal for Pedagogy, Pluralism, & Practice*. (Online: www.lesley.edu/journals/jppp/4/shor.html)

Spears-Bunton, L. (1992). Literature, literacy, and resistance to cultural domination. In C. Kinzer & D. Leu (Eds.), *Literacy research, theory, and practices: Views from many perspectives*. Forty-first yearbook of the National Reading Conference (pp. 393–401). Chicago: National Reading Conference.

Stotsky, S. (1999). *Losing our language: How multicultural classroom instruction is undermining our children's ability to read, write and reason*. New York: Free Press.

Willis, A. (1997). Exploring multicultural literature as cultural production. In T. Rogers & A. Soter (Eds.), *Reading across cultures* (pp. 135–160). New York: Teachers College Press.

Willis, A. (2000). Cultivating understandings through reader response: Dawn's responses to *The Thing They Carried* and *When Heaven and Earth Changed Places*. In N. Karolides (Ed.), *Reader response in the classroom* (pp. 269–286). New York: Longman.

The Grammatical Construction of Scientific Literacy

Zhihui Fang

University of Florida

Language is the essential condition of learning, the process by which experience becomes knowledge. (Halliday, 1993, p. 94)

Scholars of the language-based theory of learning (Christie, 1989; Halliday, 1993; Halliday & Martin, 1993; Hasan & Martin, 1989; Hasan & Williams, 1997) proposed that all learning is fundamentally a linguistic process in three interrelated dimensions: learning language, learning through language, and learning about language. As a principal resource for making meaning, language is intimately involved in the manner in which human beings negotiate, construct, organize, and change the nature of social experience (Halliday, 1978). Becoming literate is essentially an extension of the functional potential of language. It has been argued that developing students' knowledge and understanding in school science entails developing their knowledge of the linguistic forms that construct and communicate that understanding (Christie, 1989; Unsworth, 1997). In the words of Halliday and Martin (1993), "learning science is the same thing as learning the language of science" (p. 84).

In the elementary school, one of the common curricular genres is the science report. Science reports are a textual form that makes general, nonspecific statements about a class of things. They are characterized by two discursive features: conventionality and abstraction. First, science reports consist of a set of relatively small but durable constellations of text-level linguistic features that adhere to certain cultural conventions, that are appropriate for particular social and cultural occasions, and that accomplish specific communicative intents (Kamberelis, 1999; Kress, 1989). For example, science reports are usually structured into three parts: topic introduction, detailed description of the attributes of different elements around the topic, and summary statements about the information covered (Derewianka, 1990; Martin, 1989; Pappas, 1993). They use generalized participants (e.g., *cats*), rather than specific participants (e.g., *my cat*); timeless present tense (e.g., *exist, grow*); logical connectives (e.g., *because, if*) to signal reasons for or the results of general characteristics or processes, as well as logical relations among entities in the world; and relational verb phrases for defining, attributing, classifying, and comparing/contrasting (e.g., *are, have, are called, belong to, can be classified as, are similar to, are more powerful than*) (Derewianka, 1990). Second, there is greater abstraction of written language in science reports (Halliday & Martin, 1993; Unsworth, 1997). That is, in science reports there is greater use of nouns (e.g., *water conservation*) to express actions and events

© Copyright 2000 by the National Reading Conference. All rights reserved.
National Reading Conference Yearbook, 49, pp. 367–380.

(e.g., *to conserve water*). There is also greater density of information. This density is achieved partly through linguistic integration, such as the use of longer and more complex noun groups.

From the perspective of the language-based theory of learning, learning to read and write science reports means a gradual apprenticeship to the distinctive linguistic forms that index these features (i.e., conventionality, abstraction). Literacy scholars (Kamberelis, 1999; Martin, 1989; Pappas, 1993) have suggested that gaining knowledge of science reports and the typified rhetorical situation that constitutes and is constituted by them is a primary developmental task for young children as they learn to read and write. As children become literate, they are gradually reconstituting their lexicogrammar in the more scientific mode so that they can use language more effectively as a resource for constructing curricular knowledge (Christie, 1989). Because conventionality and abstraction are essential to the construction of scientific understanding, becoming communicatively competent in science reports necessarily implies building and consolidating children's knowledge of the grammatical forms that embody these features.

The purpose of this study is two-fold: (a) to identify the grammatical resources that young children use to construct science reports, and (b) to examine whether students of different grade levels demonstrate differential working knowledge of science reports. This study is unique in that, unlike much of the recent research that focuses on the *social* construction of literacy, it explores how young children's understanding of literacy is *grammatically* constructed.

Method

Participants

Participants in the study were 19 children from a newly formed, intact multigrade classroom in a socioculturally diverse, medium-sized K–5 elementary school in a southeastern state of the United States. There were 8 first graders (3 girls, 5 boys), 6 second graders (3 girls, 3 boys), and 5 third graders (4 girls, 1 boys) in the class. Nine of them (3 third graders, 3 second graders, 3 first graders) received free or reduced-price school lunch. There were 7 European Americans (2 third graders, 3 second graders, 2 first graders), 9 African Americans (1 third grader, 3 second graders, 5 first graders), 2 Asian Americans (1 third grader, 1 first grader), and 1 mixed-race child (third grader).

Pedagogical Context

Literacy instruction in the target classroom could be characterized as literature based. However, it was also supplemented by basals (Silver Burdett & Ginn), as mandated by the school. The classroom was rich with print and print-related materials. The walls were decorated with children's book posters, a variety of charts (alphabet, counting, weather, student name), calendar, children's work, and class rules and regulations, among others. The class library was equipped with over 700 authentic literature books of various genres that the teacher brought from home and students checked out periodically from the school and local libraries. The books were placed on two book shelves and in dozens of baskets subjectively labeled by the teacher as "hard, harder, hardest"; "really hard, really harder, really hardest"; and "super hard, super harder, super hardest." Next to the library were a sofa and a bathtub with pillows where students could read books independently or in pairs. There was a special chair in the front of the classroom where the teacher read to the children and where the children had the opportunity to tell experiences and share stories they had written, a colorful rug laid in front of the chair for group meetings, listening to teacher read-alouds, and minilessons. Students were grouped heterogeneously into six desks where they did individual and small-group projects. There was a kidney-shaped table in the back of the room where the teacher conducted individual or small-group instruction.

Each day, different modes of reading were used, including teacher read-alouds, independent reading, guided reading with the teacher, shared reading, partner reading, and reading along with a tape. Students engaged in journal writing and sharing at least twice per week, usually the first thing in the morning. From time to time, the teacher would assign topics related to the theme of the unit under study for students to write about. Students also regularly wrote responses to the literature books they read. A typical schedule of the daily literacy events in the classroom is presented in Table 1.

Data Collection

Two kinds of data were collected for the study as part of a larger research project: children's writing samples and contextual data related to their learning environment and literacy experiences. The researcher worked as participant observer (Spradley, 1980) and teacher aide in the classroom at least twice a week throughout the school year. The writing samples were collected during the Spring semester (end of January) after the researcher had established rapport with the children. Each child worked individually with the researcher in a quiet corner of the classroom for approximately 30–45 minutes. During the session, the child was asked to assume the role of a scientist and nonfiction book writer, and compose a science report text. If the child seemed tired or distracted, the session was terminated and rescheduled. Specifically, the following direction was used by the researcher to get the child started on the task:

> Hi, I know you've been studying sea animals recently and you've read a lot of books about them. You've been on field trips to see some of these animals. You've also had guest speakers coming to class to talk about the animals. What I'd like you to do today is to pretend that you are a scientist and nonfiction book author. And you want to write a science report about one of your familiar or favorite animals, so that other people (like your friends from another state) who do not know anything about the animal can get to know it really well. Remember that you are going to be a nonfiction book author. You can take a few minutes to think about what you want to write.

Table 1

Typical Schedule of Daily Literacy Events in the Target Classroom

Time	Agenda	Literacy Activities
7:45–8:15 a.m.	Free Choices	students turned in their take-home reading folders; students read self-selected books or wrote diaries in their journals; teacher checked students' reading reports in the folder.
8:15–8:30 a.m.	Announcements	students listened to school announcements of daily news and events through close-circuit TV and intercom.
8:30–9:00 a.m.	Circle Time	students shared their journals on the rug; teacher read one or two storybooks aloud to students; students filled in blanks in the "morning message" that focused on punctuation, capitalization and spelling; students then completed a "student-of-the-day" message that focused on practicing basic math skills, such as counting, addition, and subtraction.
9:00–9:30 a.m.	Specials	students attended PE, music, or art elsewhere in the school.
9:30–10:20 a.m.	Math & Language Arts	students worked on Saxon math and/or language arts worksheets from basals; teacher worked with individuals and/or small groups during this time on math or language arts skills.
10:20–10:40 a.m.	Recess	students had snack and went on playground recess.
10:40–11:40 a.m.	Literacy Block	students wrote about an assigned topic, read self-selected or teacher-assigned books, completed book reports or literature response, played on computers (e.g., sending e-mails to friends, reading stories), or listened to books on tape; teacher conferenced on individual or group projects during this time.
11:40 a.m.–12:15 p.m.	Book Talks	teacher read aloud and discussed one picture book or chapter book with children.
12:15–1:00 p.m	Lunch & Recess	students went for lunch and recess after lunch.
1:00–1:40 p.m.	DEAR Time	students read self-selected books (appropriate to their levels) on their own, in pairs, with the teacher, or with a tape.

Table 1 *(continued)*

Time	Agenda	Literacy Activities
1:40–1:50 p.m.	Shared Reading	teacher shared a short storybook with students.
1:50–2:00 p.m.	Preparation for Dismissal	students prepared to go home; each student had to bring home a folder that contained any unfinished math and language arts worksheets, literature books to be read at night, and a parent checklist.

Other than delivering the instructions for the writing task, the researcher provided no further "hints" about task requirements, editing, or revising. Each child was asked to read his or her text to the researcher before leaving the session. All writing sessions were audiotaped and transcribed.

To collect contextual data on children's learning environment and literacy experiences, the researcher kept records of all the books shared in class and read at home by children, audiotaped selected literacy events (e.g., book talks, writing conferences) in small groups and whole class, documented children's assigned and self-selected writing in class, conducted informal interviews with the teacher about her literacy beliefs and practices, and collected lesson plans and other artifacts (e.g., student worksheets, weekly work schedules). These contextual data were used to help make sense of the patterns that emerged from the analysis of writing samples.

Data Analysis

The children's written texts were analyzed linguistically in terms of the two fundamental features of science reports: conventionality and abstraction. Two scorers each analyzed the data independently and then cross-checked with each other. Discrepancies were resolved through thoughtful discussion in light of relevant theory and research studies. The average interrater agreement rate on all analyses was 92%.

Measures of conventionality. Because science reports have a small, distinctive set of fairly stable and conventionalized features of their own, each text was evaluated on whether it successfully incorporated these conventionalized features. Accordingly, a three-step procedure was instituted. First, each text was coded for the presence of the five conventionality markers described earlier: text structure, generalized participants, simple present tense verbs, logical conjunctions, and relational verb phrases. Second, percentages of obligatory text structures, generalized participants, and simple present tense verbs were calculated. This was done by counting the number of obligatory text structures, generalized participants, and simple present tense verbs in each text and then dividing them by the number of, respectively, obligatory science report structures (3), participants, and verbs in the text. Third, ratios of logical conjunctions and relational verb phrases per "clause" (Halliday, 1994) were computed. This was done by first counting the number of logical conjunctions and relational verb phrases in each text and then dividing them each by the number of clauses in the text. A summary score for the conventionality feature was also computed by adding up the five indices of the conventionality markers.

Measures of abstraction. Four indices were used to measure the degree of abstraction in children's science reports. The first is lexical density. According to Halliday and Martin (1993), lexical density is "a measure of the density of information in any text according to how tightly the lexical items (content words) have been packed into the grammatical structure" (p. 76). Compared to everyday talk (usually two to three lexical words per clause), there is greater density of information in scientific texts (often four to six lexical words per clause). This density is achieved partly through the use of longer and more complex noun groups. Lexical density is calculated by dividing the total number of content words (i.e., nouns, verbs, adjectives, most adverbs) by the total number of clauses in the text.

The second index of abstraction is the number of grammatical metaphors per clause. Grammatical metaphor measures the extent to which the qualities, events, and things of science are represented though "incongruent" grammatical categories. It refers to the substitution of one grammatical class or one grammatical structure (e.g., verbal group—*he departed; they are clumsy*) by another (noun group—*his departure; their clumsiness*).

The third and fourth indices are the number of nominal groups per clause and the number of words per nominal group, respectively. Nominal groups can vary from very simple structure (e.g., *we, dogs*) to structures that are long and dense (e.g., *these two grouchy goldfish with red stripes on the body*). Nominal group structure is closely linked to the use of grammatical metaphor and it measures the level of linguistic integration and sophistication in scientific writing. Finally, a summary score for the abstraction feature was computed by adding up the four indices of the abstraction markers.

Syndrome of features. A syndrome score was calculated for each text by combining the summary scores of conventionality and abstraction. In essence, this is a prototypicality score that makes it possible to see how closely the children's texts emulated prototypic science reports and, more specifically, how well the children understood the language that is central to scientific reporting.

Statistical analysis. Because certain outcome variables are correlated with others, the dependent variables were grouped into three logical sets: conventionality, abstraction, and the syndrome. The first two sets were each analyzed through multivariate analysis of variances (MANOVA). If MANOVA produced significant effects, univariate analysis of variance (ANOVA) was then conducted on each dependent variable within the set. The two summary scores (conventionality, abstraction) were each analyzed using ANOVA. The third set of variables (i.e., the syndrome) was also analyzed using ANOVA. Finally, the number of clauses for each text was calculated as a measure of textual length and subsequently submitted to ANOVA. For all analyses, grade level was the between-subjects independent variable.

Results

The descriptive statistics (i.e., means and standard deviations) for all dependent variables by grade level are presented in Table 2.

Conventionality. The children in the sample demonstrated mastery over one conventionality marker (i.e., simple present tense), considerable working knowledge of some other conventionality markers (i.e., text structure, generalized participants), and much more nascent sense of still others (i.e., logical conjunction, relational verb phrases). The children at all grade levels scored perfect for the simple present tense measure. This suggests that the children were able to use simple present tense verbs consistently throughout their science reports. The scores for generalized participants were also fairly high, albeit imperfect, across the three grade levels. This means that even though the children did not yet demonstrate complete mastery over this conventionality marker, they were largely consistent in using it during the construction of science reports. The scores for text structure were, however, not uniform among the three grade levels. The first and third graders scored fairly high, whereas the second graders scored surprisingly low. Although there were few well-developed pieces that contained all three obligatory structural elements of a science report, most texts did contain both topic statement and a list of "facts" about the topic. In contrast, the scores for other markers of conventionality were strikingly low. The children used practically no logical conjunctions to signal logical connections among different propositions, and few relational verb phrases for defining, attributing, classifying, and comparing/contrasting.

Comparing the scores across the three different grade levels, MANOVA showed no statistically significant grade level effect on the conventionality markers. Nor did ANOVA yield any significant grade-level effect for the summary measure. On the other hand, as evidenced in standard deviations, there were considerable variations within each grade level in the children's use of most conventionality markers (i.e., text structure, generalized participants, logical conjunctions, relational verb phrases).

Abstraction. The children in the sample exhibited inchoate knowledge of the abstraction feature. The scores for all abstraction markers were strikingly low. For example, none of the children used grammatical metaphors in their texts. Furthermore, the children, regardless of their grade level, employed an average of fewer than two nominal groups per clause and each nominal group contained, on average, fewer than two words. Not surprisingly, the lexical density of their texts was low (around 2.5), which is close to that of everyday spoken language (Halliday & Martin, 1993). Taken together, these indices suggest that the children's texts might

Table 2

Means (M) and Standard Deviations (SD) of Textual Measures

	Grade 1		Grade 2		Grade 3		Sample	
	M	SD	M	SD	M	SD	M	SD
Conventionality	2.71	.40	2.94	0.48	2.83	.44	2.82	.42
% of obligatory text structure	.71	.28	.50	.19	.80	.18	.67	.25
% of generalized participants	.73	.20	.87	.11	.76	.21	.78	.18
% of simple present tense verbs	1.00	.00	1.00	.00	1.00	.00	1.00	.00
# of logical conjunctions per clause	.03	.07	.07	.10	.05	.12	.05	.09
# of relational verb phrases per clause	.25	.21	.51	.25	.25	.22	.33	.25
Abstraction	6.35	1.59	6.42	1.29	6.16	.99	6.32	1.29
# of nominal groups per clause	1.83	.28	1.79	.21	1.62	.21	1.76	.25
# of words per nominal group	1.87	.95	2.08	.47	1.92	.70	1.95	.73
# of grammatical metaphors per clause	.00	.00	.00	.00	.00	.00	.00	.00
Lexical density	2.66	.74	2.55	.70	2.62	.49	2.61	.64
Syndrome of Features	9.07	1.78	9.36	1.01	9.00	.99	9.14	1.33
# of clauses per text	3.88	1.55	6.00	1.79	9.20	4.09	5.95	3.22

be more oral like and less sophisticated than expected for science reports.

Comparing the scores across the three grade levels, MANOVA showed no statistically significant grade-level effect on the abstraction markers. Nor did ANOVA turn up any significant finding for the summary measure. On the other hand, as evidenced in standard deviations, there were considerable variations within each grade level in the children's use of nominal groups and lexical density.

The syndrome. Collapsing the scores of the two summary measures (i.e., conventionality and abstraction) into one graph (see Figure 1), it is evident that the prototypicality scores for the three grade levels were quite close. In fact, ANOVA yielded a statistically nonsignificant grade-level effect for the syndrome of features. This suggests that the first, second, and third graders demonstrated comparable working knowledge of science reports. In other words, they drew upon similar grammatical resources in the construction of science reports.

Textual length. Finally, the number of clauses per text was computed as a measure of textual length. ANOVA revealed statistically significant differences between the first grade and the third grade (Scheffé, $p<0.05$). This shows that the third graders produced significantly longer texts than did the first graders.

Discussion

The data from the study suggest that the children in the sample were fairly naïve with regard to the science report genre, although there were considerable variations within each grade level in terms of their working knowledge of science

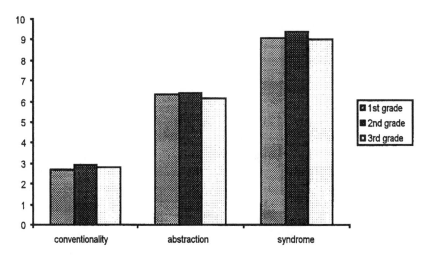

Figure 1. Comparison of summary and syndrome measures across the three grades.

reports. Except for a couple of conventionality markers (e.g., simple present tense, generalized participants, text structure), the children as a whole appeared to be quite limited in their grammatical resources for constructing science reports. Both developmental and pedagogical factors may help explain these children's performance. First, from a developmental perspective, it is possible that, unlike some of the conventionality markers (e.g., text structure, simple present tense, generalized participants) that are internalized relatively early in development, other features of science reports (e.g., logical conjunctions, relational verb phrases, grammatical metaphors, complex nominal group structure) may be so subtle and complex that they are not typically well developed in this early, "learning to read" stage (Chall, 1996). Recent research on primary-grade children (Fang, 1998; Kamberelis, 1999) has generated partially corroborating evidence in support of this hypothesis.

Second, it may also be argued that the children's lack of familiarity with science reports may be caused more by insufficient exposure to them than by any difficulty inherent in the genre. Related to this point, it must be noted that the opportunity to interact with information books in the target classroom was considerably less than that provided for storybooks. Contextual data showed that about 20% of the books in the class library were expository. In addition, over 90% of the books used in the teacher-directed reading activities (e.g., read alouds, shared reading, guided reading, book talks) were storybooks (as opposed to informational books). Further, the children had limited opportunity to engage in writing informational texts. In fact, most writing assignments were narrative. Thus, the dearth of opportunity to interact with informational texts could result in low levels of achievement in scientific literacy.

Third, the children's working knowledge of scientific language may have been influenced by the model of written language that literature books provide. As Kress (1994) pointed out, the most potent factors in a child's learning of writing are "the models of written language which the school provides, and which it encourages the child to emulate" (p. 86). In this connection, it should be pointed out that many children's books for beginning readers, particularly picture books, use vocabulary and syntax that are close to children's oral language. Moreover, they tend to laminate scientific information and elements of informational prose within the narrative discourse structure (Fang, 1998; Kamberelis, 1999), presumably to make the books more interesting and accessible (that is, "developmentally appropriate") for young readers.

An equally surprising finding of the study is that older children did not seem to possess more working knowledge of science reports, despite more years of schooling (and presumably more literacy experiences). Recall that except for textual length, the children across the three grade levels performed similarly in terms of using appropriate grammatical resources to construct science reports. This is somewhat puzzling and counterintuitive. Two recent studies help shed light on this puzzle. In a recent longitudinal study of effects of storybook experience, Meyer, Wardrop, Stahl, and Linn (1994) reported that the amount of time first-grade teachers spent reading to their students was unrelated to the reading achievement of their students and that the amount of time kindergarten teachers spent reading to kindergarten children was negatively related to the children's reading achievement in subsequent years. They posited that teachers who read the most spent the least amount of time in direct teaching activities that were positively correlated with reading achievement. They concluded that although storybook reading is important, greater benefits from such storybook experience can come only when children develop print-related awareness and skills. In another study, Senechal, LeFevre, Thomas, and Daley (1998) found that storybook exposure explained statistically significant unique variance in young children's oral language skills but not in their written-language skills; in contrast, parent's direct teaching explained statistically significant unique variance in children's written language skills but not in their oral language skills. They hypothesized that storybook exposure enhances children's oral language skills, whereas additional support in the form of explicit teaching may be necessary to enhance their written language skills. Although these researchers did not specifically address the constructs examined in this study, their findings suggest that engaging children in conscious exploration of the discursive features of book language may be both desirable and beneficial. From a developmental viewpoint, it does seem plausible that when children's literacy development reaches a certain threshold level, mere exposure to more books may not yield benefits.

Related to this point, a number of educational linguists (Carter, 1982; Cazden, 1995; Cope & Kalantzis, 1993; Hammond, 1990; Unsworth, 1997) have underscored the importance of metatextual talks that focus on the schematic and lexicogrammatical features of text. Specifically, they argued that pedagogical practices that embed "consciousness raising" (Rutherford & Sharwood-Smith, 1985; Yule, 1986), that is, intentionally drawing learners' attention to salient features of book language, may facilitate children's language/literacy development. As Derewianka (1990) argued, "Children who develop an appreciation of the characteristics of such written texts are more likely to write in ways that may be expected of them as they grow older" (p. 67). Other researchers (Fang, 2000; Kamberelis, 1999) have also suggested possible links between teacher metadiscourse and children's communicative competence in curricular genres.

In this regard, two points are worth noting. First, because of the high-stakes nature of state-mandated testing, the target teacher, like other teachers in the school, implemented a systematic, structured method of writing instruction called "Power Writing" (Sparks, 1982) toward the end of the Fall semester and conscientiously talked about elements of text structure during writing conferences. Such direct instruction might have increased the children's scores on the text structure measure. Second, except for text structure, other features of informational text (or any text) were seldom explored in class either during book talks or writing conferences. That is, the teacher rarely engaged her students in conscious examination of the grammatical resources (e.g., linguistic techniques and conventions) appropriate for constructing particular types of text for particular purposes. There was also little explicit discussion in class about the qualitative differences between oral and written language in general. Therefore, even when opportunities to interact with informational texts did arise, the quality of such interaction was not optimal.

Limitations and Implications

Like all studies, this study suffers from several limitations. First, the number of subjects in the study was small, and it is inadvisable to generalize the research findings beyond the characteristics of the present sample. Replication-extension studies using larger samples are needed, because they are a critical means for enhancing the accuracy of scientific and scholarly knowledge (Robinson & Levin, 1997).

Another potential limitation has to do with the study's task, which consisted of school-like prompts, and each text was produced during a single experimental session. It is possible that some children may have demonstrated more or less knowledge of science reports on this task than they would have under other, more naturalistic conditions. To understand such differences would require collection of multiple written samples across multiple conditions. A corollary problem is one that is inherent in all developmental studies. Specifically, it is highly unlikely that all children understood the task requirements in the same way or with the same degree of sophistication. Fortunately, the study's design included measures to minimize this problem. For example, prior to data collection, the children had studied a literature unit on sea animals, read books about these animals, gone on field trips to see the animals, had guest speakers talk to them about the animals, and engaged in discussion and tasks related to the animals. The teacher also talked in general terms about the differences between fiction and nonfiction books. A further limitation concerning task is that because the act of phonetically transcribing text is both physically laborious and cognitively challenging for young children (Gundlach, 1981; Sipe, 1998), some children might have exhibited less knowledge of science reports than they actually possessed. However, allowing the children to read their texts back to the researcher and using these reenactments of written texts in the analysis should, to some extent, help offset this potential limitation.

Finally, from a pedagogical standpoint, considering the potential relationship between children's literacy development and their learning experience in school (Duke, 1999; Fang, 2000; Kamberelis, 1999), it seems critically important that teachers provide rich opportunities for students to interact with informational/scientific texts and simultaneously engage them in conscious exploration of the linguistic technology that constructs and communicates scientific concepts, principles and processes. Indeed, recent research in the United States (Donovan, 1996), Britain (Bain, Fitzgerald, & Taylor, 1992; Carter, 1990) and, in particular, Australia (Derewianka, 1990; Rose, McInnes, & Korner, 1992; Rothery, 1994) has suggested that such a proposal has considerable merit.

References

Bain, R., Fitzgerald, B., & Taylor, M. (1992). *Looking into language: Classroom approaches to knowledge about language*. Sevenoaks, England: Hodder & Stoughton.

Carter, R. (1982). *Linguistics and the teacher*. London: Routledge & Kegan Paul.

Carter, R. (1990). *Knowledge about language and the curriculum: The LINC Reader*. Sevenoaks, England: Hodder & Stoughton.

Cazden, C. (1995, April). *Bernstein's visible and invisible pedagogies: Reading Recovery as a mixed system*. Keynote address delivered at the meeting of American Educational Research Association. San Francisco, CA.

Chall, J. (1996). *Stages of reading development* (2nd ed.). New York: Harcourt Brace.

Christie, F. (1989). *Language education*. New York: Oxford University Press.

Cope, B., & Kalantzis, M. (1993). *The powers of literacy: A genre approach to teaching writing*. Pittsburgh, PA: University of Pittsburgh Press.

Derewianka, B. (1990). *Exploring how texts work*. Victoria, Australia: Primary English Teaching Association.

Donovan, C. (1996). First graders' impressions of genre-specific elements in writing narrative and expository texts. In D. Leu, C. Kinzer, & K. Hinchman (Eds.), *Literacies for the 21st century: Research and practices*. Forty-fifth yearbook of the National Reading Conference (pp. 183–194). Chicago: National Reading Conference.

Duke, N. (1999). *The scarcity of informational texts in first grade* (Tech. Rep. No. 1-007). Ann Arbor: Center for the Improvement of Early Reading Achievement, University of Michigan.

Fang, Z. (1998). A study of changes and development in children's written discourse potential. *Linguistics and Education, 9,* 341–367.

Fang, Z. (2000, April). *Learning the storybook language in a literature-based classroom*. Paper presented at the meeting of the American Educational Research Association, New Orleans, LA.

Gundlach, R. (1981). On the nature and development of children's writing. In C. Frederiksen & J. Dominic (Eds.), *Writing: Process, development and communication* (pp. 133–151). Hillsdale, NJ: Earlbaum.

Halliday, M. A. K. (1978). *Language as social semiotic: The social interpretation of language and learning*. London: Longman.

Halliday, M. A. K. (1993). Towards a language-based theory of learning. *Linguistics and Education, 5,* 93–116.

Halliday, M. A. K. (1994). *An introduction to functional grammar* (2nd ed.). London: Edward Arnold.

Halliday, M. A. K., & Martin, J. R. (1993). *Writing science: Literacy and discursive power*. Pittsburgh, PA: University of Pittsburgh Press.

Hammond, J. (1990). Oral and written language in the educational context. In M. A. K. Halliday, J. Gibbons, & H. Nicholas (Eds.), *Learning, keeping and using language* (pp. 257–270). Philadelphia, PA: John Benjamins.

Hasan, R., & Martin, J. R. (1989). *Language development: Learning language, learning culture*. Norwood, NJ: Ablex.

Hasan, R., & Williams, G. (1997). *Literacy in society*. London: Longman.

Kamberelis, G. (1999). Genre development and learning: Children writing stories, science reports, and poems. *Research in the Teaching of English, 33,* 403–460.

Kress, G. (1989). *Linguistic processes in sociocultural practice*. Oxford, England: Oxford University Press.

Kress, G. (1994). *Learning to write*. New York: Routledge & Kagan Paul.

Martin, J. R. (1989). *Factual writing: Exploring and challenging social reality*. Oxford, England: Oxford University Press.

Meyer, L. A., Wardrop, J. L., Stahl, S. A., & Linn, R. L. (1994). Effects of reading storybooks aloud to children. *Journal of Educational Research, 88,* 69–85.

Pappas, C. (1993). Is narrative "primary?": Some insights from kindergartners' pretend readings of stories and information books. *Journal of Reading Behavior, 25,* 97–129.

Robinson, D., & Levin, J. (1997). Reflections on statistical and substantive significance, with a slice of replication. *Educational Researcher, 26*(5), 21–26.

Rose, D., McInnes, D., & Korner, H. (1992). *Scientific literacy.* Sydney: Metropolitan East Disadvantaged Schools Program.

Rothery, J. (1994). *Exploring literacy in school English.* Sydney: Metropolitan East Disadvantaged Schools Program.

Rutherford, W., & Sharwood-Smith, M. (1985). Consciousness-raising and universal grammar. *Applied Linguistics, 6,* 274–282.

Senechal, M., LeFevre, J., Thomas, E. M., & Daley, K. E. (1998). Differential effects of home literacy experiences on the development of oral and written language. *Reading Research Quarterly, 33,* 96–116.

Sipe, L. (1998). Transitions to the conventional: An examination of a first grader's composing process. *Journal of Literacy Research, 30,* 357–388.

Sparks, J. E. (1982). *Write for power.* Manhattan Beach, CA: Communication Associates.

Spradley, J. (1980). *Participant observation.* New York: Holt, Rinehart & Winston.

Unsworth, L. (1997). Some practicalities of a language-based theory of learning. *Australian Journal of Language and Literacy, 20*(1), 36–52.

Yule, G. (1986). Comprehensible notions. *Applied Linguistics, 7,* 275–283.

Author Note

The research reported in this article was made possible in part by a grant from the National Council of Teachers of English Research Foundation. The data presented, the statements made, and the views expressed are solely the responsibility of the author.

Peer Mediation Strategies of Linguistically Diverse Beginning Readers

Valerie G. Chapman
University of Memphis

L imited knowledge of the graphophonic cueing system and how to use it defines the beginning reader (Clay, 1991; Ehri, 1991; Juel, 1991). Researchers (Byrne & Fielding-Barnsley, 1991, 1993; Lundberg, Frost, & Petersen, 1988; Stahl & Murray, 1994) have studied phonemic awareness, an element of the graphophonic cueing system, in beginning readers, but these studies did not investigate how phonemic awareness develops. Neither did these studies examine how beginning readers apply knowledge about phonological aspects once the rules are mastered. Thus, the development of the graphophonic cueing system in beginning readers is not fully understood.

Many studies (Baumann & Bergeron, 1993; Fuchs, Mathes, & Simmons, 1997; Palincsar, Brown, & Campione, 1993) have demonstrated the benefits of social interaction in the classroom. In these studies the primary form of social interaction involved a teacher mediating for students, or teachers demonstrating specific techniques for students to emulate when working with peers. MacGillivray and Hawes (1994) examined the roles that first graders exhibit when working in self-selected dyads. The researchers, however, did not examine strategies that more capable peers used to assist their less capable peers (referred to here as learning peers).

The purpose of this study was twofold. The first purpose was to examine how more capable peer mediation facilitates the development of beginning readers' English literacy in a linguistically diverse classroom setting. Related to that, the second purpose was to examine how beginning readers demonstrate their understandings of the graphophonic cueing system as they read and reread texts with other beginning readers. The research question was "How do more capable beginning readers mediate for their learning peers in a first-grade classroom setting?"

Theoretical Framework

This study was guided by Vygotsky's sociocultural framework that focuses on one or more of the cultural, historical, and institutional factors of individuals' mental functioning rather than on universals of cognitive development (Davydov, 1995; Wertsch, 1990, 1991; Wertsch & Toma, 1995). For instance, each home culture has a significant historical development that influences the social and cogni-

National Reading Conference Yearbook, 49, pp. 381–391.

tive development of individuals within that home culture. In turn, students are involved in teacher-organized learning experiences in institutional settings (e.g., elementary classrooms) that influence the social and cognitive development of each student.

Vygotsky (1986) identified the zone of proximal development and mediation as elements that are present during learning. The zone of proximal development is "the distance between the actual developmental level as determined by independent problem solving and the level of potential development as determined through problem solving under adult guidance or in collaboration with more capable peers" (p. 86). The existence of the zone of proximal development is critical to understanding the need for social interaction in order for learning to occur. Learning occurs within a zone of proximal development that is unique for each individual. More capable peers are able to assist their learning peers within their zones of proximal development when classroom activities are organized to allow social interactions among students. This framework helped me examine how students used their knowledge to mediate for learning peers.

Method

This qualitative study took place in a first-grade classroom in a Title I school (Central Elementary), in the southwestern United States. This school was initially selected because of the linguistic diversity reflected in the school's census records. In the first-grade classroom where I conducted my study, linguistic diversity referred to students' knowledge of two different home languages, English and Spanish, and students' uses of various dialects. According to the Home Language Survey completed by parents, only 2 students' parents indicated that Spanish was spoken in the home. Based on information gathered during home visits, 11 of the students had some level of understanding of the Spanish language. Parents in five homes indicated that Spanish was their first language and was emphasized in their homes.

The class consisted of 5 girls and 14 boys. Three girls were European-American and 2 were Mexican-American. Four boys were European-American, 9 were Mexican-American, and 1 boy was African-American. Sixteen of the students were eligible for free or reduced lunch. The classroom teacher, Ms. Grace, and her teaching assistant, Ms. Webb, were involved in the setting, although not as participants.

The qualitative methods used for data collection include participant observation, informal interviews with each of the 19 participants, and collection of documents. Sessions were audiotaped and videotaped. Utilizing these methods of data collection allowed me to triangulate the data (Lincoln & Guba, 1985). Data were collected in a naturalistic setting from the first day of school through the middle of December. Trustworthiness is assured through the techniques of prolonged engagement, persistent observation, triangulation, peer debriefing, member checking, and the use of a reflective journal. To provide for transferability I describe the participants, setting, and instances as fully as possible. Data were analyzed using the constant comparative method. Initially data were analyzed through open coding, resulting in both emic and etic codes. These codes then were organized around axial codes allowing me to use the process of selective coding (Strauss, 1987). The codes were organized into two themes.

Results

I use excerpts from the data as illustrations that will help the reader understand my findings. For each excerpt, I identify specific characteristics of each student. Ethnicity includes European-American (E-A), African-American (A-A), and Mexican-American (M-A). For the Mexican-American participants, I also identify whether they are active bilinguals (AB) or passive bilinguals (PB). Active bilinguals understand and speak two languages; passive bilinguals understand two languages but speak one. Finally, I provide reading instructional levels from the beginning and end of the study. The instructional groups were below level (BL), low average (LA), average (AV), above average (AA), and advanced (AD).

The two themes that emerged from the data were related to the types of interactions first graders used as they mediated for one another during literacy activities: physical interactions and vocal pacing. The two themes identify several peer mediation strategies developed by the beginning readers.

Physical Interactions

Physical interactions fell generally into three types: (a) peer pointing, (b) demonstrating, and (c) elaborative gestures accompanying oral language (emic codes).

Peer pointing. When learning the correspondence between letters and sounds and written symbols and whole words, students easily got lost in the text. More capable peers mediated for learning peers by pointing to words and moving their finger forward only when a new word was read. This physical interaction helped the learning peer internalize concepts of print, such as words and spaces, punctuation marks, directionality of print, and the correspondence between oral and written language.

When reading independently, almost all the students pointed for themselves. Students sometimes got lost in the text even when they pointed to words. In these instances, more capable peers mediated for their learning peers by pointing to words in the text. The following excerpt illustrates how Regina (E-A, AV-AA) used peer pointing to assist Sally (E-A, LA-BL):

> Sally brought her ABC book about outer space to share with me. A cluster of children was waiting around me to listen to each other and for their turn to read. As Sally was reading her book, Regina looked over Sally's shoulder and joined in

her reading. On the "M" page, Sally got lost. She stopped and began rereading the page but got lost at the same place in the text. After the second time, Sally heaved a heavy sigh. Regina stopped reading and began at the first of the line with Sally. When Sally paused at the problem spot, Regina took her [Sally's] wrist and pointed her [Sally's] finger at the correct words. As soon as Sally's voice matched the words pointed to, Regina let go of Sally's wrist and continued reading aloud.

In this example, even though Sally was pointing for herself and reading her own composition, she experienced difficulty. When she wrote the text, Sally did not leave space between two of the words. Consequently, as she read, she had difficulty finding enough written words to match her spoken words. Regina held Sally's pointing finger and helped her differentiate between words and clusters of letters that did not look like separate words because they were written too closely together. At the troublesome spot, Regina silenced her own voice and mediated physically, holding Sally's pointing finger under each word, while Sally read each word. As a more capable peer, Regina was able to identify two words even though Sally left no space between them. Sally, the learning peer, needed the space to identify each cluster of letters as an individual word. The physical interaction of peer pointing provided Sally with the assistance she needed to read the text.

More capable peers also mediated by pointing across distances at reference points. In each case when more capable peers pointed the way for their classmates, pointing did not stand apart from students' use of oral language, but enhanced it. When learning peers needed assistance, more capable peers searched the room for a reference point (e.g., letter in the alphabet strip, classmate's name on the roster, learning center chart). Upon locating the reference point the more capable peers extended their arms and pointed toward it. Then more capable peers described the surroundings or the object itself.

Demonstrating. A second type of physical interaction that students used was demonstrating something unknown or unclear to learning peers. Demonstrating involved making certain movements in the air (e.g., writing letters in the air) or putting objects together (e.g., laying plastic letters together to spell a word). First graders did not use verbal descriptions to accompany demonstrations. More capable peers signaled their demonstrations by saying simple phrases, such as "like this" and "like that."

One example of demonstrating occurred in the ABC center. In this center students used a variety of manipulative letters to spell words and classmates' names. One set of letters consisted of plastic upper and lower case letters. In the following example, Gabe, David, and Regina were each using the letters to spell classmates' names. As often happened in this center, some letters appeared in classmates' names more frequently than others, creating a shortage when several students were at the center at the same time:

> Gabe (M-A, AB, AV-AV): I'm trying to find a "y." (He sorted through the pile of letters.)
> Researcher: A "y." What's a "y" look like?

Gabe: Um, kind of like a "v." Then you put a line down. (He motioned with his index finger in the air.)

David (E-A, AA-AD): Like that. (Without saying another word, David placed two letters on the floor in front of Gabe. He placed a red plastic "v" with a yellow plastic "l," which extended the right leg of the "v" at a downward slant. (Gabe shook his head.) (The researcher offered an upper case "Y" and Gabe shook his head.)

Gabe: No.

Regina (E-A, AV-AA): But I'm making it. (Without speaking another word, Regina physically demonstrated the "y" differently from David's demonstration. She placed an "i" at an angle on the left side of an "l" and touching the middle of the "l.")

Gabe: Oh! I get it! Then you put one more stick down. Kind of like a "y."

In this example, Gabe was the learning peer. David demonstrated what Gabe had orally described and drew in the air. I also offered him a capital "Y." Gabe was not satisfied with either suggestion, however. Regina, the more capable peer, demonstrated an acceptable lower case letter. Her use of the "l" emphasized the slant of the right leg of the "y," because the entire right leg of the "y" was one piece. With her demonstration it was not possible to move the lower portion of the right leg to make the letter look like an upper case "Y." Regina's demonstration provided a symbol that matched Gabe's desired letter.

Elaborative gestures accompanying oral language. Closely related to demonstrating is another type of physical interaction, elaborative gestures accompanying oral language. These were not gestures that stood on their own, such as waving farewell, nor purposeful voiceless demonstrations as described above. Instead they were hand gestures that students used to elaborate on the oral language they used. The elaborative gestures allowed students to provide a visual representation of what they were mediating for their learning peers.

One example of elaborative gestures occurred in early November when students were studying the solar system. During an interactive writing session, Gabe was clarifying an idea for the group, and he used his hands to elaborate on his description of the orbiting process:

Gabe (M-A, AB, AV-AV): The earth. I mean the moon. It moves around it. And then the earth it goes around the sun. (As he spoke, Gabe used both hands to elaborate the moon's orbit around the earth. First he extended the index finger of his right hand and made a circular path around his left fist. Then he put his right hand in his lap and moved the left fist in a larger circular path around an imaginary sun while he described the Earth's orbit.)

Ms. Grace: So, the moon goes around the Earth. But the Earth goes around
. . .

Clifton (A-A, LA-LA): The moon.

Gabe: Sun (again holding up his fist).

In this instance, Gabe explained scientific concepts to the group. He used the word "around" to describe both the moon's orbit around Earth and Earth's orbit around the sun. The gestures he used to accompany his verbal description elaborated on the relative sizes of the bodies and on the relative sizes of the orbits.

Vocal Pacing

The second theme, vocal pacing, is a term that emerged from the data. First graders' vocal pacing differed from what Ms. Grace modeled when students read jointly during shared reading, guided reading, and at learning centers. In this study, reading jointly means two or more individuals reading the same text together. In all reading settings, the more capable peers' voices remained distinctly audible; however, at learning centers, more capable peers adjusted the pace of reading and the amount of expression they used depending on their learning peer's capabilities.

Four distinct vocal patterns demonstrated individual participant's varying capabilities with the text. These vocal patterns are mumble reading, echo reading, shadow reading, and choral reading. All four patterns are similar to what many listeners experience when a new song catches their attention on the radio. When they hear the song for the first time, many listeners begin mumbling along the second or third time the chorus is sung. The mumbling is more than mere humming but distinct words are not evident. The next time they hear the song, many listeners remember some of the words but not necessarily at the exact time the performer is singing them. They echo words or phrases that stand out in importance. Echoing, in this instance, is singing complete words but about half a beat or longer after the performer. The next pattern is when listeners become more familiar with the song or parts of the song. At this point many listeners sing along as a shadow. As the performer begins each word, the initial sound triggers the memory of what the word is supposed to be, and the listener finishes the word with the performer. Finally, when the song is learned, many listeners sing along, word for word, much like multiple voices singing the same part in a chorale.

Participants repeated these four vocal patterns daily, with the more capable peer taking the role of the "singer" and the learning peer taking the role of the radio listener. More capable peers adjusted their pace and inflection depending on the vocal pattern that the learning peer exhibited at any given point in a text (see Table 1 for a summary of vocal patterns).

Four distinct vocal patterns emerged from the data: (a) mumble reading, (b) echo reading, (c) shadow reading, (emic codes), and (d) choral reading (etic code). Each pattern demonstrated the more capable peer's and learning peer's varying capabilities with a given text. Although the following examples illustrate a single pattern, it is important to note that the dyads switched among patterns as a learning peer's need arose or capability was demonstrated.

Mumble reading. Mumble reading refers to a learning peer's attempts at oral reading. During mumble reading, students sat side by side with the more capable peer holding the book. When learning peers demonstrated mumble reading, more capable peers read much like a conventional reader. For example, one day in the library center, Thomas (M-A, PB, AV-AA) exclaimed, "This book is too hard!" expressing his dissatisfaction with his book choice, *Hunky Dory Ate It* (Evans, 1989). Celia (M-A, AB, AA-AD), the more capable peer, sat on the floor next to him and offered to read it with him. She held the book on her lap as he looked on, and she began pointing to each word as she read orally. Her inflection and phrasing were like an adult would read the book. When Thomas made no sounds she looked at him and said, "You have to read it, too." He began mumble reading as she continued reading the text. Each time his voice became silent, Celia stopped, marked her place with her finger, and looked at him. She resumed reading whenever his voice was audible. Her purpose appeared to be to help him read, not to read the book to him. It did not matter that he was not reading words that matched the ones that she read. His mumbling satisfied her demand that he "read it, too." Mumble reading called for the more capable peer to model oral reading in a conventional way.

Echo reading. During echo reading, students sat side by side with self-selected partners. The more capable peer pointed at the word, read the word, and then paused. During the pause the more capable peer often turned and looked at the learning peer's face while the learning peer echoed the word. When the learning peer repeated the word, the more capable peer looked back at the text and moved his or her finger to the next word to continue reading. For example, at the buddy reading center, Regina (E-A, AV-AA) and Sally (E-A, LA-BL) read a poem from a big book they frequently chose during buddy reading. Regina led the reading as the more capable peer. The actual text read, "When I grow up, I plan to keep eleven cats." As the girls read, Regina adjusted the pace for Sally:

Table 1

Summary of Vocal Pacing

Vocal Patterns	More Capable Peer	Learning Peer
Mumble reading	Models the pacing and expression of conventional reading.	Audible noise, but no distinctly audible words. Attempting the rhythm of the text.
Echo Reading	Points to words in text. Reads with a broken pace. Reads whole words, one at a time, or reads short phrases, pausing for peer. Flat expression.	Repeats single words or short phrases read by more capable peer. Flat expression.
Shadow Reading	Points to words in text. Attempts conventional phrasing. Slows the pace, drawing out initial sounds to allow learning peer to join in. Attempts expression.	Joins in as soon as he or she realizes what the word is. Dependent on more capable peer's isolating initial sound of word.
Choral Reading	No discernible differences between peers.	No discernible differences between peers.

Regina and Sally (reading together with Regina pointing): When I grow up,
　　　I . . .
Sally:　　want (pause followed by a sigh)
Regina:　Plan. (pause)
　　　　(Sally takes a deep breath and holds it for a second. Regina moves the
　　　　pencil that serves as a pointer back to the beginning of the text.)
Regina:　When I grow up, I plan
Sally:　　Plan
Regina:　to
Sally:　　to
Regina:　keep
Sally:　　to keep

Although the girls began by reading the poem together, Sally miscued by substituting "want" for "plan." This miscue was consistent with many first graders' use of the phrase, "When I grow up I want to be . . ." Sally's sigh and pause indicate that she realized the printed word did not match the word she said. Although she miscued a word that would likely make sense, she knew the sounds for her word, "want" did not match the letters present in the text. Regina then prompted her with the correct word, "plan." Throughout the episode, Regina waited long enough after she read each word to allow Sally time to echo it. She increased the number of words in her first prompt to the entire phrase when Sally did not respond in a timely manner. Then Regina reduced subsequent prompts to single words rather than phrases. In echo reading more capable peers set a pace that focused on recognizing individual words or short phrases, mediating within a learning peer's zone of proximal development. The more capable peer did not attend to reading with expression during echo reading, but read words as if they were separate items on a grocery list. Echo reading called for a pace that broke connected text into individual words and involved peer pointing. Echo reading focused on reading whole words, rather than breaking unknown or unrecognized words into parts.

Shadow reading. During shadow reading, students also sat side by side with the more capable peer pointing to words. When first graders implemented shadow reading, more capable peers modified the pace differently from echo reading. They stretched out the initial sound of each word until the learning peer joined in. When learning peers joined in, sometimes they omitted the initial sound of the words. Sometimes, however, they produced the initial sound after their more capable peers began the word, and then they finished the word together. An example of shadow reading occurred when Julie (M-A, PB, AA-AD), the more capable peer, and Candy (E-A, AA-AD), the learning peer, were reading together at the library center. (In this example, Julie's initiating speech is represented in italics. Sounds that the girls made together are represented in regular type.) "*Da ann*nkle *bbbb*one *connected t*to *d*da *l*leg bone." Candy waited for Julie to begin each word and then joined in as she recognized what the word could be. Shadow reading called for the more capable peer's ability to draw out the pronunciation of the words as the learning peer read. During shadow reading the more capable peer attempted to set a more conventional pace, bridging words within phrases rather than the halting spaces between words that were apparent in echo reading. As this example shows, if the more capable peer's extending the initial sound was not sufficient to trigger the learning peer's recognition of the word, the more capable peer continued reading.

Choral reading. During choral reading it was no longer always possible to determine who was the more capable peer and who was the learning peer. Neither voice was conspicuously audible before the other. Students stated that they took turns pointing. Reading was conventional as evidenced by the pace, inflection, and phrasing.

Conclusions

First graders transferred, modified, and developed mediation strategies to assist their peers' literacy development. Regardless of their linguistic backgrounds, many of the ways in which beginning readers mediated for one another differed from the ways teachers often mediate for children.

First graders in this study used physical interactions as they mediated for their learning peers. The teacher in this setting did not model the use of pointing, except pointing to text during shared reading and guided reading (Clay, 1991). Although Ms. Grace allowed her students to point, she did not model the strategy beyond Clay's recommendations related to concepts of print. Interestingly, all the participants transferred that strategy to independent work as they utilized pointing to words in text as well as modifying the strategy to include pointing across a distance to a reference point to mediate for learning peers. These first graders developed the strategies of demonstrating and elaborative gestures accompanying oral language to compensate for limited oral language development, whether their learning peer's or their own.

Vygotsky's (1978, 1986) descriptions of mediation involve verbal discourse. In this study, first graders' verbal discourse took the form of vocal pacing rather than questions and explanations. As learning peers' zones of proximal development changed, more capable peers were able to alter the pace of reading. With mumble reading, learning peers were attempting the rhythm of language and attending to the meaning of a passage. More capable peers who used this pattern showed that students transferred what their teacher modeled during shared reading to their more private interactions with print. With echo reading, however, more capable peers modified their teacher's practices. Ms. Grace consistently modeled reading of extended phrases in text (e.g., subject phrases, predicate phrases) and lines of poems. All participants who were observed to be more capable peers implemented the echo reading strategy during the study. They modified their teacher's instruction to provide assistance with single words and shorter phrases. Finally, with shadow reading, students developed a mediation strategy no adult in the classroom modeled. More capable peers attempted to maintain the rhythm of the language in a given passage while modifying the pace to allow learning peers to keep up. More capable peers in this study were able to determine which vocal pacing pattern was an appropriate match between their learning peers' abilities and a text. Learning peers provided clues by hesitating or promptly responding, and more capable peers continued with the pace or altered it accordingly.

Vocal pacing patterns (and peer pointing that accompanied their joint reading) which these participants implemented also provide insight, albeit limited, about how these beginning readers demonstrate their understandings of the graphophonic cueing system as they read and reread texts with other beginning readers. Whichever vocal pacing pattern the more capable peer implemented demonstrated some aspect of a whole-to-part-to-whole process. With both mumble reading and echo reading, more capable peers focused on a whole, either a whole passage or whole words. In using these two patterns, more capable peers demonstrated use of strategies such as visual memory (Clay, 1991) and sight words (Ehri, 1991; Juel, 1991). Moreover, they made use of these strategies when learning peers seemed to require the most assistance.

It is with shadow reading that beginning readers demonstrate developing abilities to use phonemic awareness as they isolate initial sounds of words. When more capable peers prompted learning peers with initial sounds, they demonstrated their own abilities to isolate initial sounds and to expect learning peers to make use of initial sounds. When learning peers could match the initial sounds of words to appropriate-meaning words in the given text, they joined in the reading. When learning peers were not able to match the initial sounds to text, more capable peers made an adjustment. They either continued the shadow reading pattern when it was profitable with subsequent words, or they altered the pacing strategy when their learning peers were unable to use the initial sound information for several words in a row. Without modeling or direct instruction in this specific set of strategies, these first graders were able to monitor and adjust their vocal pacing patterns based on learning peers' needs.

This study holds practical significance for primary-grade classroom teachers. Although it may be beneficial to demonstrate some literacy strategies (Baumann & Bergeron, 1993; Fuchs et al., 1997; Palincsar et al., 1993), first graders are able to develop their own strategies to assist one another. They are also capable of assessing the needs of their peers and using a variety of strategies to mediate instruction for one another. Therefore, it is important that classroom organization and instruction allow students the opportunities to assist one another.

References

Baumann, J. F., & Bergeron, B. S. (1993). Story map instruction using children's literature: Effects on first graders' comprehension of central narrative elements. *Journal of Reading Behavior, 25,* 407–437.

Byrne, B., & Fielding-Barnsley, R. (1991). Evaluation of a program to teach phonemic awareness to young children. *Journal of Educational Psychology, 83,* 451–455.

Byrne, B., & Fielding-Barnsley, R. (1993). Evaluation of a program to teach phonemic awareness to young children: A one-year follow-up. *Journal of Educational Psychology, 85,* 104–111.

Clay, M. M. (1991). *Becoming literate: The construction of inner control*. Portsmouth, NH: Heinemann.

Davydov, V. V. (1995). The influence of L. S. Vygotsky on education theory, research, and practice. *Educational Researcher, 24*(3), 12–21.

Ehri, L. C. (1991). Development of the ability to read words. In R. Barr, M. L. Kamil, P. Mosenthal, & P. D. Pearson (Eds.), *Handbook of reading research* (Vol. 2, pp. 383–417). White Plains, NY: Longman.

Evans, K. (1989). *Hunky Dory ate it*. New York: Scholastic.

Fuchs, L. S., Fuchs, D., Mathes, P. G., & Simmons, D. (1997). Peer-assisted learning strategies: Making classrooms more responsive to diversity. *American Educational Research Journal, 34*, 174–206.

Juel, C. (1991). Beginning reading. In R. Barr, M. L. Kamil, P. Mosenthal, & P. D. Pearson (Eds.), *Handbook of reading research* (Vol. 2, pp. 759–788). White Plains, NY: Longman.

Lincoln, Y. S., & Guba, E. G. (1985). *Naturalistic inquiry*. Beverly Hills, CA: Sage.

Lundberg, I., Frost, J., & Petersen, O. (1988). Effects of an extensive program for stimulating phonological awareness in preschool children. *Reading Research Quarterly, 23*, 263–284.

MacGillivray, L., & Hawes, S. (1994). "I don't know what I'm doing-they all start with *B*": First graders negotiate peer reading interactions. *Reading Teacher, 48*, 210–217.

Palincsar, A. S., Brown, A. L., & Campione, J. C. (1993). First-grade dialogues for knowledge acquisition and use. In E. A. Forman, N. Minick, & C. A. Stone (Eds.), *Contexts for learning: Sociocultural dynamics in children's development*. New York: Oxford University Press.

Stahl, S. A., & Murray, B. A. (1994). Defining phonological awareness and its relationship to early reading. *Journal of Educational Psychology, 86*, 221–234.

Strauss, A. (1987). *Qualitative analysis for social scientists*. New York: Cambridge University Press.

Vygotsky, L. S. (1978). *Mind in society: The development of higher psychological processes*. Cambridge, MA: Harvard University Press.

Vygotsky, L. S. (1986). *Thought and language*. Cambridge, MA: MIT Press.

Wertsch, J. V. (1990). The voice of rationality in a sociocultural approach to mind. In L. C. Moll (Ed.), *Vygotsky and education: Instructional implications and applications of sociohistorical psychology* (pp. 111–126). New York: Cambridge University Press.

Wertsch, J. V. (1991). *Voices of the mind: A Sociocultural approach to mediated action*. Cambridge, MA: Harvard University Press.

Wertsch, J. V., & Toma, C. (1995). Discourse and learning in the classroom: A sociocultural approach. In L. P. Steffe & J. Gale (Eds.), *Constructivism in education* (pp. 159–174). Hillsdale, NJ: Erlbaum.

Integration of Academic Content Learning and Academic Literacy Skills Development of L2 Students: A Case Study of an ESL Science Class

Jingzi Huang
Monmouth University

This paper reports on a classroom action research study. It takes the view of "language socialization" (Schieffelin & Ochs, 1986) to investigate the relationship between academic content learning and literacy skills development of secondary English as a Second Language (ESL) students. Two aspects of the study are addressed in the paper. First, the relationship between linguistic skills and content knowledge is examined through discourse analysis of written texts produced by students. Second, the role of classroom instruction in integrating language and content learning is investigated from a constructivist perspective through analyzing classroom interaction and comparing student written discourse produced at different learning stages. The paper argues for the legitimacy and feasibility of integrating literacy in a content-based language program.

With "recognition of the central role of language in education, not only as a subject in the curriculum, but also as the medium in which the learning and teaching of all subjects is actually carried out" (Wells, 1997), studies in language education (Cummins, 1984; Early, Mohan, & Hooper, 1989; Mohan, 1986; Swain, 1988) have advocated the integration of language and content learning. This reflects a functional linguistic view toward language and language learning in which all language is seen as occurring in a social context. Vocal and verbal activities are socially organized and embedded in cultural systems of meaning (Bauman & Sherzer, 1974; Gumperz & Hymes, 1972). Language learning is closely related to learning about the world or learning through language (Halliday & Hasan, 1985), and it is important to examine the relationship between language learning and learning through language.

Language socialization refers to a sociocultural framework for language acquisition that incorporates linguistic knowledge, sociocultural knowledge and activity. Within this framework, classroom language activities are viewed as language practices that are "partially engendered by grammatical, discourse, sociocultural, and general cognitive structures" (Ochs, 1988, p. 17) and that are used to "create . . . and recreate . . . knowledge" (p. 16).

From the perspective of language socialization, a second-language program should facilitate the integration of content and language learning through carefully designed activities. Research has examined how integration can systematically take place (Early, 1990; Huang, 1996; Mohan, 1986) in classroom settings. A

National Reading Conference Yearbook, 49, pp. 392–000.

question that remains is how the teaching and learning of academic content knowledge is related to and interacts with the teaching and development of academic writing skills.

Many studies have addressed the relationship of literacy development and academic achievement (Black, 1998; Coleman, 1997; Coulson, 1996). However, literacy instruction and content teaching remain as two separate enterprises (Newell, 1998). The writing-to-learn and writing across the curriculum movements have had little impact on secondary schools. Moreover, there have been few empirical investigations examining the relations between academic writing and learning in the content areas, especially at the secondary level. Few studies have addressed the issue of how the learning of new registers (Halliday, 1985) and relevant subject content knowledge can be specifically integrated through classroom instruction. Since "writing activities offer something unique to specific academic subjects" (Newell, 1998, p. 178), it is important to study how writing activities play a role in content learning. And it is equally important to study how the learning of specific subject area content affects students' writing performance.

Method

This research is a qualitative, 5-week case study of a secondary, ESL science class for new immigrants in western Canada. The questions that guided the study were: (a) How are sophistication in writing and content knowledge interrelated and interdependent in ESL students' science writing? and (b) How can classroom instruction facilitate the integration of the two in a content-based language program? To investigate the relationship between the students' writing skills and content knowledge, a functional approach (Halliday, 1985; Martin, 1992; Mohan, 1986) was adopted to analyze discourse data from student written work. To address the issue of the role played by classroom instruction, the instructional processes that lead to the learning product were analyzed.

Data were collected in a secondary school where more than 50% of the student population is ESL. The school is located in a fast-developing city where the population of new immigrants, especially those from Hong Kong, is growing at an increasing speed. How to benefit the ESL students linguistically, cognitively, and academically has become the major task of educational programs in the system.

According to the ESL policy of the school district, all ESL students are annually evaluated for English proficiency to determine how much ESL support to provide for the following year. Based on the evaluation, one of the five levels, ranging from Level 1 indicating the lowest English abilities to Level 5 indicating the abilities approximating to native speakers of English, is assigned to each student. During the year of the study, content courses are offered to students at different ESL levels.

Two ESL science classes with a mixture of 23 Level 2 and 12 Level 3 students from Grade 8 to Grade 10 were involved in the study. There were roughly equal numbers of male and female students in the classes. Among the total of 35 students, 25 were from Hong Kong, 4 from Taiwan, 2 from Mexico, 2 from India, 1 from

Israel, and 1 from South Korea. Cantonese, which was spoken by 24 students, was the first language of the majority in both classes. The rest of the primary languages spoken by the students were Mandarin (5), Spanish (2), Punjab (2), Korean (1), and Hebrew (1). At Levels 2 and 3, most of the students had the abilities to communicate in English with Basic Interpersonal Communicative Skills (Cummins, 1983, 1984), though with variation in both fluency and accuracy. But in terms of Cognitive-Academic Language Proficiency (Cummins, 1983, 1984), they still had to struggle tremendously.

The researcher was the teacher of the course. As a bilingual Canadian immigrant who had been in Canada for 8 years, she had the advantage of understanding the students' difficulties in terms of linguistic and cultural barriers as she had "been there, done that." She was fully aware of the frustration caused by the huge gap between the students' limited English language proficiency and their high cognitive capabilities. As an ESL Science teacher, she was responsible for choosing the teaching/learning materials, designing lessons, giving instructions, and establishing criteria for evaluation. The teaching approach, which was based on the Knowledge Framework (Mohan, 1986), was carefully chosen to facilitate the students' language acquisition, content learning, and cognitive development.

Data Collection

The data were collected during 5 weeks of instruction. The teacher organized lessons for the *Composition of Matter* unit from an ESL science textbook, designed student tasks using graphic representations to mediate between language and content. Lesson plans were considered to be part of the data as it could help address questions of the role of classroom instruction. Field notes were taken to record content of each lesson, to examine the actual implementation of the lessons. A questionnaire was used to identify student perceptions of the learning process, so as to find out, from the students' perspective, how the understanding of academic content and the writing skills are interrelated and interdependent. Finally, student-teacher interactions and student written work were collected as data for the discourse analysis of the students' understanding of academic content and their writing skills development.

The teacher began by introducing a short reading passage that clearly entails the classification knowledge structure (KS). The message content of the passage is about the classification of matter according to its properties. Using examples from the passage, the teacher conducted a classroom discussion on how English language could be used to classify the information. Several classification trees interpreting the classification structure in the passage were used to help the students understand the message content and the classification relations in the text. A summary of the linguistic device used for classifying was also provided. Following this, students were required to write a classification passage according to the classification tree provided. The students wrote three drafts during the seven lessons. In these lessons, first, the students were asked to work on a first draft following the model text. After the draft was produced, a classroom discussion of the classification concepts and the analysis of the sample student discourse from the first draft were conducted. Through discussion, an agreed-upon understanding of the standards in terms of content and language was established for a second draft. To meet the language and content requirements, students engaged in various activities including class/group discussion, seeking information from different sources while producing the second draft. Finally, a third draft was produced after the second draft was peer-edited against the established standard.

Results

The Relationship Between Writing Quality and Content Knowledge

Knowledge Structure Analysis (Huang, 1996, 1999; Mohan, 1999) was employed to examine the integration of language and content learning. This analysis uses six basic knowledge structures or KSs (i.e., classification, description, principles, sequence, evaluation, choice). However, in this study, only classification will be analyzed. The aim of integrative assessment is supposed to assess language and content together, giving attention to intrinsic relationships between linguistic devices used and content knowledge expressed. Under the content topic *Classification of Matter,* the Knowledge Structure Analysis of students' written discourse, which has its foundation in systemic functional linguistics (Halliday, 1985, 1994), enables the researcher to explicitly evaluate (a) students' knowledge of how matter can be classified, (b) levels of sophistication in the use of the English language to demonstrate their knowledge, and (c) if the semantic relationship of classification is successfully expressed via linguistic devices.

Since the focus of the study is on the learning of the content knowledge and the development of writing skills, the analysis was focused on the first draft and the third draft of students' writing. As in Schleppegrell's (1988) analysis of students' description discourse, the present approach "views students' error within a broader textual context and recognizes the strength that learners bring to particular assignments, rather than focusing on discrete errors in isolation" (p. 183). For each draft, four steps were taken: (a) Introduce a text and identify the KS that it represents; (b) Present a graphic representation of the KS in the text; (c) Specify the main semantic relation or relations that serve to construct the KS in the discourse example; and (d) Identify the key linguistic features that express the knowledge structure in the discourse, with particular attention to reference, transitivity, conjunction, and lexis.

The following pieces of writing from Student 17 are representative of the students' first and third drafts:

Draft 1

All the things in the world are made up of matter. Anything has weight and take up space is matter.

Matter can be classified as organic and inorganic. Organic can be divided into two classes: plants and animals. Inorganic never has life.

Plants are a kind of organic, plants can be classified as bacteria, algae, and seed plants.

There are two categories of animals: vertebrates and invertebrates. Amphibians, birds, reptiles, bony fish and mammals are all classified as vertebrates. Insects are a kind of invertebrates.

Everything we know is made up of matter in organic and inorganic form.

Draft 3

All the things in the world are made up of matter. Anything has weight and takes up space is matter.

Matter can be divided into organic and inorganic. Organic is the thing that has life. Bacteria, birds, insects, mammals are all classified as organic. Inorganic never has life.

Organic can be grouped into two classes: plants and animals. Plant is that any living thing has cell that has cell wall. Trees, shrubs, fungi, algae are plant. Animal is that any living thing has cell that do not has cell wall.

Bacteria, algae, seed plants are classed as plants. Bacteria is diverse group of one-celled micro-organisms found when there is life. Algae is a large group of mainly agnostic, one-celled or multi-celled organisms traditionally are classified as plants. Any plant that bears seeds are seed plants. Animals can divided into two classes: vertebrates and invertebrates. Any animal that has a segmented spiral column is vertebrate. Any animal lacking a backbone is invertebrates.

Amphibians, birds, reptiles, bony fish and mammals are grouped as vertebrates. Amphibians is an animal that can live either on land or in water. A frog is an amphibian. Feathered creatures with two legs and two wings are birds. A cold-blooded animal that creeps or crawls is reptile for example snake. Bony fish is a fish has many bones, it has bones to prop up their body. Mammals is an female animal feeds the young with its own milk. Pigs and cows are mammals. Insects are a kind of invertebrates. Insects is a very small animal usually with three pairs of legs and two pairs of wings. Bee and butterfly are insects.

Everything in the world is made up of matter in organic form and inorganic form.

It is easy to see that the two passages are similar in terms of the KS expressed (i.e., classification of matter according to being organic or inorganic). But there exists obvious variation in both content message conveyed and linguistic sophistication. Graphic representation of the texts as in Figures 1 and 2 explicitly reveal that whereas Draft 1 contains five layers of classification, Draft 3 contains six. The one more layer added to Draft 3 provides some specific examples illustrating different groups of animals. Each draft introduced 16 scientific concepts (boxed items in the graphics), but whereas only two concepts are introduced with definitions in Draft 1, every concept is accompanied by a definition in Draft 3. It seems the use of the definition or explanation of terms and the specific examples illustrating those terms have helped make Draft 3 more elaborated in message content.

This result is significant in that it shows how this approach can address content learning. An understanding of message content is inseparable from an understanding of certain concepts. In school science concepts are fundamental to the learning of principles and are usually introduced in classification discourse. Classification is used to establish basic knowledge in a topic area including showing how things are classified, and to introduce important technical terms and show how these relate to one another (Veel, 1987). In both of these texts, some basic knowledge about matter is demonstrated and terms related to matter are classified. Furthermore, technical terms, such as vertebrates and invertebrates, are introduced and relationship between terms are illustrated.

To address issues of learning and development, I examined depth of understanding. To do this, we must start by looking into students' conceptual knowledge of terms related to *matter*. The capability to explain a concept in terms of class, critical attributes, and examples shows the level of understanding of the concepts. The learning of classification of *matter* is basically the development of conceptual knowledge related to different forms of *matter*. The more accurately a student can express the class-example relations, elaborately describe critical attributes, and specifically provide examples or non-examples, the better conceptual knowledge the student has. Extending the argument to the present study, a comparison of Figures 1 and 2 reveals how the student has progressed in terms of the development of conceptual knowledge. In both drafts, terms are classified. However, only in Draft 3, are extensive definition, description, and specific examples provided.

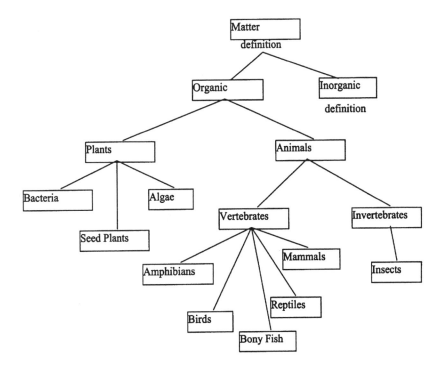

Figure 1. Graphic representation of Draft 1.

The graphics show the KS expressed in the student discourse and the degree of elaboration in terms of content conveyed. The discourse analysis helps reveal the linguistic sophistication of the drafts. Using Knowledge Structure Analysis as an approach to analyze the macro-organization of texts, the researcher investigates the various discourse realizations of a specific KS. A KS is constructed from semantic relations that have a range of linguistic realizations. At this stage, the approach draws upon ethnographic research (Werner & Schoepfle, 1987) and the work of systemic-functional linguistics that categorize linguistic systems such as reference, conjunction, and transitivity (Eggins, 1994; Halliday, 1985, 1994; Martin, 1992). In genre analysis, language systems such as reference and transitivity are analyzed to identify the features of a genre. In Knowledge Structure Analysis, they are analyzed to identify the way in which they convey the semantic macro-organization of a text. In the Knowledge Framework, Classification is used as a broader term to cover taxonomic and part-whole relations (Werner & Schoepfle, 1987. In the discourse examples presented here, the classification relations are represented through both taxonomic (the "is a" relation) and part-whole (the "has a" relation) relations.

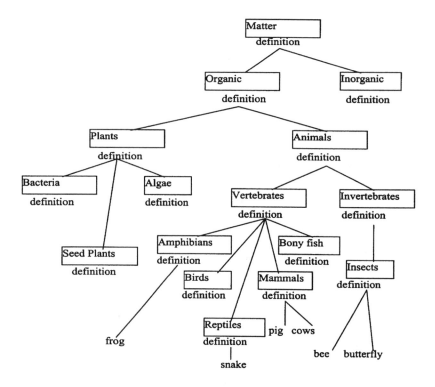

Figure 2. Graphic representation of Draft 3.

Detailed Analysis of Discourse Samples

Reference. Generic reference is identified as a linguistic feature that goes with classification (Christie, 1989; Martin, 1992). In both texts, generic reference helps build classification. So, in Draft 3, "*Anything* [that] has weight and takes up space is *matter.*" Or in Draft 1, "*Amphibians, birds* . . . are all classified as *vertebrates.*" Whereas *anything* is used as a generic reference to a set, *matter, amphibians,* and *birds,* are used as generic references to a subset of matter. Draft 3 used 15 more different generic references than Draft 1.

Transitivity. The "use of transitivity processes, relational ones in particular . . . help build . . . classification" (Christie, 1989, p. 29). Relational process are identified as "those of being" or that "something is" (Halliday, 1985, p. 112). There are two modes (i.e., attributive, identifying) for "those of being," and intensive and possessive ways of being can be particularly identified as linguistic features that realize classification. In both texts, both intensive and possessive ways of being were used. So intensive ways of being ("Anything is matter"), part-whole relations through possessive ways of being ("It has bones"), and certain classification lexis in the forms of verbs ("Plants *can be classified* as bacteria, algae, and seed plants") were all evident in these drafts. But whereas Draft 1 contains five different uses of such relational process transitivity, Draft 3 contains seven.

Conjunction. Both texts contain one kind of conjunction, *and,* which is additive, but Draft 3 shows more occasions of using it.

Lexis: classification. Another means of encoding classification is through vocabulary or word choice, using lexical items that express classification relations. In both drafts, two kinds of lexical realization are obvious. One realization is through the use of a single noun that explicitly entails classification relations, such as kind, class, group, category ("Plants are a *kind* of organic thing"). Both drafts contain three different uses of this kind of lexis. A second lexical realization of classification is through the use of two or more words that are taxonomically related ("*Pigs* and *cows* are *mammals*"). In Draft 3, there are six more such classification lexis than in Draft 1 and all of them are used when specific examples are given to illustrate terms.

Nominal groups. The nominal group is considered a major linguistic feature that realizes the semantic relation of subcategorization: "*a* is a subset of *x.*" This has usually been referred to in the grammar of the nominal group as modification (Halliday, 1985). For elaborated taxonomies, the language operates through the expansion of the noun into a nominal group by premodification. For complex nominalization, there is the postmodification in English. In both drafts, there is a frequent use of nominal groups which helped realize classification relations. But Draft 3 makes much heavier use of nominal groups and usually when a definition is given to a certain term or concept, expansion of a noun into a nominal group through pre- or post-modification is the main device employed ("Everything is made up of *matter in organic and inorganic form*").

Draft 3 is linguistically more sophisticated in the sense that more varied linguistic devices and more kinds of the same linguistic device were used. The texts get richer in generic references, taxonomically related lexis that serve to demonstrate an understanding of class membership between technical terms, and nominalization through modification. It is the elaboration of terms in the student texts that helped make the texts much richer in content.

Although Draft 3 is linguistically more sophisticated, it is also more elaborated in message content expressed. The correlation between sophistication in writing and elaboration of content knowledge expressed further supports the sociocultural view of the interdependence between linguistic skills and sociocultural knowledge.

Relationship Between Instruction and the Integration of Writing and Content Learning

As analyzed above, the improvement in Draft 3 reflects the student's development in a learning process. This development took place as a result of a series of classroom activities. Several steps were taken during the instructional process as summarized in Figure 3.

Matching these steps to student improvements are revealing of the role of classroom instruction. First, modeling appears to be necessary but insufficient to help students learn to write academically. The teacher conducted a classroom discussion to analyze a model classification text, using graphic representations to mediate between language and content. The discussion included what KS was entailed, how message content was elaborated, what linguistic features were used. The example seemed straightforward and the students expressed they understood very well after the discussion. Nevertheless, the first drafts produced by the students lacked elaboration in content and sophistication in language. It was the actual engagement in writing followed by the analysis of one's own writing that enabled the students to move closer to the criterion. The comparison between the model text and students' own writing helped raise the students' awareness of the weaknesses in their own writing.

Second, instruction has to be intentionally organized to integrate content learning and language development so as to enable the students to produce academic writing of higher quality. One of the weaknesses evident in the students' drafts was the lack of definition or explanation of terms. Another problem was the lack of specific examples. To be able to provide accurate definition and relevant examples, one needs to have the relevant knowledge. When the students were invited to define some of the terms, the teacher and students started to realize that the focus first had to be on a better understanding of the terms. For instance, many students defined plants as "any living thing that has leaves, roots, and a soft stem," whereas others used whales as an example of fish. To help the students understand the relevant academic content better, the teacher spent much time having students check in dictionaries and encyclopedia and encourag-

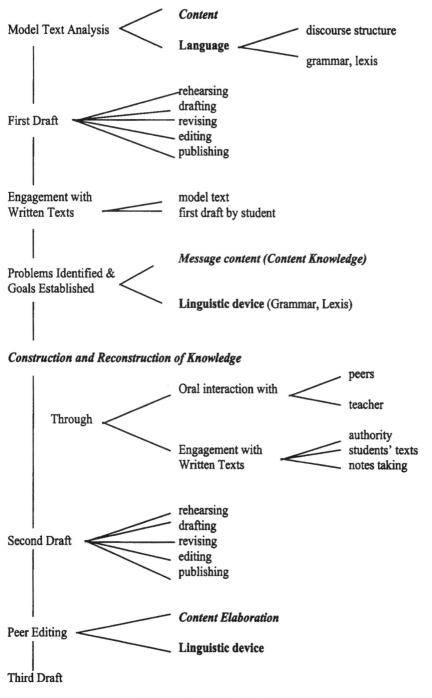

Figure 3. The instructional process.

ing them to use logic to define and exemplify. This resulted in a better understanding of certain scientific concepts.

In addition to engaging with written texts, students also participated "in living traditions and conversation through knowledge in action" (Newell, 1989, p. 198). Certain "knowledge arises out of participation in ongoing conversations about things that matter, conversations that themselves embedded within larger traditions of discourse that we have come to value" (Applebee. 1996, p. 3). The following interaction between the teacher and students illustrates how knowledge constructed or reconstructed in the class discussion.

After a student defined a plant as any living thing that has leaves, roots, and a soft stem, the teacher wrote the definition on the board:

T: Any disagreement?
S: (No answer).
T: Do we agree that all living things can be classified into plants and animals?
S: Yes.
T: So, if a living thing is not an animal, it has to be
S: (Shout) Plants.
T: What do you think a mushroom is?
S: A plant.
T: What is the definition of a plant?
S: It has to have leaves, roots, and a soft stem. Oh, oh! Then mushroom is. . . . But it is not an animal, isn't it?
T: Look at the big tree outside. It does have leaves, roots, but where is its soft stem? . . .

The discussion led to a search for information on the differences between plants and animals. Through search and discussion, the students learned relevant concepts. Conversations were on going and took place among students as well when they worked in groups. For many of them, the searching and discussing played a role of reconstructing the knowledge introduced long time ago. Engagement with written texts and the interactions with the teacher and the fellow students provided an opportunity for students to reconstruct this knowledge.

Although the learning of relevant knowledge does not necessarily enable students to successfully express their knowledge verbally, especially in a language that they are still struggling with, the activity does provide an opportunity for teaching language relevant to student needs. With the writing assignment, writing became a useful medium for practicing the ways of organizing and presenting ideas that are most appropriate to a particular conversational domain within the content area of science (Newell, 1998). Students improved from draft to draft in terms of message content expressed, but they were weak in terms of the use of the English language, a limitation they were well aware of. They actively sought help from the teacher or more capable peers. The result of the process is the students' newly gained or reconstructed knowledge and relatively more successful use of associated linguistic features in many of the students' second and third draft.

Ochs once argued that "the notion of practice or activity is central to an integrated theory of language acquisition" and "language activities are at the same time linguistic and sociocultural phenomena" (Ochs, 1988, p. 17). In this study, the findings support this sociocultural view of literacy development. The students acquire linguistic/literacy skills and scientific knowledge hand in hand as they assume various communicative and social roles within carefully planned language activities. The structures of grammatical discourse and scientific knowledge are created through students' participation in temporarily and spatially situated practices. This indicates that to enable the students to be successful in academic writing, the instruction should be organized to integrate content learning and language development through active engagement with written texts.

Conclusions

This paper reports on a qualitative, 5-week case study of a secondary ESL science class for new immigrants to examine the relationship between academic content learning and writing skills development. The results of the study further support the argument that language and content go hand in hand in the learning process. Sophistication in writing and content knowledge were found to be interrelated and interdependent in science writing. Sophistication in linguistic skills appears to enable elaboration of message content and a better understanding of content knowledge helps produce academic writing of higher quality. Classroom instruction appeared to play an important role in integrating language skills development and academic content learning.

As a 5-week study, it does have limitations. This may be too brief a period to see sufficient growth in language or content knowledge that may be due to instruction or development. Another limitation has to do with its generalizability. Although the study sheds light on the possibilities of the integration of academic content learning and language skills development and further directions for intentional planning, the findings are mainly based on an investigation of the teaching of one content unit involving one KS in one kind of ESL situation. To see how the findings apply in a broader range, studies on the teaching of other content topics in different situations are necessary.

References

Applebee, A. N. (1996). *Curriculum as conversation: Transforming traditions of teaching and learning.* Chicago: University of Chicago Press.

Bauman, R., & Sherzer, J. (1974). *Explorations in the ethnography of speaking.* New York: Cambridge University Press.

Black, M. S. (1998). Keeping the promise. *Journal of curriculum and supervision 13,* 373–379.

Christie, F. (1989). Genres in writing. In F. Christie & J. Rothery (Ed.), *Writing in schools* (pp. 3–48). Victoria, Australia: Deakin University.

Coleman, C. F. (1997). Our students write with accents. *College Composition and Communication 48,* 486–500.

Coulson, A. J. (1996). Schooling and literacy over time. *Research in the Teaching of English, 30,* 311–327.

Cummins, J. (1983). Language proficiency and academic achievement. In J. W. Oller, Jr. (Ed.), *Issues in language testing research* (pp. 321–337). Rowley, MA: Newbury House.

Cummins, J. (1984). *Bilingual and special education.* San Diego, CA: College Hill.

Early, M. (1990). Enabling first and second language learners in the classroom. *Language Arts, 67,* 567–575.

Early, M., Mohan, B., & Hooper, H. (1989). The Vancouver school board language and content project. In J. H. Esling (Eds.), *Multicultural education and policy: ESL in the 1990's* (pp. 107–124). Toronto: OISE Press.

Eggins, S. (1994). *An introduction to systemic functional linguistics.* London: Pinter.

Gumperz, J., & Hymes, D. (1972). *Directions in sociolinguistics: The ethnography of communication.* New York: Holt, Rinehart & Winston.

Halliday, M. A. K. (1985). *An introduction to functional grammar.* London: Edward Arnold.

Halliday, M. A. K. (1994). *An introduction to functional grammar* (2nd ed.). London: Edward Arnold.

Halliday, M. A. K., & Hasan, R. (1985). *Language, context and text.* Geelong, Victoria, Australia: Deakin University.

Huang, J. (1996). *Form-function relations in student discourse contextualized by classroom language activities.* Unpublished doctoral dissertation, University of British Columbia, Vancouver.

Huang, J. (1999, July). *Using KSA as a discourse analysis approach to study student's written discourse in science.* Paper presented at the meeting of the International Systemic Functional Congress 99, Singapore.

Martin, J. (1992). *English text.* Philadelphia: John Benjamins.

Martin, N. (1992). Language across the curriculum: Where it began and what it promises. In A. Herrington & C. Moran (Eds.), *Writing, teaching, and learning in the disciplines* (pp. 6–21). New York: Modern Language Association of America.

Mohan, B. (1986). *Language and content.* Reading, MA:Addison-Wesley.

Mohan, B. (1999, July). *Evaluating causal discourse.* Paper presented at the meeting of the International Systemic Functional Congress, Singapore.

Newell, G. E. (1998). "How much are we the wiser?": Continuity and change in writing and learning in the content areas. In N. Nelson & R. C. Calfee (Eds.), *The reading-writing connection.* Ninety-seventh yearbook of the National Society for the Study of Education (Pt. 2, pp. 178–202). Chicago: National Society for the Study of Education.

Ochs, E. (1988). *Cultural and language development.* Cambridge, England: Cambridge University Press.

Schieffelin, B. B., & Ochs, E. (1986). Language socialization. In B. Siegel (Eds.), *Annual review of anthropology* (pp. 163–191). Palo Alto, CA: Annual Reviews.

Schleppegrell, M. J. (1998). Grammar as resource: Writing a description. *Research in the Teaching of English, 32,* 182–211.

Swain, M. (1988). Manipulating and complementing content teaching to maximize second language learning. *TESL Canada Journal 6*(1), 68–84.

Veel, R. (1987). *Exploring literacy in school science.* Syndey: New South Wales Department of School Education.

Wells, G (1996). Making meaning with text: A genetic approach to the mediating role of writing in activity. *Dialogic Inquiry: Towards a Sociocultural Practice and Theory of Education.* Cambridge, England: Cambridge University Press.

Wells, G. (1997, November). *Dialogic inquiry in education: Building on Vygotsky's legacy.* Paper presented at the meeting of the National Council of Teachers of English, Detroit, MI.

Werner, O., & Schoepfle, G. M. (1987). *Systematic fieldwork.* Beverly Hills, CA: Sage.

Constructing Achievement Orientations Toward Literacy: An Analysis of Sociocultural Activity in Latino Home and Community Contexts

Lilia Monzó and Robert Rueda

University of Southern California

T eachers are interested in motivating students to read, especially diverse learners (Snow, Burns, & Griffin, 1998). Teachers often believe minority children lack the motivation to engage in academic tasks (Heath, 1983; Valdez, 1996). Parents are often blamed for lacking interest in their children's schooling (Valencia, 1997). Recent works suggest that these contentions can be challenged (Delgado-Gaitan & Trueba, 1991; Vasquez, Pease-Alvarez, & Shannon, 1994). Latino families have been found to place a high value on formal education and to believe that schooling is the main avenue for social and economic mobility (Goldenberg & Gallimore 1995).

In part, misunderstandings over motivation and achievement orientations can be explained by how these constructs have been conceptualized. Dominant theories view motivational processes as occurring inside the individual. This approach fails to recognize that sociocultural and historical factors shape the context within which individuals act. From a sociocultural approach, motivation and behavior are created and displayed in interactions between the individual and the environment in specific contexts (Rueda & Moll, 1994).

In this paper we examine how achievement orientations toward schooling and literacy are constructed in the home and community contexts of five low-income Latino families. We begin with a brief theoretical discussion of motivation and how our study was guided.

A Theoretical Discussion of Motivation and Reading Engagement

Task engagement is often discussed as the observable manifestation of achievement motivation. Sometimes, it is identified by on-task behavior and completion of activities. More recently, cognitive-oriented researchers argue that an engaged reader is one who is motivated, knowledgeable, strategic, and socially interactive (Gambrell, 1996; Guthrie & Wigfield, 2000). This involves actively thinking about the task, but students may act engaged while paying little attention to the task.

Defining and assessing such constructs with diverse learners is quite complicated. The way interest and motivation are displayed is culturally defined (Sivan, 1986). Vasquez et al. (1994) document how one child, utilizing his classmates as

*National Reading Conference Yearbook, **49**, pp. 405–420.*

learning resources—a common activity among the Mexicano families they studied—was reprimanded for walking around the classroom. The teacher did not understand that the child was displaying elements of task engagement by seeking knowledge and verification from his peers. Not surprisingly, existing theories attempting to explain motivational processes have not been very successful with respect to ethnic minorities (Rueda & Dembo, 1995; Rueda & Moll, 1994).

Cognitive Contributions

Dominant theories of motivation emerge from a cognitive perspective conceptualizing motivation as individual cognitive processes (for a review, see Covington, 1998). These have provided important insights into the factors that produce achievement motivation. These have been divided into three main components: (a) The students' goals and values related to the task or "Why am I doing the task?" (b) The students' self efficacy in relation to the task or "Can I do the task?", and (c) An affective component, "How do I feel about the task?" (Wigfield, 1997).

Thus, a cognitive approach proposes a relationship between beliefs, attitudes, and values as mediators of task engagement (Eccles, Wigfield, & Schiefele, 1998). Reading motivation is defined as "the individual's personal goals, values, and beliefs with regard to the topics, processes, and outcomes of reading" (Guthrie & Wigfield, 2000, p. 3). Reading engagement requires not only being motivated to read but having the conceptual knowledge needed to make sense of the text and effectively using strategies that facilitate understanding the text (Guthrie, 1996). In addition, a number of authors discuss the social aspects of engaged reading, suggesting that reading engagement involves talking about the task with others (Rowe, 1989).

Although these theories have proven helpful in explaining motivational processes in many children, they have proven less useful with respect to ethnically diverse students. The problems stem from a neglect of the cultural and historical forces that shape attitudes, beliefs, and goals and from the focus on the individual exclusive of related sociocultural factors.

A Sociocultural Approach

A sociocultural approach defines learning and development as culturally, historically, and socially mediated processes (Vygotsky, 1987; Wertsch, 1998). Although this approach has mostly been used to explain learning and cognitive activity, a few authors (Rueda & Dembo, 1995; Rueda & Moll, 1994; Sivan, 1986) have begun to apply it to affective processes such as motivation. Because activity is socially mediated, motivation does not take place in the mind of the individual, but rather is produced in social interaction.

These interactions are shaped by the context in which they take place and the sociocultural and historical nature of that context. Contextual features (operationalized as the activity setting or the who, what, when, where, why, and how) are products of sociocultural and historical forces that play an equally important role in the activity and in the interactions that take place through participation. Contexts shift from moment to moment as particular features of an activity setting change. Minority children have often been found to perform differently within different contexts even when each context requires similar skills (Heath, 1983). From this perspective, research on motivation requires observation of participation in action and consideration of the features of the context that produce the behavior.

Rogoff (1995) points out that the analysis of sociocultural phenomena incorporates three interrelated levels: the individual, the interpersonal, and the community. She suggests foregrounding these separately at times in order to facilitate analysis although they can never be considered in isolation. This framework has guided our efforts to understand how achievement motivation is produced in and out of school contexts.

Our study examined activities in home and community contexts that produced engagement with literacy or fostered a value for schooling and literacy. We were particularly interested in documenting the literacy resources that home and community contexts provide for the children and the messages that these activities carried.

Method

The study from which this paper draws examined the contexts that produce literacy engagement in low-income, Latino children. Twenty-one Spanish-dominant Latino children were observed within classroom, home, and community contexts. The children are students at the neighborhood school of one of the most impoverished, inner city, immigrant communities in Southern California. Many of the parents in our study work in the garment industry. Some earn minimum wage in these positions, but many are paid by piece and tend to earn much lower wages. All of the parents in the study are immigrants to this country and speak little or no English. Some are undocumented. All of the children were born in the United States and vary in levels of English proficiency.

Researcher Roles

As Latinos, we shared common cultural and linguistic points of reference with the families. This was crucial in gaining access to families. The researchers (bilingual Latino doctoral students) who conducted the ethnographic work often developed personal relationships with the families. Mothers often shared personal information with them and sought instrumental knowledge regarding schooling. Reciprocity was an important element in these relationships. Researchers also shared information and experiences of their own with families. While insiders in some ways, our roles as researchers also made us outsiders among the families.

We came into the project with a strong personal conviction that Latino families and communities offer important resources for learning. These convictions have been strengthened by the work of others on Latino families (Delgado-Gaitan

& Trueba, 1991; Valdez, 1996). Concerns over possible bias were minimized through descriptive data collection and consistent reflection and discussion throughout all phases of the study among the research team.

The Families

For this paper we draw primarily from data on five families: Las familias Corral, Velarde, Torres, Arellano, and Guerra. These families were targeted for greater depth in our observations of their interactions in their home and community for two reasons: (a) the mothers developed a good rapport with the research assistants that visited them which allowed for multiple visits and (b) they represented a range of important factors that we were finding among the larger sample. Table 1 provides demographic information on each family.

Table 1

Family Characteristics

Family	Parents' Birthplace	Parents' Occupation	Immigration Status	Children (Ages)	TC* Grade
Corral					
Mother	Mexico	Garment worker	Undocumented	Alisa (9)* Marisol (1)	1st
Velarde					
Mother	Mexico	Garment Worker	Undocumented	Ramón (17) Carmen (10)*	2nd
Father	Mexico	Garment worker	Undocumented	Raul (6)	
Torres					
Mother	Mexico	Garment worker	U.S. citizen	Juan (20) Lupita (9)*	1st
Father	Mexico	Dairy Packing	Permanent resident		
Arellano					
Mother	Mexico	Garment worker	Undocumented	Ricardo (9)* Veronica (6)	2nd
Father	Mexico	Demolition company	Permanent resident		
Guerra					
Mother	Mexico	Garment worker	Permanent resident	María (22) Antonio (15) Marta (13)	1st
Father	Mexico	Parking attendant	U.S. citizen	Clara (10) Carmela (9)*	

*Target Child (TC).

Data Sources

Data were collected during a 2-year period through weekly classroom observations, grade reports, interviews with teachers regarding children's reading engagement and families' involvement with school, and a focus group with teachers and another with parents exploring factors impacting reading. In addition, the "Student Motivation to Read Profile" (SMRP) (Gambrell, Palmer, Codling, & Mazzoni, 1996) measuring reading self concept and value in reading was administered to each student in the language they were most proficient. Teachers completed the "Teacher Perception of Student Motivation to Read" (Sweet, 1997) for each child.

Data collection for the five families also included ethnographic data gathered through participant observation within the home (dinner, homework) as well as in the community (visiting library, doctor's appointments). The focus of observation was on practices and interactions revealing beliefs and values on education and literacy. Generally, visits lasted approximately 3 hours. Fieldnotes were taken immediately upon leaving the site. The Corral, the Velarde, and the Guerra families were each visited seven times. The Arellano family was visited eight times. The Torres family was most accessible and was observed an average of once per week for over a year. Whereas our extended study of the Torres family gave us greater depth and detail than we were able to obtain with the other families, it was encouraging to find that the later data did not reveal conceptual inconsistencies with the earlier data.

Data Analysis

The quantitative measures were scored according to published scoring procedures. The qualitative data were analyzed using a grounded approach. The initial theme of "constructing values for literacy and schooling" developed through discussions of findings among the research team. The data were then coded with respect to this broad category and later divided into subcategories. The second theme developed as we noted the children beginning to differentiate themselves with respect to reading performance and interest in school-like literacy tasks at home. Because of this observation, we developed a number of case studies of the different families. Two of these are contrasted here. The final section on parental strategies to motivate their children emerged directly from the data by clustering related themes.

Constructing Values for Schooling and Literacy

We found that families' daily routines, the typical activities in which they engaged and the conversations they had with children and with others in the presence of children, offered rich contexts within which values for schooling and literacy were constructed.

Parents' Aspirations

Parents had high educational aspirations for their children. All wanted their children to go *"lo más que se pueda, que sea alguien"* (as far as possible, to be somebody). Parents had received little schooling as youngsters and believed this to be the cause of their low economic security. These high aspirations often translated into high expectations. All parents believed that their children would benefit from the educational system in the United States and often compared it to that in their home countries. As one parent put it, *"Es un crimen que aquí hay tantos niños que no aprovechan de todos los beneficios que tienen en las escuelas"* (It's a crime that there are so many children that don't take advantage of the benefits they have in school).

Central Role of Schools

Children's schooling played a central role in each of the households. This was evident in the many activities that centered around schooling, from the daily routine of taking children to school and making sure they completed homework assignments to discussions of school activities and listening to stories children brought home about their experiences, their teachers, and their classmates.

Parent-child discussions about future career goals were common among all families as well. Parents often boasted with respect to what their children wanted to be when they grew up, indicating their interest in such topics. One example is of Alisa who was asked what she wanted to be and responded *"cantante"* (singer). Her mother's live-in partner asked *"¿No te gustaría ser abogada o doctora?"* (Wouldn't you like to be a lawyer or a doctor?) Her mother added, *"¿No que siempre decías que querías ser maestra?"* (Didn't you always say you wanted to be a teacher?)

As in the above example, parents did not just leave questions regarding career goals up to children. They often proposed career goals. These tended to be professional goals and carried respect within the community, such as teacher and doctor. With children and parents' talk centering on education, children were constantly immersed in an environment in which they constructed a value for schooling.

The Need for Literacy

Generally in the home context, language and literacy were functional tools used to accomplish a task or gain needed knowledge. Common literacy activities involved documents and forms that needed to be interpreted or filled out, reading and writing letters from relatives in Mexico, and reading labels and signs in the community that guided what they purchased, what they ate, where they went in the community and how they got there.

Although the community is predominantly Latino and diversity is evident in the many businesses that operate and advertise in Spanish (Rueda & MacGillivray, 1999), there was much interaction with English print. This produced much frustration and difficulties for parents with little English. In practically every home the researchers were asked to translate or explain documents.

As children gain English literacy their role within the family often becomes crucial (McQuillan & Tse, 1995). For instance, during a time, Lupita was seeing a medical specialist who did not speak Spanish. Ms. Torres felt frustrated because her questions often went unanswered. Lupita's English skills were critical on these occasions. Although not fluent enough to handle more complex interactions she was able to meet basic communication needs. Managing affairs within this English culture was something all families struggled with consistently.

We observed that as children encountered the need to negotiate print to achieve daily tasks, such as ordering from menus, reading labels and signs to orient their behavior, they had many opportunities to see the importance of becoming literate. Especially salient was the observation that as they saw their parents struggle due to difficulties with English language and literacy skills, these needs became that much more obvious.

Not surprisingly, parents understood first hand the need for English literacy and expressed to us repeatedly their desire for their children to learn to speak, read, and write in English. The children also expressed a strong belief in the need for literacy, reporting in the motivation to read survey that "Knowing how to read well is important" (Ricardo, Alisa) and "very important" (Carmen, Lupita, Carmela).

We found this telling in light of the popular notion that children in bilingual education programs do not develop the motivation to learn English. English is sometimes so valued that the value of maintaining Spanish was often obscured to children, as was the case with some of our focal children. The following conversation between the researcher and Alisa took place in her room after about 30 minutes of playing during which time Alisa had spoken only in English even after repeated attempts by the researcher to engage her in Spanish:

RA: How come you are speaking to me only in English? Do you speak to your mom in English?
Alisa: No. She doesn't know English.
RA: How come you're talking to me in English?
Alisa: Because you know English.
RA: I know Spanish too.
Alisa: Yes but you know English too and English is better.

The functional nature of literacy in the home context is distinct from the decontextualized literacy of the classroom. Some children may not recognize what the book-reading and writing activities of the classroom have to do with the daily literacy tasks they encounter outside school. Even though Ricardo and Alisa reported in the SMRP that "knowing how to read well is important," the teachers' responses to the TPQSMR indicate that both rarely engaged with reading and writing activities in the classroom. Indeed, Table 2 shows that the children scored similarly in the value for reading factor regardless of differences in their reading self concepts and in their teachers' perceptions of their reading engagement and performance.

School-like Reading in the Home

Children who have had positive experiences with school literacy activities may be more likely to bring school literacy practices home. Lupita, Carmen, and Carmela described by their teachers as avid readers, felt efficacious with respect to reading. Their responses to the motivation to read survey indicate that they believed themselves to be better readers than their classmates. All three often read for pleasure at home. In contrast Ricardo who indicated that "when I read out loud I am a poor reader," rejects bringing this activity home.

Access to books is another factor in motivating children to read at home. Although the families were demographically similar, we found variance with respect to resources available to the children. Carmela, Carmen, and Lupita all had a collection of books in the home and they also visited and checked out books from the library regularly. Ricardo and Alisa, though, had few books in the home and they did not use the public library.

Instrumental knowledge seemed an important factor contributing to children's access to books at home. Ricardo's and Alisa's parents had little knowledge of the educational system and no family members from whom to access this knowledge. They were unfamiliar with the public library and its use. In contrast, Carmen, Carmela, and Lupita had older siblings who attended U.S. schools and spoke English fluently. These siblings often mediated for families.

Still broader sociopolitical constraints impact access to books. Ricardo and Alisa's primary caretakers are undocumented and do not use the library. They avoid situations that may reveal their legal status. Their fear is not unfounded given the visible role of the Immigration and Naturalization Service in the garment industry where they work and the strong anti-immigrant sentiment in the media. Amidst a sociopolitical environment that views human rights as secondary to political demarcations of power, educational achievement, and motivation cannot be purely explained within individuals. Broader constraints of society must be considered.

Table 2

Comparison of Motivation-to-Read Factors and Performance Measures

| | SMRP* | | | TQSMR** | | |
Children	Value in Reading	Reading Self-Concept	Reading Activity	Reading Autonomy	Social Reading	Reading Grade
Lupita	35	35	3.5	3.0	3.5	A
Carmen	36	29	3.3	3.0	3.5	A
Alisa	33	29	3.0	2.5	2.5	C
Carmela	36	35	3.3	2.8	3.3	A
Ricardo	35	21	2.0	2.0	1.8	F

*Student Motivation to Read Profile (Gambrell et al., 1996).
**Teachers's Questionnaire on Student Motivation to Read, 3rd ed. (Sweet, 1997).

Not surprisingly, Carmela, Carmen, and Lupita regularly read for pleasure at home. In contrast, Ricardo's and Alisa's parents discussed their frustration trying to get them to read in the home. In the case of Alisa, it was particularly clear that lack of books in the home was an important factor. Her teacher describes her as a highly motivated reader in her classroom which contained a large selection of books and a context for "open reading" for students to engage with books in any way they chose.

The teacher tells of an occasion in which families who participated in a family literacy night would receive a free book. Alisa was very interested in obtaining the book and since her mother was out of town she asked repeatedly for details on how to complete the parent form. Although she was told that the form was for parents to fill out, she persisted, completing the form on her own and accepting the invitation. This does not sound like a child who lacks motivation to read. Without access to interesting books at home, even the most motivated reader turns to other activities (Pucci, 1994).

Beyond Mechanics

Children also engaged in nonconventional forms of literacy in the home and community contexts that typically go unrecognized at school. These included the use of billboards and other community markers used for getting around within their community. Children engaged in oral activities with their families. They often shared stories about school, retold stories told to them by teachers, and told jokes. The Guerra family sometimes engaged in discussions about political issues as they watched the news in the evenings. The children showed great enthusiasm in these types of nonconventional literacy activities.

Diversity in Sociocultural Contexts Among Families

The value parents placed on schooling was evident in the sacrifices they made to ensure what they believed to be the best education for their children. Although demographically similar, each family had unique circumstances that impacted the ways they supported their children's schooling. Here we attempt to show how activities and interactions are shaped by each family's unique sociocultural experience and how they provide a context for valuing education. We stress that within each family we found rich contexts for literacy learning and motivation but our emphasis here is on the constraints and affordances provided with respect to the types of literacies valued in schools. We contrast two families to illustrate this.

The Torres Family

Mr. and Ms. Torres have two children, Juan, who lives at home and attends a state college, and the focal child, Lupita. They have lived in the United States, in the same apartment, for nearly 20 years. Both earned minimum wage in nearby garment factories, but Ms. Torres was laid off from work during the first year of the study. The family lives in a small one-room apartment. A temporary cardboard divider and a curtain separate the room in two, making a small bedroom and a small living room area.

Mr. Torres's experience entering the work force at an early age has given rise to the belief that working distracts from education and that wages make immediate gratification more attractive to youngsters than the long-term benefits of education. Mr. and Ms. Torres discourage their son from seeking employment to assist the family. This is a topic discussed often in the household and makes clear that education is a primary goal.

When Juan took late evening classes at the university, the family would insist on picking him up in their car because riding the bus home at a late hour would be dangerous. Although this was difficult after a day at work, the family took pride in supporting their son this way. When the 2-hour bus ride to and from campus began to weigh heavily on Juan, they purchased a used car with their savings. When they learned of the sometimes 2-hour waits to access a computer on campus, they purchased one on credit.

Achievement motivation is not all it takes to succeed. Real constraints exist and these limit opportunities too. These major purchases of car and computer and Ms. Torres's lay off from work required a very restricted household budget. This financial situation was exacerbated when Mr. Torres was fired from his job of 20 years over a disagreement with his boss. The anxiety that this loss of employment created was immediate and serious. Juan announced that he would be enrolling the following semester at the junior college rather than continuing at the 4-year institution he was attending.

Like the Torres family, the other families also made many adjustments in their daily lives to support their children's education. We believe these adjustments provide contexts in which a value of education and achievement orientations are constructed. Yet even among these demographically similar families we found that some families were better able than others to make these types of adjustments.

The Torres family, for instance, had some knowledge of school, having both received a few years of primary education in Mexico and having had family members who completed high school equivalence in Mexico and a brother who went on to university. Recent employment changes aside, they had maintained a steady, although minimum wage income, for years. Both were also legal residents and had established a strong, although small, social network that served as social support in negotiating within mainstream U.S. culture. Their older son also served as cultural and linguistic broker, provided childcare when needed, and served other important roles in the family. Furthermore, Ms. Torres had made an important contact with a teacher at the school who often mediated for her when she had concerns about her child's education and gave her information and advice regarding how best to support her children with their education.

The Arellanos

The Arellano family's sociocultural experiences offer an important example of the constraints that many families face in operationalizing their value for education. The Arellanos are much younger than the Torres. They come from rural areas in Mexico. Ms. Arellano immigrated without papers at the age of 13 in 1989. Upon her arrival she entered the work force. As is common among undocumented workers, she does not have steady employment but rather has to roam the garment factories on a daily basis to see if they need extra workers. Typically she is paid by the piece, making much less than minimum wage.

Mr. Arellano is a permanent resident thanks to the amnesty act of 1988. He has never attended school and cannot read or write in the conventional sense. He works approximately 12-hour days for a demolition company sometimes earning up to $10 an hour but the work is sporadic and sometimes he is out of work for months at a time. Although he is eligible for citizenship and could secure the legal status of his wife, his lack of conventional literacy impedes this from happening due to the literacy requirements of the citizenship exam.

The family includes Ricardo and his younger sister Veronica. At the time of study they lived in an apartment above a factory that rents out the rooms to different families. A common dining room, kitchen, and bathroom are shared among the families. They had recently moved to this apartment because their room has an added second small room that is used as the children's room. Ms. Arellano indicated that they thought the children were getting too old for the entire family to share the same room.

When their second child was born, the family could not afford to pay childcare for two and, consequently, Ricardo was placed in kindergarten early at the age of 3½. He was placed in an English only class from the start and although Ms. Arellano had signed permitting such placement, she seemed unsure of whether her child had received bilingual instruction. As documented by others (Valdez, 1996) it is not uncommon for non-English speaking parents to not understand about the documents they sign at school. Linguistic and cultural barriers and lack of knowledge about U.S. schools limit parents from making informed decisions about their children's schooling.

At the time of the study, Ricardo was retained in the third grade because he was having difficulty learning to read and had been referred to RSP. Teachers commented that Ricardo was easily distracted and did not participate in class discussions. Ms. Arellano remarked that she tried to get him to read at home but that he never wanted to read. He resisted initial attempts by the research assistant to engage him in reading, participating in the activity with obvious reluctance, rolling his eyes and becoming very quiet. The RSP pull out program to which he was sent daily was a clear indication to him of poor reading skills and his knowledge of this was corroborated by his responses in the motivation to read survey in which he indicated being a "poor reader" and reading "not as well as his friends."

It was only as he noted that the reading activity with the researcher was socially interactive, looking at and discussing the pictures and sharing personal stories related to the text, that Ricardo began to relax and enjoy the activity. In response to the researcher's query, he indicated that at school they did not discuss stories in this manner.

The families' lack of instrumental knowledge regarding schooling in the United States became evident as the research assistant attempted to explain some basic information, such as the three tiers in our system: elementary, middle, and high school. Ms. Arellano seemed unaware of the importance of returning homework assignments as she explained that her daughter in kindergarten had received a dissatisfactory note in her report card regarding homework completion. She remarked that she made sure that her daughter did the homework every day and that she spent time helping her, but that they stacked up because they often forgot to return them. From her perspective, homework was a home activity to be monitored by the parent. Completing the assignment was important, whereas returning the assignment was less so given that they were kindergarten-level activities that she could help her daughter learn.

Unlike the Torres family, the Arellanos did not know someone who could provide them with information about school. Often teachers did not speak Spanish and communication between parents and teachers took place only twice a year at formal parent-teacher conferences, during which time interpreters were provided. The Arellano family clearly had less resources available to make their commitment to their children's education work for them.

Parental Strategies That Motivate

Of the five families, the more successful at producing intrinsic motivation to read in a conventional sense were the Velarde and Torres families. Carmen and Lupita often chose to engage in reading and writing at home, even when it was not required homework. In this section we detail four motivational strategies that these parents described.

Modeling

The Velarde family constructs their value for education as they participate in a different set of activities, activities that surround a mother's struggle to better herself educationally. The Velarde family made many adjustments in their home in order to support her night school attendance and her time commitment to study and complete homework assignments. Toward the end of our study these efforts were rewarded as she passed the GED, high school equivalence exam. Ms. Velarde beamed, sharing that her daughter Carmen took her diploma to school for show and tell because she said she was very proud of her mother.

Ms. Torres also models reading engagement for Lupita, often reading in the evening from an old history text that was given away at her daughter's school or from other government books she borrowed from the library to help take the citizenship test. She comments, *"Mas que nada lo hago para que ella se embuye. Yo me siento a leer mis libros y asi ella se sienta y lee sus libros"* (Mostly I do it so that she will become motivated. I sit to read my books and that way she sits and reads her books).

Consejos

Offering *consejos* or advice to their children is another way in which both families support the development of an achievement orientation toward schooling. *Consejos* regarding persistence in education come from parents as well as family members who are presently enrolled in higher education. These family members offer advice in the form of instrumental knowledge as well as offering an important model of academic achievement.

In the Torres family, for example, children are active participants in stories regarding their parents' struggles in the work place. These offer a context within which parents' *consejos* make sense. *"Yo siempre les aconsejo que deben de estudiar para que no tengan que pasar las humillaciones y las verguenzas que se tiene que pasar en estos trabajos"* (I always advise them that they should study so that they don't have to take the humiliations and the embarrassments that you endure in these jobs). Indeed, Ms. Torres found her son a summer job in a tortillería *"para que aprenda lo que es trabajar en un lugar como ese"* (so that he learns what it's like to work in a place like that). This strategy of sharing their struggles at work and promoting schooling as a means to a better life was typical of all five families.

Children are often told stories of the successes that family members or others in the social network have achieved. These successes are attributed to formal schooling and the subsequent well-paying jobs they have secured. This strategy is not available to families in which no one has completed high levels of formal schooling.

Imagining Future Success

Ms. Torres shared that she tries to encourage her son when he complains of being tired of school by encouraging him to imagine his life after completing his university program. *"¡Que ganas tengo de ver a mi muchacho encorbatado, sentado en su escritorio, así grande!"* (I can't wait to see my son with a tie on, sitting at his desk, a big desk!)

Lupita has also begun to visualize herself within a high status role that includes having significant autonomy. She tells us that when she becomes a doctor she will be in her office and will tell her secretary that she will charge her other patients, but that she will not charge her mother. Ms. Torres believes that this is an important way to encourage her children to continue to strive for their educational success.

Advocating on Their Children's Behalf

Although children sometimes faced negative experiences in school, they were encouraged to believe that parents could negotiate on their behalf. The Torres family, for example, tells Lupita that if she feels mistreated or ignored by teacher that she is to immediately tell them so that they, as her parents, can speak on her behalf. Three of the five families shared stories in which they did speak up on their children's behalf. When children see that their parents can successfully mediate for them and make the school system work in their favor, they may develop an internal locus of control, that is they will begin to believe that they have control over their own success or failure.

Indeed for two children this belief was evident in their willingness to question their teachers' actions and to speak to someone regarding these concerns. Lupita the only student entering an English-only class after receiving bilingual instruction, was given a test in Spanish whereas all other students were given the same test in English. Lupita came home upset because she felt she had been discriminated against. Her mother and her older brother immediately went to school to inquire about the incident. They sought information first from the teacher who had become part of their social network and often provided them with important information and support. A teacher told us another example. Carmen had come to tell her in confidence that her family was enduring harsh economic difficulties, and seeking support for her family. "Carmen knows that I keep little snacks. She confided to me that they were eating mostly beans everyday. So together she and I filled a little bag with those snacks and then I made a point during that time to take things like lunchmeat."

Conclusion

The previous discussion suggests that home and community contexts are rich with resources from which an achievement orientation toward schooling and literacy is produced. All families were literate in ways that allowed them to function within their communities, but these forms of literacy are rarely acknowledged within school contexts and are not built upon. Furthermore, the benefits and constraints of their varying levels of conventional reading and writing produced contexts that made the importance of literacy, particularly English literacy, evident to children. Yet clear differences in the extent to which children put these orientations into practice by engaging in activities that foster conventional literacy development are evident and can be traced to the benefits and constraints that vary even among these demographically similar families.

It is also noteworthy that the interactions families have with print are based on real needs that make transparent the function of literacy. The intercultural interactions they have in the community make transparent the need to negotiate the dominant cultural and linguistic norms. These functions are often obscured in classroom activities and may be part of the reason why children often fail to recognize their value. As Lave and Wenger (1991) suggest, the transformation from peripheral participation to full participation in communities of practice require that the cultural practices and their values and goals be transparent and accessible to the novice.

Teachers must access the resources of the home and community contexts to build on the intellectual and practical skills of children developed as they participate in daily household and community activities (Moll & González, 1994). With knowledge of their students' home and community contexts teachers can provide instruction that is contextualized to children's lived experiences, making it relevant for children. Gonzalez and her colleagues (González et al., 1995) have shown that when teachers learn about the home contexts, their perceptions of Latino children and their families change dramatically and deficit orientations are challenged.

Although we have offered some interesting insights into the role of literacy and how its value is constructed within home and community contexts, there is still much research to be done in this area. Future studies that focus on specific literacy contexts within the home and community, such as storytelling, would likely reveal important insights.

References

Covington, M. V. (1998). *The will to learn: A guide for motivating young people.* New York: Cambridge University Press.

Delgado-Gaitan, C., & Trueba, H. T (1991). *Crossing cultural borders: Education for immigrant families in America.* Bristol, PA: Falmer.

Eccles, J. S., Wigfield, J., & Schiefele, U. (1998). Motivation to succeed. In W. Damon (Series Ed.) & N. Eisenberg (Volume Ed.), *Handbook of child psychology* (Vol. 3, 5th ed.; pp. 1017–1095). New York: Wiley.

Gambrell, L. B. (1996). Creating classroom cultures that foster reading motivation. *Reading Teacher, 50,* 14–25.

Gambrell, L. B., Palmer, B. M., Codling, R. M., & Mazzoni, S. (1996). Assessing motivation to read. *Reading Teacher, 49,* 518–533.

Goldenberg, C., & Gallimore, R. (1995). Immigrant Latino parents' values and beliefs about their children's education: Continuities and discontinuities across cultures and generations. *Advances in Motivation and Achievement, 9,* 183–228.

González, N., Moll, L., Tenery, M. F., Rivera, A., Rendon, P., Gonzales, R., & Amanti, C. (1995). Funds of knowledge for teaching in Latino households. *Urban Education, 29,* 443–470.

Guthrie, J. T. (1996). Educational contexts for engagement in literacy. *Reading Teacher, 49,* 432–445.

Guthrie, J. T., & Wigfield, A. (2000). Engagement and motivation in reading. In M. L. Kamil, P. B. Mosenthal, P. D. Pearson, & R. Barr (Eds.), *Handbook on reading research* (Vol. 3, pp. 422–463). Hillsdale, NJ: Erlbaum.

Heath, S. B. (1983). *Ways with words: Language, life, and work in communities and classrooms.* New York: Cambridge University Press.

Lave, J., & Wenger, E. (1991). *Situated learning: Legitimate peripheral participation.* New York: Cambridge University Press.

McQuillan, J., & Tse, L. (1995). Child language brokering in linguistic communities: Effects on cultural interaction, cognition, and literacy. *Language and Education, 9,* 195–215.

Moll, L. C., & González, N. (1994). Lessons from research with language minority students. *Journal of Reading Behavior, 26,* 439–456.

Pucci, S. L. (1994). Supporting Spanish language literacy: Latino children and free reading resources in schools. *Bilingual Research Journal, 18,* 67–82.

Rogoff, B. (1995). Observing sociocultural activity on three planes: Participatory appropriation, guided participation, and apprenticeship. In J. V. Wertsch, P. Del Rio, & A. Alvarez (Eds.), *Sociocultural studies of mind* (pp. 139–164). New York: Cambridge University Press.

Rowe, D. (1989). Author/audience interaction in the preschool: the role of social interaction in literacy learning. *Journal of Reading Behavior, 21,* 311–349.

Rueda, R., & Dembo, M. H. (1995). Motivational processes in learning: A comparative analysis of cognitive and sociocultural frameworks. *Advances in Motivation and Achievement, 9,* 255–289.

Rueda, R., & MacGillivray, L. (1999, December). *Literacy in downtown Los Angeles.* Paper presented at the meeting of the National Reading Conference, Orlando, FL.

Rueda, R., & Moll, L. (1994). A sociocultural perspective on motivation. In H. F. O'Neil & M. Drillings (Eds.), *Motivation: Research and theory.* Hillsdale, NJ: Erlbaum.

Sivan, E. (1986). Motivation in social constructivist theory. *Educational Psychologist, 21,* 209–233.

Snow, C. E., Burns, S. M., & Griffin, P. (Eds.). (1998). *Preventing reading difficulties in young children.* Washington, DC: National Academy Press.

Sweet, A. P. (1997, January). Teacher perceptions of student motivation and their relationship to literacy learning. *NRRC News,* 4–7.

Valdez, G. (1996). *Con respeto: Bridging the distance between culturally diverse families and schools.* New York: Teachers College Press.

Valencia, R. (Ed.). (1997). *The evolution of deficit thinking: Educational thought and practice.* London: Falmer.

Vasquez, O. A., Pease-Alvarez, L., & Shannon, S. M. (1994). *Pushing boundaries: Language and culture in a Mexicano community.* New York: Cambridge University Press.

Vygotsky, L. S. (1987). *L. S. Vygotsky, collected works* (R. Rieber & A. Carton, Eds.; N. Minick, Trans.) (Vol. 1). New York: Plenum. (Original work published 1934)

Wertsch, J. V. (1998). *Mind as action.* New York: Oxford University Press.

Wigfield, A. (1997). Children's motivations for reading and engagement. In J. T. Guthrie & A. Wigfield (Eds.), *Reading engagement: Motivating readers through integrated instruction.* Newark, DE: International Reading Association.

A Case for Exemplary Classroom Instruction: Especially for Students Who Come to School Without the Precursors for Literacy Success

Cathy Collins Block

Texas Christian University

For many years, educators have sought to identify means by which young children can enter the world of literacy with greater ease and success. These studies have lead to a consensus that (a) various reading curricula and philosophical approaches can produce both good and bad results depending on how well they are implemented, (b) a combination of approaches generally produces the best results, and (c) more research is needed to identify instructional approaches for students who come to school without the basic precursors to success in literacy (Allington, Guice, Michelson, Baker, & Li, 1996; Baumann, Hoffman, Moon, & Duffy-Hester, 1998; Block, 2000a; Bond & Dykstra, 1967/1997; Hoffman, McCarthy, Elliott, Bayles, Price, Ferree, & Abbott, 1998; Sacks & Mergendoller, 1997). Such research would enable more educators to provide the basic language, decoding, and comprehension abilities necessary for young children to obtain pleasure from literacy. These precursors include an enriched oral/written vocabulary, phonemic awareness, and strategies for making meaning from text.

Past studies have characterized the archetypal primary-grade teacher as one that "embraces a literature-based perspective, combines trade book reading with the reading of basal anthology selections . . . teaches phonics in the context of literature, so students learn and practice pronouncing words presented in stories, [and] practices a philosophy of disciplined eclecticism" (Baumann et al., 1998, pp. 646–647). In addition, other analyses suggest that highly influential teachers (a) have distinct personal characteristics (i.e., they are risk-takers, energetic, committed, passionate, warm, caring, and flexible), (b) understand learners' potential, (c) possess positive attitudes toward the subject(s) they teach, (d) are concerned about learners' lives, and (e) develop quality-based instructional repertoires. Good teachers also provide individual students with the instruction that they need (Block & Mangieri, 1995a, 1995b, 1996), promote students' high levels of self-esteem (Berliner & Tikunoff, 1976; Medly, 1977), support pupils in their initial attempts to learn new literacy concepts (Block, 1995b, 2000b; Cazden, 1994; Porter & Brophy, 1988); and, maintain high expectations of themselves and their students (Block, 1995a; Erickson, 1993; Leibert, 1991; Ruddell, 1997). Their instructional repertoires include clear purposes and directions (Block, 1993; Good &

*National Reading Conference Yearbook, **49**, pp. 421–440.*

Grouws, 1975; Porter & Brophy, 1988), and teachers do not predominate students' interpretations of what they read (Almasi & O'Flahavan, 1997; Barnes, 1996/1997).

Despite all that has been learned about teaching, studies have not provided understanding of how effective teachers differ from less effective ones or how they create highly effective literacy programs for students who enter first grade without the necessary precursors for literacy success. The purpose of this study was to provide a detailed analysis of more versus less effective Grade 1 literacy instruction that significantly increased less able readers' achievement. The specific questions asked were: What beliefs and instructional actions distinguish exemplary from typical first-grade teachers? How do exemplary teachers transform a basic curriculum into one that meets the needs of students who do not enter first grade with the precursors for literacy success? Such research holds promise to uncover the artful, informed, and instantaneous interactions that are at the core of good teaching.

This study focused on the power of the teacher to contribute to literacy growth for less prepared beginning readers. This focus does not minimize the belief that students play an active role in the construction of their own literacy (Vygotsky, 1967; Wertsch, 1991). What students do, however, does depend greatly on the instruction they receive; the classroom context driven by their teacher, and the materials available to support the development of their literacy (Block, 2000a, 2000b; Pressley, 1998). Inherent in this theory is the belief that teachers' philosophies and actions go far in determining the nature of instructional episodes.

Method

The present study began in 1996 and continued until the end of 1998. It involved 30 teachers, and began as one component of a national study at the National Center for English and Literacy Achievement at the State University of New York–Albany. The national study was designed to study literacy instruction in five U.S. locales. The 8 teachers in the present study are from one of these five locales, representing 30% of the teachers in the national sample. This investigation extended the work in the larger study by (a) continuing the study of first-grade student achievement until the end of second grade, (b) providing more intensive measures of teaching effectiveness in first grade, and (c) collecting pre- and posttest data to describe students' literacy achievement after they left the classrooms of exemplary first-grade teachers.

Setting and Participants

Teachers. This study was conducted in four school districts in the state of Texas. Because of its large size, varied student populations, and its influence on policy, curricular issues, and educational publishing, Texas provided a rich cross-section of the main issues affecting first-grade teaching (Bowler, 1978; Farr, Tulley, & Powell, 1987; Hoffman et. al, 1998). Each school had received the highest academic ranking (i.e., Exemplary) given by the Texas Educational Agency. An Exemplary School Ranking meant that a school had (a) at least 90% of its students passing all subtests of the Texas Assessment of Academic Skills, regardless of the socioeconomic level of students served by the school; (b) no more than a 1% dropout rate; and (c) at least a 94% daily student attendance. That is, the study was conducted in schools meeting high standards. Classes were not larger than 22 because of state law, nor smaller than 18 students. Schools varied in size from 300 to 750 students.

In the high socioeconomic school (District 1), Grade 1 teachers met as a team, planned interdisciplinary units, and integrated mathematics with language arts by selecting children's literature that could be used in mathematics classes to strengthen instruction. Three times a year, these teachers also conferred with other teams in their building to develop and coordinate curricula for schoolwide thematic units. In the middle socioeconomic school (District 2), when the Grade 1 team gathered, one teacher (the exemplary teacher in this study) was its leader. In reality, other team members borrowed and implemented the units created by the team leader. In the middle-to-low (District 3) and low (District 4) socioeconomic schools, teachers planned independently and no interdisciplinary units were used.

All teachers had a B.S. of Education degree, and one nominated-exemplary and one nominated-typical teacher had an M.S. All teachers had prior first-grade teaching experience (from 2 to 17 years) and 4 to 23 years of total teaching experience. All used a districtwide basal and children's literature as instructional materials. All classrooms had (a) shelves filled with children's literature and basal textbooks, (b) posters lining the walls, (c) a center rotation system, (d) many supplemental teaching aids, and (e) at least one computer. All materials in the participating classrooms fell within the range identified as typical of first-grade classrooms in the 1990s (Baumann et al., 1998). Literacy instruction occurred through blocks of time in which children interactively engaged with and responded to quality children's literature and basal readers.

Students. All districts served diverse racial and ethnic populations. District 1's school served 80% Caucasian, 7% Asian-American, 4% African-American, and 9% Hispanic students. District 2's school consisted of 30% Caucasian, 48% Hispanic, and 22% African American. District 3's school was composed of 67% Hispanic, 14% Caucasian, and 19% African American. District 4's school was composed of 65% Caucasian, 8% Hispanic, 17% African American, and 10% Asian. One hundred ninety-eight students were observed in the eight classrooms.

Prior to beginning the study, each teacher identified six children from her class who would receive more formal assessments (hereafter referred to as "target students"). In each classroom, two of these students were among the highest achieving, two were working on grade level, and two were among the lowest performing in the class. A portfolio was constructed for each target student, including the student's end-of-first-grade and end-of-second-grade written compositions; pre–first grade Observation Survey (Clay, 1984); a list of the books that each student self-selected to read during May of Grade 1; end-Grade 1 reading level as determined by the readability level of books that students self-selected to read during the last month of Grade 1; standardized test scores of end-Grade 1 literacy ability, as computed from the composite score on *Terra Nova Basic Battery* Word Analysis, Vocabulary, Language Arts, and Reading Subtests; and, *Gates MacGinitie Reading Achievement Test* end-Grade 2 test scores.

Selection of Participants

Once a school was selected, the researchers asked the language arts director at the central administration office of the district to nominate two Grade 1 teachers from that school to participate in the study. One was to be truly exceptional at promoting literacy, as identified by that district's standards. The second Grade 1 teacher was to be one whose instructional methods and practices would be classified as typical of solid Grade 1 literacy instruction in that district. No participating teacher was characterized by the district as below average or deficient in professional competence.

The school officials were asked to make their nominations using a variety of indicators. These could include standardized test performances, student writing performance, student enthusiasm in the classroom, teachers' use of best practices, teaching awards, and teacher involvement in continuous professional development. Researchers in the study were not told which teachers were nominated as exemplary or typical by their districts. Even so, initial observations confirmed variability in behaviors between the teachers in each school and district.

Data Collection and Analysis

Five researchers collected data using a variety of measures, including multiple-person observations, two formal and several informal interviews, video- and audiotaped transcriptions, standardized test scores, student reading records, and writing samples. Observations were made by two researchers at a time for two visits, complemented by five visits to each classroom by researchers one at a time. When in the classroom, researchers adhered to the privileged observer approach (Wolcott, 1988). Observers tried to be unobtrusive by minimizing their interactions with teachers and students to (a) take detailed fieldnotes, (b) attend to the teaching process, and (c) record student performances as objectively and thoroughly as possible. Their purposes were to document what occurred during a typical day of beginning reading and writing instruction.

Methodological triangulation occurred in several ways. First, two or more researchers visited each classroom and agreed upon the conclusions derived from the observational data. Data were also member checked by teachers, as they (a) were asked their rationale for specific classroom actions and (b) read the observation reports and interview data to verify that the contents accurately reflected their intentions for specific instructional episodes. Whenever teachers suggested alternative rationales for actions or variations in their philosophical belief statements, the wording was altered to match the teachers' intentions.

Data analysis was ongoing, using the method of constant comparison (Strauss

& Corbin, 1990). The first strand of analysis focused on identifying categories of what teachers and students did and said as part of literacy instruction. There were no a priori determinations made to search for specific types of actions to the exclusion of others, nor were observers asked to pay special attention to particular dimensions of literacy instruction (Lincoln & Guba, 1985). Categories were refined and gaps in information were filled as subsequent observations occurred, until no new categories emerged. The audio- and videotapes for each class, as well as the interview data, permitted analyses of the social roles adopted by teachers as they led small group literacy and one-to-one interactions with children. These data revealed distinctive patterns between children and teachers as they jointly constructed a shared view of the nature, content, and purposes of literacy. We were particularly interested in the instructional actions and verbal interactions that occurred between first-grade teachers and readers with the fewest precursors for literacy success.

We were also interested in philosophical differences between teachers who were more versus less effective in promoting literacy. Thus, two in-depth interviews were conducted. The first, completed 6 months into the study, contained 14 questions concerning teaching philosophies. The second, completed 8 months into the study, contained 17 questions concerning instructional practices. (All questions are contained in Appendix A.) Answers to all questions were typed by a research assistant. Each answer was on a separate sheet. The answers were typed so that the researchers who rated the answers could not identify the respondents through recognition of the handwriting. That is, the researchers who rated interview answers were blind to the identities of the respondents. Two researchers independently considered every answer for each of the 31 questions and rank ordered the answers with respect to the number of valid points made in each answer. A point was judged to be valid if it answered the question and was not repetitive of a point made earlier in that specific answer.

After the two researchers made their independent ratings, they compared their ratings and resolved discrepancies. Even before the discrepancies were resolved, the ratings were very similar with the interrater reliability being .91. After a total number of points was determined for each teacher for every answer, an analysis of variance between these totals was conducted.

Results

Assessing the Relationship Between the Quality of Teaching and Student Performance

Teacher effectiveness was determined by seven measures of efficacy. The first and second measures were subjective ratings of effectiveness made independently by two researchers who observed each teacher's literacy instruction for eight hours or more on at least four different occasions during the school year. These researchers defended their ratings based on a variety of factors, including teacher-to-student rapport, the creation and implementation of effective lessons, stimulation of student learning; high student expectations, high student engagement, ability to meet individual pupil needs, and the competence to create readers and writers who exceeded Grade 1 achievement standards. The first researcher's ranking of every teacher did not deviate by more than one rank from the second researcher's ranking, with most rankings being identical.

The third measure of teacher effectiveness was the average percent of students who were on-task in each teacher's class during two, 1-hour visits by two researchers who visited at the same time in the Fall and Spring. Fall data were collected within a 14-day period as were the spring data so that data for all teachers were collected at approximately the same time during the school year. To compute the percent of students on-task, both researchers counted, at 15-minute intervals for one hour, the number of students who were on-task. Off-task behavior was defined as fidgeting, not attending to the current objective, or displaying repetitive task-avoidance behaviors (e.g., walking around the room aimlessly, talking to a classmate about a subject unrelated to curricular objectives). After each count of on-task behavior, the researchers divided the number of students engaged by the total number present in the class to determine the percentage of the class that was on-task. When each observation ended, researchers compared their 15-minute on-task percentages. Discrepancies were resolved by the observers consensually estimating the percentage, consulting the fieldnotes for information relevant to the estimation. Only two such discrepancies needed to be resolved.

Because the students of more effective Grade 1 teachers can read more advanced books by the end of Grade 1 (e.g., Pressley, Wharton-McDonald, Allington, Block, & Morrow, 1998), the fourth measure of teaching effectiveness was the average reading level of books that the six targeted students self-selected to read at the end of Grade 1. Similarly, since good teachers stimulate their students to read more (Morrow, 1992; Stanovich, 1986) the fifth measure was the average number of books read by the six targeted students during the last month of Grade 1. The sixth measure was the average of the six targeted students' literacy scores on the *Terra Nova Basic Battery*.

The seventh measure was the average writing ability of the six targeted students, based on the coherence of stories they wrote and the percentage of sentences that were free of grammar, punctuation, spelling, and capitalization errors. Two examples follow. The first is an example of a high-scoring composition, and the second is an example of a low-scoring composition. Errors are underlined, and the scoring of each is explained:

> One trillion years ago there were 4 martians named jared, mitt, cullen and cheyne ___ were playing on Jupiter. Then, weird aliens landed. Shannon, the leader of all the aliens said, "Get off my planet!" Matt tried to blast Shannon, but she blocked it. then she hit him with her hair. She screamed so loud it shook the planet. She said, "smack will come after you." They ran so hard that the sand got kicked up behind them. a smoke cloud appeared behind them, and it turned in_to a robot. Matt noticed, and he turned around and fried him with his x-ray vision. I sid, "7h4t was closed." They said, "Where do we go?" Jared said, "We need some where to hide!", I put out my spikes and made a bomb shelter, but

when we got in, another machine that looked like <u>smock</u> was at the door. Cheyne ran toward him, grabbed him, jumped over him, and then threw him as far as he could. Then Jared said, "Way to go <u>c</u>heyne!" We went out of the bomb shelter, and there was a space ship. Mat zapped it, and Jared shot it with his <u>hedd</u>. Cheyne and I got on the ship. We never had problems again.

This sample contained 19 sentences and each sentence contained a subject and predicate (100% correct on sentence structure). This story had 7 sentences with incorrect punctuation at some points (63% correct). This story had 213 words. Nine were in the incorrect case (96% correct), and 6 were misspelled (97% correct). The story had no coherency problems, and sentences were not out of sequential, temporal, or spatial order (100% correct). The sum of percentages of correct writing choices that this sample indicates is 456. The second illustration follows:

I <u>hav</u> a <u>qun</u> on <u>mi woll</u> and <u>mi dds rks</u> for <u>Peskkuntr</u>

This sample contains one sentence, and this sentence has a subject and predicate (100% correct). The sentence has two of two punctuation errors (0% correct). The sample contains 12 words and 1 is incorrectly capitalized (the word "Peskkuntr" should be "pest control"). This is a 92% correct rate on capitalization. There are 8 misspelled words (33% correct). The sentence lacks coherence (0% correct). The sum of percentages of correct choices in this sample is 225.

Students taught by nominated-exemplary teachers descriptively and statistically outperformed students taught by nominated typical teachers on all measures of effectiveness. The most striking differences between student performance among the two group of teachers was that the lowest achieving students in the most effective teachers' classrooms outscored their peers in the more typical classrooms to a significant degree on three key standardized subtests at the end of first and at the end of second grade (as shown in Table 1). The gains low-achieving students made during the first-grade year not only enabled them to pull ahead of their peers at the end of first and second grades, but to equal, or in some cases, to surpass the achievement of "average" students in the more typical classrooms. The most significant differences were in these students' word analysis skills. Despite the small number of classrooms, it is striking that five of the seven achievement measures in Table 1 were statistically significant. Most striking was the high correlation between the researchers' ratings of teacher competence and student engagement, the average reading level of the books selected by targeted students, and the number of books read by targeted, low-performing students. Researchers observed more engaging teaching in the classrooms of exemplary, as compared to typical, teachers.

Literacy Performance at Grade 2 of Students Taught by Exemplary Versus Typical Grade 1 Teachers

The end-Grade 2 writing and reading test scores of children who had been targets in Grade 1 were collected. What is most striking is that there is a clear effect of the quality of Grade 1 teacher, with all comparisons of former students of nominated-exemplary and nominated-typical teachers descriptively favoring the

Table 1

Teacher Rankings by Seven Measures of Teaching Effectiveness

Group	Researcher #1 Ranking	Researcher #2 Ranking	Student Engagement Ranking	Average Reading Level	Number of Books Read	Standardized Test Scores Ranking	Writing Scores Ranking	Overall Mean Ranking	Aggregate Group Mean
High									2.83a*
NE-(DIST2)	2	1	1 (99.5%)	3 (2.0)	1 (25)	2 (71)	3 (75%)	1.86	
NE-(DIST3)	1	2	2 (95.5%)	1 (2.6)	3 (20)	5 (67)	2 (77%)	2.29	
NE-(DIST1)	3	3	3 (91.5%)	2 (2.4)	2 (24)	2 (71)	1 (78%)	2.29	
NE-(DIST4)	4	5	4 (90.5%)	3 (2.0)	5 (7)	6 (52)	7 (47%)	4.86	
Low									6.07
NT-(DIST1)	6	6	6 (78.5%)	5 (1.9)	4 (9)	4 (70)	5 (64%)	5.14	
NT-(DIST3)	5	4	5 (82.5%)	6 (1.8)	6 (6)	7 (48)	8 (45%)	5.86	
NT-(DIST2)	8	7	8 (62.5%)	8 (0.7)	7 (3)	1 (74)	6 (62%)	6.43	
NT-(DIST3)	7	8	6 (78.5%)	7 (1.4)	8 (1)	8 (41)	4 (69%)	6.86	

*a t-test comparing *High* (M=2.83) and *Low* (M=6.07) groups, p<.01.

students who had exemplary teachers. Eleven of these comparisons were amenable to statistical analyses, and were found to be statistically significant, as described below.

Three distinctive beliefs. Exemplary teachers had more complete literacy understanding. In responding to questions concerning instruction, the nominated-exemplary teachers expressed more beliefs ($M=6.18$, $SD=.50$) per question than did typical teachers ($M=3.42$, $SD=.75$). For example, an exemplary teacher answered to, "What do you believe is the purpose of independent reading?": "For students to become more independent in their decoding, to learn to self-correct, to be able to predict, to understand the elements of the story, recognize problems, generate solutions, analyze characters, and place themselves in the setting. For them to enjoy it, to be comfortable with reading. I want them to build their confidence, that they can do it. I want them to have a can-do attitude" [Lines 445–447].

In contrast, a typical teacher's answer to the same question was: "I'm not real sure what the purpose of independent reading is. I think the children need to learn to read independently by themselves, but I think that independent reading is more profitable when they're a little bit older. What I view is that right now they kind of just sit and look at the book" [Lines 176–178].

Moreover, while typical and exemplary teachers knew the latest literacy terminology, nominated-exemplary teachers, more freely and consistently inserted very specific examples of how they were applying research with individual children than did nominated-typical teachers. To illustrate, we can contrast answers from such teachers to the question "What do you believe to be the role that a child's social and emotional development plays in literacy development?" An exemplary teacher responded:

> Crucial. I think that if they relate well to each other, they're going to be better readers and teach other children to read, they're going to be 'contagious' if you will. For instance, Amy came to me with weak interpersonal skills, but she had an extremely high verbal intelligence. I asked Amy to stay after school for three days a week, during the first month of school and I taught her to use Holloway's seven functions of language as she interacted one-on-one with me. Then, I invited Angela to stay after school and work with Amy and I on some special projects. The next week I invited Angela, Samantha, and Amy to work together after school on a special project for the class, as I assisted and then gradually reduced my level of support until Amy became the peer-leader of this cooperative group. By October, Amy had overcome her social deficits and was leading a group of children by reading orally every day during "free reading choice" time. Developing the emotional confidence in literacy in first grade is also crucial. Even if a child isn't developmentally ready to read, they feel like they're a reader if that confidence is there. If they don't have confidence they've really lost half the battle and they're going to have some real repercussions with literacy later in life [Lines 332 –339].

In contrast, a typical teacher's answer was:

> I think social and emotional development plays a big role, because if they're not ready to read, they're not going to read. I don't think there's anything you can

do as a teacher, short of planting that seed. But, until they're socially and emotionally ready, that seed is not going to flourish. It may not flourish until second grade. [Lines 568–570]

Second, exemplary teachers believed that they had the skill to adapt instruction to meet students' special needs. They averaged 4.15 (*SD*=.50) instructional modifications a day for students with special needs compared to .50 (*SD*=.25) for typical teachers. In general, exemplary teachers believed that no barrier to students' literacy was greater than their professional competencies. This greater flexibility was clearly evident during observations, as one researcher stated:

> I have noticed that exemplary instructors do not wait until the second half of the year for the 'lights to go on' in a child. These teachers start from day one to empower each child with the ability to succeed in their classrooms. Exemplary teachers created a 'can do attitude' in each and every student, were sensitive to all their varying levels of literacy development, and modified or adapted instruction accordingly. I have yet to have an exemplary teacher tell me that 'they do not know what to do' for a given child (Although, I heard this many times from typical teachers). Exemplary teachers found ways to teach each and every child. (Nelson, 1997, p. 3)

Third, exemplary teachers had strong beliefs about how their instructional program contributed to students' superior literacy growth. Nominated-exemplary teachers believed they knew what part of their actions, instructional programs, and teaching repertoires built their less prepared readers' literacy successes. For example, an exemplary NE-District 3 teacher stated, "My children do a great job of expanding their reading and writing because we study many new concepts and words every day. Students compose and construct their own written communications for at least 45-minutes every afternoon in my classroom" [Lines 862–863]. Conversely, nominated-typical teachers didn't hold as high a level of self-efficacy. They did not judge their programs or their teaching repertoires to be special. As volunteered by a typical NT-District 2 teacher: "I do not feel that there is anything in my classroom which I would nominate for an award or television feature because I am just doing my job as is any other teacher in my building and thousands of others in this state" [Lines 59–61].

Aside from the above beliefs, nominated-exemplary and nominated-typical teachers' thinking about teaching differed little, including the number of types of new materials that they wanted to add to their programs, aspects of the program that they desired to change, how and why they planned the instruction, general philosophical approach to beginning reading instruction, commitment to phonics and/or whole language, or the types of assessments that they used (see Appendix A).

Eight distinctive instructional actions. Eight instructional characteristics distinguished the exemplary from the typical first-grade teachers. First, exemplary teachers "cast a larger literacy net." They used more variety in literacy instruction to meet individual student needs than did typical teachers. For example, in response to the question, "Describe literacy instruction in your first grade classroom," exemplary teachers reported more types of instruction (*M*=12.23, *SD*=2.50) on a typical day than typical teachers (M=5.00, SD=.25), and this difference was statistically significant, $t(7)$=2.89, p<.05. In addition, exemplary teachers averaged eight grouping systems (that they varied each week), and typical teachers used only three (tending to use these three in the same order every day)—reading aloud to students; holding small-group, homogeneous instructional meetings; and, asking students to copy, complete worksheets, or read alone until the whole class came together again. Exemplary teachers also varied the membership of small-group lessons to reteach concepts in new ways for those who needed more practice on specific objectives.

Second, exemplary teachers covered more content. For example, on September 17, during only the first 45 minutes of a 2½-hour literacy block that morning, an exemplary District 1 teacher reviewed 31 new words in a student-generated KWL chart, from which all students were to select 15 words to include in stories that they created individually [because this activity was the introduction to adjectives and the use of more descriptive nouns and verbs when writing]. She also taught the "r controlled vowel" phonetic generalization, structural analysis, and how to blend words which have /ch/, /sh/, and /sch/ as beginning or ending consonant digraphs. On the same day, during the same amount of time, however, the typical teacher in the same school taught only the letter "h" and its sound. Also, exemplary teachers averaged four books or stories read by, with, and to students, and two student-composed writings per week. Typical teachers focused a week's instruction around no more (and often less than) one story from a basal or children's book. And, students in typical classrooms averaged less than one student-written composition a week.

Third, exemplary teachers regularly integrated reading and writing instruction into content areas. Typical teachers did not incorporate objectives for literacy growth into their content material as frequently, and this difference was statistically significant, as exemplary teachers reported (and were observed to perform) almost twice as many integrations (M=9.00, SD=.75) as typical teachers (M=5.00, SD=1.25, $t(7)$=4.9, p<.01).

Fourth, exemplary teachers asked parents to perform more (up to seven) roles in their children's literacy development (M=5.07, SD=.45) whereas typical teachers averaged only one (M=1.08, SD=.25). This difference was statistically significant ($t(7)$=3.69, p<.01). Exemplary teachers asked guardians to (a) sign that their child had read a book that the teacher sent home, (b) help their child identify and bring their favorite books and literacy samples to school to share, (c) send common household items to be used in teaching reading and writing, (d) re-administer a spelling or sight word list (learned during the week) that night at home with the results to be returned to the teachers the next day, and (e) supervise their child's journal writing about experiences at home that would be read in class the next day. Exemplary teachers also scheduled parents to read regularly at school with students in small groups and in one-to-one settings. They, and not their principals or reading coordinators, initiated this involvement.

Fifth, exemplary teachers held high expectations for all children. They regularly urged less-prepared readers to attempt tasks a little more difficult than they were already accomplishing (e.g., reading a slightly more advanced book). While doing so, exemplary teachers also were ready and available to provide assistance, in the form of personalized, tailored instruction as needed by these students, and, in fact, the teachers provided such assistance throughout the day. They monitored the students as they read and wrote, alert for moments to intervene so that students could overcome an obstacle at the moment that the difficulty arose. When students had studied the concept for some time, exemplary teachers require perfectly completed work. They scaffolded with a PWI cycle. This cycle included Praise (for sections of a skill that a student had mastered); Why (question asked as to why the student performed the skill in the way he or she did); and Instruction as to the next step that the student could take to achieve even greater levels of success and broader applicability of that literacy skill.

In contrast, typical teachers unintentionally communicated lower expectations through their direction-giving, instructional talk, and teaching actions. To illustrate, a typical District 2 teacher always began big book lessons by saying: "Read along with me *if you like,*" and with this freedom to choose, most students' eyes wandered around the room instead of focusing on the words in the book. Similarly, before making writing assignments, she would say: "You don't have to write that much *if you don't want too,* only two paragraphs *if you can.*" Also, she allowed students to guess randomly before she told them answers to questions that she asked, and she did not describe how to generate the thinking processes, unaided, in the future to find such answers for themselves.

Sixth, exemplary teachers stimulated pupil initiative. For example, an NE-District 3 teacher allowed (up to but usually no more than) six students to express their reasoned judgements to open-ended questions (such as "Why do you think this author picked this title?") before they summarized the group's thinking and moved the discussion forward. Similarly, when writing assignments were made, exemplary teachers in District 1, 2, and 3 prefaced these assignments with high-level brainstorming sessions (see Block, 2000b, for specific examples of these prereading lesson differences). When compared to their peers, these teachers offered more flexible topic choice and broader parameters for students' writing, while simultaneously directing students' attention to two different writing conventions to be mastered during each composition activity. In addition, exemplary teachers spent less than 5 minutes of a reading period in non-textually related activities, such as drawing pictures or cutting and pasting without reading. They also used student ideas and words in prewriting semantic web activities.

In contrast, typical teachers more often (a) gave sentence starters to begin every student writing activity, (b) read most of the words for students when they were in small group sessions, (c) did not provide time for students to figure out words independently, and (d) allowed middle-to-low achieving students to spend as much as 50 minutes of the morning literacy block in nontext related activities, such as coloring a worksheet and cutting and pasting sheets of paper that did not require students' reading of words. Typical teachers did not use student-generated words or writings in their instruction, preferring to use the preprinted ones that accompanied the basal.

Seventh, exemplary teachers maintained discipline continuously. They did so by (a) establishing and following routines consistently, (b) tying reasons for stopping misbehavior to a learning objective, and (c) building students' self-efficacy and self-esteem. Exemplary teachers could be discerned by the predominance of instructional over disciplinary statements that they made during literacy lessons. Exemplary teachers tied the importance of self-management to the role it played in increasing students' literacy. For example, an exemplary District 2 teacher, stated at mid-lesson (during her December 10th observation): "Larry, would you sit up straight for me so I'll know that you are ready to learn and your mind is focused on our next learning goal. Thank you. I see that you are ready now."; and, on February 4, 1997, she stated to the entire class, "All you need is your journal, a pencil, a cover sheet, and your listening ears."

To sum up, the classroom management of exemplary teachers was systematic and unquestioned by less-able students, with very few comments ever being made about individual student misbehavior before the entire group. Things went more smoothly in classrooms headed by exemplary teachers. Movement routines took less time and were student-monitored. Students knew that it would do them no good to attempt to delay their instruction. Exemplary teachers would not delay future instruction to give them more time because they had wasted class time, nor would they diminish the quality of the work that they expected.

Eighth, exemplary teachers provided specific feedback to less prepared readers. Their feedback targeted a specific area in which an individual had grown, or could grow by exerting a little more effort, learning, or thought. Exemplary teachers did so by providing just enough guidance so that students did not give up in frustration, and yet at the same time, not so much as to deny students' personal satisfaction and growth because all of the thinking was done for them by their teachers. exemplary teachers described exactly what literacy growth students' samples demonstrated. For example, an exemplary District 2 teacher commented, "I like the way you wrote your summary to begin with the main idea, and when you see the words 'in summary' when you read, they will be a clue to you that the author is about to summarize just like you did" [Lines 222–224].

Also, exemplary teachers stopped their lessons to give feedback as soon as a child asked for it. For example, Andy wanted an exemplary District 2 teacher to check his writing as she walked to the chalkboard to signal the end of center time. Instead of asking the student to wait, she placed this student's need first, stopped immediately, and allowed Andy to read it to her. It took only 45 seconds. She focused intently on that writing. Then she said, "Good job. I want to tell you one thing. Look at the word 'saw.' That was one of your spelling words. You should be spelling that word correctly now. Good job." Andy picked up his pencil, found that word on the wall, and wrote it correctly. Then, his teacher said: "What I liked about your reading was that you read it just like you talk, and such expression-filled reading will make it very interesting when you read aloud to others as an adult" [Lines 377–382].

In contrast, typical teachers frequently corrected students' compositions without teaching students how to revise: "This would be one sentence; this would be a second sentence."; and, more often than exemplary teachers, directed feedback to the entire class rather than to single individuals.

Discussion

Data in this study suggest that Grade 1 instruction (that is effective for poorly prepared students) contains 11 distinctive qualities; is multifaceted, informed, textualized; and, blends well-managed skills instruction with rich, challenging, and continuously varied reading and writing experiences, as summarized in Table 2. We observed that both code and meaning were emphasized, literature sometimes drove instruction and sometimes did not, both choice and challenge occurred, and various forms of grouping were used, depending on the task and circumstances.

In exemplary classrooms, we saw instruction that was thick, deep, and rapid. Student engagement was sustained through the variety of activities, and by the enthusiasm generated by the continuous interactions less-prepared readers had with their teacher, peers, books, literacy, and varied learning opportunities. Literacy instruction also continued into the afternoon hours through integration with content area instruction. There was a consistent, efficient, and reliable classroom management system. Parents were involved with their children's literacy development. The classroom schedule enabled teachers to spend the most time with students who needed the most instruction. There was much opportunistic teaching and re-teaching. In short, exemplary classrooms demonstrated an interaction of eleven instructional factors.

There are many implications of this study for typical teachers. First, educators who seek to better address the needs of students who enter school without the precursors for literacy success have a model to follow that appears to develop these foundations for children. Specifically, teachers of young children can employ the eleven qualities in Table 2 to enhance the chances that their children will achieve initial literacy success with greater ease. Second, those who conduct professional development sessions for educators can turn to Table 2 as a guide in planning such professional enrichment experiences. When more teachers use the eleven variables in Table 2, more students might begin their journeys on the road to literacy more successfully. Third, educators can begin to document specific statements and actions that exemplary teachers employ to enact each of these eleven qualities of classroom instruction. Such work is beginning and will be reported in future research by this author (Block, in press; Block, 2000b).

A critically unanswered question, however, is whether other teachers can be developed to teach like exemplary teachers teach. There certainly are reasons to be skeptical for it is clear exemplary teachers had a vast knowledge about classroom management, print as code and how decoding can taught, children's literature, writing, and elementary science and social studies content. Beyond knowledge of the primary canon, exemplary teachers also had detailed knowledge

Table 2

Summary of 11 Indicators of Exemplary First-Grade Literacy Instruction

Beliefs that Distinguish Teachers Whose Students Significantly Outperformed Their Peers

1. Exemplary teachers had a more complete understanding of reading and writing processes. They could describe specific incidents in which they applied research in their instruction and interaction with individual students.
2. Exemplary teachers had the skills to adapt instruction to meet individual students' special needs. These teachers adapted instruction four times more frequently than typical teachers, employing up to four different methods of instruction each day to meet special students' needs.
3. Exemplary teachers had strong beliefs about how their instruction programs contributed to students' superior literacy growth. They knew what they were doing for their classes (as a whole group and individual students) that was leading to the largest gains in literary abilities.

Instructional Actions that Distinguish Teachers Whose Students Significantly Outperformed Peers

1. Exemplary teachers used greater variety in daily literacy instruction. They used 12 different types of literacy-related activities in a typical day as compared to three, literacy-related activities that were employed each day by less effective teachers.
2. Exemplary teachers covered more content in a typical day's lesson. Such teachers would teach many decoding and comprehension cueing systems in a single day while typical teachers tended to emphasize only one.
3. Exemplary teachers integrated reading and writing into content areas. These teachers taught reading and writing in the afternoon classes as well as in their morning literacy blocks.
4. Exemplary teachers asked parents to perform up to seven, distinct roles to enhance their children's literacy development. These roles included methods that exemplary teachers used in the classroom, as parents served as volunteers during the day, and activities that were assigned to be completed at home, together with their children.
5. Exemplary teachers held high expectations for all children. They communicated that no child was less able than peers; some merely had less practice with specific concepts and in this class they would be provided with the practice necessary to achieve success. They scaffolded individually using Praise, Why, and Instruction (PWI Cycle of Feedback). When students had studied a concept for some time, they were required to display perfect duplication of the concepts learned.
6. Exemplary teachers stimulated pupil initiative to learn literacy. They engaged students through open-ended, reflective questions and statements.
7. Exemplary teachers maintained discipline by creating consistent routines, tying discipline statements to the role that self-discipline played in enhancing literacy abilities, and sustaining student engagement through expectations that students would manage their own movement patterns.
8. Exemplary teachers provided specific feedback to individual students. They stopped to answer questions as soon as they were asked, and challenged students to move to the next higher level ability as soon as one stage of understanding had been mastered.

of their students, that they used fluidly to guide their instructional decision making. Clearly, exemplary teachers started every day with a plan (often encoded in a daily schedule that was on the chalkboard), but the plan was just a beginning. There were many mini-lessons, and numerous occasions when individual, less prepared children were prompted to engage in one activity over another. Can such teachers be developed through some form of teacher education? Is there some way to identify individuals with the talents to become such teachers? The principal investigators involved in the initial national study are exploring these questions. At present, we do not know. However, by illuminating just how complex good Grade 1 teaching is, we believe that we are better prepared to address such questions intelligently.

This study also deepened our understanding of just how great the need is to improve Grade 1 literacy instruction. We assume that there are many classrooms that are not much different from the typical classrooms in this study. There is an urgent need to identify mechanisms that might improve Grade 1 instruction—an urgent need to move on to research on teacher development or personnel selection that might result in better Grade 1 teachers.

References

Allington, R. L., Guice, S., Michelson, N., Baker, K., & Li, S. (1996). Literature-based curriculum in high-poverty schools. In M. Graves, P. van den Broek, & B. Taylor (Eds.), *The first r: Every child's right to read* (pp. 73–96). New York: Teachers College Press.

Almasi, J., & O'Flahaven, J. (1997, December). *Analysis of peer-led student reading response groups.* Paper presented at the meeting of the National Reading Conference, Scottsdale, AZ.

Barnes, B. (1996/1997). But teacher you went right on: A perspective on Reading Recovery. *Reading Teacher, 50,* 284–293.

Baumann, J. F., Hoffman, J. V., Moon, J., & Duffy-Hester, A. (1998). Where are teachers' voices in the phonics/whole language debate: Results from a survey of U.S. elementary teachers. *Reading Teacher, 50,* 636–651.

Berliner, D. C., & Tikunoff, W. J. (1976). The California beginning teacher evaluation study: Overview of the ethnographic study. *Journal of Teacher Education, 27,* 24–30.

Block, C. C. (1993). Strategy instruction in a literature-based program. *Elementary School Journal, 93,* 123–145.

Block, C. C. (2000a). *Teaching the language arts: Expanding thinking through student centered instruction* (3rd ed.). Boston, MA: Allyn & Bacon.

Block, C. C. (2000b, May). *How first-grade teachers employ developmentally appropriate practices in instruction.* Paper presented at the meeting of the International Reading Association, Indianapolis, IN.

Block, C. C. (in press). *Teaching reading comprehension.* Boston: Allyn & Bacon.

Block, C. C., & Mangieri, J. N. (1995a). *Reason to Read: Volume I.* Palo Alto, CA: Addison-Wesley.

Block, C. C., & Mangieri, J. N. (1995b). *Reason to Read: Volume II.* Palo Alto, CA: Addison-Wesley.

Block, C. C., & Mangieri, J. N. (1996). *Reason to Read: Volume III.* Palo Alto, CA: Addison-Wesley.

Bond, G. L., & Dykstra, R. (1967/1997). The cooperative research program in first-grade reading instruction. *Reading Research Quarterly, 32,* 345–428.

Bowler, M. (1978). Textbook publishers try to please all, but first they woo in the heart of Texas. *Reading Teacher, 31*, 514–518.

Cazden, C. (1994). *Whole language plus*. Portsmouth, NH: Heinemann.

Clay, M. (1984). *Observation survey*. Portsmouth, NH: Heinemann.

Erickson, J. (1993). *Teachers' voices: An interview project*. Unpublished master's thesis, Fresno Pacific College, CA.

Farr, R., Tulley, M., & Powell, D. (1987). The evaluation and selection of basal readers. *Elementary School Journal, 87*, 267–282.

Good, T. & Grouws, D. (1975). *Process-product relationships in fourth grade mathematics classes*. Columbia: University of Missouri College of Education.

Hoffman, J. V., McCarthy, S. J., Elliott, B., Bayles, D., Price, D., Ferree, A., & Abbott, J. (1998). The literature-based basals in first-grade classrooms: Savior, Satan, or same-old, same-old? *Reading Research Quarterly, 33*, 168–197.

Leibert, R. E. (1991). The Dolch List revisited. *Reading Horizons, 31*, 217–227.

Lincoln, Y. S., & Guba, E. G. (1985). *Naturalistic inquiry*. Newbury Park, CA: Sage.

Medley, D. M. (1977). *Teacher competence and teacher effectiveness: A review of process-product research*. Washington, DC: American Association of Colleges for Teacher Education.

Morrow, L. M. (1992). The impact of a literature-based program in literacy achievement, use of literature, and attitudes of children from minority backgrounds. *Reading Research Quarterly, 27*, 250–275.

Nelson, E. (1997). *The glass bottom boat*. Unpublished master's oral discussion paper, Texas Christian University School of Education, Fort Worth.

Porter, A., & Brophy, J. (1988). Synthesis of research on good teaching. *Educational Leadership, 45*, 74–85.

Pressley, M. (1998). *What is a balanced reading program?* New York: Guilford.

Pressley, M., Wharton-McDonald, R., Allington, R., Block, C., Morrow, L., Tracey, D., Baker, K., Brooks, G., Cronin, J., Nelson, E., & Woo, D. (1998). *The nature of effective first-grade literacy instruction* (Report Series 11007). Albany, NY: National Research Center on English Learning and Achievement.

Ruddell, R. B. (1997). Researching the influential literacy teacher: Characteristics, beliefs, strategies, and new research directions. In C. K. Kinzer, K. A.. Hinchman, & D. J. Leu (Eds.), *Inquiries in Literacy Theory and Practice*. Forty-sixth yearbook of the National Reading Conference (pp. 37–53). Chicago: National Reading Conference.

Sacks, C. H., & Mergendoller, J. R. (1997). The relationship between teachers' theoretical orientation toward reading and student outcomes in kindergarten children with different initial reading abilities. *American Educational Research Journal, 34*, 721–739.

Stanovich, K. E. (1986). Matthew effects in reading: Some consequences of individual differences in the acquisition of literacy. *Reading Research Quarterly, 21*, 360–406.

Strauss, A., & Corbin, J. (1990). *Basics of qualitative research*. Newbury Park, CA: Sage.

Vygotsky, L. (1967). Play and its role in the mental development of the child. *Soviet Psychology, 12*, 62–76.

Wertsch, J. (1991). *Voices of the mind*. New York: Harvard.

Wolcott, H. F. (1988). Ethnographic research in education. In R. M. Jaeger (Ed.), *Complimentary methods for research in education* (pp. 187–249). Washington, DC: American Educational Research Association.

Author Note

This research was supported in part (a) under the Research and Development Centers Program (Award Number R305A60005) as administered by OERI; and (b) The Block Foundation. However, the contents do not necessarily represent the positions or policies of the Department of Education, OERI, or the Institute on Student Achievement.

Appendix A

Written Questions About Philosophical Beliefs
Answered 6 Months into the Study

1. What do you want to see more of in your classroom and why?
2. What do you want to see less of in your classroom and why?
3. What part of your classroom program would you nominate for a state or national recognition award or want to feature in a local television program and why?
4. To what do you most attribute your students' success and why?
5. What would you describe as the most distinguishing characteristics of first grade instruction that has high student literacy success rates?
6. From your experience, how would you define emergent literacy?
7. Using an example from one of your students, please describe how you witnessed their transition into conventional literacy.
8. What is the latest review of literacy research you have read and what was your reaction to it?
9. Have you been influenced by any major researcher or theory and if so, how has he/she/it influenced your teaching?
10. Please describe how you determined your placement of group reading levels in your classroom.
11. How is your planning time spent? What do you plan for students?
12. What are your beliefs, skills, and practices regarding adaptations and planning for students with learning disabilities or special literacy needs?
13. To what extent do you view yourself as effective in meeting the needs of diverse learners?
14. Please respond to the following two research quotes:
    (a) Observations of students "in low reading groups taught in traditional 'skills' programs indicate that less-proficient readers not only receive even more instruction in isolated skills than their more proficient peers, but also receive less specific instruction about how to transfer these skills into other reading tasks."
    (b) "It is not the program that makes the difference, it is the teacher who makes the difference."

Oral Questions about Instructional Practices
Answered 8 Months into the Study

1. How are children assigned to classrooms in your school?
2. Describe literacy instruction in your first grade classroom.
3. Describe your philosophy of literacy instruction for first graders.
4. What do you judge to be the most important components of reading instruction?
5. What skills, knowledge, attitudes did your students come to your classroom with?
6. How do you make decisions about what to teach?
    —which skills and how much instruction do you allocate to skill instruction, and what materials do you use?

—how much time do you allocate to various activities, when do you group for reading instruction, whom do you group together and why?

—what are your room arrangements and why?

7. Would you explain how your reading groups work, specifically how you group your students, how often do groups meet, what activities, and differences that exist between the activities that you engage for students who are above and below the average ability in literacy for first grade?

8. What role do you see children's social/emotional development playing in their literacy development?

9. What role do you see writing playing in reading development?

10. Do you attempt to integrate content area curricula into your reading and writing instruction? Can you give me an example?

11. Typically, how long do your lessons extend over time, e.g., over several days, weeks, or months?

12. What role do you see parents playing in your literacy instruction and in children's literacy development?

13. How do you adapt instruction for weaker/stronger readers?

14. What do you intend as the purpose of reading aloud to students, students' reading aloud, students' independent reading, reading in partners, reading groups, journal writing, morning letters, and centers?

15. To what extent are your practices determined by district mandates?

16. What do you judge to be the most important barriers to providing effective literacy instruction?

17. What do you judge to be your students' greatest strengths when they leave your room at the end of first grade?

Teachers' and Students' Suggestions for Motivating Middle-School Students to Read

Jo Worthy

University of Texas at Austin

T he time that students spend reading is important because of its strong relationship to academic achievement (Anderson, Wilson, & Fielding, 1988; Mullis, Campbell, & Farstrup, 1993) as well as cognitive growth (Stanovich, 1986). According to researchers and educators, students develop resistance and negative attitudes toward reading as they move beyond the primary grades (McKenna, Ellsworth, & Kear, 1995). Particularly for upper elementary and middle school students, negative attitudes and conflicting interests often lead to a decline in voluntary reading (Anderson, Tollefson, & Gilbert, 1985; Cline & Kretke, 1980), as illustrated in the comment below:

> When I was a little girl I loved to read. I mean I was so smart. I was excellent. I was reading the newspaper when I was eight. When I was a little girl I would just read and read every night. I would read a whole book every night. . . . But then when I got older I got interested in a lot of other things and I just put that aside and I started forgetting how to read. . . . When I got older, I just hated to read. (Marta, end of fifth grade, 1997)

Researchers who have interviewed students in depth about their reading attitudes, habits, and preferences have suggested that negative attitudes often arise from how reading is presented in school, and that many so-called reluctant readers feel differently about the reading they do on their own (Bintz, 1993; Worthy & McKool, 1996). However, for many students, academic and recreational reading are inextricably intertwined as, for many students, school is a major source of their ideas and attitudes about reading, as well as their reading materials. Thus, it is important to address school reading instruction in discussions of reading attitudes and motivation. The purpose of this study was to examine and compare middle school teachers' and students' suggestions for how language arts instruction can help motivate students to read. I also wanted to compare the suggestions with current research in motivation and interest.

Review of Research

Much of the current research about voluntary reading focuses on the role that motivation plays in students' decisions to read or not to read. According to current theories of motivation, when a person is motivated to learn, he or she

National Reading Conference Yearbook, 49, pp. 441–451.

requires no incentive other than the enjoyment, interest, and satisfaction that accompanies the learning (Csikszentmihalyi, 1990; Deci, 1992). Young children rarely lack motivation for learning, and most children come to school intrinsically motivated to learn. All that is needed for motivation to continue is an environment conducive to exploration and engaged learning (Condry, 1977). Yet, judging from the "middle school slump," that time during which many students' voluntary reading decreases, such environments may be limiting.

Rewards for Reading

Educators have tried every trick imaginable to entice students to read, from contests and rewards for students who read the most, to the threat of pop quizzes and bad grades for students who choose not to read. More recently, a rash of commercial programs offering rewards for reading have appeared in schools. These programs feature time for reading and access to books, both widely recognized as important to reading progress (Allington, 1981; Anderson, Wilson, & Fielding, 1988; Morrow; 1992). Yet the reward structure, in which students are awarded points that are exchanged for prizes, is based on the theory that motivation is imposed on individuals by outside forces (Bandura, 1977). According to recent research in learning and motivation, external incentives rarely work for reluctant learners or for intrinsically motivated learners. Rewards, which may be interpreted as bribes, do not increase and may even diminish the learner's natural desire to participate in the activity (Lepper, Greene, & Nisbett, 1973). Further, there can be damaging consequences of a work-for-pay system that may not be immediately apparent. In classrooms employing extrinsic reward systems, children tend to select easier problems than they would in the absence of rewards, work quicker with less focus on quality, and are less creative than students not offered extrinsic rewards (Lepper et al., 1973). Kohn (1993) noted that "when individuals are working for a reward, they do exactly what is necessary to get the reward and nothing more." Students who are given rewards for reading, then, may eventually come to view reading as an undesirable task, one they must be paid to do.

The Role of Interest in Motivation

Beyond the intrinsic/extrinsic dichotomy, a student's decision to read is often based on the availability of interesting materials and instruction. Early pioneers of education considered interest to be of paramount importance in learning (Dewey, 1913; James, 1890/1950), and later researchers showed that when students are interested in what is taught and have access to materials that interest them, learning, motivation, effort, and attitudes improve (Hidi, 1991; Schiefele, 1991). Csiksentmihalyi (1990) insisted, "there cannot be any learning unless a person is willing to invest attention" (p. 116). Recent researchers have approached interest as a broader construct that involves an interaction between a person and the environment or context. Interest is an "important resource for learning" (Schiefele, 1991, p. 316) that is related to cognition and intrinsic motivation, but that has distinct properties and additional effects on learning. Interest is content-specific; personal interest in a subject motivates and facilitates the learner in going beyond surface level information to a deeper level of processing.

Two focus areas of recent research that relate to classroom instruction and reading motivation are situational interest and individual interest. Situational interest focuses on how the learning environment can capture or create interest. Instructional approaches or materials that are motivating, as well as teachers who show interest and enjoyment in the subject they teach, can facilitate temporary interest in a subject or activity, and can sometimes lead to the development of long term interest (Schiefele, 1991). Individual interest involves (a) a person's inclination or disposition toward a particular subject or domain and (b) the actualization or realization of that personal interest through an environment with conditions and stimuli that are conducive for the learner (Hidi & Baird, 1986). These conditions may include social relationships and characteristics of instruction as well as materials or objects that are personally interesting. Actualized individual interest can lead to a psychological state characterized by "increased attention, greater concentration, pleasant feelings of applied effort, and increased willingness to learn" (Krapp, Hidi, & Renninger, 1992, p. 9), as in Csikszentmihalyi's (1990) description of "flow" and Nell's (1988) description of "ludic reading." Students' personal interests can be actualized in the classroom through provision of materials in which students can become personally engaged (Fink, 1995/96; Rucker, 1982). In a study of adults who had been identified as dyslexic in childhood, Fink (1995/96) found that her informants had reached the highest level of reading competence through voluntary reading in areas of personal interest.

Social and cultural perspectives on motivation. Social relationships, important for learning at every age, focus heavily on peers during preadolescence and adolescence (Hynds, 1997). Middle school students in particular enjoy opportunities to read and talk with their friends about what they are reading. Instructional activities such as literature circles and informal book conversations can aid learning and motivation (Almasi, 1997; Raphael & McMahon, 1994). Another important issue for instruction is to consider students' backgrounds and interests when providing experiences and materials (Sleeter & Grant, 1999). Unfortunately, there is often a mismatch between students' interests and what schools provide (Pucci, 1994; Worthy, Moorman, & Turner, 1999).

Method

Participants and Data Gathering Procedures

Teachers. This research was part of a larger study conducted in middle schools in a large, ethnically and economically diverse school district in the southwestern United States. Principals of the 13 district middle schools housing sixth-grade students were invited to participate in the study and 9 accepted. Of the 9 schools, 6 serve predominantly low-income areas of the city and three serve middle-income areas. Of the 44 sixth-grade language arts teachers in the 9 schools, 35 (80%) agree to participate in the study. There were 33 women (10 Latina, 4 African American, 19 European American) and 2 men (1 African American, 1 European American), all from middle-income backgrounds, with a range of 2 to 22 years in teaching experience. The teachers responded to interview questions about their language arts instruction, about materials in their classrooms (Worthy, Moorman, & Turner, 1999), and about motivating students to read. The specific question of interest for this study was "What do you think are the best ways of motivating students to read?" Teachers spoke at length about this topic and each had multiple suggestions.

Students. The second phase of the study involved surveying students from three of the schools. These schools were chosen because, together, they included a range of ethnic and socioeconomic groups. Cedar Trails Middle School is located in a rapidly growing, middle-income suburb and serves mostly European-American students. Baker Middle School serves a low- to middle-income, ethnically diverse area just south of the city's center, and Garza Middle School is located in a low-income, predominantly Latino/Latina community, 10 minutes from downtown. For data analysis and results, I combined the responses from the three schools.

Across the 28 language arts classes in the three schools, there was a potential pool of 614 students; 419 of these students secured parent permission to participate in the study. There were 125 students from Cedar Trails (67 girls, 58 boys), 149 from Garza (80 girls, 69 boys), and 152 from Baker (82 girls, 70 boys).

Student participation involved responding to surveys about reading attitudes, habits, and preferences. The current study focused on an open-ended question in which students were asked, "What could your language arts teacher do to make students more motivated to read?" Students were asked to write up to 3 suggestions; they made a total of 506 suggestions.

Analysis

I began by analyzing 20% of the student and teacher suggestions, looking for recurring patterns and grouping comments into categories by way of constant comparative analysis (Strauss & Corbin, 1990). This first round of analysis and discussion yielded six categories. I analyzed an additional 20% of the suggestions using the six categories, refining and combining them into three, as follows: (a) *classroom modifications* consisted of all suggestions that related to changing instructional activities (e.g., reading aloud, responding in journals), physical atmosphere (e.g., pillows in the reading center), or teacher actions (e.g., showing more excitement); (b) *reading materials* consisted of all suggestions related to what students read; and (c) *incentives* included tangible rewards (e.g., treats) and intangible incentives (e.g., competition, setting a goal of reading a certain number of award winning books).

After constructing these working categories, I returned to the data to test their validity and refine them. When I was satisfied that category descriptions reflected and described all the data, I enlisted the help of a colleague who is an experienced qualitative researcher to establish interrater reliability. I showed the data to her, described the categories, and we independently categorized 25% of the reflections that had been set aside. Interrater reliability was 92%. Tables 1 and 2 present the suggestions by category and in order of frequency for both teachers and students.

Results

Classroom Modifications

Suggestions for classroom modifications accounted for the largest percentage of students' (46%) and teachers' comments (36%). Students' recommendations focused mainly on how to change instruction to increase the enjoyment of self-selected reading time through choice, more time to read, and a more comfortable, fun atmosphere. A large number of students requested that teachers allow them to "just read" at least part of the time rather than to always require that they write journal responses or answer questions about what they read. Students also

Table 1

Students' Suggestions for Motivating Students to Read

Category	Number of Suggestions
Classroom Modifications	Total: 232 (46%)
Choice in books	52
More time to read	39
No requirements	34
Read aloud and introduce books	32
Make reading more fun/interesting	21
Make reading center comfortable	20
Let students act out books; do readers' theater	19
Other (suggested by fewer than 5 students)	10
Reading Materials	Total: 229 (45%)
Horror, scary books or stories	64
Interesting, good, great, better, cool books	51
Magazines	28
Sports	17
Comedy, funny, jokes	17
Comics	18
Mystery	17
Science fiction	5
Other (suggested by fewer than 5 students)	15
Incentives	Total: 45 (9%)
Treats, rewards, prizes, or money	45

made it clear that they would like to hear their teachers read aloud more and introduce books and authors that they might enjoy reading. Examples of the most common student comments are shown below:

> Let us always choose what we want to read!
>
> Let us read every day so we get a habit of it.
>
> Do we have to do journal entries every time we read?
>
> She could get some couches and beanbag chairs so we can be more relaxed when we read.
>
> Find an exciting book, read a little bit of it. And I will read it.
>
> Let us talk to our friends about the books we're reading so we can hear how good the books are.

Many teachers were aware of the kinds of instructional modifications that were motivating to students as the comments below illustrate:

> They seem to enjoy when I read out loud. I thought middle school kids would not, but they still like the read-aloud.

Table 2

Teachers' Suggestions for Motivating Students to Read

Category	Number of Suggestions
Classroom Modifications	Total: 84 (36%)
Read aloud and introduce books	19
Get to know and respect students, provide instruction that relates to their lives	18
Let students choose what they read	15
Model enthusiasm about reading	11
Make the atmosphere successful, positive	11
Other	10
Reading Materials	Total: 83 (35%)
Horror, scary books or stories	20
Books at students' reading levels	17
Interesting, good, great, better, cool books	16
Comics, comedy, funny, jokes	13
Magazines	9
Other	9
Incentives	Total: 67 (29%)
Requirements, grades, extra credit	37
Rewards, prizes	13
Recognition	9
Reminders, warnings, nagging	8

People in later years are only going to read what they want to read. So why try to force them into something that they don't want to read? It just turns them against it altogether. And as long as it's appropriate to school, then they should be allowed to read it.

Teachers also spoke of the importance of getting to know students, respecting their interests and concerns, and providing instruction, materials, and a positive, enthusiastic atmosphere in which students could feel successful: As they explained:

You've got to get to know them a little bit better. Establish rapport, get to know who they are. What they want from life. What they want to read. Why they don't want to read. Once you find that out it's easier to get them interested.

I want them to know "Hey, you can be yourself in here. You can take a risk." And gradually, as they get to know me, they realize that I want them to learn and that I'm on their side. And I think that really helps when they know that I care about them and I'm not just here to grade them.

Reading Materials

For students and for teachers, this category received virtually the same number of suggestions as the instructional modifications category (45% for students; 35% for teachers). Students suggested that their classroom book collections needed an overhaul, and they had a variety of recommendations for the types of books that should be provided to stimulate their interest. First, students simply wanted more books in the classroom. Specific kinds of materials suggested were scary books, comics, and magazines, as well as more recent, "fun for our age" materials. Examining student suggestions across ethnic, gender, and socioeconomic subgroups yielded few differences in suggestions, except that low-income students (that is those eligible for free or reduced price lunch) ranked books about animals higher than non low-income students. Boys ranked cars and trucks and almanacs higher than girls, whereas girls ranked funny novels and series books higher. No students specifically mentioned multicultural materials. In their own words, students said:

We could tell her what kinds of books that we like to read and everybody could help buy some books for our classroom. The more books there are, the more we want to read.

Those interesting books that would keep us readers in the book.

Get some new books in the room. Hers are from the 1960s!

Scary and mystery books. Also ones with imagination.

Get magazines. Order some from the mail (not the X-rated kind).

Let me read comics.

Many teachers were aware of what students liked to read, including scary book, comics, humorous materials, and magazines. Although students did not mention text difficulty, many teachers suggested that students needed more materials that they could read successfully. Only two teachers (one Latina woman and one African-American woman) specifically mentioned providing students with multicultural materials, although many commented that students should have materials that interest them. Below are examples of typical teacher comments:

> They like Calvin and Hobbes and comic books and they like R. L. Stine. That's a biggy—like *Goosebumps*. And mysteries.

> All children are different so they all like a variety. But sixth graders just love gross, disgusting things.

> A lot of the girls bring like a star magazines or some kind (17). Usually that motivates them pretty much. . . . I've got a lot of *Sports Illustrated* [in my classroom].

Many teachers felt responsible for providing these reading materials for their students, particularly those who did not have access to many reading materials at home. As one teacher said, "A lot of the problem is that they can't read, it's too high level, so you've got to find something that's on their level and interesting at the same time." Another remarked, "Some of these kids have no books in their homes. Absolutely nothing to read." Because most schools did not provide enough of such materials (Krashen, 1992; Worthy, Moorman, & Turner, 1999), about a third of the teachers used their own money to buy books from book clubs, garage sales, or bookstores, and some brought their own magazines into their classrooms (this information was gathered from other interview questions). Several teachers elicited the help of their students in building their classroom libraries. One who worked in a school serving a low-income area was pleasantly surprised when her students began to donate their own books. Another teacher offered to pay students a small sum of her own money for books that would be kept in the classroom library. Teachers said that student book donations served a dual purpose; the library holdings increased quickly, and the peer-donated books were the most popular in these classroom libraries.

Incentives

Teachers and students made strikingly different suggestions regarding incentives. Although 29% of teacher suggestions were focused on rewarding or coercing students to read (i.e., grades, "nagging"), only 9% of students' suggestions fell into this category, and often their suggestions were obviously facetious (e.g., "Give us $10 for every page we read").

Although most teachers spoke of the importance of developing intrinsic motivation to read, more than half said that they used external motivators as inducements to reading. The most common incentives were grade points and other recognition. As one teacher said, "Grades are real important to my sixth graders. . . . I grade their [reading] journals every three weeks and they should have nine entries for an A." Other teachers assigned grades based on the number of points earned in a computer-based reading incentive program or on the number of pages read outside of class.

More tangible motivators, such as prizes and candy, were also used. Some teachers also made a distinction between their honors and basic classes. Of the 35 teachers, 18 taught sections of both honors and basic classes. Of these 18, ten specifically commented that the students in their honors classes were more intrinsically motivated to read, whereas their basic students required more external motivators:

> They respond real well to the carrot at the end of the string. They respond to instant gratification. . . . You know I have to use the candy jar with that class and I do. It kind of went against my grain in the beginning to bribe with candy, but at this point I decided, "O.K., everyone else does it, I guess I will too." And it does work.

Other external motivators included setting goals, reminding or nagging students to read, and bargaining:

> There are 43 Bluebonnet books. And I told them our goal was to see if someone could read them all.

> I'm constantly nagging them about it. They know what I'm going to say when I open my mouth.

> I have a lot of artists that would draw for hours on end and never read. . . . And if I let them do a certain amount of art work and drawing then they have to give me a certain amount of reading. So that's another bargaining tool I have.

Discussion and Implications

Research reviewed for this study suggests that motivation to read can be bolstered by engaging instruction, a positive, supportive atmosphere, opportunities for social interaction, and experiences and materials that match students' interests and cultural backgrounds. In language arts instruction, this includes frequent opportunities for students to choose and read personally interesting and meaningful texts (Carson, 1990; Turner, 1995), time for students to read "just for fun," and share with their peers what they are reading (Manning & Manning, 1984; Palmer, Codling, & Gambrell, 1994), and opportunities to hear engaging texts read aloud. The majority of students' and teachers' suggestions could have come directly from the articles cited above, although suggestions with a sociocultural slant were limited.

Fewer than 10% of the student suggestions were related to extrinsic incentives, a surprise considering the reading incentives programs that are now so common in schools. However, nearly one-third of the teacher suggestions were based on the assumption that students' motivation to read is enhanced by external rewards. Even if they also provide engaging instruction and materials, it is possible that teachers who make such assumptions may give students the subtle impression that reading is not a highly valued activity, but is something one would do only if rewarded (Kohn, 1993).

Unfortunately, schools are becoming increasingly reliant on programs that offer rewards for reading. If current motivation theories are correct, these programs may have long-term negative effects on students' attitudes, time spent reading, and achievement (Kohn, 1993; Lepper et al., 1973). Such programs back their claims of effectiveness with research about the importance of sustained reading and access to books; yet, the emphasis on rewards speaks louder than words. Even if they are not harmful, are these expensive programs worthwhile? The students in this study suggested that the answer is no. To have a positive impact on students' motivation to read, one suggestion for schools is to listen to students and follow their suggestions.

References

Allington, R. L. (1981). Poor readers don't get to read much in reading groups. *Language Arts, 57*, 872–877.

Almasi, J. A. (1997). A new view of discussion. In L. B. Gambrell & J. Almasi (Eds.), *Lively discussions! Fostering engaged reading* (pp. 2–24). Newark, DE: International Reading Association.

Anderson, M. A., Tollefson, N. A., & Gilbert, E. C. (1985). Giftedness and reading: A cross-sectional view of differences in reading attitudes and behaviors. *Gifted Child Quarterly, 29*, 186–189.

Anderson, R., Wilson, P., & Fielding, L. (1988). Growth in reading and how children spend their time outside of school. *Reading Research Quarterly, 23*, 285–303.

Bandura, A. (1977). *Principles of behavior modification.* New York: Academic.

Bintz, W. P. (1993). Resistant readers in secondary education: Some insights and implications. *Journal of Reading, 36*, 604–615.

Carson, B. (1990). *Gifted hands.* Grand Rapids, MI: Zondervan.

Cline, R. K. L., & Kretke, G. L. (1980). An evaluation of long-term SSR in the junior high school. *Journal of Reading, 23*, 502–506.

Condry, J. (1977). Enemies of exploration. Self-initiated versus other-initiated learning. *Journal of Personality and Social Psychology, 35*, 459–477.

Csikszentmihalyi, M. (1990). Literacy and intrinsic motivation. *Daedalus, 119*, 115–140.

Deci, E. L. (1992). The relation of interest to the motivation of behavior: A self-determination theory perspective. In K. A. Renninger, S. Hidi, & A. Krapp (Eds.), *The role of interest in learning and development* (pp. 43–70). Hillsdale, NJ: Erlbaum.

Dewey, J. (1913). *Interest and effort in education.* New York: Houghton-Mifflin.

Fink, R. (1995/96). *Journal of Adolescent and Adult Literacy, 39*, 268–280.

Hidi, S. (1991). Interest and its contribution as a mental resource for learning. *Review of Educational Research, 60*, 549–571.

Hidi, S., & Baird, W. (1986). Interestingness—A neglected variable in discourse processing. *Cognitive Science, 10*, 179–194.

Hynds, S. (1997). *On the brink: Negotiating literature and life with adolescents.* Newark, DE: International Reading Association, and New York: Teachers College.

James, W. (1890/1950). *The principles of psychology* (2 vols.) New York: Dover. (Original work published 1890)

Kohn, A. (1993). *Punished by rewards: The trouble with gold stars, incentive plans, A's, praise, and other bribes.* Boston: Houghton Mifflin.

Krapp, A., Hidi, S., & Renninger, K. A. (1992). Interest, learning, and development. In K. A. Renninger, S. Hidi, & A. Krapp (Eds.), *The role of interest in learning and development.* Hillsdale, NJ: Erlbaum.

Krashen, S. (1992). *The power of reading.* Englewood, CO: Libraries Unlimited.

Lepper, M. R., Greene, D., & Nisbett, R. E. (1973). Undermining children's intrinsic interest with extrinsic rewards: A test of the overjustification hypothesis. *Journal of Personality and Social Psychology 28,* 129–137.

Manning, G. L., & Manning, M. (1984). What models of recreational reading make a difference? *Reading World, 23,* 375–380.

McKenna, M., Ellsworth, R., & Kear, D. (1995). Children's attitudes toward reading: A national survey. *Reading Research Quarterly, 30,* 934–957.

Morrow, L. M. (1992). The impact of a literature-based program on literacy achievement, use of literature, and attitudes of children from minority backgrounds. *Reading Research Quarterly, 27,* 250–275.

Mullis, I., Campbell, J., & Farstrup, A. (1993). *NAEP 1992: Reading report card for the nation and the states.* Washington, DC: U.S. Department of Education.

Nell, V. (1988). *Lost in a book: The psychology of reading for pleasure.* New Haven, CT: Yale University Press.

Palmer, B. M., Codling, R. M., & Gambrell, L. B. (1994). In their own words: What elementary students have to say about motivation to read. *Reading Teacher, 48,* 176–178.

Pucci, S. (1994). Supporting Spanish language literacy: Latino children and free reading resources in schools. *Bilingual Research Journal, 18,* 67–82.

Raphael, T. E., & McMahon, S. I. (1994). Book Club: An alternative framework for reading instruction. *Reading Teacher, 48,* 102–116.

Rucker, B. (1982). Magazines and teenage reading skills: Two controlled field experiments. *Journalism Quarterly, 59,* 28–33.

Schiefele, U. (1991). Interest, learning, and motivation. *Educational Psychologist, 26,* 299–323.

Sleeter, C., & Grant, C. A. (1999). *Making choices for multicultural education* (3rd ed.). Upper Saddle River, NJ: Merrill.

Stanovich, K. (1986). Matthew effects in reading: Some consequences of individual differences in the acquisition of literacy. *Reading Research Quarterly, 21,* 360–406.

Strauss, A. & Corbin, J. (1990). *Basics of qualitative research: Grounded theory, procedures, and techniques.* Thousand Oaks, CA: Sage.

Turner, J. (1995). The influence of classroom contexts on young children's motivation for literacy. *Reading Research Quarterly, 30,* 410–441.

Worthy, J., Moorman, M., & Turner, M. (1999). What Johnny likes to read is hard to find in school. *Reading Research Quarterly, 34,* 12–27.

Worthy, J., & McKool, S. (1996). Students who say they hate to read: The importance of opportunity, choice, and access. D. J. Leu, C. K. Kinzer, & K. A. Hinchman (Eds.), Literacies for the 21st Century: Research and Practice. *Forty-fifth yearbook of the National Reading Conference* (pp. 245–256). Chicago: National Reading Conference.

What Happened When Kindergarten Children Were Reading and Writing Information Text in Teacher- and Peer-Led Groups?

Riitta-Liisa Korkeamäki
University of Oulu

Mariam Jean Dreher
University of Maryland

several authors (e.g., Dreher, 2000; Duke, 2000) have expressed their concern about the scarce use of information text in reading education in the United States. Stories are used extensively as a context for learning to read. Many have assumed that young children prefer narrative or even that exposition is "unnatural" for young children (see Pappas, 1993, for a summary of these arguments). However, researchers have documented that young children respond favorably to information text (Bissex, 1980; Harste, Woodward, & Burke, 1984; Pappas, 1993). Similarly, Newkirk (1987) has shown that children's early writing is not limited to stories.

The same concern about story-based literacy instruction applies to Finnish reading education. For example, of the two most widely used books for first-grade instruction, one has no information text and the other includes only a few information text pages at the end. Decoding skills and stories are emphasized in Finnish first-grade reading books. Yet projects requiring the use of information books are very popular in Finnish first- and second-grade classrooms. These projects require children to read information on their own from books, including encyclopedias, which often are not written for young readers. As a result, children have problems reading and comprehending the text and end up copying it (Dreher, 1995). It has been taken for granted that when decoding skill has been achieved, children can decode, comprehend, and learn from information text without any further instruction. Thus, there is gap between what children are expected to do and the instruction they receive.

The study reported here is a part of a larger, whole-year project in which we implemented a meaning-based approach to teaching literacy to Finnish kindergartners. Because literacy instruction is not part of the kindergarten curriculum in Finland (Korkeamäki & Dreher, 1995), we were free to experiment with an innovative approach in teaching literacy with meaningful print and balanced attention to stories and exposition without risking children's achievement. We included information texts for children to investigate so that they could learn about things they were interested in.

National Reading Conference Yearbook, 49, pp. 452–463.

Our purpose in the current study was to investigate what happened in kindergarten when students read and wrote information text in teacher- and peer-led groups. The nature of the text is not the only important factor when engaging children in reading and writing. Equally important is the way children are guided in their interaction with the text. Drawing on Vygotsky's (1978) social constructivist and Rosenblatt's (1978) transactional theory, many have argued that collaborative interaction is an important part of literacy instruction and that children benefit cognitively, socially, and emotionally from small-group collaboration (Gambrell & Almasi, 1996; Paratore & McCormack, 1997). Collaboration entails construction of shared meaning, resulting from the process of achieving consensus and intersubjectivity (Webb & Palincsar, 1996).

However, the role of the adult or teacher in such collaborative interaction is complex. Research demonstrates that peer collaboration is effective (Tudge, 1992). Still other studies show that collaboration with adult assistance results in better performance than collaboration without an adult (Rogoff, 1991). Yet according to a Piagetian perspective (Tudge & Rogoff, 1989; Webb & Palincsar, 1996), adult-child discussions lead to asymmetrical interactions because the adult has the power and the child cannot really share the adult's point of view. As a result, the child agrees with the adult and abandons his or her own ideas. In such interactions, children do not learn how to examine and verify their points of view. Although adults function as models for appropriate behavior for children's later collaboration and strategies (Rogoff, 1991), it is also possible that in some cases children are better explainers for their peers than are adults because peers' language is on the same level and they may provide more relevant explanations than adults (Webb & Palincsar, 1996).

Vygotsky (1978) emphasized the more competent partner, peer or adult, in a social interaction. Adults are more competent in scaffolding appropriately than children. They are able to use more verbal explanations and elicit active participation from children (Korkeamäki, 1996; Tudge & Rogoff, 1989). According to the Vygotskian view, however, it is important that these partners have intersubjectivity which means shared understanding rather than power (Wertsch, 1985). Unfortunately, this situation does not always characterize real classrooms. Almasi (1995) found that fourth graders in teacher-led literature discussions used less complex language, posed fewer questions, and were less active than in peer-led discussions. The teachers dominated the episodes by talking most and asking the most questions. The episodes demonstrated "unnatural conversations patterns in which an authority figure is prominent" (Almasi, 1995, p. 341).

Given the complexity of the adult role in collaborative literacy episodes, it seems likely that optimal literacy learning may depend on teachers' flexible use of varying collaborative structures depending on the desired outcome (Seidenstricker, 1999). Consequently, we organized instruction that allowed kindergarten children to be engaged in both teacher-led and peer-led small groups. These small groups involved children with stories and information texts, though this study emphasizes only the use of information texts. Because our instruction was inquiry based, the information text about animals offered an excellent context for exploring interesting animals and making their own "encyclopedia" based on their search. That way the children would have a real purpose for their reading and writing.

Three research questions were the focus of our investigation: (a) What happens when kindergartners read and write information text in a teacher-led small group? (b) What happens when kindergartners read and write information text in a peer-led small group? and (c) What patterns are evident in the information text kindergartners produce during small-group work? To answer these question we examined first how two children and a teacher, and then how three kindergarten children, worked collaboratively while they read, wrote, and painted in the context of searching for information about snakes. We analyzed transcribed, videotaped interactions, and written texts produced during these interactions. In particular, we noted patterns of social interaction and guidance, and the patterns evident in the written texts that were produced in each situation.

Method

Participants and Setting

The study took place in a Finnish kindergarten with 21 children, two kindergarten teachers, and a nurse. In Finland, kindergartens are freestanding day-care centers with children of all ages up to and including age 6. In our group, there were both 5- and 6-year-old children. Here we report data only from three 6-year-old boys (their pseudonyms are Sami, Pasi, and Hannu) and from one teacher in two separate events.

The Finnish kindergarten curriculum does not focus on teaching academic skills but rather emphasizes developing children's social skills and free play. In this classroom, however, we implemented literacy episodes such as those described by Korkeamäki and Dreher (1995). In this report, we examine data collected during the spring term of the school year in a situation in which children were working on a project about animals. The children had visited a zoological museum a few days earlier. In the museum they drew and made notes, and most of the children copied texts from the displayed labels. Back in the kindergarten classroom, the children discussed their observations, drawings, and notes. Some children asked teachers to add information about the animals to their notes. Based on these observations or their interests, children were encouraged to explore books about animals and to choose one or two animals about which they could write a contribution to the class "encyclopedia." For this task, the children were to illustrate and write a text with the help of an adult.

An assessment conducted just before the episodes reported here showed that Sami was a reader as measured by pseudo-word reading. In other words, he had reached the alphabetic phase (Ehri, 1991) and he was able to decode any Finnish word. But neither Pasi nor Hannu were able to read or write independently. Hannu recognized 10 letters. Although Pasi recognized considerably more—23 letters, which is enough for reading and writing the Finnish words—he was not able to decode. (The Finnish alphabet has 28 letters—all the English letters, except v and w, which are not counted as separate letters, plus å, ä, and ö. Note that 21 letters are required to spell Finnish words; the remaining 7 letters are needed for spelling foreign borrowings.)

Data Sources and Analysis

The data come from two working periods on 2 days which were a few days apart from each other (April 7 and 11). On the first day, the teacher and two of the boys (Sami and Pasi) read about snakes using five books as a source of information. Four of the books were children's information books and one of them was an ordinary encyclopedia. The children authored a page and illustrated it with the teacher's help. On the second day, three boys authored and illustrated another page among themselves. The data were collected by videotaping both events. We also used the products of the children's writing in our analysis.

To address the first two questions, the data from the videotapes were transcribed verbatim in three columns. In the first column were lines of dialogue, in the second were what the children were writing while they were speaking, and in the third was a listing of nonverbal activity such as turning the pages. These transcriptions were first carefully read several times and then coded for social interaction and guidance. First, the topics of discussion were coded. A topic unit included a conversational meaning. A new topic unit began when the topic of discussion shifted. As Linell (1990) noted, utterances are understandable only in context which means that each utterance is a response to a previous one and a new utterance follows the current one. Thus, the first coding within each topic unit allowed us to identify the nature of the dialogues. Second, the data were coded at the message unit level. A message unit is a single comment contributed by one participant. This procedure was necessary to identify the nature of each interlocutor's contribution in the dialogue and actions. These comments were coded for instances of guidance, and the following categories were identified: (a) motivating by encouraging, suggesting, and so on; (b) assisting by acting, such as reading further or dictating letters; and (c) directing attention to relevant spots of the text.

To address the third question, artifacts of children's writings were analyzed by using a diagram system similar to that used by Newkirk (1987) and Cox, Shanahan, and Tinzmann (1991). Using clause as unit of analysis, a diagram was created for each of the children's writings. Clauses were used as units because such an approach made apparent relationships between clauses within sentences. Thus, the diagrams show the hierarchical structure of each text and the relationship of individual clauses and their length.

Results

What Happened When Children Searched for Information About Snakes with the Teacher?

The teacher, Sami, and Pasi were studying about snakes. Because Sami was a fluent reader, the teacher asked him to read aloud which he did with speed (note that the extracts are translated from Finnish and that italics indicate reading):

> T: Let's stop here for a while. That's how the snake strangles. What does this poor mouse [do]? (pointing to the picture)
> S: Yes, and big snakes do [strangle]. They don't bite. But look, they twist in different positions around the animal . . . some snakes
> T: What do we have here [in a picture]?
> S: *Snakes don't wink their eyes because they don't have moving eyelids.* [laughter]
> T: Lets read this with Pasi!
> P: I don't know how to.
> T: Let's do it together!
> T & P: *Fresh food. Many snakes eat their victim when it still is alive.*

Sami continues reading with speed.

The teacher was the leader of the team by directing actions, discussions, and children's attention. In doing so, she ignored what Sami was saying several times. The teacher tried to draw Pasi from a peripheral position to a more central position and invited him to join her as she read the book. But because it was difficult for Pasi, the teacher did not bother Pasi with decoding, having him read along with her. The teacher also focused on making the discussion balanced and hence she directed her questions to Pasi:

> T: Pasi, what do you know about a snake's skin?
> P: They can remove it and then they . . .
> S: Yeah, and and the adder . . . me too, I saw removed skins of snakes in the museum.
> T: Did you see them too, Pasi?
> P: Yes.
> T: It says here that a snake's skin consists of hundreds of small scales.
> S: Same as the fishes have.
> T: A bit like the tiles on the roof, they overlap each other. Such small scales and there are so, so, so many of them.
> S: Just like fishes' [scales].
> T: Just like tiles on the roof.
> S: And fishes' [scales].
> T: And the fishes' [scales], too.
> S: Just like honeycombs.
> T: It says here [reads further].

Assisting was not easy because the teacher had to deal with wide variation in the children's literacy knowledge as well as in knowledge about snakes. During the discussion, it became apparent that Sami's knowledge about snakes was quite advanced based on his earlier readings at home (one of the books being used was his). Sami's knowledge was so advanced that the teacher did not realize it when they discussed the snakes' skins. As a result, a lack of intersubjectivity appeared between him and the teacher. Instead of noting Sami's view, the teacher stuck with the roof tile analogy presented in the book which was far less developed than Sami's understanding about the snakes' skins.

Although the teacher directed her attention to Pasi, she also acknowledged Sami's skill and asked him to read further. However, Sami was so eager to learn that he read unprompted. At times, the teacher had to restrain him from reading because it was obvious that important information about snakes would otherwise pass without comprehension.

The discussion was very intense, and occasionally the boys argued with the teacher. For example, they argued about what is inside the eggs:

S: What is inside eggs?
T: Indeed, what's inside eggs?
S: Baby chickens, of course, or baby birds.
T: Is it really? What's inside? What's inside a hen's egg?
P: Such small black lumps.
S: Really, yes that's right!
P: There are such, such black, such black lumps.
T: Have you sometimes seen it? Did you break such a bird's egg some time?
P: No, but I know, I know.

Arguing about eggs and snake skins demonstrates that young children do not necessarily abandon their views just because adults have power. In fact, they were quite persistent with their views and the teacher often had to verify her points by reading from the book. This session clearly showed what a powerful tool reading was for gaining information and initiating new topics of discussion not only for the teacher, but also for Sami. Altogether, 13 topics with several subtopics about snakes were read and discussed.

How Was the Information Transferred into Text and Pictures?

Pasi was the illustrator and Sami was the author. They did not want to change their roles because they were aware of what each was able to do. Pasi was willing to paint because "Sami is such a good writer." Later during the event, when the roles were renegotiated, changing the roles did not work because Sami still had so many things to write about; further, Pasi stated that "I'll continue with this (painting)." Such clear roles could have led the children to work separately but the teacher ensured their cooperation. All through the event she encouraged the boys to make shared decisions by saying, "You boys have to decide."

Because Sami was so much more competent in reading and writing, it was natural that he contributed most of the ideas for writing the page. But the teacher did not allow Sami to put them into practice without consulting Pasi. Instead she asked Pasi's opinion about the idea:

S: Poison or strangle. I'll write that.
T: Yes, but what about Pasi. Do we write about the poison? Wait, let's decide.

Pasi what do you want to write about this king snake? How does it look?
What could we write?

P: Black and white.

S: Yes, I'll write, see, see, I'll start here.

But it was not always easy for Sami to get the right words for his sentences from the discussion and he sometimes went back to the text: "Wait I'll read here. *An adder catches mice and moles.* I'll write that. [An adder-snake] is a compound word, right?" Although the teacher and Sami took turns in dominating the situation by reading and talking the most, their intention was to have a page as a result of collaborative work as evident in the examples above. In fact, while coding it was necessary to go back to the videotapes to listen to the prosodic cues such as stress and the tone of voices; doing so indicated that the teacher did not take the role of commander. Rather, she invited and suggested in an effort to maintain a balance in discussion between the boys.

Sami, in turn, was very enthusiastic about the task and eager to complete it. Note that Sami was equally confident in spelling as in reading. In fact, during the entire event he asked for help only twice in spelling. His role in the second event gives more evidence of his developed social behavior.

What Happened While Writing a Page Without the Teacher?

When the boys were working without the teacher, their interaction was very different from that described above. A third child, Hannu, was willing to join the group:

H: Can I also start making snakes for you, please?

P: No, no, don't. I'm so good at making these, so don't come. There is no space for more than one [snake]. Or maybe we should make a third page.

H: All right!

S: O.K.!

H: I'll help you.

Soon the boys were working and the following discussion took place:

P: Did you write anything about how snakes shed their skin?

S: No, not yet. But wait I'll write

P: I can't do anything because . . .

H: Here is more about snakes. Did you write this?

H: Do you need help? (He asks Sami.)

S: No. (Hands the pen over to Pasi.)

P: Do I start writing, so you can take a break?

With these words "you can take a break" the children created a new rule for working together. That is, changing from writing to painting meant break and resting. However, Sami's breaks did not allow him to get rid of the responsibility for segmenting the words into their sounds and letters because the other boys were not skillful enough to write independently:

S: *Anaconda, the giant snake of South America is not the longest snake of the world, but it is the thickest snake.* This is the anaconda (points to the picture). Write anaconda here, like so: A, A (repeats because P is pondering), N, A, K, O. [The word is anakonda in Finnish].

P: How does O look like?

S: A round one like zero (draws in the air).

S: Ana, anako N. Do you remember how D looks like?

P: D, D was (draws in the air).

S: Yeah, that's it, D, A.

The extract depicts the difference in Sami's and Pasi's literacy knowledge. Sami read fluently but Pasi did not even remember the letter shapes which Sami provided appropriately and gently. However, Pasi printed only this word after which Sami again took the writer's role. As a result of the role change and the change in the wording Sami did not control the structure of the sentence. Consequently, the children's page says: "Anaconda the thickest snake of South America and the world."

A little later the following discussion emerged:

P: Did you write about this (he asks Sami)?

S: What is it? This one is a sea snake.

P: Write!

S: Phew!

P: You have to carry on!

H: Phew!

P: You have rested for so long, start working now!

S: Rested? I just finished writing.

   . . .

S: Phew. I'm too tired of spelling these words.

H: I get it.

P: Let's continue tomorrow!

H: No, in the afternoon!

P: In the afternoon!

The two less knowledgeable children, Hannu and Pasi, dominated the more knowledgeable child, Sami, who carried the burden of authoring the text. Even Sami's breaks turned into tiring dictations instead of more relaxing painting. During this event, no more extensive reading or discussion took place. The page was produced based on memorization, scanning the books to look for illustration, and occasionally reading captions underneath. The event was action driven, which did not allow space for wide reading, nor did they have the same resources as in the earlier event to do so since Sami was the only reader. Interestingly, the boys were on task without the adult's control because their motivation was very high. They were ready to author a "hundred pages or at least fifteen," they said.

What Patterns are Evident in the Two Pages About Snakes?

Overall the two pages authored are excellent examples of 6-year-olds' cooperative work. The amount of text is quite impressive and the texts and illustrations match. Also, the spelling of the words is very good, due to the fact that Sami worked as the writer in both situations. But there are also differences between the written pages and illustrations.

The first page, which was authored with the teacher, has more text: 14 sentences and 68 words. The text includes six subtopics, with three of the subtopics elaborated by using a few additional explaining sentences. The tree diagram in Figure 1 shows the organization of the text and the way the children related individual statements to the topic "snakes" and the subtopics. As is evident from the diagram, the clauses within each subtopic are linked to the preceding and following statements. However, the location of the fifth sentence is not optimum because it is semantically linked to the second sentence.

The text includes many sentences similar to the books the children used. As described earlier, Sami tended to draw what to write from the books. However, he was not allowed to copy all the information from the books, and some books were even closed when he was writing. Several sentences share many words with the books' sentences but also include substitutions of synonyms. This finding suggests that Sami internalized quite well what was read and that he was able to recall sentences literally, but also that he used his own wording. Evidence of his good memorization skill comes from the fact that he recalled the page numbers for where to find certain information. At the bottom of the page there are sentences that include information from several books. This information was gained both from pictures and their captions.

The illustration is simple, two snakes and a tree. Pasi has labeled the snakes, but despite the help he received, the spelling is not quite correct. Despite the simplicity of the pictures, Sami praised them: "Quite good looking snakes." "Pasi draw a good one." "Wow!"

The second page the boys created looks different from the first page, just as the circumstances of creating the pages were different. The text is shorter than the

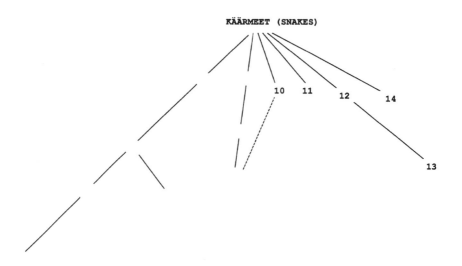

Figure 1. The organization of the text on the first page.

first page, with 10 sentences and 45 words. The organization of the text is also different, as Figure 2 shows. The sentences are in random order and not related to each other. Thus, they could be reorganized with no loss of meaning. The text is a list of sentences each describing a fact about one snake. These sentences are shortened versions of the captions in the books.

There is a clear explanation to the text structure. There were two painters who looked for a model for their pictures from the books' illustrations. When they finished their drawing of each snake they asked: "Did you already write about this snake?" Because it was faster to paint than write, Sami had to limit the length of his writing to keep up with his peers' painting. Thus, creating the text for the second page was driven by painting whereas the first text was authored based on discussion and reading.

There was one exceptional sentence that contained erroneous information due to incorrectly combining facts found in the encyclopedia in two separate sentences. The children's sentence said: "The deadly bite of a snake is seldom dangerous." Evidently, Sami was in such a rush while writing the text that he did not have time to think over the ideas and monitor his writing. In the earlier event, the teacher took the final responsibility for creating sensible sentences.

The illustrations on the second page are much more attractive than those on the first page. The snakes resemble the snakes in the books. Sami was so overloaded with the work, he did not have time to praise the drawings this time. The snakes are labeled as in the first picture, but this time Pasi and Hannu made Sami label them by using the excuse that he was so much more competent.

Discussion

The two literacy events documented here can be interpreted in light of the research and theory reviewed earlier. On one hand, the teacher was an excellent assistant. This is evident both from the discussion and the text the children produced with her assistance. On the other hand, she tended to dominate the situa-

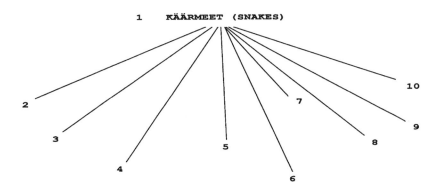

Figure 2. The organization of the text on the second page.

tion by talking the most (cf. Almasi, 1995). When children were left on their own they were able to solve the problems themselves and the two less knowledgeable children performed well beyond their own abilities with a more competent peer as Vygotsky (1978) suggested. The findings, however, contrast with Piaget's notion that children abandon their ideas before the adult's power (Tudge & Rogoff, 1989). In the first event, the children were very persistent, but they were not necessarily good at verifying their views.

These two events can also be evaluated from the perspective of using information text as a context for literacy. It became clear that the children were interested in learning about snakes as well as working on authoring their contribution to the class "encyclopedia." That the children authored the second page, when only one was necessary, strongly supports that interpretation. Perhaps their motivation was also supported by the use of small-group work. This small-group work helped them make sense of what was going on and gave them opportunities to be active contributors. While working this way in a small group, the children used humor, laughter and engaged behavior, and language typical of natural discussion. Working with the teacher resulted in more formal interactions.

We think that the teacher's role, despite the flaws in the interaction and her dominance, was necessary for children to learn strategies for working with such a demanding task. We suspect that both the first text and the second text were so advanced due to the thorough discussion about the first text and experiences related to it. The data suggest that the children's interactions with their peers may have been influenced by the teacher's model in the earlier episode. While working with the first text, the children acquired both a social and cognitive model for their next event.

Further research should extend these findings by further examining the interplay between teacher- and peer-led small-group episodes. Teachers' flexible use of varied collaboration appears to be rich topic for investigation (Seidenstricker, 1999). Moreover, additional research on young children's interaction with information text seems particularly promising, in view of its apparent potential for creating motivating literacy contexts.

References

Almasi, J. F. (1995). The nature of fourth graders' sociocognitive conflicts in peer-led and teacher-led discussions of literature. *Reading Research Quarterly, 30,* 314–351.

Bissex, G. L. (1980). *Gnys at wrk: A child learns to write and read.* Cambridge, MA: Harvard University Press.

Cox, B. E., Shanahan, T., & Tinzman, M. B. (1991). Children's knowledge of organization, cohesion, and voice in written exposition. *Research in the Teaching of English, 25,* 179–218.

Dreher, M. J. (2000). Fostering reading for learning. In L. Baker, M. J. Dreher, & J. T. Guthrie (Eds.), *Engaging young readers: Promoting achievement and motivation* (pp. 68–93). New York: Guilford.

Dreher, M. J. (1995). *Sixth-grade researchers: Posing questions, finding information, and writing a report* (Reading Research Report No. 40). College Park, MD: University of Maryland, National Reading Research Center.

Duke, N. K. (2000). 3.6 minutes per day: The scarcity of informational texts in first grade. *Reading Research Quarterly, 35,* 202–224.

Ehri, L. (1991). Development of the ability to read words. In R. Barr, M. L. Kamil, P. Mosenthal, & P. D. Pearson (Eds.), *Handbook of reading research* (Vol. 2, pp. 383–417). New York: Longman.

Gambrell, L. B., & J. F. Almasi (Eds.). (1996). *Lively discussion! Fostering engaged reading.* Newark, DE: International Reading Association.

Harste. J. E., Woodward, V. A., & Burke, C. L. (1984). *Language stories and literacy lessons.* Portsmouth, NH: Heinemann.

Korkeamäki, R.-L. (1996). *How first graders and kindergarten children constructed literacy knowledge in the context of story reading and meaningful text* (ACTA Universitatis Ouluensis series E 21). Oulu, Finland: University of Oulu.

Korkeamäki, R.-L., & Dreher, M. J. (1995). Meaning-based reading instruction in a Finnish kindergarten. In K. A. Hinchman, D. J. Leu, & C. K. Kinzer (Eds.), *Perspectives on literacy research and practice.* Forty-fourth yearbook of the National Reading Conference (pp. 235–242). Chicago: National Reading Conference.

Linell, P. (1990). The power of dialogue dynamics. In I. Markova & K. Foppa (Eds.), *The dynamics of dialogue* (pp. 147–177). New York: Harvester.

Newkirk, T. (1987). The non-narrative writing of young children. *Research in the Teaching of English. 21,* 121–144.

Pappas, C. C. (1993). Is narrative primary? Some insights from kindergartners' pretend readings of stories and information books. *Journal of Reading Behavior, 25,* 97–129.

Paratore, J. R., & McCormack, R. L. (Eds.). (1997). *Peer talk in the classroom: Learning form research.* Newark, DE: International Reading Association.

Rogoff, B. (1991). Guidance and participation in spatial planning. In L. Resnick, J. Levin, & S. Teasley (Eds.), *Perspectives on socially shared cognition* (pp. 349–383). Washington, DC: American Psychological Association.

Rosenblatt, L. (1978). *The reader, the text, the poem: The transactional theory of the literary work.* Carbondale: Southern Illinois University Press.

Seidenstricker, L. S. (1999). *The comparative effects of small group peer-led discussion on the strategic reading comprehension, literary interpretation, and engagement of seventh grade readers.* Unpublished doctoral dissertation, University of Maryland, College Park.

Tudge, J. (1992). Processes and consequences of peer collaboration: A Vygotskian analysis. *Child Development, 63,* 1364–1379.

Tudge, J., & Rogoff, B. (1989). Peer influences in cognitive development: Piagetian and Vygotskian perspectives. In M. H. Bornstein, & J. S. Bruner (Eds.), *Interaction in human development* (pp. 17–40) Hillsdale, NJ: Erlbaum.

Webb, N. M., & Palincsar, A. S. (1996). Group processes in the classroom. In D. C. Berliner & R. C. Calfee (Eds.), *Handbook of educational psychology* (pp. 841–873). New York: Macmillan.

Wertsch, J. V. (1985). *Vygotsky and the social formation of mind.* Cambridge, MA: Harvard University Press.

Vygotsky, L. S. (1978). *Mind in society: The development of higher psychological processes.* Cambridge, MA: Harvard University Press.

How is Technology Really Used for Literacy Instruction in Elementary and Middle-School Classrooms?

Douglas Fisher, Diane Lapp, and James Flood
San Diego State University

S tudents from yesteryear would hardly recognize some of the "smart" class rooms of the present. Imagine the fourth-grade class of 1965 visiting their alma mater today. Many would be awestruck at seeing high-tech computer labs, student groups working on computers in the classroom, and teachers assigning work that required students to access the World Wide Web not only for research but also for interaction with experts across content areas. Lessons would now be assigned, including the *Triton* project, based on thematic units about the ocean (e.g., http://edtech.sandinet/triton/), *Earth Day,* offering environmental activities (e.g., http://earthday.wilderness.org/), and *MayaQuest: Mysteries of the Rainforest,* a site where students and teachers accompany explorers on archeological trips through Mexico and Central America (e.g., http://www.classroom.com/mayaquest/default.html).

Whereas the question of the 1960s and 1970s might have been whether or not to have typewriters and calculators in every classroom, technology in the last half of the century has galloped far beyond the predictions of many. During the past decade, the number of computers used in classrooms has significantly increased. In 1997, schools averaged one computer for every 6 students nationwide (Education Week, 1998); 10 years ago there was approximately one computer for every 30 students. The annual budget for school computers topped $5 billion (Education Week, 1998). As computers and other forms of technology (e.g., CD-ROMs, video laser discs) become more common in the classroom, educators are asking for evidence of the effectiveness of technology (Fisher, Lapp, & Flood, 1999).

Current research indicates a positive relationship between electronic environments and literacy (Baines, 1998; Beach & Lundell, 1998; Kieffer, Hale, & Templeton, 1998). Reading and writing instruction and performance in an electronic literacy environment differs from those found in traditional classroom activities. Typically, when students are asked to write papers, they have an understanding of their audience and the expectations of the teacher. However, in writing something for the web that anyone can read, students "place a premium on the paper's accuracy, use of technical and specialized vocabulary, and degree of coherence" (Alvarez, 1998, p. 45).

Dahl and Farnan (1998) point out in their book, *Children's Writing,* that computers and technology have significantly altered the ways in which people expe-

National Reading Conference Yearbook, 49, pp. 464–476.

rience the world. Researchers have attempted to document positive outcomes when students use computers as part of their writing process program. As Dahl and Farnan further note, the research results are complex. For example, Russell (1991), in her meta-analysis, found that the relationship between technology and writing was significantly influenced by the social interactions that students had in the computer lab although the writing was higher quality when students used word processing software and computers.

In a study of first graders' use of word processing software, Jones and Pellegrini (1996) found that the use of technology facilitated the students' writing of narratives. These researchers hypothesized that the use of the computer shifted the focus from the mechanical aspects of writing to focus on words and ideas. Similarly, in a case study of a 5-year-old writer, Cochran-Smith, Kahn, and Paris (1990) noted that the computer provided a mechanism that supported the child's writing. More specifically, the computer allowed the child to focus more directly on her words and ideas than on her handwriting, letter formation, and alignment of words.

Similar results have been documented for older students as well. In their study of middle school students, Owston, Murphy, and Wideman (1991) found that students wrote higher quality essays when using word processing software than when they wrote their essays in cursive. The students in their study were all experienced computer users. The researchers hypothesized that the reason for the high quality was related to the number of times students revised their work on the computer. Odenthal (1992) found similar results among second-language learners. Haas (1989) also documented similar results when she found that easy-to-use software programs facilitated the revision process. The results of these studies indicate that technology positively impacts literacy and that teachers can effectively use technology in literacy instruction.

It may very well be, as Cuban (1999) noted that "teachers use computers at home more than at school" (p. 68). As computers and other forms of technology flood our classrooms, it seems reasonable to study how teachers have incorporated technology into their literacy instruction. In our study, we examined the ways in which technology was used in order to understand: (a) the types of technology used, (b) the comfort and confidence teachers have with technology use, (c) the contextualization of computers—how they are used, and (d) the reasons teachers give for their practices. More specifically, we were interested in learning from larger numbers of teachers about their actual practices.

Method

The purpose of this study was to investigate the current practices of classroom teachers relative to the integration of technology into their literacy instruction. Teachers were surveyed and observed to determine their: (a) insights about issues affecting language-arts instruction, (b) the current use of technology, (c) their beliefs about effective instruction using technology, and (d) their comfort with technology.

Participants

One hundred and thirty-seven teachers from Southern California were randomly selected from a pool of teachers who met the following criteria: (a) teaching in one of the 30 urban schools in which San Diego State University and San Diego Unified School District are partners in the preparation of new teachers; this spread of schools afforded the opportunity to study issues related to literacy instruction for children from many cultures, language backgrounds, and socioeconomic levels; and (b) either a master's degree or current enrollment in a graduate program after having completed a credential program. Selected teachers ranged in experience from 1 to 29 years, with an average of 5.5 years. The number of teachers per grade level included 55 kindergarten to second-grade teachers, 35 third- and fourth-grade teachers, 28 fifth- and sixth-grade teachers, and 19 seventh and eighth-grade teachers. All but 6 teachers indicated that they had a computer at home (96%), all (100%) had e-mail at school, and 119 (87%) had e-mail and access to the World Wide Web at home.

Measures

Two measures were designed to survey and observe the participants.

Survey. This instrument, which contained demographic questions and 10 content-specific questions, was divided into four sections. Section 1—Demographic data: In this section participants were asked to indicate years of teaching, grade taught, and at-home personal technology use of computers, e-mail, and World Wide Web. Section 2—Technology use: This section consisted of three questions, the first of these was open-ended and focused on the types of technologies available for use in the classroom. The next two questions were Likert-type questions related to concern about and confidence in using technology for literacy instruction. Section 3—Student assessment and instruction: This section consisted of four questions, each of which focused on student needs and methods of instruction, such as the importance of integrating technology instruction into the language arts program. Choices on these 5-point, Likert-type questions ranged from "not at all important" to "very important." The final question in this section was open-ended and asked for information about the ways in which technology was used during literacy instruction. Teachers were asked to expand on their answers and provide examples. Section 4—Classroom logistics and management included three questions about grouping strategies used during language arts time and the amount of time spent in literacy instruction per day.

The survey was piloted with five teachers who taught at schools not in the study. Minor changes in wording were made based on the feedback from these five teachers.

Classroom observations. The second measure consisted of classroom observations. The 137 teachers who completed the survey agreed to possible selection for a classroom observation. This allowed the researchers to observe a randomly selected subset of the teachers who completed surveys, 6 from each grade level (*n*=54). We were interested in how teachers actually used technology for literacy instruction and the amount of time they allotted to literacy instruction. The observations were unannounced and occurred during the literacy block of time. Fieldnote forms (LeCompte & Preissle, 1993) were used to create a record of classroom events and conversations. To ensure consistency and interrater reliability, teachers were always observed by at least two researchers. All researchers have experience with ethnographic and qualitative research. Teachers were observed twice each, and classroom observations typically lasted between 60 and 100 minutes.

Analysis

Survey responses were quantified to determine frequency of responses made by teachers regarding how they used technology as well as the amount of time they allotted to literacy instruction. Data from the surveys were used for measures of central tendency and to create frequency tables. Differences were identified and grade levels collapsed for ease of presentation. Observational data were categorized using a constant comparative method (Bogdan & Biklen, 1992). The observation notes were independently reviewed by the researchers. A number of coding categories were identified following multiple reviews of the data (LeCompte & Preissle, 1993). The final categories and representative quotes were agreed on by the researchers. Each of these categories was named, and quotes that typified the category were identified. For example, as the researchers reviewed the data, it became clear that the data clustered into four main categories: technology used in learning centers, technology integrated into whole-class instruction, technology used during separate instructional times, and other uses of technology such as for Spanish-language instruction. Discussion of each category continued until consensus was reached. In addition, direct quotes were obtained from the surveys and during the observations.

Results

The results from the 137 surveys and 54 observations were combined into several areas related to literacy instruction, including: technology materials used, concern and confidence relative to technology, the ways in which technology was used, and grouping practices and time allocated for literacy instruction.

Technology Material Availability and Use

In section 2 of the survey, teachers were asked to indicate availability and use of technology in their classroom. Computers were the most common; 83% of the teachers indicated they used them for tasks such as word processing, Internet access, and phonics skills training. Fifty-seven percent of the teachers indicated that they used listening posts so that students could access books on tape. TV/VCRs were used in 52% of the classrooms for showing videos and watching the news for current events. CD-ROMs were also common in these classrooms and

46% of the teachers indicated that they used them to access information sources such as encyclopedias and interactive learning programs. Overheads, film projectors, records, and video cameras were used in 37%, 22%, 8%, and 2% of the classrooms, respectively. These types of technology were used for presentations, poetry reading, and as information sources.

Consistent with survey responses, classrooms were filled with various types of technology, including computers, CD-ROMs, TV/VCRs, listening posts, CD players, overheads, calculators, and the like. The technology seemed to be strategically placed around the room. For example, in a third-grade classroom, a group of four students were sitting on the floor using an overhead projector to project poems on the wall as they took turns reading them to one another. In a fifth-grade classroom, five students seated at a table were listening, via headphones, to a cassette tape recording of the biography of Frederick Douglass while they read along. The observational and survey data indicate that teachers had a wide range of materials available. Interestingly, no classroom had more than five computers (including the teacher's computer), no more than one listening station, and no more than one TV/VCR. Thus grouping situations were influenced by the technology available.

Concern, Confidence, and Use for Assessment and Instruction

Teachers were asked about their use of, concern for, and their confidence in teaching using technology during literacy instruction. We were interested to see if our observations matched teachers' beliefs about their assessment and instruction practices. Teachers became increasingly concerned about their students technological literacy once the students had developed a basic level of reading literacy. Interestingly, the more teachers integrated the use of technology the more they worried about doing so in a manner that promoted reading and writing literacy (see Table 1). Teachers saw themselves as teachers of reading and writing with technology as a means to accomplish this, rather than teachers of technological literacy.

Observational data supported these findings. Teachers in the upper grades were pleased to have visitors observe their lessons and talked freely about the

Table 1

Concern, Confidence, and Use Regarding Technology for Literacy Instruction

Grades	% Very Concerned	% Very Confident	% Who Use Technology Often
K–2	8	20	40
3rd & 4th	18	20	63
5th & 6th	52	35	71
7th & 8th	75	42	85

ways in which they used technology during literacy instruction. A sixth-grade teacher said, "You've come at a great time. The students are just starting their webquests and I'm working with a small group on webpage design. You'll see that we only have five computers, so I have to have a lot of different reading and writing activities going on." However, the primary-grade teachers were worried that they were not performing in some way that the researchers expected. As a first-grade teacher said, "I'm not sure what you are looking for. I'm really focused on reading instruction and I use my computer for the language development program that the district purchased. I haven't yet introduced the web to my students, but I'm sure some of them know about it. I have to get them to read before I can concentrate on the use of technology."

One of the most common concerns voiced by the teachers related to the reliability of the technology. A third-grade teacher said, "I'd feel more confident using technology if I knew what to do when something went wrong. At home, I can call someone. In the middle of a lesson or group activity, I really can't call anyone for help. When I do call, help may not arrive for a few days!" It may very well be that teachers would like to further incorporate technology into their literacy instruction, but lack the technical skills to problem-solve hardware and software failures. Similarly, some of the teachers who are less confident may have had experiences like the kindergarten teacher who said, "I love technology, but I've had it go really bad in the middle of a lesson, so I don't use it much. One time, I planned this very interactive lesson with videos, recordings, and a slide show on the computer. When I was ready to do it, the program on my school computer wasn't the same version as the one at home. Nothing worked and my students sat and watched me fuss with the computer for about 15 minutes. What a waste of their time and mine." This sounded reminiscent of teacher's stories of lost hours of instruction because of broken reel-to-reel films and burnt out overhead projector bulbs. Perhaps an on-staff technology aide who could be available to teachers when problems with hardware occur could provide a feeling of greater security that appears to be needed as teachers attempt to integrate technology throughout their instruction.

The Implementation of Technology: Contextualized or Isolated

Teachers were also asked to respond to a question about the ways in which they used technology during literacy instruction. The results differed by the grade level taught. Teachers who taught kindergarten through fourth grade used technology most often during learning centers or rotations (47%). Examples included listening stations, writing centers, phonics skills instruction on computers. Thirty-six percent of the teachers integrated technology into their instruction through the use of VCRs, overheads, and video projections of the read-aloud material. Another 25% of the teachers indicated that technology was used during separate instructional times such as computer labs and pull-out programs. Finally, 6% of the K-4 teachers indicated that they did not use technology in their classrooms.

In the upper grades, fifth through eighth, learning centers and rotations were also the most common place in which technology was used—as indicated by 76% of the teachers. Fifty-four percent of the upper grade and middle school teachers indicated that they integrated technology into their instruction, whereas 35% indicated that their students used technology during separate instructional times at labs, 22% for pull-out, and 9% for Spanish instruction. Some written examples of these approaches include:

> Learning centers: "I ask students to find current information about the topics we are studying on the web. I have bookmarked several different sites that they can use to find this information. I have to be careful that they don't just play or look for inappropriate sites. There is a lot of good information for students to find." (Grade 4)

> Integrated into lesson: "Given that our district has a standard that students will use technology, I think it is important that they see me using it. I try to use some form of technology every day—computers and video projection, websites, email, overheads, etc. I especially like to email with my students and for them to email one another." (Grade 4)

> Separate instructional times: "I think it is important to have students learn specific skills on the computer. I only have 3 computers in my class so we go to the lab several times a week. Students get individual attention from the programs and from my aide and me." (Grade 2)

The observational data also supported these survey results. Learning centers and rotations were the most common way in which students accessed technology. We observed a number of classrooms in which students were working in groups of four or five and, as part of that work, were using technology. We also observed teachers integrating technology into their whole-class instruction. Interestingly, we observed four teachers who were so comfortable with technology and who so completely understood how to meaningfully use technology during their instruction that the technology became transparent. The point of these lessons was not the computer. Nor was it a fancy way of doing something that could have been done another way—like answering test questions on the computer. These four teachers had transcended the technology—the focus was on learning, and it was clear that the technology was essential for that learning.

We also observed students using technology as part of a lab. The lab situations were limited to computers and most often were related to direct instruction of reading or math. The purpose of these lessons was not to make technology transparent, but to engage students in specific tasks via the computer. The programs that the students used varied, but each of them involved graphics, sound, and immediate feedback. The tasks were designed to be completed individually, and group interactions were not observed during computer lab time. Students seemed engaged in their work and printed their review sheets at the end of the times. Some of the software offered points at the end of the session that students could later redeem for prizes.

Although we did not observe any classroom void of technology, including computers, VCRs, and overheads, there were two classrooms in which the technology was not used either time while we were there. The first was a primary-grade teacher who indicated that she "did not use much technology, but rather focused on individual student's reading." She also indicated that she did use the VCR "as a reward to watch videos on some Fridays." The other teacher, a fourth-grade teacher, indicated that she did use technology during her instruction, but that the particular thematic unit they were studying (growth of the rainforest) did not require technology. However, she indicated that her next thematic unit (saving the rainforest) involved significant use of technology.

Grouping Practices

In addition to the methods and materials used, we were also interested in the grouping strategies that teachers used during the literacy block. It should be noted that California has reduced class size in Grades K–3 to a maximum of 20 students. The upper-grade classrooms still contained 32–36 students. Teachers across grades differed widely in their grouping strategies for literacy instruction. For example, class time in the primary grades included: 52% homogeneous groups, 25% whole group, and 23% heterogeneous groups. In contrast, the upper-grade teachers reported their use of class time to be 25% homogeneous groups, 30% whole class, and 45% heterogeneous groups.

This was clearly displayed in the observations. The primary-grade teachers in this study often grouped students homogeneously based on reading instruction needs. These were not permanent ability groups for the entire day but were fairly consistent across literacy block time. Students in the primary grades worked in small homogeneous groups most often with other students with similar needs who the teacher had identified. Teachers in the primary grades used whole-class instruction to read aloud to students and complete shared writing activities. In observations at the same schools in which ability grouping was occurring in the primary grades, the upper-grade teachers were using much more heterogeneous grouping patterns. However, it should be noted that the upper-grade teachers still had a wide range of reading levels and a range of opinions regarding grouping practices. As a fourth-grade teacher said, "I think that ability grouping is dangerous. I know that some of the first-grade teachers at this school group by ability. However, they only have 20 students, I have 36 this year. There is also more difference in reading fluency by the time they are in fourth grade. So, I mix up the groups and plan activities for the students to do together that push all their learning."

One of the fifth-grade teachers highlighted the relationship between the technology he had access to and his grouping patterns. "I have a listening post with four headphones. I have four computers in my class. I have one TV/VCR with only one headphone. You see, the technology dictates my grouping. While I may want to have six students listen to the read aloud on tape, I can only have four at a time. I may want to have five or seven students at the computer station, but then they'd have to pair up."

Time Allocations

The final question in section 4 related to the amount of time that teachers spend on literacy instruction. All of the elementary school teachers used a 3-hour literacy block as mandated by district office. This means that, for 3 hours each day, students were engaged in reading, writing, speaking, listening, and viewing. All teachers provided students with independent reading time, a read aloud, and writing instruction during the literacy block. Most often, teachers' lessons came directly from the basal that the class was using. The primary-grade teachers often set aside time during this block for phonics instruction. This translates to about 45-minutes per day of, as one teacher said, "working with words."

The observational data supported the information from the survey. Teachers in Grades K–8 were observed spending significant amounts of time on reading, writing, and word study activities. Their philosophical orientation toward technology was the greatest predictor of the ways that they used this time. In other words, teachers who were more comfortable with technology used it more often during literacy instruction. As students got older, they were also more likely to see technology used as part of their literacy instruction.

Discussion

The results indicated that the majority of teachers in the study integrated technology into their literacy instruction. However, we did not obtain information about the use of technology at other points during the day. It may very well be that teachers use technology differently for other content areas. The use of technology by these teachers seemed related to: (a) the degree of importance assigned to it by them as well as their confidence in using it to teach, (b) the availability of it in their classroom and its role in instruction, (c) the grouping strategies that they used, and (d) the support they received for technology failures.

Technology Available

Teachers in this study reported a wide range of technology at their disposal. When we first considered this study, we were most interested in the use of modern, high technology devices such as computers and CD-ROMs. However, the concept of "technology" to many teachers includes CD players, record players, overhead projectors, video projection systems, listening stations, calculators, and the like. We would be wise to address all of these forms of technology when talking with classroom teachers about literacy instruction. Because, to many teachers computers were just one type of technology, we believe that the preparation of future teachers should include the appropriate use of all kinds of technology during literacy instruction and assessment, including overheads to read poetry, listening stations during group rotations, and webquests on the computer.

Concern and Confidence

Data indicated that there was a strong relationship between concern about technology, confidence expressed by teachers, and actual amount of technology used. Primary-grade teachers were less concerned, had less confidence, and used technology less. They believed that their basic responsibility was to teach their students to "read and write." As one teacher stated, "They can't read yet, so they really need direct instruction from me because I don't have any early literacy software." Once this was accomplished, this teacher as well as others felt that they could add other dimensions such as technology into the curriculum. As we talked with them, it became obvious that if they had early literacy software (e.g., phonemic awareness, alphabet and word recognition), they would use it in a technology center to reinforce their instruction.

Upper- and middle-grade teachers were more confident, more concerned, and used technology more often. This seems logical given the heavy focus on learning to read in the primary grades. It would be interesting to know if the heavy emphasis phonics instruction has received in the media has had any influence on this aspect of professional practice (Collins, 1997; McQuillan, 1998). We believe that classroom technology use would increase if schools provided a technology resource teacher who apprised teachers of existing software and supported classroom technology maintenance and use.

This group of teachers could not be considered technophobic. They had significant access to computers, e-mail, and the World Wide Web both at school and at home. We were impressed with the level of access these teachers had, and even with the amount of technology use we saw during literacy instruction. However, the findings do support Cuban's (1999) position: although most teachers use technology in their own life, they may not be as adroit in using technology as part of their instructional repertoire simply because they need maintenance support. The preparation of future teachers should address the ways in which technology can be meaningfully integrated into instruction. As Cuban (1999) points out, we no longer need to teach future teachers BASIC programming. We believe that instead teachers need to be continually inserviced regarding available technology that supports that literacy programs. As Poftak (1999) pointed out, teachers today are learning about the integration of technology into the curriculum and managing technology in the classroom. We believe teachers are doing well using the technology they have and will continue to expand this use if they are given local school support to do so.

The Methods of Technology for Literacy Instruction

The methods used by these teachers did not differ much by grade level. At all levels, teachers reported and were observed using technology most often for learning centers. Given the numbers of upper- and middle-grade teachers who used technology, it can be assumed that teachers use more technology as students get older, and our observations confirmed this. These teachers often used technology during literacy instruction because they felt comfortable that these students could read the information found on the Internet and in the software.

The teachers in this study raised a very interesting point. Many felt that their instruction, especially in learning centers, was dependent on the available technology. For example, in one classroom there was only one listening station with two headphones. This influenced the planning of group activities and rotations. Computers in classrooms ranged from one to five. This forced some intermediate-grade teachers to use a separate instructional lab time to ensure that all students had "seat time" in front of a computer. The schools were in various stages of being Internet ready. We found that in spite of these limitations teachers were successfully using the available technology.

The Pervasive Nature of Technology

Perhaps even more interesting than the approaches used to integrate technology was the fact that the 54 teachers we observed (93%) were observed using technology in their classrooms during random visits. Although the methods varied based on the teachers' philosophical orientation, each provided students with instruction that required them to use technology. This finding is significant given the focus of the media attention on the need for students to experience technology during their school years and the new technology standards (e.g., Rosenthal, 1999). Although educators may need to agree upon best practice methods of instruction via technology, it is clear that students in these classrooms were learning that technology was a valuable and important part of life.

Summary

This study adds to the growing body of evidence that classroom teachers are concerned about technology for their students and that they do provide this instruction regularly in the classroom. As one teacher said, "I provide a balanced language arts program for all of my students. As part of that balance, they need to see that technology is a tool. It is a tool that allows them to find information. It also gives them another authentic reason for reading. When they get into the websites, they really want to know what's there." Although the survey data indicated that primary-grade teachers were less confident about their use of technology and appropriate literacy software, the observational date indicated that most of these teachers in Grades K-8 were quite skilled at designing instruction that was appropriate for their students and that integrated the use of a wide array of technology. We believe that policy makers and politicians could benefit from listening not only to classroom teachers describe their strategies for meaningfully integrating technology into the classroom but also to the specifics on their needs.

References

Alvarez, M. C. (1998). Developing critical and imaginative thinking within electronic literacy. *NASSP Bulletin, 82*(6), 41–47.

Baines, L. (1998). The future of the written word. In J. S. Simmons & L. Baines (Eds.), *Language study in middle school, high school, and beyond* (pp. 190–214). Newark, DE: International Reading Association.

Beach, R., & Lundell, D. (1998). Early adolescents' use of computer-mediated communication in writing and reading. In D. Reinking, M. C. McKenna, L. D. Labbo, & R. D. Kieffer (Eds.), *Handbook of literacy and technology* (pp. 93–112). Mahwah, NJ: Erlbaum.

Bogdan, R. C., & Biklen, S. K. (1992). *Qualitative research for education* (2nd ed.). Needham Heights, MA: Allyn & Bacon.

Cochran-Smith, M., Kahn, J., & Paris, C. L. (1990). Writing with a felicitous tool. *Theory Into Practice, 29,* 235–247.

Collins, J. (1997, October 27). How Johnny should read. *Time Magazine,* pp. 78–81.

Cuban, L. (1999, August 4). The technology puzzle. *Education Week, 18*(43), pp. 68, 47.

Dahl, K. L., & Farnan, N. (1998). *Children's writing: Perspectives from research.* Newark, DE: International Reading Association and National Reading Conference.

Education Week. (1998, October 1). *Technology counts '98: Putting school technology to the test.* Bethesda, MD: Author.

Fisher, D., Lapp, D., & Flood, J. (1999). Technology and literacy: Is there a positive relationship? *California Reader, 32*(4), 35–38.

Haas, C. (1989). Does the medium make a difference: Two studies of writing with computers. *Human Computer Interaction, 4,* 149–169.

Jones, I., & Pellegrini, A. D. (1996). The effects of social relationships, writing media, and microgenetic development of first-grade students' written narratives. *American Educational Research Journal, 33,* 691–718.

Kieffer, R. D., Hale, M. E., & Templeton, A. (1998). Electronic literacy portfolios: Technology transformations in a first-grade classroom. In D. Reinking, M. C. McKenna, L. D. Labbo, & R. D. Kieffer (Eds.), *Handbook of literacy and technology* (pp. 145–164). Mahwah, NJ: Erlbaum.

LeCompte, M. D., & Preissle, J. (1993). *Ethnography and qualitative design in educational research* (2nd ed.). San Diego, CA: Academic.

McQuillan, J. (1998). *The literacy crisis: False claims, real solutions.* Portsmouth, NH: Heinemann.

Odenthal, J. M. (1992). *The effect of a computer-based writing program on the attitudes and performance of students acquiring English as a second language.* Unpublished Doctoral dissertation, San Diego State University & Claremont Graduate University, San Diego, CA.

Owston, P. D., Murphy, S., & Wideman, H. H. (1991). On and off computer writing of eighth grade students experienced in word processing. *Computers in the Schools, 8,* 67–87.

Poftak, A. (1999). Technology and learning surveys schools of education. *Technology and Learning, 19*(8), 26–27.

Rosenthal, I. G. (1999). New teachers and technology: Are they prepared? *Technology and Learning, 19*(8), 22–27.

Russell, R. G. (1991, April). *A meta-analysis of word processing and attitudes and the impact on the quality of writing.* Paper presented at the meeting of the American Educational Research Association, Chicago.

Appendix A

Technology Questionnaire

How many years have you been teaching? _____

What grade do you currently teach? _____ For how long? _____

What grades have you taught, and for how many years at each grade?_____

_____

Describe your technology use at home (e-mail, websites, word processing, games, etc.)

_____

_____

_____

1. What types of technology are available for use by students in your classroom?

2. What level of concern do you have about integrating technology into the classroom?
   1 = none   2 = low   3 = average   4 = high   5 = very high

3. How would you rate your confidence in integrating technology into the classroom?
   1 = none   2 = low   3 = average   4 = high   5 = very high

4. How important is integrating technology into your language arts curriculum?
   1 = none   2 = low   3 = average   4 = high   5 = very high

5. How important is technology in your assessment and grading system?
   1 = none   2 = low   3 = average   4 = high   5 = very high

6. How important is technology in your instructional decisions?
   1 = none   2 = low   3 = average   4 = high   5 = very high

7. Please describe how you use technology in the classroom (give us lots of examples)

8. When do you group your students? For what part of the day?

9. Which of the following best describes your student groupings?
   a. I use both heterogeneous and homogeneous grouping.
   b. I use only heterogeneous grouping.
   c. I use only homogeneous grouping.
   d. I use only whole-class instruction.
   e. Other

10. How much time each day do you spend on literacy instruction?

A Study of the Effectiveness of an Intervention Program Designed to Accelerate Reading for Struggling Readers in the Upper Grades

J. David Cooper
Ball State University

Irene Boschken
San Juan Unified School District

Janet McWilliams
Literacy Consultant

Lynne Pistochini
San Juan Unified School District

The purpose of this study was to test the effectiveness of a reading intervention model designed specifically for upper grade students who are struggling readers. This model, known as Project SUCCESS, is designed to accelerate reading for students using authentic literature sequenced in complexity, reciprocal teaching, graphic organizers, and scaffolded instruction with 40-minute daily lessons that are delivered *in addition to* quality classroom instruction.

Theoretical Framework

Project SUCCESS is based on the following research-based conclusions:

1. There are upper grade students who need intervention, but the focus of this intervention should be on the application of decoding skills and strategies and developing comprehension (Palinscar & Brown, 1984a, 1984b; Rosenshine & Meister, 1994).
2. The structured, fast-paced lessons used in early intervention seem appropriate for upper grade students (Allington & Walmsley, 1995; Clay, 1985; Hall, Prevatte, & Cunningham, 1992; Hiebert, Colt, Catto, & Gury, 1992; Pinnell, Fried, & Estice, 1990; Slavin et al., 1996; Taylor, Frye, Short, & Shearer, 1992).
3. Reciprocal teaching and graphic organizers are instructional strategies that have been proven effective in accelerating the reading of upper grade students. Scaffolding is an important part of this successful instruction (Collins, Brown, & Newman, 1986; Heimlich & Pittelman, 1986; Palincsar, 1984; Palincsar & Brown, 1984a, 1984b, 1986; Pearson, 1984; Pehrsson & Robinson, 1985; Rosenshine & Meister, 1994).
4. The materials for upper grade intervention should be authentic literature sequenced from simple to complex to help students accelerate their reading (Allington & Walmsley, 1995; Collins et al., 1986; Harris, 1961; Huck, 1989; Peterson, 1991).

National Reading Conference Yearbook, 49, pp. 477–486.

In spite of the successes of early intervention programs, reports of individual teachers and national studies of reading achievement (Mullis, Campbell, & Farstrup, 1993; National Assessment of Educational Progress, 1995) show that many students in Grade 3 and above are reading considerably below their age-appropriate level. Attempts to help such students in Grade 3 and higher have focused heavily on a remedial model using high-interest, easy-reading materials with controlled vocabulary (Harris & Sipay, 1985). Lessons accompanying these texts usually follow a pattern of introducing vocabulary, reading to answer questions, and teaching one or more skills. Research has demonstrated that this type of instructional approach has not been effective in helping upper grade readers achieve success. The gap between the less able readers and the more capable readers continues to widen across the grade levels (Allington & Walsmley, 1995).

Method

During the 1995–96 school year, we developed and revised the model used in this study based on experiences with two teachers, and 11 fourth-grade students who were reading considerably below level. One teacher was a fourth-grade classroom teacher and the other was a Title 1 Instructional Specialist. The students gained an average of 3.0 levels in retelling and 2.4 levels in oral reading as measured by the *Basic Reading Inventory* (Johns, 1994). It was concluded that with this amount of growth, the model should be tested more carefully to see if similar gains could be obtained in a more controlled situation.

Persons attending a national presentation of Project SUCCESS in May 1996 were invited to submit proposals to become research sites for the 1996–97 national research study. The proposals submitted had to include a description of need, background of teachers, commitment of school or district, and a coaching plan to support teachers during the project. Thirteen sites submitted plans that were accepted.

Population and Sample

The population for the study was the fourth-grade students identified as reading one to three years below level in 24 different schools within the 13 sites. Sites ranged from major metropolitan locations to rural areas throughout the United States. A total of 38 teachers taught Project SUCCESS.

Teachers identified the pool of subjects for the study on the basis of students reading one to three years below level, having basic decoding skills, and showing signs of potential for improvement as shown by listening comprehension, IQ, or math problem solving ability higher than computation. All students in the pool had problems in comprehending and constructing meaning.

The samples for the Project SUCCESS groups and the control groups were randomly selected from the pool of subjects identified. The number of students in the initial sample (409) was reduced due to mobility of students and inaccurate scoring of tests. The final sample consisted of 345 students (185 Project SUC-CESS group, 160 control group).

Testing

Two instruments were selected to use for pre- and post-testing, the *Qualitative Reading Inventory-II* (QRI-II) (Leslie & Caldwell, 1995) and the *Gates-MacGinitie Reading Tests* (MacGinitie & MacGinitie, 1989a, 1989b). These tests were selected for their validity, reliability, and wide use in reading programs for struggling readers. The pretesting occurred within the first three weeks of the 1996 school year; posttesting took place during the first two weeks of March 1997.

The QRI-II was given as a silent reading test in which students did a retelling and answered questions. This procedure was followed by oral reading of the passages to determine a fluency level.

The retelling protocol was marked with key items for each passage so that a score could be obtained. The criterion for acceptable retelling was 75% of the items in the passage being retold.

The second measure used was the *Gates-MacGinitie Reading Tests;* Form K was used as a pretest and Form L as a posttest. These tests were used to obtain a standardized measure of vocabulary and comprehension.

Instructional Plan for Project Success: Description and Rationale

The instructional plan for Project SUCCESS is a five-part, fast-paced plan that requires 40 minutes per day in addition to the regular classroom reading program. The five parts of the lesson are Revisiting (5 minutes), Reviewing (5 minutes), Rehearsing (10 minutes), Reading (15 minutes), and Responding/Reflecting(5 minutes). These parts were selected for the model because each has considerable support in existing research. The fast pace of the lessons is achieved by giving a designated amount of time for each part of the lesson and keeps students actively engaged in the reading process.

During Revisiting, students reread alone or with a partner a previously read Project SUCCESS book or discussed books they were reading independently outside the Project SUCCESS time. This builds fluency and develops comprehension (Anderson, Wilson, & Fielding, 1988; Samuels, 1979/1997). In Reviewing, students used their graphic organizers to summarize the previous day's reading and talk about the reciprocal teaching strategies (summarize, clarify, question, predict) they used. This helps to build comprehension and keeps students focused on the strategies. During the Rehearse step, students previewed the text to develop background for the specific text (Clay, 1985). During Reading, students silently read a meaningful chunk of the text and engage in reciprocal teaching with the teacher. These activities lead to application of comprehension strategies and develop their abilities to construct meaning (Palincsar, 1984; Palincsar & Brown, 1984a, 1984b, 1986; Pearson, 1984). In the final step of the lesson, Responding/

Reflecting, students write about what they have read and reflect on the strategies they have used to develop their comprehension and continued use of the strategies (Sweet, 1993).

Students were taught in groups of five to seven using authentic literature, with accompanying graphic organizers and reciprocal teaching. The books used for instruction were sequenced from simple to complex using criteria developed to go beyond those used in early intervention programs (Peterson, 1991). Posters were displayed during the lessons to help keep the pace fast and to remind students to use the strategies during the reciprocal teaching. A poster for each graphic organizer was provided. The story map or event map was used for narrative texts; semantic maps, main idea/supporting detail frames, and other appropriate organizers were used for expository texts.

Training, Treatment, and Monitoring

Certified teachers who were to be Project SUCCESS teachers were given 2 days of intensive training. During this training, teachers were taught how to use the Project SUCCESS instructional model, reciprocal teaching, and the lessons provided for each of the books designated for fourth grade (see Figure 1 for a list of books). Ongoing coaching was provided for each teacher throughout the study.

The treatment began at different times due to variable starting dates for each school. Each teacher was asked to teach the Project SUCCESS group for 40 minutes per day for 4 or 5 days per week. Project SUCCESS teachers kept a record of the number of days taught and the number of books completed. The Project SUCCESS groups were taught as pullout groups, in-class groups, and extended day groups. In addition, they received their regular classroom reading instruction. The control groups also received instruction in their regular classroom reading

Level I	Book 1	*Tippu*, Abigail Pizer, Barrons, 1993
Level I	Book 2	*The Paper Crane*, Molly Bank, Greenwillow Books, 1985
Level II	Book 3	*A Field Full of Horses*, Peter Hansard, Candlewick Press, 1993
Level II	Book 4	*The Relatives Came*, Cynthia Ryland, Scholastic, Inc., 1985
Level II	Book 5	*Whales*, Gail Gibbons, Holiday House, 1991
Level II	Book 6	*Sharks*, Gail Gibbons, Holiday House, 1992
Level II	Book 7	*The Cut-ups*, James Marshall, Puffin Books, 1984
Level II	Book 8	*Blaze and the Mountain Lion*, C. W. Anderson, Aladdin Paperbacks, 1959
Level III	Book 9	*The Popcorn Book*, Tomie dePaola, Holiday House, 1978
Level III	Book 10	*Amazing Grace*, Mary Hoffman, Scholastic Inc., 1991
Level III	Book 11	*The Paper Bag Princess*, Robert Munsch, Annick Press Ltd., 1980
Level III	Book 12	*The Bicycle Man*, Allen Say, Houghton Mifflin, 1982
Level III	Book 13	*Cam Jansen and the Mystery of the Dinosaur Bones*, David Adler, Puffin Books, 1991
Level IV	Book 14	*John Muir: Man of the Wild Paces*, Carol Greene, Childrens Press, 1991
Level IV	Book 15	*Penguins*, Emilie Lepthien, Childrens Press, 1983
Level IV	Book 16	*Bill Clinton: Forty-Second President of the United States*, Carol Greene, Childrens Press, 1995
Level IV	Book 17	*Yosemite National Park*, David Petersen, Childrens Press, 1993
Level IV	Book 18	*Shaquille O'Neal: Shaq Attack*, Ted Cox, Childrens Press, 1993
Level V	Book 19	*The Seven Treasure Hunts*, Betsy Byars, Harper/Trophy, 1991
Level V	Book 20	*The Bathwater Gang*, Jerry Spinelli, Little, Brown and Company, 1990

Figure 1. Project SUCCESS Books—Grade 4.

program, but did not receive the Project SUCCESS treatment. Some of the control group students were given additional support through Title 1 or other support programs; no attempt was made to control this factor.

Data Sources

Data from this study were analyzed using raw scores. The use of raw scores avoids many of the problems associated with interpreting transformed scores.

The control and Project SUCCESS groups including the two location subgroups, in-class and pullout, were compared relative to the pretest scores using the Hotelling T^2 statistic (reported as an F statistic). This same procedure was used to test differences between subgroup posttest means. Univariate F statistics were interpreted if multivariate F statistics were significant. A strength of relationship index was computed where appropriate. Finally, a t statistic was used to compare time means for the pullout and in-class subgroups. There were not sufficient numbers of teachers and students in the extended day group to allow for an analysis of that data.

Results

In order to test the hypotheses of this study, the means and standard deviations on all dependent measures were calculated. The number of instructional days for the groups varied from site to site; the average amount of instructional time was 75.8 days.

The pretest scores for the Project SUCCESS (PS) group and the control group were compared to determine whether the Project SUCCESS and control groups were equivalent at the beginning of the study. It was possible to compare the posttest scores without using the pretest scores as covariates because the Project SUCCESS and control groups did not differ at the beginning of the study.

The multivariate F-ratio was significant at the .05 level ($F_{5,339}=17.445, p<.001$). Therefore, the univariate F statistics were interpreted to determine which of the dependent measures contributed to the differences. Differences were noted for QRI-II retelling ($F_{1,343}=75.95, p<.001$), questions ($F_{1,343}=69.61, p<.001$), oral reading ($F_{1,343}=26.95, p<.001$), and the *Gates-MacGinitie* comprehension subtest ($F_{1,343}=4.99, p<.03$). No difference was found for the *Gates-MacGinitie* vocabulary subtest. The Project SUCCESS group significantly outperformed the control group in retelling (PS=63.4, C=45.4), answering questions (PS=38.0, C=29.1), oral reading (PS=1,626.5, C=1,398.8) as measured by the QRI-II, and comprehension (PS=20.8, C=18.9) as measured by the *Gates-MacGinitie* subtest after an average of 75.8 days of instruction (see Figures 2 and 3).

The pretest mean scores for the in-class and pullout groups were compared to determine whether the two groups were equivalent at the beginning of the study. It was possible to compare the posttest scores without using the pretests as covariates because the two groups did not differ initially. The multivariate F-ratio was not significant at the .05 level ($F_{5,173}=2.16, p<.058$). Therefore, the univariate F statistics were not interpreted. The researchers were unable to say that the pullout group performed differently from the in-class group.

Secondary Analyses of Data

Two secondary analyses of the data were conducted. One looked at the relationship of the amount of time with the treatment location and the other examined the percentage of students reading on grade level or higher at the conclusion of the treatment period. The teachers who taught Project SUCCESS as a pullout program and those teaching Project SUCCESS as an in-class model did not devote significantly different amounts of time to instruction.

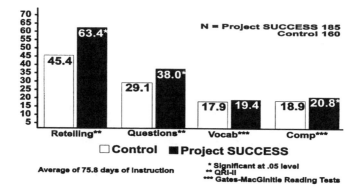

Figure 2. Posttest raw score comparisons by treatment.

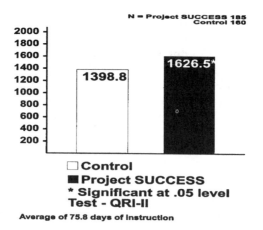

Figure 3. Posttest oral reading raw score comparison by treatment.

The second analysis was undertaken to determine the percentage of students who were reading at grade level or higher at the conclusion of the treatment period. This analysis was done using the QRI-II scores. Operationally, for a student to be reading on level, he or she had to be at an instructional level of fourth grade or higher in retelling or answering questions *and* oral reading. For the 12 sites where the data were usable, the Project SUCCESS groups had from two to seven times as many students who were reading on level or higher at the conclusion of the treatment (see Figure 4).

The findings from this study are limited to the populations from which the samples were drawn. The inability to control any additional instruction given the control groups beyond the classroom reading program is another factor that must be considered in interpreting the results reported.

Conclusions

Based on the results of this study, the following conclusions are warranted:

The results are generalizable to the fourth-grade population studied. Because the research sites represented a variety of geographic regions and locations, the results should be representative of the country as a whole. Furthermore, because the randomization procedures resulted in equivalent research and control groups at the beginning of the study, it is safe to assume that these results can be replicated in other situations.

It is possible to accelerate the reading of struggling fourth graders in a relatively short amount of time. The lessons required for this intervention used authentic literature sequenced from simple to complex. They were fast-paced, incorporated reciprocal teaching, graphic organizers, and scaffolded instruction. They were taught 40 minutes per day over and beyond the regular classroom reading instruction that was provided, and these lessons followed the lesson model developed in this study. The gains made by students in this study are consistent with the findings of other researchers who have incorporated reciprocal teaching as a part of the instructional model (Palincsar & Brown, 1984a, 1984b, 1986; Rosenshine & Meister, 1994).

The intervention instruction is likely to be equally effective if delivered as an in-class program or as a pullout program. There was not enough evidence to draw conclusions about the extended day model. The in-class model poses challenges relative to classroom management for some teachers. The pullout model poses challenges in deciding when to pull students from the classroom. It is important to note that students in this study were not pulled from the classroom during the classroom reading program.

Teachers who become upper grade intervention teachers must be selected with care because teachers do not all respond equally well to the structured process of intervention instruction.

Training and coaching are essential components in helping teachers learn the type of model utilized in Project SUCCESS.

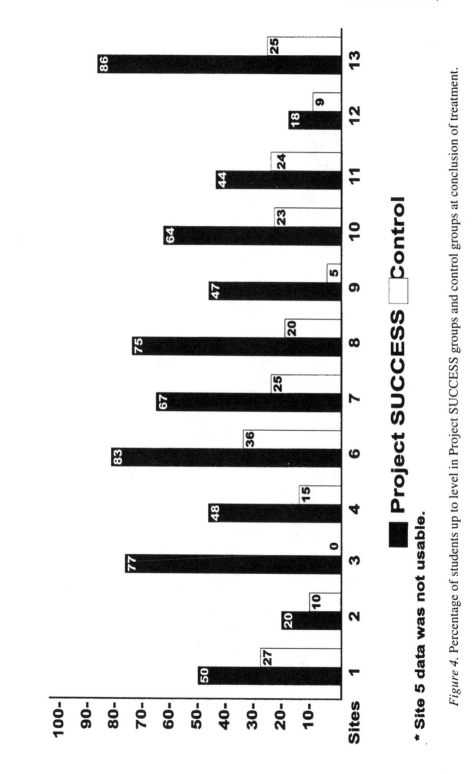

Figure 4. Percentage of students up to level in Project SUCCESS groups and control groups at conclusion of treatment.

This research supports the conclusion that the Project SUCCESS model is a promising one for helping struggling readers in the upper grades accelerate their reading to an age-appropriate level. This research should be replicated using students from other grade levels and special populations.

References

Allington, R. L., & Walmsley, S. A. (Eds.). (1995). *No quick fix: Rethinking literacy programs in America's elementary schools.* New York: Teachers College Press.

Anderson, R. C., Wilson, P. T., & Fielding, L. G. (1988). Growth in reading and how children spend their time outside of school. *Reading Research Quarterly, 23,* 285–303.

Clay, M. M. (1985). *The early detection of reading difficulties* (3rd ed.). Auckland: Heinemann.

Collins, A., Brown, J. S., & Newman, S. E. (1986). *Cognitive apprenticeship: Teaching the craft of reading, writing and mathematics* (Report No. 6459). Cambridge, MA: BBN Laboratories.

Hall, D. P., Prevatte, C., & Cunningham, P. M. (1992, December). *Eliminating ability grouping and failure in the primary grades.* Paper presented at the meeting of the National Reading Conference, San Antonio, TX.

Harris, A. J. (1961). *How to increase reading ability* (4th ed.). New York: David McKay.

Harris, A. J., & Sipay, E. R. (1985). *How to increase reading ability* (8th ed.). New York: Longman.

Heimlich, J. E., & Pittelman, S. D. (1986). *Semantic mapping: Classroom applications.* Newark, DE: International Reading Association.

Hiebert, E. H., Colt, J. M., Catto, S. L., & Gury, E. C. (1992). Reading and writing of first-grade students in a restructured Chapter I program. *American Educational Research Journal, 29,* 545–572.

Huck, C. S. (1989). No wider than the heart is wide. In J. Hickman & B. E. Cullinan (Eds.), *Children's literature in the classroom: Weaving Charlotte's web* (pp. 252–262). Needham Heights, MA: Christopher-Gordon.

Johns, J. L. (1994). *Basic reading inventory* (6th ed.). Dubuque, IA: Kendall Hunt.

Leslie, L., & Caldwell, J. (1995). *Qualitative reading inventory-II.* New York: HarperCollins.

MacGinitie, W. H., & MacGinitie, R. K. (1989a). *Gates-MacGinitie Reading Tests.* Chicago: Riverside.

MacGinitie, W. H., & MacGinitie, R. K. (1989b). *Technical summary: Gates-MacGinitie Reading Tests.* Chicago: Riverside.

Mullis, I. V. S., Campbell, J. R. & Farstrup, A. (1993). *National Assessment of Educational Progress reading report card for the nation and the states.* Washington, DC: U.S. Department of Education, National Center for Educational Statistics.

National Assessment of Educational Progress (1995). *NAEP 1994 reading, a first look: Findings from the National Assessment of Educational Progress* (rev. ed.). Washington, DC: U.S. Department of Education, National Center for Educational Statistics.

Palincsar, A. S. (1984). The quest for meaning from expository text: A teacher-guided journey. In G. Duffy et al. (Eds.), *Comprehension instruction: Perspectives and suggestions* (pp. 251–280). New York: Longman.

Palincsar, A. S., & Brown, A. L. (1984a). Reciprocal teaching of comprehension-fostering and comprehension-monitoring activities. *Cognition and Instruction, 2,* 117–175.

Palincsar, A. S., & Brown, A. L. (1984b). *A means to a meaningful end: Recommendations for the instruction of poor comprehenders.* Champaign: University of Illinois at Urbana-Champaign, Center for the Study of Reading.

Palincsar, A. S., & Brown, A. L. (1986). Interactive teaching to promote independent learning from text. *Reading Teacher, 39,* 771–777.

Pearson, P. D. (1984). *Reading comprehension instruction: Six necessary changes* (Reading Ed. Rep. No. 54). Champaign: University of Illinois at Urbana-Champaign, Center for the Study of Reading.

Pehrsson, R. S., & Robinson, H. A. (1985). *The semantic organizer approach to writing and reading instruction*. Rockville, MD: Aspen Systems.

Peterson, B. (1991). Selecting books for beginning readers. In D. E. DeFord, C. A. Lyons, & G. S. Pinnell (Eds.), *Bridges to literacy* (pp. 119–147). Portsmouth, NH: Heinemann.

Pinnell, G. S., Fried, M. D., & Estice, R. M. (1990). Reading Recovery: Learning how to make a difference. *Reading Teacher, 43,* 282–295.

Rosenshine, B., & Meister, C. (1994). Reciprocal teaching: A review of research. *Review of Educational Research, 64,* 479–530.

Samuels, S. J. (1979/1997). The method of repeated readings. *Reading Teacher, 50,* 376–381.

Slavin, R. E., Madden, N. A., Dolan, L. J., Wasik, B. A., Ross, S., Smith, L., & Dianda, M. (1996). Success for All: A summary of research. *Journal of Education for Students Placed At Risk, 1*(1), 41–76.

Sweet, A. P. (1993). *State of the art: Transforming ideas for teaching and learning to read.* Washington, DC: U.S. Department of Education, Office of Research.

Taylor, B. M., Frye, B. J., Short, R., & Shearer, B. (1992). Classroom teachers prevent reading failure among low-achieving first-grade students. *Reading Teacher, 45,* 592–597.

Learning To Teach and the Pedagogy of Adult Community Mentors in an Urban After-School Program

William McGinley, Shuaib Meacham, Christina DeNicolo, and Katanna Conley
University of Colorado–Boulder

This study explores the forms of literacy-related educational knowledge that adult community members enacted in the contexts of teaching young children and mentoring preservice teachers in an urban after-school literacy program called Literacy and Learning for Life. The purpose of the study was to understand more about the possible educational identities and roles that adult community members might assume, as well as the kinds of literacy-related knowledge and instructional insight they might offer as mentors of preservice teachers who were working with young children in an urban after-school program. Specifically, we sought to document the pedagogies and literacy-related knowledge that the adult community members recommended and practiced as part of their participation in the after-school program. In addition, we investigated how preservice teachers used the pedagogical knowledge that these adults provided.

An assumption underlying this work is that adults from culturally diverse communities and varied educational backgrounds have deep experientially based understandings of children and of cultural factors related to language, society, and education essential to improving the educational experiences of young children (e.g., Cruz, 1997; McLaughlin, 1996; Moll, 1992, in press). As McLaughlin (1996) reminds us, theories about education or everyday social and political life are not the exclusive domain of an epistemological elite. Rather, they are also the practice of "ordinary citizens" working and theorizing in settings where "survival is most contested—in the workplace, in churches, in the media, and in family and personal life" (p. 164).

Literacy researchers have long emphasized the need to understand and learn from the cultural practices and local language conventions of individuals from diverse cultural and linguistic backgrounds. In short, this research has emphasized that the study of literacy and the preparation of literacy teachers ultimately requires an understanding and awareness of social groups and institutions within which children and adults are socialized and enculturated to value, interpret, and use literacy in particular "local" ways (Delgado-Gaitan, 1990; Ladson-Billings, 1994; Reyes, 1992). Affirmation and support for the value of "ordinary" experience and the community-based knowledge of "everyday people" can also be

National Reading Conference Yearbook, 49, pp. 487–499.

found in the work of academic theorists from many disciplinary perspectives (Baker, 1984; West, 1993).

Despite the contemporary and historical basis for valuing vernacular forms of knowledge and educational theorizing, teacher education programs seldom draw upon this community knowledge in preparing new teachers (Ladson-Billings, 2000; Mahan, 1982). This is especially true with respect to programs designed to prepare teachers for urban educational settings where knowledge of cultural and community life is so essential to the educational success of school children (Cruz, 1997; Gay, 1993). As Ladson-Billings (1994) explained, the most successful teachers of African-American children are those that "see themselves as part of the community" (p. 25), and who develop relationships with children that extend beyond the classroom, and who draw upon their knowledge of cultural and community practices in their teaching.

A significant area of research designed to address the cultural and community knowledge base of preservice teachers has focused on the role of exemplary cooperating teachers who not only teach diverse children, but also encourage preservice teachers to communicate with caregivers and other community members (Cochran-Smith, 1995; Gay, 1993; Haberman, 1996). Although current research suggests that mentoring relationships significantly influence the professional practices of new teachers (Hawkey, 1997), this research has primarily examined the mentoring influence of more experienced professional teachers. Although this approach affirms what McLaughlin (1996) has called the "epistemological privilege" of those with whom we wish to work and affiliate, we might also explore the knowledge that parents and other community members could contribute to a mentoring relationship. Involving adult community members in the mentoring of preservice teachers could provide these young teachers with additional knowledge relevant to the development of their professional identities in ways not previously considered.

The overall goal of this study is to extend our knowledge of the possible identities and roles that adult community members might assume, as well as the diverse kinds of literacy-related knowledge they might share while mentoring preservice teachers in an urban after-school literacy program. As such, it provides insight into the efficacy of teacher preparation programs in literacy education that draw upon the insight of a relatively unacknowledged community of theorists and questioners who represent a variety of educational backgrounds and experiences.

Methods

After-School Program and Participants

This study took place in an urban community center located in a major metropolitan area in a western state. Founded in 1980, the mission of the community center is "to bring hope to our neighborhoods and the Gasoline Point Community. By mentoring, training, and nurturing youth, our mission is to prepare them that they might become the leaders of the next generation." In the fall of 1999, we began a partnership with the community center staff aimed at developing an after-school literacy program designed to complement existing educational programs at the center. Together with the center staff, we began exploring curricular plans, identifying possible teachers, and recruiting children. As it pertains to the literacy education of children, it was important to community center staff that we offer an instructional program that would help children understand the importance of literacy as it pertained to understanding personal and social issues in their community (McGinley & Kamberelis, 1997). Additionally, the community center staff was concerned that children also acquire broader, socially valued, literate competencies associated with learning to read and write.

The after-school program faculty included one Latino woman, two African-American males, one African-American female, and five preservice teachers. The community mentors, Chico (71), Joe (71), Josie (64), and Loretta (40) were all longtime residents of the area with a variety of life experiences related to local community issues, one of which was the education of young children. We first met Joe, Josie, and Loretta as a result of their involvement in a local tutoring program entitled Project LINK (Literacy In the Neighborhood is Key). Chico became involved by virtue of his friendship with Joe. Although the extent of their experience varied, each had a history of community or school involvement aimed at improving the educational experiences of urban youth. The five participating preservice teachers, Ruchi, Amanda, DJ, Stephanie, and Sarah were all first-year students in an elementary teacher licensure program with little or no formal teaching experience. Each student volunteered for the program at the start of the fall semester. This was also their first "school-like" teaching experience in an urban setting.

As part of their participation in the program, the following four teams of community mentors and preservice teachers met once a week for 15 weeks both to plan and provide literacy instruction for children: Monday (Chico, Ruchi, Amanda), Tuesday (Joe, Stephanie, DJ), Wednesday (Josie, Sarah), and Thursday (Loretta, Erin). Teaching sessions were attended by a university researcher who, in addition to collecting data, often facilitated mentor and preservice teacher collaboration. Eighteen Latino and African-American children (ages 6–8) enrolled in the program in the fall of 1999. These children (11 girls and 7 boys), who represented a wide range of academic abilities, were neither the highest nor the lowest achieving students in their school classrooms. They did, however, vary in their literacy-related needs. Two groups of nine children attended the program 2 days a week on alternating days for a total 4 hours weekly. During this time, they participated in a wide range of literacy-related instruction and activities developed by preservice teachers and the adult community mentors.

The specific curriculum in the after-school program revolved around a common interest in connecting reading and writing instruction to children's lives in the community. As a result, literacy instruction took place primarily in the context of oral storybook reading that was thematically related to issues in children's lives. Related activities included journal writing in response to reading and everyday experiences; vocabulary and spelling development; writing, revising, and publishing creative work about family and community activities; collaborative dramatization of selected stories and life experiences; opportunities for reading with peers and to larger audiences; instructional support for reading, writing, and speaking in a second language; and artistic responses to the content of storybooks and other community-based projects (i.e., field trips, neighborhood tours, library visits).

Although the preservice teachers were primarily responsible for the development of daily instructional plans and classroom organization, they consulted weekly with their cooperating community mentor on topics related to the activities they sought to provide for children. In addition to these weekly meetings, university researchers, mentors, preservice teachers, and a community center staff member met bimonthly as a group to address specific literacy-related issues, as well as to raise other concerns related to teachers and mentors work with the children.

Data and Data Collection

Data for this study were collected during classroom visits made 4 days a week from September to January for 15 weeks. In all, we observed approximately 60 hours of instruction involving mentors, perservice teachers, and children. During these visits, we worked as participant-observers in the classrooms of community members and preservice teachers. Over the course of the study, we engaged in several modes of data collection, including interviewing community mentors about their life and work histories; interviewing preservice teachers and community mentors about their respective roles and relationships in the after-school program; interviewing staff members at the community center about the school community and development of the program; collecting copies of preservice teachers' daily lesson plans/journals, community mentor's research logs, and children's creative work; tape-recording bimonthly meetings involving community mentors, preservice teachers, and community center staff; and composing fieldnotes of classroom activities. In addition, we made occasional visits to other sites in the community where adults often spent time (e.g., restaurants, homes, local clubs).

Data Analysis

We sought to conduct our research in ways that respected and made use of the practical and theoretical knowledge of community members, preservice teachers, and staff at the community center. Our goal as researchers was to attend to the theories and practices produced by "insiders who speak the vernacular of the practice," devising their own interpretive strategies and local theoretical questions in ways that might extend our definition of theory and the process of learning to teach (McLaughlin, 1996, p. 165). We viewed our research as a collective endeavor with community mentors and preservice teachers, and we worked to involve them in as many aspects of data collection and analysis as possible.

We explored the teaching-related knowledge and pedagogical practices of community mentors from an interpretive perspective (Erickson, 1986). Specifically, we conducted a content-based analysis of our data for the kinds of knowledge and insight related to children's literacy instruction that seemed to underlie the teaching approaches that adult mentors practiced or recommended. During periodic meetings over the course of the study, we discussed findings, examined emerging trends, and identified possible themes among ourselves and with preservice teachers and community mentors (Glaser & Strauss, 1967). Working as a team of four university researchers, we repeatedly read and compared notes on the transcribed interviews, mentors' research logs, preservice teachers' journals, and fieldnotes. We then shared our interpretations with the mentors and preservice teachers who helped us to further revise and refine our understanding of the kinds of insight and support that mentors offered. This process was recursive and ongoing, continuing until we were satisfied that we had identified a collection of perspectives or categories adequate to the task of describing the teaching-related knowledge that mentors' seemed to provide. Drawing upon the wealth of data collected over the semester, we identified several major themes or pedagogical orientations that described the mentors' participation. We use the term *pedagogy*, or pedagogies, to refer to the kinds of the collective social, intellectual, and experiential knowledge that adult mentors brought to bear in their work with the preservice teachers. We chose this term because it seemed to capture a quality of lived-through theoretical understanding or praxis that characterized adult community members' disposition toward mentoring and teaching children.

Results

This study examined the diverse kinds of literacy-related knowledge that four adult community members used in the context of mentoring preservice teachers in an urban after-school literacy program. In this paper, we focused primarily on the mentoring practices of Joe, Chico, and Josie. Analyses of interviews, written texts, and classroom practices revealed five primary pedagogical orientations. These included the pedagogy of integrity and personal commitment; the pedagogy of self-worth; the pedagogy of power and access; the pedagogy of hope and personal transformation; and the pedagogy of personally and culturally relevant literacy skills.

The Pedagogies of Community Mentors

For Chico, Joe, Josie, and Loretta, involvement in the program originated, in some measure, with a belief in the possibility that people can change their lives, and an understanding of the kind of hope that is necessary to actualize such change. In most cases, this belief was linked to their own life histories and experiences with change and the hope that made it possible. In other words, the literacy-related ideas and instructional activities adults recommended were always an extension of their personal commitments and experiences with respect to human possibility and the desire to make a difference in the community. Joe and Chico, friends for over 50 years, made this point during an early meeting of community mentors and university researchers. Joe began by articulating his interpretation of the role that he and other mentors might assume in their relationship with the preservice teachers:

Joe: Well see, this is where Josie, Chico, Loretta, and myself—this is where we've become involved. The way I understand it, we are to put our input into this program based on past experiences and things that we're transferring back over to the student teacher. We are saying, look, this what we went through. We've been through it—grade school, junior high, high school, some college, military, a work history of 35 or 40 years on the job, and these things like this can be transferred to the student teacher, and then let them work off that.

Chico: I gotta hear that. I think any problem a child in the age range we work in might bring to that building and that class can be saved even if they're on the way to being lost because they can still be influenced. . . . They can overcome. So any kid that comes into the class that myself, Ruchi, and Amanda are working with, as far as I'm concerned, they've got a future. Dante and the other boy, Tory, they can be saved. There's as much difference in those two kids when they're not together as night and day. So it tells you right there that they're not destined, as such, to fail. What changed me was a teacher. A teacher changed me.

The pedagogical approaches that Chico, Joe, and the other mentors personified in the program grew out of a fundamental commitment to improving the educational lives of the children in their community. Within such a framework, their participation as mentors in the after-school literacy program was conceptualized as a specific extension of their commitment to the educational potential of all children regardless of the struggles they might face in their classrooms or communities. Such a commitment was consistently embodied in the mentoring activities and the specific pedagogies they enacted throughout their interaction with preservice teachers and children.

Pedagogy of integrity and personal commitment. The community mentors enacted a pedagogy of integrity and personal commitment. In short, they conceptualized literacy instruction as having a moral and ethical component. This imperative was reflected in a commitment to reconcile theory and practice, to resolve instructional inconstancies, and to hold themselves accountable for the learning opportunities provided to children. Nowhere was this pedagogy of integrity more apparent than in Josie's work with Kenny, a 7-year-old boy who, on one very memorable occasion, said he could not write because his letters were "too ugly." Later that evening at home, literally unable to sleep until she developed a way to respond to his problem, Josie called Sarah. Soon after their conversation, Sarah wrote in her journal about the experience and the commitment it conveyed as she evaluated her own development as a teacher:

Josie called me tonight. She said that last night she couldn't sleep because she kept thinking about Kenny. She wanted to think of a way to help him. She thought that maybe if I made up a story with half-formed letters and had him close the letters up and then draw a related picture it might help. . . .

Pedagogy of self-worth. Adults also practiced a pedagogy of self-worth wherein literacy learning was theorized as deeply related to and reflective of children's conception of themselves. This pedagogical orientation involved a commitment to understanding how children's physical, emotional, intellectual, and cultural backgrounds influenced their disposition to learn. Additionally, it required that teachers nurture the unique qualities of individual children while also engaging in honest affirmation of their work. For example, in discussing how they might influence the behavior of Veronica, a child who was having difficulty participating in class, Chico suggested that placing her in a leadership position might affect her self-image and her participation in subsequent literacy activities:

> It is possible. It's probably possible... How would you go about taking a child like Veronica and in a way, subtly, put her in a leadership role to bring out what you see in her. And then she would be doing it [participating] with the other kids too. And then you get this feedback—[other children] thinking, "Well, I'd like to be like Veronica." They don't say that to us, but in their mind their taking note mentally of what Veronica is doing that's just a tad above what they're doing or how they're participating.

Pedagogy of power and access. Adults' instructional recommendations and practices also reflected a desire to make connections between literacy and personal/social empowerment. In their interactions with preservice teachers, they emphasized how literacy might provide access to more socially prominent literate competencies and greater cultural capital. A compelling example of this pedagogy involved the often taken-for-granted value of a public library card. When recommending ways to improve the existing after-school program, Chico made the following suggestion regarding library cards for children:

> If through this organization, this program, we were to get these kids library cards, what would be one of the peripheral types of results from it? Kids ask their parents to take them to the library. Now you've got the parents going to the library. "Mom, Dad, can you take me to the library Saturday, Friday, whatever?" Through that activity, they also become a little closer to their parents.

Pedagogy of hope and personal transformation. Another strong current in the literacy instruction of adult mentors was an unwavering belief in children's ability to succeed and use literacy in order to lead productive lives. Even when helping preservice teachers to teach children with challenging social and family backgrounds, adult mentors worked from a perspective of hope and possibility regarding the learning potential of all the children in the program. Joe conveyed this pedagogical disposition in the following statement:

> But see, this is what we don't want. See, we don't want to lose one of these children that's in this program if at all possible. We want every one of these children, if at all possible, to finish this class this year and if you do that we've been successful. . . . There is no such thing as a "lost" child. I truly believe that.

Pedagogy of personally and culturally relevant literacy instruction. This pedagogy involved an approach to literacy instruction that portrayed literacy activities as having personal relevance to those who engaged in them. In exploring the relevant uses of literacy, adults focused on some of the ways that stories enhanced personal and cultural identity, as well as on additional uses of reading and writing. When discussing the behavior of Mark (second-grade boy) who preferred to daydream rather than read because certain literacy activities had little to do with his life outside of school, Josie recommended an approach that enabled Mark to draw upon that "life" as the topic of his writing:

> A teacher brings him "down" and says, "It's O.K. to be lost up there but come on down and use what you are thinking. [Ask the student] What are you think-ing? Let's write what you're thinking about. What do you do out there? Do you play football? Do you play in the mud pile? What are you doing out there?" That's a story.

Community Pedagogies in Action: Exploring the "Pedagogy of Self-Worth"

Each of the pedagogical orientations we describe abides complex connec-tions between adults' lived experiences, their classroom literacy practices, and their relationships to preservice teachers. In order to more fully render the com-plex nature of these pedagogies, we present findings related to the pedagogy of self-worth as it was employed with both preservice teachers and children.

In their first days in the after-school program, preservice teachers were struck by what they reported to be children's lack of confidence in their literacy abilities, readily lamenting the fact that many children responded to activities by saying, "I can't." Ironically, children's sense of inadequacy regarding their literacy created a situation where student teachers had to confront their own lack of understanding regarding how to effectively respond to such a problem. As Stephanie reflected during an early interview: "Yeah, I would say for some of them [the children], it wouldn't matter what you did. They'd say they couldn't do it as the first re-sponse. . . . We never expected that and didn't know what to do."

As the issue of confidence grew more salient, building children's self-worth emerged as one of the primary goals of the preservice teachers. Moreover, com-munity mentors were faced with the delicate instructional task of simultaneously building the self-esteem of the children while also bolstering the preservice teach-ers own sense of confidence in their ability to teach children who, like themselves, were questioning their abilities. In essence, adult mentors responded to the needs of both children and preservice teachers with a pedagogy of self-worth. Although cultivation of self-worth is often thought to be outside of or tangential to what counts as knowledge related to literacy instruction, neither children's literacy or preservice teachers' instructional knowledge would have developed without it. In short, the pedagogy of self-worth constituted an approach to instruction that conceptualized the personal development of children as fundamental to, if not requisite for, more formal literacy learning.

In relation to this point, community mentors always seemed to respond to what they perceived to be children's literacy abilities and potential rather than their more immediate, and sometimes less than cooperative, behaviors. This practice was evident in the manner that Joe dealt with Dante (first-grade boy) on the second evening of class. Dante was disrupting Stephanie as she attempted to read a story to the children. When she paused and asked him to quiet down, he immediately left the group in anger. As Stephanie continued to read, Joe joined Dante in the corner of the room. Once there, he focused on the activity, redirecting Dante's attention to the book and offering him help with the literacy activity he was resisting:

> Joe: [Pointing to the book] See that sloth? When do sloths come out?
> Dante: [Discouraged] I don't want to draw about him, dude.
> Joe: What if you draw and I help you write something about it? What do you say about that?

Later, in a lesson-planning meeting with Stephanie and DJ, Joe addressed more fully the difficulties they were having with Dante and the consequences their decisions might have regarding his self-worth:

> . . . that's the type of child that you really need to help, you know. Of course sometimes it's tough, because if you don't—Well, if you look at everybody else we have in here, they pretty much pay attention to what's going on... But, what's going to happen is that he's [Dante is] going to adopt the attitude where's he's going to feel that the whole world is against him, [and think] "why are they pulling me out [of class] all the time," [because] he doesn't see himself as disrupting everything else they were trying to do around here. . . .

These perspectives from Joe with regard to Dante and the pedagogy of self-worth were further reflected in much of what both DJ and Stephanie had to say about other children and their teaching experiences in general. For example, several weeks into the program, Joe's hopefulness and the language of self-worth he consistently embodied were adopted in DJ's discussion of children and literacy instruction:

> I think [we are here] to help build their confidence. To give them the ability to know that they can. So many times in school they're shut down because of the way they present their literacy. And so we're saying that literacy is a broad range. . . . but also we're talking about the one child, Mark or Dante, who wouldn't try anything cause he was worried about, "I'm not good at this. I'm not good at that." Getting him in an environment where he's not afraid to go out and try to, you know, to just write something on a sheet of paper.

More than any skill or instructional technique that Joe employed, he personi-fied a sense of assurance, evoking both trust and faith from the preservice teach-ers. In this sense, Joe functioned as a kind of "dramatic resource" (MacIntyre, 1981) for DJ and Stephanie—able to verbally articulate his knowledge, as well as practice it in challenging educational circumstances. As DJ and Stephanie tried to explain, regardless of what may have been happening, Joe was able to create a nurturing environment that reinforced both their own self-confidence, as well as the children's. His influence led to productive literacy-related experiences for everyone:

DJ: Joe, again, has an ability to assess a situation really well, to see what a problem might be, what a solution might be, you know.

Stephanie: He's so calm, too. I think that's what he gives to the children. . . . It's just this calm, quiet, never raises his voice. I mean, it's like he can have twenty things going on with the kids moving around and you don't notice he's doing it.

DJ: Something about his manner demands a lot of respect from the kids without it being an overbearing way, too. I think.

Much like Joe, Josie also embodied a pedagogy of self-worth that was reflected not only in her interactions with children, but in her collaboration with Sarah. In her research journal, where she regularly reminded us that she would "tell all," Josie provided detailed accounts of conversations with Sarah, as well as specific instances attesting to Sarah's development as a teacher of young children. As she wrote: "Sarah's making them talk. She's bringing those kids out. I tell her everyday, 'Sarah, Sarah' and she does it."

Sarah, a young teacher experiencing her own struggles connected with learning to teach in an urban setting, recognized and acknowledged this pedagogy of self-worth and its impact on her own development. She, too, wrote about her relationship with Josie in her journal:

I can't even find words to express how impressed I am by Josie. She has such a kind and generous heart. She thinks the world of these kids and wants what's best for them. What an amazing human being. Surely a lesson for me. . . . I am learning a lot from Josie just by observing her interactions with the kids. . . . I feel much more confident in my ability to manage a classroom and teach children, thanks to my experience with Josie.

For Josie, the act of helping a child role-play a story character or to read their writings to others were not activities peripheral to becoming a reader. Rather, they were central to a view of literacy learning that conceptualized school-like reading, writing, and especially talking as tantamount to self-completion:

"It's giving them a worth," she said, "a worth in literacy . . . bring them up here [to the community center] and let them see what reading, writing, or talking do and that they [the children] are worth something."

Clearly, Josie drew a direct connection between one's self-worth and the ability to express oneself. As she conceived it, talking was synonymous with being present, having power, and making a difference in the world. By contrast, not asserting one's right to speak about issues that affected the quality of one's life could lead to powerlessness and vulnerability in matters of personal importance. This belief was rooted in her own experiences as an active community member, a mother, and a woman who had first-hand experience with how her words and opinions were not always valued in community institutions:

I listen to people and I want people to listen to me. . . . I don't always get along with my priest. At my church he wants to do things his way only and he doesn't give parishioners a word to say. Well, he's gonna paint and we haven't even talked about the color! And I said, "Oh this man!" . . . So that's why I say learning how to talk to people [or read and write] and not being afraid. I've never been afraid to talk to a congressman or anybody that comes to the community. "You'll listen to me! Reading, writing, and talking is what's life's all about."

Not surprisingly, in the classroom Josie and Sarah developed projects in connection to particular storybooks that engaged children in talking and role-playing. As Josie explained more fully:

And we'll act it out. I like it because you're talking and you're talking. One girl is doing a whole bunch of sentences and talking, and then the other one, the other one, and the other one. It's talk, talk, talk, the role. You have a responsibility to talk. Like I had my girls coming off the school bus and each one came and said. "Mommy, Mommy! This happened today." And then I comfort them and tell them, "We'll we'll do this fix that problem." And with Sarah, it's just like I'm working with one of my children because she goes along with my say and I go along with her say . . . it's like being a mother and a grandmother only teaching.

As Josie suggested, her emphasis upon the importance of talk as an act of self-worth also grew out of her efforts to raise her daughters to be assertive and express their views and opinions. This was evident as Josie recalled a conversation in which Sarah made several remarks that did not reflect the same sense of children's progress that she recognized. Josie began by urging Sarah to look more carefully at what the children had accomplished:

Sarah said something [about the problems she was having with the children], and I said, "Listen, look at the kids and look at that girl how she's really got better and talking more." I like talking because they don't get that at home or maybe even at school. . . . My two daughters, we'd talk and talk. And like I say, they're different. But we'd talk. . . . And my daughters, they both have good jobs and they said, "Mom, if we wouldn't have had a good Mom like you, I don't know what would have happened." Because a lot of their friends are into drugs or whatever and mine aren't. So I'm really on talking. Talking, talking, talking. That's what helped my daughters make it through the troubles and the street mess.

Conclusions

In the present study, we examined the pedagogical knowledge that a group of adult community members recommended and practiced in the process of mentoring several preservice teachers working in an urban after-school program. Our findings illustrate that community mentors involvement with preservice teachers engendered five pedagogical orientations important to the preparation of new teachers and to the educational experiences of the young children in the program. Although adult mentors differed in both the specific manner and extent to which they embodied these pedagogies, preservice teachers consistently developed instructional approaches aimed at addressing the intellectual and social needs of children that reflected these five pedagogical stances. However, much like the community mentors with whom they worked, preservice teachers adopted some pedagogical approaches more readily than others. For example, Josie's commitment to encouraging children to talk and express oneself (a practice she associated with "saving" her daughters from "the streets") was often reflected in the manner and extent to which Sarah sought to engage children in story discussions. Indeed, Sarah's decision to regularly involve children in dramatizing story characters and events developed from Josie's concerns about the limited opportunities for conversation at home and perhaps even in their school classrooms. Additionally, Josie's relentless desire to reconcile theory and practice (to "walk the talk") and to hold both herself and Sarah accountable for children's learning opportunities, enabled Sarah to envision a level of personal integrity and commitment to teaching rarely described in the pages of popular textbooks on literacy pedagogy.

Joe also embodied a pedagogy of integrity and personal commitment as it pertained to reconciling theory and practice. However, even more significantly, his mentoring practices often reflected a pedagogy of hope or faith—dispositions that resulted from struggles he experienced in his own personal and professional life, and that he saw as essential to understanding how children's personal histories not only explained their behavior, but also explained their sense of self-worth in relation to literacy learning. This orientation was reflected in many of the comments about children and the instructional practices of both DJ and Stephanie as they sought to "build confidence" and understand more fully the meaning of helping some children to "just write something on a sheet of paper."

In sum, we wish to argue that community mentors and the knowledge they offered to preservice teachers raise some important questions about the relationship between community knowledge and the preparation of young teachers. As teacher mentors, these adults challenged our collective educational imaginations with the intellectual insights and moral authority they brought to conceptual issues related to the teaching of literacy, as well as to the development of practical strategies aimed at improving the education of children. It safe to say that as a society and as members of the educational community, we have grown comfortable with certain assumptions regarding the preparation of literacy teachers and the instructional frameworks conducive to effective literacy learning. We assume the primacy of academic disciplinary preparation for preservice teachers, as well as practicing teachers. We assume that school-based learning contexts with certified mentors as pedagogical role models will optimize teacher preparation. In short, a large preponderance of our collective imagination regarding how one learns to teach focuses on activities that take place in universities and schools with individuals who are officially authorized to work in those domains.

However, as West (1993) reminds us, "People don't live on [academic] arguments. . . . They live on love, care, respect, touch and so forth" (p. 24). Integrity, self-worth, hope, power and access, and meaning could also be added to West's description of factors that foster and sustain community and educational life. However, as we suggested, the pedagogies that community mentors brought to bear in the after-school program, are seldom a part of our educational imagination, especially as it concerns the preparation of preservice teachers (Liston & Zeichner, 1991). Perhaps as we search for strategies to close our literacy "gaps," and assist young teachers in contributing to this process, we might draw upon the history that lives in our midst, incorporating lived experiences alongside academic knowledge, grace alongside statistical probabilities, and human understanding along-side content standards and proficiency testing.

References

Baker, H. (1984). *Blues, ideology, and Afro-American literature: A vernacular theory.* Chicago: University of Chicago Press.

Cochran-Smith, M. (1995). Color blindness and basket making are not the answers: Confronting the dilemmas of race, culture, and language diversity in teacher education. *American Educational Research Journal, 32,* 493–522.

Cruz, B. C. (1997). Walking the walk: The importance of community involvement in preservice urban teacher education. *Urban Education, 32,* 394–410.

Delgado-Gaitan, C. (1990). *Literacy as empowerment: The role of parents in children's education.* New York: Falmer.

Erickson, F. (1986). Qualitative methods in research on teaching. In M. C. Wittrock (Ed.), *Handbook of research on teaching* (3rd ed., pp. 145–158). New York: Macmillan.

Gay, G (1993). Building cultural bridges: A bold proposal for teacher education. *Education and Urban Society, 25,* 285–299.

Glaser, B. G., & Strauss, A. (1967). *The discovery of grounded theory: Strategies for qualitative research.* Chicago: Aldine.

Haberman, M. (1996). Selecting and preparing culturally competent teachers for urban schools. In J. Sikula (Ed.), *Handbook of research on teacher education* (2nd ed., pp. 747–760). New York: Simon & Schuster.

Hawkey, K. (1997). Roles, responsibilities, and relationships in mentoring: A literature review and agenda for research. *Journal of Teacher Education, 48,* 325–335.

Ladson-Billings, G. (1994). *Dreamkeepers: Successful teachers of African American children.* San Francisco: Jossey-Bass.

Ladson-Billings, G. (2000). Fighting for our lives: Preparing teachers to teach African American students. *Journal of Teacher Education, 51,* 206–214.

Liston, D., & Zeichner, K. (1991). *Teacher education and the social conditions of schooling.* New York: Routledge.

McIntyre, A. (1981). *After virtue.* Notre Dame, IN: University of Notre Dame Press.

Mahan, J. (1982). Native Americans as teacher trainers: Anatomy and outcomes of a cultural immersion project. *Journal of Educational Equity and Leadership, 2,* 100–110.

McGinley, W., & Kamberelis, G. (1997). Maniac Magee and Ragtime Tumpie: Children negotiating self and world through reading and writing. *Research in the Teaching of English, 30,* 1–39.

McLaughlin, T. (1996). *Street smarts and critical theory: Listening to the vernacular.* Madison: University of Wisconsin Press.

Moll, L. (1992). Funds of knowledge for teachers using a qualitative approach to connecting homes and classrooms. *Theory into Practice, 31,* 132–141.

Moll, L. (in press). The diversity of schooling: A cultural-historical approach. In M. Reyes, & J. Halcon (Eds.), *The best for our children: Critical perspectives in literacy education for Latino students.* New York: Teachers College Press.

Reyes, M. de la Luz. (1992). Challenging venerable assumptions: Literacy instruction for linguistically different students. *Harvard Educational Review, 62,* 427–446.

West, C. (1993). *Beyond Eurocentrism and multiculturalism: Prophetic thoughts in Postmodern Times.* New York: Common Courage.

America Reads: Teachers' Perceptions of the Program

Pamela Ross
San Diego State University

In August 1996, President Bill Clinton proposed the America Reads Challenge in an effort to insure that all children will read independently and well by the end of third grade. Guidelines for the America Reads Challenge proposed the establishment of a local reading partnership between two agencies or organizations. In October 1996, Congress approved a bill to substantially increase Federal Work-Study funds, earmarking the increase for college and university work-study students to serve as reading tutors for elementary school children 5–8 years of age under the America Reads umbrella. Unlike other work-study programs, the usual 30% match required of work-study employers was waived. This meant tutoring was to be provided by colleges at no cost to the schools, although the tutoring was not actually performed by volunteers in the purest sense. In short, the program affords college students an opportunity to provide individualized literacy tutoring to elementary school children in high-poverty schools while earning money to defray the cost of their own university education.

According to Federal statistics, 1,000 colleges and universities have joined America Reads. Although millions of dollars have been allocated for possible use by college campuses nationwide, no funding for infrastructure and few guidelines for implementation, delivery, or evaluation accompany the program. However, research indicates that successful literacy tutoring programs require a structure for providing ongoing training and coaching of tutors, quality materials for tutoring, consistent service to the students being tutored, and monitoring of students' progress (Erickson & Anderson, 1997; Neumann, 1994; Pinnell & Fountas, 1997; Schine, 1997; Wasik, 1998). Managing an America Reads tutoring program on a shoestring budget is a challenge and innovation is a necessity since external sources of support must be identified and utilized.

Preliminary research on America Reads Programs has been highly positive both for those tutored (Morrow & Woo, 1998) and for the tutors themselves (Adler, 1999; Fitzgerald & Wolery, 1998; Gambrell, Dromsky, & Mazzoni, 1998). This paper describes the approach to the America Reads Challenge developed at a large, urban university in southern California. It documents the evolution of the program's successive approximations during its first 2 years, provides a description of the program training, and discusses strategies employed to manage the instructional delivery associated with the endeavor. In addition, a research component summarizes data collected concerning teachers' practices related to tutor assignments as well as their perceptions of the program, including its effects on student achievement.

National Reading Conference Yearbook, 49, pp. 500–510.

Description of the Program

Background

In spring 1997, the university's College of Education and Financial Aid Office met with representatives from the California Literature Project and school district staff in two partner districts to design and implement an America Reads Program. Approximately $250,000 in work-study money was committed to the project. This was the maximum allowable amount the institution could dedicate to the initiative and the Financial Aid Office seemed bent on creating the largest impact possible while at the same time meeting overall requirements for providing visible community service with its federal funds. On the other hand, the academic side of the house was concerned with developing a quality program that would go beyond presence in the community to support achievement gains in target schools. It was also interested in recruiting potential teacher candidates from underrepresented groups on campus who might be likely to apply for assistance through federal work-study. As a result of these differences in goals, the university partners often worked at cross-purposes and insufficient attention was given to the broad ramifications of launching and monitoring such a large tutoring program.

Year One

Coordination. In year one of the program, district representatives from central administration selected the schools that would receive the tutors. Sites served highly diverse student populations and were low-performing schools based on standardized test scores. A point person was designated for each district to serve as a liaison with the university. In turn, these individuals selected site coordinators, generally the reading teacher, for each target school. The financial aid coordinator, the university academic coordinator, district liaisons, and the site coordinators met throughout the spring to establish routines for payment of tutors, guidelines for tutoring, and a mechanism for problem solving issues that might arise.

Tutors. In addition to being work-study eligible, potential tutors were required to complete an application describing special qualifications to serve as a tutor. Applications were reviewed by financial aid staff based on educational goals (a major related to future teacher preparation was a plus), tutoring experience, and experience working with children. Acceptable candidates were sent for placement to a school site where they were assigned by the site coordinator to classrooms. Ultimately, over 160 undergraduate tutors worked with over 1,000 children in 25 schools within two districts.

Training. In the absence of funding for training, a number of school sites planned to provide support for tutors connected with other volunteer programs such as Rolling Readers. At the last minute, after serious campaigning by the academic coordinator, funding was obtained from the university's Academic Affairs office to offer two sections of a credit-bearing tutor-training course. The California Literature Project, a state-funded subject matter program, agreed to supply funds for a third. Three instructors, all practicing reading specialists, worked with the academic coordinator to develop a course that students were encouraged to but not required to take, due to inadequate notice about its existence. The majority of students did opt to enroll. Two sections were taught in English; a third section for bilingual university students emphasized Spanish language literacy.

The tutor-training course consisted of two units of instruction in the first semester focusing on the reading process, simple diagnostic tools (word lists, running records, phonics inventory), and a variety of literacy strategies such as guided reading, shared reading, language experience (writing), repeated readings, reciprocal questioning, think alouds, K-W-L, phonemic awareness/phonics activities, and use of predictable books. In general, the content of the course matched the key components for tutoring sessions recommended in the literature (Invernizzi, Juel, & Rosemary, 1997; Pinnell & Fountas, 1997), as well as instructional approaches for struggling readers supported by research (Juel, 1996; Pinnell, Lyons, DeFord, Bryk, & Seltzer, 1994; Wasik, 1998; Wasik & Slavin, 1993). Because of the number of English-language learners in local schools, some information on stages of second-language acquisition was also included. Students were required to keep a reflective journal containing lesson plans and to complete a case study on one child. However, tutors had considerable latitude in development of lessons and were encouraged to experiment with strategies.

In the second semester, students took a one-unit follow-up course that presented opportunities to discuss their tutoring experiences with peers as well as extend knowledge about strategies previously introduced. A handbook containing federal and financial aid guidelines associated with the program, list of key personnel, and course materials was developed and distributed to all students and site coordinators. Specific guidelines for host teachers were included in a letter that tutors transmitted at the beginning of the semester. The letter clarified responsibilities, mentioned the tutor-training course and requirements, and detailed federal restrictions on the types of activities tutors could perform.

Assessment. In order to assess the effectiveness of the program and make revisions, informal data were collected from tutors by course instructors and from site coordinators by financial aid. The greatest areas of need identified from this feedback included clearer communication and more support for the tutors. Not surprisingly, a comparison of tutors enrolled in the course versus those who were not revealed much greater satisfaction with the America Reads experience for those who received training.

Year Two

Coordination. Based on analysis of the initial year, in 1998–99 additional support for tutors was provided by two graduate student tutor-training coordinators paid by financial aid through work-study funds. The tutor-training coordinators became conversant with the tutoring class, conducted on-site visitations, met with district staff, offered ad hoc training sessions, and kept office hours for tutors seeking individualized help. The site coordinator monitored the mechanics of time cards, placed tutors with teachers, established tutoring schedules, and served as a liaison between tutors, the district, and the university tutor-training coordinators. Unfortunately, site coordinators were not compensated for extra duties associated with America Reads. Articulation meetings involving university faculty, financial aid staff, and district reading coordinators took place at least twice a semester. Procedures for evaluating tutors at least once each semester and a termination policy for unsatisfactory performance were established.

Tutors. During the second year of the program, nearly 1,000 children in 25 schools had contact with 110 America Reads tutors. This time, applications were reviewed by the tutor-training coordinators and scored on a scale of 1 to 4 based upon willingness to enroll in a tutor-training course as well as the other characteristics used the previous year. Candidates with the highest scores were identified and referred to a school district where they were interviewed by the reading coordinator before a final decision was made. A suggested list of interview questions was supplied to the site coordinators.

Training. Tutors were required to enroll in and complete the tutor-training course. Students who were unable to enroll in the course at the times it was offered were required to attend three Saturday workshops and to plan to enroll in the course the following semester. They were encouraged to seek assistance from the tutor-training coordinators during office hours.

Assessment. The tutor-training coordinators conducted a survey of tutors to ascertain the nature of their classroom assignments. Most tutors reported working at least 10 and up to 20 hours a week at their school sites; the number of hours varied according to individual financial aid eligibility. Tutors sometimes failed to monitor their hours and used up their awards months before the end of the academic year. In order to stay within our total America Reads allocation and because with so many tutors it was difficult to predict when this would happen, financial aid would not allow us to replace tutors who expended their awards early. This situation concerned the university academic coordinator because it affected consistency of contact with children and sometimes left teachers without tutors a month or two before the end of the year. Although tutors were expected to work one-to-one with at least some children on a regular basis, they were told they might work with small groups (up to three students). Some tutors reported working in more than one classroom with a variety of children and in large groups.

Despite written guidelines, then, how teachers chose to use the services of the tutors was ultimately their decision and, in a program of this size, very difficult to oversee. In light of gaps in communication that surfaced between the university and the schools, a study was designed to determine teachers' perceptions of America Reads and how the program was implemented in classrooms.

Study of Teachers' Practices and Perceptions

Data Collection and Analysis

Teachers who hosted America Reads tutors in 1998–99 were the subjects of this study. In the spring of 1998, approximately 160 surveys were distributed through the school site coordinators to K–3 teachers hosting one or more America Reads tutors. Up to this point, site coordinators had been the main point of contact and source of information about the program for the teachers. Aside from the tutors, teachers had little direct contact with university personnel and did not attend the broader coordination meetings. A total of 68 surveys were returned for a response rate of 43%.

The five-part teacher survey included questions related to tutor assignments, quality of the tutors, consistency of tutor contact with the same children, degree and nature of interactions between teachers and tutors, strategies most frequently used by tutors, and the appropriateness of these strategies to tutor abilities. Fifteen teachers were randomly selected to be interviewed in greater depth about the program using a structured interview format. Question probes included topics related to (a) contacts with site and tutor-training coordinators, (b) awareness of the training the tutors received, (c) details related to the nature of interactions with tutors, (d) selection criteria employed in assigning tutors to children, (e) degree to which teachers monitored progress of children as a result of tutoring, (f) the match between strategies covered in tutor training and the school curriculum, (g) beliefs about the impact of the program on the children tutored, (h) overall strengths and weakness of the program, and (i) suggestions for improving the program.

The 15–20 minute interviews were conducted by the academic coordinator of the program at the teacher's convenience. Fieldnotes from the interviews were entered on the computer immediately following the contact. Statements for each question were analyzed and response categories were developed for each item. In some cases, multiple responses to questions were supplied by teachers. For these items, all nonredundant responses were tallied and results reported as a percentage of the total number of responses rather than as a percentage of the teachers who gave a specific response. All results are reported descriptively.

Survey Results

Of the teachers who responded to the survey, 42% taught Grade 3, 27% taught Grade 2, 19% taught Grade 1, and 12% taught Kindergarten. The great majority of teachers (90%) assigned tutors to work on a one-to-one basis at least part of the time. Many teachers (49%) also assigned tutors to work with pairs of children, or in small groups of no more than three (47%). However, 32% reported that tutors also worked with more than three children at a time. Tutors worked consistently ("always" or "most of the time") with the same children in 88% of classrooms. However, 13% of the respondents indicated that tutors "sometimes" worked with the same children.

Teachers were asked to rate the tutors in terms of reliability, professionalism, potential for teaching, and overall quality on a scale of 1 to 5. Results indicate that, on the whole, teachers were favorably impressed with the quality of the tutors. Table 1 summarizes these ratings.

Teachers were asked to estimate the time in minutes they spent each week interacting with tutors giving directions related to instructional materials, discussing broader needs of the children receiving tutoring, discussing strategies to be used in instruction, observing interactions between the tutor and children, and discussing teaching as a profession. The amount of time devoted to each of these activities ranged from 0 to more than 20 minutes. On average, however, teachers indicated they spent 7–12 minutes a week communicating with tutors for each type of interaction. Overall, then, teachers spent more than 30 minutes a week supporting tutors in the classroom.

Finally, a list of strategies drawn from the tutoring course outline was provided and teachers were asked to check all activities they observed tutors using. Responses revealed that six strategies were employed by more than 50% of tutors: guided reading (84%), shared reading (70%), phonemic awareness activities (65%), phonics activities (62%), repeated readings (59%), and language experience (51%). When queried about the appropriateness of these strategies to the tutors' ability level, 88% of teachers deemed them "highly appropriate" or "appropriate."

Interview Results

Results of individual interviews with teachers significantly enhanced the snapshot of the America Reads Program produced by this investigation. Teachers were asked to describe the extent to which they had contact with their site coordinator and the university tutor-training coordinator assigned to their school. Most (60%) indicated that they had little or no contact with the site coordinator. About 40% indicated the coordinator "checked in" with them periodically or held some sort of formal meeting once or twice a semester. It became obvious that a number of other tutoring programs coexisted in project schools and that there was a lack of clarity about the source of the America Reads tutors. Uniformly, the interviewees had little or no contact with the university tutor-training coordinator

Table 1

Teacher Ratings of Tutor Quality

Variable	High (4–5)	Average (3)	Low (1–2)
Reliability	74%	14%	12%
Professionalism	88%	8%	4%
Potential for Teaching	77%	17%	4%
Overall Quality	77%	17%	6%

whose role was to observe and meet with the tutors when they were on site tutoring. Although awareness of the training provided by the university for the tutors was high (87%), 13% knew nothing about the training. However, one-third of the tutors discussed the course with their teachers, sharing information about the strategies they were learning. Despite awareness of the training, 60% of the teachers said they had never seen the course syllabus or the handbook, copies of which were supplied to the site coordinators.

Through question probes about the nature of teacher-tutor interactions and the criteria used to select the children to be tutored, it became clear that the use made of the America Reads tutors varied widely from classroom to classroom. According to teachers, most tutors (87%) worked with a small number of children on a one-to-one basis at least part of the time. However, nearly half worked with all children in the class as well. Sometimes tutors functioned as aides, working with every group during the reading rotation established by the teacher. Sometimes tutors worked with all children on a specific task such as computer based phonics lessons, listening to oral reading, or working on proofreading skills during writing. To determine the children most in need of one-to-one tutoring, many teachers (75%) used all or part of a "Directed Reading Activity" consisting of a sight-word list (San Diego Quick), a running record, and a comprehension measure. About 60% of teachers specifically mentioned supplying all the materials the tutor used and designating a spot for the tutor where these materials were housed. Fluctuation in tutor attendance due to conflicts with university course schedules was an issue that emerged quite often.

Teachers were asked to what extent they were able to monitor the progress of the children in their classroom as a result of tutoring. About 40% of teachers made no attempt to do so or felt that this was difficult at best since progress could be attributable to other sources of instructional assistance such as the classroom aide, the school reading teacher, other tutors, and teachers themselves. Several teachers (27%) reported using running records or the district DRA, and another 20% relied on tutor notes, folders containing work completed with the tutor, or other forms of tutor feedback. One teacher used growth in English language fluency as an index of success with a non-English speaking child who worked intensely with a tutor who spoke the child's native language. Suggestions for simple ways to monitor progress more closely included activity logs or portfolios containing products of activities done with tutors, running records, and criterion-referenced measures or observations. Most teachers (60%) felt there was a good match between strategies the tutors learned in their university training and the demands of the school curriculum. Once again, a large portion (40%) said they did not know about the content of the tutor training and therefore could not comment on the compatibility of strategies with the curriculum.

The majority of teachers (66%) believed that the America Reads Program had substantial impact on the achievement of the recipients. Another 26% saw some benefits, and one teacher saw no benefit. Several mentioned again that because the program was just one factor among many, it was difficult to determine its direct outcomes. When teachers were asked to list the strengths of the program, a total of 21 responses fell roughly into five categories: provision of one-to-one instruction (28.6%), regular/consistent contact with children (20%), supplemental help for the teacher (19%), positive interactions with children (19%), and tutor training (19%). Weaknesses of the program most frequently mentioned included scheduling (27%), communication (27%), and lack of teacher familiarity with content of training (17%).

When asked to suggest ways to improve the program, Most (50%) responses centered on building better communication between the university and host teachers, and on ways to enhance tutor training (17%) by emphasizing such things as a continuum of skills for emergent readers, basic reading terminology, and phonics background. Finally, the opportunity to provide any other input produced positive statements about the program such as "great," "wonderful," or "excellent" and requests for more tutor time. Although teachers liked the autonomy and consistency of the tutors, they referred to scheduling problems. Specifically, it was noted that tutors tended to arrive and leave during instructional time when the teacher was occupied and unable to converse with them. In addition, tutors' schedules did not necessarily coincide with the block of time in the morning dedicated to literacy instruction.

Discussion and Conclusion

Overall, teacher response to the America Reads Program was positive, even in the absence of hard data that it improved student achievement. Teachers' ratings of tutor quality were generally high, indicating that the screening process and procedures for evaluating tutors worked reasonably well. However, important concerns related to tutor assignment, communication, training, and the monitoring of student progress surfaced as a result of this study.

Given the guidelines supplied for the use of tutors and the documented success of early intervention programs, it was expected that most tutors would be assigned to K–1 classrooms by site coordinators. Surprisingly, this was not the case. One rationale supplied by teachers for placing tutors predominantly in Grades 2 and 3 was the availability of other services for first graders such as Reading Recovery. New mandates for third-grade achievement levels in one of the districts also may have influenced these decisions. Furthermore, it was discovered that some tutors were placed in multiple classrooms and many frequently worked more as instructional aides than tutors. It is likely that the number of hours tutors spent in classrooms each week (up to 20) influenced broader tutor assignments. It would be wise for teachers, site coordinators, and the university academic coordinator to revisit this issue in order to develop firmer guidelines. Scheduling, grade placement, and assignment within classrooms should be discussed periodically by the partners and revised as necessary.

There is evidence that in successful tutoring programs a certified reading specialist needs to supervise tutors (Wasik, 1998). Currently, school site coordinators who might serve in this capacity are not compensated for the extra work associated with America Reads. Therefore, beyond monitoring time cards and attending infrequent meetings, many do not attempt to promote communication between the university and the district and have minimal contact with tutors regarding instruction. Ways to provide release time for site coordinators or reward them for their efforts in some other fashion should be explored. Meanwhile, to improve dissemination of information, it appears that the academic director of the program or designee may need to visit each school to meet with the site coordinator and all teachers hosting America Reads tutors. At these meetings, she could share the course syllabus, handbook and other guidelines, as well as collect feedback to help improve services.

Teachers repeatedly mentioned schedule conflicts. Several solutions to this problem come to mind. Prior to beginning instruction, tutors should meet with their host teachers to discuss the content of training, shape a workable schedule, and plan conference times. Tutors and teachers might sign contracts with agreements about responsibilities and hours; teachers might initial weekly training logs to assure awareness of the strategies the tutors are learning.

The addition of tutor-training coordinators in the second year of the program certainly eased burdens in the financial aid office, helped improve communication, and provided support to tutors. However, paying tutor-training coordinators out of work-study funds proved to be a poor solution as coordinator salaries absorbed dollars that could have been allocated to tutors, federal guidelines severely restricted the nature of coordinator activities, and bureaucratic procedures made salary payments erratic. In 1999–2000, University Academic Affairs agreed to support two graduate student coordinators out of its own budget. Although this development has alleviated many difficulties, coordinator turnover from year to year is bound to impact the program and will need to be resolved.

Despite our best efforts to keep track of tutors in training, it appears there are always a few who are unable or avoid enrolling in the tutor-training course. The Saturday workshops scheduled later in the semester help solve the problem of tutors whose schedules prevent enrollment in the training course or who transition into the program after the start of the semester. Nonetheless, a few untrained tutors are in classrooms for periods of time. To solve this problem, we are exploring putting the tutor-training course on line and requiring three mandatory Saturday workshops as part of the package. In addition, to improve the match between teacher needs and tutor knowledge, initial instruction in the university classroom will be revised to include self-guided or programmed phonics knowledge materials for tutors and more emphasis on the scope and sequence of skills in early literacy. Given the small number of strategies employed in the schools, we are considering concentrating on more structured tutoring sessions employing fewer techniques as have other tutoring programs described in the literature (Juel, 1996; Many, Elliot, Howard, & Hiltbrand, 1999; Wasik, 1998).

In its urgency to use all available funds allocated for America Reads on the university's campus, the financial aid office with the complicity of the College of Education may have created a behemoth. Monitoring over 100 tutors in 25 schools is a full-time job with no compensation for most district or university staff time.

Although the tutor-training coordinators helped close some gaps, university staff need to communicate with host teachers throughout the year. The addition of an Americorps Vista volunteer to the coordination team in January 2000 whose primary function will be to meet with teachers at each site may help alleviate some of the communication and monitoring problems.

Under current procedures for assigning tutors, hundreds of children receive help from our America Reads Program, a fact that makes monitoring progress extremely unwieldy. Presently, although tutors select one child for pre/post evaluations as part of their course requirements, progress of remaining children may not be documented. A system for monitoring gains of those tutored on a one-to-one basis needs to be developed and standardized. The involvement of teachers and site coordinators in creating a workable system will be key to success of this plan. In addition, many tutors (almost 50%) return to tutor for a second year and do not re-enroll in the course. Ongoing support mechanisms for continuing tutors need to be established.

The magnitude of America Reads programs and their potential to impact literacy instruction and achievement in K–3 classrooms is substantial. Any tutoring program can create positive reactions without producing real achievement gains for its recipients. Developing strategies to deliver programs as effectively as possible in order to maximize impact on achievement is essential. Research and dialogue with others operating similar programs need to be encouraged if we are to develop procedures that are fiscally sound, provide opportunities for recruiting potential teachers from the undergraduate ranks, and simultaneously help achieve the goal that all children will read independently and well by the end of Grade 3. To attain these goals without making unrealistic demands on the professionals who agree to support initiatives like America Reads is a balancing act we have yet to master.

References

Alder, M. (1999). *The America reads challenge: An analysis of college students' tutoring* (CIERA Rep. No. 3-007). Ann Arbor: University of Michigan.

Fitzgerald, J, & Wolery, R. (1998, December). *An exploratory close-up look of two tutors.* Paper presented at the meeting of the National Reading Conference, Austin, TX.

Erickson, J., & Anderson J. (Eds.). (1997). *Learning with the community: Concepts and models for service-learning in teacher education.* Washington, DC: American Association for Higher Education.

Gambrell, L., Dromsky, A., & Mazzoni, S. (1998, December). *Tutor successes and frustrations.* Paper presented at the meeting of the National Reading Conference, Austin, TX.

Invernizzi, M., Juel, C., & Rosemary, C. A. (1997). A community volunteer tutorial that works. *Reading Teacher, 50,* 304–311.

Juel, C. (1996). What makes literacy tutoring effective? *Reading Research Quarterly, 31,* 268–289.

Many, J. E., Elliot, L., Howard, F., & Hiltbrand, R. (1999, December). *Redesigning a volunteer tutoring program: Participants' implementation of and reaction to a research-based literacy curriculum.* Paper presented at the meeting of the National Reading Conference, Orlando, FL.

Morrow L., & Woo, D. (1998, December). *The effect of "America reads" tutoring on achievement and attitude of children.* Paper presented at the meeting of the National Reading Conference, Austin, TX.

Neumann, A. (1994). *Volunteer tutor's toolbox.* Newark, DE: International Reading Association.

Pinnell, G. S., & Fountas, I. C. (1997). *A coordinator's guide to help America read: A handbook for volunteers.* Portsmouth, NH: Heinemann.

Pinnell, G. S., Lyons, C. A., DeFord, D. E., Bryk, A. S., & Seltzer, M. (1994). Comparing instructional models for the literacy education of high-risk first graders. *Reading Research Quarterly, 29,* 9–39.

Schine, J., (Ed.). (1997). *Service learning: Ninety-sixth yearbook of the National Society of the Study of Education.* Chicago: University of Chicago Press.

Wasik, B. A. (1998). Using volunteers as reading tutors: Guidelines for successful practices. *Reading Teacher, 51,* 562–570.

Wasik, B. A. & Slavin, R. E. (1993). Preventing early reading failure with one-to-one tutoring: A review of five programs. *Reading Research Quarterly, 28,* 178–200.

Is Narrative Primary? Well, It Depends . . .

Laura B. Smolkin
University of Virginia

Carol A. Donovan
University of Alabama

Richard G. Lomax
University of Alabama

I n his December 1999 address to the National Reading Conference, Jerome Bruner revisited many of the themes and topics that have delighted reading researchers for the past 25 years. As he extolled the wonders of the narrative, many in the audience thought back to a seminal study of children's approximations of the linguistic patterns of two distinct written forms. Examining narrative (story) and nonnarrative (information books) genres, Pappas (1993) questioned the "validity of the common assumption in literacy development that narrative, or story, is somehow primary—that children's abilities to understand and compose stories precede their capabilities to understand and use non-story, informational written language" (p. 97). This "common assumption" of the primacy of narrative, explained Pappas, was readily detectable in the writings of Wells (1986), Bruner (1986), and Egan (1988), and was attached to the stance that narrative is the primary mode of thought. For Bruner (1992), life itself is a narrative, and thought is the interpretation and reinterpretation of life experiences. Egan (1988), too, has asserted the importance of narrative; children use this form to make sense of the world by making content more meaningful and accessible. Moffett (1968), an even earlier proponent of the primacy of narrative, has even suggested that young children "must make narrative do for all" (p. 49).

Pappas's (1993) question was followed by her results of kindergartners' pretend rereadings of picture storybooks and information books. These suggested that even young children were capable of developing control over written informational language structures as well as written story language structures, leading to her contention that favoring narrative texts over nonnarrative, informational texts, was a wrongheaded approach to literacy instruction in the early grades. And, this deletion of informational texts seemed even more inappropriate given the children's responses to the two study books, *Tunnels* and *Poppy the Panda;* the children, asserted Pappas, preferred the informational text to the storybook. This she found to be true for both girls and boys, despite teachers' suggestions to her that if anyone did prefer information books, it would be boys.

National Reading Conference Yearbook, 49, pp. 511–520.

Pappas's question and initial research in this area have led to increased interest in children's exposures to a range of written genre structures with many researchers now engaged in related investigations (Chapman, 1995; Donovan, 1996; Donovan, Smolkin, & Lomax, 2000; Duke, 1999; Duthie, 1996; Oyler, 1996; Smolkin & Donovan, 2000). We now know that children can comfortably produce both narrative and nonnarrative oral texts (Pappas, 1993), even though they may have little chance to do so in classrooms dominated by teacher-selected narrative materials (Duke, 1999). Still, we have no study that examines whether early readers themselves consider narrative their preferred mode of textual presentation. Given our increased attention to the types of texts that belong in first-grade classrooms (Brown, 1999; Gunning, 1997; Hiebert, 1999), this question merits an answer. In this paper, looking at the role of gender, text type (genre) and text structure (narrative vs. nonnarrative), we return to the question of narrative's "primacy" by examining children's own choices from a well-designed classroom library.

"But, what is narrative? Isn't it just a story?"

Before examining young children's preferences, some basic elements in the definition of narrative warrant consideration. In this paper, we are adopting what Bamberg (1997) views as a Cognitive Perspective in examining narrative, in which knowledge of the basic structure of narratives is the focus. As Hasan (1984) would put it, we are considering which elements are obligatory to a narrative text.

For many, the critical obligatory element that must be addressed to determine narrative genre is the complication (or the "troubles," as Bruner so delightfully dubbed this element in his talk). Whether the troubles are present or not is often viewed as determining whether a particular text may be considered narrative (Christie, 1986; Hasan, 1984; Mandler & Johnson, 1977; Martin & Rothery, 1986; Stein & Glenn, 1979). Narrative, story, is the genre that entails fictional events during which characters engage in action that heightens conflict and calls for resolution.

For others, such as Labov and Waletsky (1967), temporality is the element that determines narrative. However, examination of many informational texts reveals that temporality is frequently critical to these texts. Consider, for example, procedural texts such as instructions (e.g., Martin, 1989) in which sequence is particularly critical. Therefore, temporality alone, the stringing together of events so commonly heard in young children's narration of what has occurred ("and then . . . and then . . . and then . . ."), is insufficient to determine the genre of a particular text. It does, however, supply critical information on how a text has been structured (see e.g., Britton & Black, 1985, or Meyer, 1975, for discussions of text structures). Information books as described by Pappas (1987) generally describe the attributes and characteristics of a single topic. This information can be structured in a nonnarrative fashion, as in Knight's (1977) *Dinosaur Days* that presents characteristic attributes of dinosaurs in general. The information can also be set within a narrative structure, as in Lavies's (1989) *Tree Trunk Traffic,* which chronicles the events of a family of squirrels. Or, the information can be presented within texts that have been termed "fuzzy" (Pappas, Kiefer, & Levstik, 1995), grey (Leal, 1993), or blended (Skurzynski, 1992). Joanna Cole's original "Magic School Bus" books, narrative tales of Ms. Frizzle's class's fantastic, science-related adventures in which nonnarrative informational representations abound, exemplify a particular subgenre of these hybrid forms, which, because of authors' intentions to entertain and inform, we have now termed "dual purpose" texts (Donovan & Smolkin, 2000). That informational texts may have narrative or nonnarrative structures makes them an especially fertile ground for examining whether it is narrative, temporality in macrostructure, or whether it is story, with its element of complication, that leads to primacy, if, in fact, such a primacy exists. Making this distinction between a narrative structure and a story genre allows us to take a finer-grained look, then, at the issue of narrative as "primary" in the literacy lives and preferences of primary-grade children. In this paper, therefore, we return to Pappas's question "Is narrative primary?" by examining children's own choices from a well designed, first-grade classroom library.

Method

The data presented in this paper are part of a study of genre in first-grade classrooms in which both teacher presentations of and children's self selections of and interactions with informational and story genres were examined. The same methodologies were employed for 2 consecutive years of a teacher's career, as she moved from a lower-to-middle SES public school on a military base to a middle-to-upper SES, suburban public school. Particular attention was given to children's self-selections during recreational reading time to explore selections by genre, gender, and socioeconomic status of the students (Donovan, Smolkin & Lomax, 1998), by readability (Donovan et al., 2000), and by "quality," topics, and features (Donovan, Smolkin & Lomax, 1999). In this paper, we focus on the selections of the first cohort of the study. Descriptive and statistical measures have been employed to examine the data presented in this paper.

Participants

The participants were in one first-grade class of 11 boys and 10 girls located in a large public school adjacent to a military base. The population was diverse in terms of children's socioeconomic and racial backgrounds as well as reading abilities.

The Reading Program

The reading program in this classroom included two different self-selected reading periods each school day. The first supplied time for children to practice fluent reading with books targeted to their assessed reading levels. The second, the focus of this study, was a 30-minute block for social, recreational reading of books self-selected from any materials in the classroom library. As the self-selected recreational reading block had been established early in the year, children were familiar and comfortable with the recreational routine that included the stipulation that they be actively engaged with their self-selected books. Although off-task behaviors had occurred occasionally during the fall, by the time of the intensive study, redirection by the teacher (and often peers) had virtually eliminated such behaviors. Teacher read alouds (Smolkin & Donovan, 2000) of informational and story trade books occurred at least twice daily. The trade books were also incorporated into daily language arts and content lessons.

The Classroom Library

The classroom library, consisting of 632 volumes, was unique in its attention to the inclusion of informational texts. Of all books in the library (632 total), 405 (64%) were storybooks and 227 (36%) were information books. A graduate student and at least one of the researchers coded each book for genre and text structure. Of the 227 information books, 35 (15%) were coded as narrative, 187 (82%) were coded as nonnarrative, and 5 (2%) were coded as dual purpose texts.

Our coding of the books was heavily influenced by the work of functional linguists (Halliday & Hasan, 1989; Hasan, 1984; Martin, 1989; Martin & Rothery, 1986) in which linguistic elements specific to different types of texts are closely examined. Following Hasan's (1984) work identifying elements specific to the story genre, Pappas (1987) identified elements specific to the information book. Those two papers most heavily influenced our text analyses as we examined text features. For this paper's particular analysis, we have attended closely to temporality. Texts with sequencing across time have been coded as narrative; those with no temporal sequencing have been coded as nonnarrative (Hasan, 1984; Pappas, 1987; Newkirk, 1987). Each of the books had been assigned a number that appeared inside the front cover on the bottom left corner.

Data Collection

So that we could track their self-selections for this study, the children were instructed to record the number of each selected book in a class log. When they chose to read with a buddy or to read with a group, children were instructed to record all names of those reading the book. Students were introduced to the sign-in procedure the week prior to the study and the teacher monitored children's accuracy in recording their selections. During a practice week, the teacher demonstrated the procedure daily and checked each child's recording efforts. Children took great pride in entering their selections in the class log, and few discrepancies were found. During the six weeks of the study, as children left the group to choose books, the teacher reminded them to record their books carefully, did a daily check of the records and visual sweeps of the children's actual reading to help ensure accuracy. The data collection period, which commenced in March of a school year that had begun in late July, lasted for six weeks.

Data Analysis

The data were analyzed in two ways. First, descriptive statistics (i.e., counts, percentages) were generated to examine one categorical variable at a time. Second, chi-square tests of association were conducted to determine the relationship between two categorical variables. Variables included gender, genre (information book) and text structure (narrative, nonnarrative, dual-purpose).

Results

During the 6 weeks of the study, boys recorded 609 total selections and girls recorded 458 selections. The analyses we report below explores the content of those selections relative to gender, genre and text structure.

Children's Book Selections by Genre and Gender

Informational texts, constituting 36% of the classroom library, were chosen 384 times (36%) overall. Storybooks, constituting 64% of the classroom library, were selected 683 times (64%) overall. We conducted a chi-square analysis to determine the relationship between gender and genre. There was a significant relationship shown ($\chi^2=7.20, df=1, p<.01$). Specifically, of the 609 texts selected by the boys, 240 (39%) were information books and 369 (61%) were storybooks. Of the 458 texts selected by the girls, 144 (31%) were information books and 314 (69%) were storybooks. Thus, the boys selected a significantly higher percentage of information books than did the girls and the girls selected a significantly higher percentage of storybooks than the boys.

Information Book Selections by Text Structure and Gender

To more carefully scrutinize the children's selections of narrative and nonnarrative texts, we analyzed the information books selections separately, attending to text structure and then to gender (see Table 1). We conducted a chi-square analysis to determine the difference between selections of narrative and nonnarrative information books, eliminating the "fuzzy" texts from the analysis because of their relatively small numbers. The difference was significant ($\chi^2=130.75$, $df=1, p<.0001$). More specifically, 280 (81%) nonnarrative information books were selected, and 67 (19%) narrative information books were selected. Therefore, the children selected significantly more information books with a nonnarrative text structure than information books with a narrative text structure.

We conducted a second chi-square analysis to determine the relationship between gender and text structure of information books selected; there was no significant relationship ($\chi^2=1.32, df=1, p>.05$). When considering only information book selections, the difference between boys' and girls' selections of the narrative and nonnarrative texts was not significantly different.

Discussion

Before we discuss our results, we wish to address the limitations of this study. Given that only one group of children's choices from one classroom library has been examined, generalizability of these findings is limited. Because this was not an experimental design, and because of the close alignment of selections with availability, which can be seen in the results, there is also a possibility that percentages of selections of each genre occurred by chance. Finally, the methodology relied on children to record their own selections. Although this procedure was monitored daily, it is possible that not all selections were recorded. Then, too, the way in which the boys of the class often shared multiple selections in small groups, recording each boy's name for each selected book may have produced the higher number of selections for boys than girls.

Having acknowledged the limitations of the study, we see the picture that arises from this exploration of children's preferences for narrative or nonnarrative texts as complex, but informative. We discuss our findings and their implications below.

Genre and Gender

As comes as little surprise to those who have followed the literature on children's reading preferences, an area of reading research more than 100 years old (e.g., Wisler, 1898), we found genre preference differences by gender. In a classroom library in which attention had been given to the inclusion of information books so that such texts constituted 36% of the total content, boys' selections of information books were significantly greater than girls', whereas girls' selections of storybooks were significantly greater than boys'. Indeed, boys'

Table 1

Information Book Selections by Text Structure and Gender

Gender	Narrative Count	Narrative %	Nonnarrative Count	Nonnarrative %	Dual Purpose Count	Dual Purpose %	Total Count	Total %
Girls	30	20.8	104	72.2	10	6.9	144	
		44.8		37.1		27.0		
		7.8		27.1		2.6		37.5
Boys	37	15.4	176	73.3	27	11.3	240	
		55.2		62.9		73.0		
		9.6		45.8		7.0		62.5
Total	67	17.4	280	72.9	37	9.6	384	
		100.0		100.0		100.0		
		17.4		72.9		9.6		100.0

Note. Within each cell, the first percentage represents percentage for that gender. The second percentage represents percentage of selection for that type. The third percentage represents percentage of total selections.

preferences for informational texts are exactly what teachers had suggested to Pappas (1991) might be the case. It is interesting to look more closely at the topics of the informational texts that the boys and the girls selected. Elsewhere (Donovan et al., 1999) we have discussed these differences. Girls' information book selections most frequently were on the topic of animals, particularly baby animals, although they did also choose books on weather and an occasional "Magic School Bus" book. Boys' top information book selections represented a much greater range of topics. Although they, too, liked books about animals and "The Magic School Bus" series, their favorites included books about planets, machines, and Michael Jordan. As there were many books on these topics, we do not believe that topic availability constrained the selections of either gender. Certainly, though, it is safe to say that both boys and girls like to read stories, as over 69% of both boys' and girls' selections were story texts. If, then, we define narrative as the story genre, it seems that children themselves find narratives to be their primary choice.

Text Structure

If, on the other hand, narrative is seen as the temporal structuring of a text, then the primacy of narrative evaporates. Given the very pronounced preference by children for stories, and given the key role temporality plays in those texts, we expected that children, particularly girls, would be drawn to the temporally organized informational texts. This, however, was not the case. Approximately three-fourths of both boys' and girls' selections of informational text were classified as nonnarrative in structure. These results supply additional support to positions expressed by Pappas (1993) and Newkirk (1987, 1989) that even young children have considerable facility and comfort with a range of text structures. We take these findings on text structure to support previous research indicating that information presented to young children need not appear in a "story-like" form such as a child's visit to the dairy farm or a fantastic bus ride to learn about the senses (Jetton, 1994; Maria & Junge, 1994; Smolkin & Donovan, 2000).

Availability

The classroom library in which this study was conducted clearly differs significantly from those described by Duke (1999). When a teacher makes informational texts available, and reads them aloud as frequently as stories are read aloud, our study indicates that children, both boys and girls, will spend time with those texts, even if it is less time than they spend with the stories Bruner stresses that children so dearly love.

In this classroom, where information books constituted over one-third of available texts, girls selected information books slightly under one-third of the time, whereas boys selected information books slightly over one-third of the time. Although our findings are limited by the single sample, we cannot help but note how very closely children's information book selections parallel availability. This same parallel of selections to availability is seen in the children's choices of nonnarrative vs. narrative structured information books. Of the information books in the library, over 80% had nonnarrative structures; both boys and girls made over 70% of their information book selections from these nonnarrative texts. Still, even if the children's selections were no more than a reflection of availability, a possibility we noted in our limitations discussion, our findings must then be interpreted as indicating that what teachers actually choose to place in their libraries really does affect what Pappas (1991) considers a "full access to literacy" (p. 126).

Conclusion

Our study raises many questions about the presence of information books and children's selections. How do children interact with the different genres they select? How do they interact with the texts if they are looking at their selections in small groups? How do they make sense of the books they peruse? What, in fact, is the influence of the teacher read aloud on a book's selection?

Returning to our original question "Is narrative primary?" we must respond "Well, it depends . . ." We take our data to suggest that given the available selections if narrative means story, then it seems to be children's primary choice. But when narrative means temporality in informational presentation, the answer appears to be "no." We readily acknowledge that only experimental designs with libraries controlled for availability of different genres and text structures will ultimately resolve this question. Until then, however, though we revel in the "troubles" of stories, we must set the stage for children's future school success. Simplistic as this may sound, what is not present in classroom libraries does not get selected, thought about, or discussed.

References

Bamberg, M. (1997). *Narrative ability and human development.* Hillsdale, NJ: Erlbaum.

Britton, B. K., & Black, J. B. (Eds.). (1985). *Understanding expository text: A theoretical and practical handbook for analyzing explanatory text.* Hillsdale, NJ: Erlbaum.

Brown, K. J. (1999). What kind of text—for whom and when? Textual scaffolding for beginning readers. *Reading Teacher, 53,* 292–307.

Bruner, J. (1986). *Actual minds, possible worlds.* Cambridge, MA: Harvard University Press.

Bruner, J. (1992). The narrative construction of reality. In H. Beilin & P. B. Pufali (Eds.), *Piaget's theory: Prospects and possibilities* (pp. 28–37). Hillsdale, NJ: Erlbaum.

Chapman, M. L. (1995). The sociocognitive construction of written genres in first grade. *Research in the Teaching of English, 29,* 164–192.

Christie, F. (1986). Learning to mean in writing. In N. Stewart-Dore (Ed.), *Writing and reading to learn* (pp. 21–34). Rozelle, Australia: Primary English Teaching Association.

Donovan, C. A. (1996). First graders' impressions of genre-specific elements in writing narrative and expository texts. In D. J. Leu, C. K. Kinzer, & K. A. Hinchman (Eds.), *Literacies for the 21st century.* Forty-fifth yearbook of the National Reading Conference (pp. 183–194). Chicago: National Reading Conference.

Donovan, C. A., & Smolkin, L. B. (2000, April). *Reading in elementary science instruction: An examination of teachers' trade book selections.* Paper presented at the meeting of the American Educational Research Association. New Orleans, LA.

Donovan, C. A., Smolkin, L. B., & Lomax, R. G. (1998, December). *Exploring first graders' book selections from a well-designed classroom library.* Paper presented at the annual meeting of the National Reading Conference. Austin, TX.

Donovan, C. A., Smolkin, L. B., & Lomax, R. G. (1999, April). *But do they pick "good literature"? First grade boys' and girls' book selections from a well-designed classroom library.* Paper presented at the meeting of the American Educational Research Association, Montreal, Canada.

Donovan, C. A., Smolkin, L. B., & Lomax, R. G. (2000). Beyond the independent level text: Considering the reader-text match in first graders' self-selections during recreational reading. *Reading Psychology, 21,* 309–333.

Duke, N. K. (1999). *The scarcity of informational texts in first grade* (Report No. 1-007). East Lansing: Center for the Improvement of Early Reading Achievement, Michigan State University.

Duthie, C. (1996). *True stories: Nonfiction literacy in the primary classroom.* York, ME: Stenhouse.

Egan, K. (1988). *Primary understanding: Education in early childhood.* New York: Routledge.

Gunning, T. (1997). *Best books for beginning readers.* New York: Allyn & Bacon.

Halliday, M. A. K., & Hasan, R. (1989). *Language, context, and text: Aspects of language in a social-semiotic perspective.* New York: Oxford University Press.

Hasan, R. (1984). The nursery tale as a genre. *Nottingham Linguistic Circular, 13,* 71–102.

Hiebert, E. H. (1999). Texts matter in learning to read. *Reading Teacher, 52,* 552–566.

Jetton, T. L. (1994). Information-driven versus story-driven: What children remember when they are read informational stories. *Journal of Reading Psychology, 15,* 109–130.

Knight, D. C. (1977). *Dinosaur days.* New York: McGraw-Hill.

Labov, W., & Waletsky, J. (1967). Narrative analysis: Oral versions of personal experience. In J. Helm (Ed.), *Essays on the Verbal and Visual Arts* (pp. 12–44). Seattle: University of Washington Press.

Lavies, B. (1989). *Tree trunk traffic.* New York: Dutton.

Leal, D. (1993). Storybooks, information books, and informational storybooks: An explication of the ambiguous grey genre. *New Advocate, 6,* 61–70.

Mandler, J. M., & Johnson, N. S. (1977). Remembrance of things parsed: Story structure and recall. *Cognitive Psychology, 9,* 111–151.

Maria, K., & Junge, K. (1994). A comparison of fifth graders' comprehension and retention of scientific information using a science textbook and an informational storybook. In C. K. Kinzer & D. J. Leu (Eds.), *Multidimensional aspects of literacy research, theory, and practice.* Forty-third yearbook of the National Reading Conference (pp. 146–152). Chicago: National Reading Conference.

Martin, J. R. (1989). *Factual writing: Exploring and challenging social reality.* Oxford, England: Oxford University Press.

Martin, J. R., & Rothery, J. (1986). What a functional approach to the writing task can show teachers about "good writing." In B. Couture (Ed.), *Functional approaches to writing: Research perspectives.* Norwood, NJ: Ablex.

Meyer, B. J. F. (1975). *The organization of prose and its effects on memory.* Amsterdam: North-Holland.

Moffett, J. (1968). *Teaching the universe of discourse.* Boston: Houghton Mifflin.

Newkirk, T. (1987). The non-narrative writing of young children. *Research in the Teaching of English, 21,* 121–144.

Newkirk, T. (1989). *More than stories: The range of children's writings.* Portsmouth, NH: Heinemann.

Oyler, C. (1996). Sharing authority: Student initiations during teacher-led read-alouds of information books. *Teaching and Teacher Education, 12,* 149–160.

Pappas, C. C. (1987). *Exploring the generic shape of "information books": Applying typicality notions to the process.* Paper presented at the meeting of the World Conference of Applied Linguistics, Sydney.

Pappas, C. C. (1991). Fostering full access to literacy by including information books. *Language Arts, 68,* 449–462.

Pappas, C. C. (1993). Is narrative "primary"? Some insights from kindergartners' pretend readings of stories and information books. *Journal of Reading Behavior, 25,* 97–129.

Pappas, C. C., Kiefer, B. Z., & Levstik, L. S. (1995). *An integrated language perspective in the elementary school: Theory into action.* White Plains, NY: Longman.

Skurzynski, G. (1992). Up for discussion: Blended books. *School Library Journal, 38*(10), 46–47.

Smolkin, L. B., & Donovan, C. A. (2000). *Information book read alouds, comprehension acquisition and comprehension instruction.* East Lansing: Center for the Improvement of Early Reading Achievement, Rep. No. 2-009, Michigan State University.

Stein, N. L., & Glenn, C. G. (1979). An analysis of story comprehension in elementary school children. In R. O. Freedle (Ed.), *New directions in discourse processing* (Vol. 2, pp. 53–120). Norwood, NJ: Ablex.

Wells, G. (1986). *The meaning makers: Children learning language and using language to learn.* Portsmouth, NH: Heinemann.

Wisler, C. (1898). Interests of children in reading in the elementary school. *Pedagogical Seminary, 5,* 523–540.

Stories About Literacy and Learning: Students Talk About Their Best and Worst

Jodi Dodds Kinner, Wendy C. Kasten,
Nancy Padak, and Jackie Peck
Kent State University

Chris McKeon
Walsh University

Mary Styslinger
University of South Carolina

This year in language arts. . . . I found out that mythology was the base of most of the English language. And every day we were told stories about each god and what they did and what they stand for. I learned a lot. I learned how to tell what words mean just by looking at them. . . . Breaking up words isn't as boring as it used to be. It can be more fun. Words have more meaning than they seem. . . . [The] stories were not even true, but they were so fascinating. And our teacher made it fun, and we ended up having fun AND learning something. (Emily, Grade 7)

What I've noticed from the first grade up to the fourth grade [is] like in first grade we also learned the same thing in second grade . . . and in third grade we learned the same thing we learned in second grade. Now in fourth grade we learned a little bit of what we learned in third grade. Now we're learning a little bit of new things, but still at the beginning of the year we learned a lot of what we learned in third and second grade. That did get kind of boring after studying it for two years. (Josh, Grade 4)

Students like Emily and Josh have much to teach us about effective and ineffective learning experiences. They are, as Alvermann et al. (1996) remind us, experts on the topic of their own experiences. Yet few educational policy-makers place student experiences with schooling at the center of explorations of educational reform. Indeed, students and the quality of their everyday experiences often seem lost in the demand for longer school days or years, more standardized testing, school accountability, and other educational "improvement" efforts.

Part of the reason for this lack of "student presence" in calls for educational reform may be that few researchers have placed students' perceptions and experiences at the center of attention (Erickson & Schultz, 1992). Researchers have sought student opinions about their best teachers (McCabe, 1995; McDowell & McDowell, 1986). Attitudes about certain subjects and types of or contexts for

National Reading Conference Yearbook, 49, pp. 521–533.

instruction have also been examined (Fouts & Meyers, 1992; Maroufi, 1989; Oldfather, 1993, 1995; Shug, Todd, & Beery, 1984).

Two studies with broader focus on student experiences provide beginning looks into this critical ingredient in educational reform. Taylor and Roselli (1993) asked students to identify things that made the school day more pleasant; students reported preferences for hands-on approaches, computers, outdoor activities, science labs, and audiovisual presentations. Wasserman (1995) asked students about their most memorable experiences in middle school. These students focused on engagement and problem solving: They loved challenges and found them satisfying; they hated busywork.

Clearly, students' ideas about learning, including literacy learning, and interests have not been mined for their value in informing educational practice. The studies reported here begin to fill this gap.

Method

Since 1996, a collaborative research group at Kent State University consisting of professors from Kent State and several other nearby institutions, school-based colleagues, and doctoral students has been working on the research problem of gathering students' perceptions of effective and ineffective instruction. All aspects of the design and piloting of the research protocol have been joint decisions (Kasten et al., 1997), but individual members of the research team conducted their own studies. Student participants in the studies were selected based on researchers' personal interests and research agendas. In brief, the research protocol involves individual interviews or surveys with students. We use the critical incidents technique, a qualitative data gathering tool that asks informants to "tell the story" of two incidents, one the best example of the construct under study and the other the worst example (Patton, 1990). For this study, the interview/ survey questions asked participants to describe fully their best and worst educational experiences. We defined *best* as "I enjoyed myself and I really learned a lot" and *worst* as its opposite. We also asked students to articulate desired changes in schools or schooling. Interviews were audio taped and transcribed for analysis.

Our analysis scheme was primarily inductive. First, each researcher looked for domains and categories in her data using the constant-comparative method (Glaser & Strauss, 1967). Bimonthly meetings during and following this process enabled us to cross check each other's findings, identify and solve analysis-related problems, and decide on a framework for discussion of results. Because of our interest in commonalities among students' stories, the discussion framework focused on common elements from students' stories, such as role of the teacher and other students, steps and stages in the experience, content area/uses of literacy, and themes emanating from the stories. In addition, each researcher determined the frequencies and percentages associated with particular themes in her data in order to organize and summarize abstractions and to make the report of the research easier to comprehend.

In this paper we first summarize the results of five separate studies (see Table 1). The studies are reported according to the age of the children interviewed/surveyed, beginning with the elementary students. The sections are written to reflect what the participants said when they described their best and worst learning experiences, as well as to reflect the lead researcher's voice and writing style. To identify lessons learned from the study, we conducted a cross-study analysis (Patton, 1990).

Results

Study A: Fourth-Grade Students on Learning

Data analysis of the fourth graders' interviews, which were obtained as part of an ongoing project in a fourth-grade classroom, revealed two preliminary observations. First, the children consistently mentioned specific teachers by talking about what "Miss" or "Mrs." did, said, or allowed them to do before elaborating on the actual learning experience. Very often these comments referred to choices that the teachers gave students: "we would get to pick out a book from the center"; "I can use my own mind and think of creative things. . . . I [like to] pick my own topic because it would be easier to stick to because I know more about what I want to write."

The second overall observation was that the fourth graders enjoyed providing vivid, detailed descriptions about their best and worst learning experiences. For example, one child remembered:

> Mrs. [S] passed out materials of what we were going to need and then she started talking, which is when I learned how sound traveled and stuff like that. It was called a tuning fork, and we had to figure out if we could get it louder other than hitting the wooden blocks, and, um, I came up with a solution that none of the other students had come up with—that one tuning fork against the other would make it real loud. I learned a lot [about how] you could generate sound.

All of the children appeared eager to tell about their experiences and were proud to share what they remembered learning.

Table 1

Description of Student Participants in the Individual Studies

Study	Number	Grade	Community
A	9	4	Urban; mixed SES
B	52	Intermediate, multiage	suburban; middle, upper-middle SES
C	23	7	Rural; lower-middle SES
D	28	11	Suburban; lower-middle SES
E	9	12	Urban; lower-middle SES

Three themes emerged regarding children's best and worst learning experiences: learning new information and skills (42% of the 94 interview segments that addressed this issue), activity-based learning including projects and field trips (39%), and home-school connections (13%). A fourth theme related to children's ideas about changing school; these were primarily time and schedule related, with students sharing concerns about not having enough time to eat lunch or talk with their friends.

Regarding learning new information and skills, one child reported that she "liked the time in second grade when [we] did a biography on the presidents . . . because I like to learn new things." Another recalled learning multiplication facts: "I always wanted to know how to do that . . . it's challenging." A third child cited learning to read as the best experience because "I always wanted to know how to read and because I always had to have my dad or mom read my books. Now I . . . read most of them. It's like when you first learn how to read, it's like starting off on a new thing, a big step."

Within this same category, when asked about their worst learning experiences, the children talked about the boring nature of lessons that did not present new information, were too repetitive, and were not challenging. In reference to doing math examples at the chalkboard, one student recalled that "we did that for maybe two weeks, and...once I learned it I didn't need to learn it anymore. But we still kept doing it." Another child used this same reasoning to conclude, "In fact, I probably learned more in kindergarten than I've ever learned in all my days of school because you learn the basic facts . . . and letters. In fact, I know I learned more in kindergarten than in any other grade."

The value children placed in doing projects was reflected in such comments as "we were working on Chinese masks, and we were wearing Chinese masks, and I learned a lot there"; "we were making globes out of papier maché . . . it was fun and it was messy and I like stuff like that"; and "we did an e-mail project . . . and you could write letters on the computer and you could send them." Additionally, all but one child recalled field trips as among their best learning experiences, often providing detailed descriptions of what they remembered learning. For example, one child remembered a trip to an invention museum: "We learned a lot about science . . . what we did was the electrical current from a radio; if it's close and there's this special thing, the lead will move to music." Collaboration was another aspect of these hands-on learning experiences; often children's comments referred to working with a partner or with a small group.

The third theme, home-school connections, was a subtle one that ran throughout the interviews. The children all mentioned learning experiences that either involved things they did with their families as a result of school assignments or were related to prior family experiences. These comments were distinctly positive. The children recalled reading books at home with family members, going to the library to research topics with family members, and doing projects at home. One child remembered a home project as "a family thing. We don't spend that much family time together. . . . I thought it was special because it was family time and we don't do that very often." On the other hand, another student complained that too much traditional homework took away from family time.

These children were both willing and able to talk about school and their prior learning experiences. Based on the characteristics of their stories, school should be challenging and children are curious and like to learn new things. They want to be active learners, to experience learning. They learn best when provided opportunities to connect home and school experiences and knowledge.

Study B: Intermediate Multiage Students on Learning

Perceptions of children enrolled in multiage classrooms were sought because of a continuing research interest in multiage settings. Teachers in the three multiage classrooms that are the focus of this study used no textbooks, used library resources consistently, and believed strongly in the practice of incorporating multiple intelligences (Gardner, 1993) into the curriculum. In these classrooms, students' responses to best learning fell into four categories. The most popular response (39%) related to assignments or experiences that reflected original research in which students collected data or various other kinds of hands-on learning experiences, such as projects. Many students (32%) cited examples of literacy in learning, such as using writing-to-learn strategies (content-related journals) or having time to read for pleasure. A third category reflected responses that involved choice or areas of personal interest (16%). Other miscellaneous responses (12%) were concerned with specific assignments that students liked, such as current events, teachers reading aloud, or assignments they were "good at."

With regard to worst learning experiences, 43% of children's responses involved critiques of teacher practice or pedagogy, such as lecturing; work that was too hard, too easy, or redundant; learning things only for tests; few opportunities to discuss anything; or unclear teacher expectations. Students also identified a collection of practices that they considered ineffective or embarrassing (23%). Included in these responses were comments about work being boring, doing worksheets, being rushed, disinterest in a topic, or lack of rigor.

Most suggestions for changes in school addressed facilities and scheduling (44%); students criticized the design of the school and the playground, wanted more recess and longer school days or years. Students (38%) also wanted more real-world experiences, such as projects, research, more math, more writing, more visitors, more choices, and more teacher feedback and attention. One category, miscellaneous (12%), was a potpourri of unrelated suggestions, such as wanting a suggestion box for the principal, a place to sell books in the school, updated technology, and less reading and writing. The smallest category (6%) was complaints about individual needs not being met, such as the ability to move at one's own pace, wanting to set personal goals, and wanting ability grouping.

These students were highly satisfied with school and admitted (sometimes quietly because it might not be too popular to say it aloud) that they liked school a great deal. They were especially effusive about transforming classroom space as part of content area study, collecting authentic data in a subject area, interviewing real people such as World War II survivors, and having choices in what to learn. They readily expressed awareness of when they were and were not learning effectively; they proved to be good informants.

Study C: Middle School Students on Learning

The 23 seventh graders in this study were preparing to enter a technologically enriched learning environment as part of another study. The interview data served the additional purpose of establishing students' learning preferences in more traditional educational settings. These students were academically successful; some of them had been identified to participate in their school's "gifted and talented" program. Students indicated a definite preference for group activities: seven (58%) of the boys and nine (82%) of the girls identified a best learning experience that involved working in groups. Only two worst experiences, one from a boy and one from a girl, involved working in groups.

A closer look at students' best learning experiences revealed five characteristics. First, these experiences took time; 21 (91%) of the students described activities that ranged from 2 weeks to an entire school year in duration. Students (43%) were also actively involved in these best experiences. They described such activities as building rockets, conducting science experiments, outdoor education experiences, making bridges out of toothpicks, and making elevation maps. Most of these activities featured an integration of more than one "subject." For example, the rocketry project involved reading, science, math, and writing. Three (13%) students described inquiry-oriented experiences, such as learning about the rain forest or a foreign country. Three also mentioned experiences that focused on learning by connecting the past and the present, such as learning mythology or local history. Finally, three best experiences were game-like: playing Carmen San Diego, foreign language guessing games, or scavenger hunts on the World Wide Web.

Reading played a part in 18 (78%) of these best experiences, usually before (e.g., science experiments, outdoor education) or during (e.g., inquiry projects, elevation maps) other activity. Writing was part of 14 (61%) experiences, usually in the form of note-taking or preparing for a final project. Reading and writing were tools for completing larger projects rather than the instructional goals themselves. The instructional cycle that was evident in these best learning experiences involved reading, doing (sometimes more reading and note-taking), and presenting results (sometimes writing).

Students' worst learning experiences had seven common characteristics. Eight (35%) students complained about situations when they were "taught" things they already knew. Students also disliked teachers making assignments without explaining how to complete them (22%) and spending class time doing homework or "busy work" (13%); math classes and worksheets in science and social studies were frequently mentioned in these complaints. Three (13%) students described experiences when they had no choice of groups or of tasks as being their least favorite. Two students decried round robin reading of content textbooks, and two others recalled experiences when they were embarrassed or punished as a result of their learning.

Round robin reading was the only type mentioned in these worst learning experiences. Completing worksheets and doing homework were the only examples of writing. In contrast to students' best experiences, reading and writing in the worst experiences were the end goals of the learning.

Most (14; 61%) students' ideas for changes in school involved more engagement and "less worksheets. Less sit-down, worksheets, sit in a chair, be quiet . . ."; "learn how to do it instead of looking it up in a book . . . [with activities] it's easier to understand because you have some fun"; "I would have more hands-on activities. Because just working out of books, it's real boring and I just feel like falling asleep. . . . Cause in social studies we read out of the book every day. . . . We have to read it out loud. It takes a long time. . . . He picks people out of the grade book. He just looks for a name and picks one. . . . [Q: Do you learn anything?] A little bit, but when you're bored the information doesn't stick."

Students (7; 30%) had advice about other teaching methods as well. For example, they want teachers to teach concepts thoroughly: "Well most of the bad ones, they think we already know something and we really don't know it that well. So they try to go ahead, or they like assume we understand it and give us a test on it. The ones that are good, they make you think about what you're doing." They also advise attention to relevance and choice: "Make things more having to do with the outside [of school] and more imagination, more room for group kinds of learning and also what you want to learn individually." As might be expected, they suggest that teachers not address concepts students already know: "In math, see, there's things we already know and then we have to keep going over them again [because one or two students] don't get it. . . . It wastes all of our time because everybody else knows it."

After 7 years experience with formal schooling, these students know what they prefer as learners. They also know what they do not.

Study D: 11th Graders on Learning

Twenty-eight 11th graders wrote descriptions of their best and worst learning experiences. These students were enrolled in a college-prep American literature class at a fine arts magnet high school in a Midwestern city. Participants were students of the teacher-researcher who volunteered to take part in the study. Data were organized and examined by looking at separate elements of the students' learning stories: setting, teachers, and curriculum. Prevailing themes in each of these areas follow.

These students desire an intimate, respectful, challenging, engaging, multicultural, and technological environment that allows for freedom of choice. They value smaller class sizes, which, they believe, allow for more personal opportunities and freedom. Flexibility in assignment deadlines and completion formats are important. Fifty percent of students wrote of the importance of choice in their school environment. Most of the participants are eager for independence from too much imposed structure, wanting instead to develop and share their own ideas: "[the teacher] gave us a list of activities we got to choose from like going on a first date, changing the oil in a car, keeping track of the bills. We chose one and wrote a couple of pages on the experience. It was cool."

These students resist aspects of the academic setting that do not allow for much choice. Unlike many of the other students included in this collection of studies, these high school students do not regard group work positively, perhaps because they are often denied the opportunity to select their own partners. Twenty-five percent wrote disparagingly of the experience. "Seldom am I paired with people that [sic] want to work and who care about their grade," one student revealed. Another complained, "The teacher put us in groups so if anybody didn't understand, they could get help. We would have to teach this obnoxious boy who slept in class and didn't listen." And yet another pleaded, "When teachers assign groups, they often put together people who don't get along hoping that by sticking them in the same group, their attitudes toward each other will change. It doesn't work that way." Three students also revealed their discomfort specifically with group assessment. They are concerned about their grades and think it unfair when all group members receive the same score, especially when they "get stuck with others who won't do anything."

The most dominant characters encountered in the educational environment are teachers, and 50% of students shared opinions about them in their stories. Students are aware of and appreciate those teachers who "try new things." They enjoy open-minded instructors who use innovative and personal teaching styles—who tell stories, for example. Their desires of teachers seem to parallel their wants in setting as both reflect the themes of personal freedom and academic choice.

Students do not enjoy teachers who "lecture all the time" or those who "do problems for you." Eighteen percent of participants described unfavorably those teachers who created a passive learning environment. Students want to be engaged themselves in the classroom; they do not desire the role of inactive recipients of knowledge. They are aware when teachers are not well enough prepared, and they certainly do not like it. They also do not appreciate teachers who "rush through everything," preferring those who seek quality rather than quantity in their approach to curriculum.

Many curricular wants and desires were evident in student responses. Creative projects top the list as 39% of students reminisce about positive learning experiences related to book making and debating. A desire for drama was evident, and 14% of students wrote longingly of play writing and role-playing in past classrooms. Eleven percent of students wrote favorable descriptions of review games, suggesting that competition can be a motivating factor.

Specifically pertaining to literacy, 21% of these participants mentioned enjoying individualized reading and expressive writing opportunities, another indication of the importance of the personal and choice. Interestingly, 14% of students yearn for experiences that they can escape into: "when I read I like to get swept away in the story"; "I love popping into someone else's life when reading"; "I like to read the types of stories that you can actually feel what the characters are feeling. It can be a great escape to be put into another place and time."

In contrast, students resist being forced to do things. Journal writing is not appreciated by 14% of students. "Journals about a book is [sic] dumb. I don't have time to do busy work." Another student shared his frustration about requirements for reports: "I hate big reports especially when there has to be a certain amount of pages, words, etc."

To summarize, these secondary students want freedom to choose. They desire flexibility in assignments, groups, and expression. They respect those—like themselves—who are willing to make choices and are open to new ideas. They want to be engaged in the classroom; they reject the passive; and they desire personal approaches and expressive means. Technology, competition, and multiculturalism are also welcome, as are stories.

Study E: Senior Humanities Students on Learning

These nine high school seniors—five males and four females—were students in an inquiry-based, team-taught humanities course, which has an advanced level designation in the college preparatory program. This classroom was the site of ongoing collaborative research on the teachers' curricular innovations. The interviews focused on students' perceptions of course experiences and were conducted near the end of the academic year.

Analysis of students' stories yielded several interesting patterns. The strongest themes emerged from analysis of the best experiences. Comments regarding connections, the most prevalent theme, appeared in six (67%) stories, most often relating to personal life experience. Sally stated, "You have to research the background and why the artist painted [the picture] and other peoples' views on it, and then your own view, of course." Rebecca said, "Other research [I've done], it's more focused; it's not with ideas. Other research is like facts. This is more emotional or personal application." Jeremy discovered "you know a lot when you get to apply it outside of school . . . like your parents are talking about political things and [you think] 'Yeah, yeah. We studied that.' We were learning how the system works, how voting works, basic things." Less frequently, students described connections to their peers' ideas; for example, Jeremy noticed "one person would make a suggestion and then everybody'd build off of it."

The next most prevalent theme of best experiences, depth, emerged from 4 students' comments (44%). They described various aspects of in-depth study and how it promoted their learning. Molly reflected, "I just found that having to do the research . . . you have to choose your own examples. [The teachers] give you the question, but you have to choose your own examples. So that made me look into the arts deeper where I normally wouldn't have." Sam found that "most of the [projects] were with the ideas of art, which I really liked. . . . 'What is a masterpiece?'. . . I think that's sort of what has always fascinated me about art. I think it adds depth to art. That's what makes art interesting. Just looking at an object or something for aesthetic purposes isn't as satisfying as realizing there's a thought behind it." Jeremy said, "[This class] doesn't teach you how to make [art], but it shows you why and how important it is, why it's so painstaking, how hard it was to do. I find it much more interesting to learn art this way than just to draw."

To a lesser extent, teacher/peer support of learning also appeared as a theme of best learning experiences. Three students (33%) identified this as a critical factor in their learning. Brad described teacher support by saying, "If you ever had a problem or didn't understand something, you could just ask [the teachers] and they'd explain it to you until you got some kind of concept in what was going on." Sally found group work with her peers supportive because "sometimes the work load can be hard on one student and to get other people's ideas and concepts really helps a lot." Jeremy felt comfortable giving critical response to trusted peers because "it's a lot easier to work with people that you know . . . you don't want to upset people with kind of an emotional statement . . . and even if they don't like your suggestion . . . [they] take it well because it's from a friend."

As supportive as working with peers seemed to be, group work emerged as problematic for some students, as evidenced in their worst stories. Jeremy described frustration when "we had a meeting at my house, and everyone was supposed to come over . . . there were 5 in the group; 2 showed up." Unlike Jeremy, Rebecca found it was sometimes hard to work with friends because "you knew who would do the work and who wouldn't, but they were your friends. . . ," implying it was hard to make friends do their part if they were reluctant or disinterested.

Two (22%) of the students' worst stories included comments that surface learning was not helpful, which further supports their perception that in-depth study promoted their learning. Two other students said that unclear purposes were a factor in their worst experiences. Other comments about worst experiences included working with assigned topics that were not of interest and not learning new things.

Few patterns appeared in students' comments about changes they would make in the course. Two students wanted longer time, either through block scheduling or by extending the course over a 2-year period. Other comments included making the class smaller, letting students select their own groups, letting groups work at their own pace and in their own ways, and getting more examples from the teachers. One student, who believed she learned best via lecture, desired "more tests so we memorize more."

These students advise that learning is more likely to occur when they have opportunities to make connections between the concepts under study and their personal life experience and also between their understandings and those of their peers. Working with concepts in depth is also important, as is teacher and peer support. However, more investigation of working with peers is also indicated; students have mixed feelings about working with friends.

Looking Across the Stories

These studies seek to legitimize student voices as a major factor in debates about educational reform. The picture of especially effective instruction portrayed by these 121 students parallels many educators' descriptions of best practices (e.g., Baker, Afflerbach, & Reinking, 1996; Zemelman, Daniels, & Hyde, 1998) and provide concrete examples of instruction that reflect the IRA/NCTE Standards for the English Language Arts (1996). Unfortunately, their descriptions of especially ineffective instruction parallel conventional educational practices used in many classrooms (e.g., Oldfather, 1995). We believe these studies to be important because of the paucity of other work on students' perceptions. Moreover, the use of a common design by the research team allows for a sample size sufficient for generalizing, a rarity in qualitative research.

So, then, what generalizations about learning are evident? Table 2 presents constructs apparent in students' best and worst learning experiences. In describing their best learning experiences, students spoke of the importance of choice, sometimes free choice, as in selecting one's own reading material or writing topic, and sometimes choice of how to proceed with a task or what aspect of a broad topic to focus upon. These students also described challenging learning situations. They want to learn new things; they describe a feeling of pride in learning something they consider both challenging and important.

Table 2

Summary of Cross-Study Findings

			Studies		
	A	B	C	D	E
Constructs: Best Learning					
Choice	x	x	x	x	x
Challenge	x	x		x	x
Hands-on	x	x	x	x	
Connected	x	x	x		x
Collaborative	x		x		x
Lengthy, deep		x		x	
Inquiry-oriented		x	x		
Game-like			x	x	
Creative				x	
Constructs: Worst Learning					
Not challenging	x	x	x	x	x
Repetitive	x	x	x		
Too much lecture		x		x	
No choice			x	x	
Unclear purposes					x

The best learning experiences offered students hands-on, active opportunities to learn, sometimes from an inquiry-oriented stance, although students also mentioned game-like experiences and creative experiences. These activities often featured connections among content areas, with peers, or between home and school. In this regard, they echoed findings from literacy researchers, such as Oldfather (1993) who found connections among choice, inquiry learning, and motivation to learn.

Worst learning was, in many cases, no learning at all. Students spoke of how boring it is to do work that is not challenging, that they do not understand because of unclear purposes, that is "busy work," and that focuses on surface-level issues. Many complained about repetitive situations, either over-practicing something new or reviewing things they had already learned. They dislike listening to too many lectures. They dislike situations that offer them few choices.

It is evident from these studies that students are, indeed, wonderful and wise informants about their own school experiences. Like Zemelman et al. (1998), these literacy learners say they learn best if their experiences are student-centered, experiential, challenging, and authentic. As literacy educators, we would be wise to listen to what these students are telling us and to conduct future research into many of the dimensions of learning that these students noted.

References

Alvermann, D., Young, J., Weaver, D., Hinchman, K., Moore, D., Phelps, S., Thrash, E., & Zalewski, P. (1996). Middle school and high school students' perceptions of how they experience text-based discussions: A multicase study. *Reading Research Quarterly, 31,* 244–267.

Baker, L., Afflerbach, P., & Reinking, D. (1996). *Developing engaged readers in school and home communities.* Mahwah, NJ: Erlbaum.

Erickson, F., & Schultz, J. (1992). Students' experiences of the curriculum. In P. Jackson (Ed.), *Handbook of research on curriculum* (pp. 465–485). New York: Macmillan.

Fouts, J., & Meyers, R. (1992). Classroom environments and middle school students' views of science. *Journal of Educational Research, 85,* 356–361.

Gardner, H. (1993). *Frames of mind.* New York: Basic.

Glaser, B., & Strauss, A. (1967). *The discovery of grounded theory.* Chicago: Aldine.

International Reading Association and National Council of Teachers of English. (1996). *Standards for the English Language Arts.* Newark, DE and Urbana, IL: Authors.

Kasten, W., Kinner, J., McKeon, C., Newton, E., Padak, N., Peck, J., Styslinger, M., & Wuthrick, M. (1997, December). *Student perspectives of learning to read and write: A collaborative study between schools and universities.* Paper presented at the meeting of the National Reading Conference, Scottsdale, AZ.

Maroufi, C. (1989). A study of student attitude toward traditional and generative models of instruction. *Adolescence, 24*(3), 65–72.

McCabe, N. (1995). Twelve high school eleventh grade students examine their best teachers. *Peabody Journal of Education, 70,* 117–126.

McDowell, E., & McDowell, C. (1986). *A study of high school students' expectations of the teaching style of male and female English and science instructors.* (ERIC Document Reproduction Service No. ED 278 074)

Oldfather, P. (1993). What students say about motivating experiences in a whole language classroom. *Reading Teacher, 46,* 672–681.

Oldfather, P. (1995). Commentary: What's needed to maintain and extend motivation for literacy in the middle grades. *Journal of Reading, 38,* 420–422.

Patton, M. Q. (1990). *Qualitative evaluation and research methods* (2nd ed.). Newbury Park, CA: Sage.

Shug, M., Todd, R., & Beery, R. (1984). Why kids don't like social studies. *Social Education, 48,* 382–387.

Taylor, K., & Roselli, H. (1993). *Results of student survey: Thos. E. Weightman Middle School.* Unpublished manuscript.

Wasserman, P. (1995). What middle schoolers say about their schoolwork. *Educational Leadership, 53*(1), 41–43.

Zemelman, S., Daniels, H., & Hyde, A. (1998). *Best practice: New standards for teaching and learning in America's schools.* Portsmouth, NH: Heinemann.

Representing Insight: Mapping Literary Anthropology with Fractal Forms

Dennis Sumara and Brent Davis
York University

Rebecca Luce Kapler
Queen's University

The process of coming to see other human beings as one of "us" rather than as "them" is a matter of detailed description of what unfamiliar people are like and of redescription of what we ourselves are like. This is a task not for theory but for genres such as ethnography, the journalist's notebook, the comic book, the docudrama, and, especially, the novel. (Rorty, 1989, p. xvi)

Understanding the complexity of human experience, argues Rorty, can only emerge from interpreting the relationships among necessary differences: of situations, of languages, of belief. From this perspective, any representation of "others" requires consideration of how such acts describe and create both "us" and "them." Humans do not come into being in isolation from one another but, rather, co-emerge with the complex relations of communities.

The problem for researchers of human experience is thus one of representation: How does one use the limitations of language, particularly print forms of language, to represent the complex ways researchers' lives and interests become complicit with processes and products of research? Moreover, how can ideas that emerge from shared research experiences be adequately portrayed within the confines of academic expository forms?

These questions challenged us as we attempted to represent our research involvements with a group of teachers. Developed around reader-response methods that Sumara (1996, 2000) following the work of Iser, (1989, 1993), has called "literary anthropologies," this research aimed to learn how teachers who self-identify as gay, lesbian, or transgendered interpret their and others' responses to literary fiction, to one another, and to experiences of pedagogy. As we discovered, during the research and in the periods of interpretation that followed, it became impossible to report results by such conventional strategies as representing participants' individual or collective thinking, developing case studies, or extracting ideas developed during the research, without some discussion of our interpersonal and intertextual involvements within and outside the research. While still in process, we have begun to develop new ways of reporting insights from research that we believe have the potential to show how ideas, researchers, re-

National Reading Conference Yearbook, 49, pp. 534–549.

search subjects, and matters occurring prior to, alongside, and following formal data-gathering processes continue to influence one another.

In this article, we use the image of the fractal to explore literary anthropology. We begin with an overview of literary anthropology as an idea and as a research method. Next, we introduce fractal geometry, contrasting it to the more familiar Euclidean geometry. We then provide one example of an interpretation of some insights emerging from within and from outside one research project. We believe this writing represents the complexity of the relations of knowledge generated through literary anthropological methods.

Using Literary Anthropology in Literacy Research

Iser (1989, 1993) suggests that all interpreted engagement with literary fiction is an anthropological event: the literary experience becomes a window into the complex relations among humans, cultural artifacts, social situations, and historical circumstances. Primarily organized by the reader's identifications with literary characters and their situations, these anthropologies are structured by experiences the reader has had both with real persons and fictional characters. Through identifications with characters and situations not usually encountered in his or her daily life, the literary experience offers an elaborated aesthetic space within which the reader is able to reflect on past, current, and projected experiences in new ways. Iser suggests that it is within this elaborated literary location that interesting and productive interpretations can occur—not merely interpretations of the text, the reader's experiences, or the contexts of reading but, also, of the complex ways these intertwine during and following the act of reading.

Like all anthropological forms of research, literary anthropology aims to develop an understanding of culture. Specifically, it seeks to develop and interpret literary locations as sites of learning and analysis. It assumes that the relations organized by literary fictions are attached to, but not identical to, other cultural relations. Literary anthropological methods are organized by the belief that shared reading of literary fiction has the potential to create sites of learning that facilitate the collection of cultural knowledge that, in some cases, has become obscured by familiarity. Because the literary aesthetic space requires readers to identify with fictional characters and to maintain already developed out-of-text relations the site of reading becomes a place where thinking is elaborated.

The aesthetic space of the text (Iser, 1989) described can be compared to Bakhtin's (1981) understanding of chronotopes. He imagined chronotopes as indissoluble matrices of space and time that can serve as a metaphor to explore the relations between art and life. His conception of chronotope arose from his understanding that organisms rely on a variety of rhythms that differ from each other and from those of other organisms. According to Bakhtin, time and space vary in qualities, and different activities and representations of those activities presume different kinds of time and space. These chronotopes of living serve as the source of representation for chronotopes in literary fictions where, as Bakhtin (1981) explained, "Time, as it were, thickens, takes on flesh, becomes artistically visible; likewise, space becomes charged and responsive to the movements of time, plot and history" (p. 84).

Where Bakhtin focuses on the potential of a text to represent living, Iser describes how such potential plays out in the relation between reader and text. When the reader becomes involved in such an aesthetic location, multiple opportunities for interpretation arise. And, because the reader-and-text relationship is always complexly involved in a context that is historically weighted the interpretations that emerge always exceed the personal response of the reader. All literary interpretation is, from a literary anthropological perspective, interpretation of culture.

In research conducted in a large urban center, two university researchers (Sumara and Davis) used literary anthropological reader-response practices to structure interpretations of the experiences of a group of gay, lesbian, and transgendered teachers. The research had two main objectives: First, working with the researchers, participants would help one another interpret ongoing responses to fiction, either written by gay, lesbian, or transgendered authors, or with themes and topics that were likely of interest to gay, lesbian, or transgendered adult readers. Second, the researchers were interested in how these literary responses might help the research group interpret the ways in which gay, lesbian, and transgendered teachers negotiate their minority identities within their daily public school teaching practices. Including the researchers, 10 persons were involved in the research: 6 men, 3 women, and 1 male who, during the course of the research, completed gender reassignment and became legally female.

The research was structured with monthly half-day meetings developed around discussions of preassigned novels (e.g., Gowdy, 1995; MacDonald, 1996), and hybrid memoir/fiction (e.g., White, 1997; Lorde, 1982). In addition, a short anthology of fiction and nonfiction, edited by Califia and Fuller (1995), was read.

Following reader-response methods outlined by Sumara (1996), group members were encouraged to jot their impressions directly in copies of their texts while reading, to keep short response journals, or to write notes on the back blank pages of their books. Each half-day meeting began with an oral reading of favorite passages from whatever was being discussed that day, followed by response to and discussion of the passages read. The researchers participated as reading group members, sharing their notes and favorite passages. During Year 2 of the research, Rebecca Luce-Kapler, an experienced writer of fiction, became involved in the project as a consultant. Because she identified as a heterosexual woman, it was believed that her presence in some group activities would be helpful in encouraging more complex interpretations of issues. To facilitate these interpretations, Luce-Kapler's primary role was to assist group members in structuring fictional writing practices. These exercises were designed to focus attention, while helping to elaborate insights emerging from the research. Most important, Luce-Kapler assisted with the further development of literary anthropological methods by helping the research group members make use of their own fictionalized experience as a means to develop critical understanding. Most of this work was accomplished during a 3-day retreat near the end of the project. At this retreat, participants learned how to structure interpretations of experience by using responses to literary fiction, to memoirs, and to familiar objects (e.g., stones from the beach outside the retreat cottage, photographs provided by Luce-Kapler).

At the end of the 2 years of research, considerable data had been collected. While all data were compelling, the researchers were concerned that they were too complex to be reduced to themes or conclusions. Further, it was clear that emergent ideas were less-than-subtly influenced by events that occurred outside (but alongside) the research and by experiences (including reading experiences) that occurred before and after the research. In the end, the shape of insights gained seemed too complex to be contained by traditional forms for research reporting.

Rejecting Euclid

At about the time that these problems with interpretation and representation were presenting themselves, one of the researchers (Davis) was reading and writing about "fractals," a new form of geometry that deals with figures and forms that are more complex than those previously examined by mathematics. As he shared ideas with the other two researchers, it became clear that the images being offered by fractal geometry would be helpful to thinking about how to organize and represent some of the results of this research project. In particular, we were attracted to certain qualities of fractal forms and how they might be used to structure reports of the complexities of our research group's literary and non-literary engagements. In this section, we provide a brief overview of fractal geometry, beginning with a short historical overview of Euclidean geometry.

For most, the word "geometry" evokes images of triangles, circles, and so on. Such forms were first gathered together into a coherent field of study by Euclid in the third century BCE. Euclid, however, did not invent geometry. In fact, in retrospect, his contribution was actually a narrowing of a somewhat richer and broader understanding of the term. A century earlier, Plato had identified geometry as the hallmark of scholarly thought. Plato's geometry was not focused on figures drawn on the plane, but on a mode of reasoning that he felt could be used to uncover the deepest secrets of the universe. Specifically, geometry was understood as that manner of inquiry that aimed at a totalized understanding of the universe through the systematic reduction of all phenomena to fundamental particles, root causes, and originary principles.

Euclid's major contribution was to assign a visual form to this manner of inquiry with the refinement of the case of planar geometry. Using 23 definitions (e.g., "A point is that of which there is no part") and five axioms (e.g., a straight line can be drawn from any point to any point), he demonstrated the power of logical argumentation for deriving and linking a diversity of known forms. In so doing, he contributed to a transformation of the meaning of geometry. However, the transition in meaning did not in any way diminish the place of Plato's geometry. On the contrary, Euclid's contributions helped to entrench the formal logical argument in Western mindsets—to the point that it has since become the invisible backdrop of most claims to knowledge in academia.

This is a point that has been thoroughly developed in certain postmodernist, feminist, ecological, critical, and culturalist discourses. What has been less well developed, however, is the manner in which Euclid's geometry continues to structure our thinking, even while the pervasiveness of Plato's geometry has been uncovered. Many alternatives to logical argumentation have been presented, including narrative, metaphoric, analogical, and metonymic possibilities. Yet, few alternatives have been proposed and even fewer have been developed in ways that are useful to discussions of research into reader response.

This is not a small point. It is now well established that human thinking is enabled and constrained by the conceptual tools that are available. In terms of the visual references that are most often used, one need only glance at human living spaces to notice that the forms of classical geometry are overwhelming in their presence. The influence of Euclid is perhaps most obvious in our homes and offices, in our rectangulated cities, and in our linearized conceptions of time and development. In schools, Euclid is present in the grids used to lay out curriculum, to order the school day, to organize learners in rooms, to structure their experiences, and to mark their progress. In research methodologies, Euclid is present in the practices and structures that insist upon the categorizing of data, in the desire to specify causal relationships, and in the imperative for straightforward reports. So dominant is this geometry that the unruly and organic are often surprising and even unwelcome. What tend to be preferred are narratives of control, predictability, and efficiency, such as is demanded by Plato's logic and embodied in Euclid's images.

Of course, several alternatives to Euclid's geometry have arisen over the past few centuries, most of which play on the fact that a change in definition or axiom can prompt a whole new set of forms and assertions. Such developments, however, have served to bolster the logical argument rather than to disrupt it, as the resulting systems continue to obey the rigid logical architecture of Plato's geometry. More recently, however, fractal geometry has risen to prominence. Although new, it is important to emphasize that fractal geometry is utterly reliant on what has come before. It is not a break from, but a dramatic elaboration of Euclid. That being said, it also interrupts much of what has preceded it by presenting a very different sort of object.

Embracing Fractals

The history of fractal geometry is one of sudden turns and unexpected developments. (See Gleick, 1987, for an account of the emergence of the field.) Among their unusual qualities, fractal images are scale independent. That is, whether one moves in on or pulls back from a fractal image, the bumpiness of detail stays the same. Unlike Euclidean objects that become simpler under close inspection (e.g., a portion of circle appears more and more like a line segment as it is magnified), fractal images are more like natural forms than classical geometric objects in this regard. As such, a fractal image might serve as an apt visual metaphor for those emergent conceptions of knowing and knowledge that pull away from classical logic and its implicit linearities. In particular, such images as foundations, structures, and hierarchies are challenged by notions of infinite regress, nestedness, and implicate orders. Moreover, fractal geometry presents an alternative to the often-unquestioned assumption that complex phenomena can be reduced to root causes. There is no "simplest level" in a fractal image. Each is as complicated as the one that preceded it and the one that follows it.

Partly because of this quality, fractal geometry has been described as "far closer to the flexibility of life than it is to the rigidity of Euclid" (Stewart, 1998, p. 23). This description is also prompted in part by the uncanny resemblances of many fractal images to natural forms—which, in turn, highlight a second important quality of fractal images. Such forms tend to demonstrate a degree of self-similarity, meaning that the form might be seen as being assembled of reduced copies of itself. Riverbeds, clouds, trees, mountains, skin—along with virtually every natural form or structure—demonstrate some sort of self-similarity.

The qualities of scale independence and self similarity raise the possibility of regarding any aspect of a fractal image as a whole with its own proper integrity, as an element of a larger whole, or as a collectivity of smaller forms. Within this frame, such oppositional dyads as part-versus-whole or simple-versus-complex are untenable. Rather, what is highlighted is an inevitable partiality in the act of viewing, where partiality is understood both in terms of the fragmentary nature of any observational act and in terms of the biases implicit in all events of perception.

Fractal geometry has been embraced by researchers from many domains, from physics to the humanities, as being descriptive of the sorts of phenomena that are now being studied (Capra, 1996). Awarenesses of scale independence and self-similarity in particular seem to have opened up possibilities for seeing a much broader range of phenomena as patterned—literally ranging from subatomic space to the distribution of matter in the universe. Phenomenon that were previously thought to be random and formless—which is to say, forms that did not conform to Euclid's geometry—are now coming to be seen as elegantly patterned. This is *not* to say that such patterns are determinable and, hence, reducible. On the contrary, they are seen as irreducible unfoldings, forms subject to incomprehensible arrays of subtle and imposing influence. What fractal geometry brings is not a renewed effort to colonize the disorderly, but an appreciation of the universe as complex, ever unfolding, self-transcending, and relational.

It is also the case that such dynamic complexities may well spring from surprisingly simple beginnings, and fractal geometry has helped to illustrate how this might happen without invoking a reductive logic or causal notions of development. Fractal images are the products of recursive procedures. Briefly, a recursive process is a repetitive one in which, at any particular level of computation, the new input is the output from the previous level and the subsequent output is the input for the next round. A familiar example of a recursive process is the calculation of compound interest. Interest earned in one term is dependent on interest earned in previous terms and will affect interest earned in later terms. Although recursive, this particular example is not fractal, as it lacks an important quality. Those recursive processes that lead to fractal images differ from other repetitive calculations in that there are no shortcuts for determining the outcomes for fractals. The calculations are nonreducible; there is no compact process or theory that can anticipate the details of the unfolding. (In contrast, compound interest many seasons hence can be calculated directly.)

Diverse applications have been developed for such processes. Within popular media, for example, convincing imitations of dinosaur skin, planet surfaces, cloud formations, and mountain vistas have been created by mimicking nature's habit of recursively playing on what has already been generated. Medicine, economics, chemistry, and other domains are also finding productive uses of such recursive processes as they seek to address complex, emergent problems in their respective domains. The discovery that certain recursive functions can give rise to cryptic order—and, moreover, that such order often resembles familiar forms—has come as a surprise to many. It has also supported the use of fractal patterns as important visual metaphors in the recently emergent field of Complexity Theory. Focused on the ways that order often emerges for free when dynamic forms are allowed to interact with one another, complexivists have demonstrated that life itself seems to be organized fractally. Put somewhat differently, complexivists (e.g., Kauffman 1995; Waldrop 1992) have problematized a modern-day habit of drawing analogies between mechanical objects and living forms. The former obey a Euclidean geometry, both structurally (forms) and operationally (logical interconnections of those components). Machines are the sums of their parts, designed deliberately to fulfill particular functions in particular ways.

Living systems seem to adhere more to a fractal geometry—again, both structurally (in terms of the scale-independent qualities of their subsystems) and operationally (in terms of the recursive processes that guide the interactions of these systems). Like a fractal image, the aspects of a living system seem to be hazily bounded and nested. A human, for instance, might be seen as a coherent unity, as a higher order that emerges in the joint activity of subsystems with their own particular integrities, or as a form that participates in such transcendent forms as social grouping, cultures, and so on. To understand the nature of a human, then, would require one to look across such nested levels as biology, context, and society.

With regard to the rules that guide the interactions of a complex form, a fractal image can also be illustrative. In fact, a somewhat surprising suggestion arises when a more recursive logic is applied to the interactions of complex forms. Departing from the Platonic/Euclidean notion that complete knowledge of an event relies on the possibility of reducing it to its most basic parts, a more holistic sensibility is suggested. Stewart and Cohen (1997), mathematician and biologist, describe the shift in thinking in this way:

> Traditional science saw regularities in nature as *direct* reflections of regular laws. That view is no longer tenable. Neither is the view that the universe rests

> upon a single fundamental rule system, and all we have to do is find it. Instead, there are—and must be—rules at every level of description. . . . The universe is a plurality of overlapping rules. (p. 76)

In other words, as might be illustrated with reference to a fractal image, emerging views of the universe suggest that it is scale independent. It does not much matter which order of phenomenon one chooses to study, the same bumpiness of detail will present itself. Conversely, with a reconceptualization of the relationships between part and whole—again, supported by a fractal image—one is freed from having to study or to interpret everything in order to understand something. The part is not simply a fragment of the whole, it is a fractal out of which the whole unfolds and in which the whole is enfolded. This different imagery has been a fecund source for rethinking the natures of time, memory, identity, words, reading, interrelation, and so on. Understood not in terms of isolated elements, such phenomena are coming to be discussed in terms of *nodes* in *webs of possibility* that, when examined more closely, are shown to be themselves similar webs of possibility, and so on.

As researchers who felt limited by traditional forms of representation, we wondered how we could take images and ideas from fractal geometry and create a text which depicted the complex way in which texts, researchers, research participants, texts and experiences within and outside the research collected to help generate insight. Following writing practices suggested by Luce-Kapler, the three researchers began to experiment with the creation of texts that seemed to embody *scale independence, recursivity, self-similarity,* and *complexity.* In each case, these writings were meant to show how such literary experiences, as responding to novels, writing, and sharing personally written texts (fictional and autobiographical), could serve as nodes of interpretation that might illuminate insights emerging from the research.

Before presenting this fractally-inspired text, it is important to note that its content emerged from heated debates among reading group members about the intersection of the biological and the cultural—particularly, the relationships among physiology, experience, and culture in the production of men and women. The female group members were disturbed that Terry, a middle-aged male-to-female transsexual discussed her gender as "female" without having had a biological or cultural history as a female. These discussions of what constitutes "man" and "woman" required all members of our group to reconsider how other categories, including "heterosexual," "gay," and "lesbian," were organized—and, particularly, whether any of these signifiers were able to capture the uniqueness and complexity of each of our lived experiences. Although all members of the research group believed at the outset that we could gather in solidarity under the banner of our minority sexualities to develop interpretive insights, we came to understand the deep significance of Sedgwick's (1990) assertion, "people are different from one another" (p. 22). Identities cannot be confined to predetermined cultural or biological categories.

These debates continued for most of our second year, supported and fueled by our reading of memoir and fiction that continually called into question commonsense beliefs we held about our own sexualities, our place in gay, lesbian, heterosexual, and transgendered communities, and our own identities as males and females. In responding to fictionalized memoir, for example, we continually came to realize that each of our identifications to gay, lesbian, transgendered, and heterosexual characters and personas were largely influenced by the particularities of our personal histories and, as such, allowed very little interpersonal identification among members. At the same time, our reading of erotic fiction prompted us to notice how each of our familiar erotic identifications could be troubled and surprised by literary identifications. In short, while our research aimed to develop insight into ways that persons identifying with minority sexualities were similar, we learned, instead, that life within any category is incredibly (and necessarily) diverse, adaptable, and complex.

In order to highlight some of the debates and insights sponsored by involvement with the research group and, additionally, to show how these insights became intertwined with personal history, and recent reading in the fields of neuroscience, memoir, and literary fiction, one of the researchers (Sumara) prepared the following report. Meant to be orally performed, the writing in the following section aims to function as autobiography, as ethnography, as theory, and as fiction.

Troubling Bodies

It is 3 a.m. and I can't sleep because my mother is having another night of asthma in the next room. She has joined my partner Brent and I on our one-week retreat to a small cabin by the sea on Vancouver Island. Six months ago when I made plans for this trip I loved my mother and had forgotten she had this terrible disease. Now, as I lie awake for another night, I do not love her. She is interrupting our vacation. Even though I know better, I think this disease is her fault. Her body is troubling to me.

In her book *Breathless,* Louise DeSalvo (1997) interprets her own experience with the sudden onset of chronic asthma. An accomplished Virginia Woolf scholar and biographer, DeSalvo uses her critical abilities to learn how her body has become troubling to her. She writes:

> When I work, I'm often oblivious to my body; it doesn't exist. This has all changed since I've been sick, and my body now makes me aware of itself with every stroke of my pen, every strike of the keys. I'm writing through my body in a way I haven't before. I wonder what this will mean? If my work will change? (p. 19)

It is the middle of the night and I can't sleep because I am thinking about Terry's sex change. I have thought about this a great deal since Terry joined our Queer Teachers' Study Group last year. Tonight it becomes interesting to me that we are having our final retreat in the same place that Brent and I brought my mother last year. As I listen to the waves break in front of our cabin I realize I am angry with Terry. Why must she continually talk about her sex change experiences? She is preventing us from talking about the novels we are studying, from the work I think we should be doing. But, then again, she is making our work more interesting. Her body is troubling to me.

In her review of the literature on trauma, DeSalvo suggests that diseases like asthma are likely, in part, the body's specific response to remembered traumas from childhood. Many asthmatics have reported chronic depression, substance abuse, anorexia, and morbid obesity. They have also described a conflicted relationship with their body, often wishing it would disappear.

In his book *Phenomenology of Perception,* Maurice Merleau-Ponty (1962) explains that all humans are doubly-embodied creatures. The fleshly body is, at once, a biological structure and a phenomenological structure. In recent years, Merleau-Ponty's theorizing about double embodiment has been confirmed by studies in neuroscience that have shown we are unable to enact experience without becoming biologically effected. Having these thoughts, rather than those thoughts, alters the brain, the nervous system, the immune system, the structure of DNA. It could be imagined, then, that the act of thinking might change what is genetically passed to children. Maybe there is a closer relationship between sex and knowledge than most of us have considered.

During our time at the cabin, my mother continues her reading habit. She only reads fiction, usually very long epic novels. She does not talk about her reading other than to say that she wonders what would become of her if she could not read. She always reads sitting since asthma makes reading in bed impossible. When she reads I notice her breathing improves, and there are long stretches with no coughing or wheezing. It may be that reading is, literally, saving her life.

On the second day of our retreat Terry participates in a writing practice that asks her to make associations between our location by the sea and her past experience. Like others, she chooses to read some of her writing to the group, something that we have done many times before. Today she talks about her childhood, describing herself as a "puny asthmatic runt." Although she has mentioned this before, it is only today that this becomes significant to me. I think that, perhaps, I am noticing this more now because, as I look at Terry stretched out in her chair, she is anything but puny. She is Amazon, leggy, using a lot of space. Puny is not what I see. I realize that Terry is sitting in the same place that my mother sat last year when she was here, one eye cast to the horizon out the window. A shock of recognition occurs: Terry said she was asthmatic. My mind races to collect what else I remember from our past meetings: a distant father, a lonely childhood, a severe education, boys' schools where she was ridiculed. Plenty of trauma.

DeSalvo (1997) writes:

> I believe that asthma is a breathing disorder that is caused by abuse and that it is probably a manifestation of post-traumatic stress. I believe that asthma tells us

that the person who has it is, or once was, so terrified that s/he feared s/he would die. (p. 147). . . . The body remembers. The body communicates. (p. 131)

Although reading *Breathless* convinces me that there is a relationship between the conditions that support my mother's chronic asthma and Terry's childhood asthma, I resist this knowledge, since I do not want to flatten the complexity of the biological/phenomenological relationship. Rather, I am interested in what can be learned about learning by studying and interpreting DeSalvo's interpretation of her chronic illness, my mother's ways of living with hers, and Terry's decision to change her body.

I realize I have adopted my mother's penchant for reading. For as long as I can remember, literary relationships have been important to me. Recently, I have learned that these have also been important and interesting ways to not only learn new things, but to increase one's capacity for learning. As DeSalvo and other literary workers such as Toni Morrison (1996) and Jeanette Winterson (1995) have suggested, involvement with literary forms creates necessary conditions to learn to perceive in more expansive ways. Literary relations are sites of interpretation. They are places where the work of art happens. And I mean this as the work of art *and* as the object of representation that this work creates. For me, literary engagements have interrupted what has become familiar to me in my non-literary experiences. The bodies of knowledge they have announced have been troubling to me.

DeSalvo argues that those who write, who make works of art, are able to use these as sites to interpret the relations between past traumatic experiences and current experiences. The work of art, then, is the work of critically interpreting the relationality that makes identity. It may be argued that Terry's sex change is a work of art, not unlike the work of performance artist Orlan who undergoes and documents plastic surgery that transforms her face and body in relation to dominant and idealized images of women. Making one's own body the site of creation can become a place where critical interpretation is possible, not just for Terry, but for those who are relationally involved with her. Working with Terry in our study group forced us all to reconsider what makes man, woman, gay, lesbian. We became troubled by what her body suggested about ours.

It is four years since my cabin experience with my mother and her asthma, three years since our retreat with our study group, two years since I first read DeSalvo's *Breathless*. As I write this I am rereading Hilton Als' (1997) book *The Women,* a strange genre that is all-at-once memoir, fiction, and theory. Most provocative to me is his theorizing of his identification with his mother, and of the complex ways in which her experience is continued in his. While all humans live out the historically conditioned past in their present, what strikes me as significant in Als' experience is that his mother understood her child's need to interpret these relations and, most important, that he needed interpretive conditions and tools. For her, this meant supplying him with fiction to read and notepads to write in. In creating art with words Hilton Als, like other literary workers, learned what

DeSalvo suggests, "That works of art make the act of listening to the testimony of human suffering possible" (p. 78). And this includes one's own suffering.

Hilton Als and Louise DeSalvo write biography, literary criticism, and memoir. Terry studies biology and writes poetry. My mother reads fiction and studies asthma. I read theory and fiction and invent ways to think about reading. Curiously, all of us experience some relief from our symptoms when engaged in these works of artistic production and representation. The symptoms may or may not be asthma. There are other symptoms that, because they are less physically insistent, are, perhaps, more insidiously damaging.

The commonsense discourse of curriculum usually ignores the fact that we are, all-at-once, biological and phenomenological creatures. It does not believe, for example, that what is learned requires that our biological bodies adapt to that learning. It forgets that identity is relational, that it is mediated by biological bodies and by human-made and other objects, including language. It mistakes the acquisition of knowledge for learning, rather than understanding that learning that matters to anyone emerges from the hard work of interpretation. It fails to remember that the work of art is not really the making of interesting representations of experience—the work of art is, as Suzanne Langer (1957) suggested forty years ago in her little book *Problems of Art*—the need to reformulate the already formulated, to make the transparent less so, to interrupt certainty, to make trouble. For me, and for those artists with whom I engage, the work of art creates a gathering location for the usually unnoticed relationship between the biological and the phenomenological. Making a novel, a painting, a memoir, reading fiction, writing essays—all these create possible conditions where troubling bodies collect to engage in the necessary work of interpretation.

It is Sunday evening and I am talking to my mother on the telephone. The miracle of this form of communication means that I can hear her congestion, although she tries to disguise it. I have learned that it is important for us to discuss what she is learning about asthma through her ongoing study of this disease. I share what I have heard about new therapies. She tells me she has made cabbage rolls for dinner. I tell her we are having chicken. She tells me she has been rereading some of my work, and continues to wonder if some of my ideas are helpful. She is a fan, but not an uncritical one. I realize we are familiar and strange to one another. She has a spell of coughing that lasts for a minute. She tells me she must hang up. I know she will soon be reading. I know I will soon be writing.

Interpreting Fractal Forms

This example of research writing aims to show how insight emerged from the writer's involvement in various textual and social communities. What was learned about engagement with literary fiction and about the experience of identifying as gay, lesbian, heterosexual, or transgendered became, for this writer, entangled in other experiences. Collected within and around the official locations of "research," then, were events that continued to influence emergent insights. In presenting these insights as we have, we hope to have shown one way that the complexity of these personal, textual, and communal involvements can be represented. Specifically, we would like to draw on the four characteristics of fractals mentioned earlier that describe the structure of this writing: recursive, scale independent, self-similar, and complex.

Recursivity

Each section of this writing elaborates and folds back on other sections. For example, connections between Terry's childhood asthma and the writer's mother's asthma were suddenly brought to attention by three circumstances: the shared cabin experience, the writer's reading of DeSalvo's book, and the various acts of reading that were occurring within the research group. Although definitive conclusions are not drawn in the writing, implied are the ways that understanding about matters related to research data colluded with other experiences of the writer. And although the text appears to move forward in a linear fashion, the sections are not representations of events as they occurred chronologically. Nor is each section necessarily meant to be an elaboration of prior sections. Each part is included not so much to add more detail, but to compel reinterpretation and elaboration of what has already been written, giving rise to new interpretive possibilities. Each new section requires a revising of how previous sections are read, not unlike the ways many modern novels evolve their plots. Further, the text, as presented, makes no pretense of completeness. Instead, it aims to invite the reader into an interpretive process. Again, like engagements with literary fictions which demand that readers continually interpret their relationship to characters and events, this text aims to create structural possibilities for readers to do what humans must do in their everyday lives—weave together seamless worlds from fragments and imaginings.

Scale Independence

The structure of the writing attempts to show how knowledge about the individual is not less complex than knowledge about the collective. In thinking about the individual biological body, for example, the writing tries to show how the act of reading, as a private event, can relieve asthmatic symptoms. Another section describes how DeSalvo analyzes a relationship between childhood trauma and chronic asthma in adulthood. Understood as systems in themselves—ones which are comprised of other systems (immune, respiratory, reproductive)—and systems attached to larger systems (the research group, family, society)—the biological bodies represented in this writing are as detailed as the systems to which they are attached. The writing, then, aims to perform the ways in which different levels of biological and cultural systems unfold from and are enfolded in one another—and especially how acts of language use including reading and writing contribute to such processes. In reporting "what happened" or "what is learned" from research practices, it is important to show how the shift in focus from the collective to the individual or from the biological to the cultural is problematic. There are no clear boundaries separating the "I" from the "we," the "he" from the "she," the "biological" from the "cultural," or "reading" from "not reading."

Self-Similarity

Although structurally unlike most research reports, this one maintains an order that is, in part, organized by a definite rhythm and pattern. Structures are repeated for effect and emphasis and, while transitions between individual passages are deliberately absent, there is a cadence to the writing that suggests a relational flow to the images and ideas presented. In terms of content, this rhythm and pattern is represented by the ways in which nodes of similarity occur in seemingly unrelated contexts and across different levels of social engagement. Consider, for example, how some of the reported traumas impacted on different individuals' bodies and how these, in turn, affected and were affected by the social collectives. For instance, Terry believed (and had considerable medical evidence to support her belief) for example, that her male genitals were in conflict with other systems of her physiological body and, at the same time, resulted in gender shaping that she felt isolated her from comfortable social functioning. At the same time, the physical and social effects of her biological imbalances dramatically affected her interactions with the reading group. Just as Terry's biological systems were in conflict, so too were the social systems within which Terry necessarily chose to participate. At each node of relationality, then—whether biological, social, individual, or collective—a range of similar and associated phenomena is presented. In alternating paragraphs and sections that deal with different sites of similarity (biological, social, individual, collective), the writing attempts to show how these self-similar structures are caught up in one another. Importantly, the writing aims to demonstrate how the activities of reading and writing function to knit together and harmonize the body (biological and social) on personal and collective levels.

Complexity

Finally, this example of research writing attempts to show how understanding cannot be traced to a particular event or a particular strategy. What is learned from research cannot be confined to what occurs during official data-gathering or data-analysis procedures. Insight that emerges from involvement in research is intimately and unavoidably entwined in the complexity of the researchers' and the research participants' shared experiences. The research location that conditions the production of insight cannot be reduced to the particularities of the data collected, the methodologies employed, or the analytic procedures and theories applied. Just as the individual sections of the experimental research report presented earlier yield a final form that is greater than the sum of its parts, research insight emerges from the complexity of multiple and shifting levels of remembered, lived, and imagined experience.

The insights presented in this report are not representations of data gathered from the reading group. They are not autobiographical accounts of the writer's personal experiences. They are not reviews of theory and philosophy. They are not representations of literary involvements. They are not *one* of these. They represent *all* of these and, in interesting ways, because they are the product of multiple contexts and involvements, the insights presented in this paper exceed their sources. Although we do not feel that this report can successfully exist without the contextualizing writing we have provided with it, we do feel that, like a novel, poem, comic book, or docudrama, this research report presents the shape of some insights that emerged from our involvement in literary anthropological research. We offer this example of research reporting and our analysis of it as an alternative to Euclidean forms of report-writing that often eliminate the interesting bumpiness of experience and complexity of thinking. We believe that inventing these new forms is necessary if research into human experience is to continue to develop. As Rorty (1989) suggests, "To change how we talk is to change what we are" (p. 19).

References

Als, H. (1997). *The women*. New York: Farrar, Straus, Giroux.

Bakhtin, M .M. (1981). *The dialogic imagination* (C. Emerson and M. Holquist, Trans.). Austin: University of Texas Press.

Califia, P., & Fuller, J. (Eds.). (1995). *Forbidden passages: Writings banned in Canada*. San Francisco: Cleis.

Capra, F. (1996). *The web of life: A new scientific understanding of living systems*. New York: Anchor.

DeSalvo, L. (1997). *Breathless: An asthma journal*. Boston: Beacon.

Gleick, J. (1987). *Chaos: Making a new science*. New York: Penguin.

Gowdy, B. (1995). *Mister sandman*. Toronto: Somerville House.

Holquist, M. (1990). *Dialogism: Bakhtin and his world*. London and New York: Routledge.

Iser, W. (1989). *Prospecting: From reader response to literary anthropology*. Baltimore, MD: Johns Hopkins University Press.

Iser, W. (1993). *The fictive and the imaginary: Charting literary anthropology*. Baltimore, MD: Johns Hopkins University Press.

Kauffman, S. (1995). *At home in the universe: The search for the laws of self-organization and complexity*. New York: Oxford University Press.

Langer, S. (1957). *Problems of art*. New York: Scribner's.

Lorde, A. (1982). *Zami: A new spelling of my name*. Freedom, CA: Crossing.

MacDonald, A. M. (1996). *Fall on your knees*. Toronto: Knopf.

Merleau-Ponty, M. (1962). *Phenomenology of perception*. London: Routledge.

Morrison, T. (1996). *The dancing mind*. New York: Knopf.

Rorty, R. (1989). *Contingency, irony, solidarity*. New York: Cambridge University Press.

Sedgwick, E. (1990). *Epistemology of the closet*. Berkeley: University of California Press.

Stewart, I. (1998). *Life's other secret: The new mathematics of the living world*. New York: Wiley.

Stewart, I., & Cohen, J. (1997). *Figments of reality: The evolution of the curious mind*. New York: Cambridge University Press.

Sumara, D. (1996). *Private readings in public: Schooling the literary imagination.* New York: Peter Lang.

Sumara, D. (2000). Learning to say something true about the world. In B. Barrell, & B. Hammett (Eds.), *Contemporary issues in Canadian secondary English education.* Toronto: Irwin.

Waldrop, M. (1992). *Complexity: The emerging science at the edge of order and chaos.* New York: Simon & Schuster.

White, E. (1997). *The farewell symphony.* New York: Knopf.

Winterson, J. (1995). *Art objects: Essays on ecstasy and effrontery.* Toronto: Knopf.

Author Index